RECCHIONI - MAMMUCARI

ORPHANS

VOLUME THREE
TRUTH

ORPHANS series created by Roberto Recchioni and Emiliano Mammucari

Original lettering by Marina Sanfelice
Original logo created by Paolo Campana
Original book design by Officine Bolzoni with Cosimo Torsoli

English translation by Valeria Gobbato and Elena Cecchini
Localization, layout, and editing by Mike Kennedy

MAGNETIC™   **LION™ FORGE**

ISBN: 978-1-942367-85-7
Library of Congress Control Number: 2018931325

Printed in China.

10 9 8 7 6 5 4 3 2 1

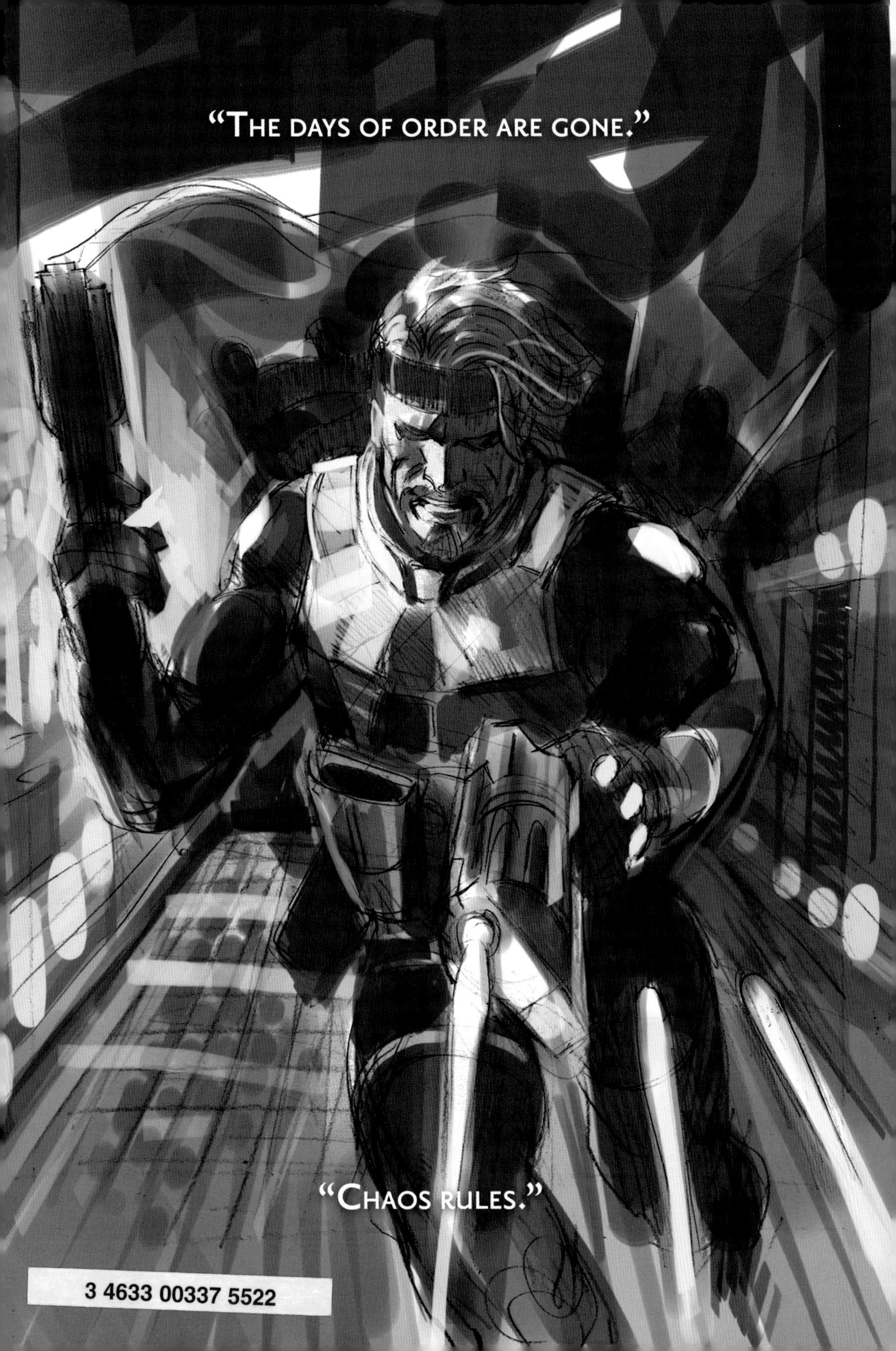
"The days of order are gone."
"Chaos rules."

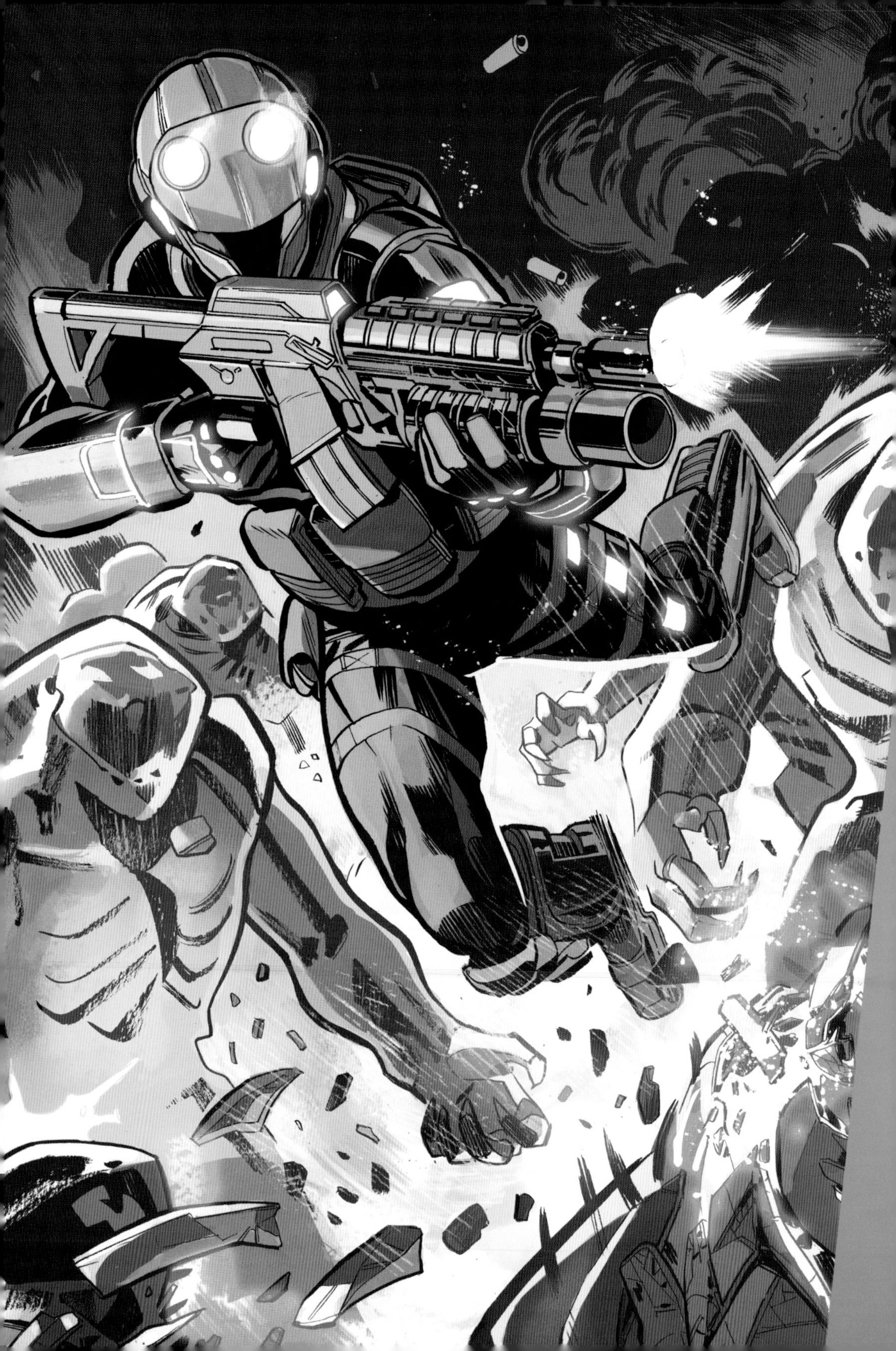

START

Color has been used by artists, film makers, costume designers, and photographers to convey mood and emotion for ages. It could be said that, in the context of visual language, color is the fourth dimension, defining an entirely unique context within an image. While a black and white image can accurately portray the subject matter of a scene, color can give it an entirely different feel. Take the image on the left -- the red, yellow, and orange hues clearly convey the heat and energy of a fiery explosion, but if it were instead colored with blue and white tones, it could just as easily be interpreted as a freezing ice storm. Hot becomes cold with a simple shift in palette.

The creative team working on *Orphans* developed specific narrative codes and design rules, doing a monumental amount of preparatory work that's often unprecedented for a comic series. In this volume, we wanted to explore the color aspect, starting with Roberto Recchioni and Emiliano Mammucari's initial intentions through the different colorists' palette choices per scene. As so much of this series is based on the shifting emotional states and surprises the characters (and readers) experience, it only seems fair to spotlight the artists that achieved such an effective goal.

Previous page: illustration by Emiliano Mammucari, colors by Annalisa Leoni

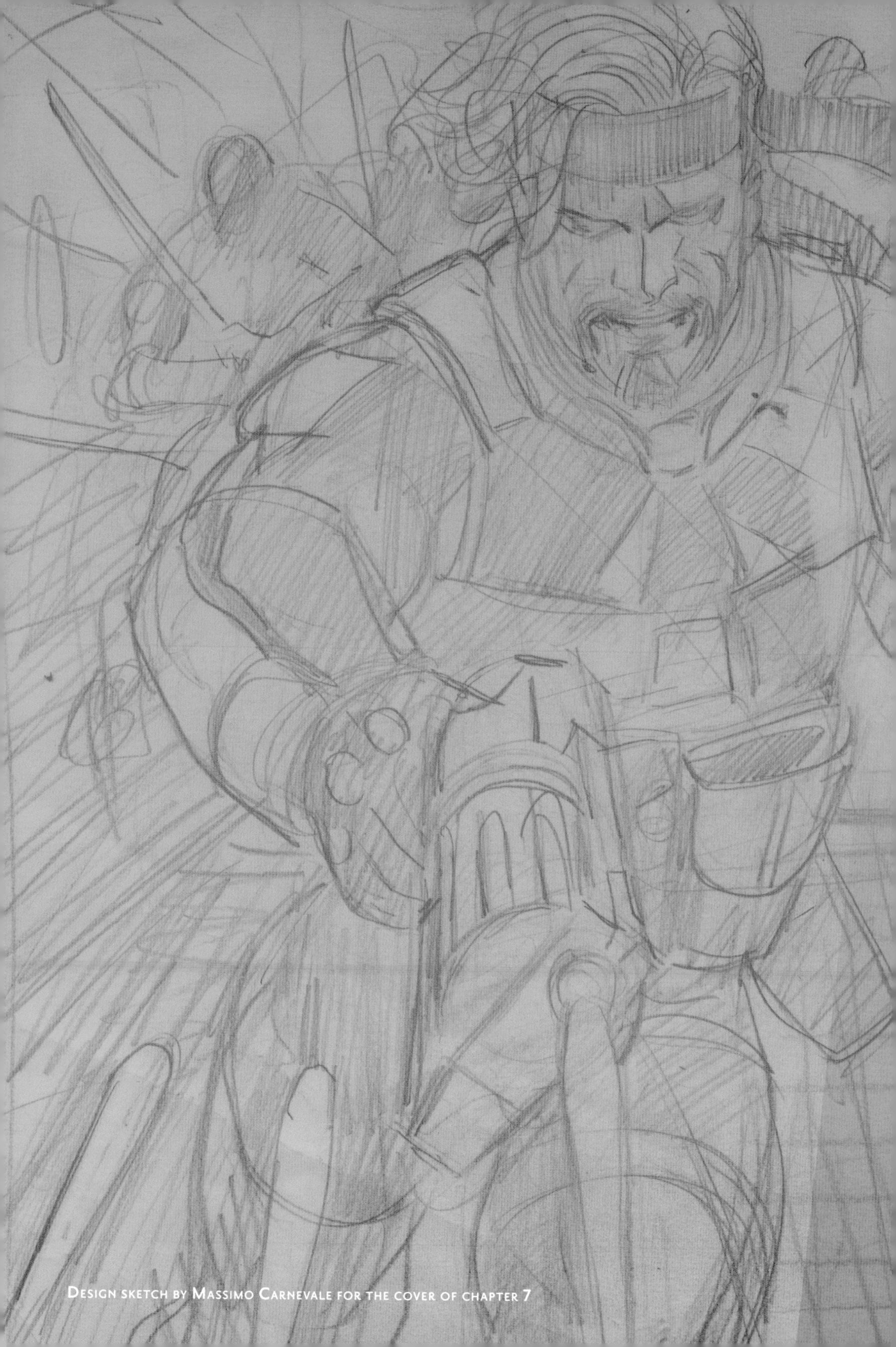

Design sketch by Massimo Carnevale for the cover of chapter 7

BULLETS AND LIES

ORPHANS: CHAPTER 7

story: ROBERTO RECCHIONI
art: GIORGIO SANTUCCI and ALESSANDRO BIGNAMINI
colors: LUCA BERTELÈ and GIOVANNA NIRO
cover: MASSIMO CARNEVALE

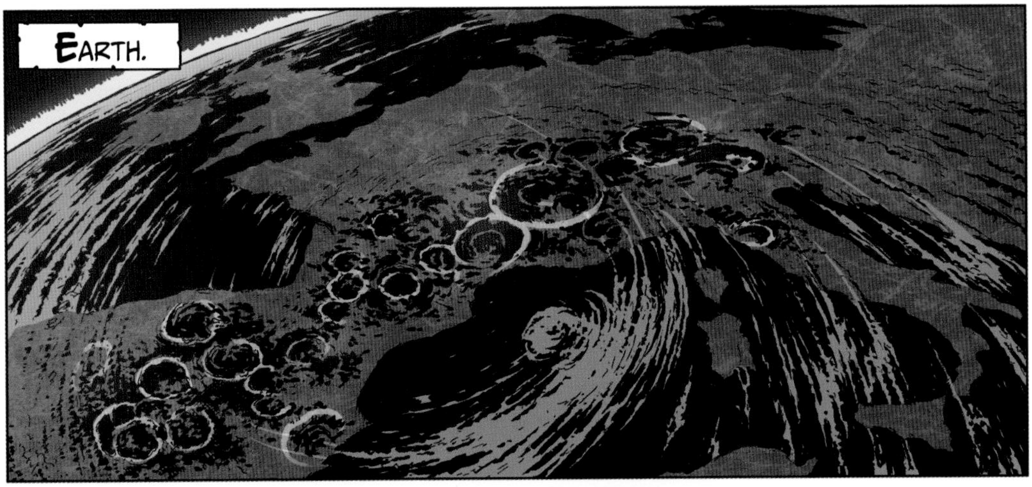
EARTH.

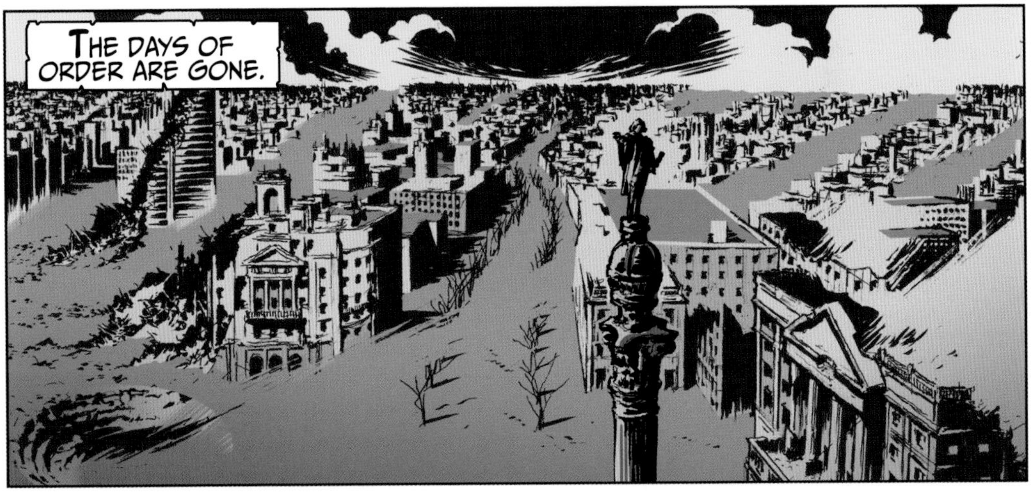
THE DAYS OF ORDER ARE GONE.

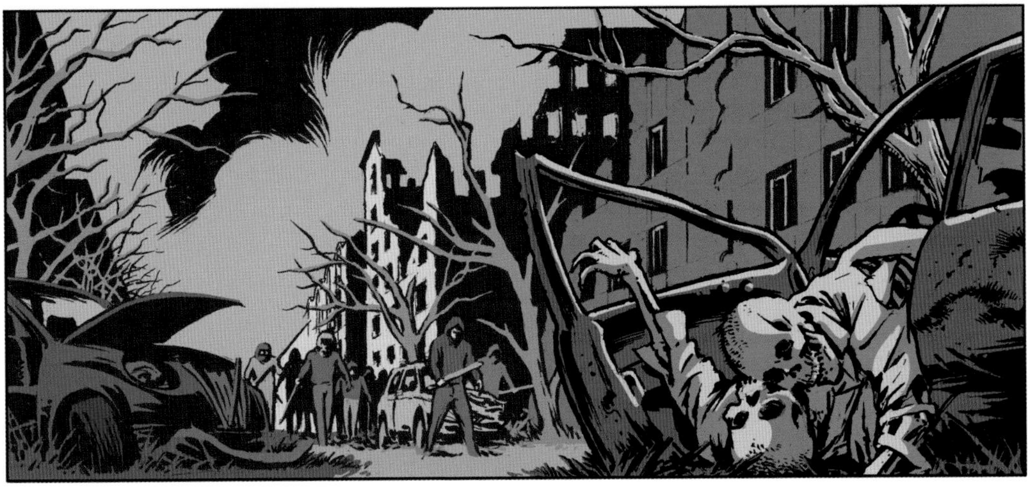

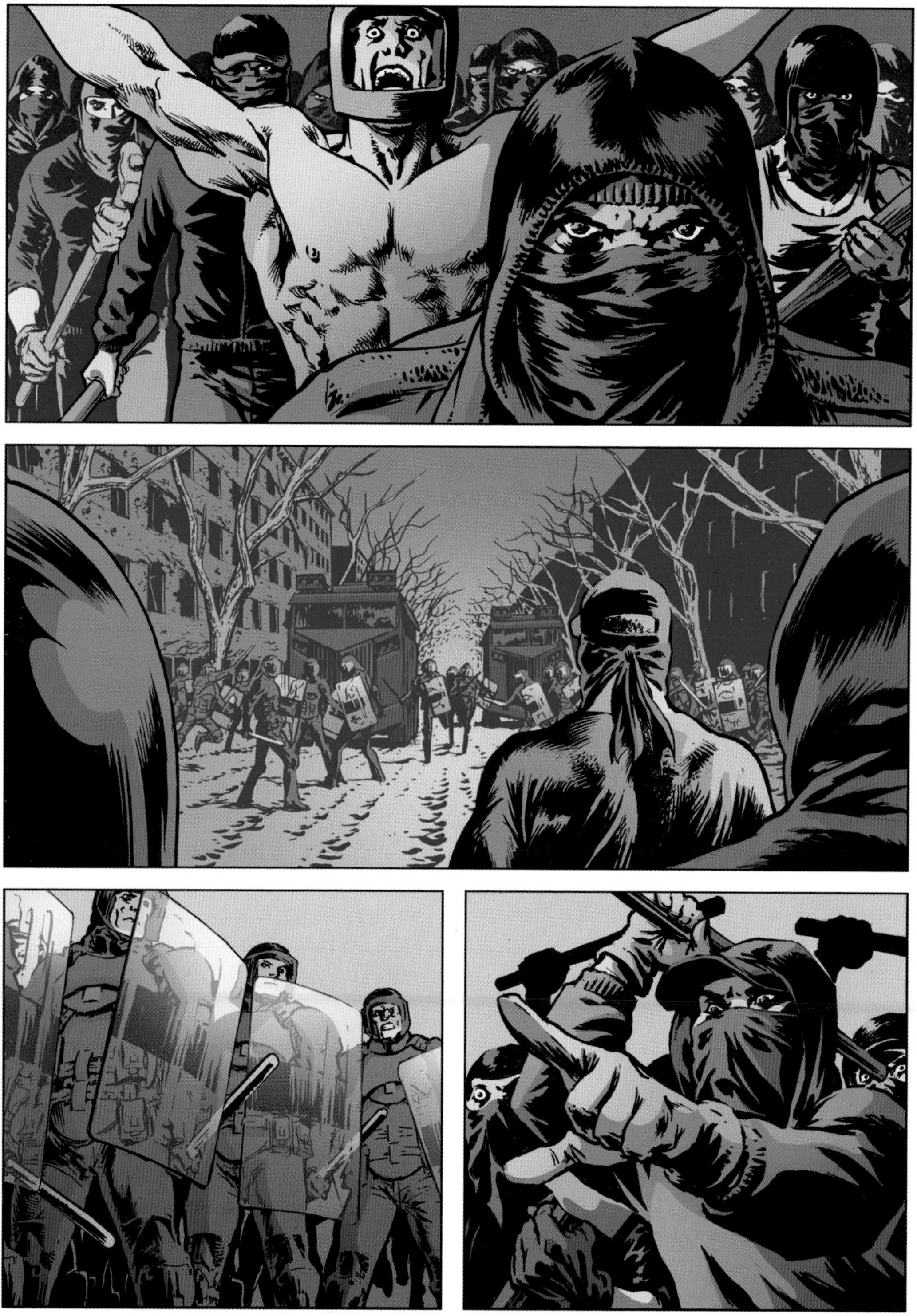

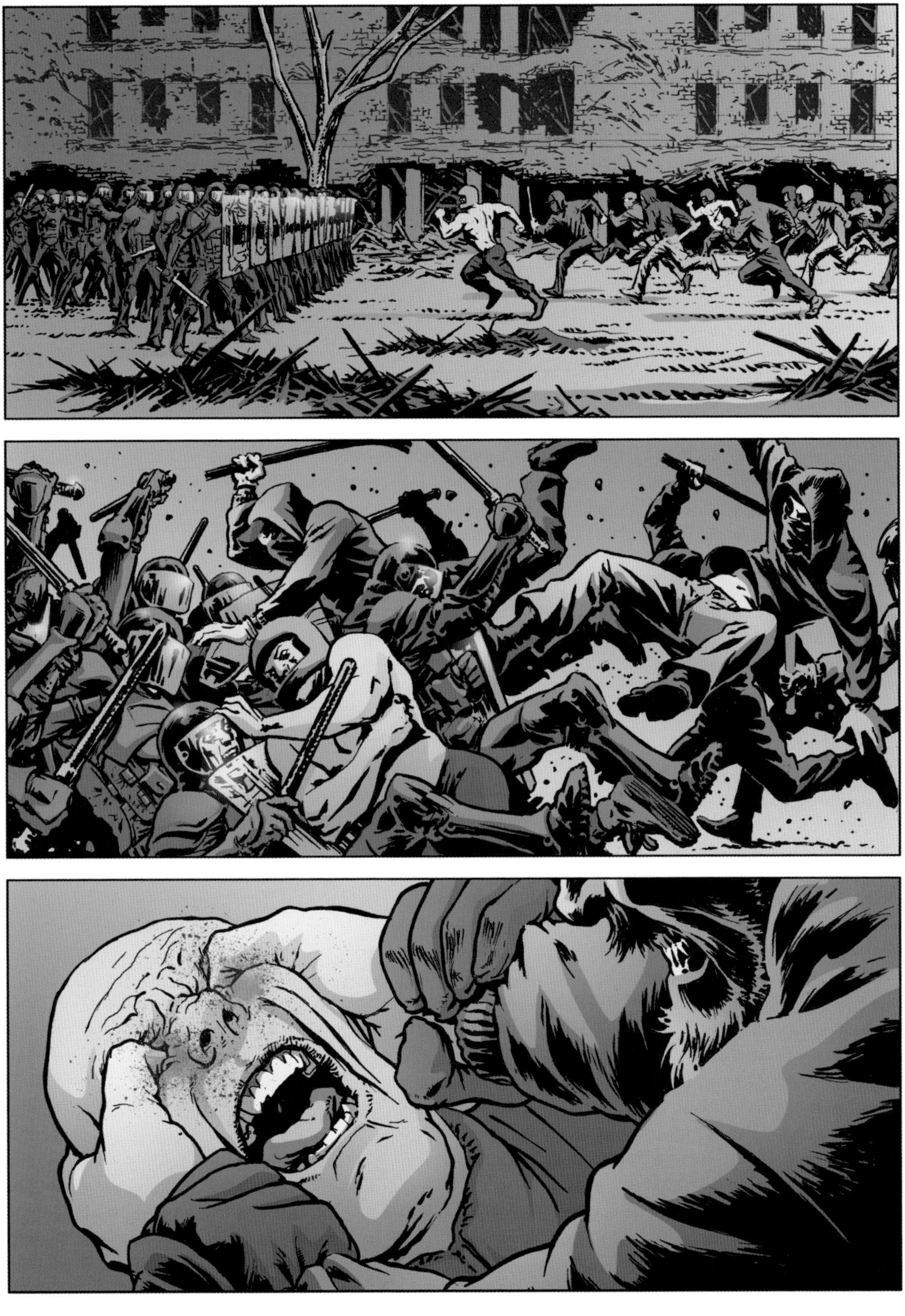

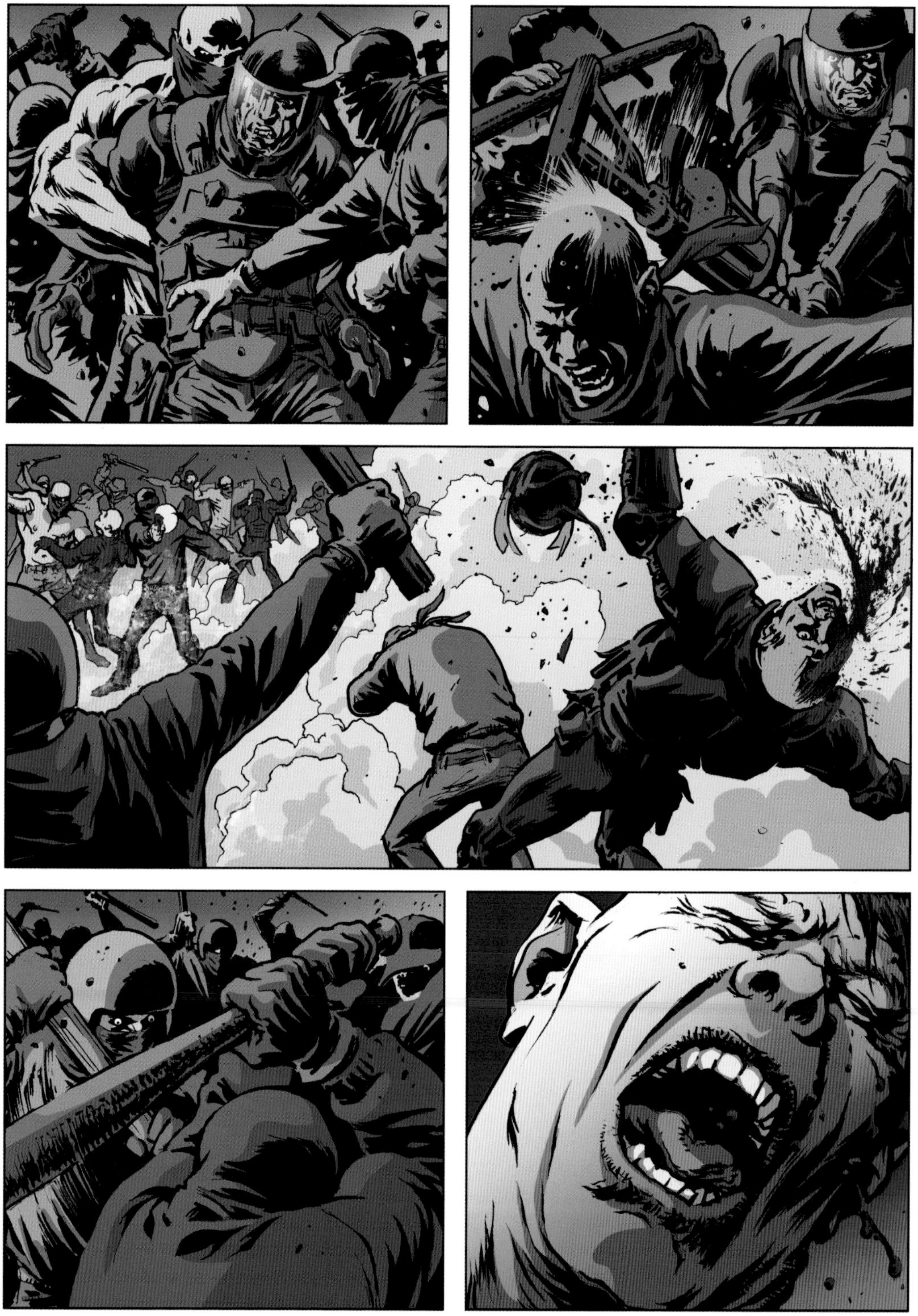

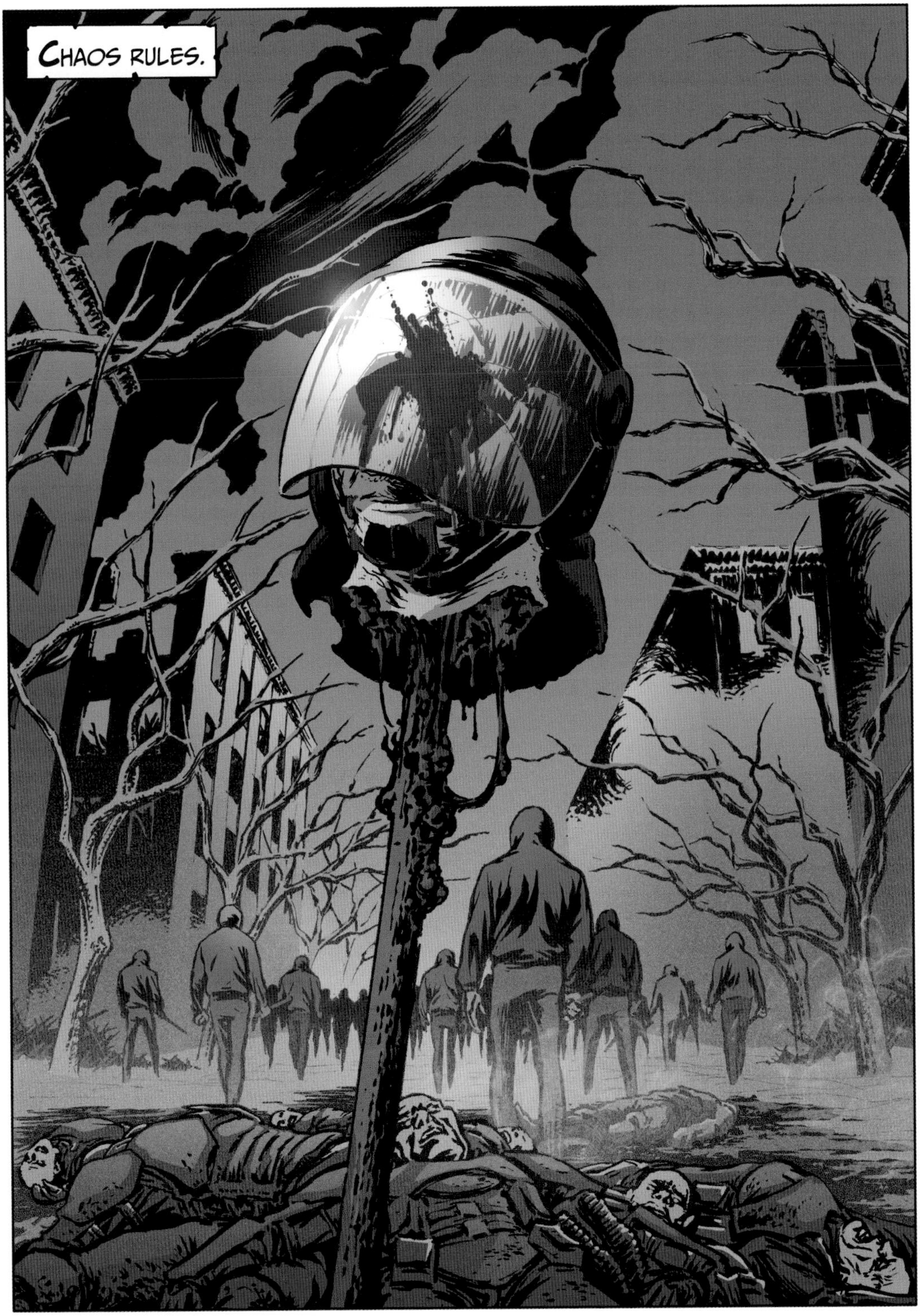
CHAOS RULES.

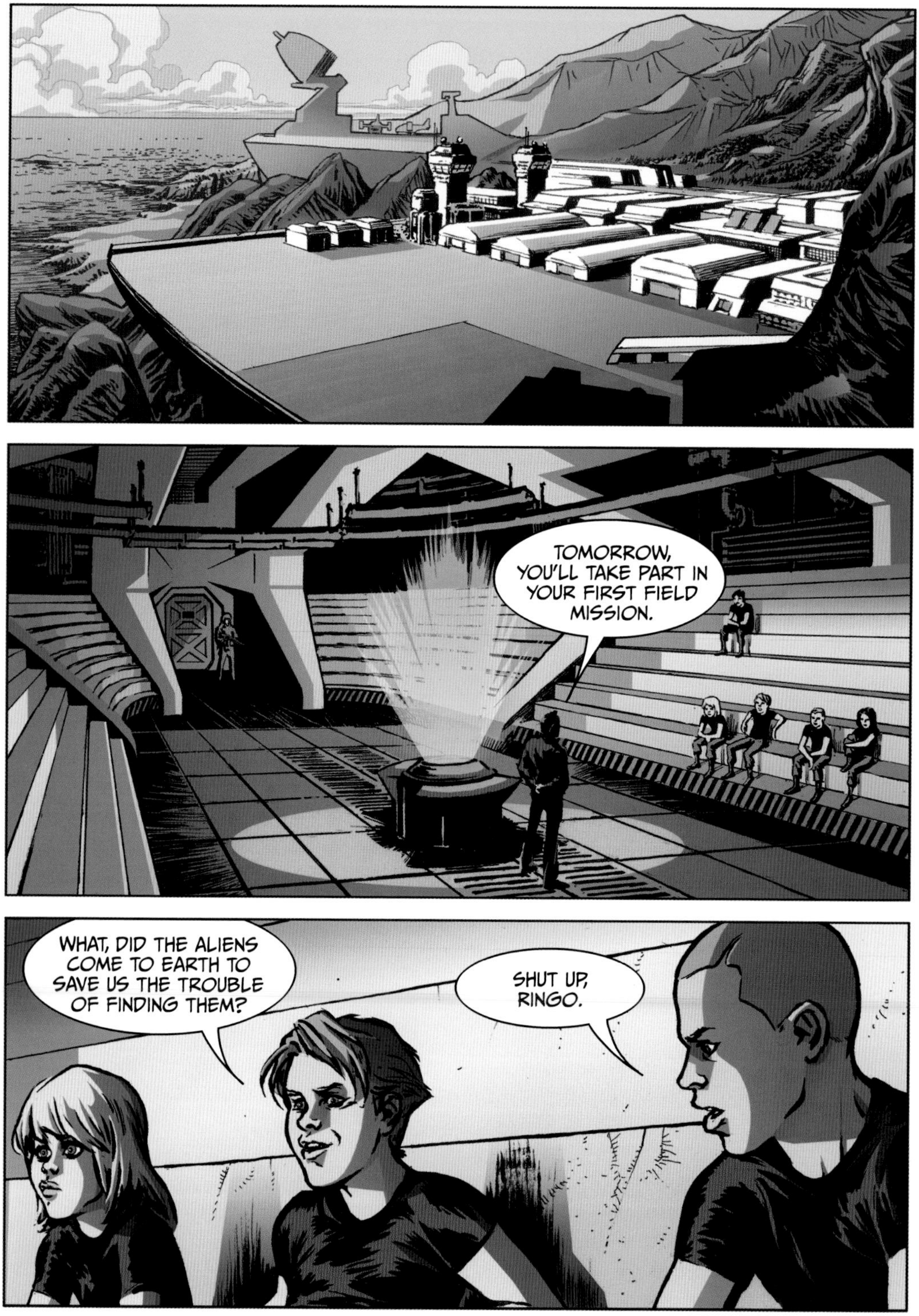
TOMORROW, YOU'LL TAKE PART IN YOUR FIRST FIELD MISSION.
WHAT, DID THE ALIENS COME TO EARTH TO SAVE US THE TROUBLE OF FINDING THEM?
SHUT UP, RINGO.

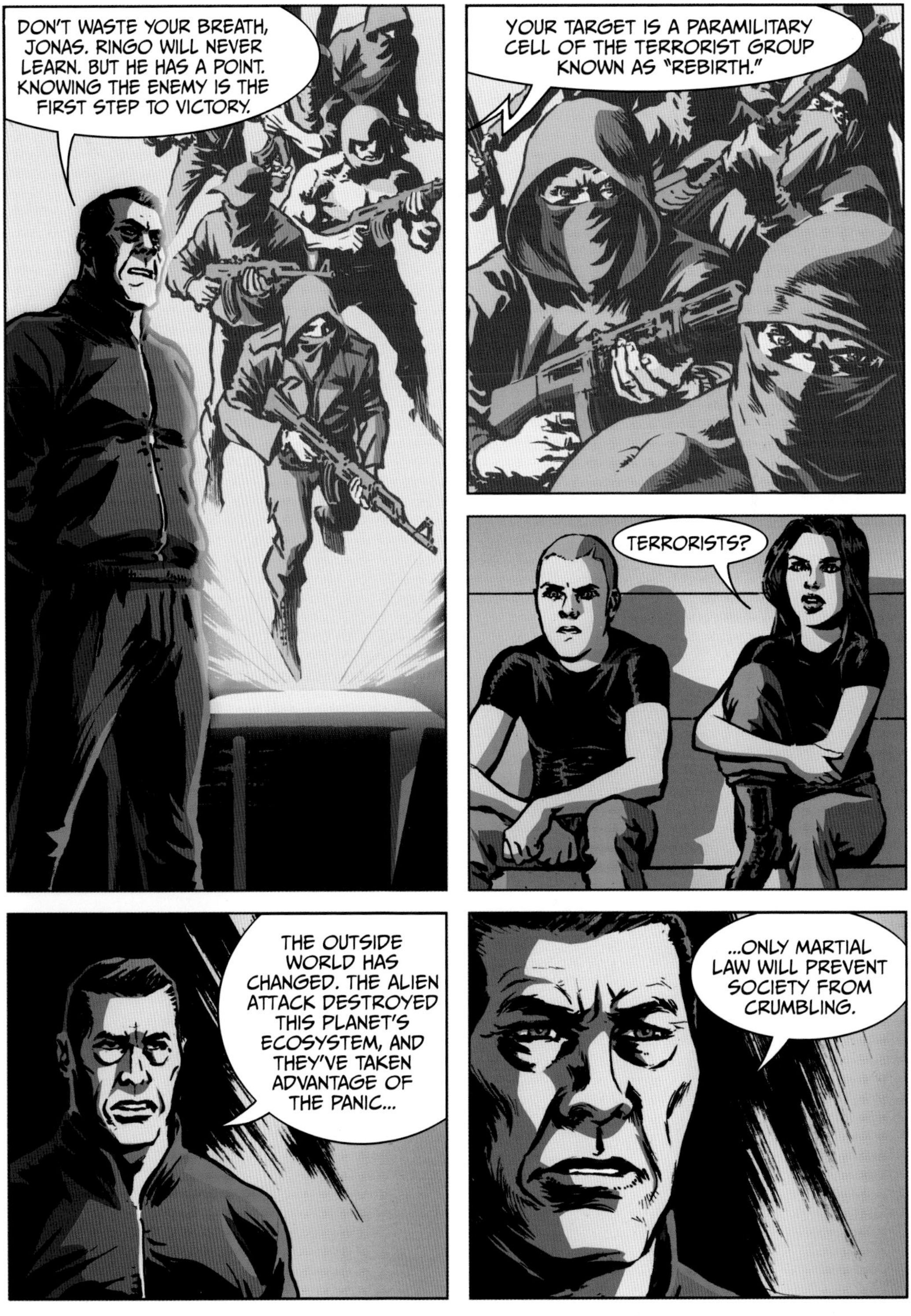
DON'T WASTE YOUR BREATH, JONAS. RINGO WILL NEVER LEARN. BUT HE HAS A POINT. KNOWING THE ENEMY IS THE FIRST STEP TO VICTORY.
YOUR TARGET IS A PARAMILITARY CELL OF THE TERRORIST GROUP KNOWN AS "REBIRTH."
TERRORISTS?
THE OUTSIDE WORLD HAS CHANGED. THE ALIEN ATTACK DESTROYED THIS PLANET'S ECOSYSTEM, AND THEY'VE TAKEN ADVANTAGE OF THE PANIC...
...ONLY MARTIAL LAW WILL PREVENT SOCIETY FROM CRUMBLING.

AND IF THAT FAILS... LINE UP THE FIRING SQUADS.

PRECISELY. YOU SHOULD UNDERSTAND WHY, RAUL.

I THOUGHT YOU WERE TRAINING US TO FIGHT THE ONES WHO DESTROYED OUR PLANET AND KILLED OUR FAMILIES. WHAT ARE WE NOW, HITMEN?

THIS IS TAMESHIGIRI.

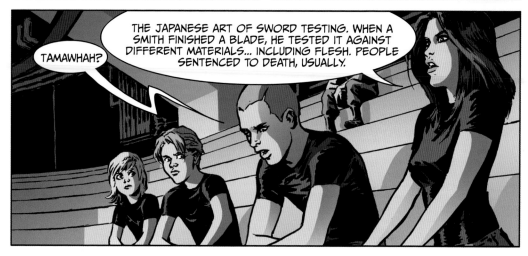

TAMAWHAH?

THE JAPANESE ART OF SWORD TESTING. WHEN A SMITH FINISHED A BLADE, HE TESTED IT AGAINST DIFFERENT MATERIALS... INCLUDING FLESH. PEOPLE SENTENCED TO DEATH, USUALLY.

WAIT... YOU MEAN WE'RE--

WE'RE THE BLADES, DUMMY!

THUD

AOW!

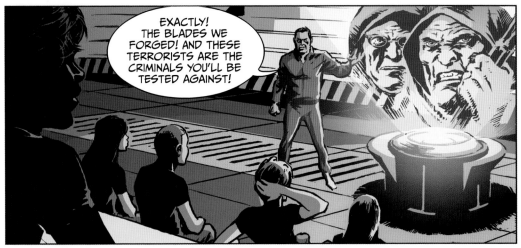

EXACTLY! THE BLADES WE FORGED! AND THESE TERRORISTS ARE THE CRIMINALS YOU'LL BE TESTED AGAINST!

NOT PRISONERS?

THAT WOULD BE POINTLESS.

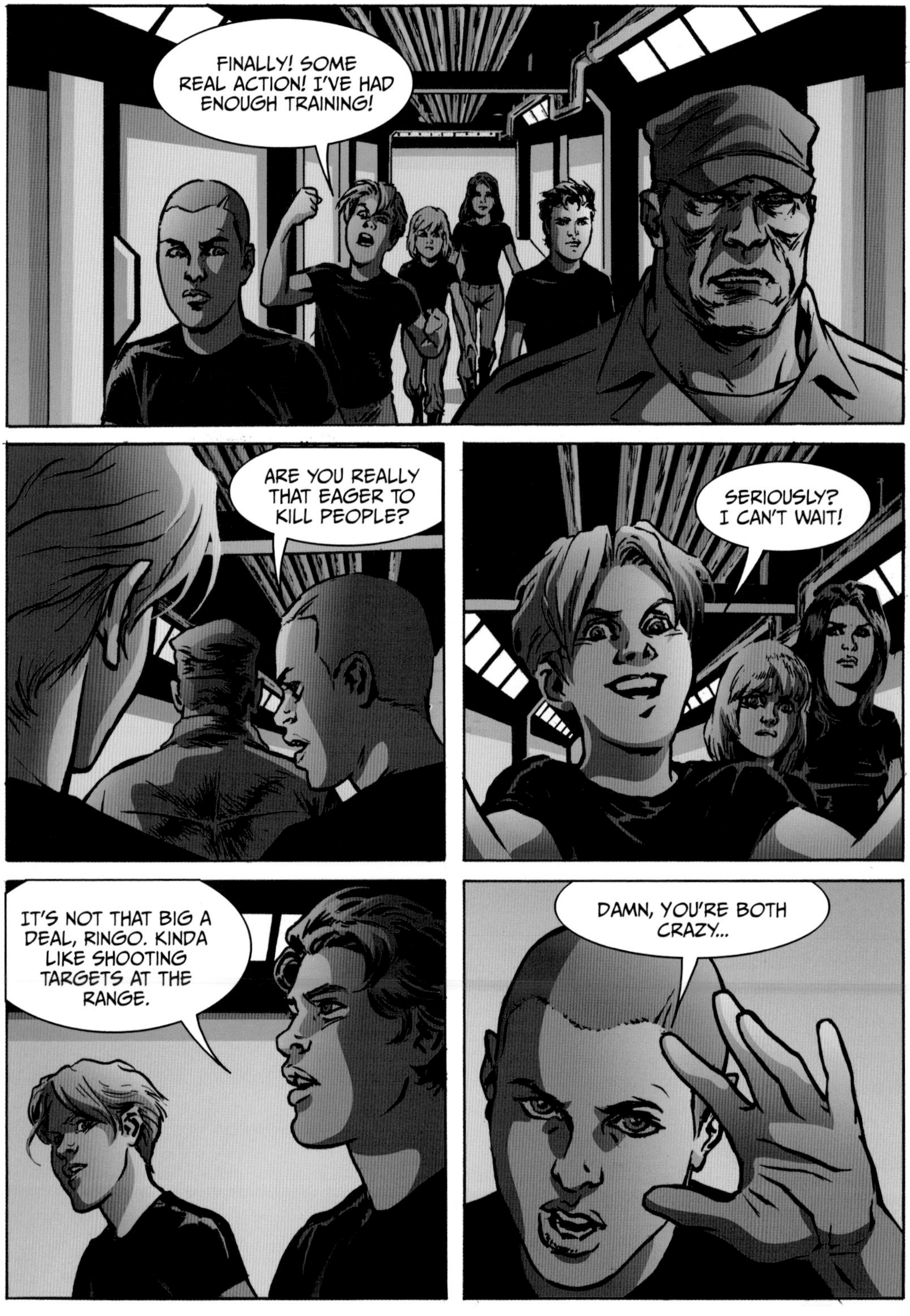
FINALLY! SOME REAL ACTION! I'VE HAD ENOUGH TRAINING!
ARE YOU REALLY THAT EAGER TO KILL PEOPLE?
SERIOUSLY? I CAN'T WAIT!
IT'S NOT THAT BIG A DEAL, RINGO. KINDA LIKE SHOOTING TARGETS AT THE RANGE.
DAMN, YOU'RE BOTH CRAZY...

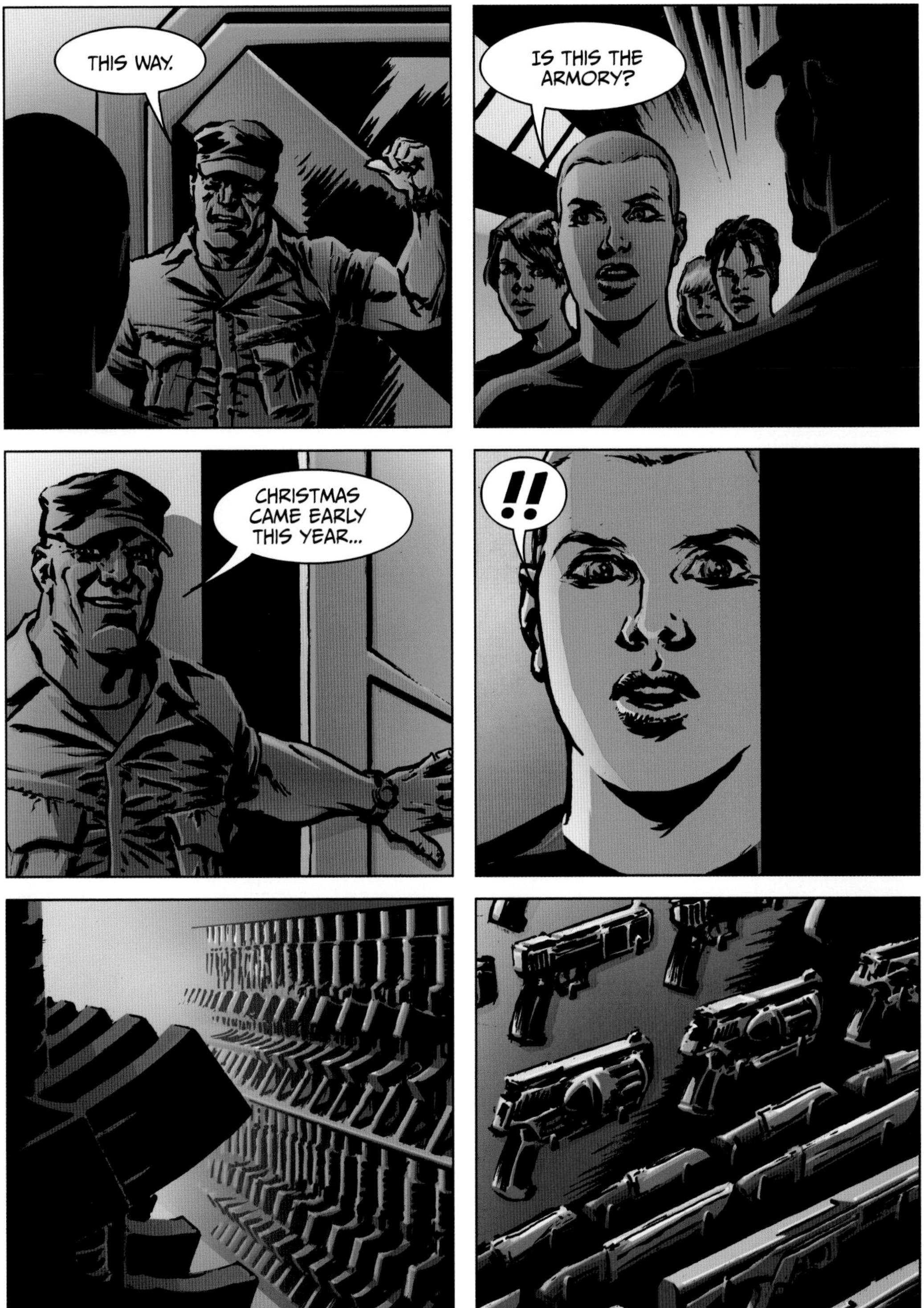
THIS WAY.
IS THIS THE ARMORY?
CHRISTMAS CAME EARLY THIS YEAR...
!!

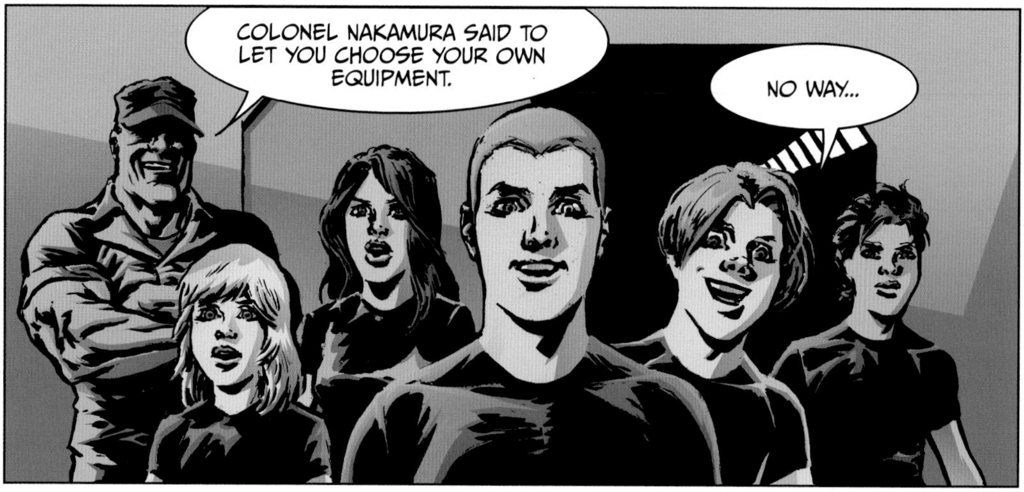
COLONEL NAKAMURA SAID TO LET YOU CHOOSE YOUR OWN EQUIPMENT.
NO WAY...

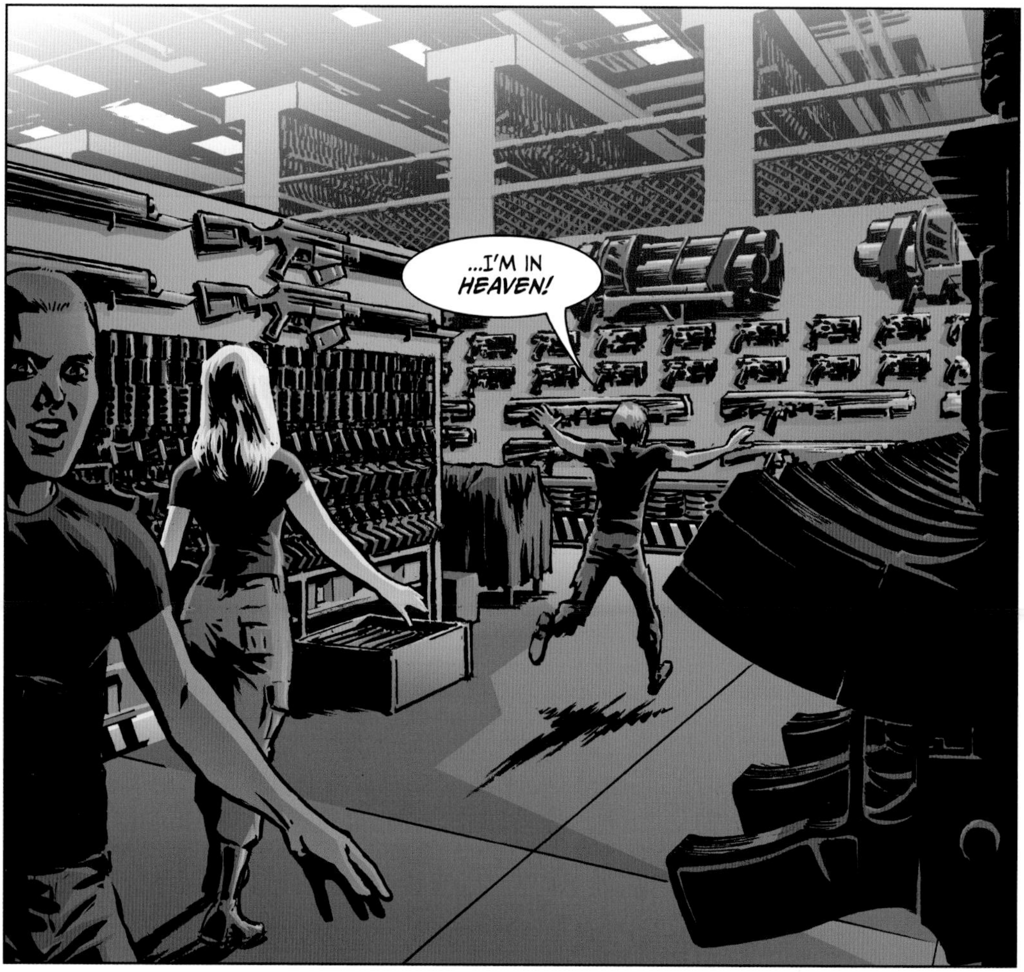
...I'M IN HEAVEN!

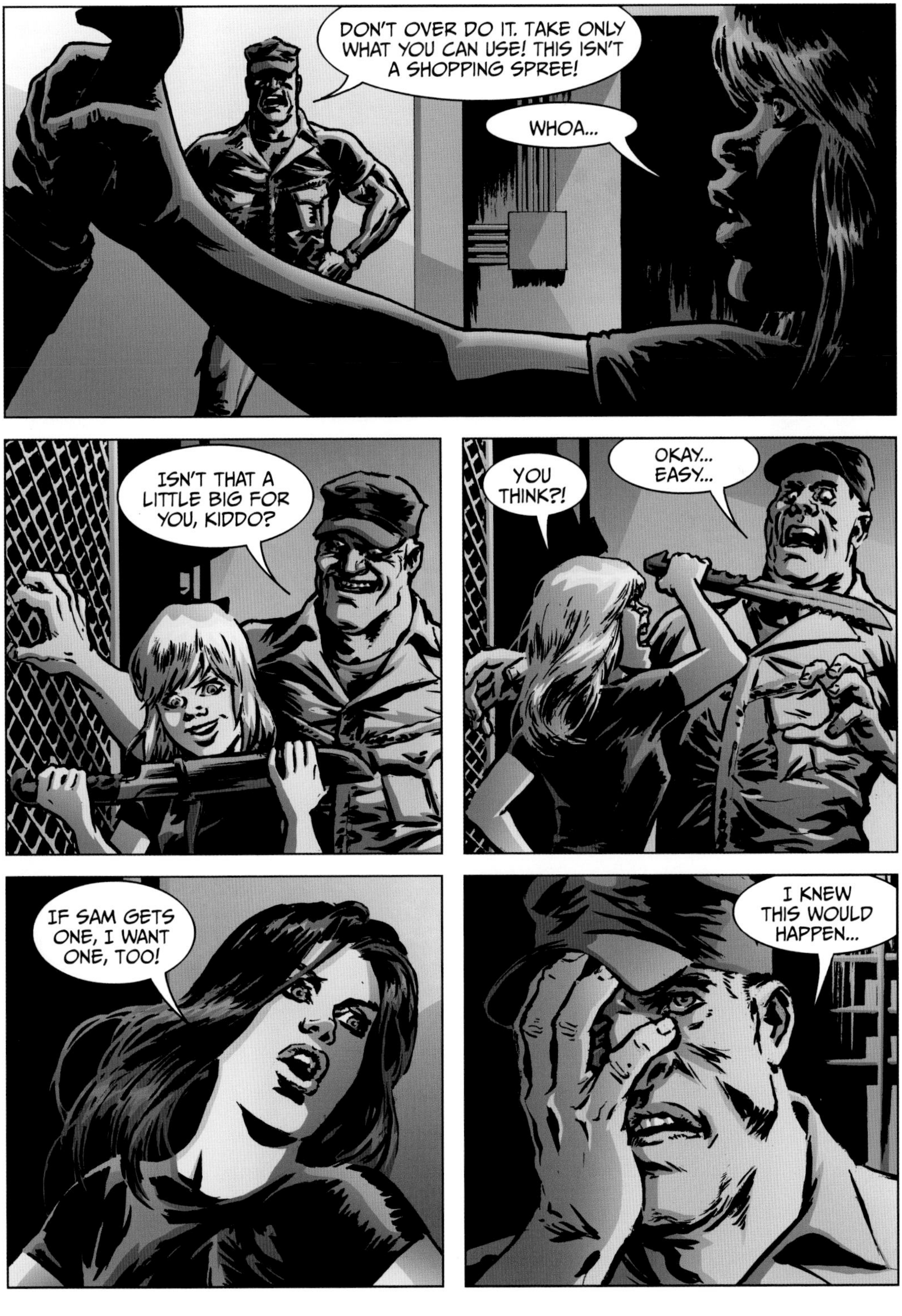
DON'T OVER DO IT. TAKE ONLY WHAT YOU CAN USE! THIS ISN'T A SHOPPING SPREE!
WHOA...
ISN'T THAT A LITTLE BIG FOR YOU, KIDDO?
OKAY... EASY...
YOU THINK?!
IF SAM GETS ONE, I WANT ONE, TOO!
I KNEW THIS WOULD HAPPEN...

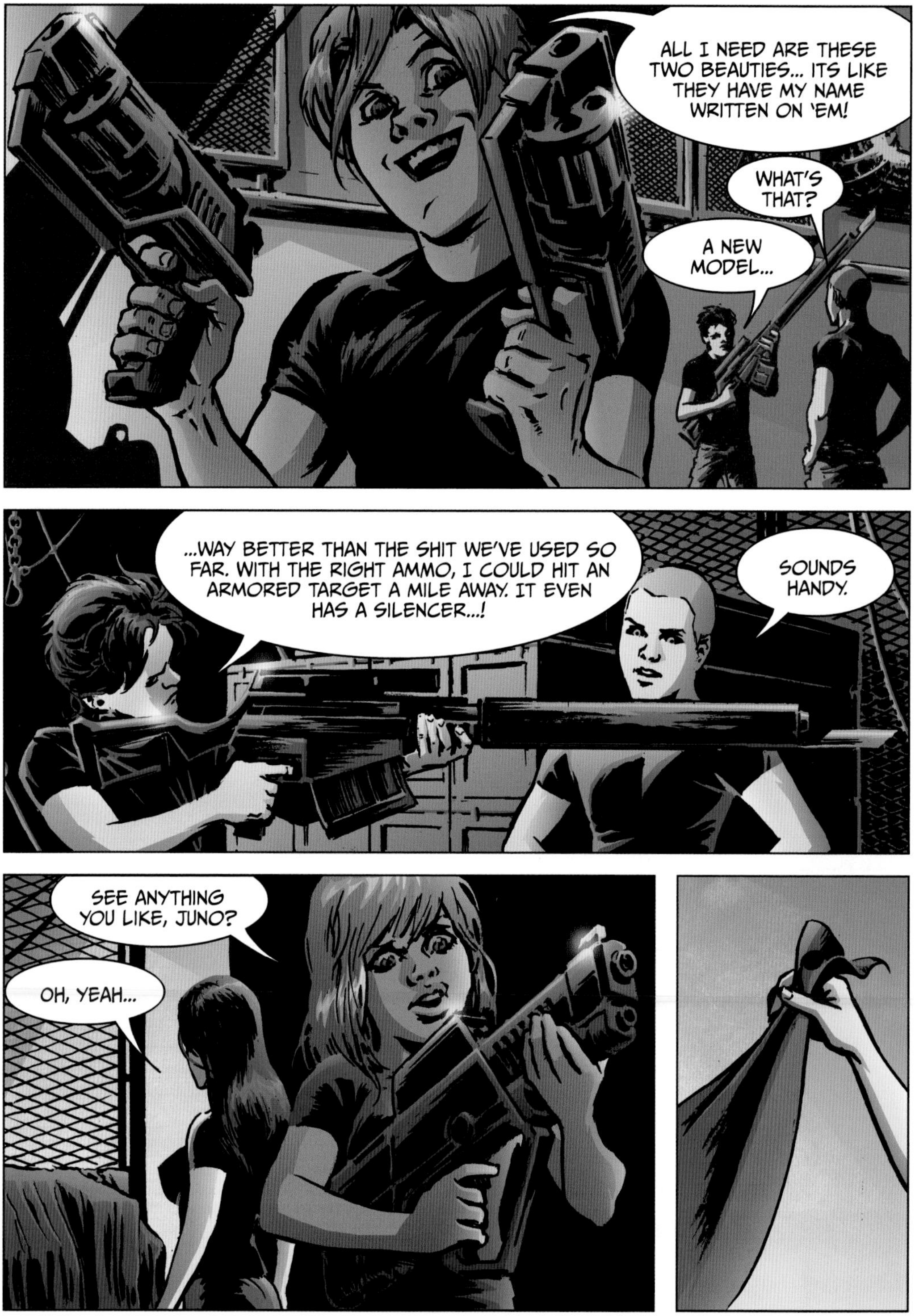
ALL I NEED ARE THESE TWO BEAUTIES... ITS LIKE THEY HAVE MY NAME WRITTEN ON 'EM!
WHAT'S THAT?
A NEW MODEL...
...WAY BETTER THAN THE SHIT WE'VE USED SO FAR. WITH THE RIGHT AMMO, I COULD HIT AN ARMORED TARGET A MILE AWAY. IT EVEN HAS A SILENCER...!
SOUNDS HANDY.
SEE ANYTHING YOU LIKE, JUNO?
OH, YEAH...

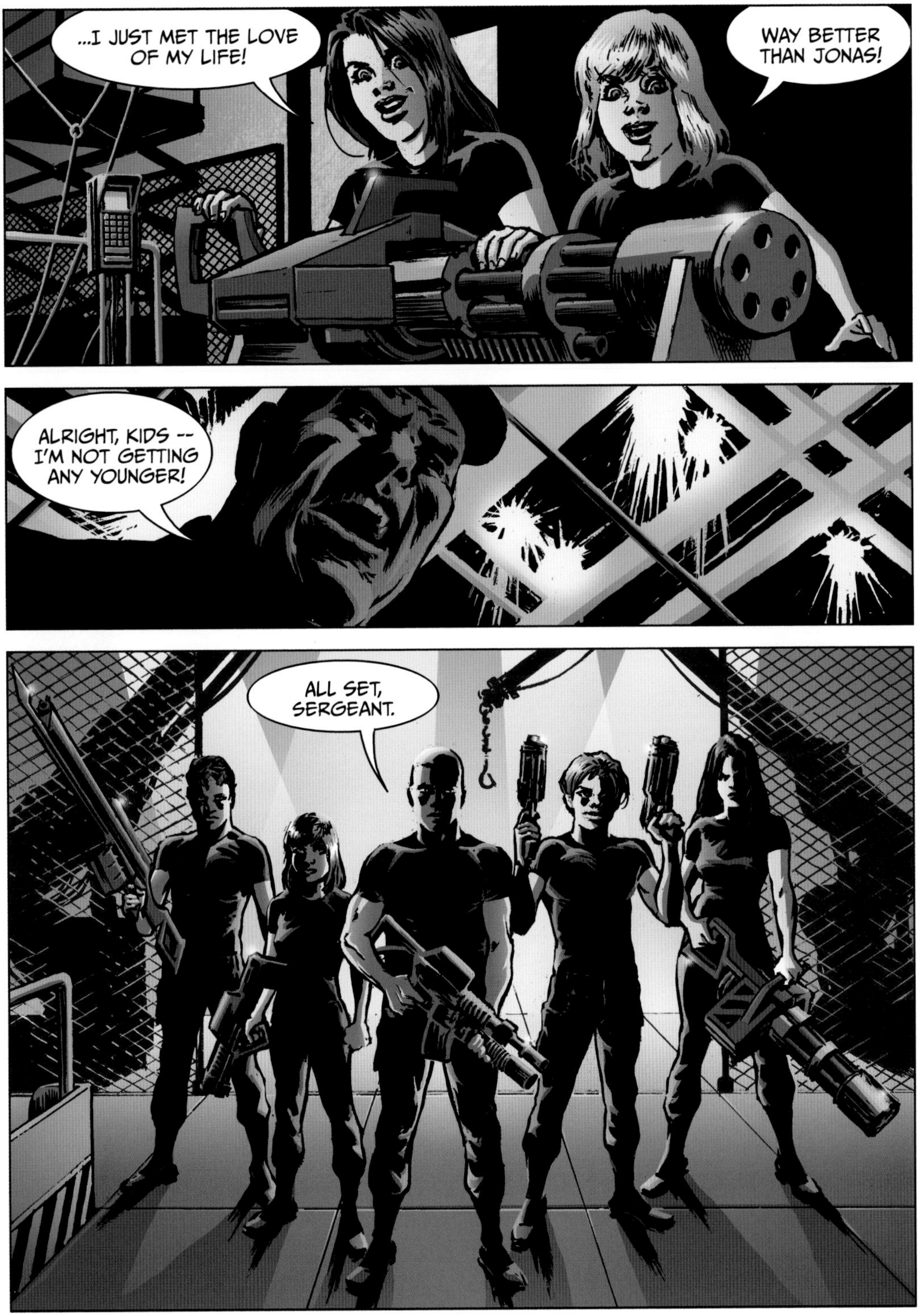
...I JUST MET THE LOVE OF MY LIFE!
WAY BETTER THAN JONAS!
ALRIGHT, KIDS -- I'M NOT GETTING ANY YOUNGER!
ALL SET, SERGEANT.

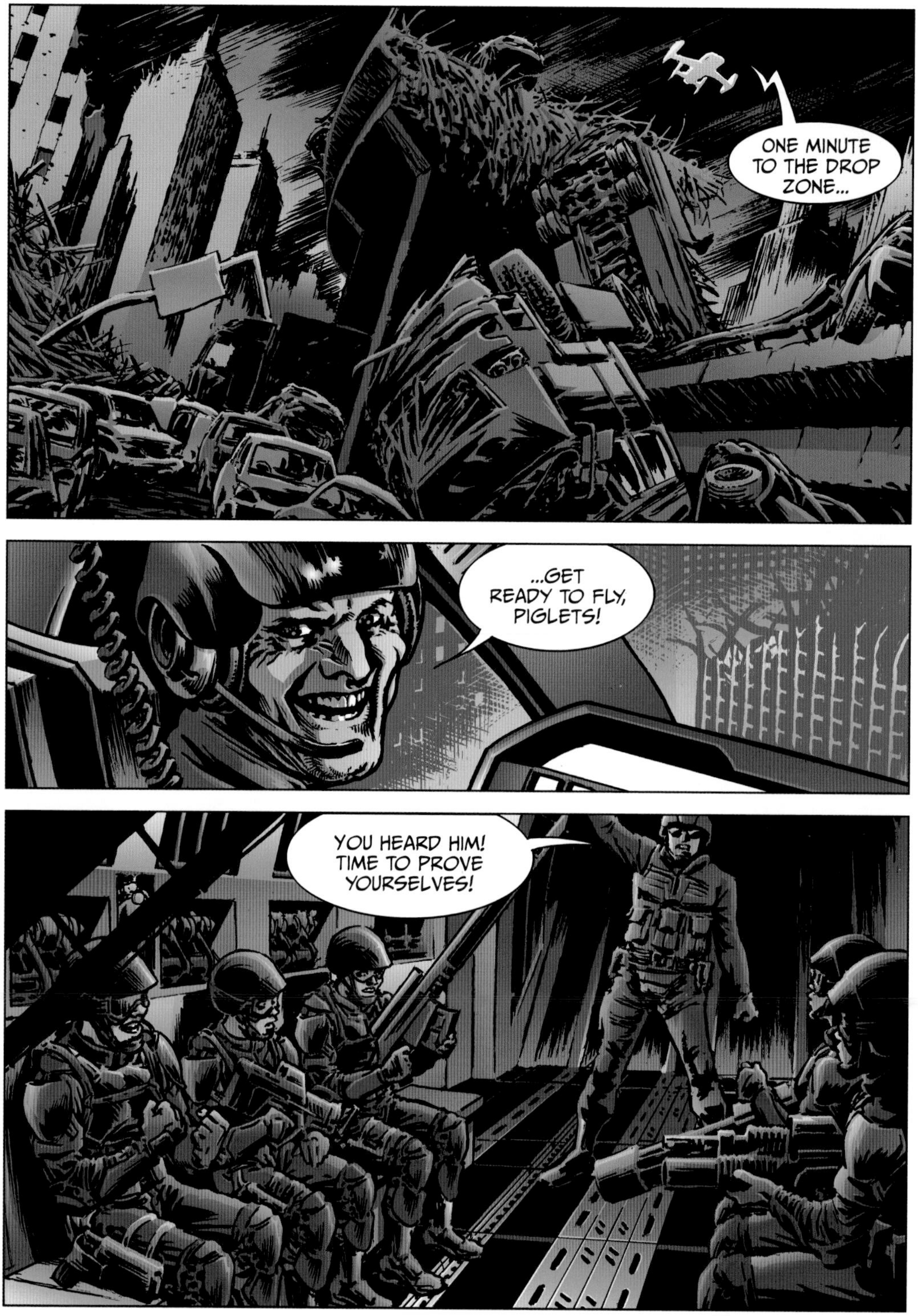
ONE MINUTE TO THE DROP ZONE...
...GET READY TO FLY, PIGLETS!
YOU HEARD HIM! TIME TO PROVE YOURSELVES!

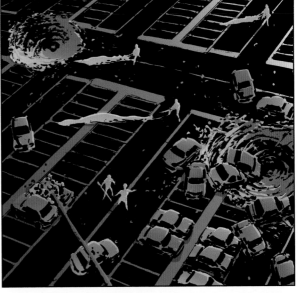

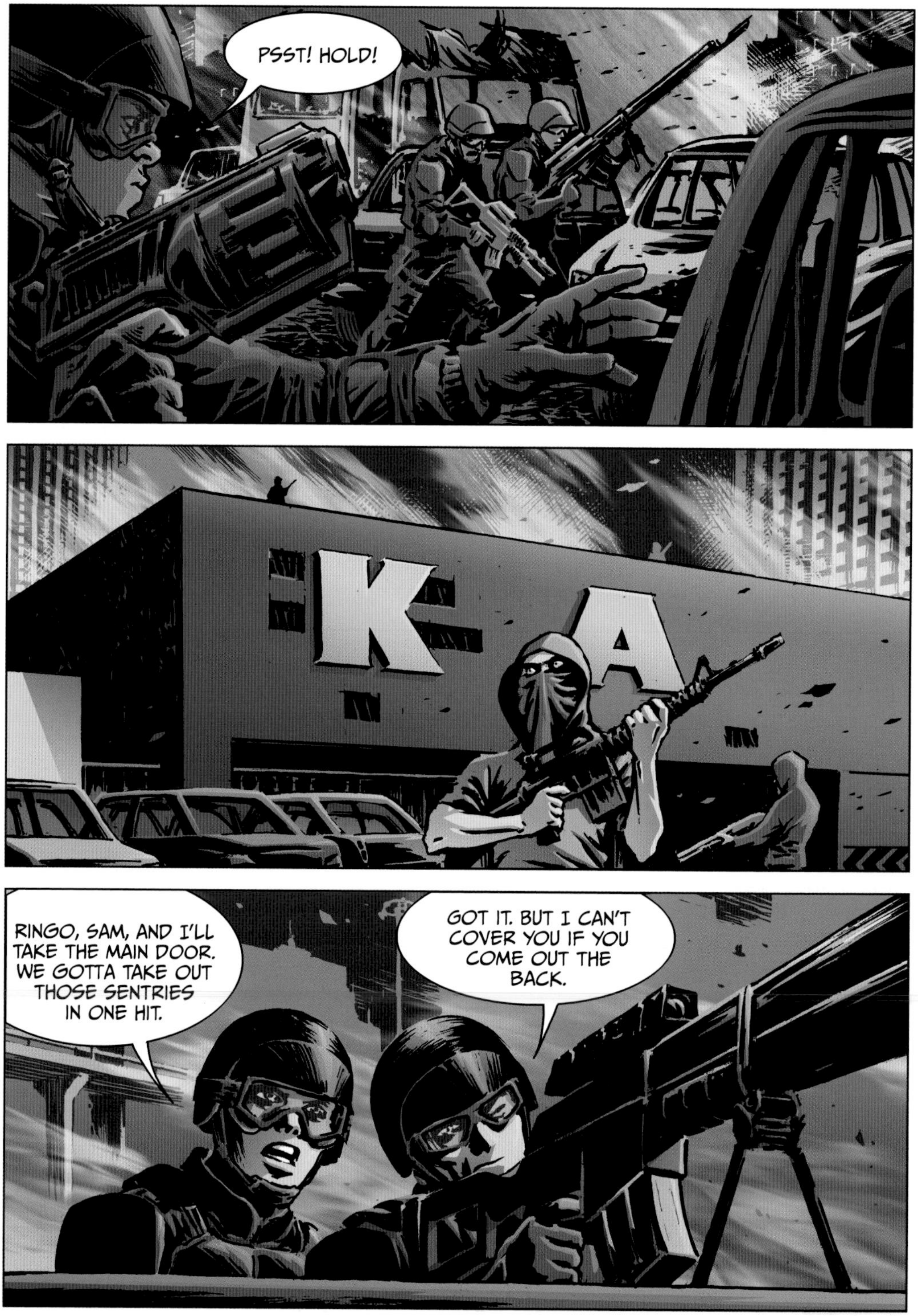
PSST! HOLD!
K A
RINGO, SAM, AND I'LL TAKE THE MAIN DOOR. WE GOTTA TAKE OUT THOSE SENTRIES IN ONE HIT.
GOT IT. BUT I CAN'T COVER YOU IF YOU COME OUT THE BACK.

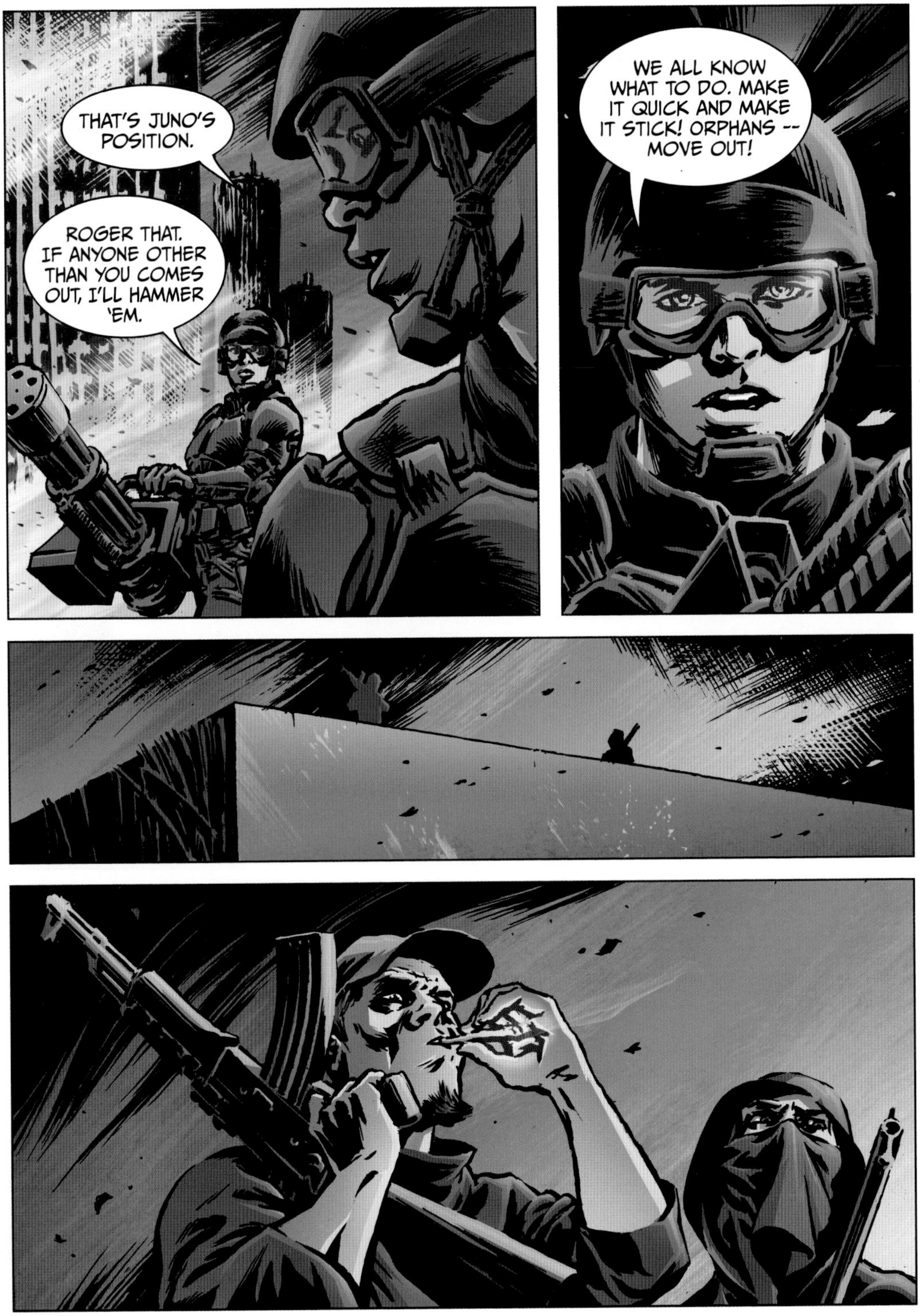
THAT'S JUNO'S POSITION.
ROGER THAT. IF ANYONE OTHER THAN YOU COMES OUT, I'LL HAMMER 'EM.
WE ALL KNOW WHAT TO DO. MAKE IT QUICK AND MAKE IT STICK! ORPHANS -- MOVE OUT!

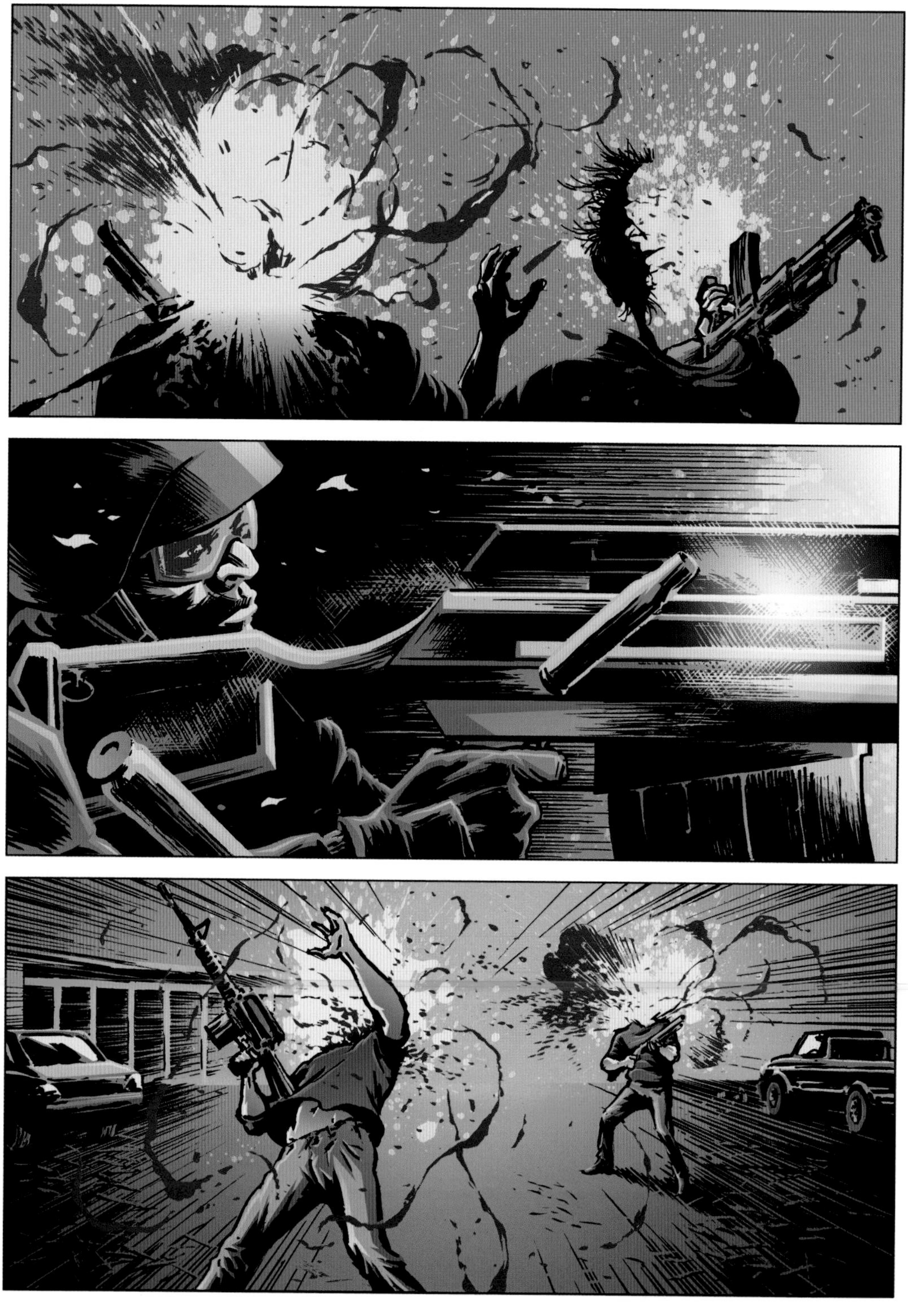

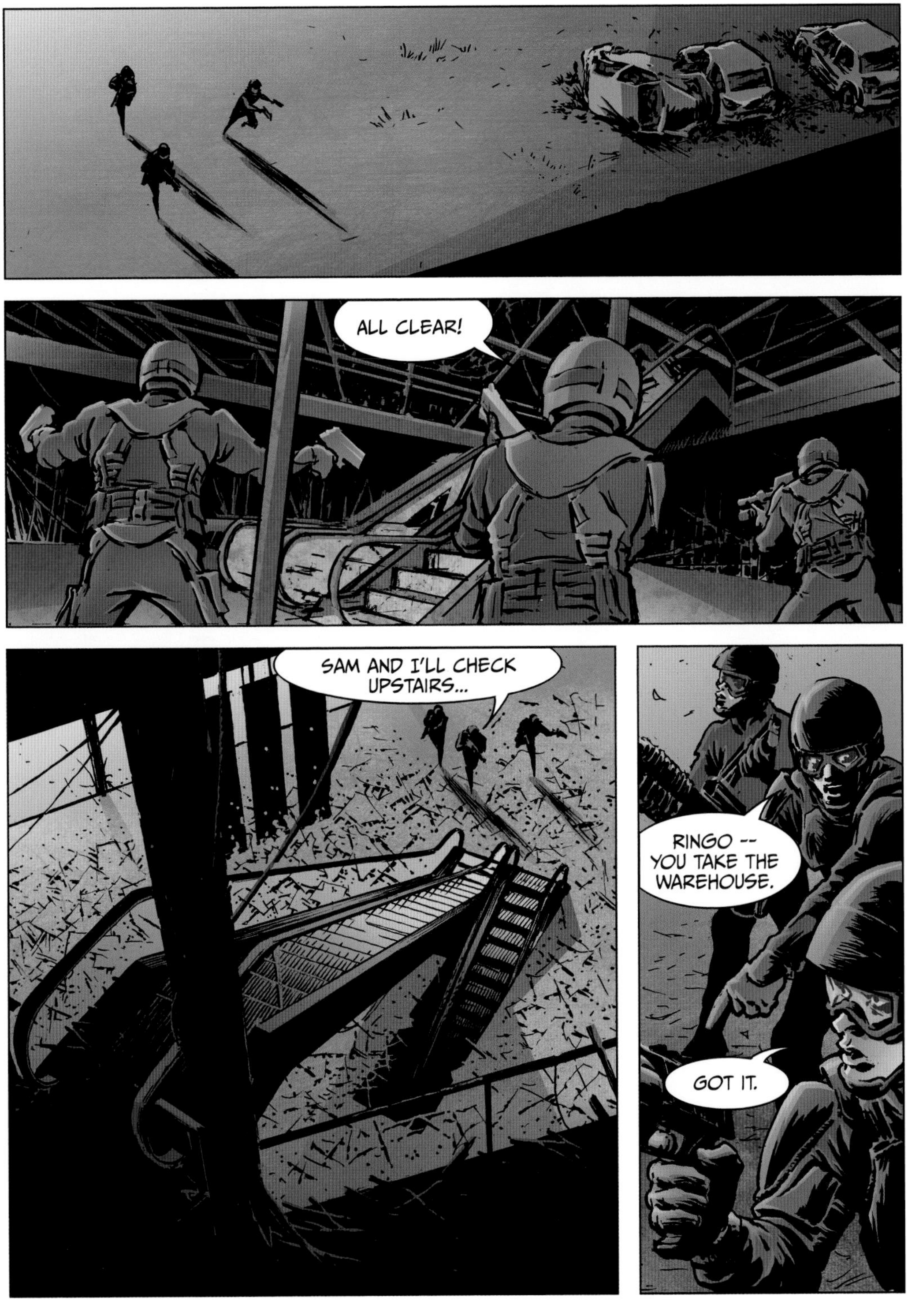
ALL CLEAR!
SAM AND I'LL CHECK UPSTAIRS...
RINGO -- YOU TAKE THE WAREHOUSE.
GOT IT.

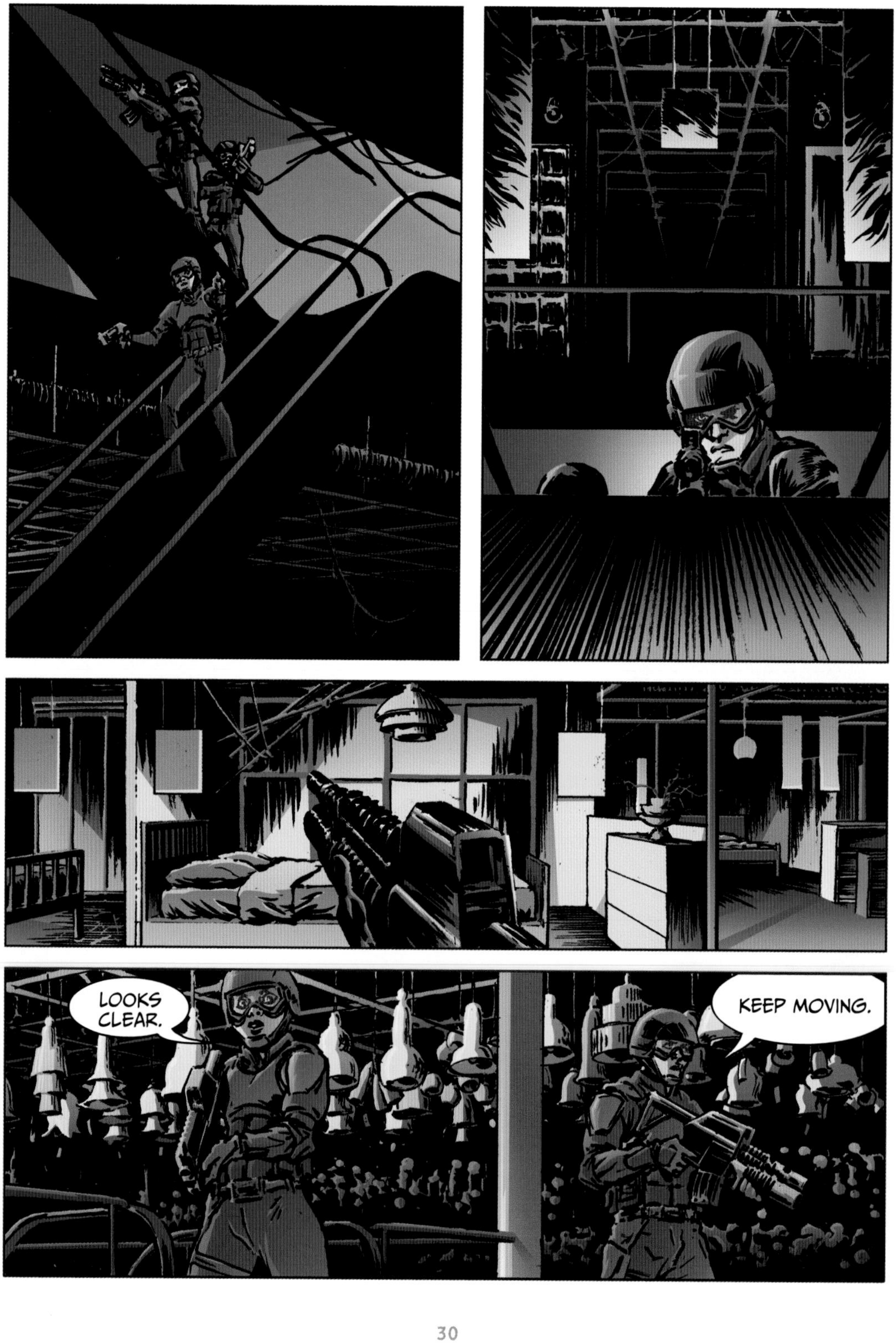
LOOKS CLEAR.
KEEP MOVING.

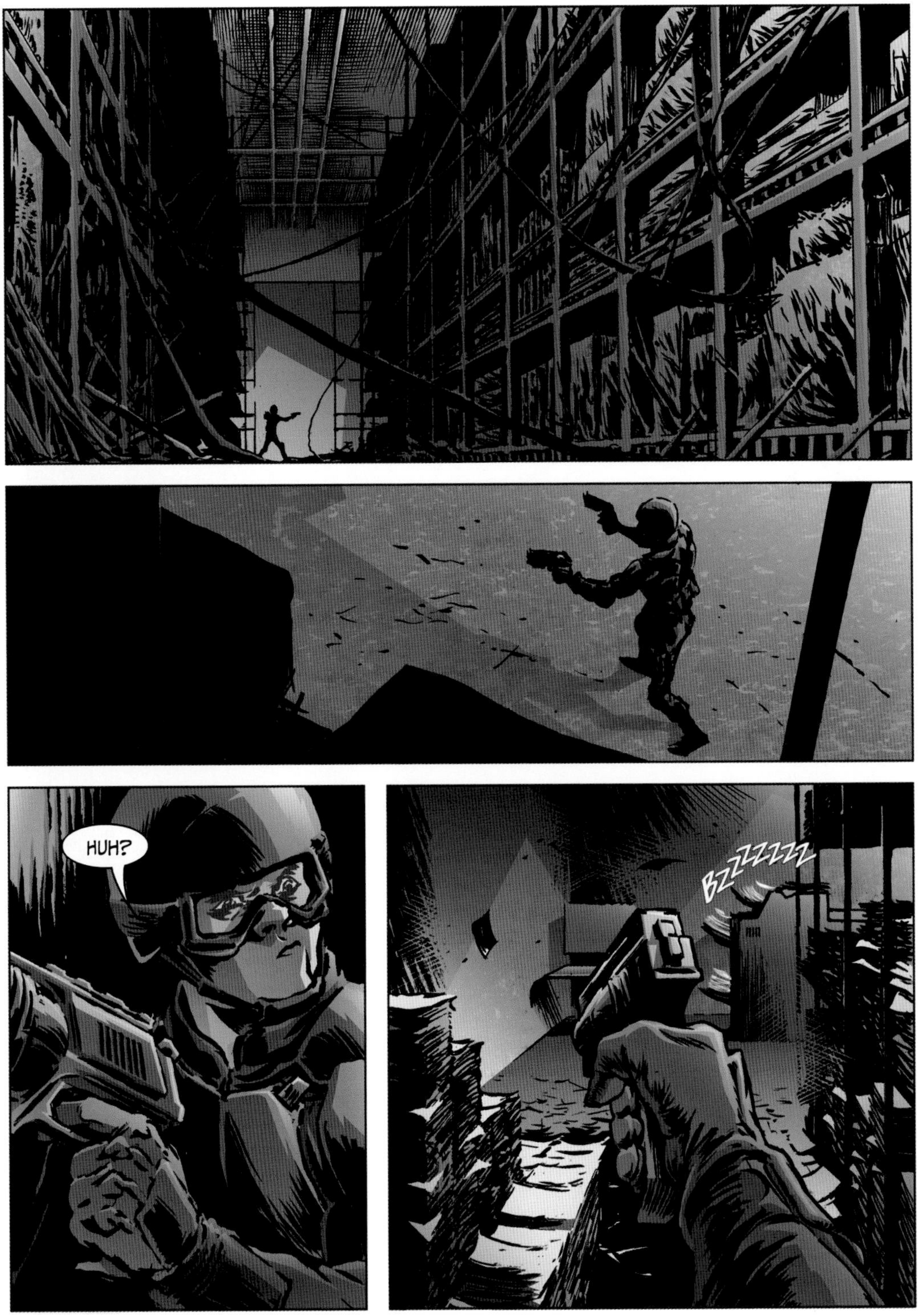
HUH?
BZZZZZZZ

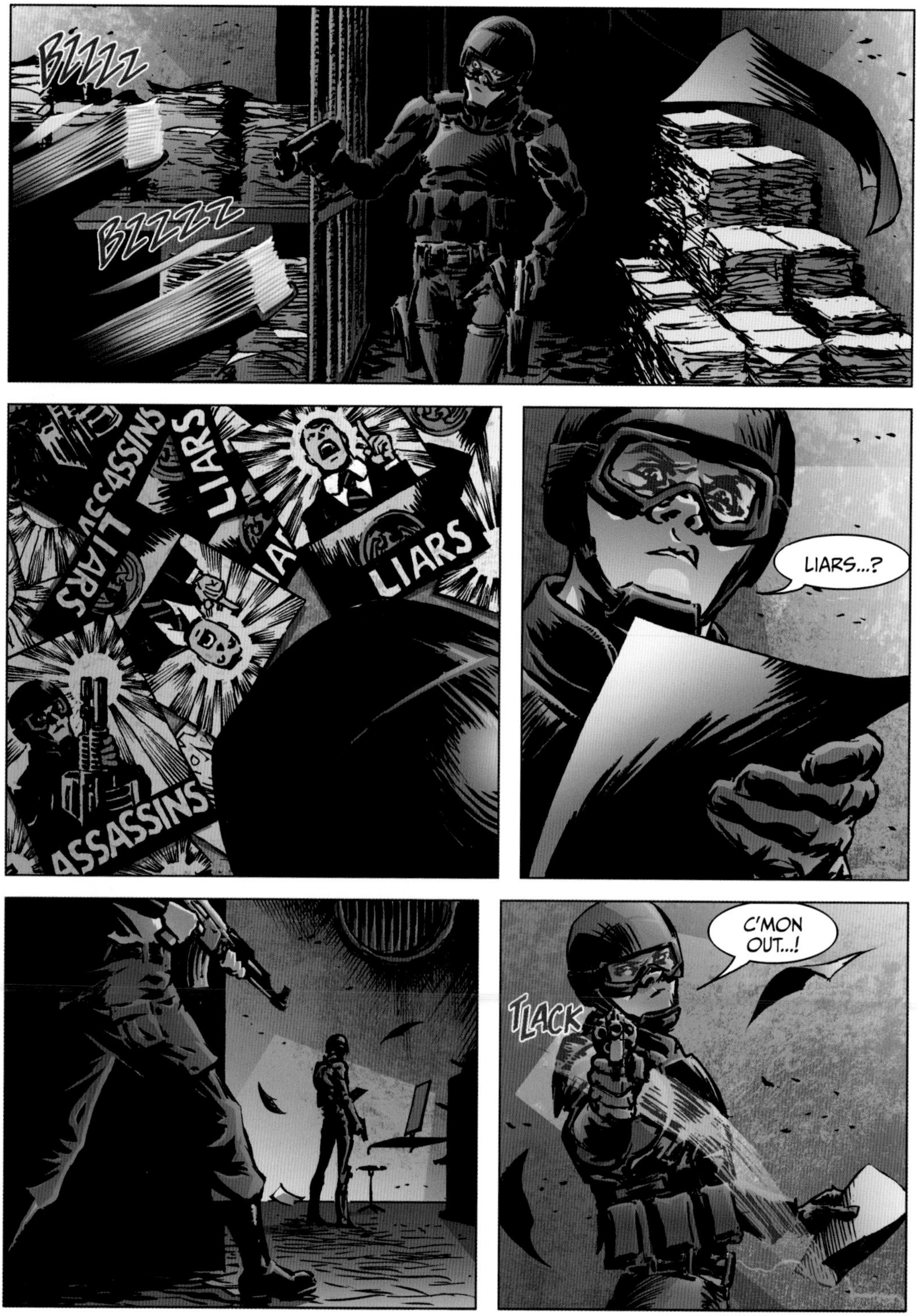
BZZZZ
BZZZZZ
ASSASSINS
LIARS
LIARS
LIARS
ASSASSINS
LIARS...?
TLACK
C'MON OUT...!

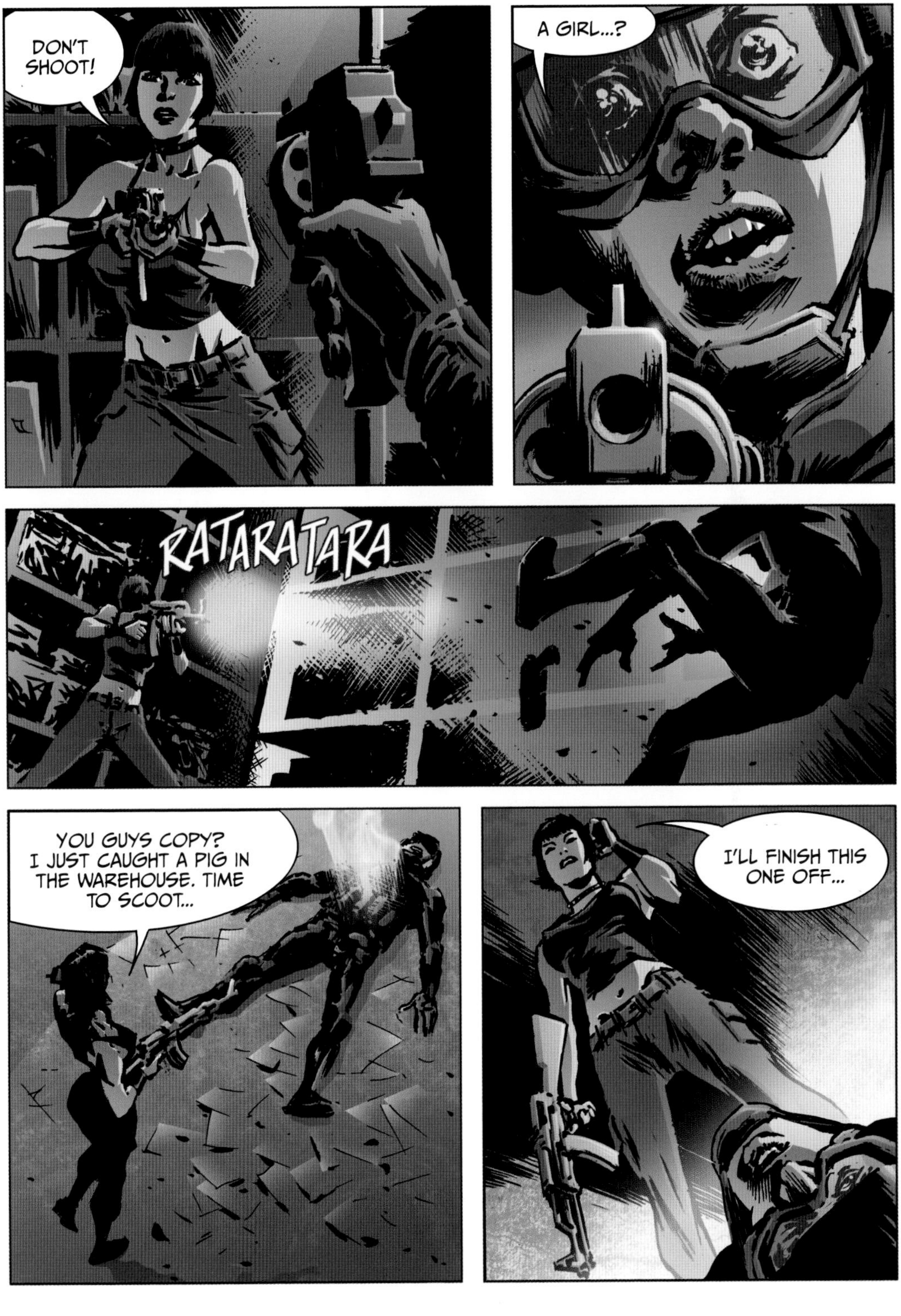
DON'T SHOOT!
A GIRL...?
RATARATARA
YOU GUYS COPY? I JUST CAUGHT A PIG IN THE WAREHOUSE. TIME TO SCOOT...
I'LL FINISH THIS ONE OFF...

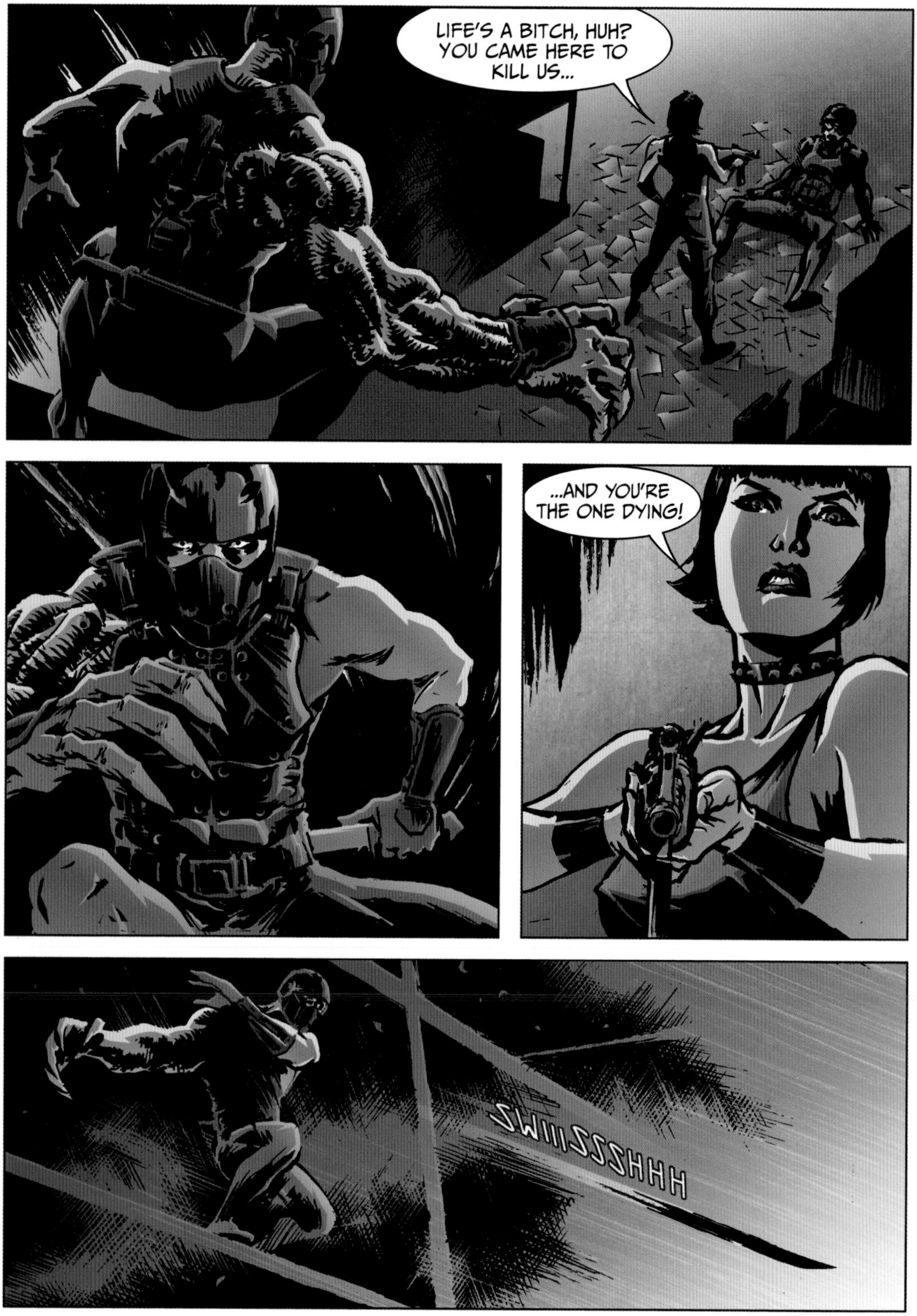
LIFE'S A BITCH, HUH? YOU CAME HERE TO KILL US...
...AND YOU'RE THE ONE DYING!
SWIIISSSHHH

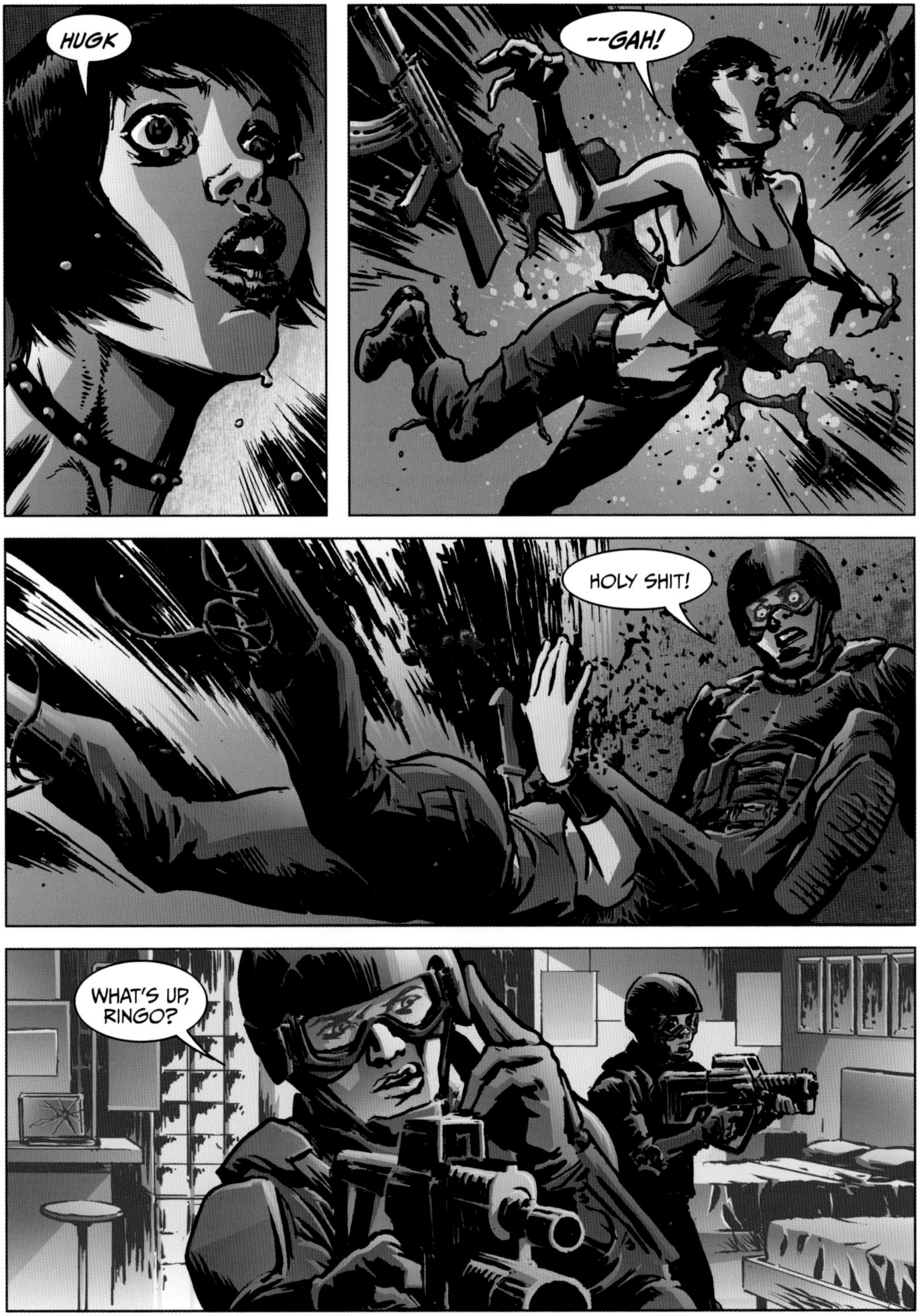
HUGK
--GAH!
HOLY SHIT!
WHAT'S UP, RINGO?

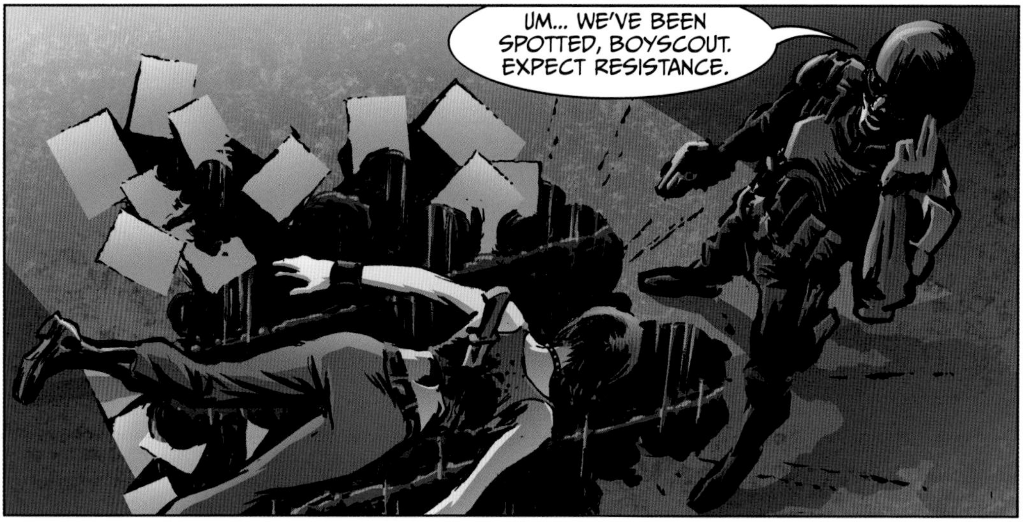
UM... WE'VE BEEN SPOTTED, BOYSCOUT. EXPECT RESISTANCE.

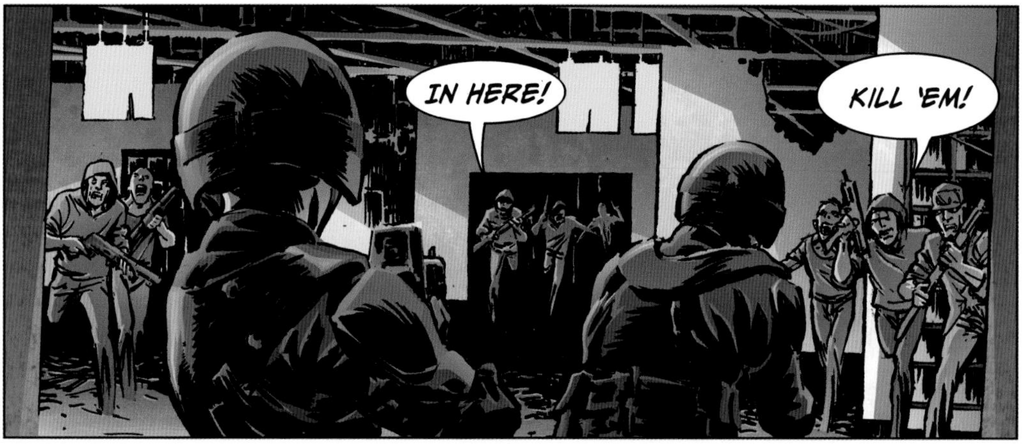
IN HERE!
KILL 'EM!

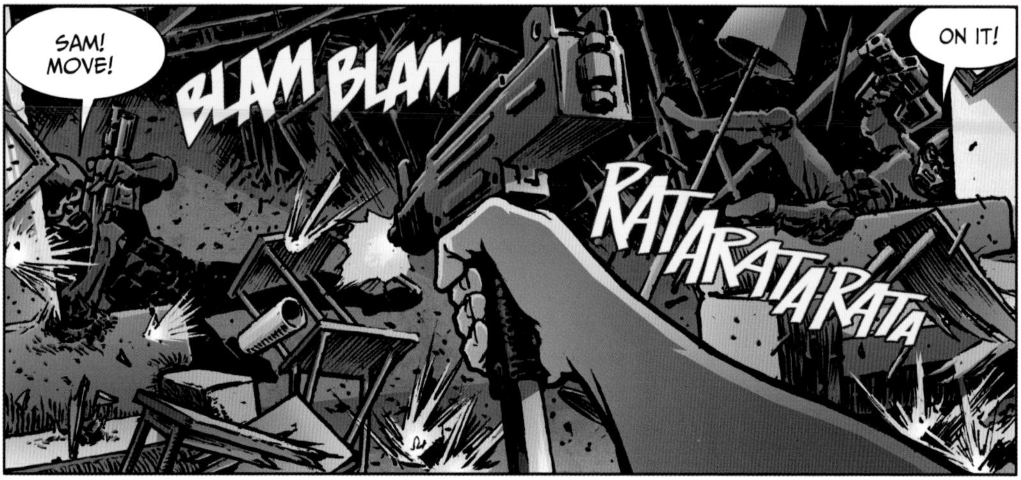
SAM! MOVE!
BLAM BLAM
ON IT!
RATATATARATATA

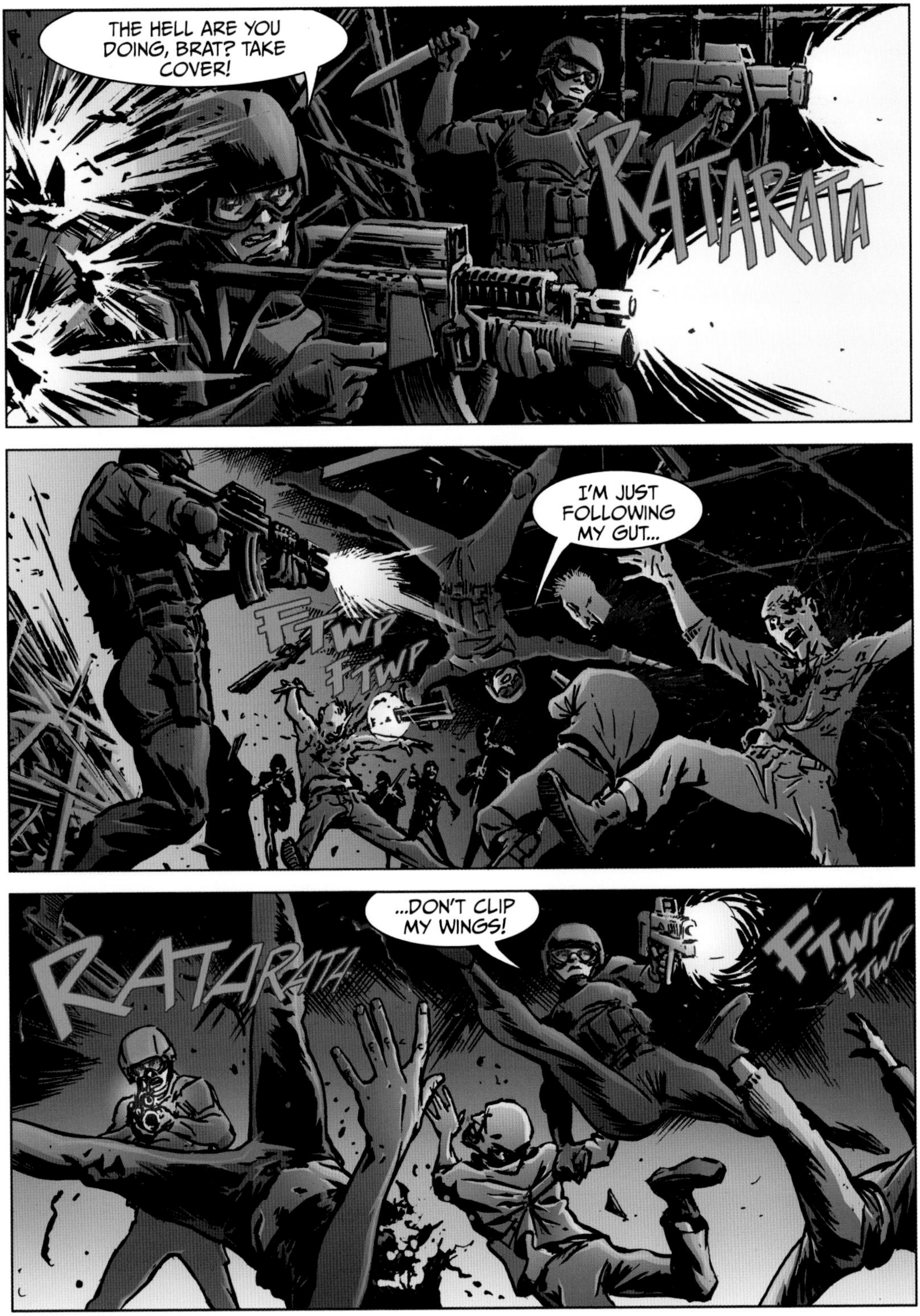
THE HELL ARE YOU DOING, BRAT? TAKE COVER!
RATARATA
I'M JUST FOLLOWING MY GUT...
FTWP
FTWP
...DON'T CLIP MY WINGS!
RATARATA
FTWP
FTWP

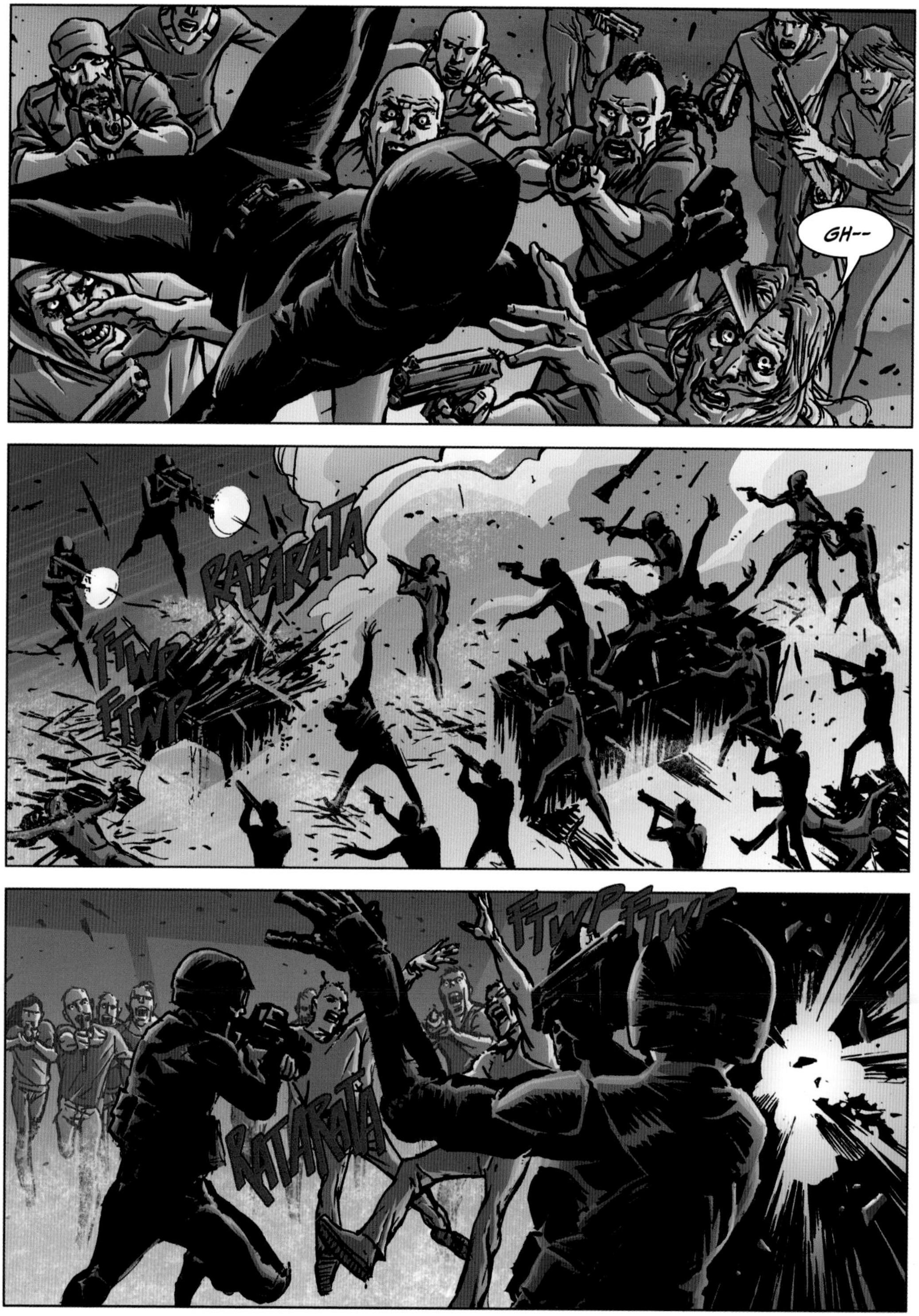
GH--
RATARATA
FTWP
FTWP
FTWP FTWP
RATARATA

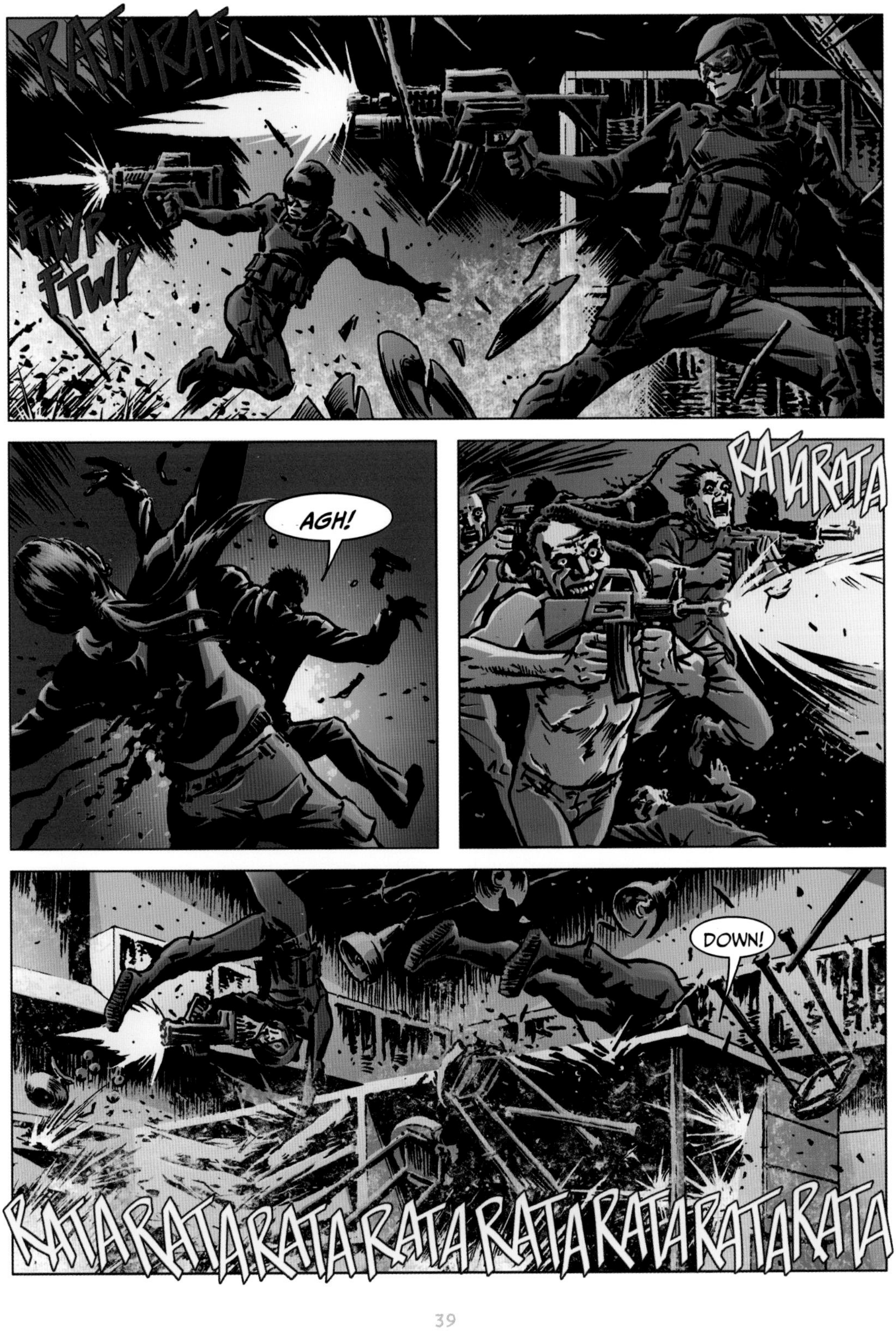
RATARATA
FTWP FTWP
AGH!
RATARATA
DOWN!
RATARATARATARATARATARATARATARATA

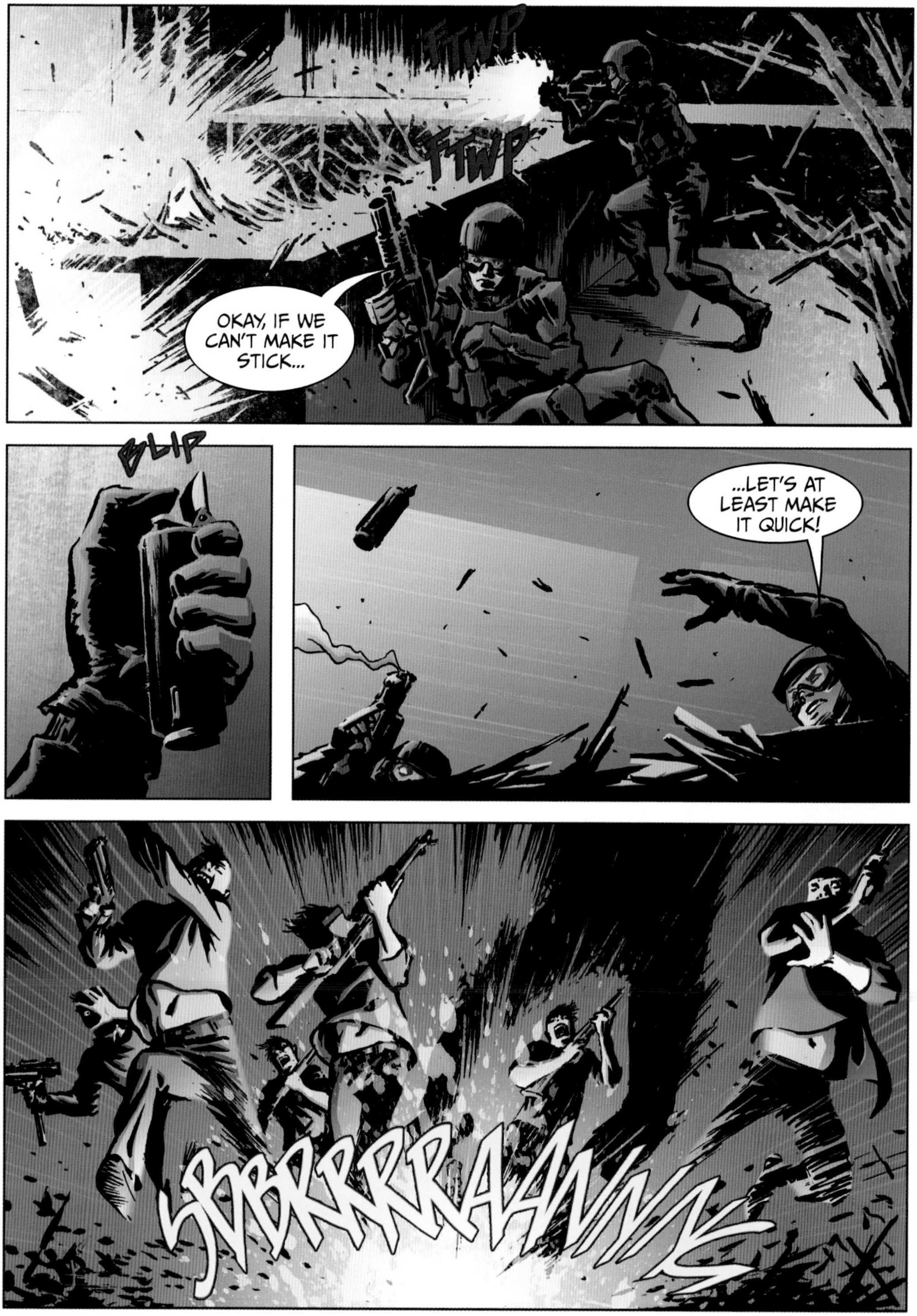
FTWP
FTWP
OKAY, IF WE CAN'T MAKE IT STICK...
BLIP
...LET'S AT LEAST MAKE IT QUICK!
SPBRRRAANNK

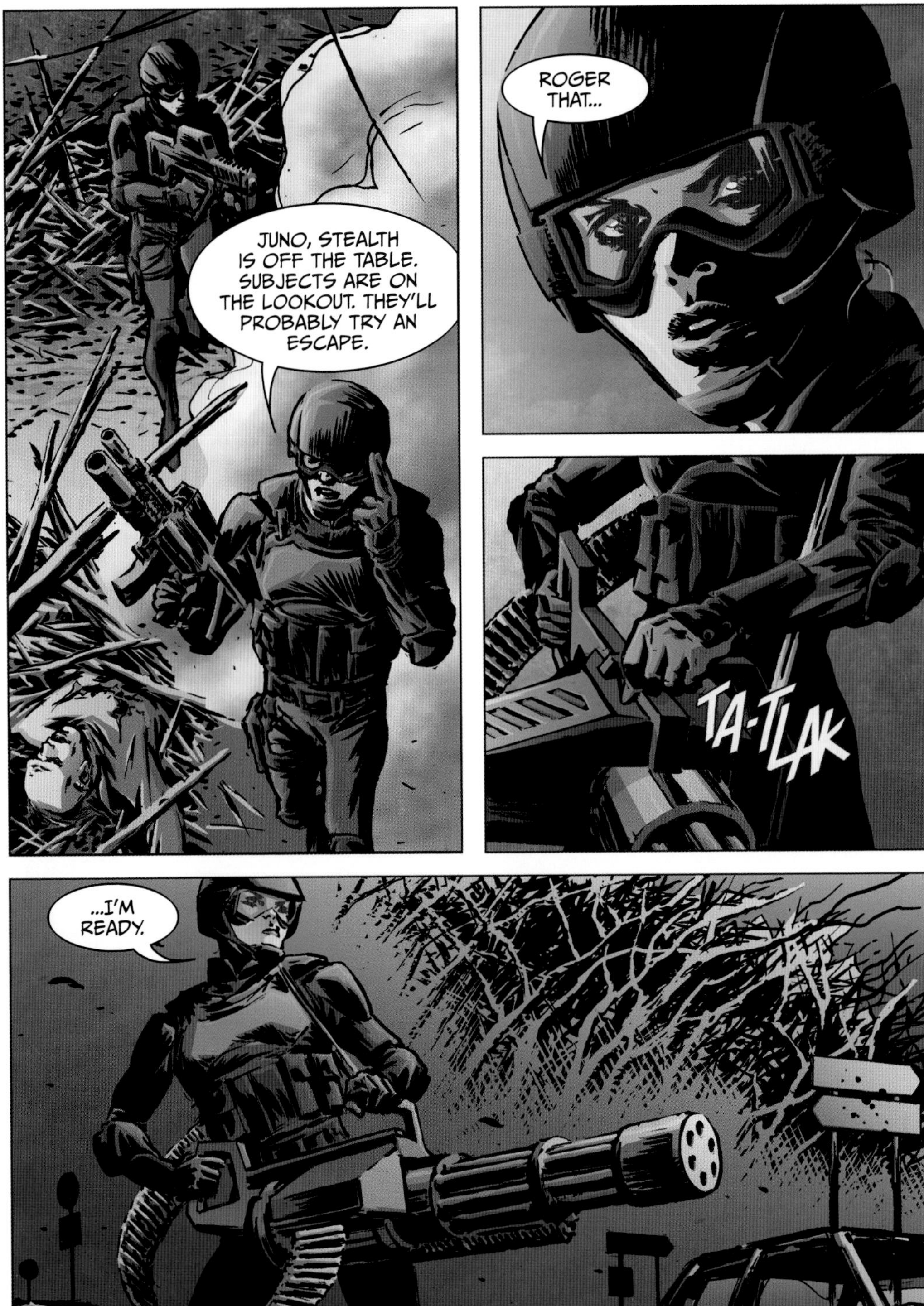
JUNO, STEALTH IS OFF THE TABLE. SUBJECTS ARE ON THE LOOKOUT. THEY'LL PROBABLY TRY AN ESCAPE.
ROGER THAT...
TA-TLAK
...I'M READY.

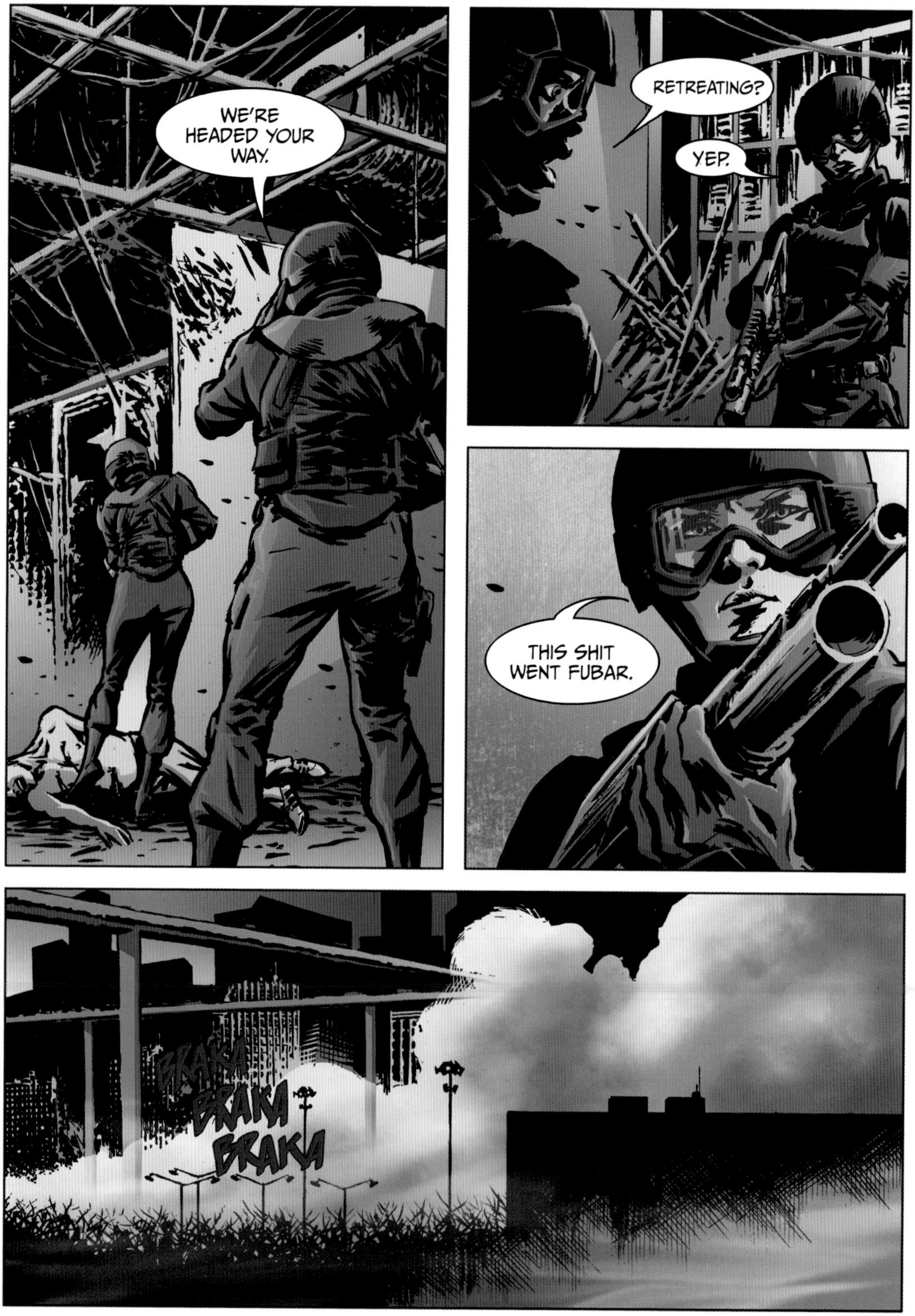
WE'RE HEADED YOUR WAY.
RETREATING?
YEP.
THIS SHIT WENT FUBAR.
BRAKA
BRAKA
BRAKA

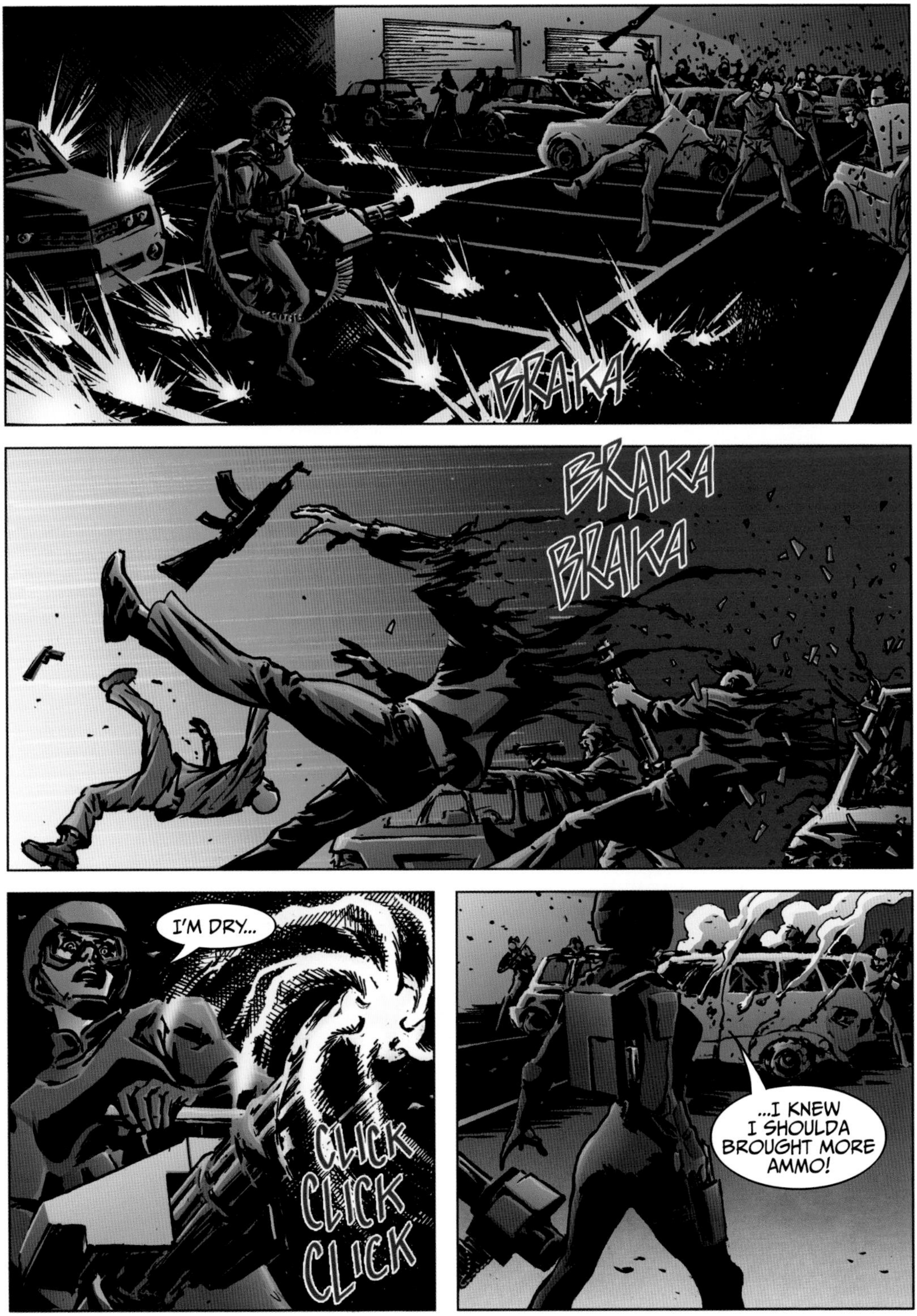
BRAKA
BRAKA
BRAKA
I'M DRY...
CLICK
CLICK
CLICK
...I KNEW I SHOULDA BROUGHT MORE AMMO!

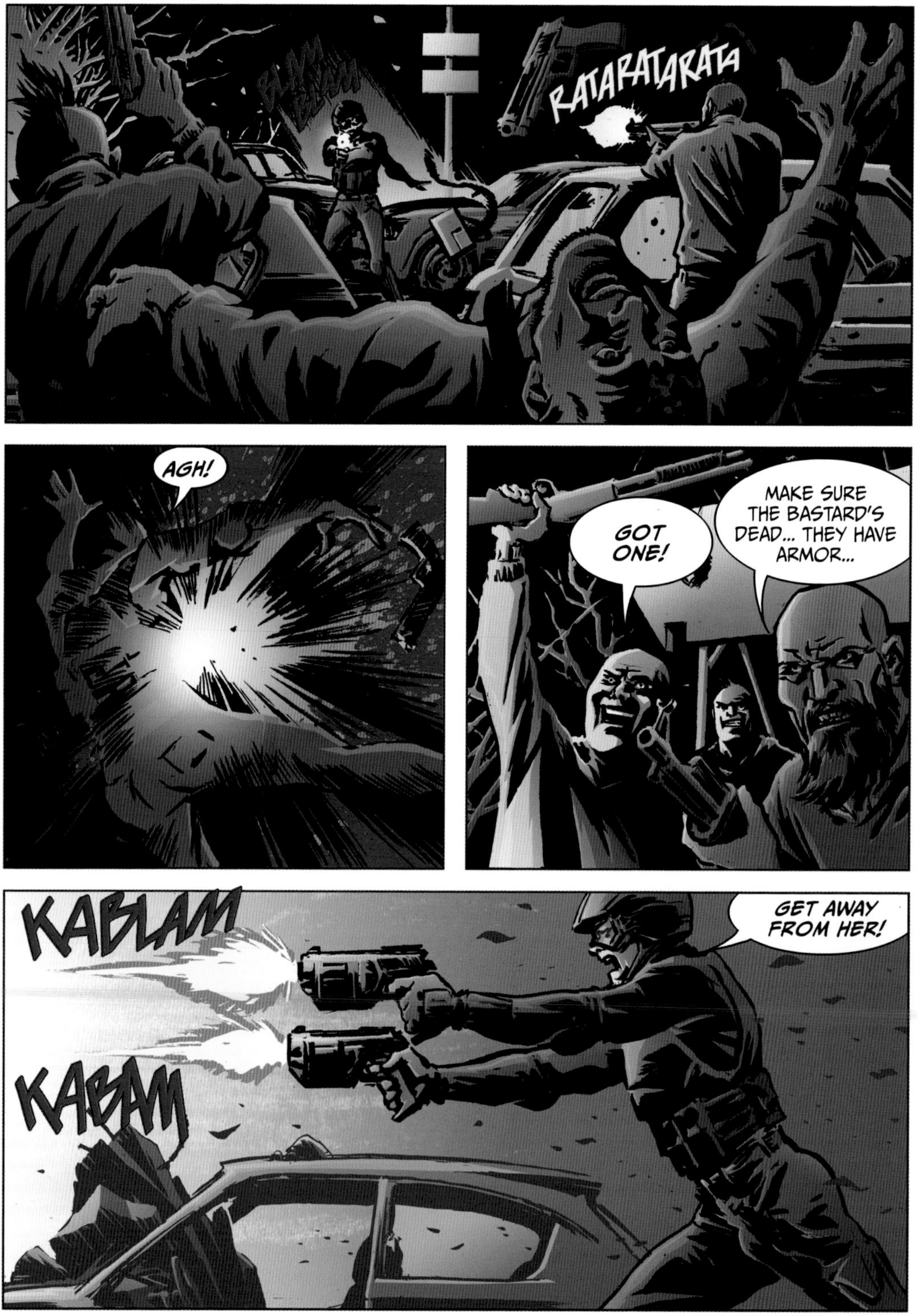
RATARATARATA
AGH!
GOT ONE!
MAKE SURE THE BASTARD'S DEAD... THEY HAVE ARMOR...
KABLAM
KABAM
GET AWAY FROM HER!

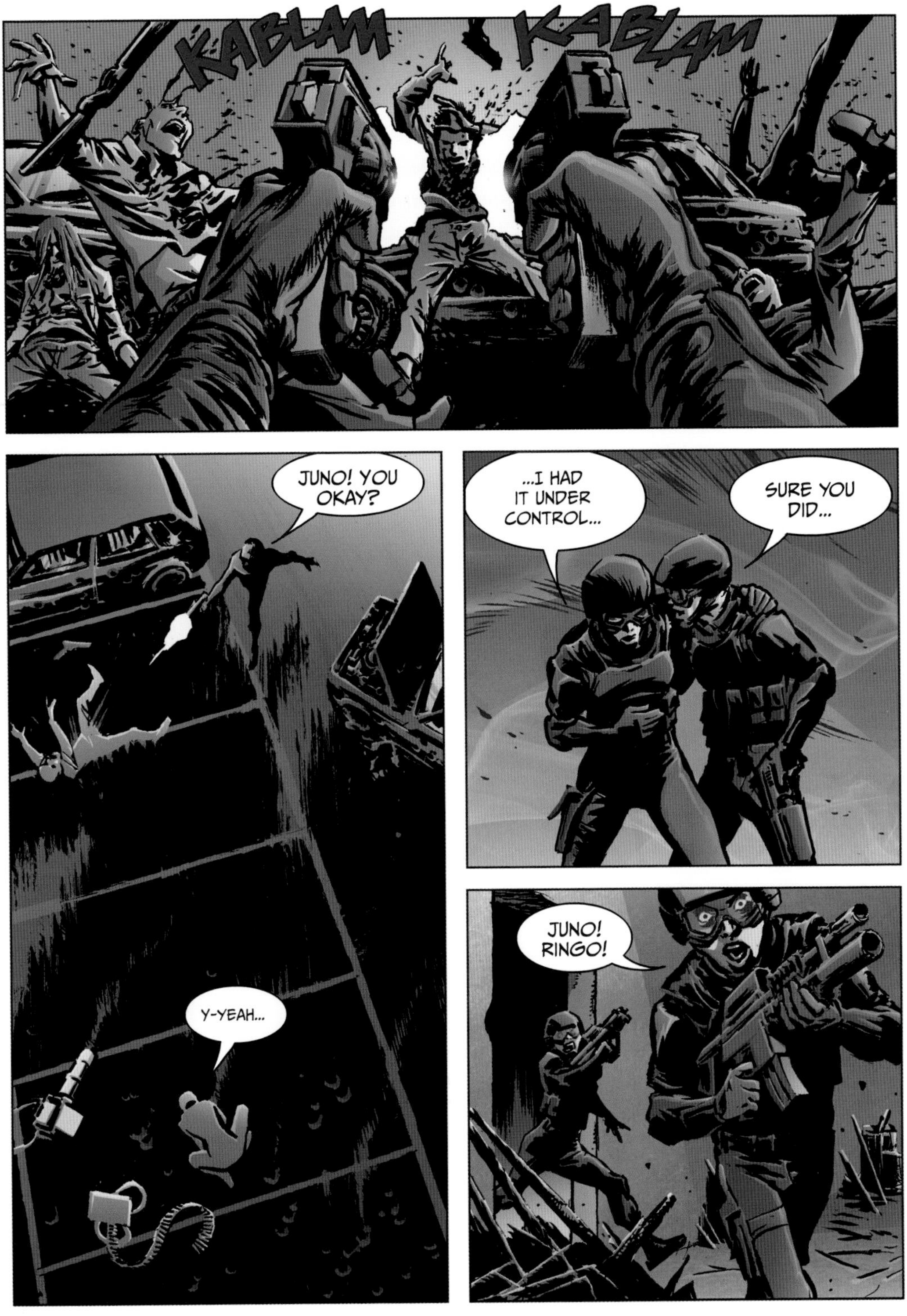
KABLAM
KABLAM
JUNO! YOU OKAY?
Y-YEAH...
...I HAD IT UNDER CONTROL...
SURE YOU DID...
JUNO! RINGO!

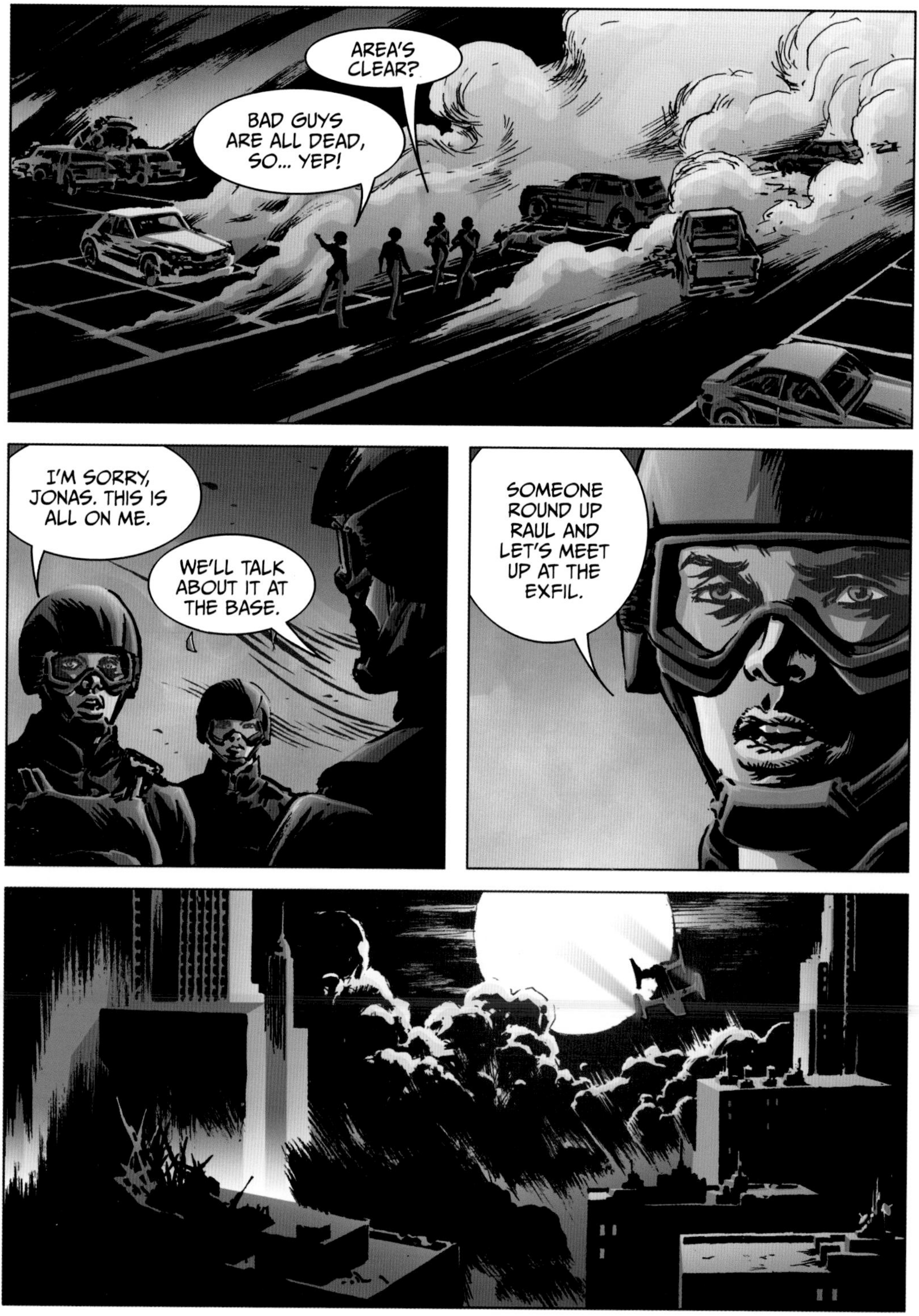
AREA'S CLEAR?
BAD GUYS ARE ALL DEAD, SO... YEP!
I'M SORRY, JONAS. THIS IS ALL ON ME.
WE'LL TALK ABOUT IT AT THE BASE.
SOMEONE ROUND UP RAUL AND LET'S MEET UP AT THE EXFIL.

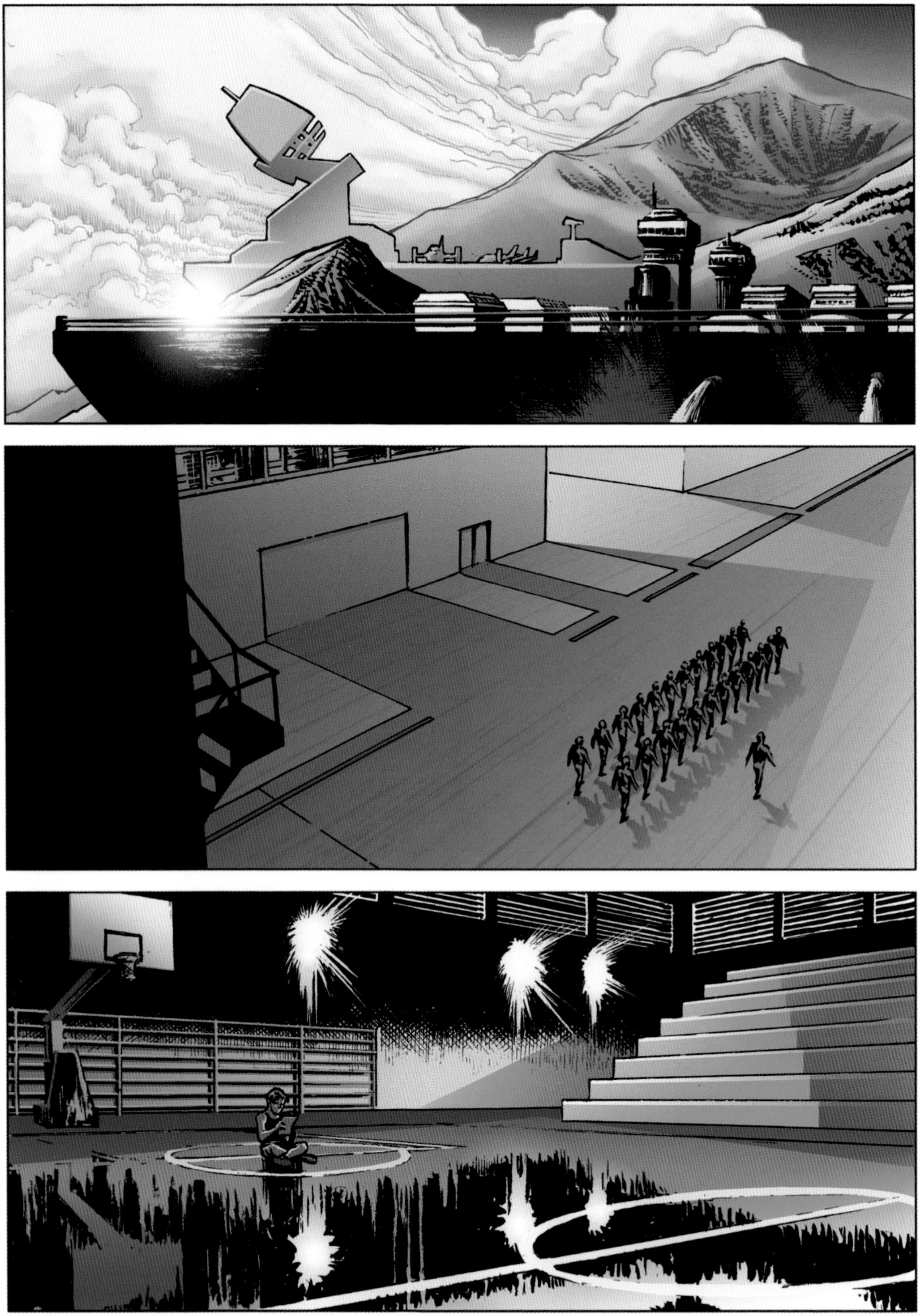

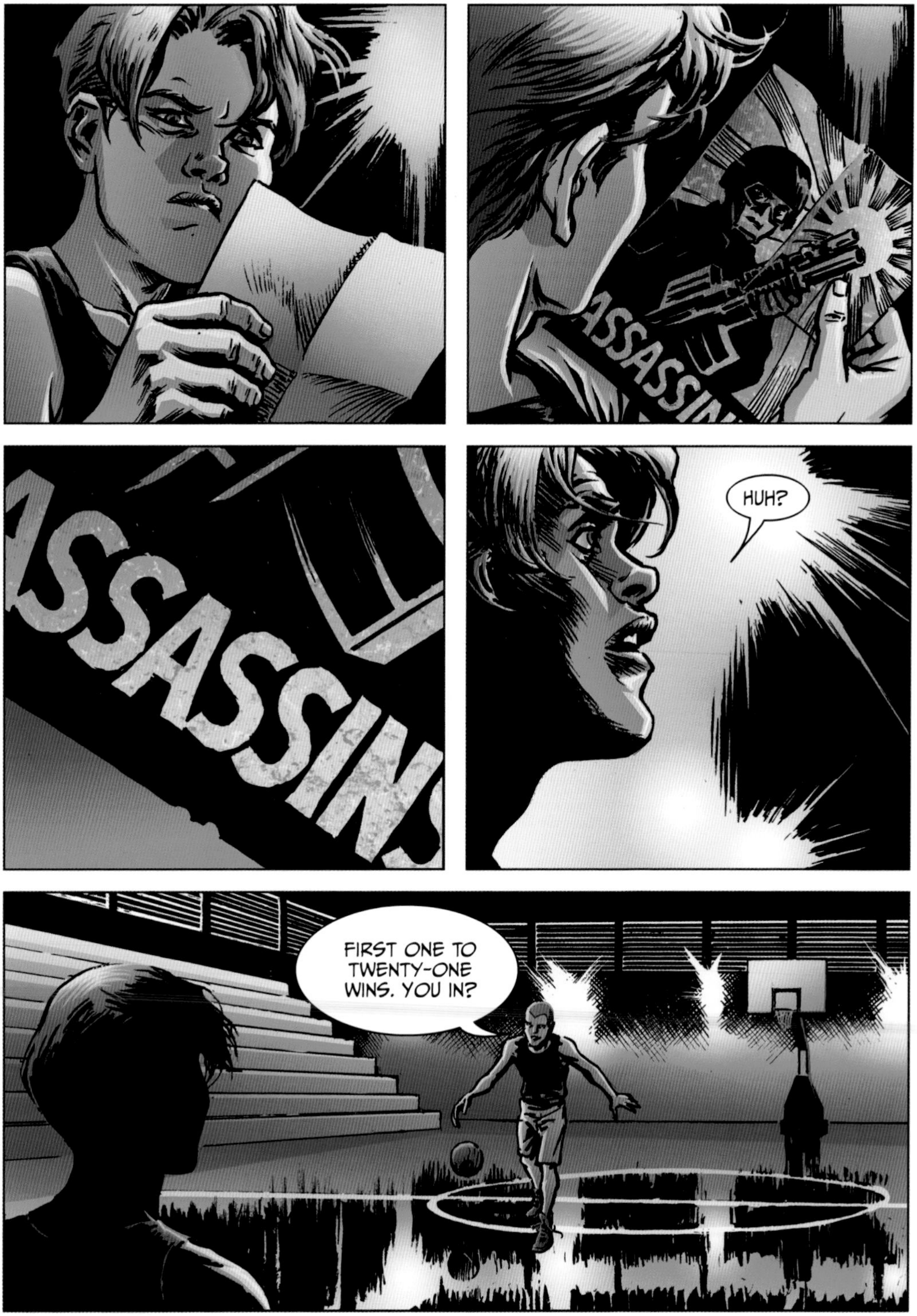
ASSASSIN
ASSASSIN
HUH?
FIRST ONE TO TWENTY-ONE WINS. YOU IN?

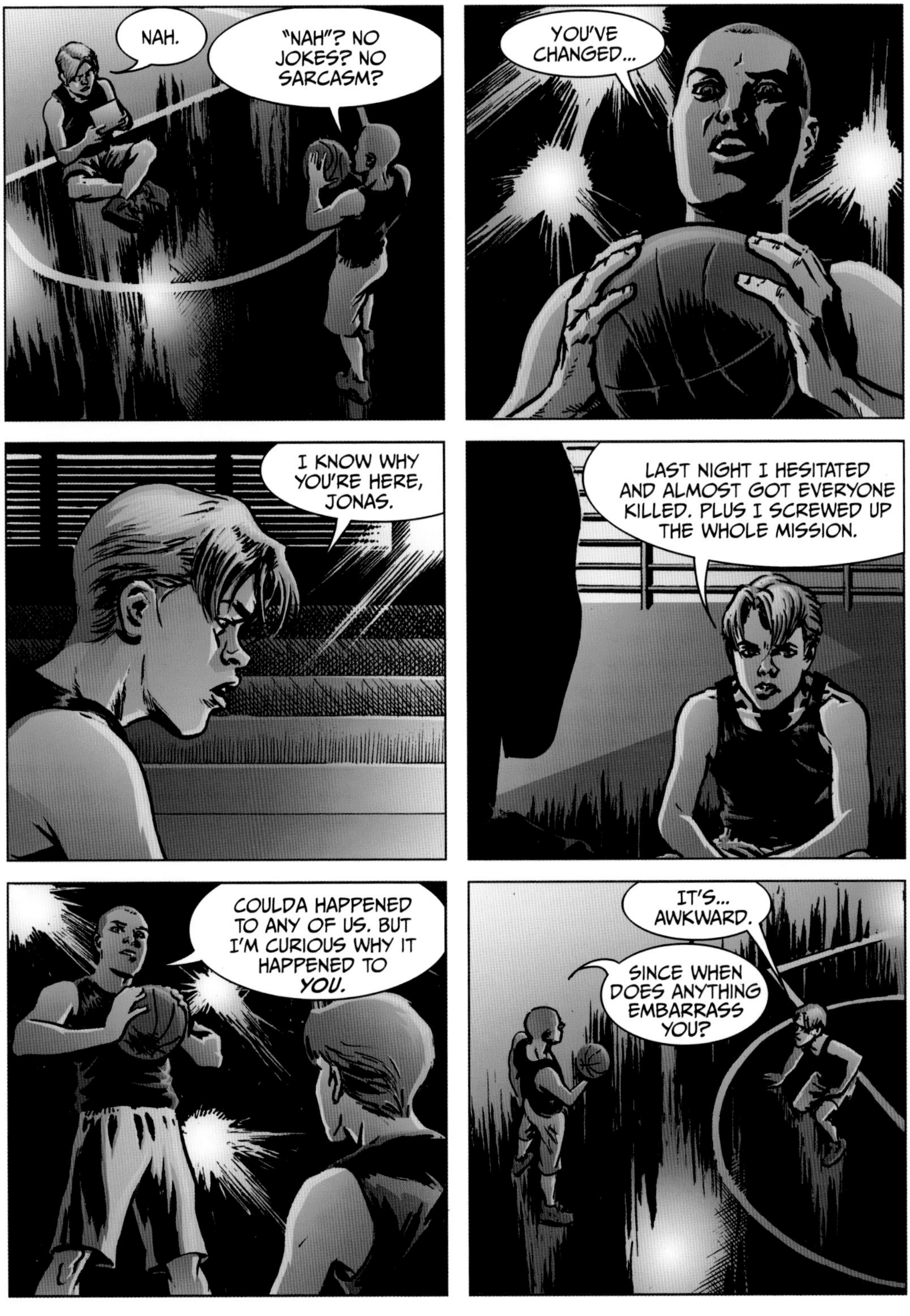
NAH.
"NAH"? NO JOKES? NO SARCASM?
YOU'VE CHANGED...
I KNOW WHY YOU'RE HERE, JONAS.
LAST NIGHT I HESITATED AND ALMOST GOT EVERYONE KILLED. PLUS I SCREWED UP THE WHOLE MISSION.
COULDA HAPPENED TO ANY OF US. BUT I'M CURIOUS WHY IT HAPPENED TO *YOU*.
IT'S... AWKWARD.
SINCE WHEN DOES ANYTHING EMBARRASS YOU?

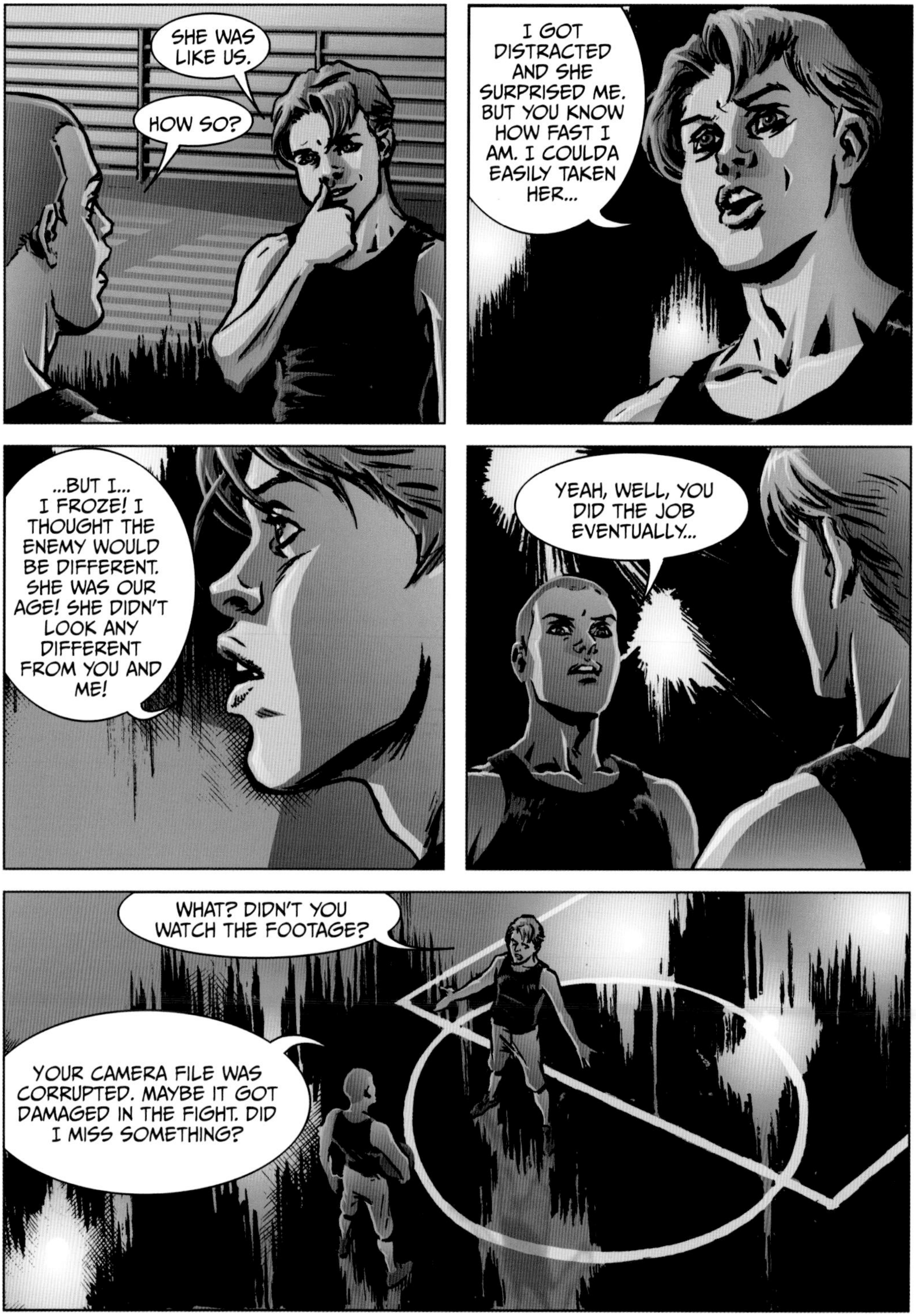
SHE WAS LIKE US.
HOW SO?
I GOT DISTRACTED AND SHE SURPRISED ME. BUT YOU KNOW HOW FAST I AM. I COULDA EASILY TAKEN HER...
...BUT I... I FROZE! I THOUGHT THE ENEMY WOULD BE DIFFERENT. SHE WAS OUR AGE! SHE DIDN'T LOOK ANY DIFFERENT FROM YOU AND ME!
YEAH, WELL, YOU DID THE JOB EVENTUALLY...
WHAT? DIDN'T YOU WATCH THE FOOTAGE?
YOUR CAMERA FILE WAS CORRUPTED. MAYBE IT GOT DAMAGED IN THE FIGHT. DID I MISS SOMETHING?

SHE HAD ME, JONAS! IF SOMEBODY HADN'T PUT A KNIFE IN HER BACK, I'D BE DEAD!

WHAT? WHO?

I DUNNO. I THOUGHT IT WAS SAM, BUT SHE WAS WITH YOU THE WHOLE TIME.

YEAH. AND JUNO AND RAUL WERE IN POSITION TOO...

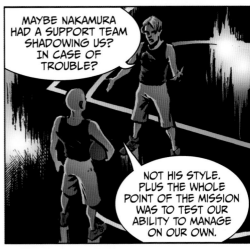

MAYBE NAKAMURA HAD A SUPPORT TEAM SHADOWING US? IN CASE OF TROUBLE?

NOT HIS STYLE. PLUS THE WHOLE POINT OF THE MISSION WAS TO TEST OUR ABILITY TO MANAGE ON OUR OWN.

THEN I'VE GOT NO IDEA. YOU'RE THE BRAINS, MAN. I JUST SHOOT STUFF.

CAN YOU KEEP DOING THAT?

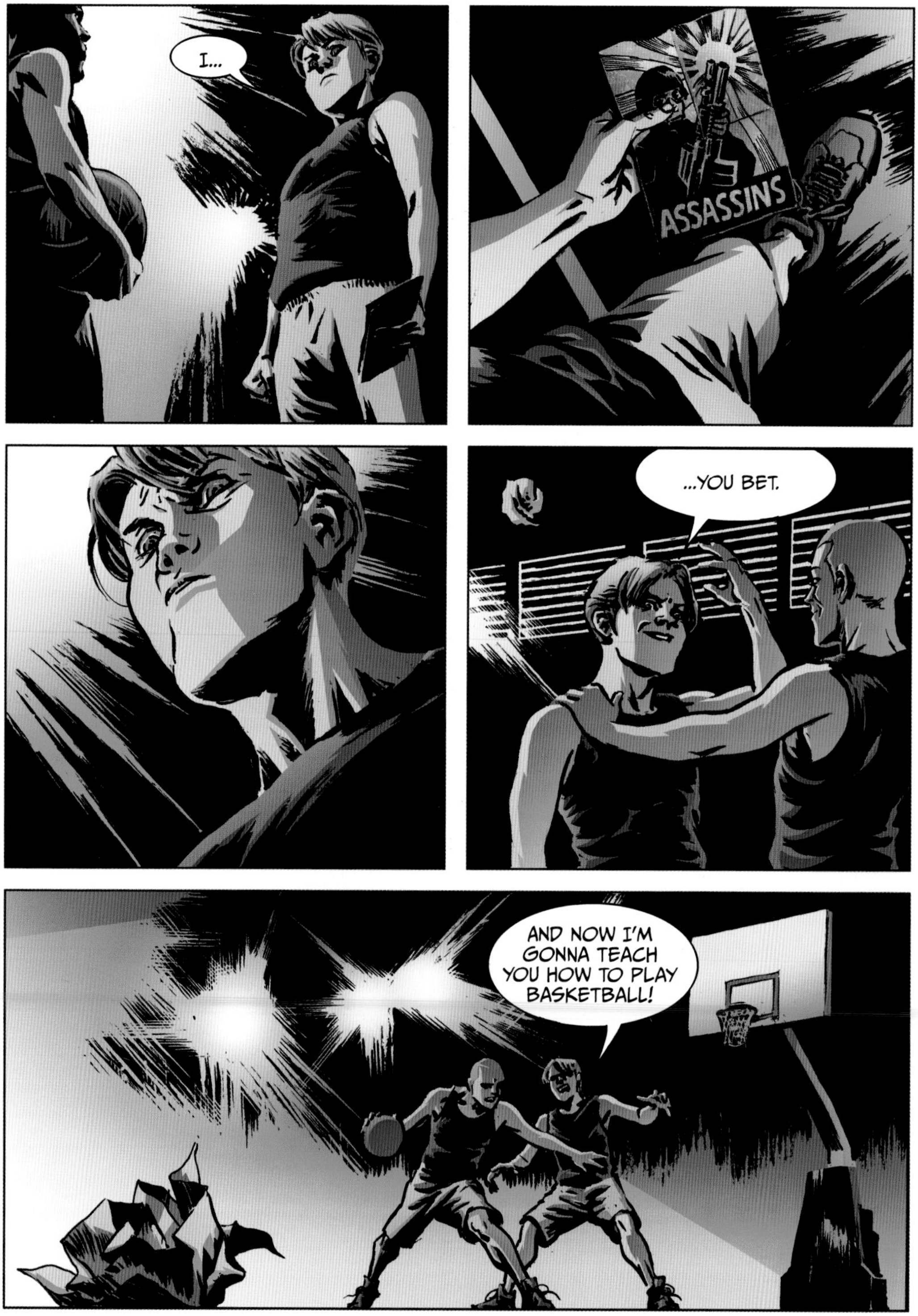
I...
ASSASSINS
...YOU BET.
AND NOW I'M GONNA TEACH YOU HOW TO PLAY BASKETBALL!

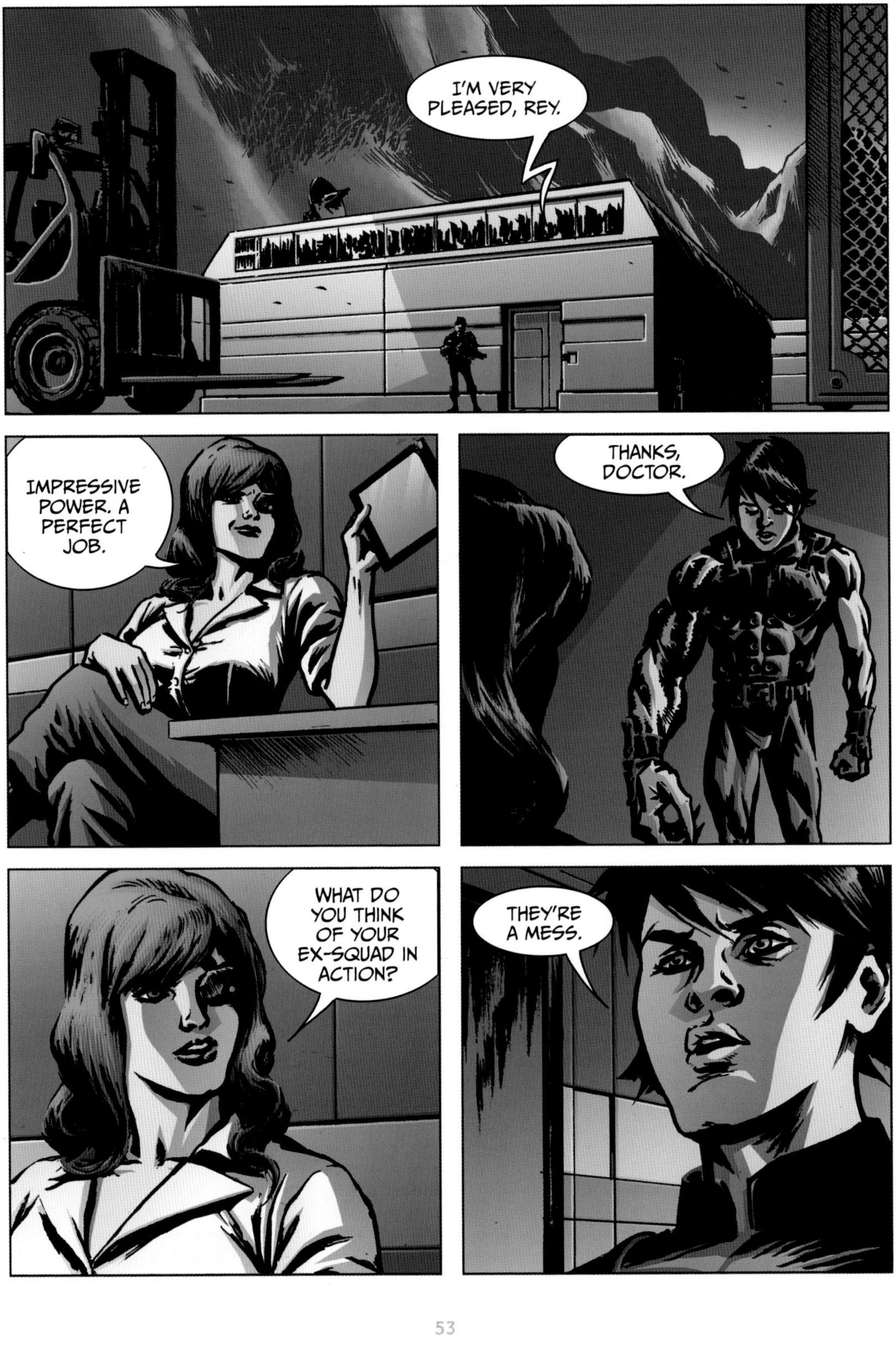
I'M VERY PLEASED, REY.
IMPRESSIVE POWER. A PERFECT JOB.
THANKS, DOCTOR.
WHAT DO YOU THINK OF YOUR EX-SQUAD IN ACTION?
THEY'RE A MESS.

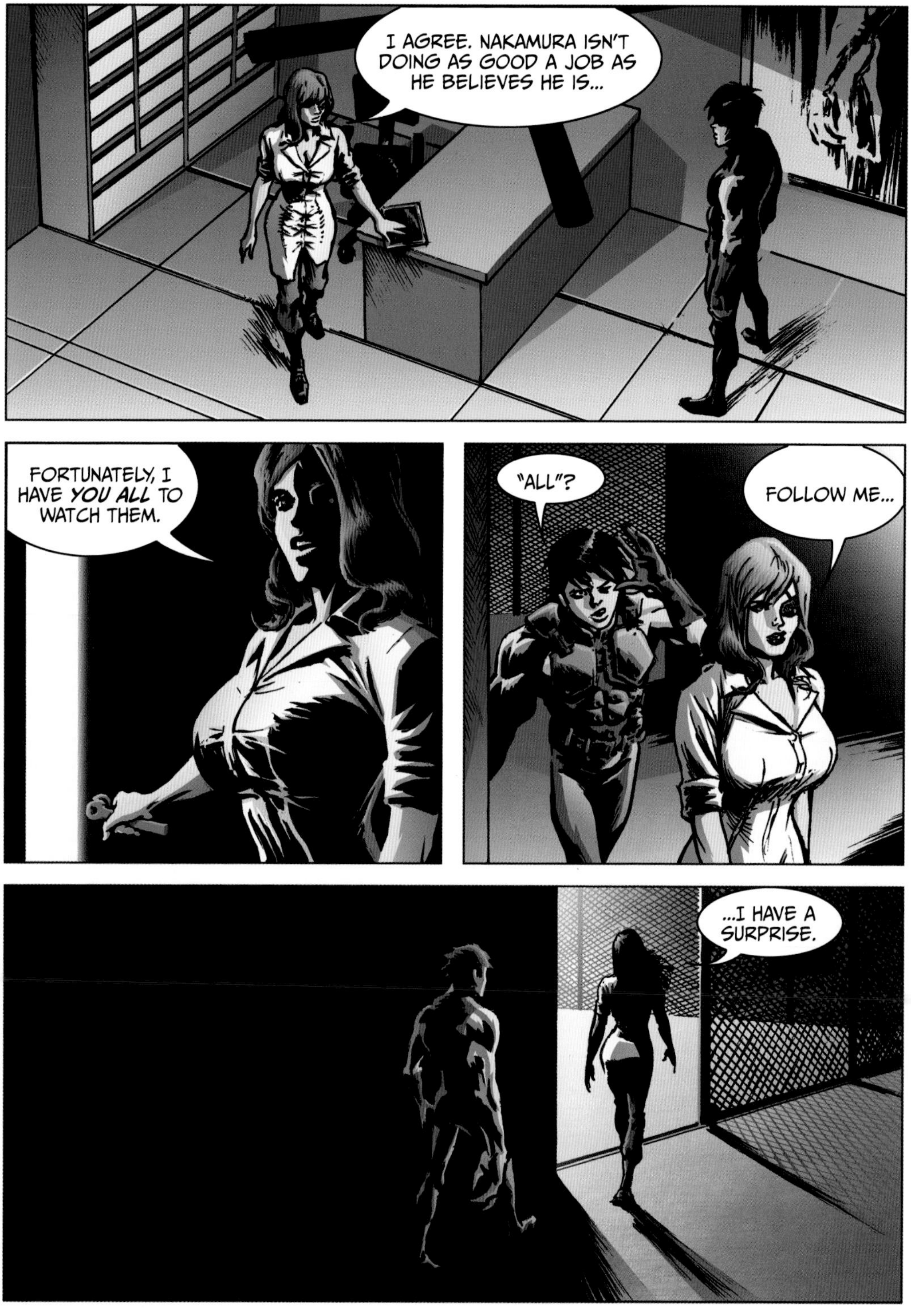
I AGREE. NAKAMURA ISN'T DOING AS GOOD A JOB AS HE BELIEVES HE IS...
FORTUNATELY, I HAVE *YOU ALL* TO WATCH THEM.
"ALL"?
FOLLOW ME...
...I HAVE A SURPRISE.

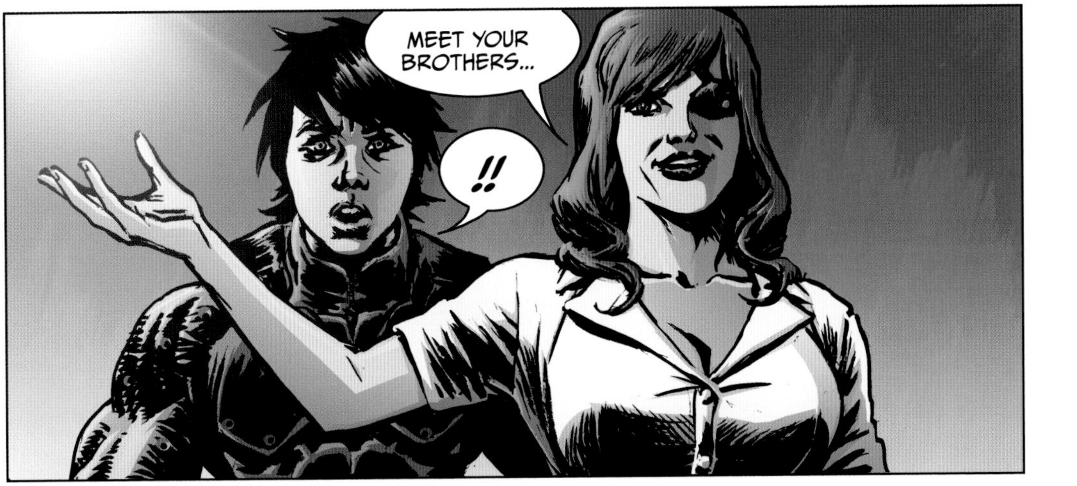
MEET YOUR BROTHERS...
!!

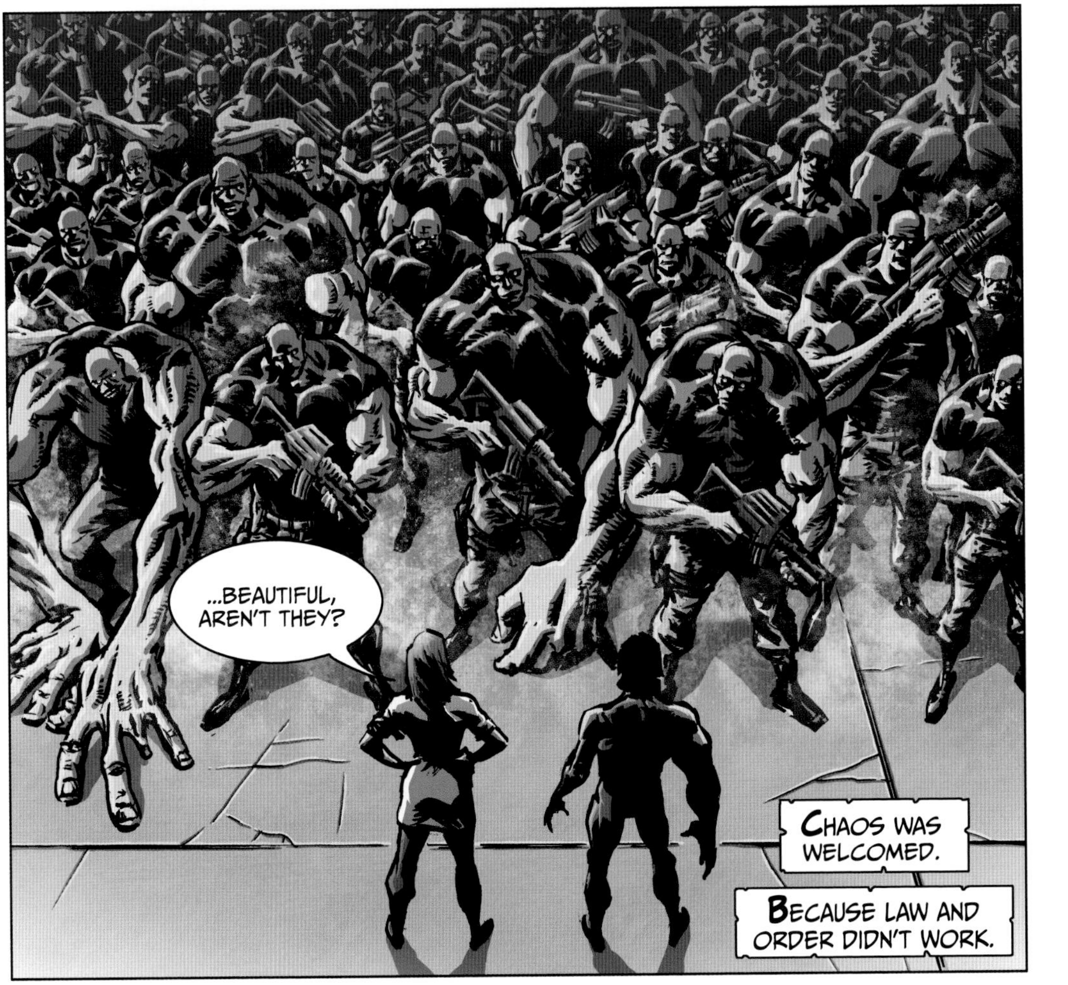
...BEAUTIFUL, AREN'T THEY?
CHAOS WAS WELCOMED.
BECAUSE LAW AND ORDER DIDN'T WORK.

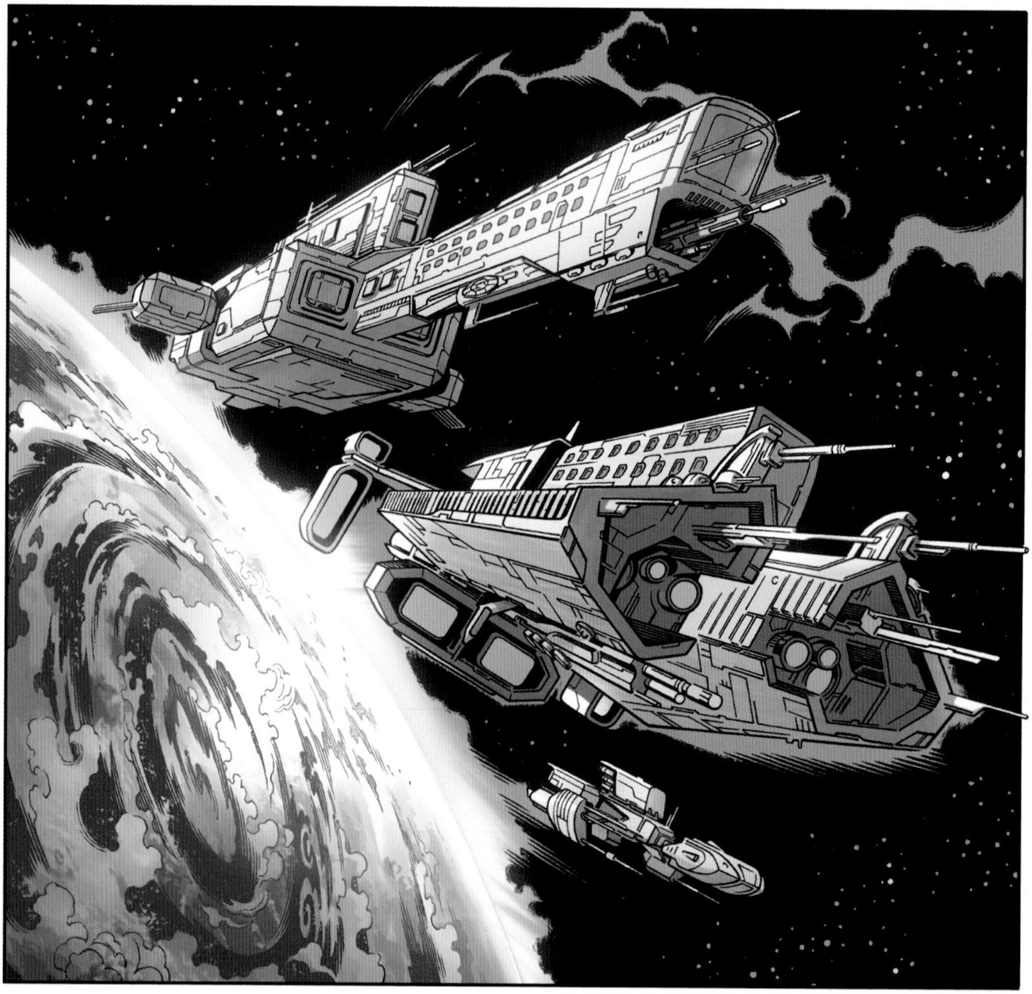

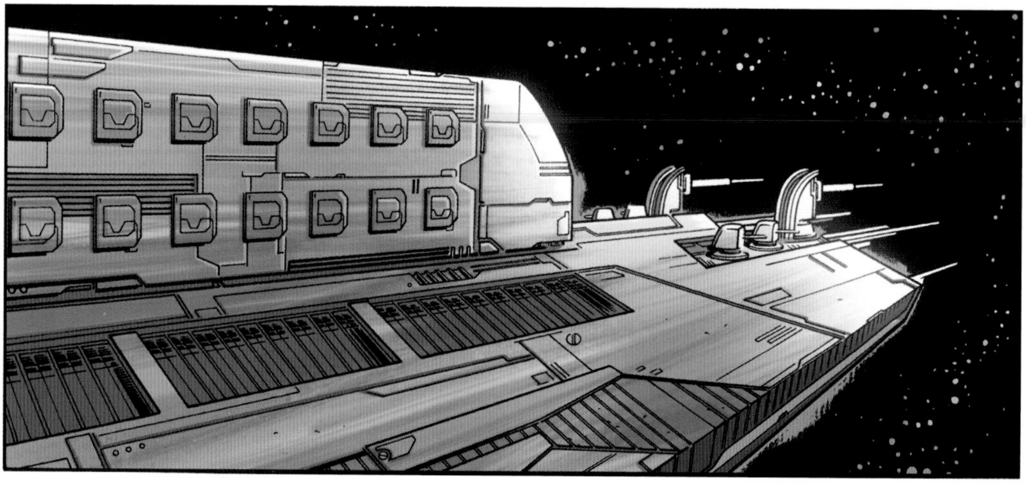

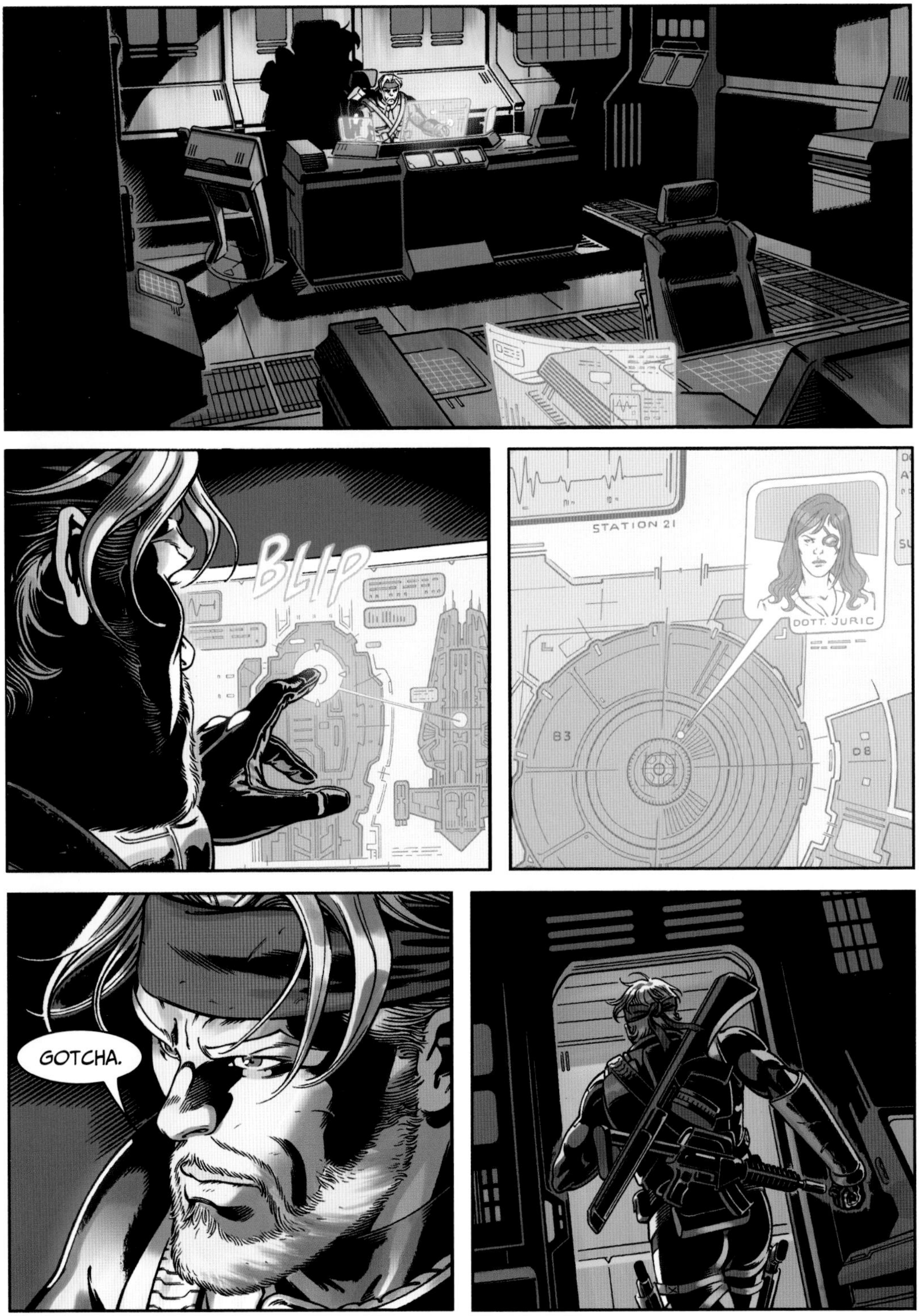
BLIP
STATION 21
DOTT. JURIC
B3
D8
GOTCHA.

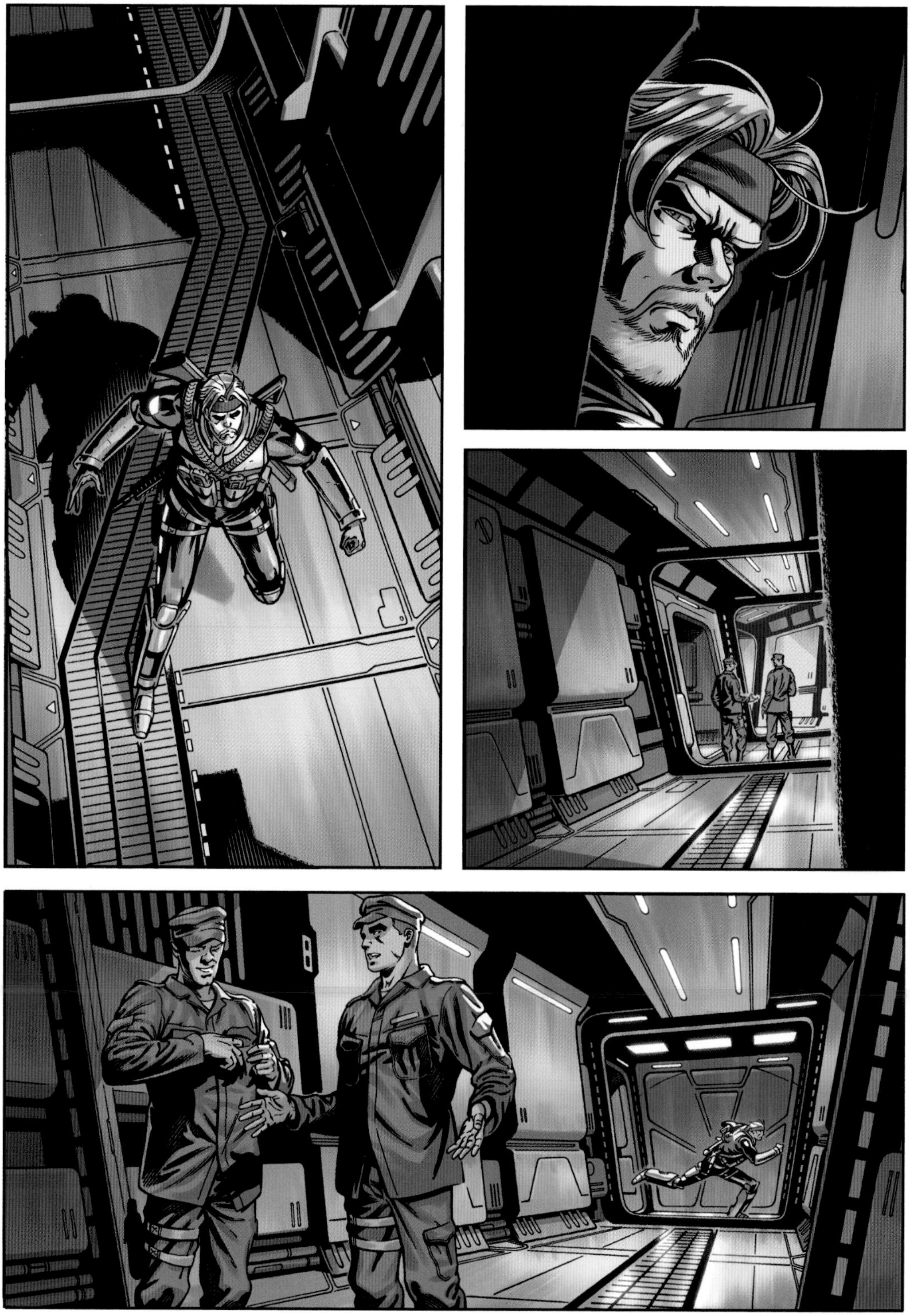

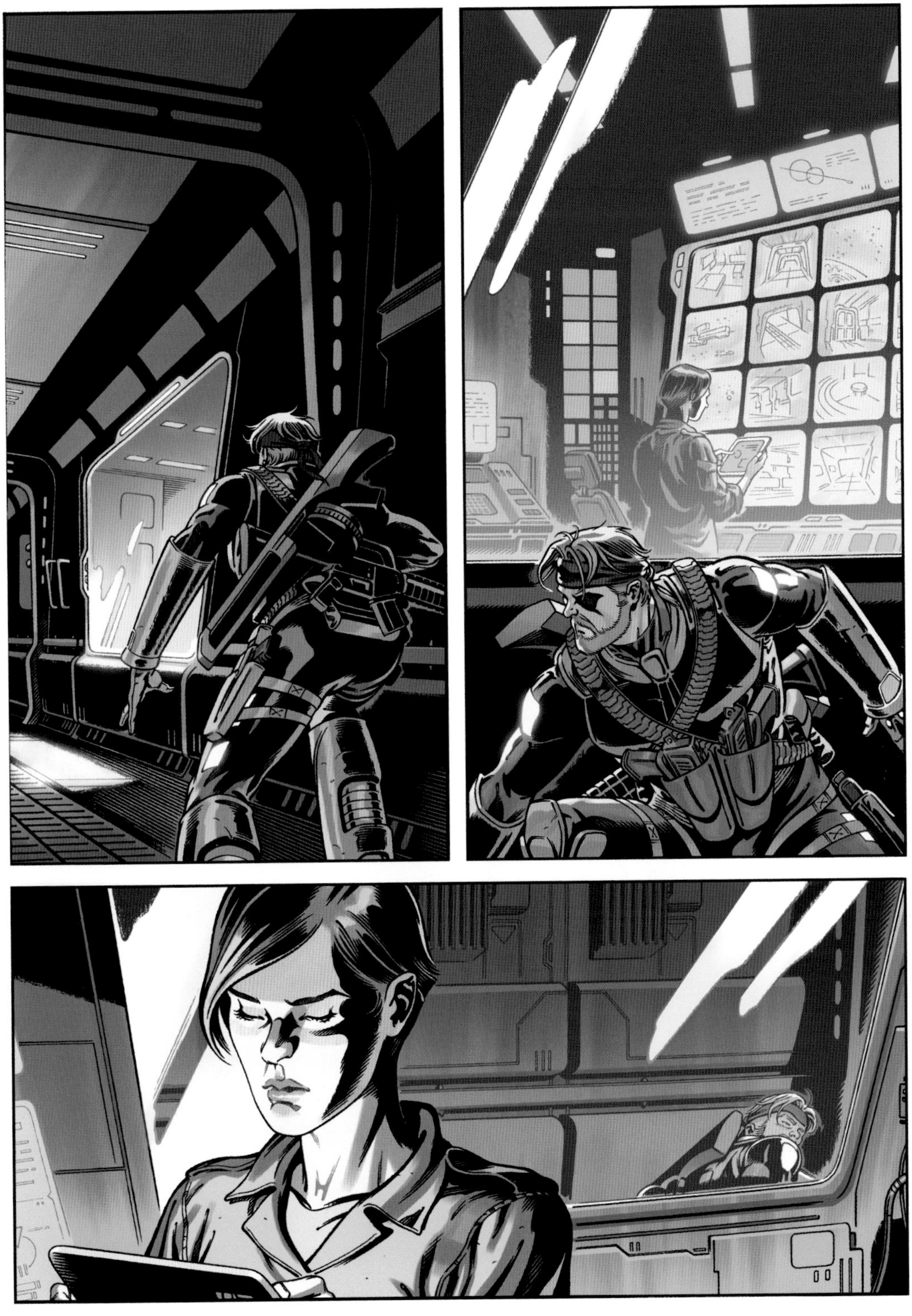

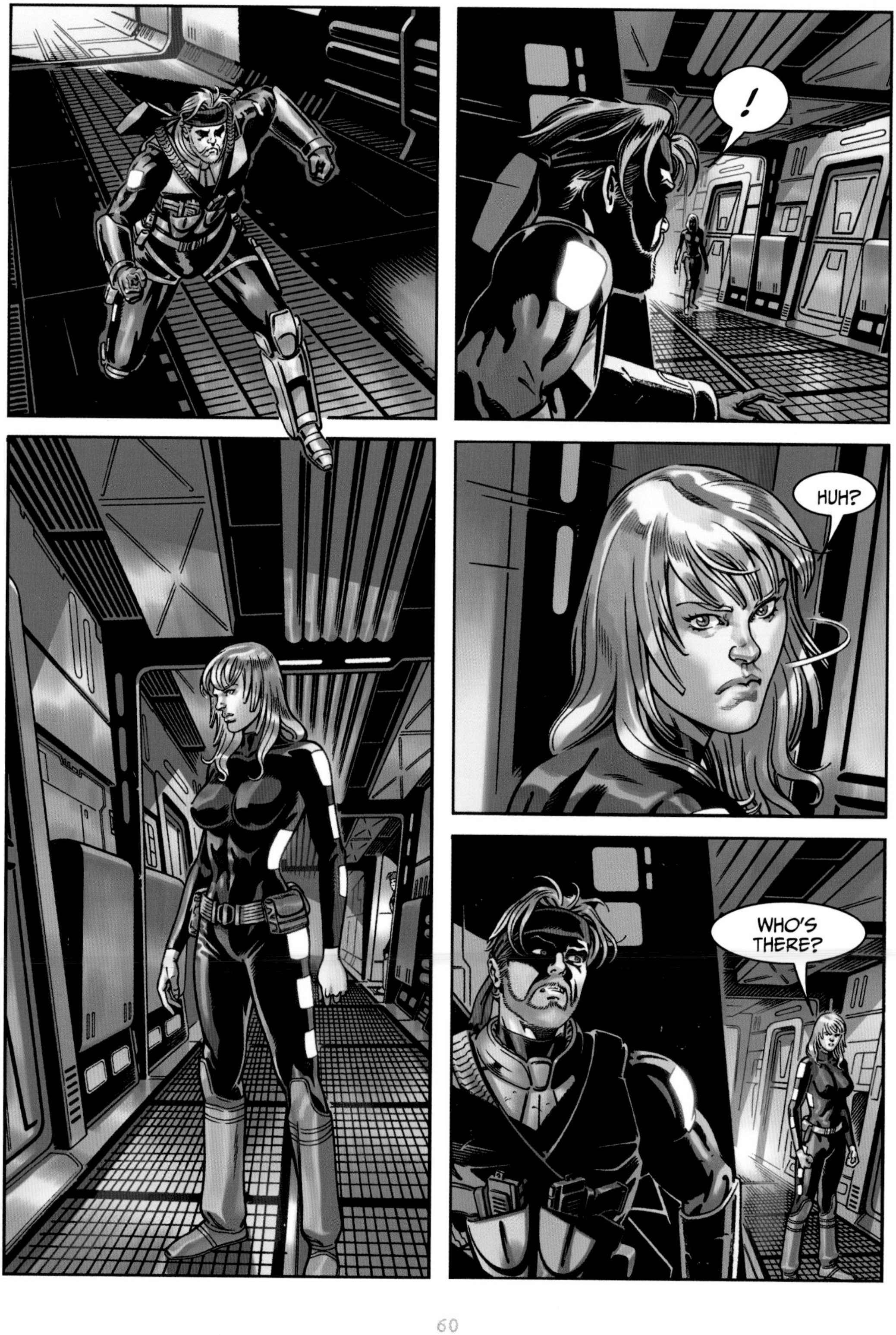
!
HUH?
WHO'S THERE?

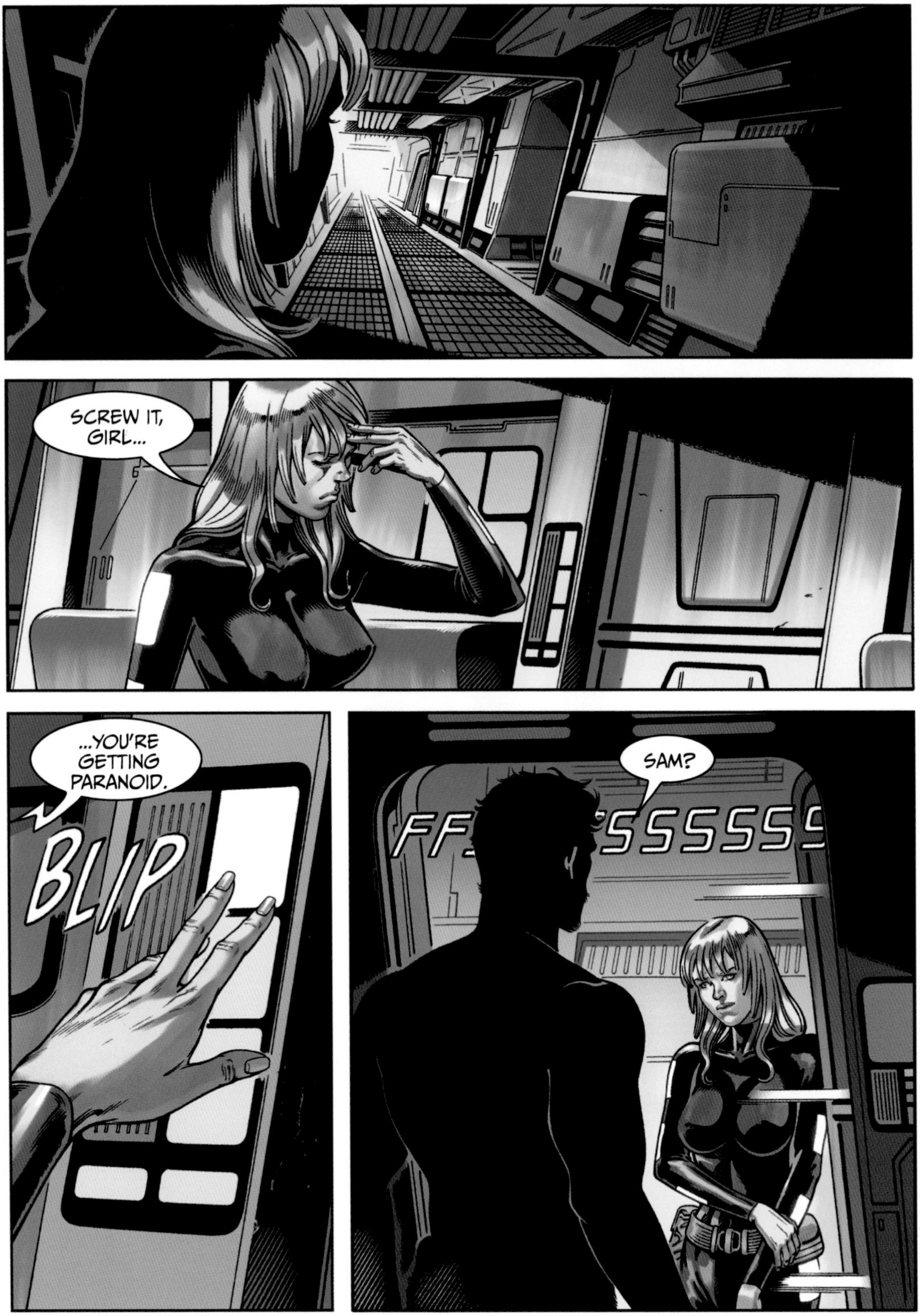
SCREW IT, GIRL...
...YOU'RE GETTING PARANOID.
BLIP
SAM?
FF
SSSSSS

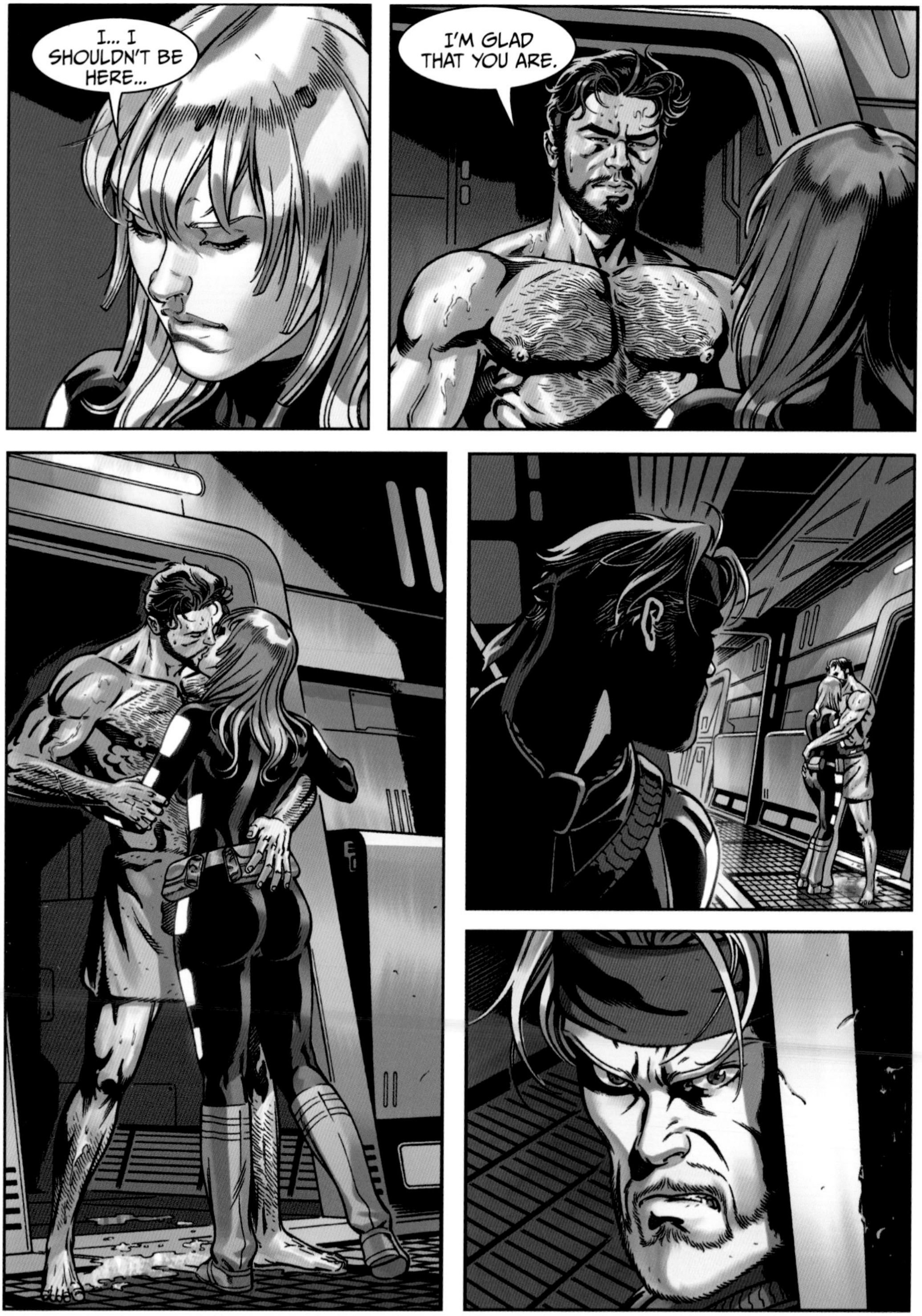
I... I SHOULDN'T BE HERE...
I'M GLAD THAT YOU ARE.

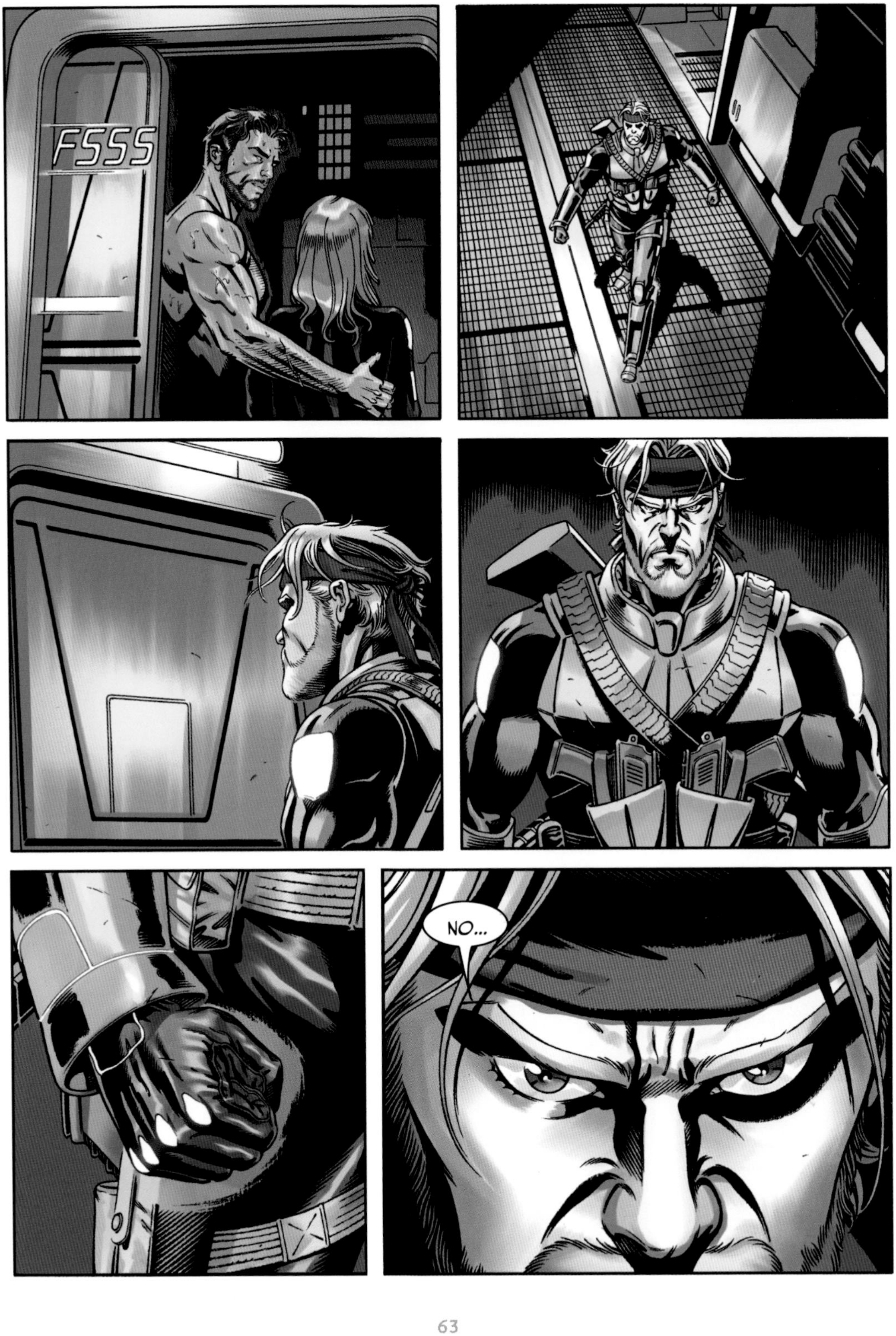
FSSS
NO...

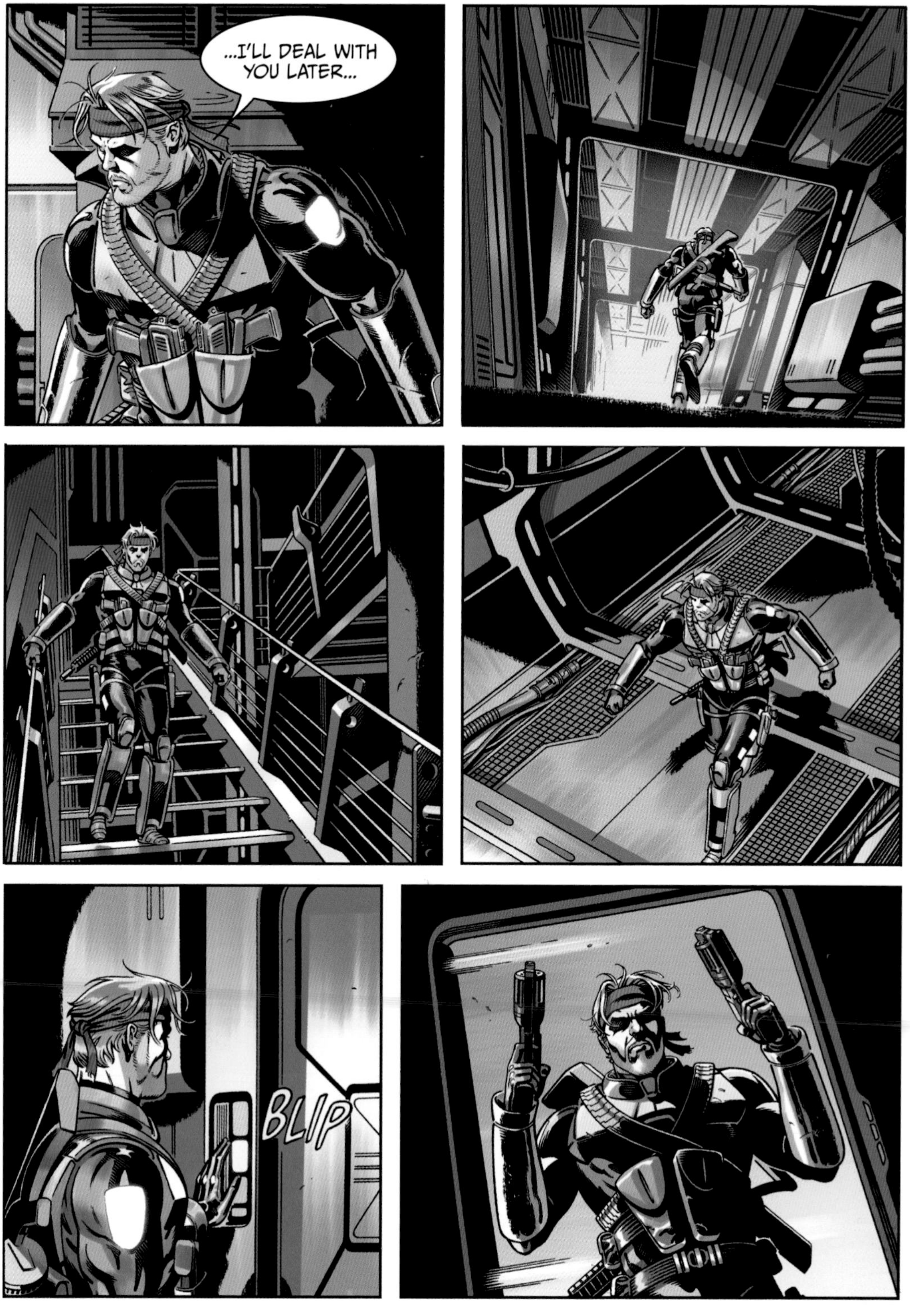
...I'LL DEAL WITH YOU LATER...
BLIP

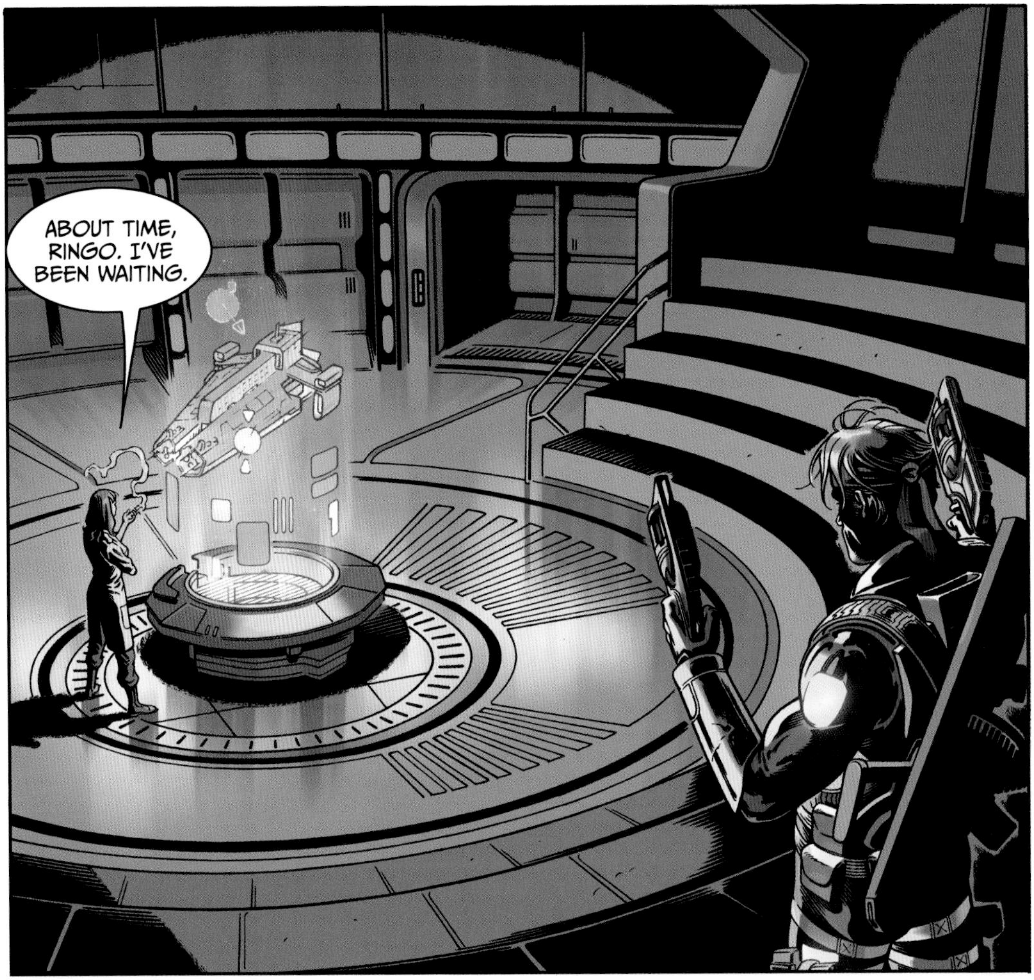
ABOUT TIME, RINGO. I'VE BEEN WAITING.

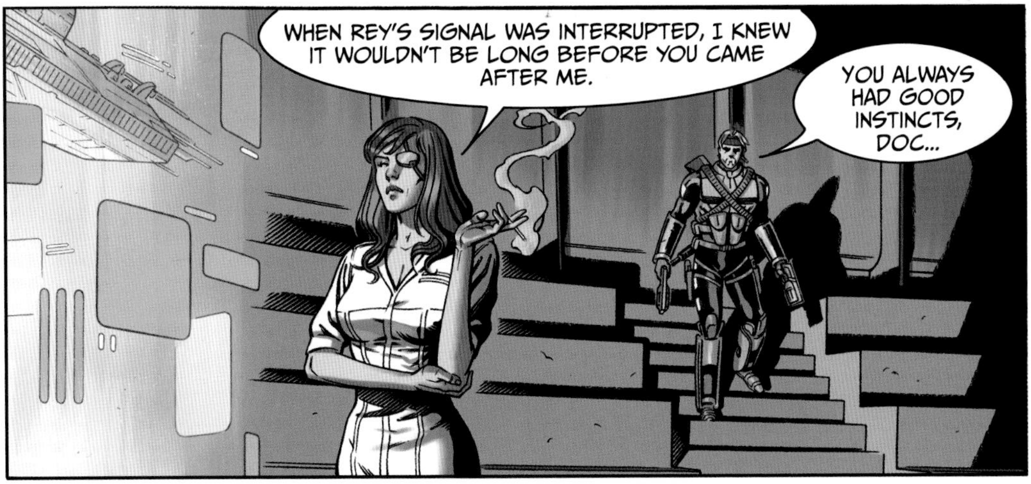
WHEN REY'S SIGNAL WAS INTERRUPTED, I KNEW IT WOULDN'T BE LONG BEFORE YOU CAME AFTER ME.
YOU ALWAYS HAD GOOD INSTINCTS, DOC...

...BUT HONESTY WAS NEVER YOUR THING.

I'M JUST DOING MY JOB.

AS A SCIENTIST?

A COMMON MISUNDERSTANDING...

...I'M A SOCIOLOGIST. AN EXPERT IN THE FIELD OF SOCIAL CONTROL. AN AUTHORITY, IN FACT. DOES THAT START TO EXPLAIN THINGS...?

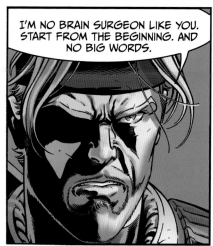

I'M NO BRAIN SURGEON LIKE YOU. START FROM THE BEGINNING. AND NO BIG WORDS.

DO YOU REMEMBER THE ATTACK ON EARTH?

IS THAT A RHETORICAL QUESTION?

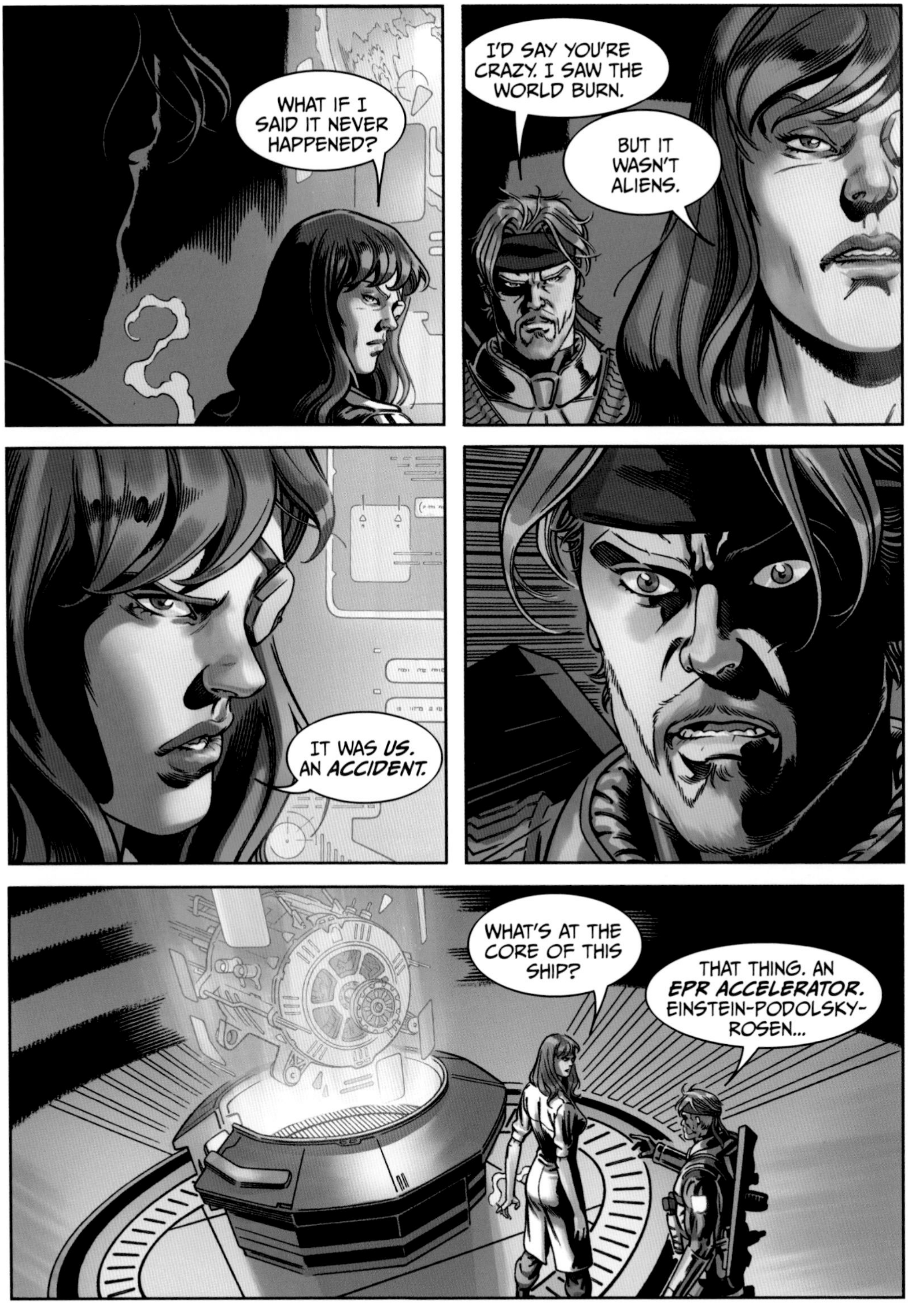
WHAT IF I SAID IT NEVER HAPPENED?
I'D SAY YOU'RE CRAZY. I SAW THE WORLD BURN.
BUT IT WASN'T ALIENS.
IT WAS US. AN ACCIDENT.
WHAT'S AT THE CORE OF THIS SHIP?
THAT THING. AN EPR ACCELERATOR. EINSTEIN-PODOLSKY-ROSEN...

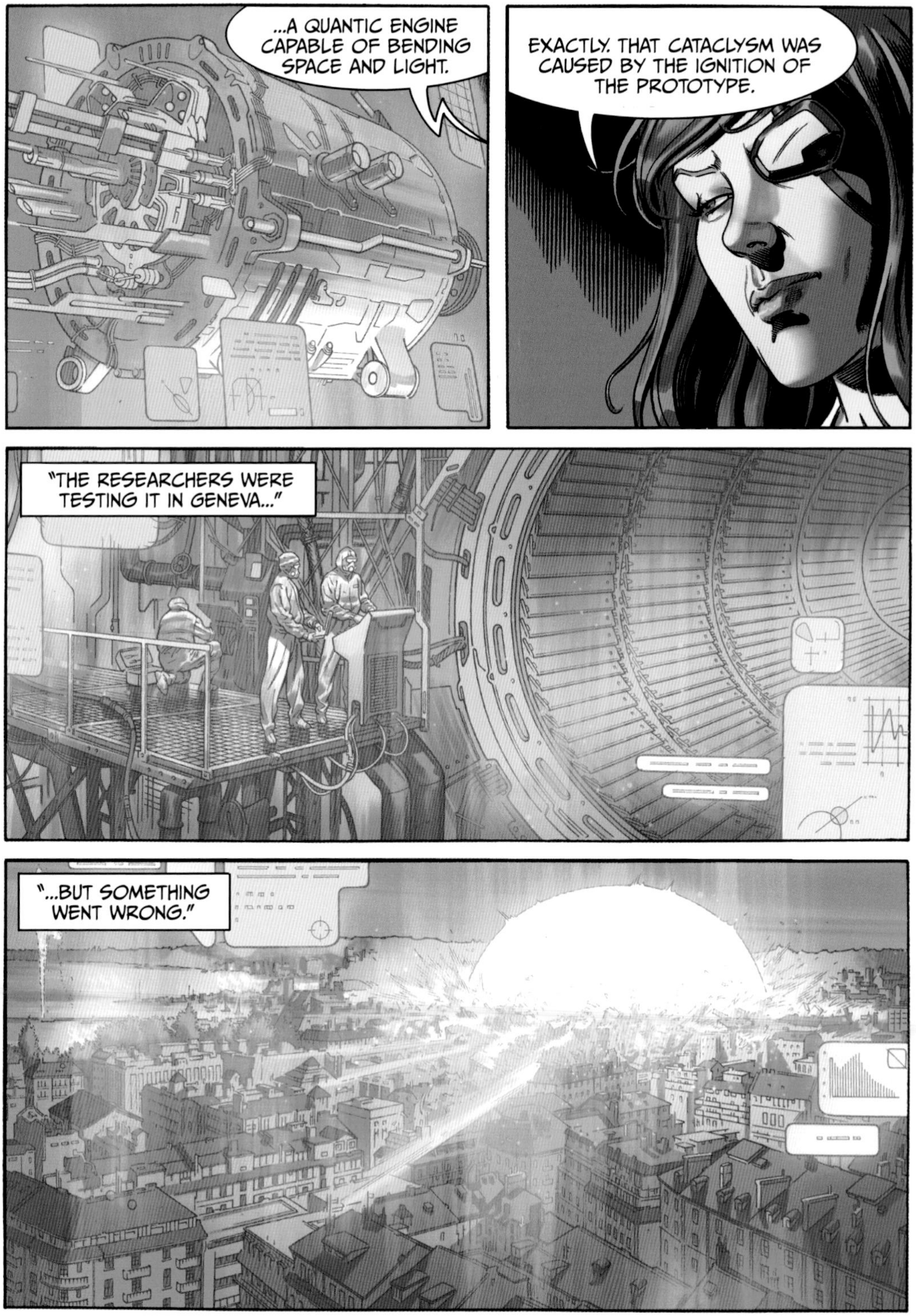
...A QUANTIC ENGINE CAPABLE OF BENDING SPACE AND LIGHT.
EXACTLY. THAT CATACLYSM WAS CAUSED BY THE IGNITION OF THE PROTOTYPE.
"THE RESEARCHERS WERE TESTING IT IN GENEVA..."
"...BUT SOMETHING WENT WRONG."

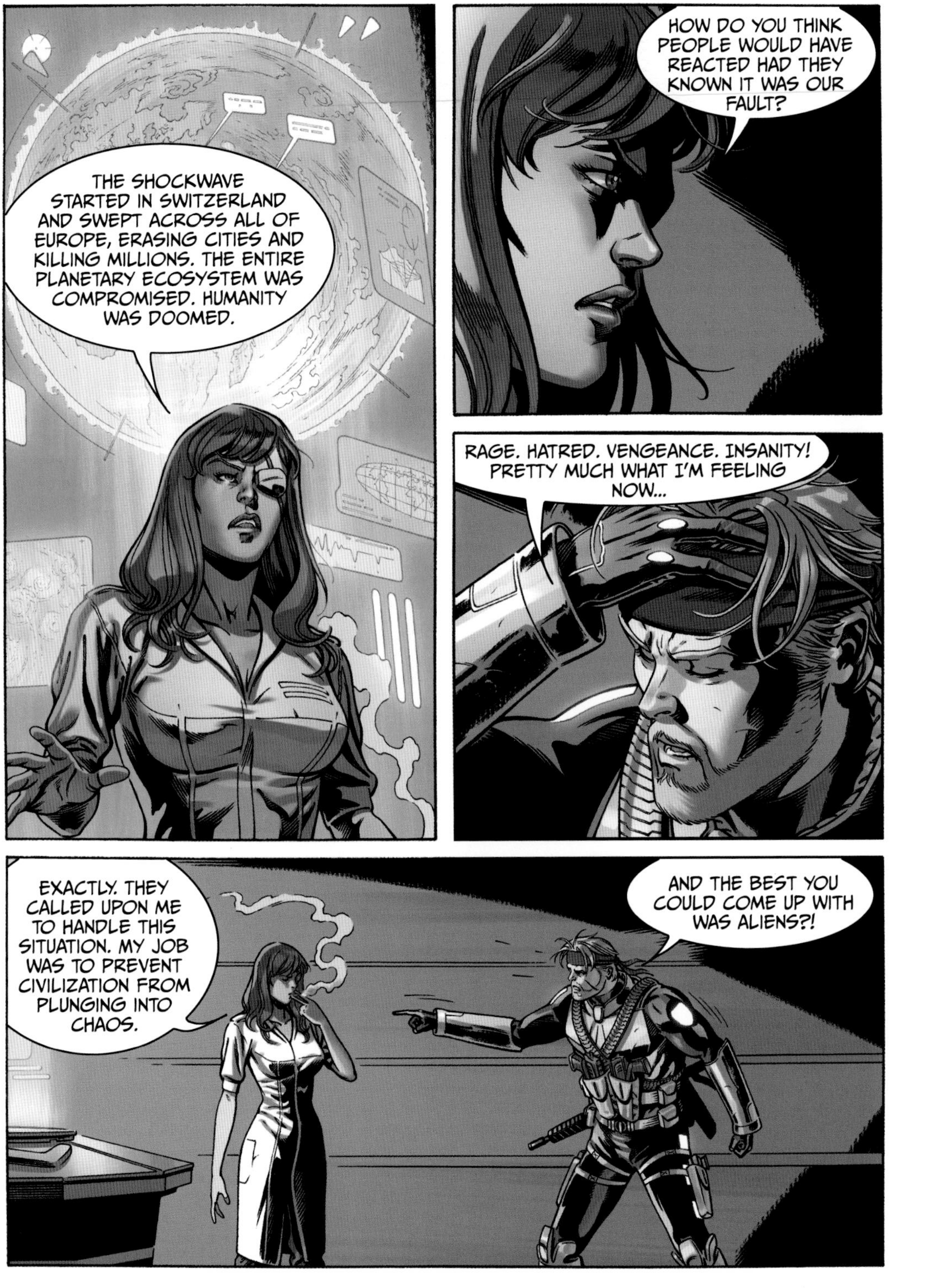
THE SHOCKWAVE STARTED IN SWITZERLAND AND SWEPT ACROSS ALL OF EUROPE, ERASING CITIES AND KILLING MILLIONS. THE ENTIRE PLANETARY ECOSYSTEM WAS COMPROMISED. HUMANITY WAS DOOMED.
HOW DO YOU THINK PEOPLE WOULD HAVE REACTED HAD THEY KNOWN IT WAS OUR FAULT?
RAGE. HATRED. VENGEANCE. INSANITY! PRETTY MUCH WHAT I'M FEELING NOW...
EXACTLY. THEY CALLED UPON ME TO HANDLE THIS SITUATION. MY JOB WAS TO PREVENT CIVILIZATION FROM PLUNGING INTO CHAOS.
AND THE BEST YOU COULD COME UP WITH WAS ALIENS?!

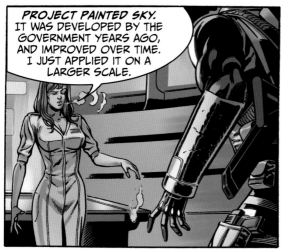

PROJECT PAINTED SKY. IT WAS DEVELOPED BY THE GOVERNMENT YEARS AGO, AND IMPROVED OVER TIME. I JUST APPLIED IT ON A LARGER SCALE.

THINK ABOUT IT -- THE SURVIVING POPULATION WAS EXHAUSTED. MILLIONS OF PEOPLE NEEDED A JOB, A FUTURE, HOPE... WE HAD TO GIVE THEM SOMETHING... A PURPOSE...

AN ENEMY TO FIGHT.

NOT JUST ANY ENEMY...

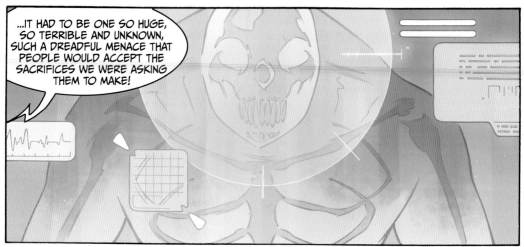

...IT HAD TO BE ONE SO HUGE, SO TERRIBLE AND UNKNOWN, SUCH A DREADFUL MENACE THAT PEOPLE WOULD ACCEPT THE SACRIFICES WE WERE ASKING THEM TO MAKE!

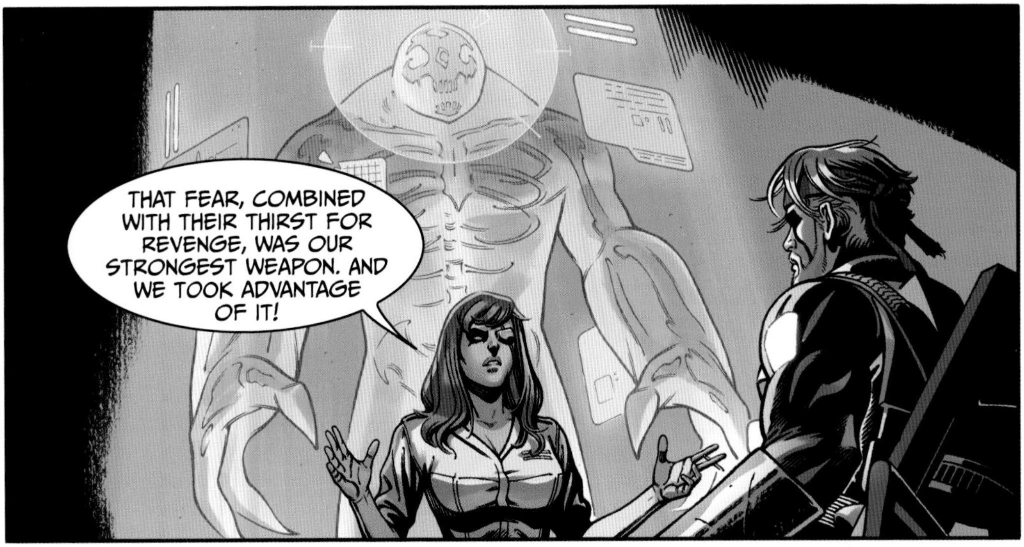
THAT FEAR, COMBINED WITH THEIR THIRST FOR REVENGE, WAS OUR STRONGEST WEAPON. AND WE TOOK ADVANTAGE OF IT!

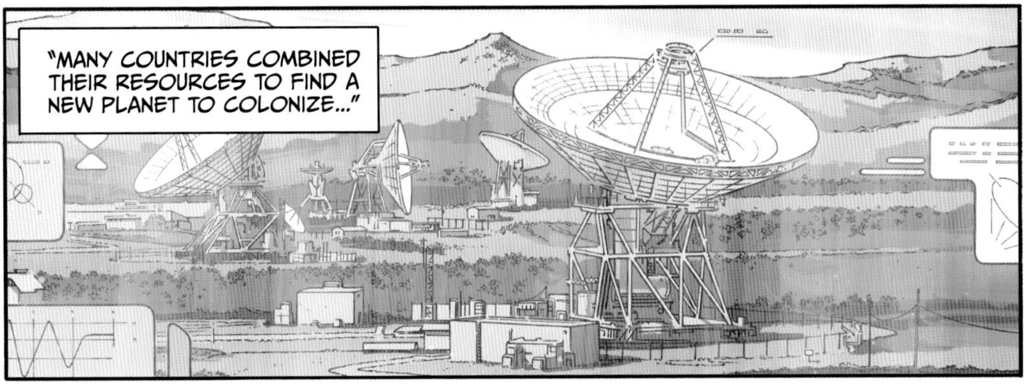
"MANY COUNTRIES COMBINED THEIR RESOURCES TO FIND A NEW PLANET TO COLONIZE..."

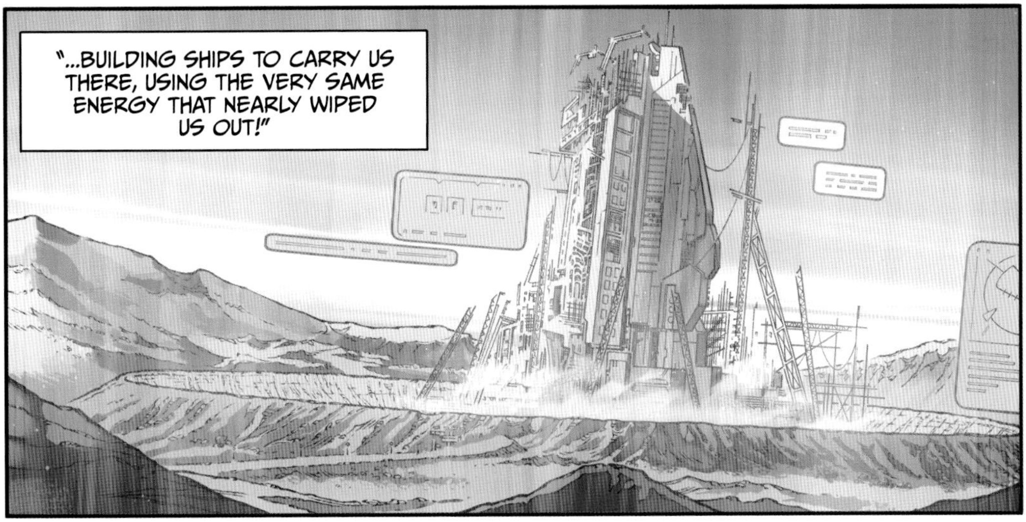
"...BUILDING SHIPS TO CARRY US THERE, USING THE VERY SAME ENERGY THAT NEARLY WIPED US OUT!"

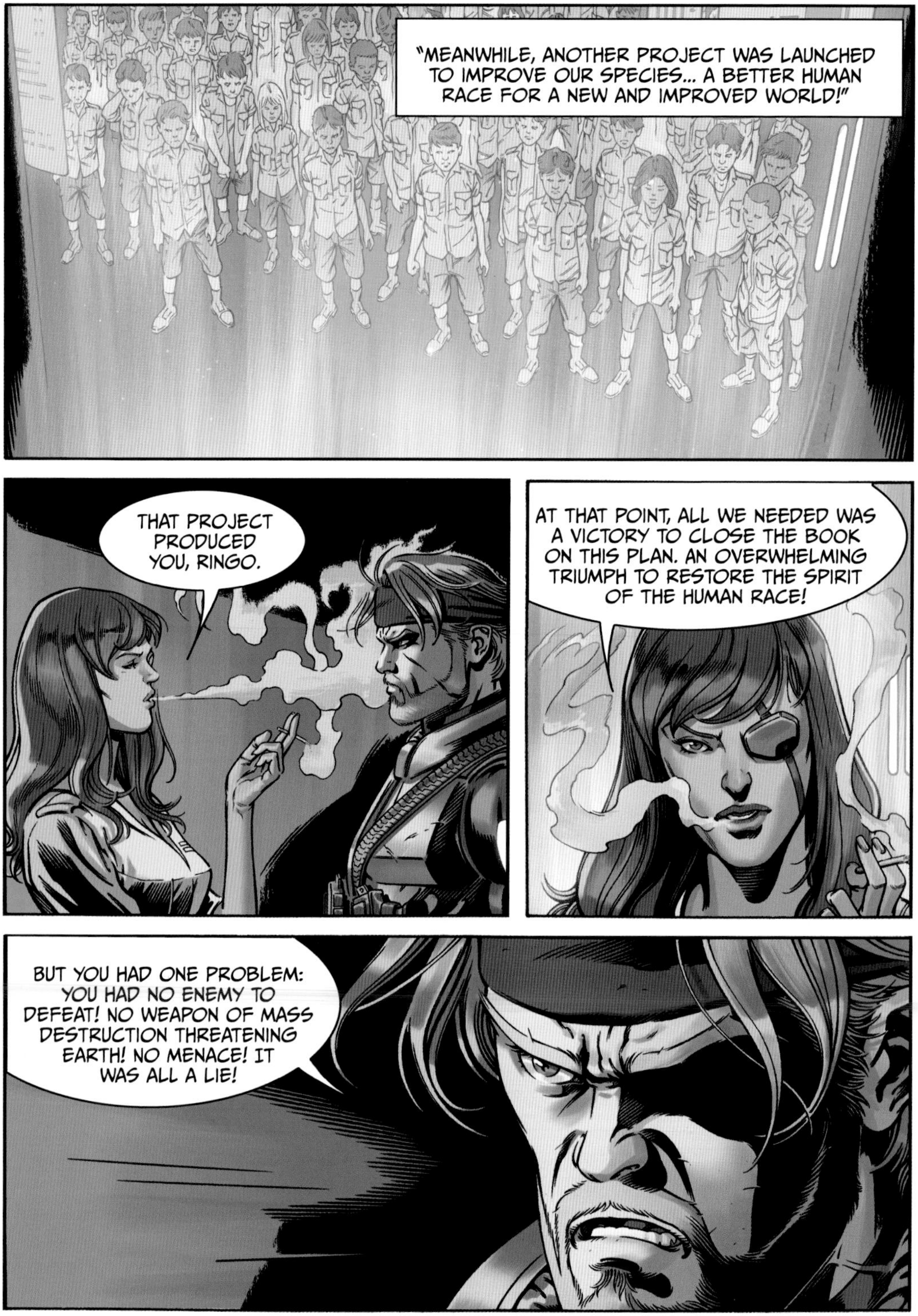
"MEANWHILE, ANOTHER PROJECT WAS LAUNCHED TO IMPROVE OUR SPECIES... A BETTER HUMAN RACE FOR A NEW AND IMPROVED WORLD!"
THAT PROJECT PRODUCED YOU, RINGO.
AT THAT POINT, ALL WE NEEDED WAS A VICTORY TO CLOSE THE BOOK ON THIS PLAN. AN OVERWHELMING TRIUMPH TO RESTORE THE SPIRIT OF THE HUMAN RACE!
BUT YOU HAD ONE PROBLEM: YOU HAD NO ENEMY TO DEFEAT! NO WEAPON OF MASS DESTRUCTION THREATENING EARTH! NO MENACE! IT WAS ALL A LIE!

SO YOU USED DRUGS, RIGHT? THAT PLANET ISN'T REALLY RADIOACTIVE -- THE ANTIDOTE YOU HAD US INJECT WAS A HALLUCINOGEN!

WELL, NANOBOTS.

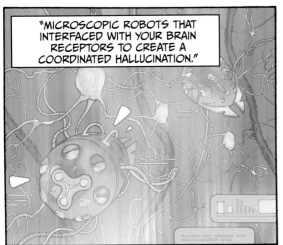

"MICROSCOPIC ROBOTS THAT INTERFACED WITH YOUR BRAIN RECEPTORS TO CREATE A COORDINATED HALLUCINATION."

BUT YES: THE PHANTOMS WERE ONLY IN YOUR MINDS. DREAMS, REALLY.

DREAMS DON'T KILL PEOPLE!

EVERY WAR HAS A PRICE, RINGO...

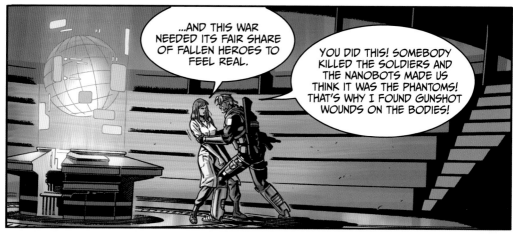

...AND THIS WAR NEEDED ITS FAIR SHARE OF FALLEN HEROES TO FEEL REAL.

YOU DID THIS! SOMEBODY KILLED THE SOLDIERS AND THE NANOBOTS MADE US THINK IT WAS THE PHANTOMS! THAT'S WHY I FOUND GUNSHOT WOUNDS ON THE BODIES!

...REY!

HE KILLED THOSE MEN... DESTROYED OUR VEHICLES...

YES, WELL... REY COULDN'T DO IT ALL ON HIS OWN...

HUH?

THE ARMY WASTES NOTHING, RINGO...

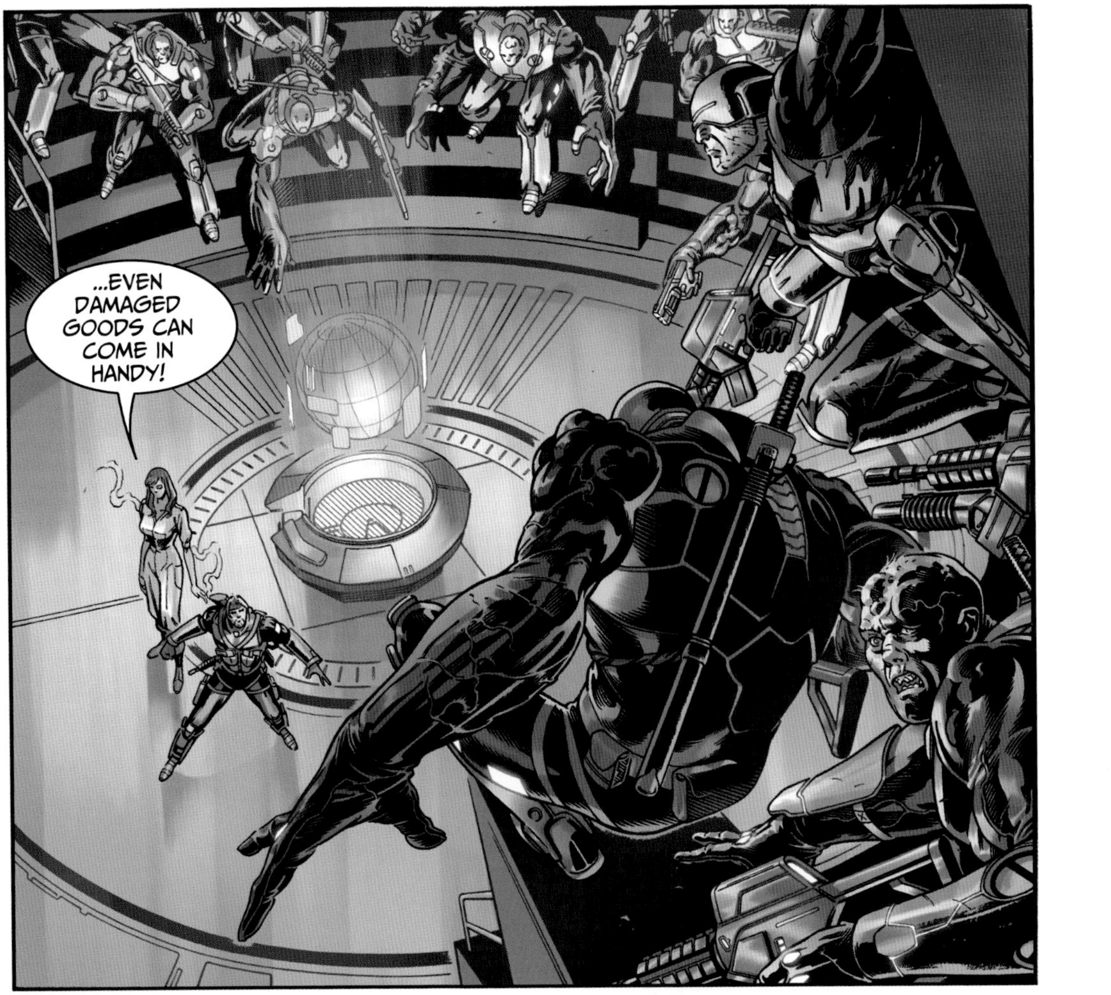
...EVEN DAMAGED GOODS CAN COME IN HANDY!

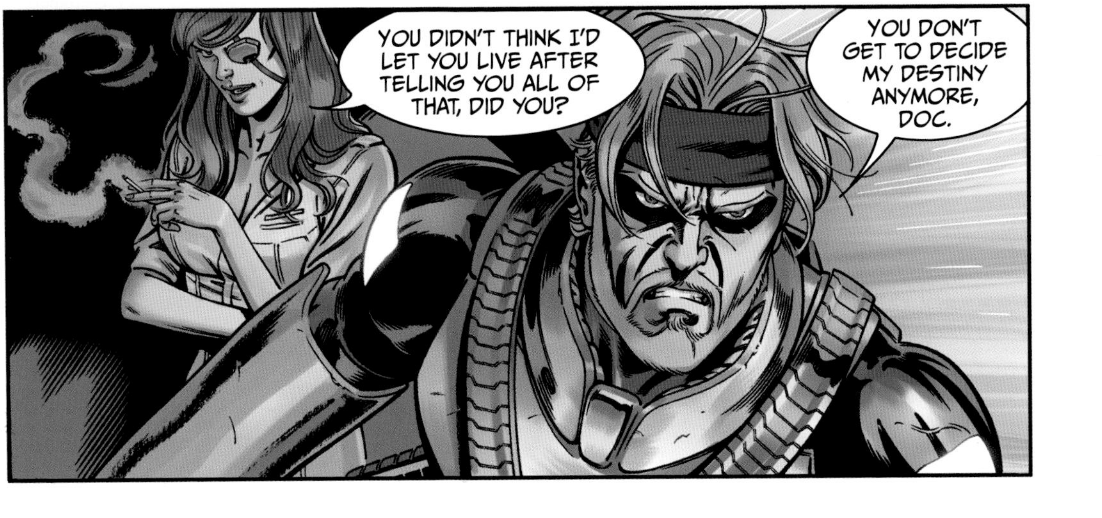
YOU DIDN'T THINK I'D LET YOU LIVE AFTER TELLING YOU ALL OF THAT, DID YOU?
YOU DON'T GET TO DECIDE MY DESTINY ANYMORE, DOC.

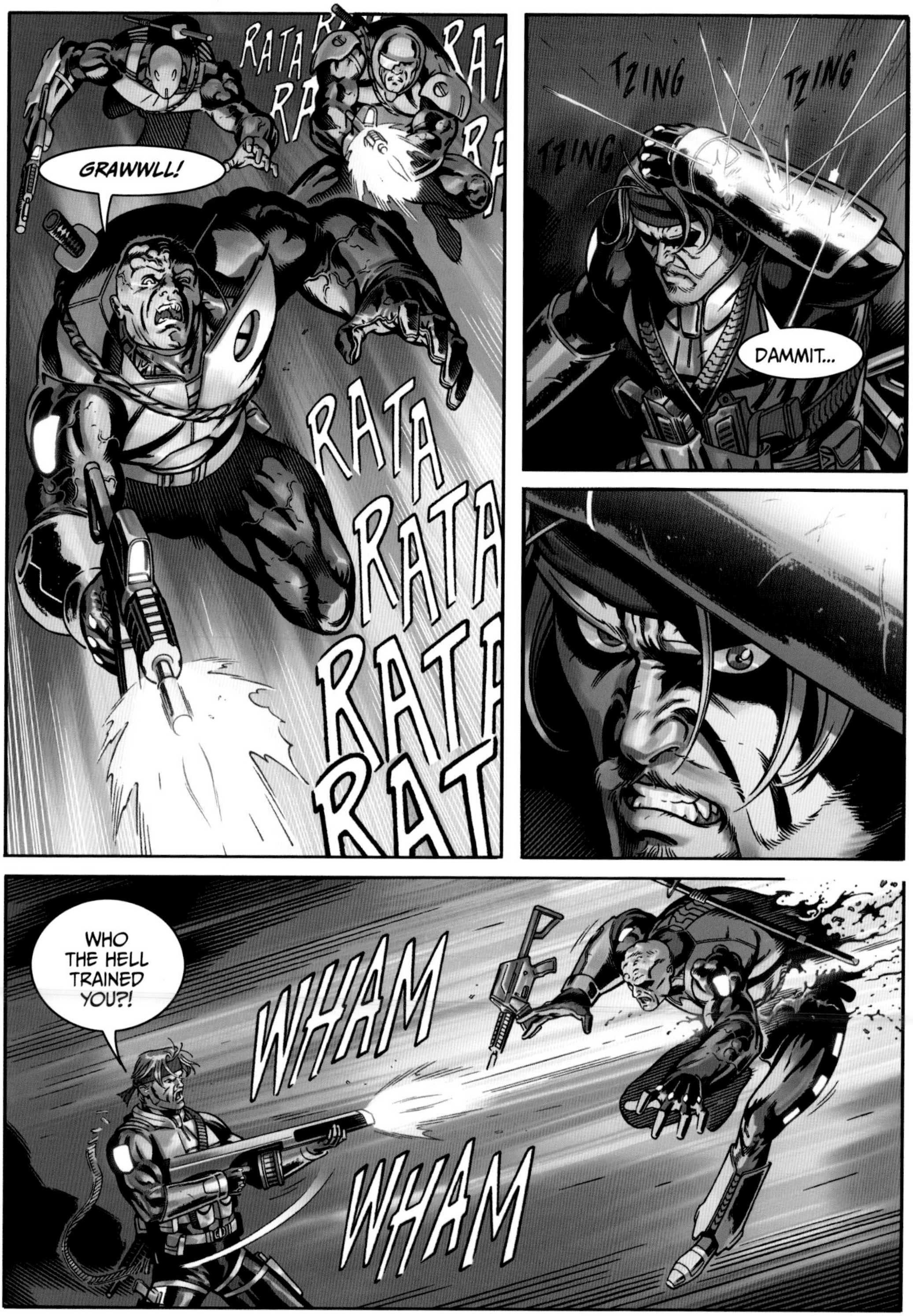
RATA
GRAWWLL!
RATA
RATA
RATA
TZING
TZING
TZING
DAMMIT...
WHO THE HELL TRAINED YOU?!
WHAM
WHAM

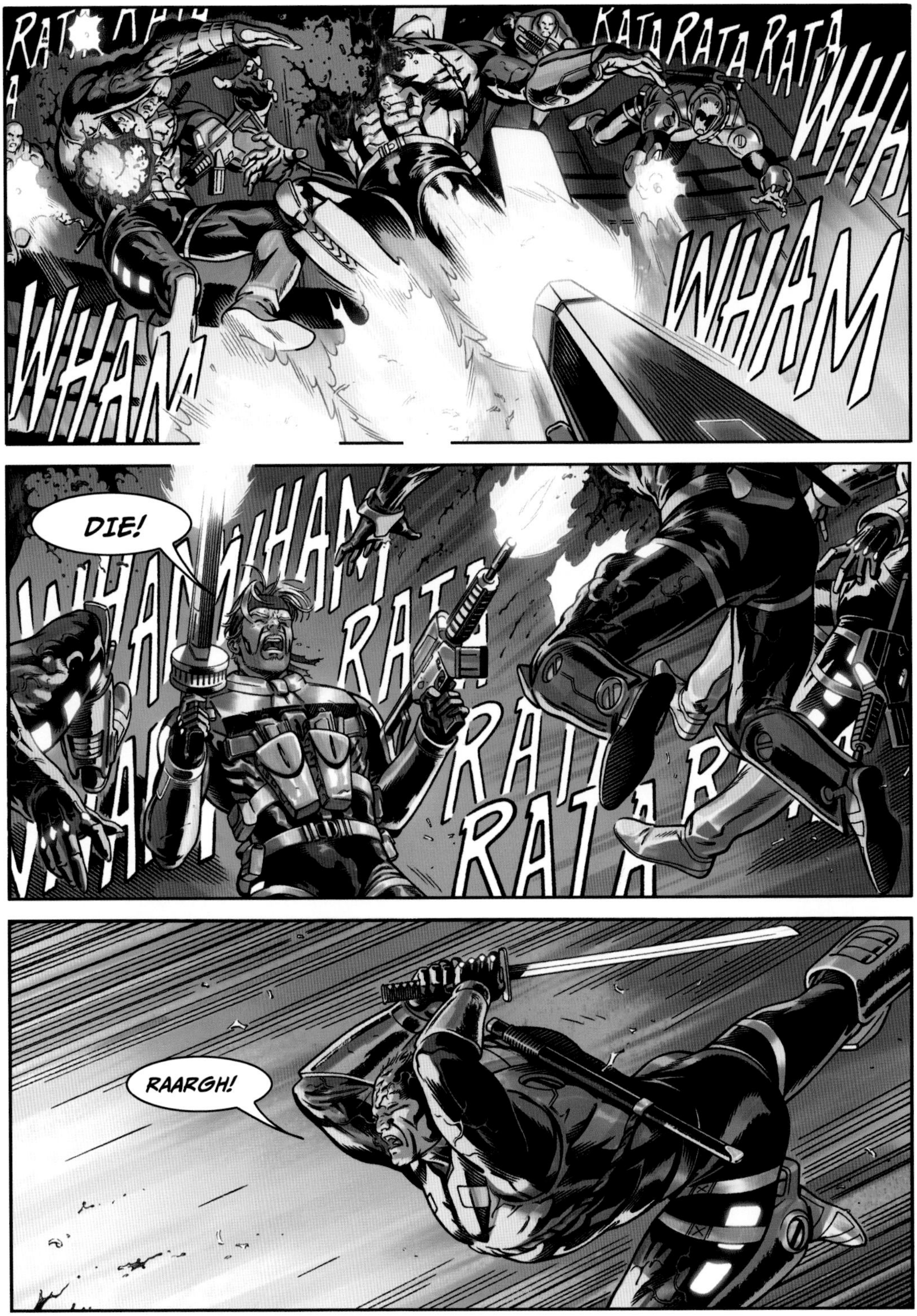
RATA RATA RATA
WHAM
WHAM
DIE!
WHAM WHAM
RATA
RATA
RATA
RAARGH!

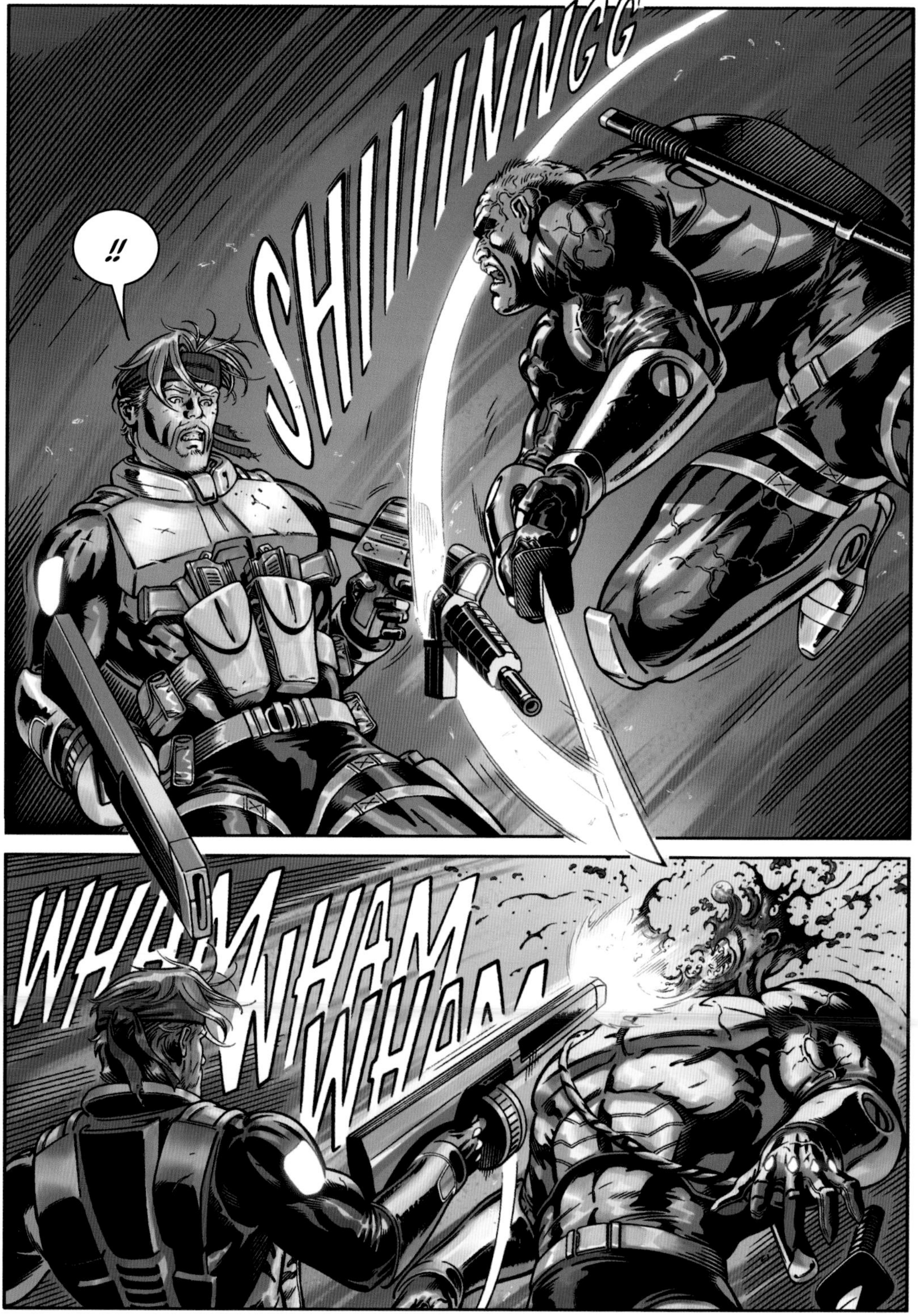
SHIIIINNGG
!!
WHAM
WHAM

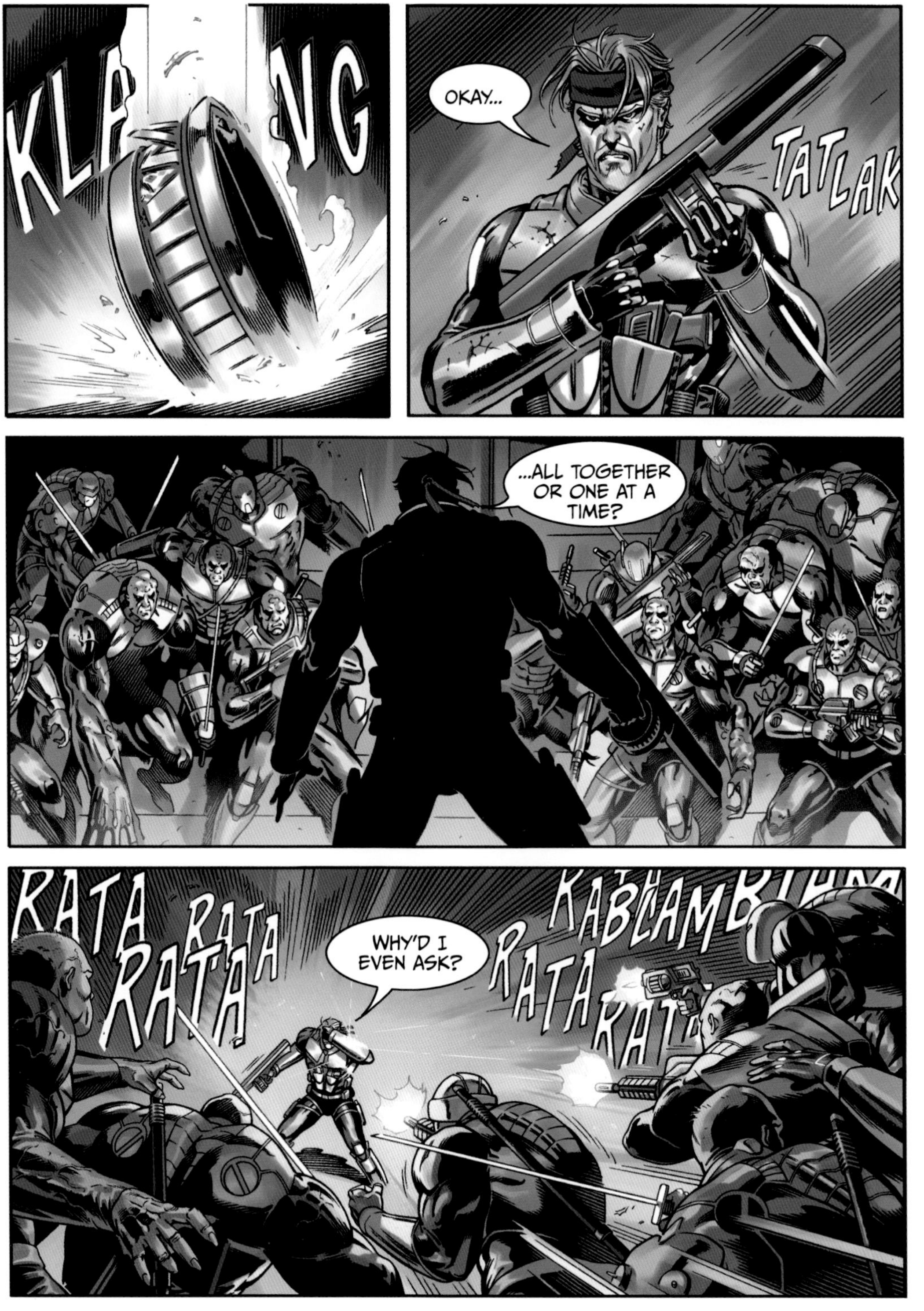
KLANG
OKAY...
TATLAK
...ALL TOGETHER OR ONE AT A TIME?
RATA RATA RATA
WHY'D I EVEN ASK?
KABLAM
RATA RATA

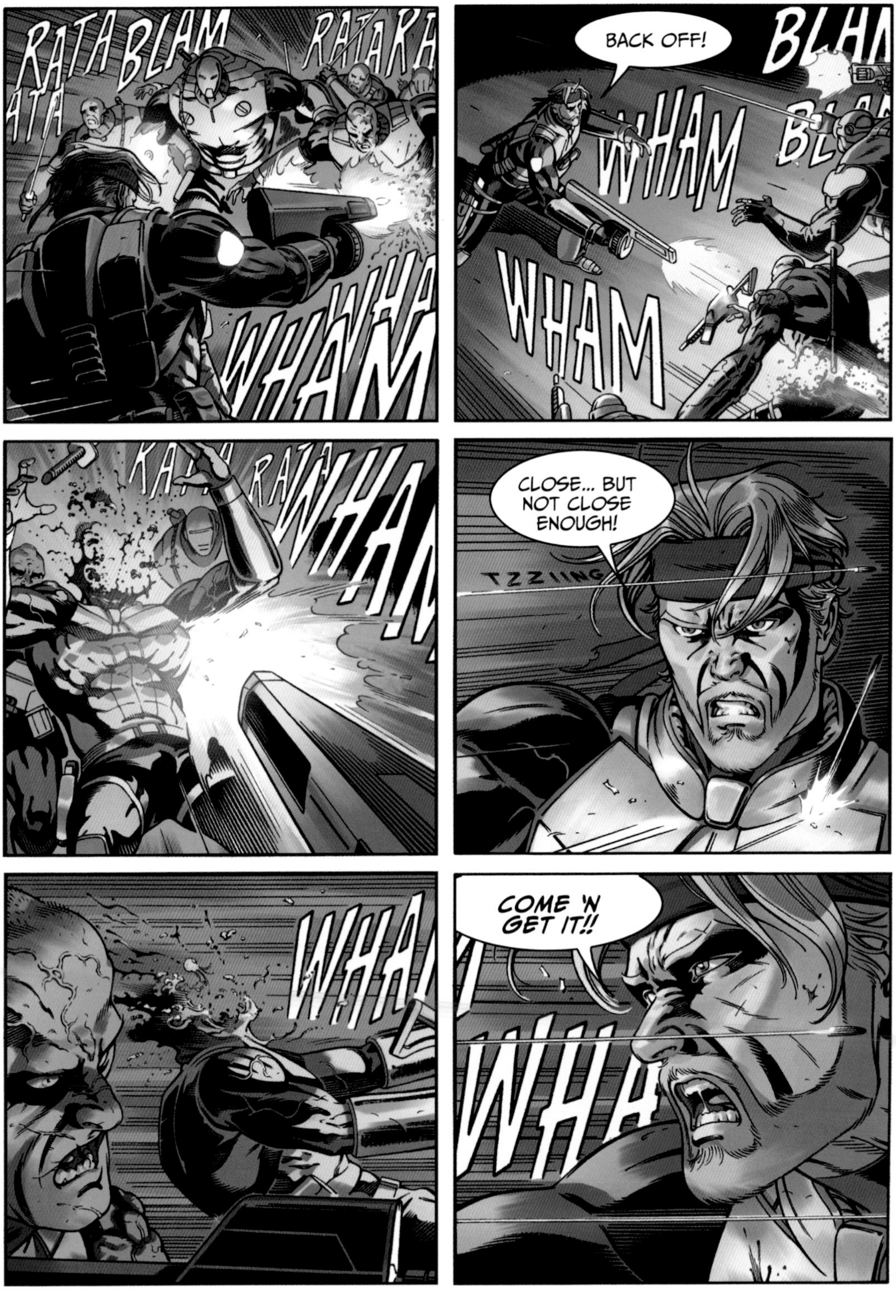
RATA BLAM
RATA
RATARA
WHAM
WHAM
BACK OFF!
BLAM
BLAM
WHAM
WHAM
RATA RATA
WHAM
CLOSE... BUT NOT CLOSE ENOUGH!
TZZIING
WHAM
COME 'N GET IT!!
WHA

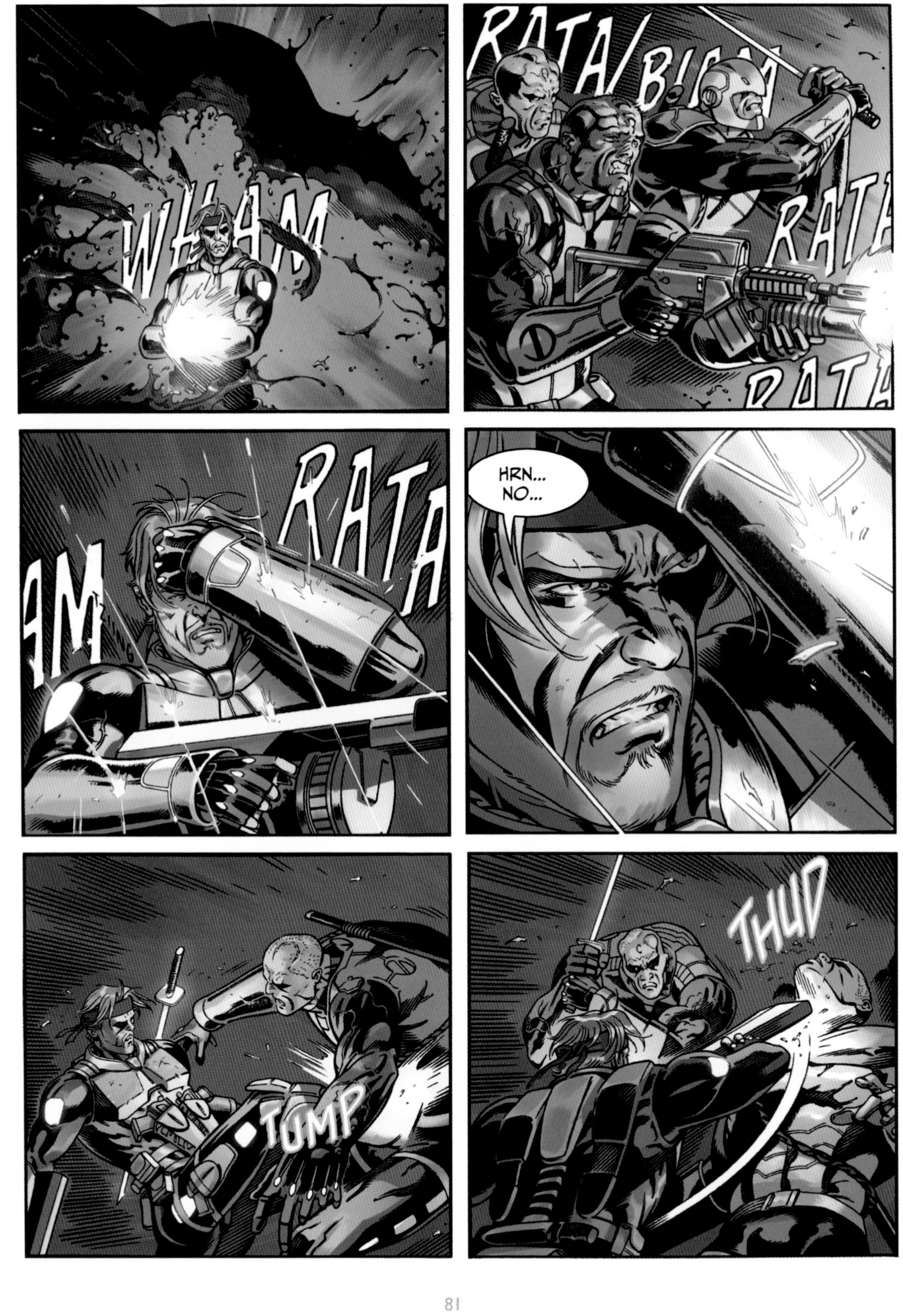
WHAM
RATA
RATA
RATA
HRN...
NO...
TUMP
THUD

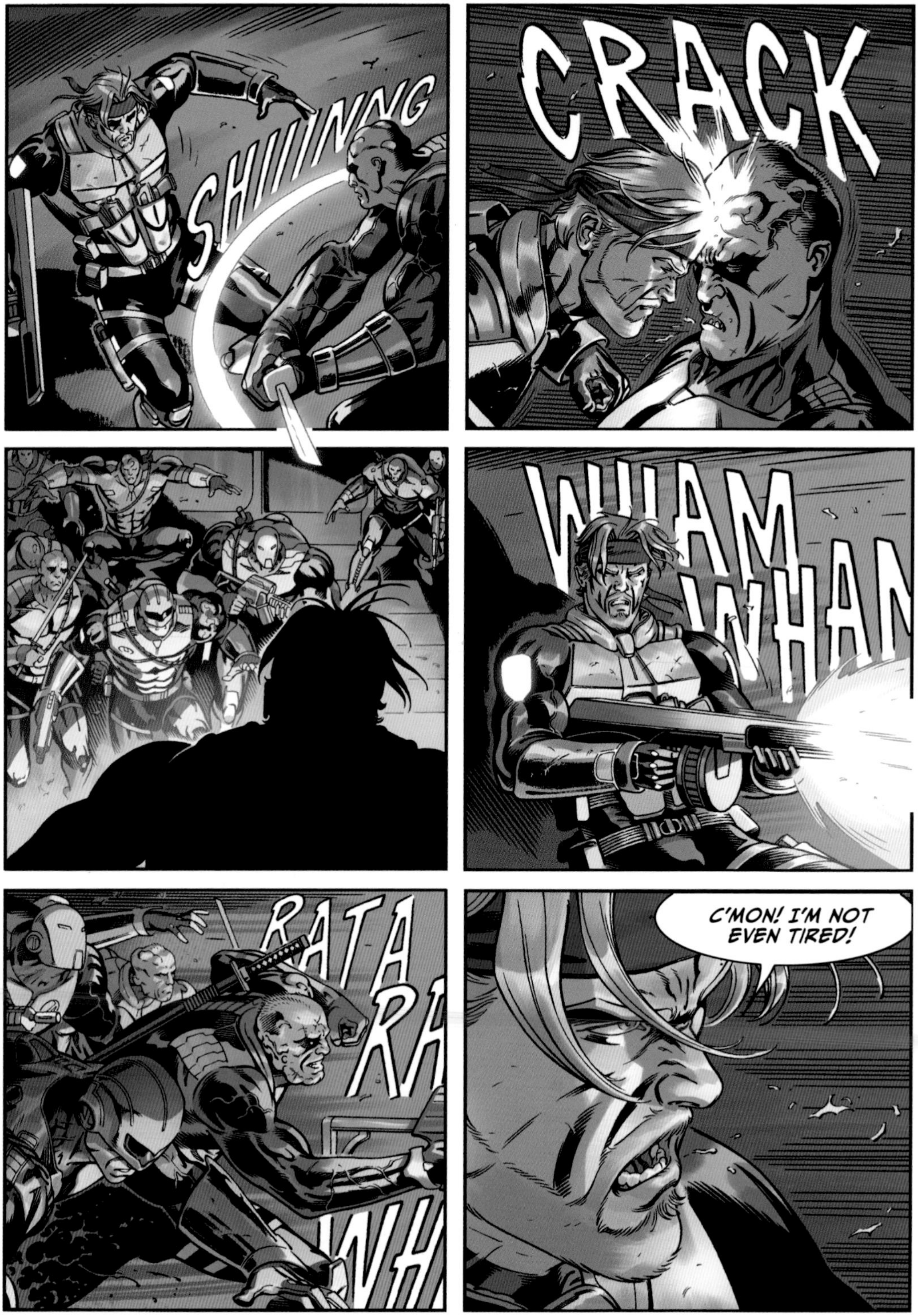
SHIIINNG
CRACK
WHAM
WHAN
RATA
RA
WH
C'MON! I'M NOT EVEN TIRED!

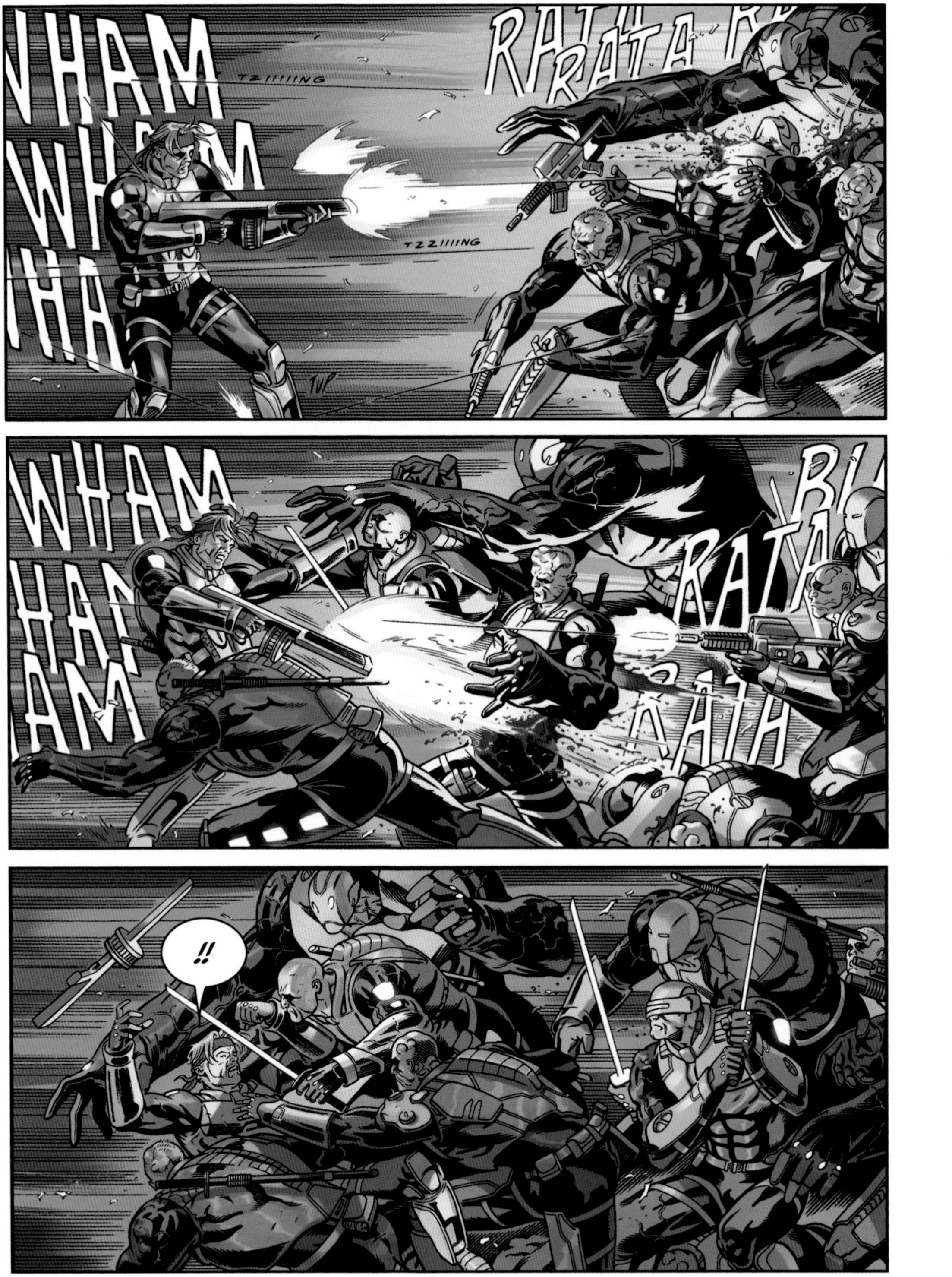
WHAM
TZIIIIING
RATA
RATA
TZZIIIING
WHAM
RATA
!!

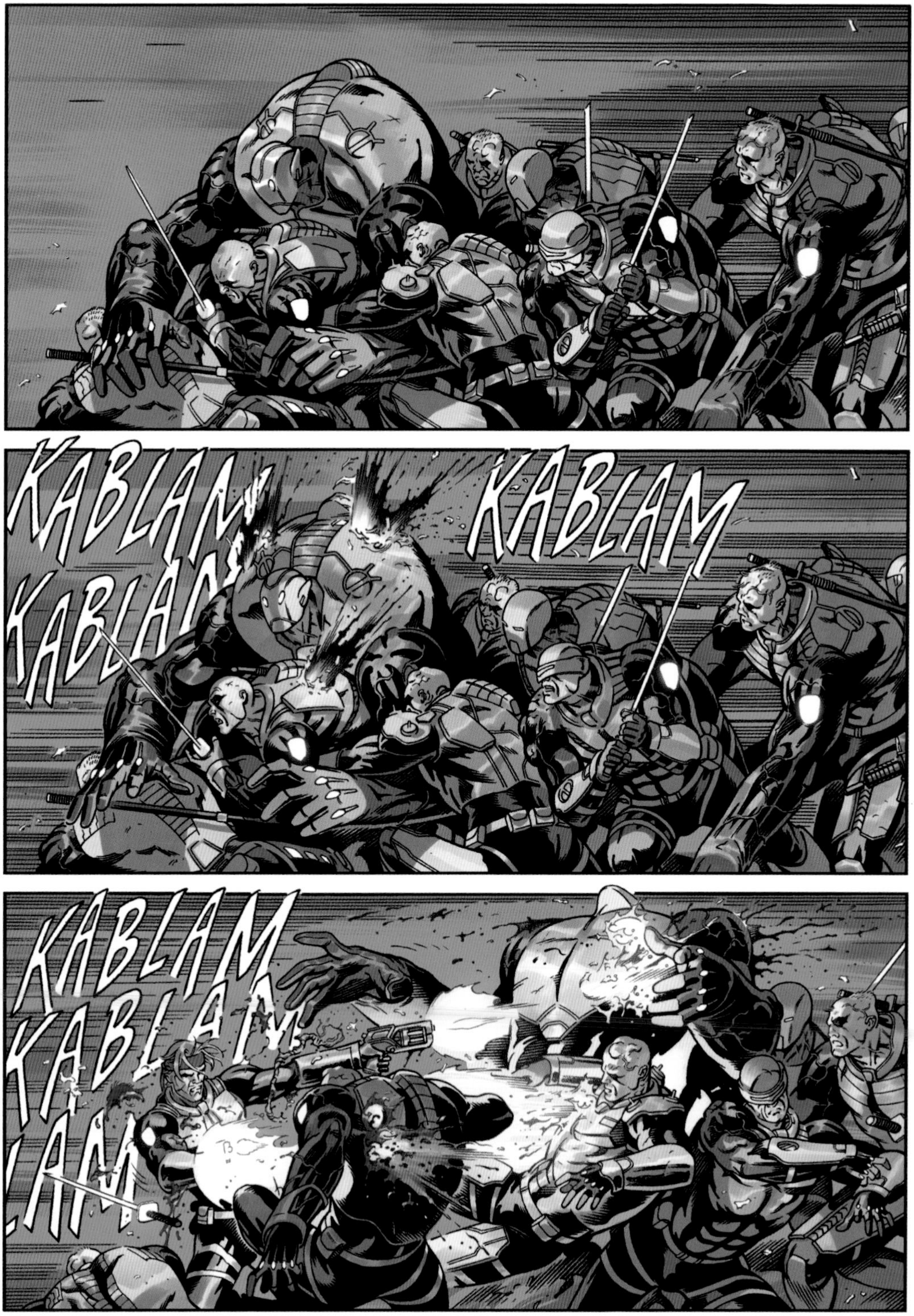
KABLAM
KABLAM
KABLAM
KABLAM
KABLAM
LAM

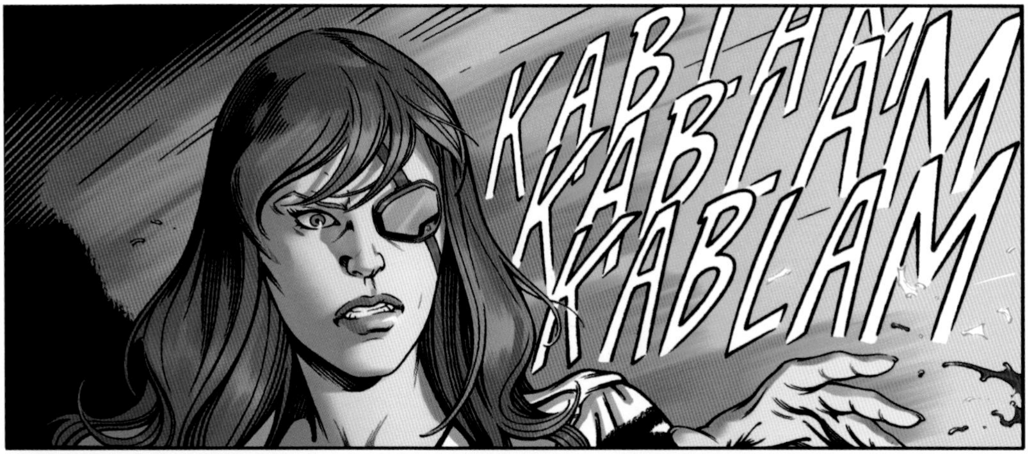
KABLAM
KABLAM
KABLAM

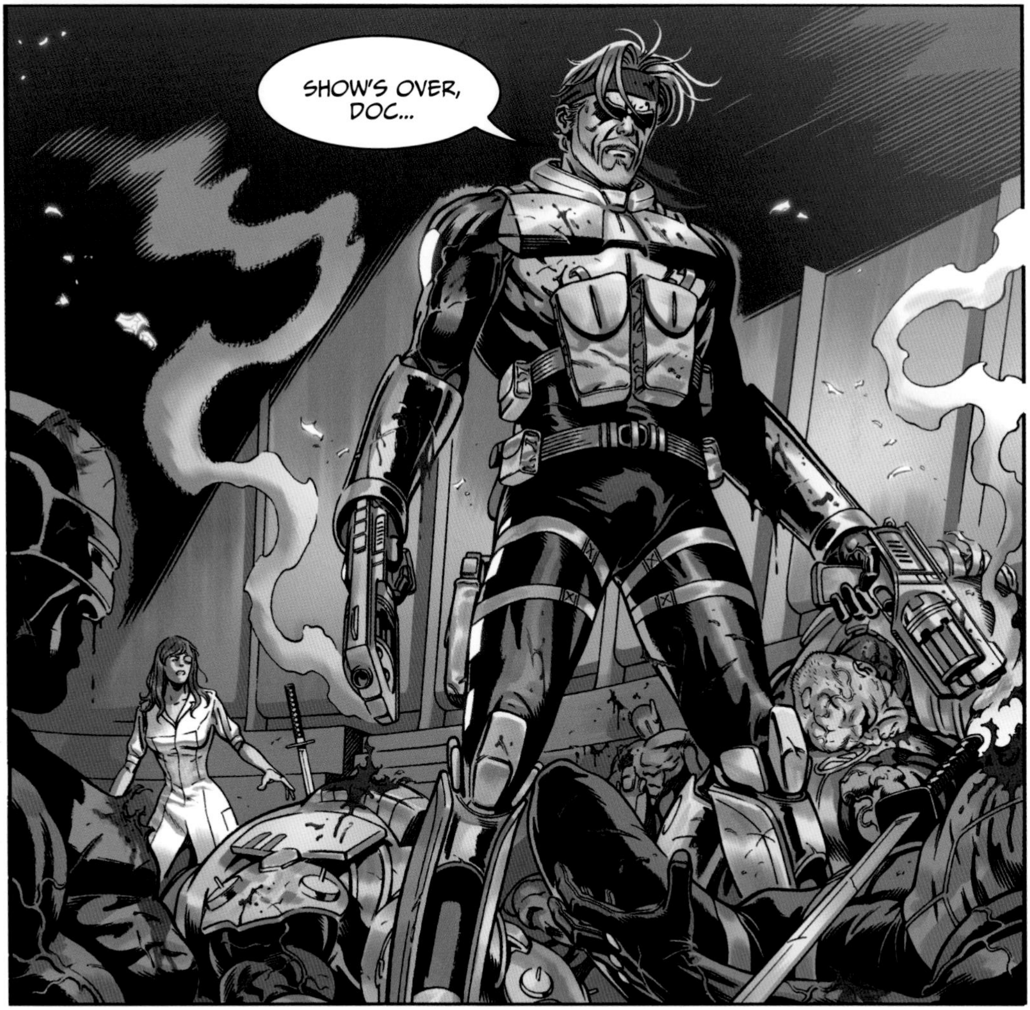
SHOW'S OVER, DOC...

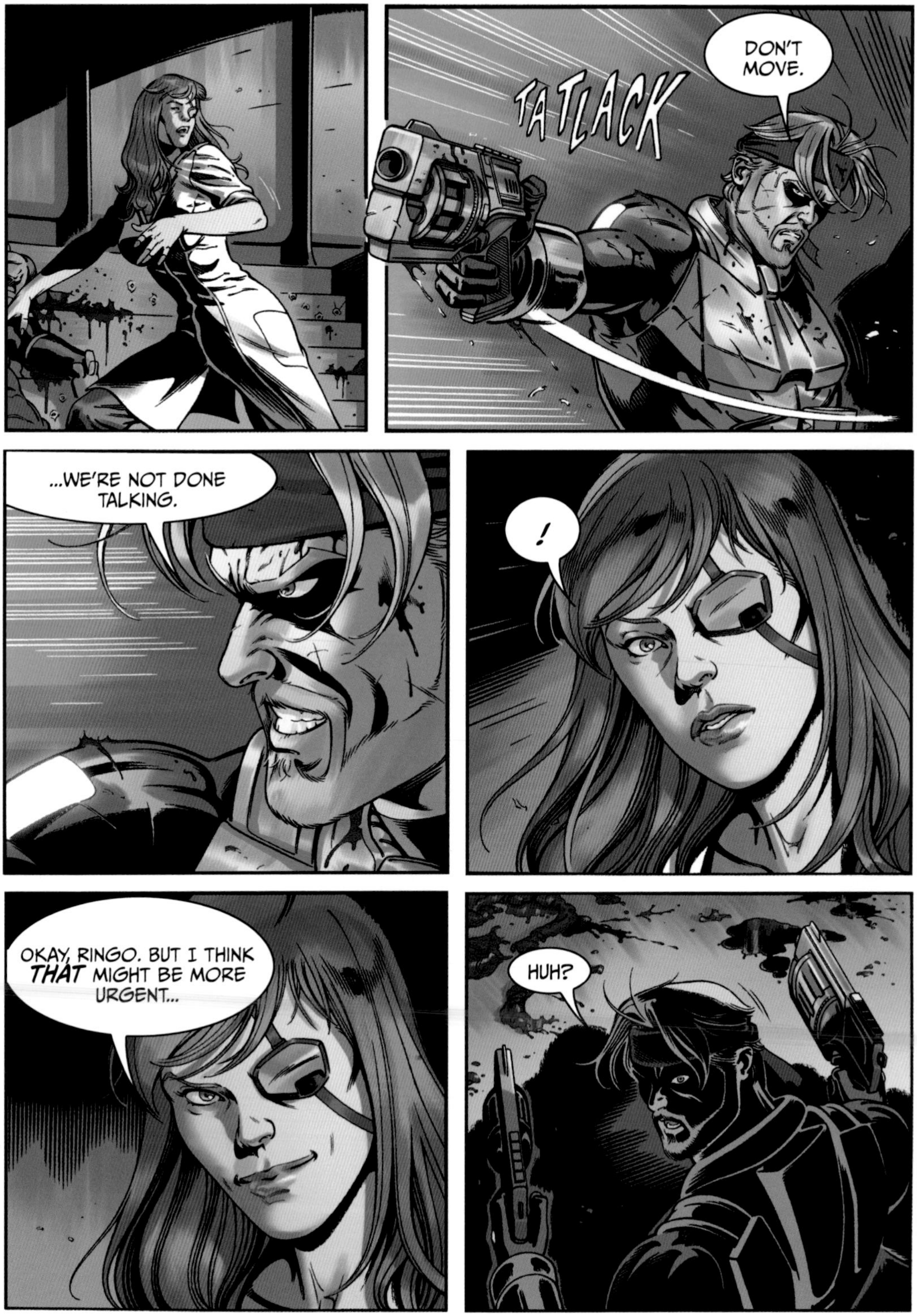
TATLACK
DON'T MOVE.
...WE'RE NOT DONE TALKING.
!
OKAY, RINGO. BUT I THINK ***THAT*** MIGHT BE MORE URGENT...
HUH?

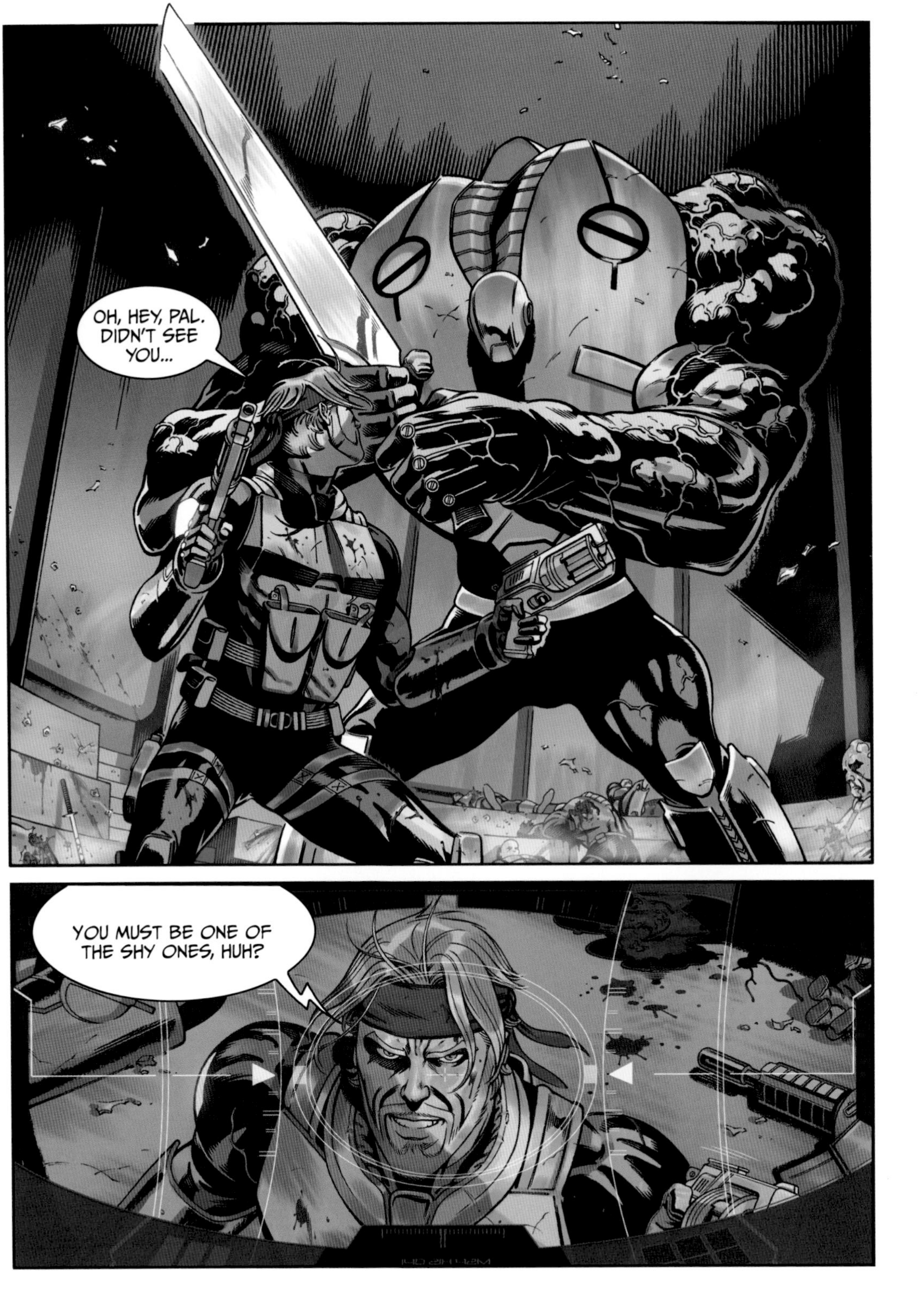
OH, HEY, PAL. DIDN'T SEE YOU...
YOU MUST BE ONE OF THE SHY ONES, HUH?

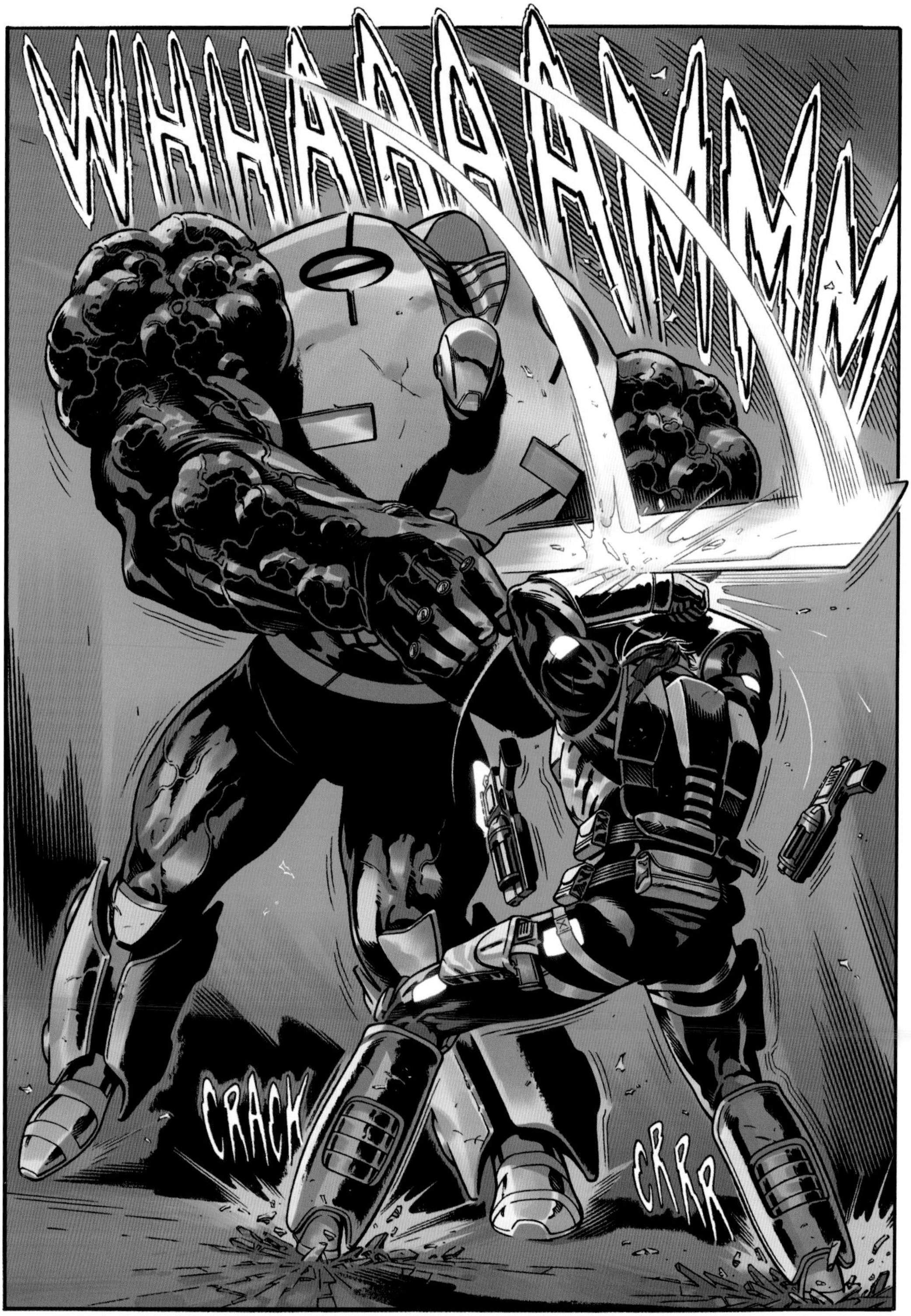
WHHAAAAMMM
CRACK
CRRR

HNGH!

CRACK

GOODBYE, GUNSLINGER.

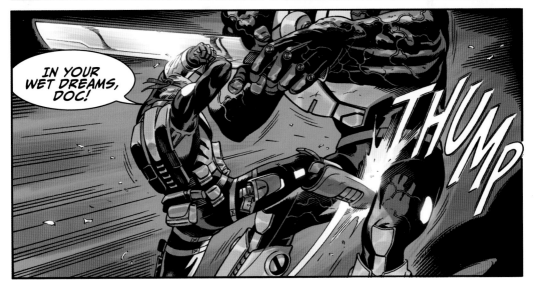

IN YOUR WET DREAMS, DOC!

THUMP

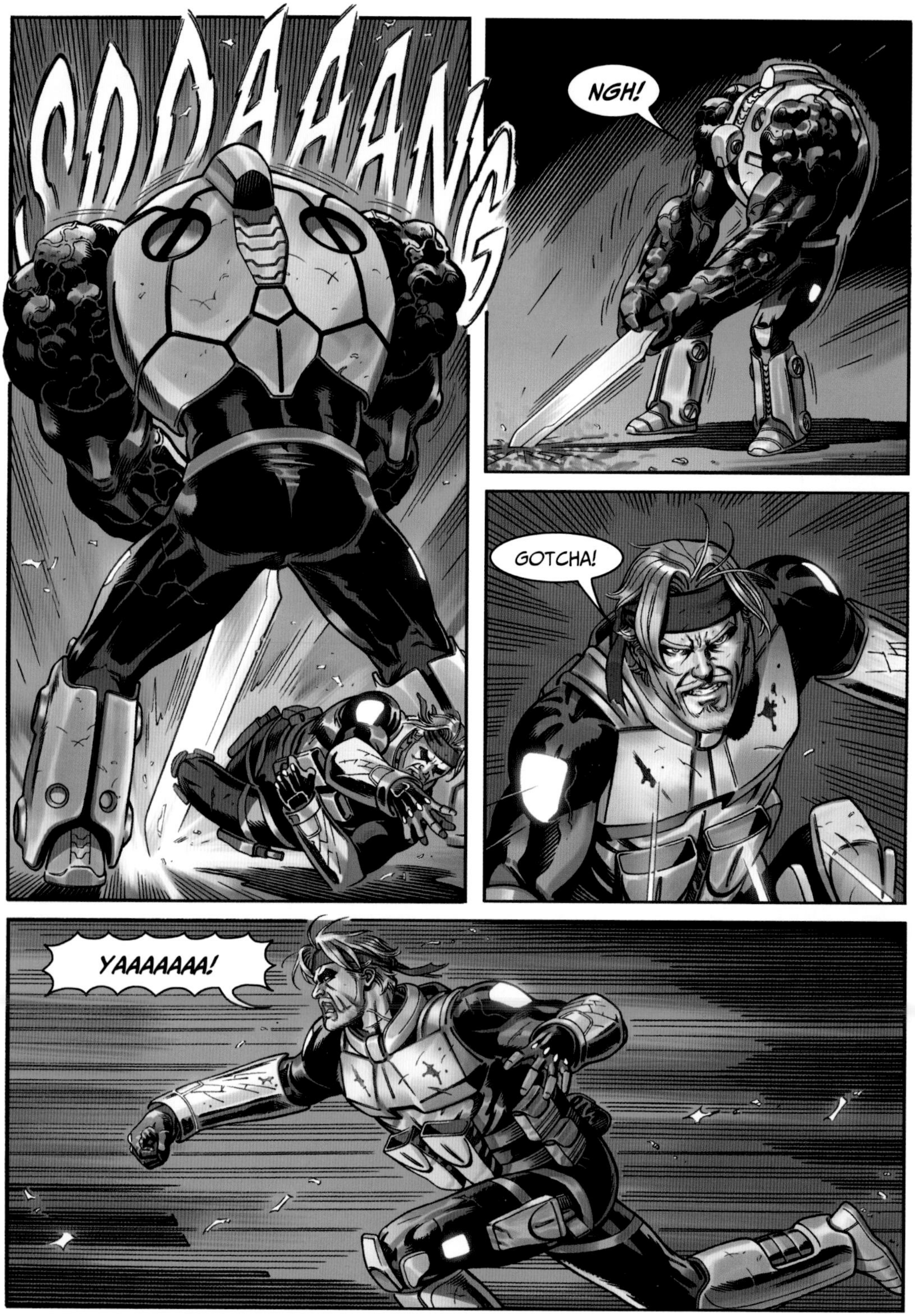
SCRAAANG
NGH!
GOTCHA!
YAAAAAAA!

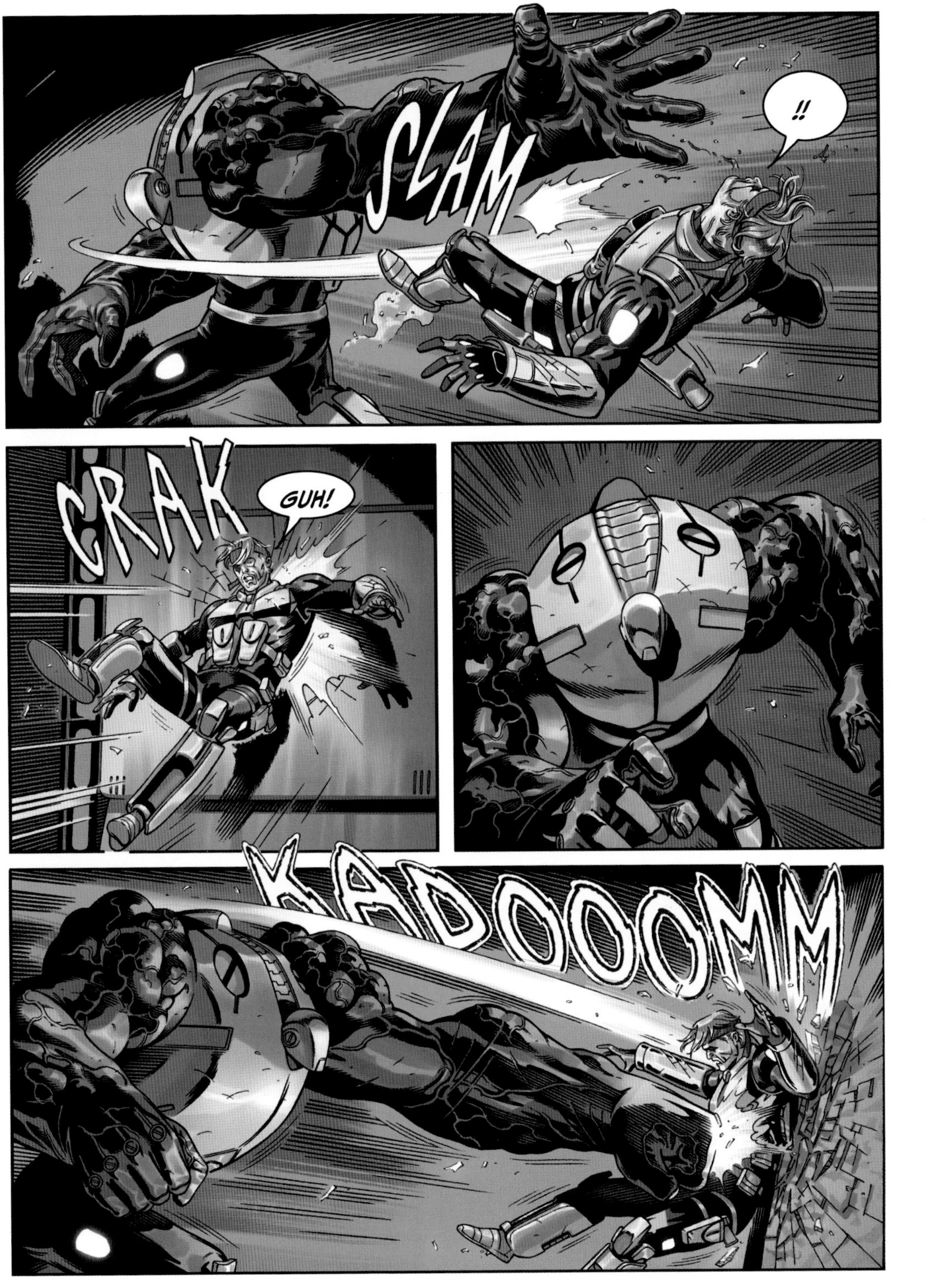
SLAM
!!
CRAK
GUH!
KADOOOMM

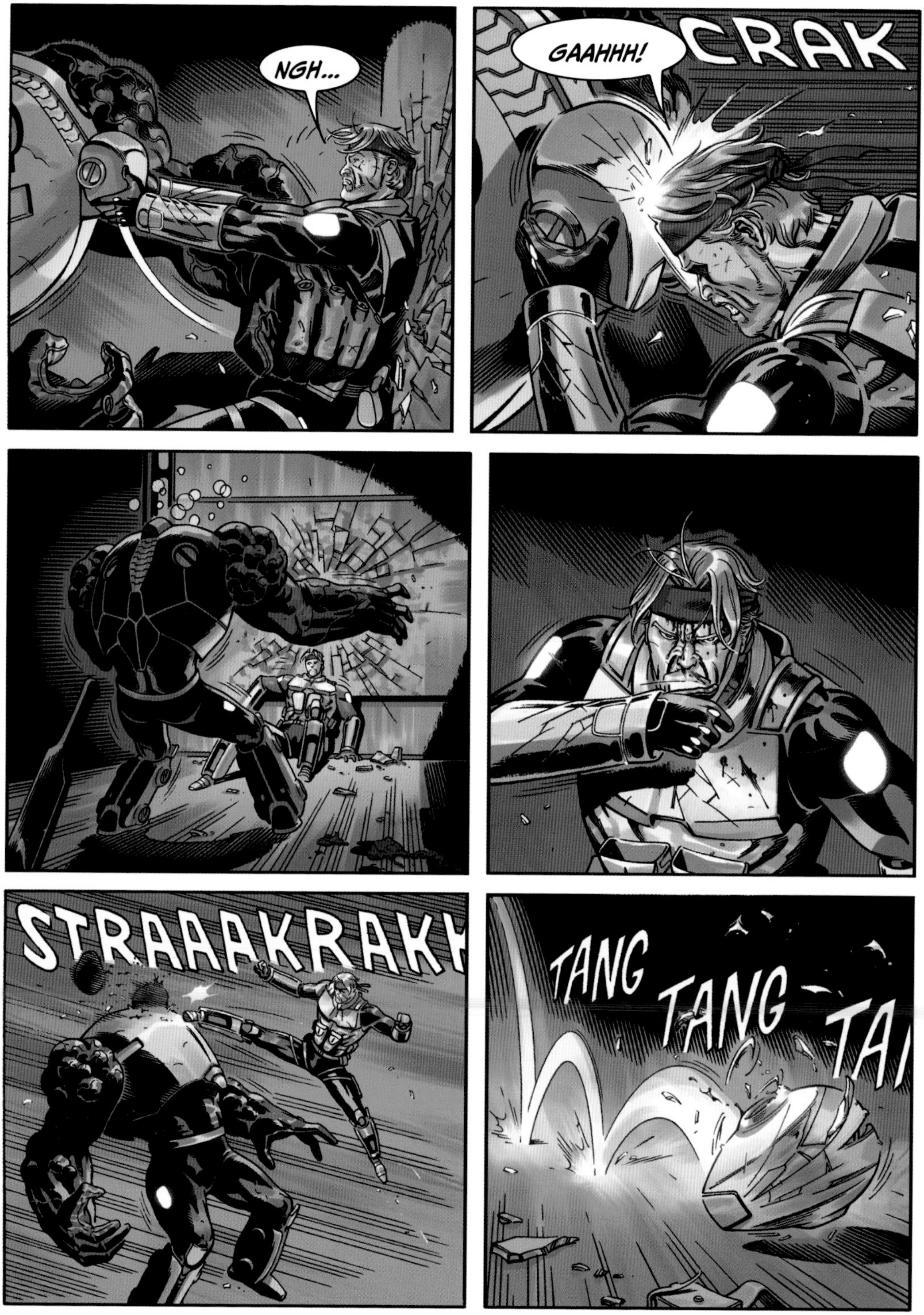
NGH...
GAAHHH!
CRAK
STRAAAKRAKK
TANG
TANG
TA

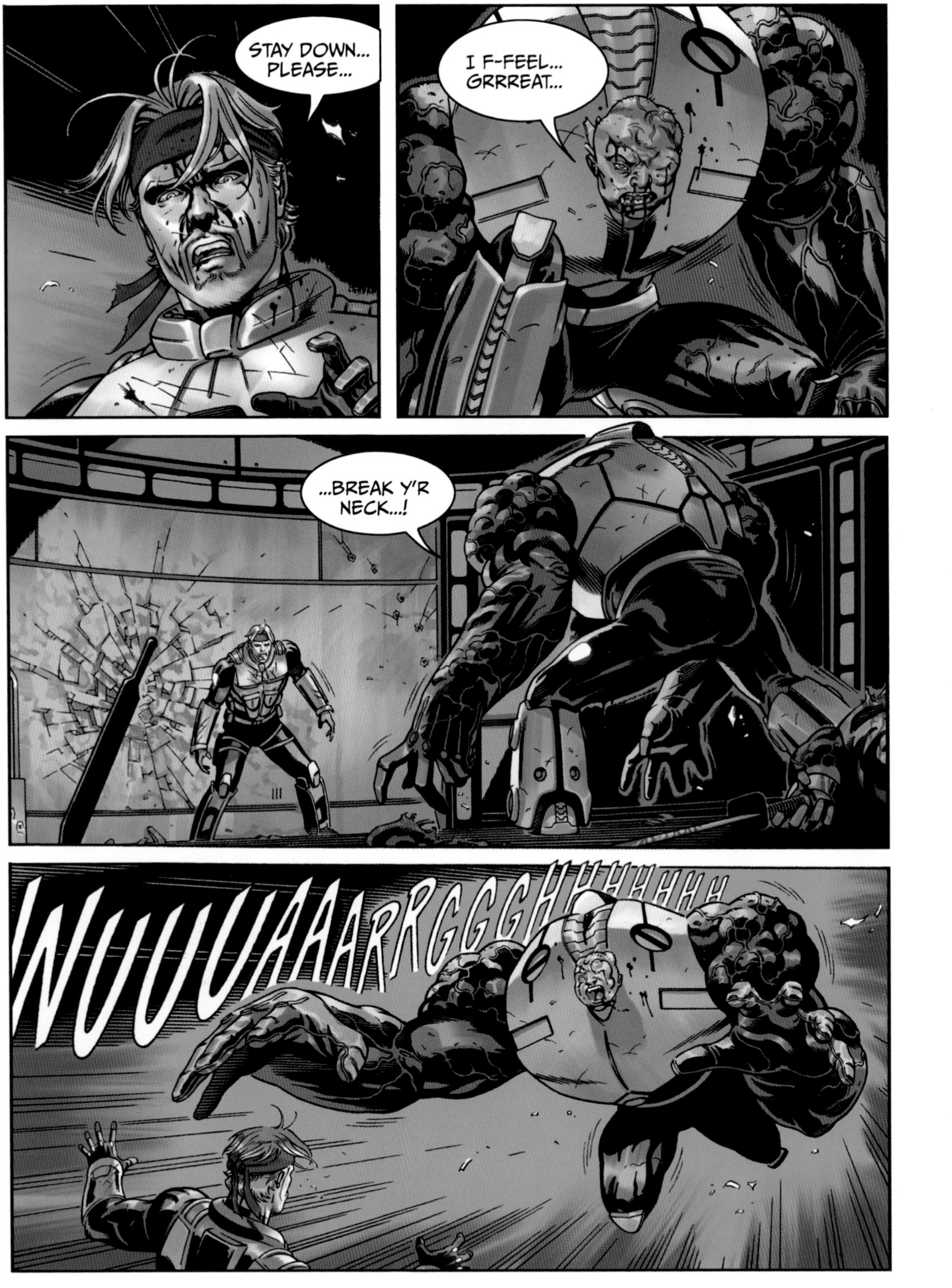
STAY DOWN... PLEASE...
I F-FEEL... GRRREAT...
...BREAK Y'R NECK...!
WUUUAAARRGGGHHHHHHHH

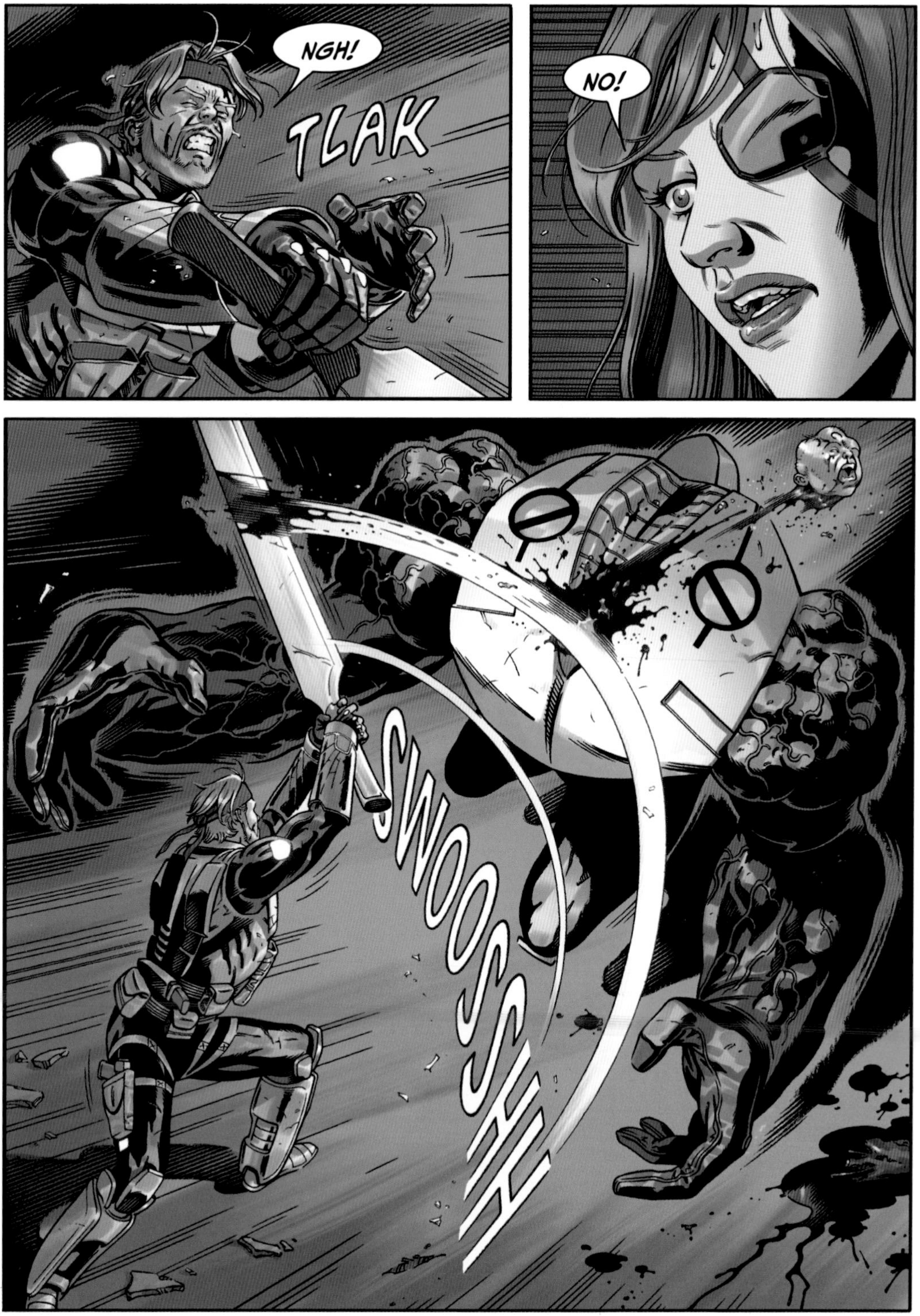
NGH!
TLAK
NO!
SWOOSHH

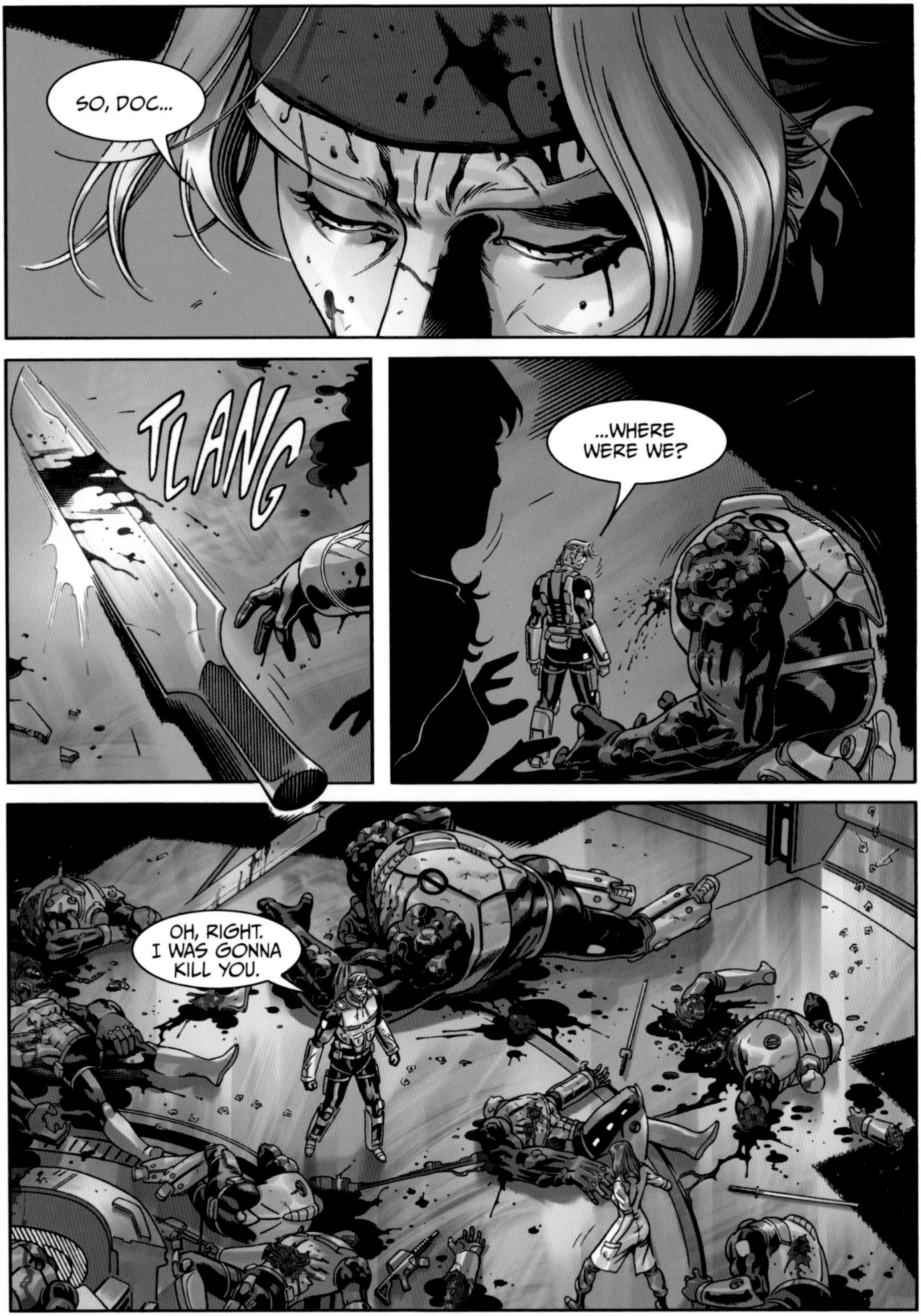
SO, DOC...
TLANG
...WHERE WERE WE?
OH, RIGHT. I WAS GONNA KILL YOU.

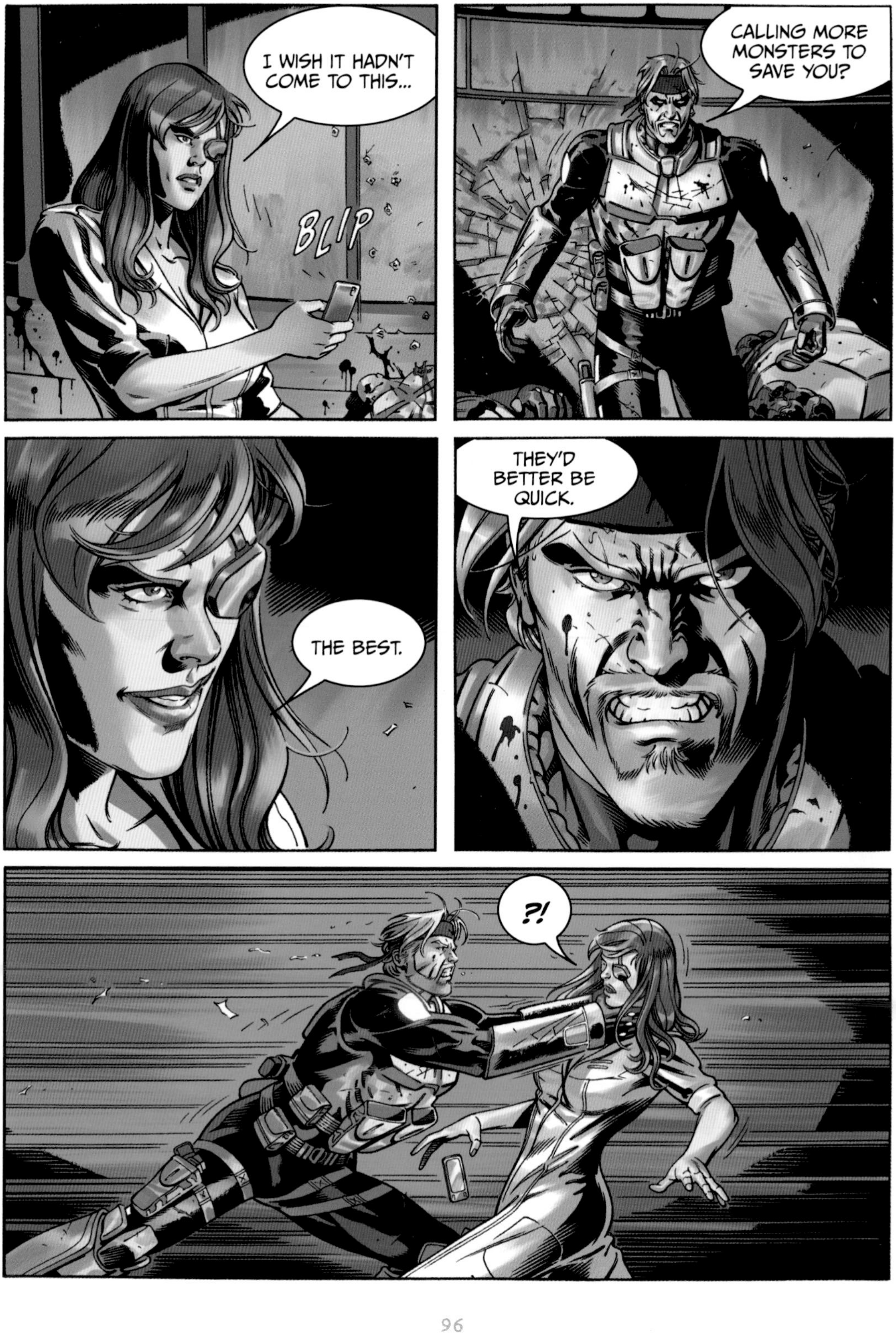
I WISH IT HADN'T COME TO THIS...
BLIP
CALLING MORE MONSTERS TO SAVE YOU?
THE BEST.
THEY'D BETTER BE QUICK.
?!

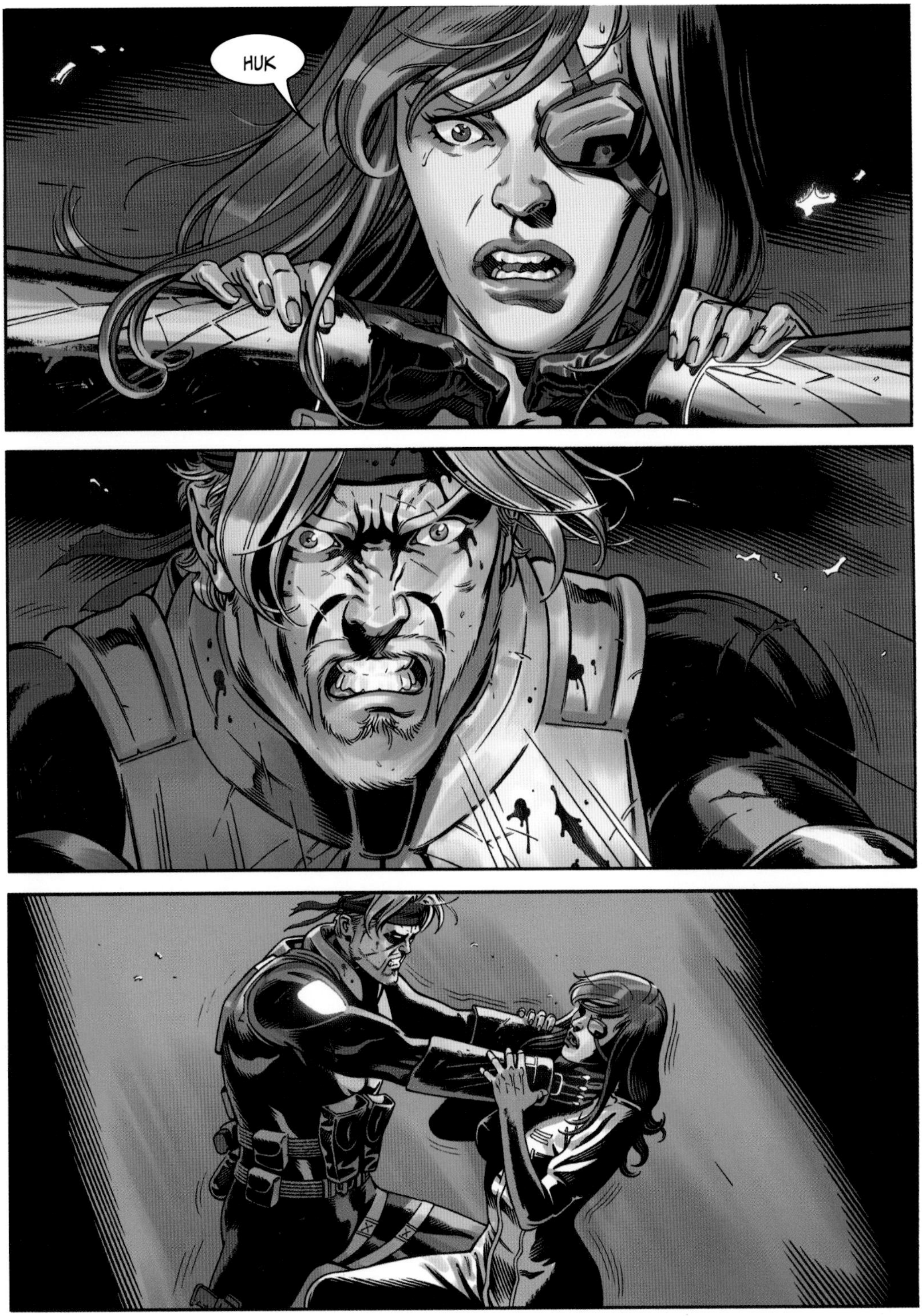
HUK

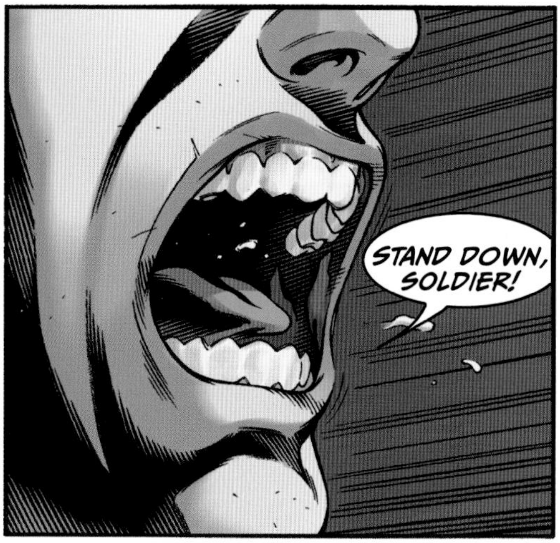
STAND DOWN, SOLDIER!

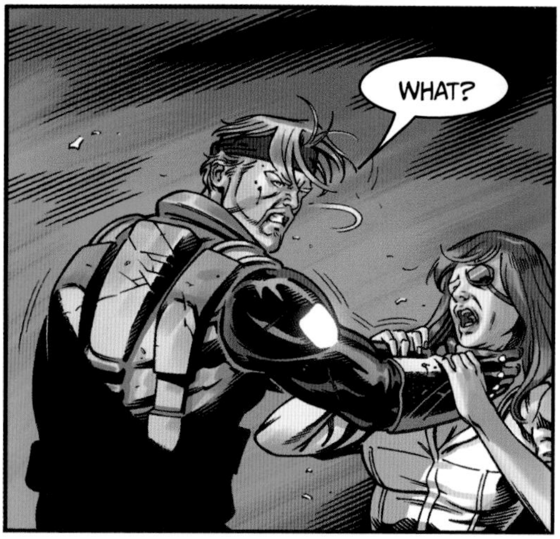
WHAT?

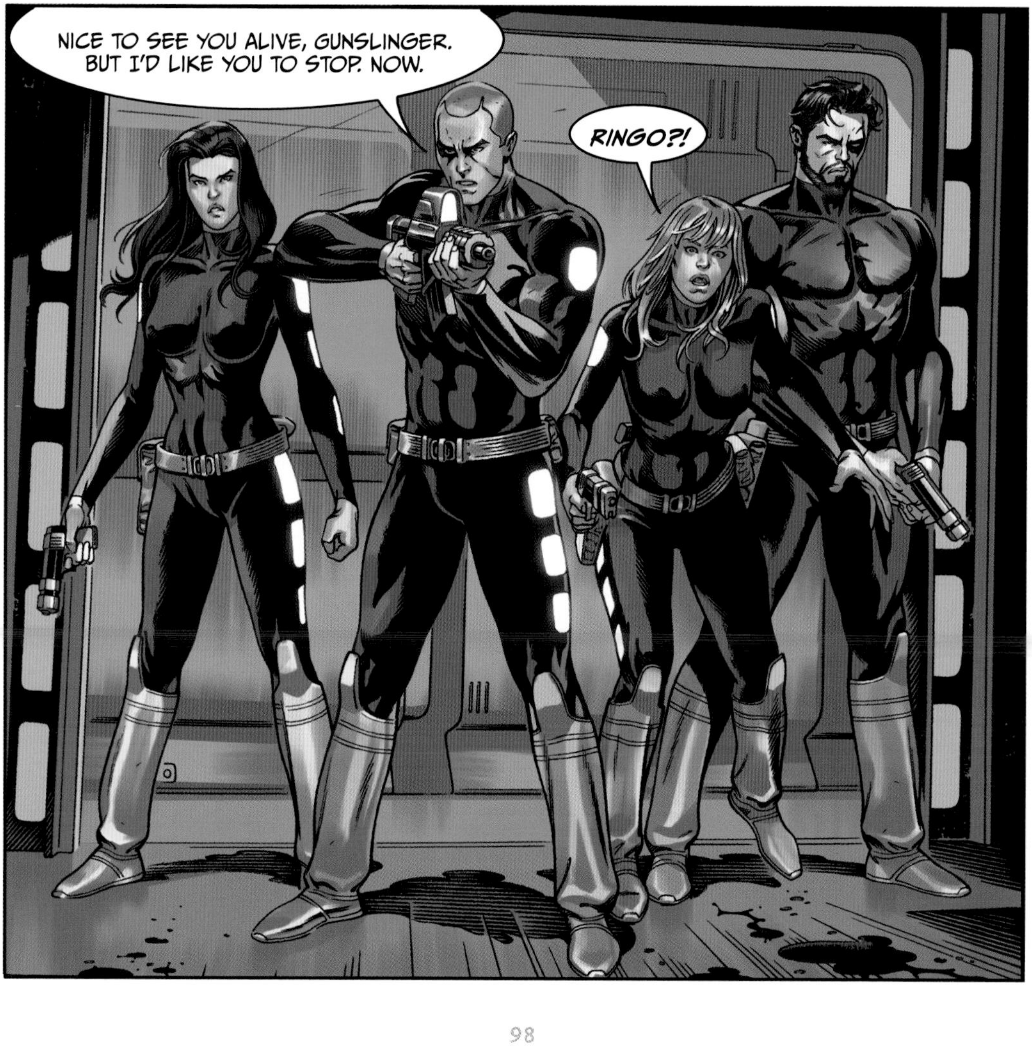
NICE TO SEE YOU ALIVE, GUNSLINGER. BUT I'D LIKE YOU TO STOP. NOW.
RINGO?!

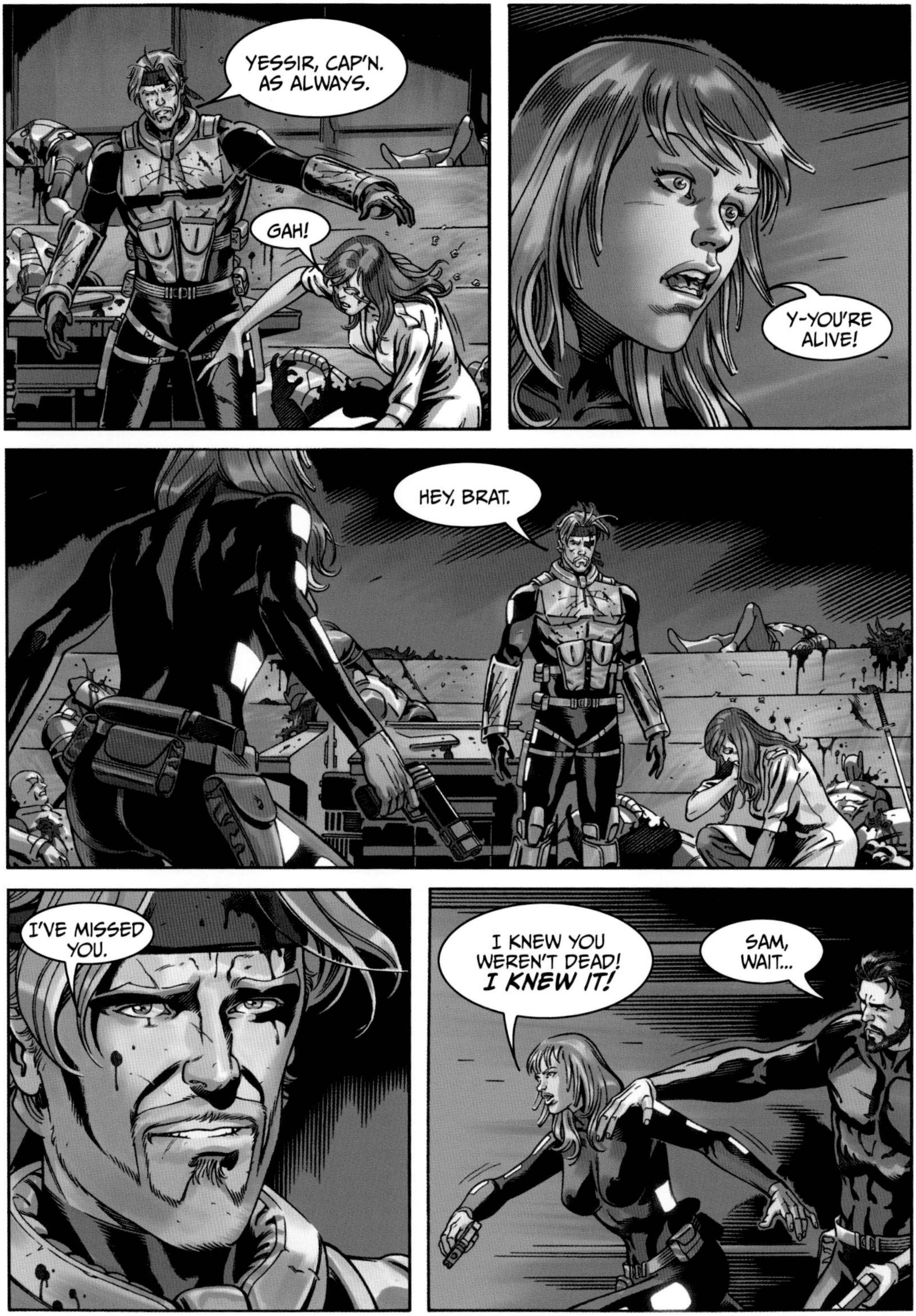
YESSIR, CAP'N. AS ALWAYS.
GAH!
Y-YOU'RE ALIVE!
HEY, BRAT.
I'VE MISSED YOU.
I KNEW YOU WEREN'T DEAD! I KNEW IT!
SAM, WAIT...

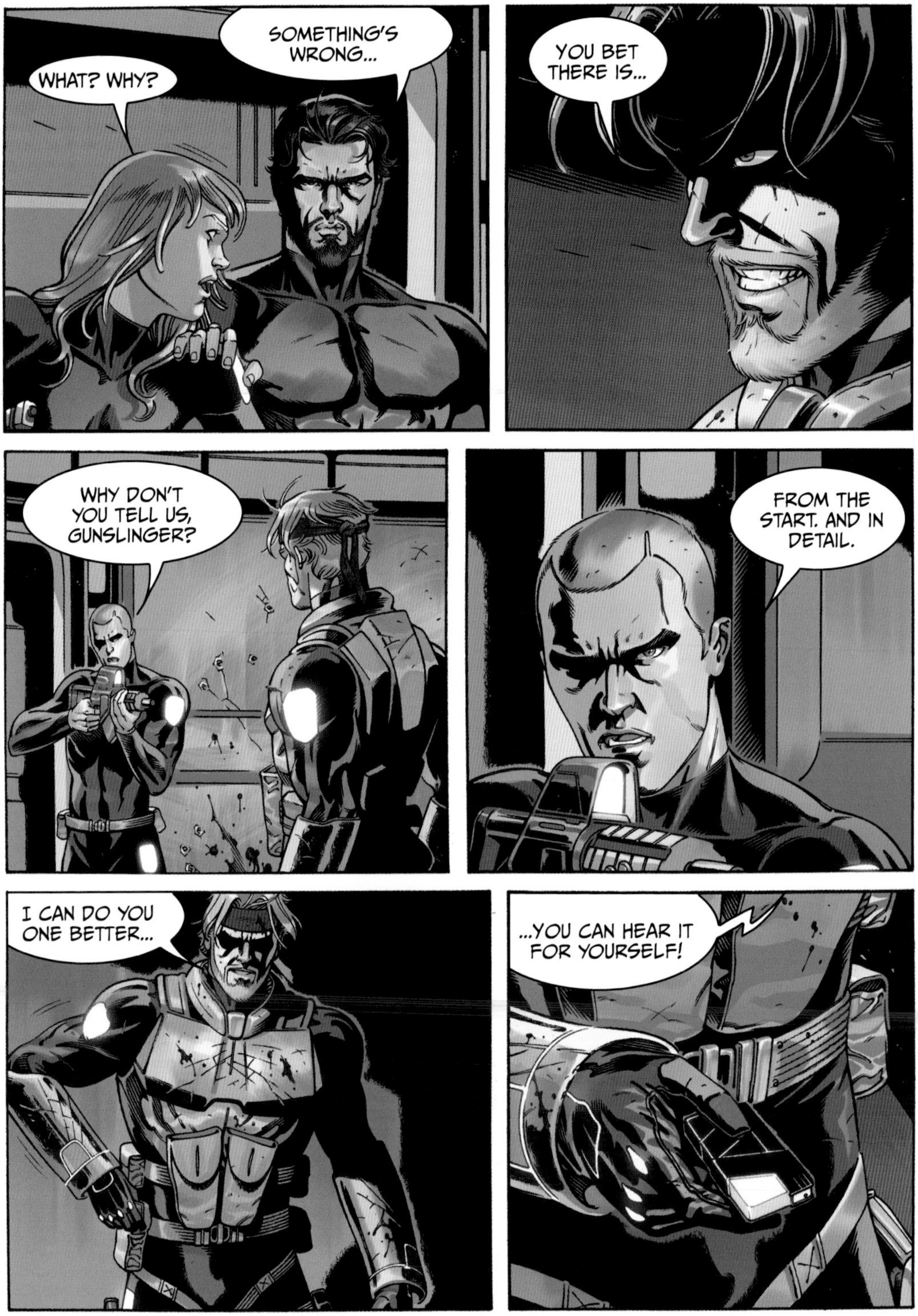
SOMETHING'S WRONG...
WHAT? WHY?
YOU BET THERE IS...
WHY DON'T YOU TELL US, GUNSLINGER?
FROM THE START. AND IN DETAIL.
I CAN DO YOU ONE BETTER...
...YOU CAN HEAR IT FOR YOURSELF!

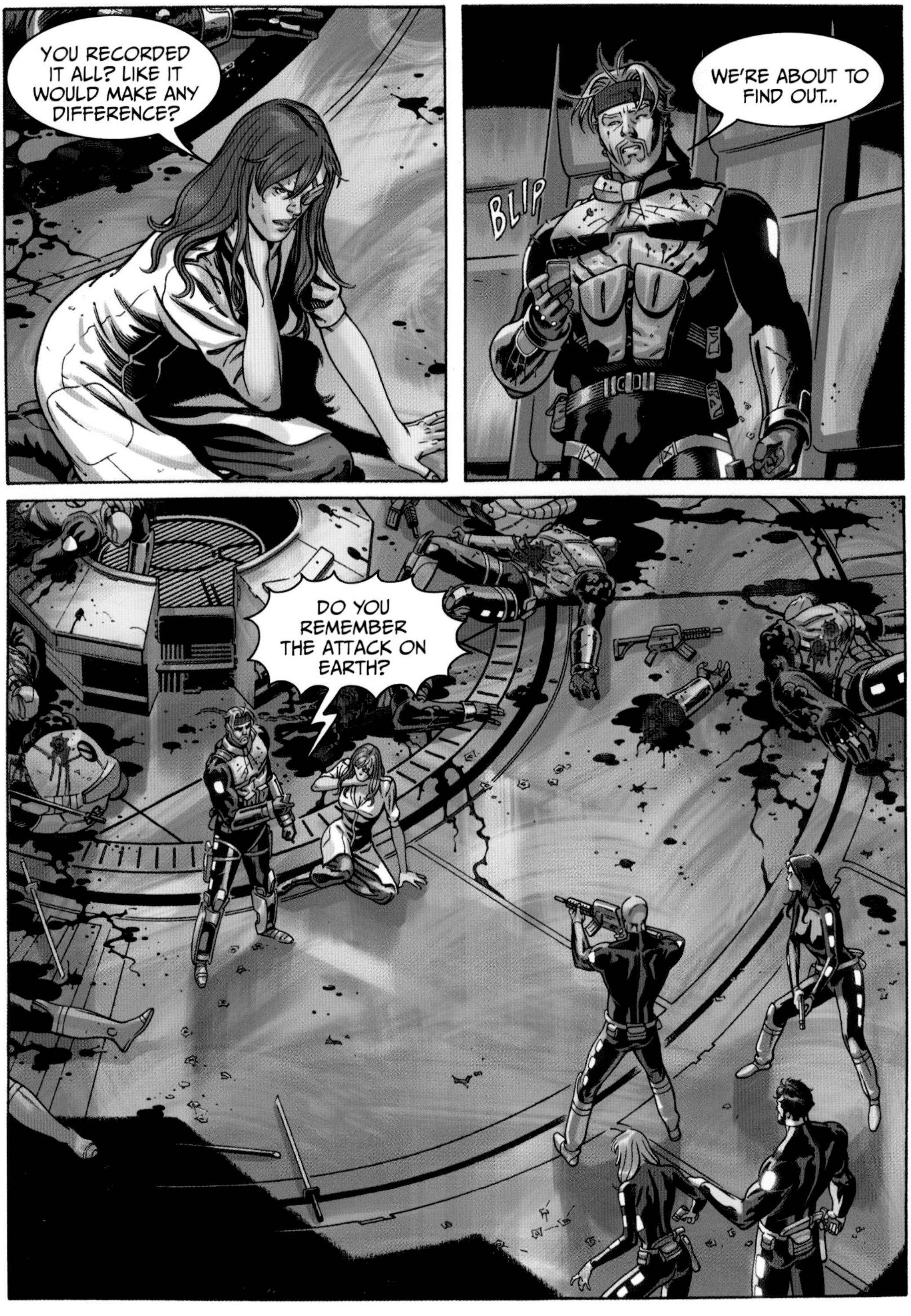
YOU RECORDED IT ALL? LIKE IT WOULD MAKE ANY DIFFERENCE?
WE'RE ABOUT TO FIND OUT...
BLIP
DO YOU REMEMBER THE ATTACK ON EARTH?

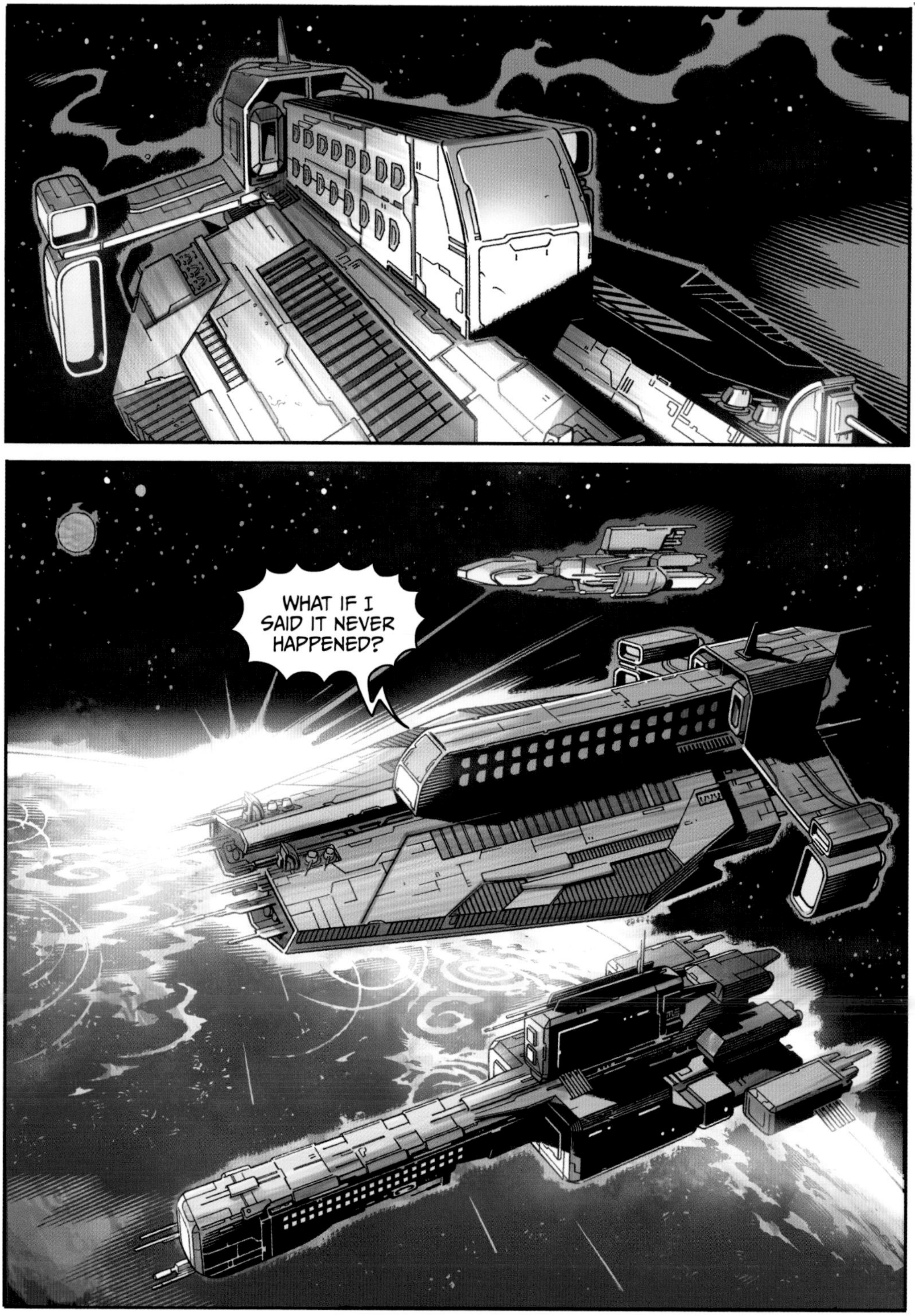
WHAT IF I SAID IT NEVER HAPPENED?

GIORGIO SANTUCCI **ARTIST**

When and where were you born? Where do you live now?
Viterbo in 1971, I still live here.

What sort of artistic education did you have?
Versatile, curious, greedy. With a fascination for everything "extreme."

Tell us about your previous works, before Orphans.
You can find them on Google.

When did you start working on Orphans, and when did you finish drawing this chapter?
It was my first work for Sergio Bonelli Editore, I took my time to get comfortable.

What tools did you use?
Paper, pencil, ink.

What was the most difficult scene and which one did you have to redraw more times?
I didn't find anything particularly difficult, but having to draw children for so many pages was new to me. Of course, the pages I enjoyed the most were the action/destruction ones.

If you could go back in time, what would you change about this chapter?
Everything and nothing.

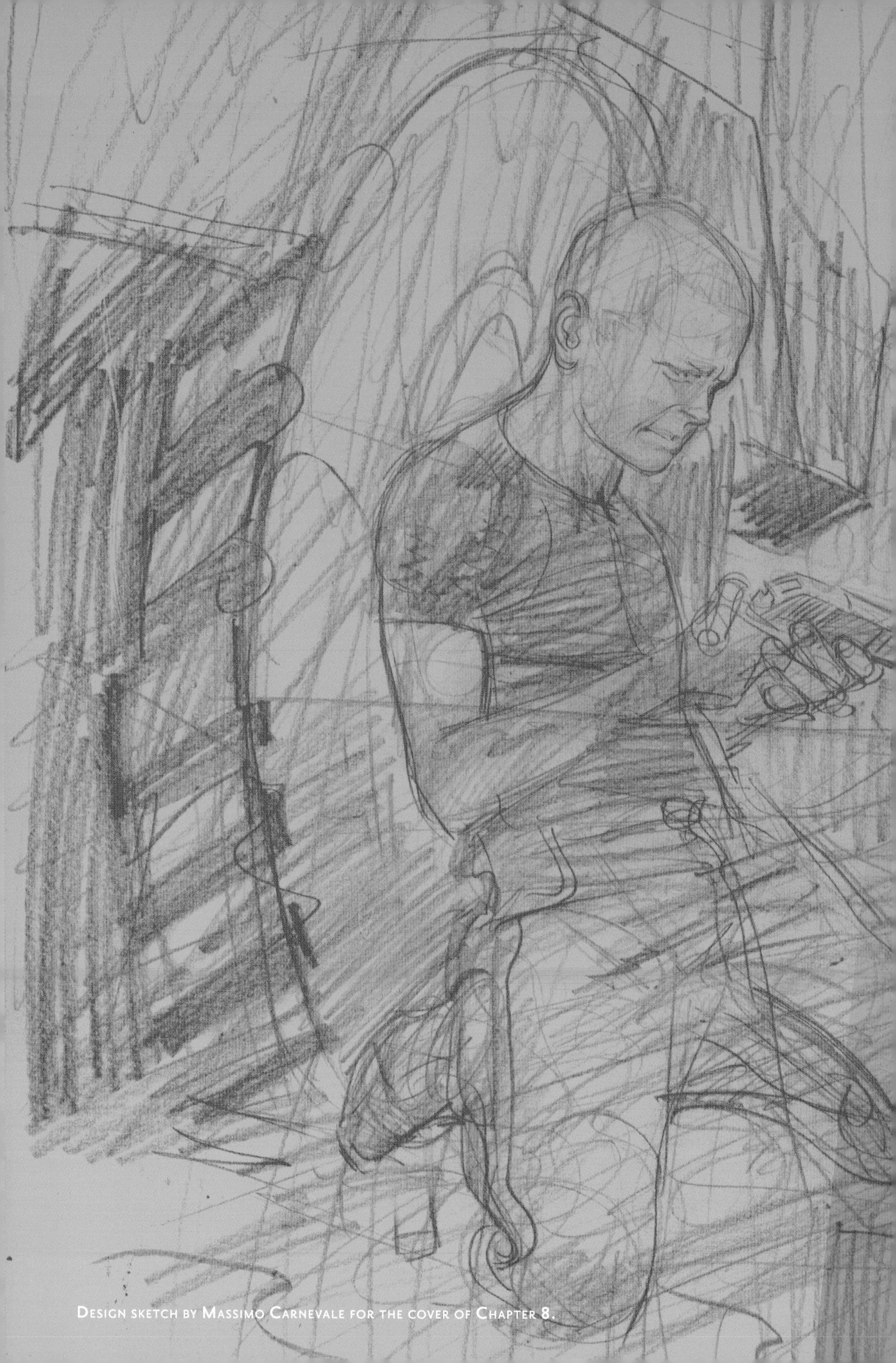

Design sketch by Massimo Carnevale for the cover of Chapter 8.

WAR PIGS

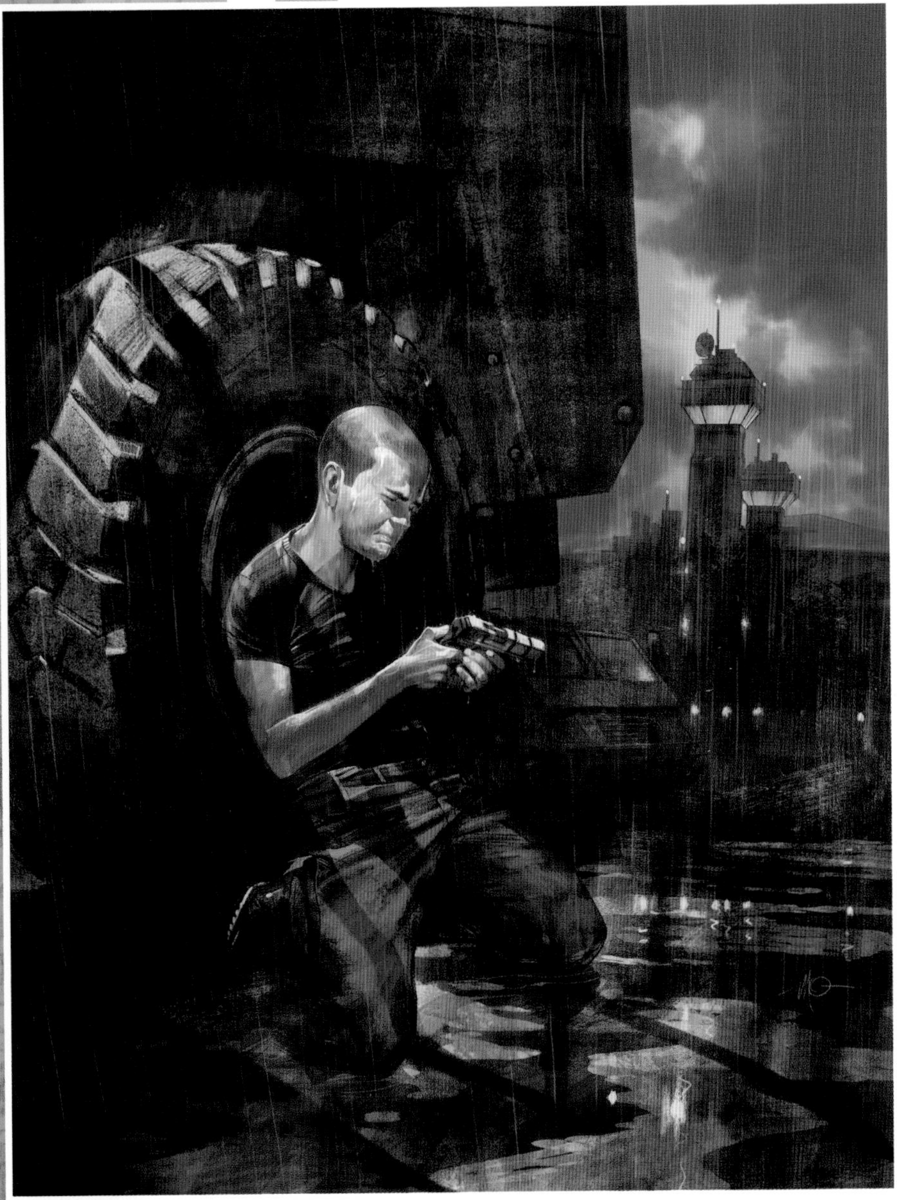

ORPHANS: CHAPTER 8

story: ROBERTO RECCHIONI
art: DAVIDE GIANFELICE
colors: STEFANO SIMEONE
cover: MASSIMO CARNEVALE

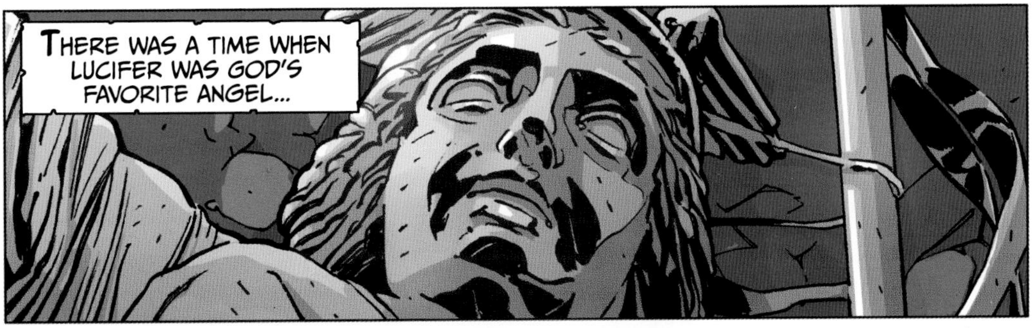
THERE WAS A TIME WHEN LUCIFER WAS GOD'S FAVORITE ANGEL...

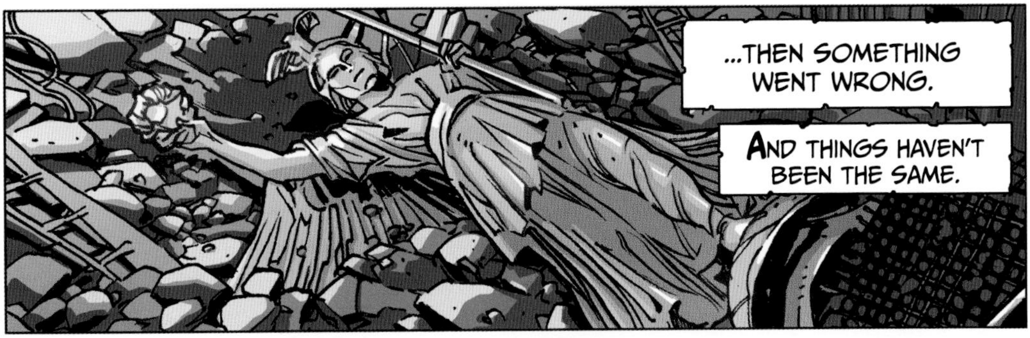
...THEN SOMETHING WENT WRONG.
AND THINGS HAVEN'T BEEN THE SAME.

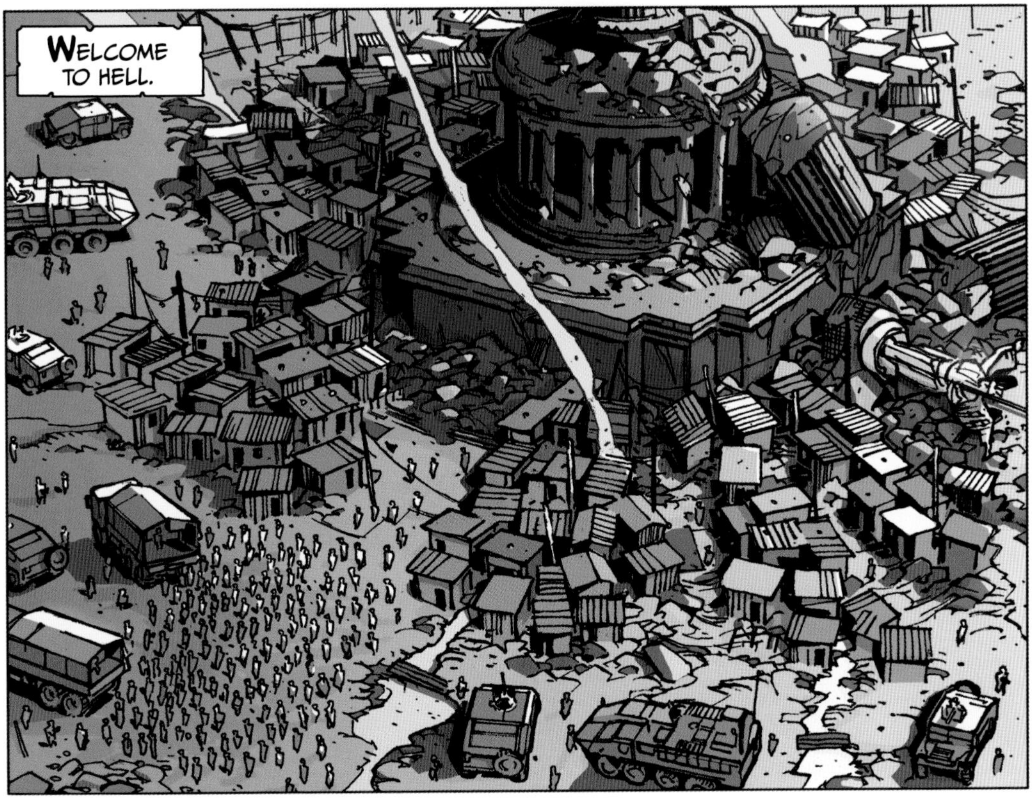
WELCOME TO HELL.

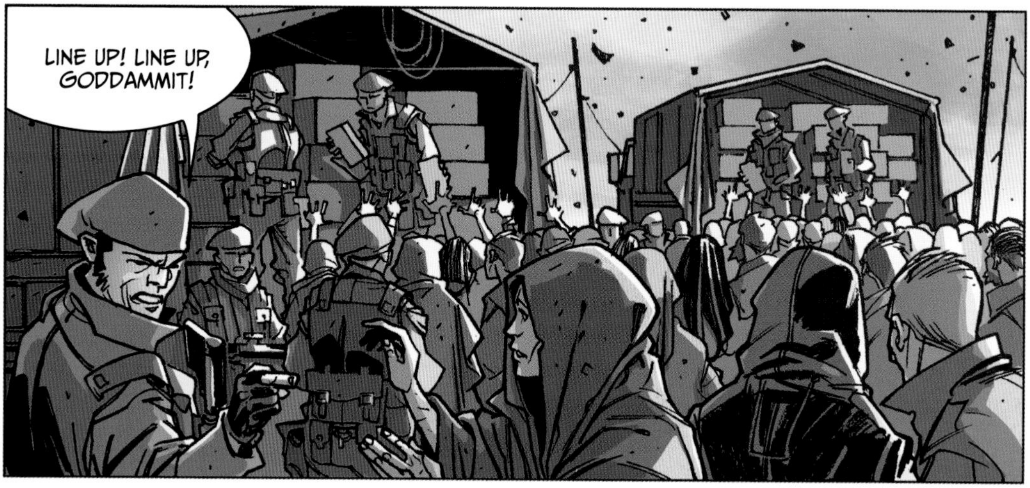
LINE UP! LINE UP, GODDAMMIT!

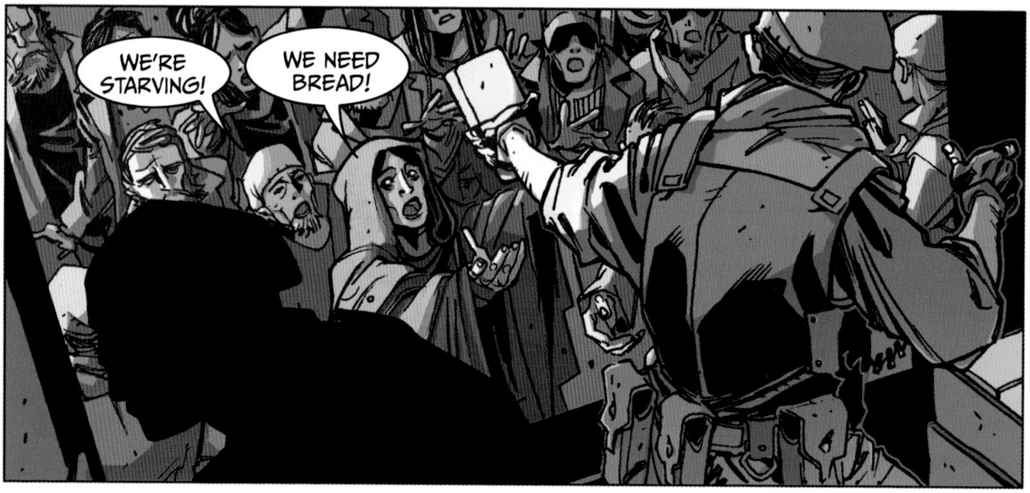
WE'RE STARVING!
WE NEED BREAD!

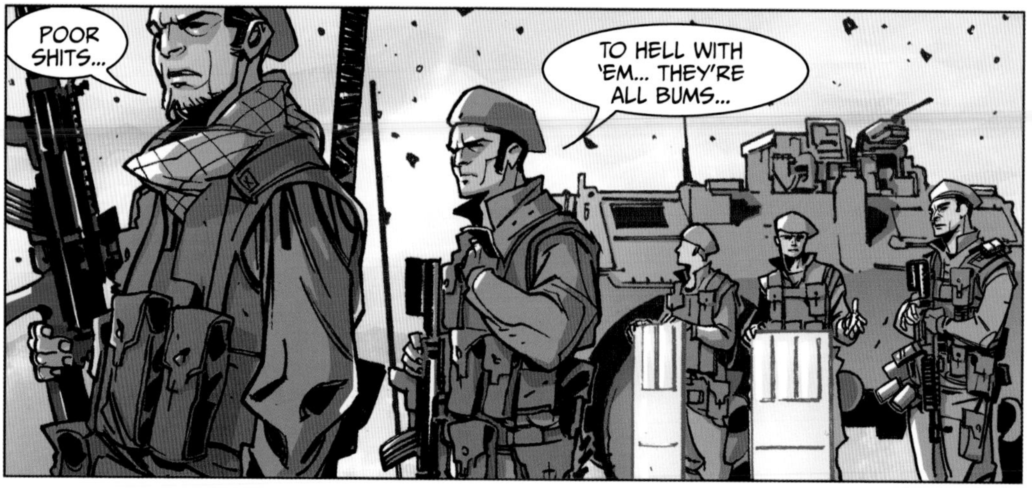
POOR SHITS...
TO HELL WITH 'EM... THEY'RE ALL BUMS...

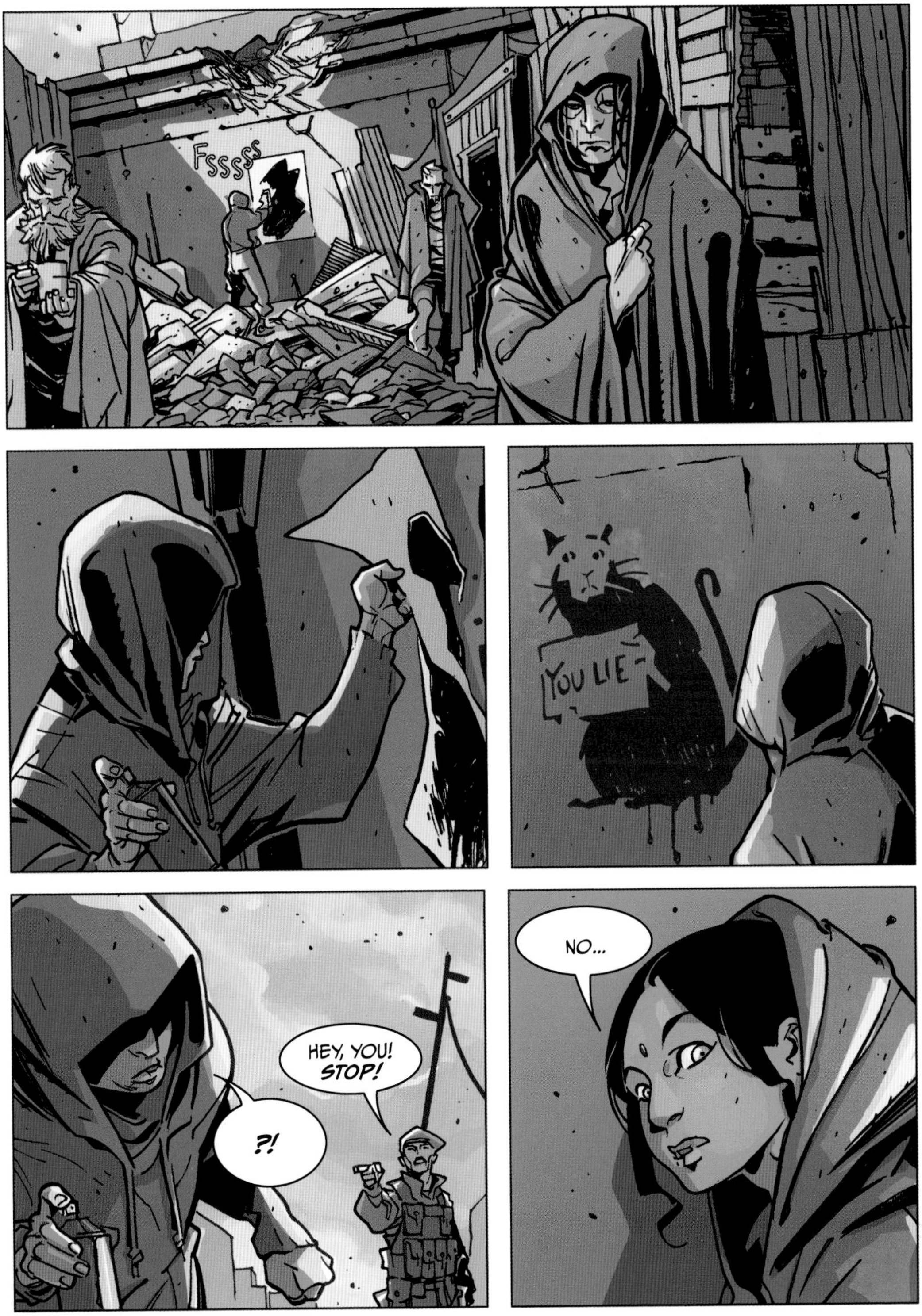
FSSSSS
YOU LIE
?!
HEY, YOU! STOP!
NO...

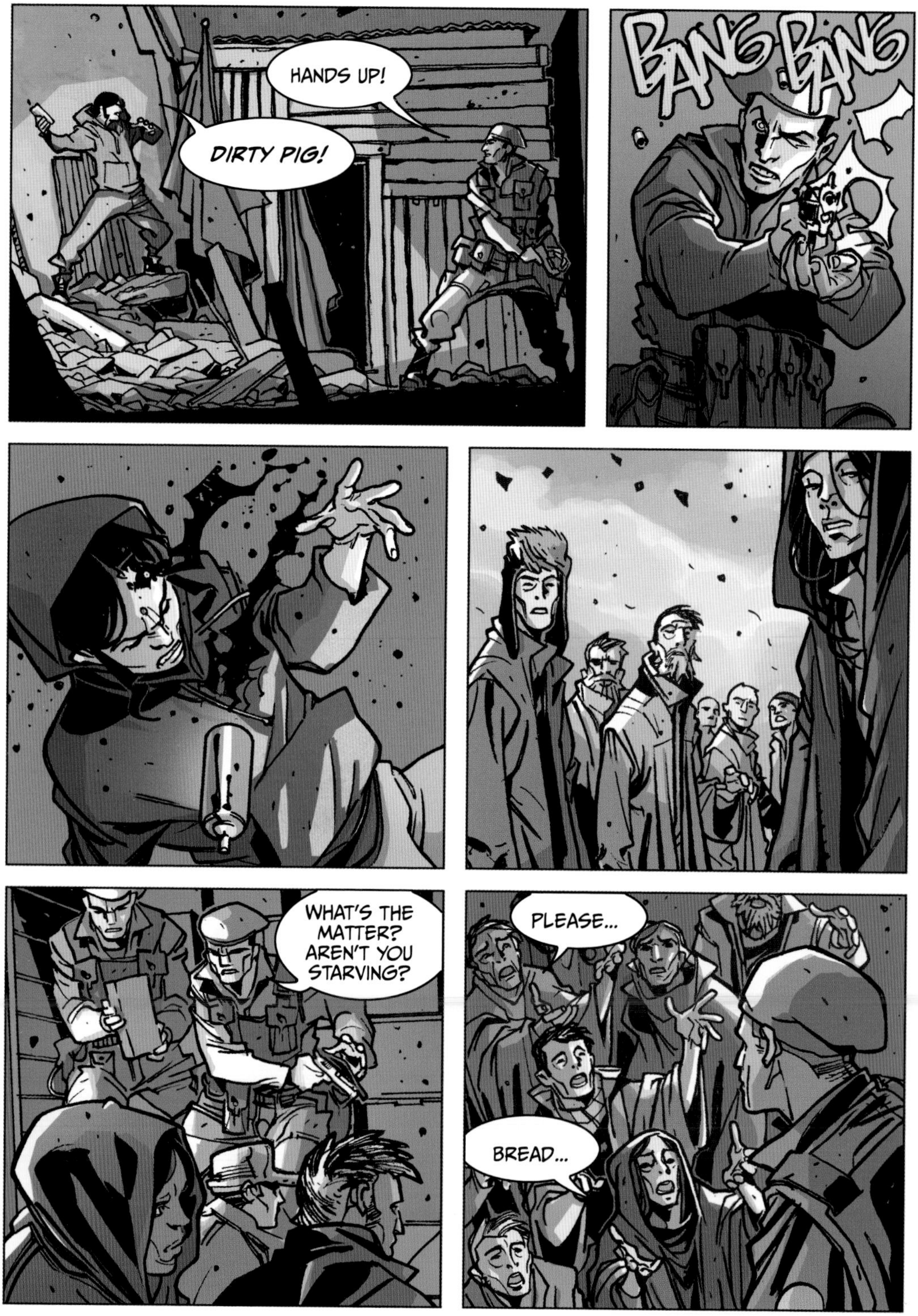
HANDS UP!
DIRTY PIG!
BANG BANG
WHAT'S THE MATTER? AREN'T YOU STARVING?
PLEASE...
BREAD...

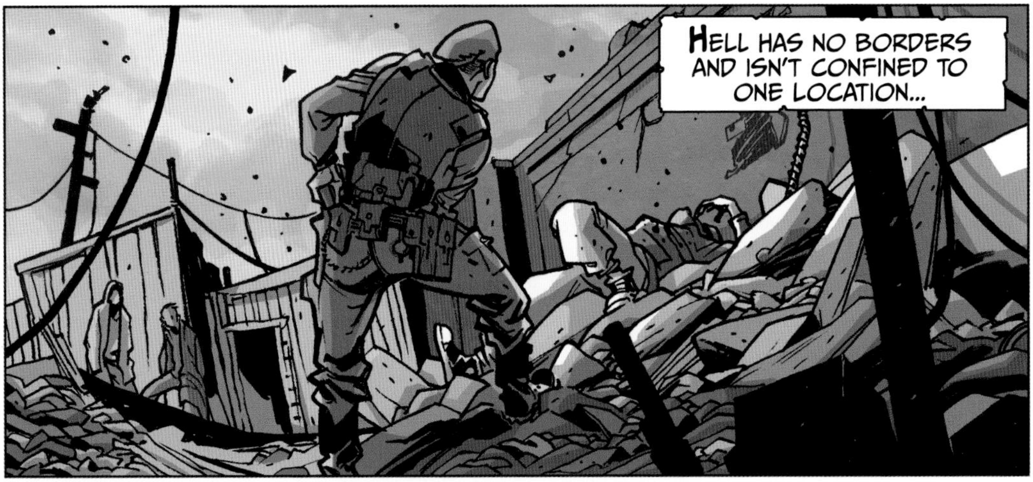
HELL HAS NO BORDERS AND ISN'T CONFINED TO ONE LOCATION...

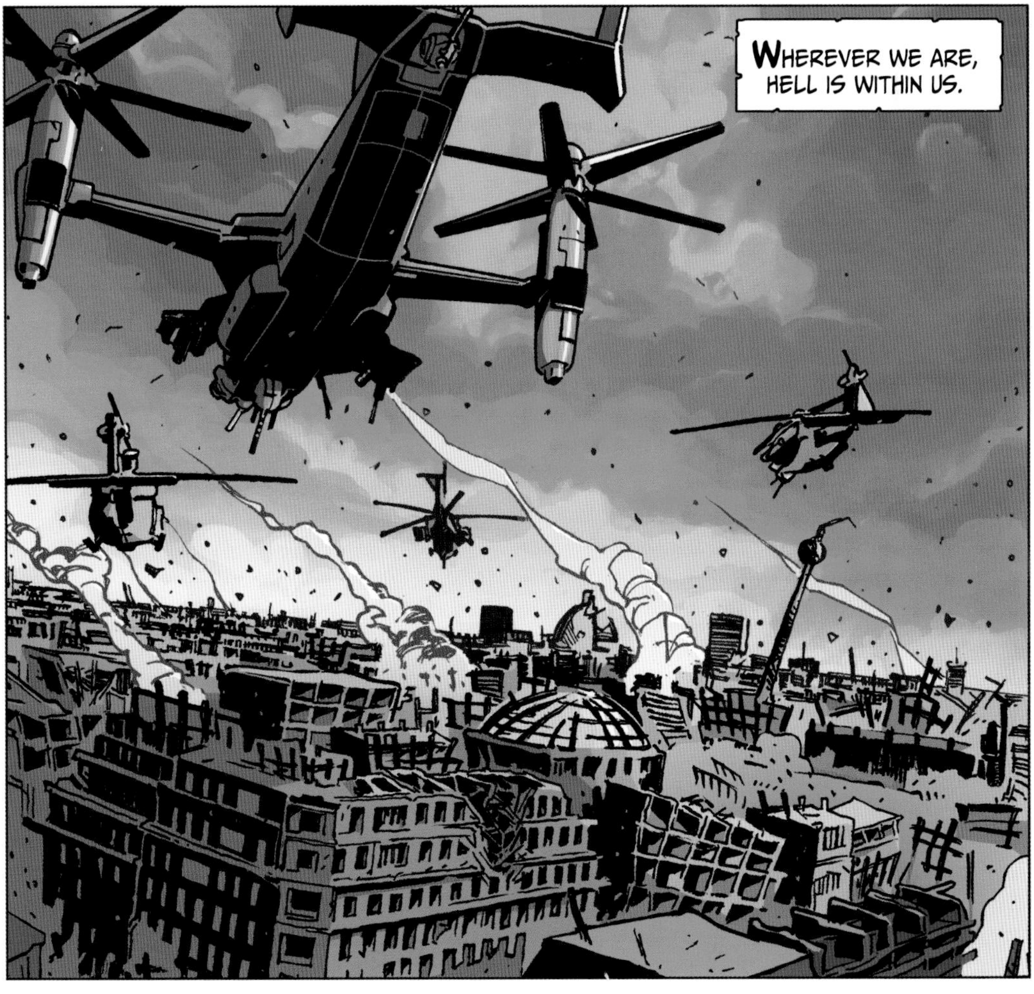
WHEREVER WE ARE, HELL IS WITHIN US.

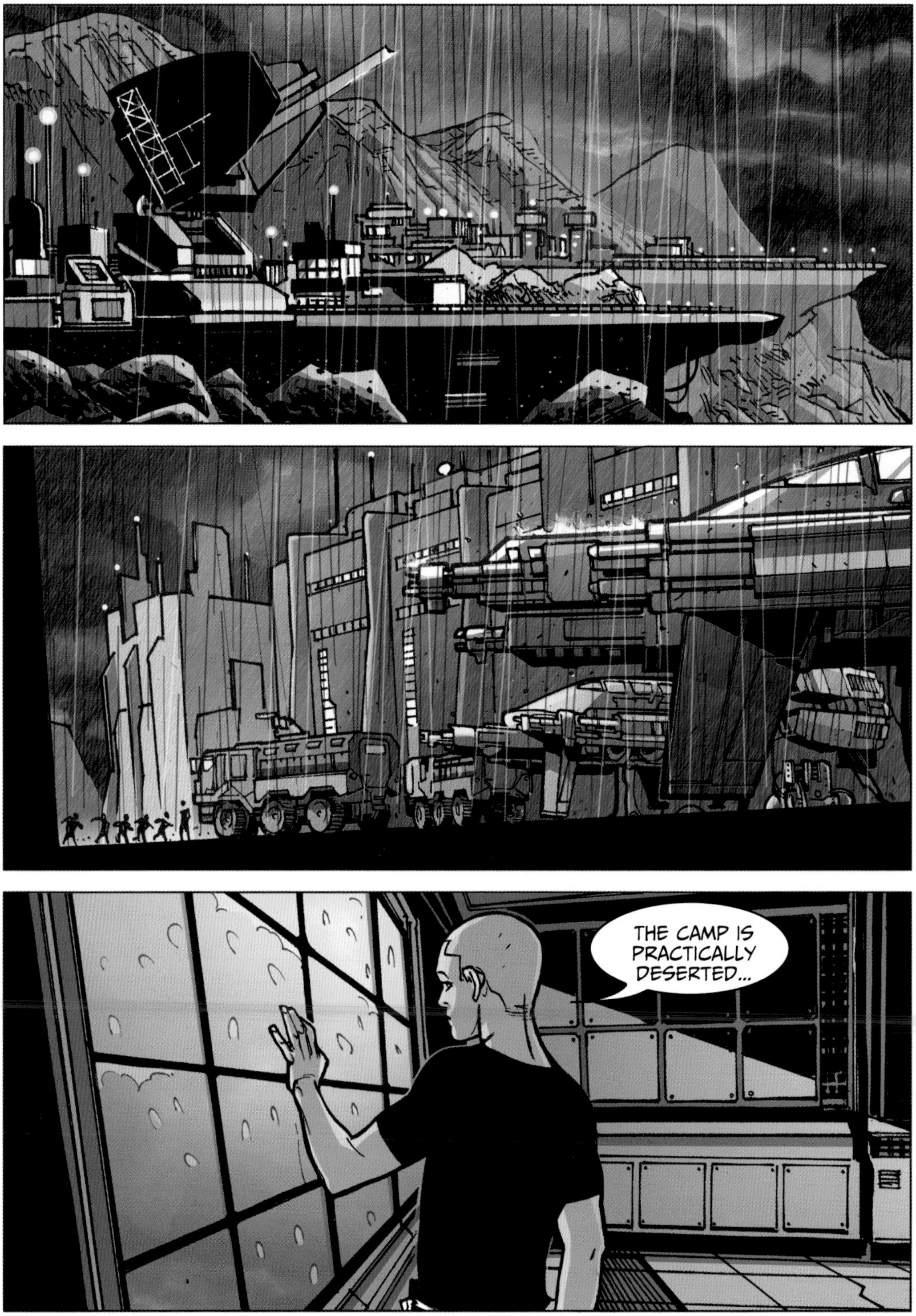
THE CAMP IS PRACTICALLY DESERTED...

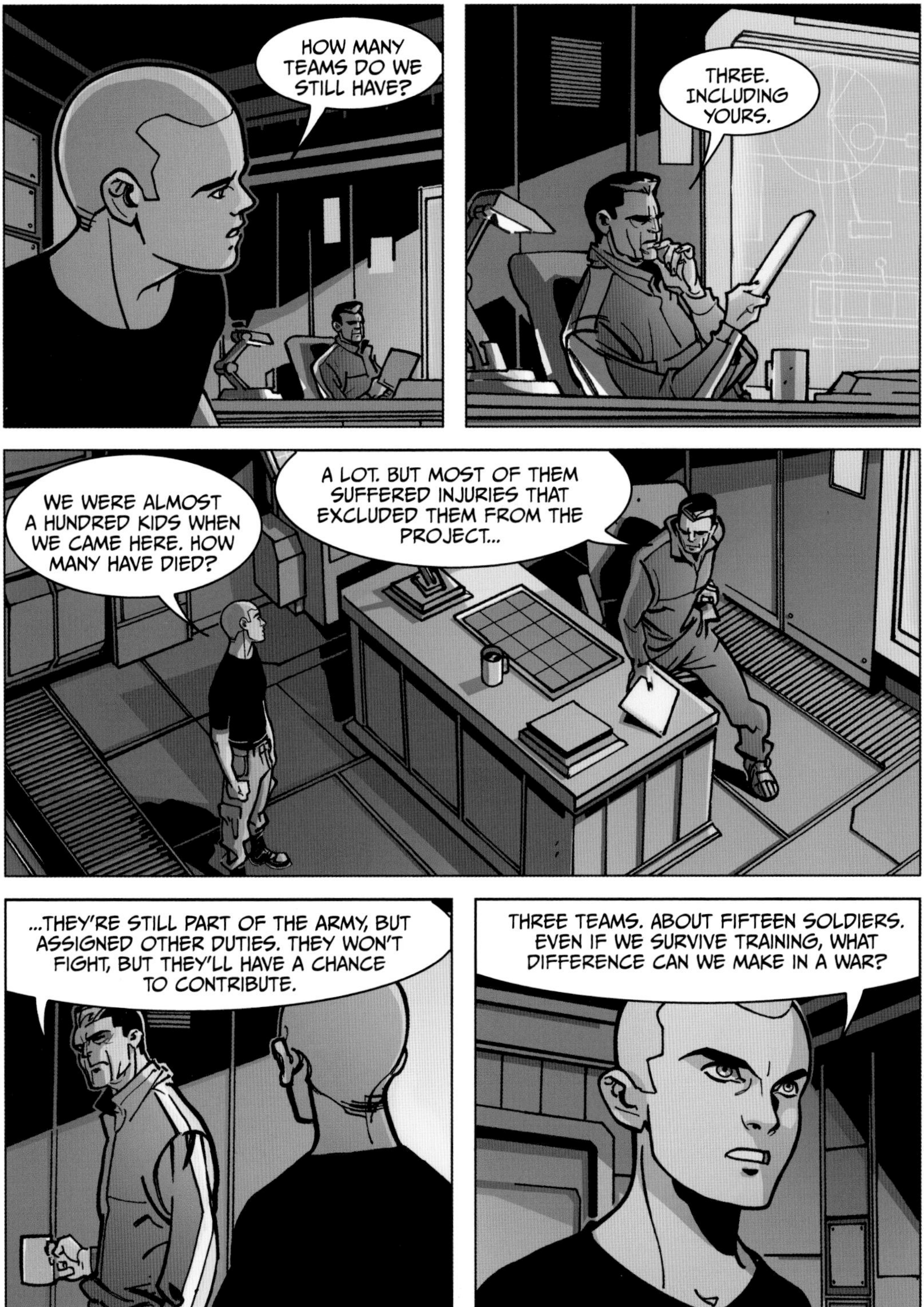
HOW MANY TEAMS DO WE STILL HAVE?
THREE. INCLUDING YOURS.
WE WERE ALMOST A HUNDRED KIDS WHEN WE CAME HERE. HOW MANY HAVE DIED?
A LOT. BUT MOST OF THEM SUFFERED INJURIES THAT EXCLUDED THEM FROM THE PROJECT...
...THEY'RE STILL PART OF THE ARMY, BUT ASSIGNED OTHER DUTIES. THEY WON'T FIGHT, BUT THEY'LL HAVE A CHANCE TO CONTRIBUTE.
THREE TEAMS. ABOUT FIFTEEN SOLDIERS. EVEN IF WE SURVIVE TRAINING, WHAT DIFFERENCE CAN WE MAKE IN A WAR?

IT'S NOT WHAT YOU DO THAT COUNTS, BUT WHAT YOU REPRESENT.

MEANING?

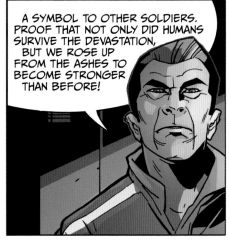

A SYMBOL TO OTHER SOLDIERS. PROOF THAT NOT ONLY DID HUMANS SURVIVE THE DEVASTATION, BUT WE ROSE UP FROM THE ASHES TO BECOME STRONGER THAN BEFORE!

I THOUGHT WE'D FIGHT!

YOU WILL.

IN THE FRONT LINE, LEADING EVERY ATTACK! YOU'LL PAVE THE WAY AND OTHERS WILL FOLLOW!

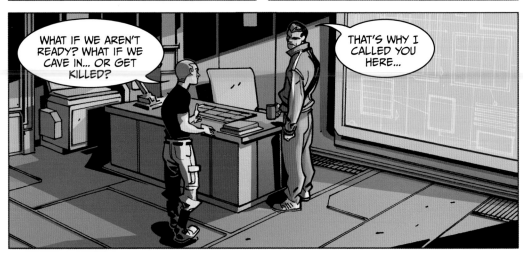

WHAT IF WE AREN'T READY? WHAT IF WE CAVE IN... OR GET KILLED?

THAT'S WHY I CALLED YOU HERE...

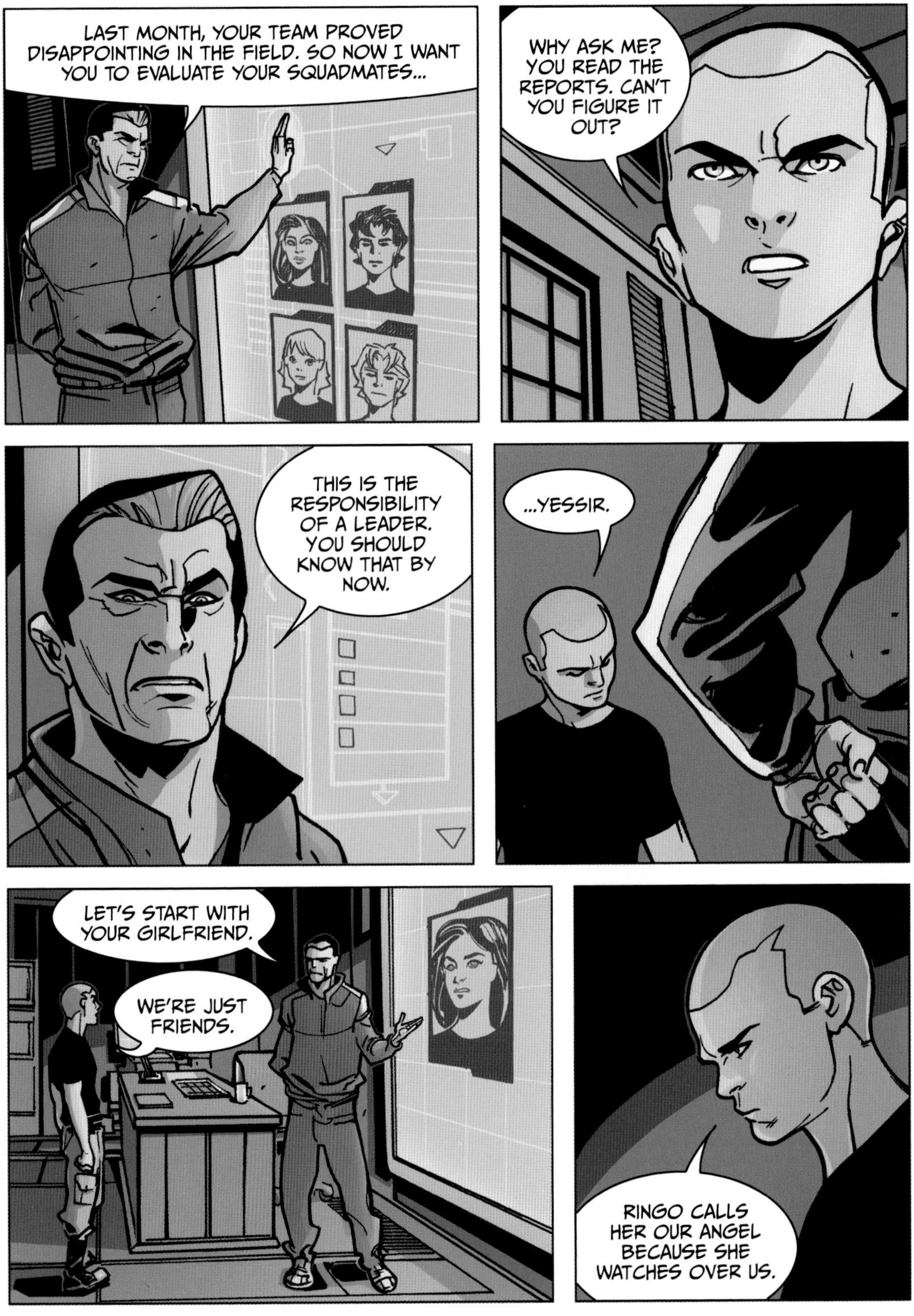
LAST MONTH, YOUR TEAM PROVED DISAPPOINTING IN THE FIELD. SO NOW I WANT YOU TO EVALUATE YOUR SQUADMATES...
WHY ASK ME? YOU READ THE REPORTS. CAN'T YOU FIGURE IT OUT?
THIS IS THE RESPONSIBILITY OF A LEADER. YOU SHOULD KNOW THAT BY NOW.
...YESSIR.
LET'S START WITH YOUR GIRLFRIEND.
WE'RE JUST FRIENDS.
RINGO CALLS HER OUR ANGEL BECAUSE SHE WATCHES OVER US.

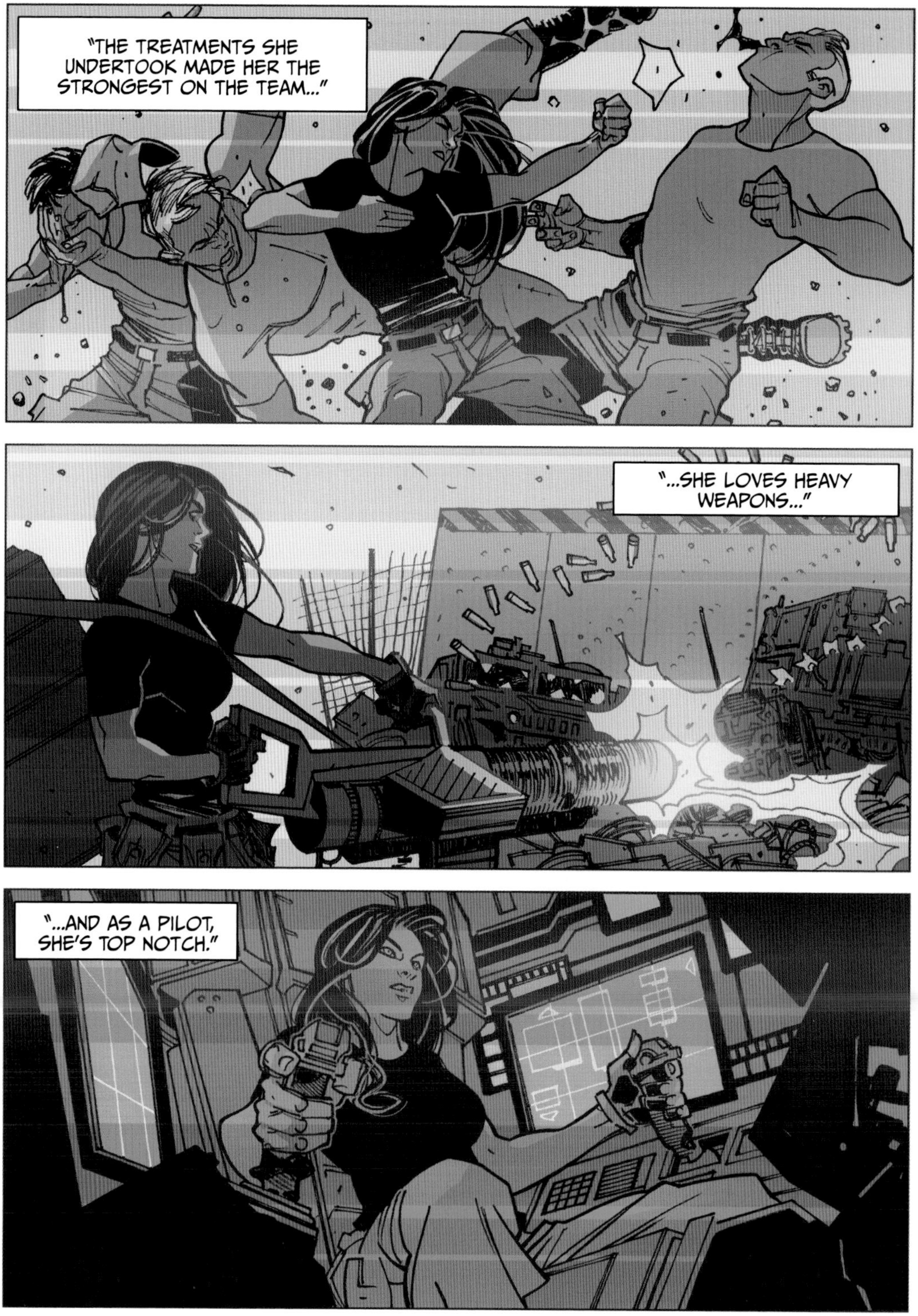
"THE TREATMENTS SHE UNDERTOOK MADE HER THE STRONGEST ON THE TEAM..."
"...SHE LOVES HEAVY WEAPONS..."
"...AND AS A PILOT, SHE'S TOP NOTCH."

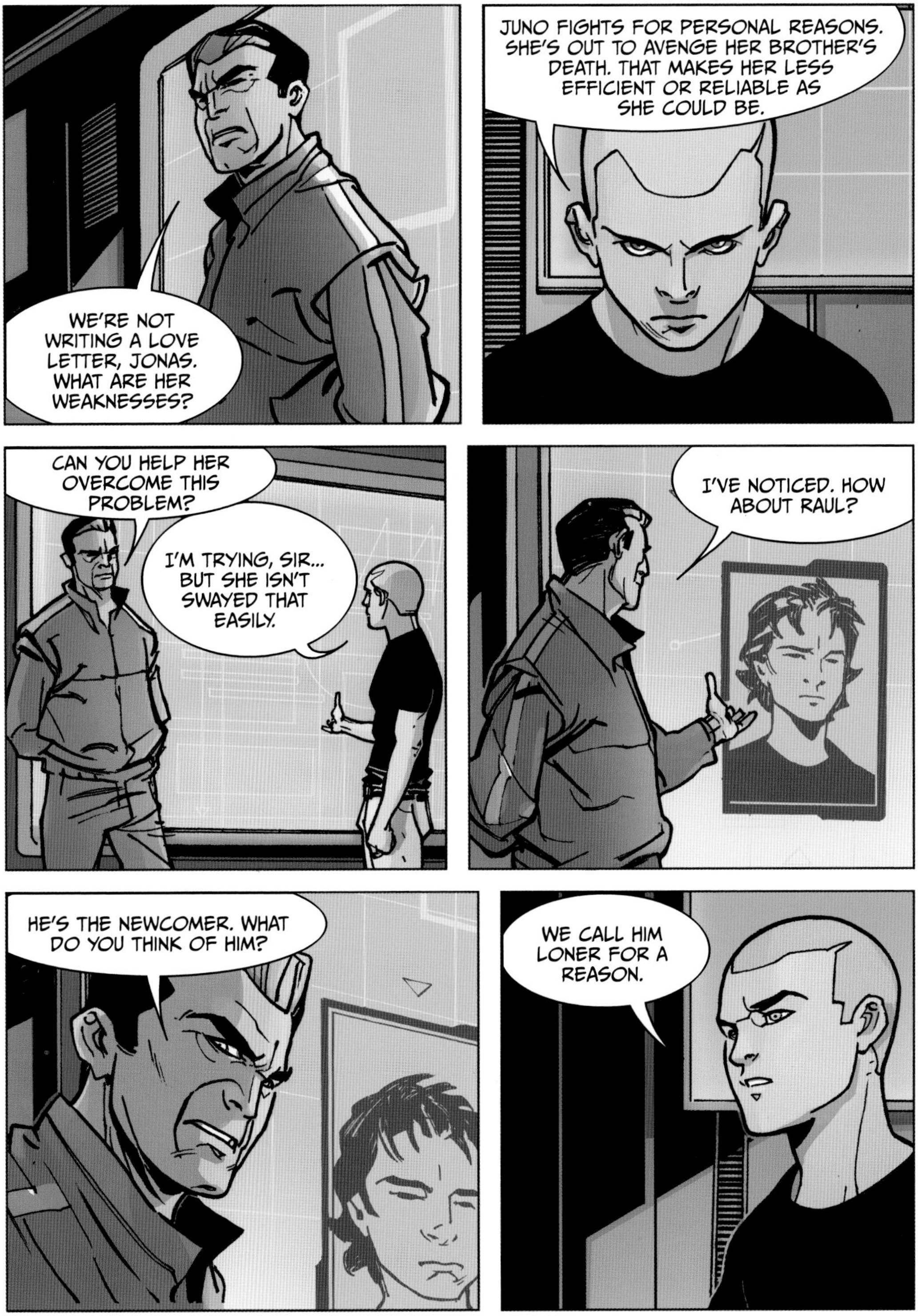
WE'RE NOT WRITING A LOVE LETTER, JONAS. WHAT ARE HER WEAKNESSES?
JUNO FIGHTS FOR PERSONAL REASONS. SHE'S OUT TO AVENGE HER BROTHER'S DEATH. THAT MAKES HER LESS EFFICIENT OR RELIABLE AS SHE COULD BE.
CAN YOU HELP HER OVERCOME THIS PROBLEM?
I'M TRYING, SIR... BUT SHE ISN'T SWAYED THAT EASILY.
I'VE NOTICED. HOW ABOUT RAUL?
HE'S THE NEWCOMER. WHAT DO YOU THINK OF HIM?
WE CALL HIM LONER FOR A REASON.

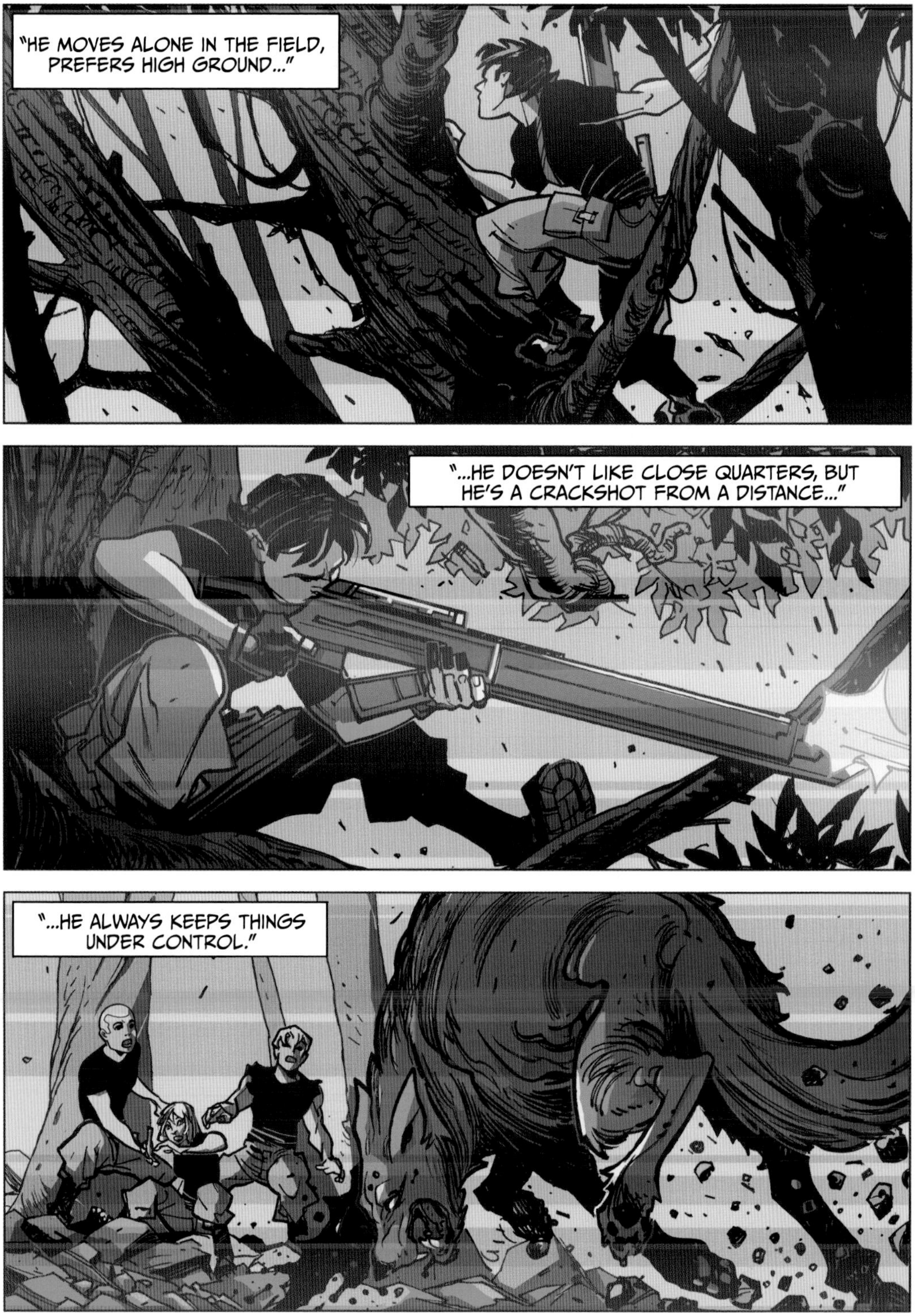
"HE MOVES ALONE IN THE FIELD, PREFERS HIGH GROUND..."
"...HE DOESN'T LIKE CLOSE QUARTERS, BUT HE'S A CRACKSHOT FROM A DISTANCE..."
"...HE ALWAYS KEEPS THINGS UNDER CONTROL."

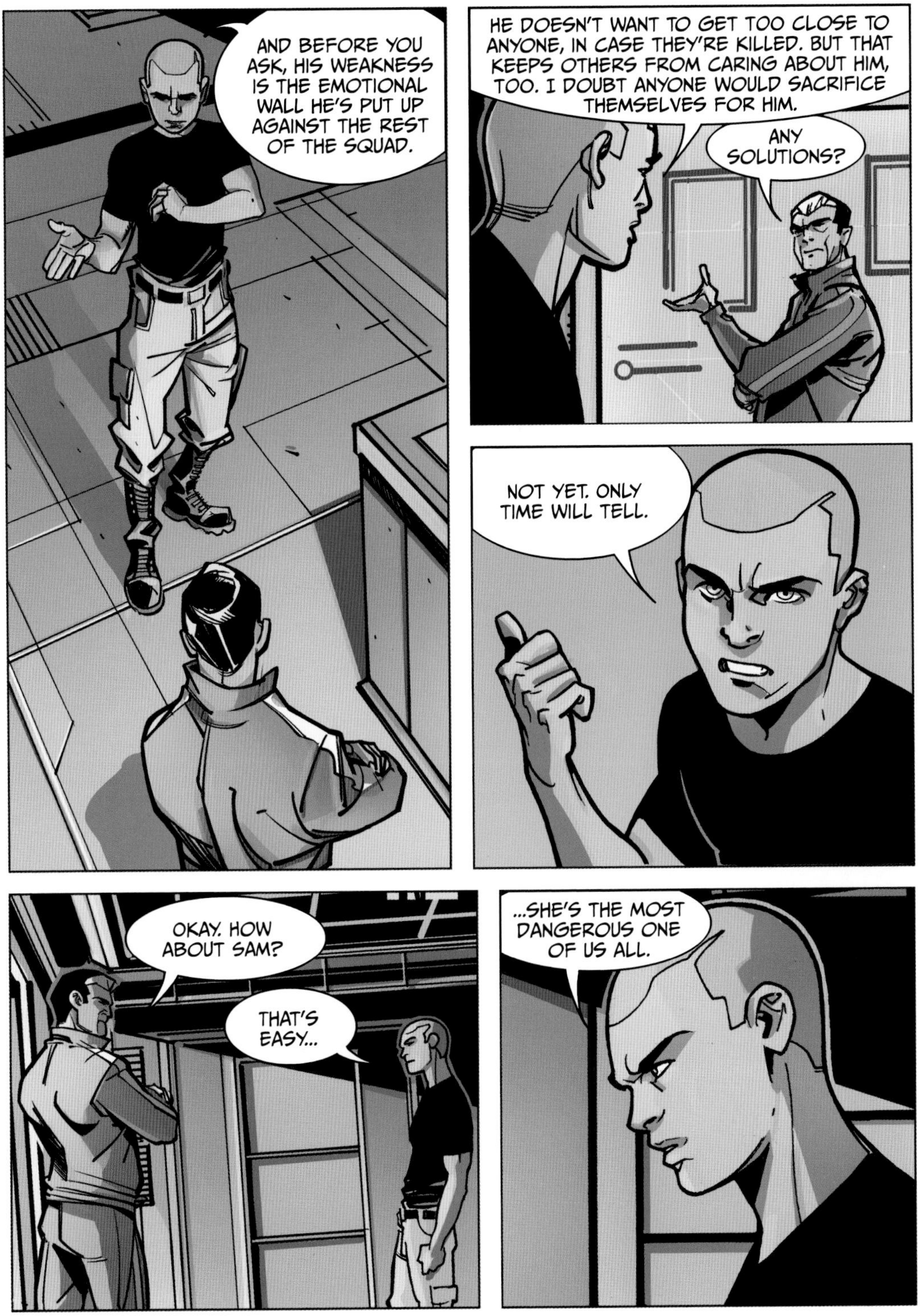
AND BEFORE YOU ASK, HIS WEAKNESS IS THE EMOTIONAL WALL HE'S PUT UP AGAINST THE REST OF THE SQUAD.
HE DOESN'T WANT TO GET TOO CLOSE TO ANYONE, IN CASE THEY'RE KILLED. BUT THAT KEEPS OTHERS FROM CARING ABOUT HIM, TOO. I DOUBT ANYONE WOULD SACRIFICE THEMSELVES FOR HIM.
ANY SOLUTIONS?
NOT YET. ONLY TIME WILL TELL.
OKAY. HOW ABOUT SAM?
THAT'S EASY...
...SHE'S THE MOST DANGEROUS ONE OF US ALL.

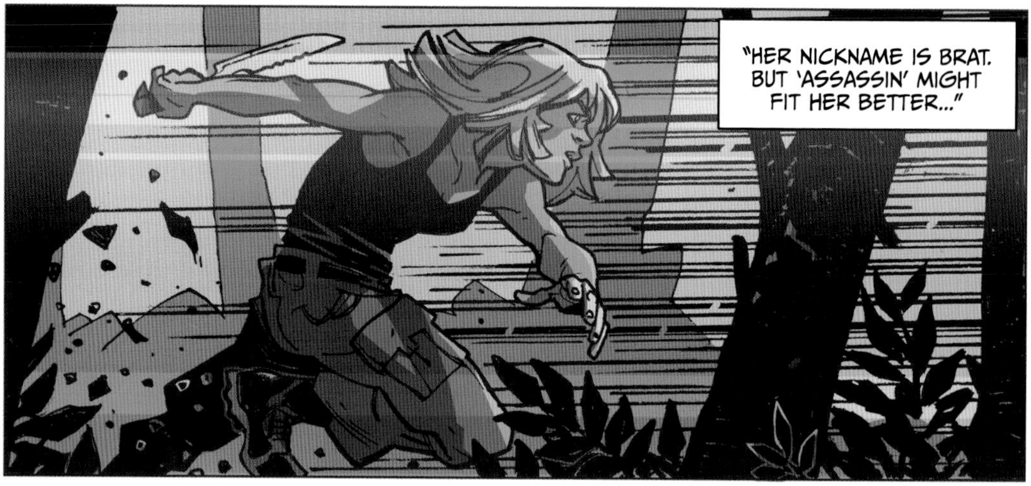
"HER NICKNAME IS BRAT. BUT 'ASSASSIN' MIGHT FIT HER BETTER..."

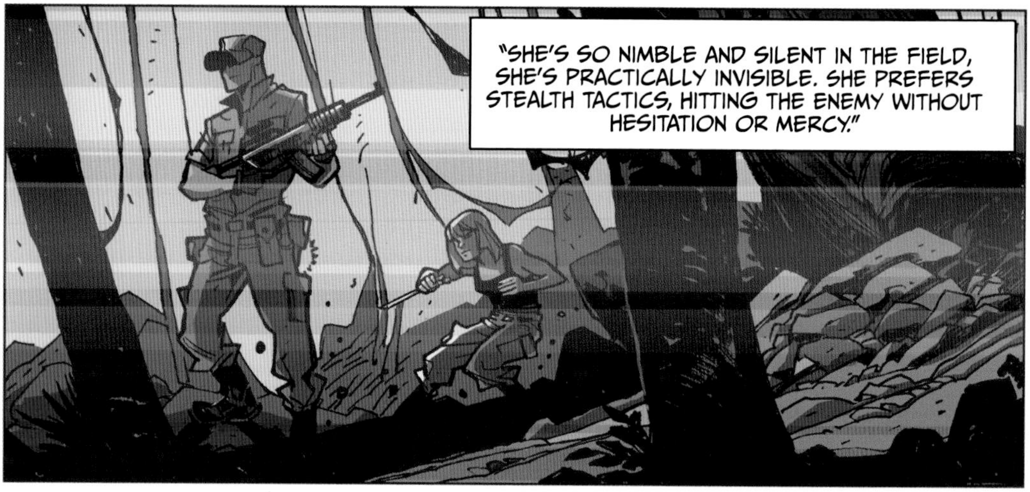
"SHE'S SO NIMBLE AND SILENT IN THE FIELD, SHE'S PRACTICALLY INVISIBLE. SHE PREFERS STEALTH TACTICS, HITTING THE ENEMY WITHOUT HESITATION OR MERCY."

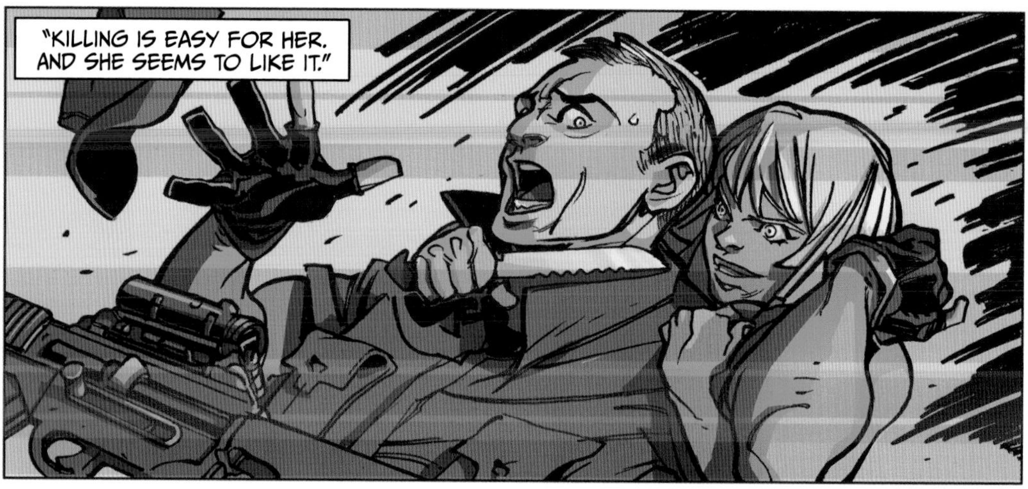
"KILLING IS EASY FOR HER. AND SHE SEEMS TO LIKE IT."

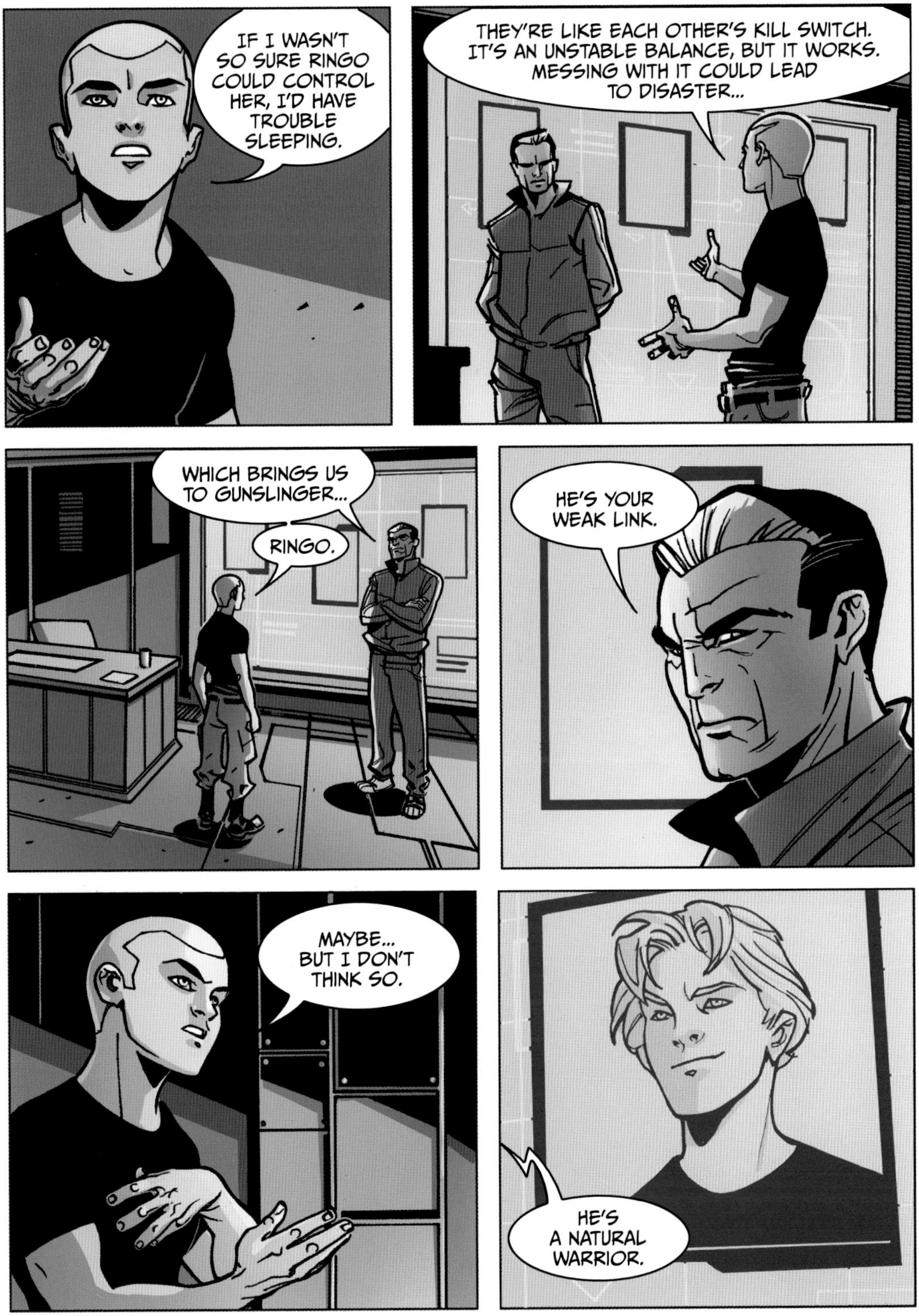
IF I WASN'T SO SURE RINGO COULD CONTROL HER, I'D HAVE TROUBLE SLEEPING.
THEY'RE LIKE EACH OTHER'S KILL SWITCH. IT'S AN UNSTABLE BALANCE, BUT IT WORKS. MESSING WITH IT COULD LEAD TO DISASTER...
WHICH BRINGS US TO GUNSLINGER...
RINGO.
HE'S YOUR WEAK LINK.
MAYBE... BUT I DON'T THINK SO.
HE'S A NATURAL WARRIOR.

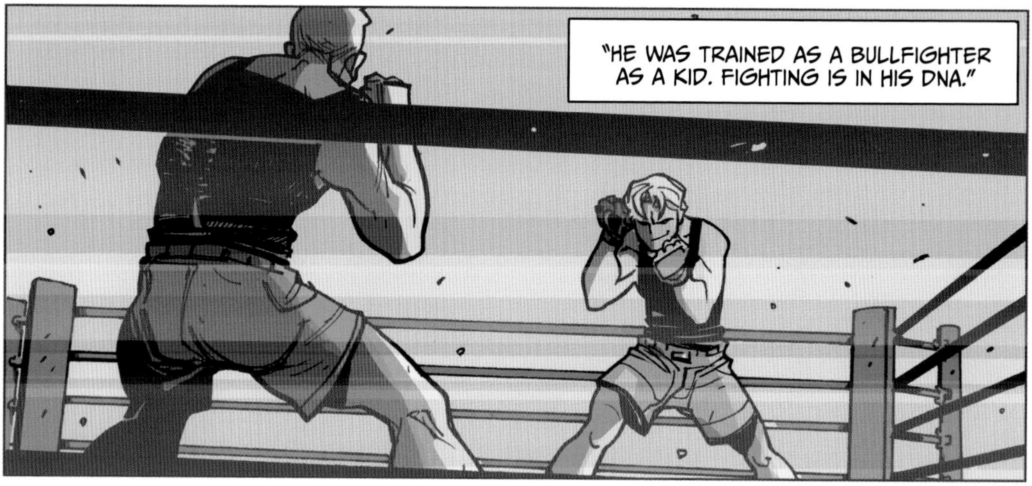
"HE WAS TRAINED AS A BULLFIGHTER AS A KID. FIGHTING IS IN HIS DNA."

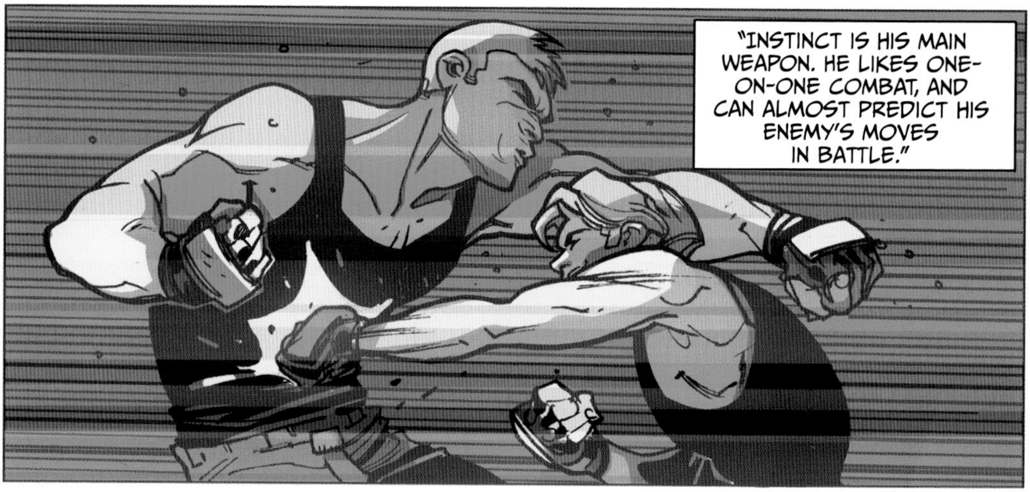
"INSTINCT IS HIS MAIN WEAPON. HE LIKES ONE-ON-ONE COMBAT, AND CAN ALMOST PREDICT HIS ENEMY'S MOVES IN BATTLE."

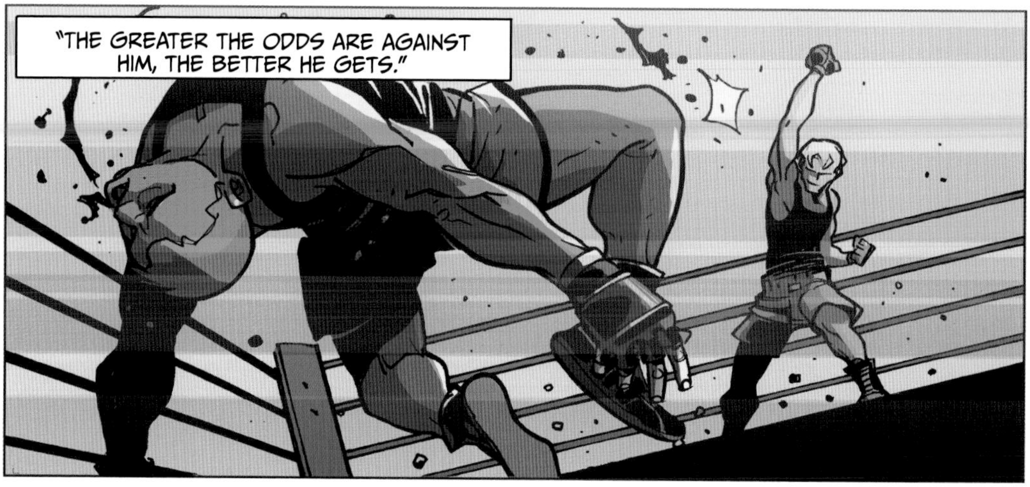
"THE GREATER THE ODDS ARE AGAINST HIM, THE BETTER HE GETS."

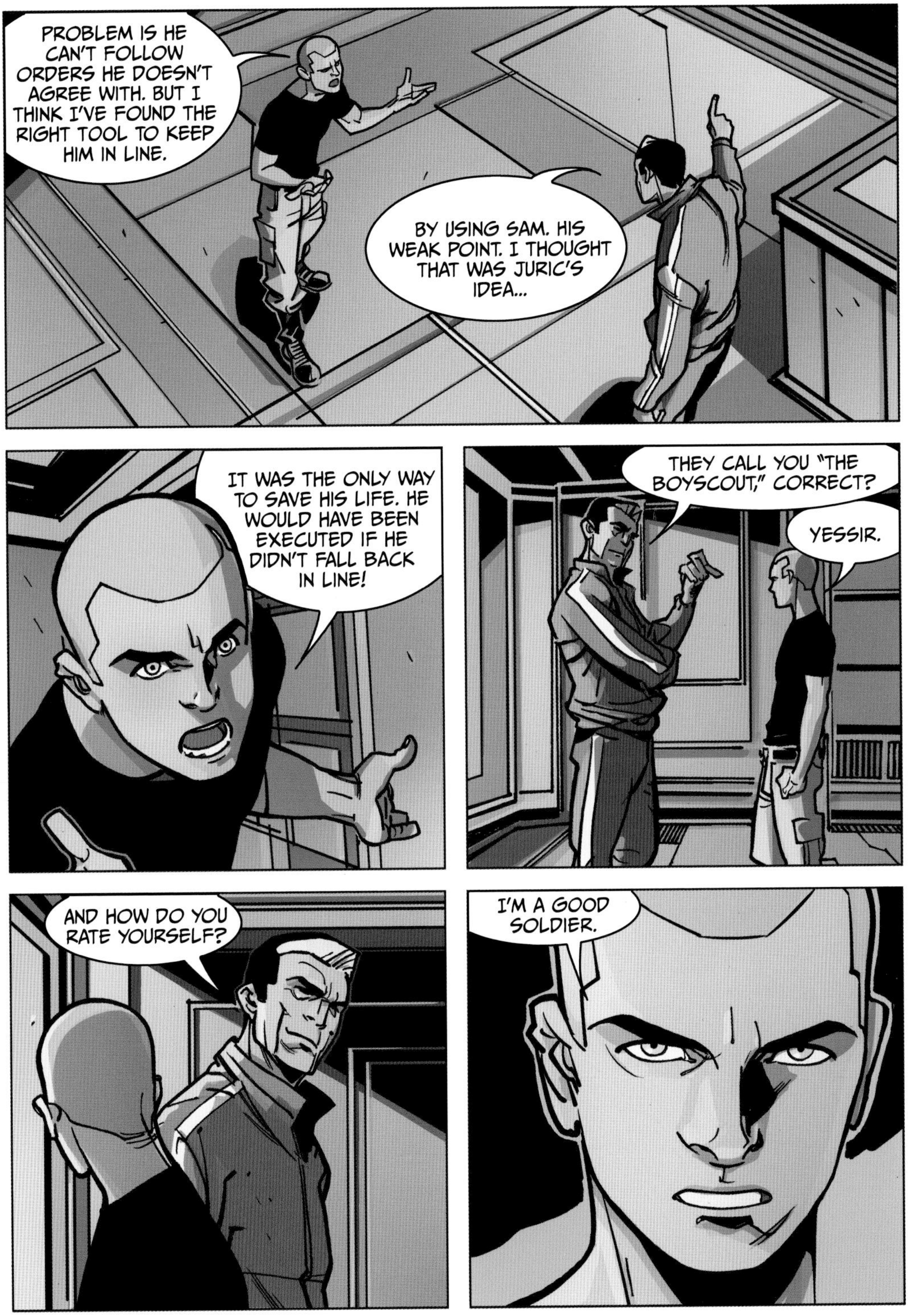
PROBLEM IS HE CAN'T FOLLOW ORDERS HE DOESN'T AGREE WITH. BUT I THINK I'VE FOUND THE RIGHT TOOL TO KEEP HIM IN LINE.
BY USING SAM. HIS WEAK POINT. I THOUGHT THAT WAS JURIC'S IDEA...
IT WAS THE ONLY WAY TO SAVE HIS LIFE. HE WOULD HAVE BEEN EXECUTED IF HE DIDN'T FALL BACK IN LINE!
THEY CALL YOU "THE BOYSCOUT," CORRECT?
YESSIR.
AND HOW DO YOU RATE YOURSELF?
I'M A GOOD SOLDIER.

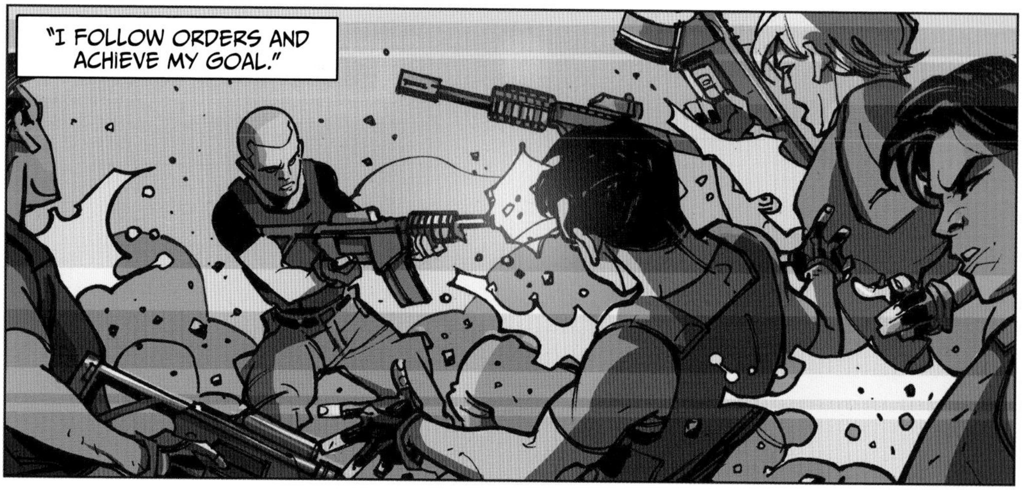
"I FOLLOW ORDERS AND ACHIEVE MY GOAL."

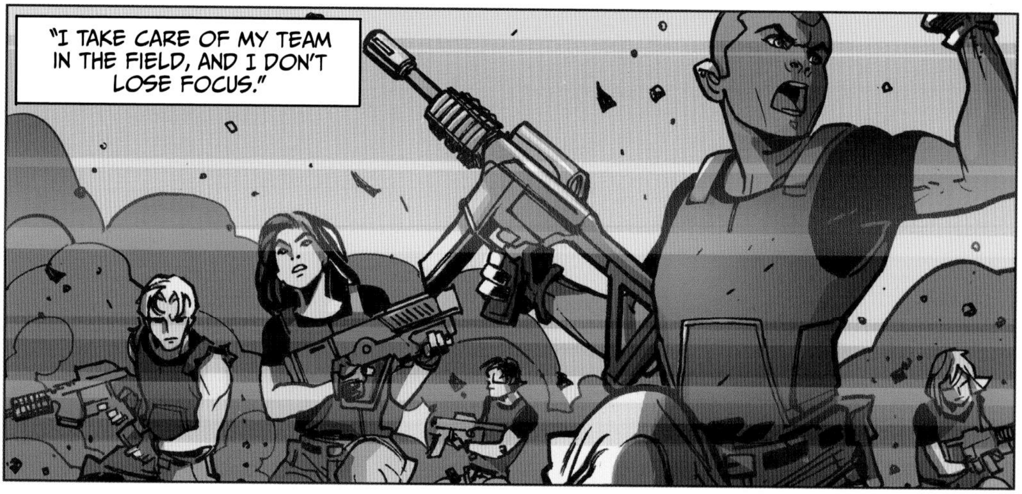
"I TAKE CARE OF MY TEAM IN THE FIELD, AND I DON'T LOSE FOCUS."

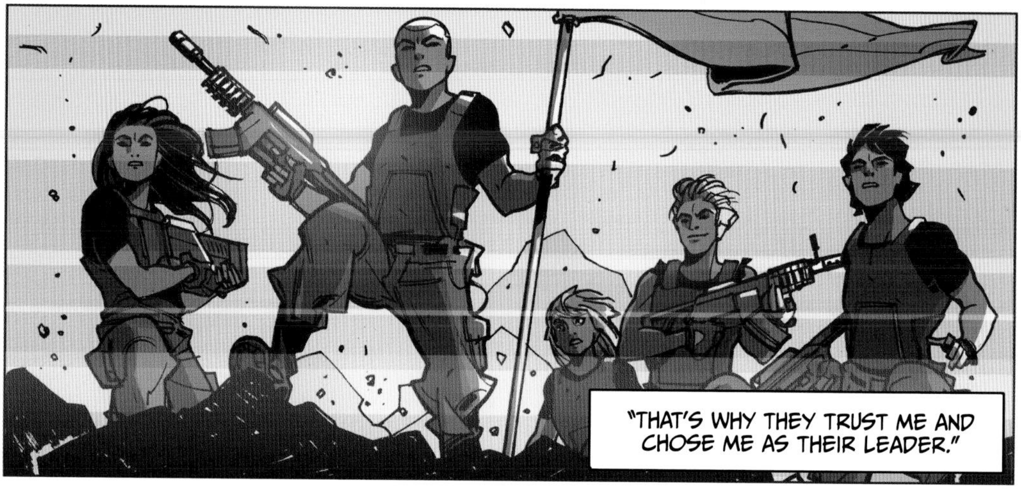
"THAT'S WHY THEY TRUST ME AND CHOSE ME AS THEIR LEADER."

DO YOU LIKE THAT ROLE?

IF HECTOR HADN'T DIED, HE'D HAVE BEEN LEADER. BUT THINGS WENT DIFFERENTLY AND I DO WHAT I NEED TO DO.

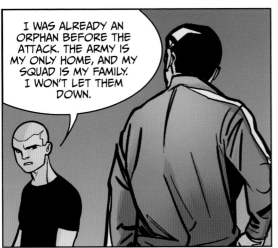

I WAS ALREADY AN ORPHAN BEFORE THE ATTACK. THE ARMY IS MY ONLY HOME, AND MY SQUAD IS MY FAMILY. I WON'T LET THEM DOWN.

THINGS AREN'T ALWAYS SO EASY.

TAKE THIS FIREARM. THERE'S ONE BULLET IN THE CHAMBER.

WHAT FOR?

KILL ONE OF YOUR SQUADMATES. YOU CHOOSE WHICH. I TRUST YOU. YOU KNOW BETTER THAN ANYONE WHO YOU CAN DO WITHOUT.

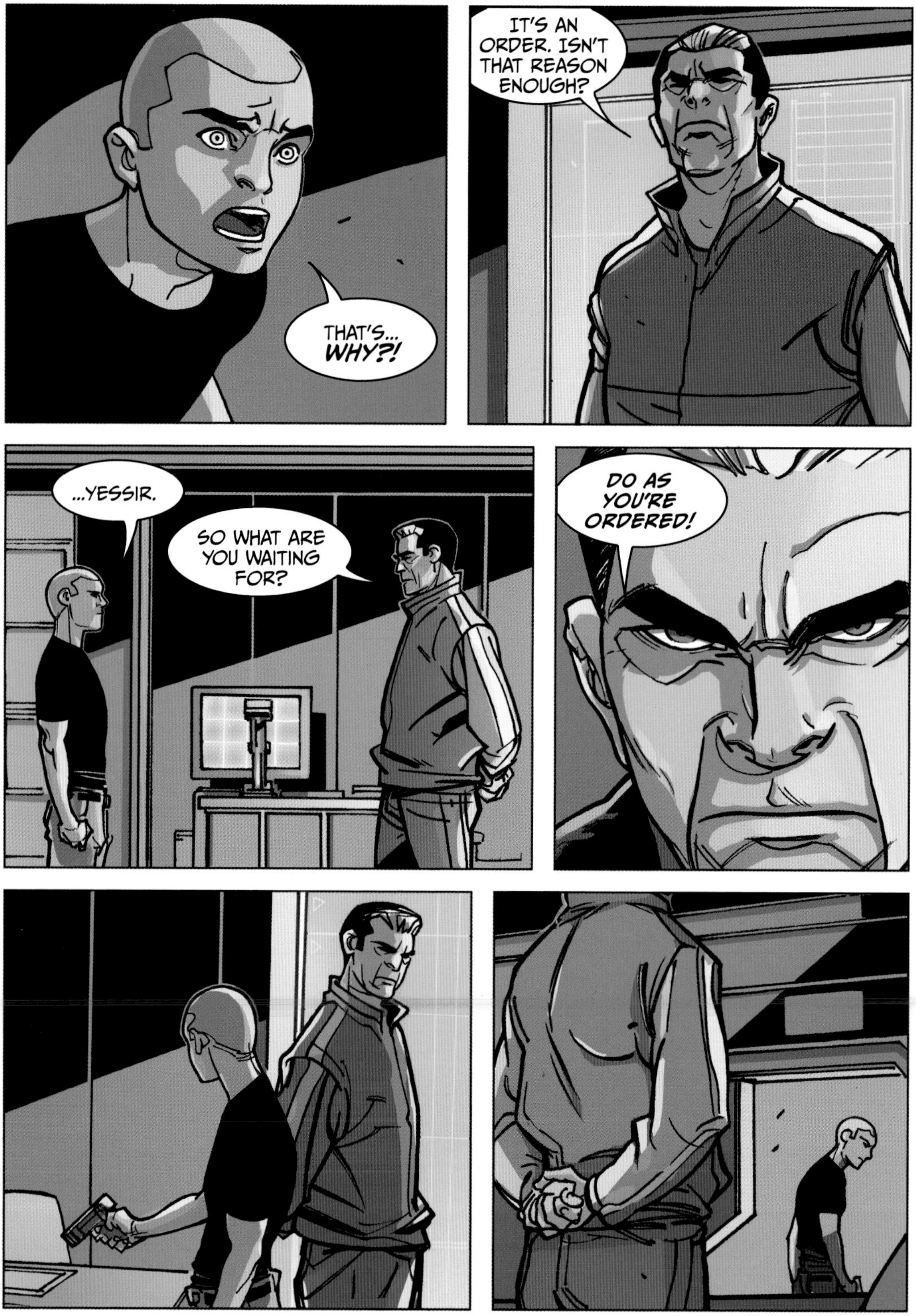
THAT'S... WHY?!
IT'S AN ORDER. ISN'T THAT REASON ENOUGH?
...YESSIR.
SO WHAT ARE YOU WAITING FOR?
DO AS YOU'RE ORDERED!

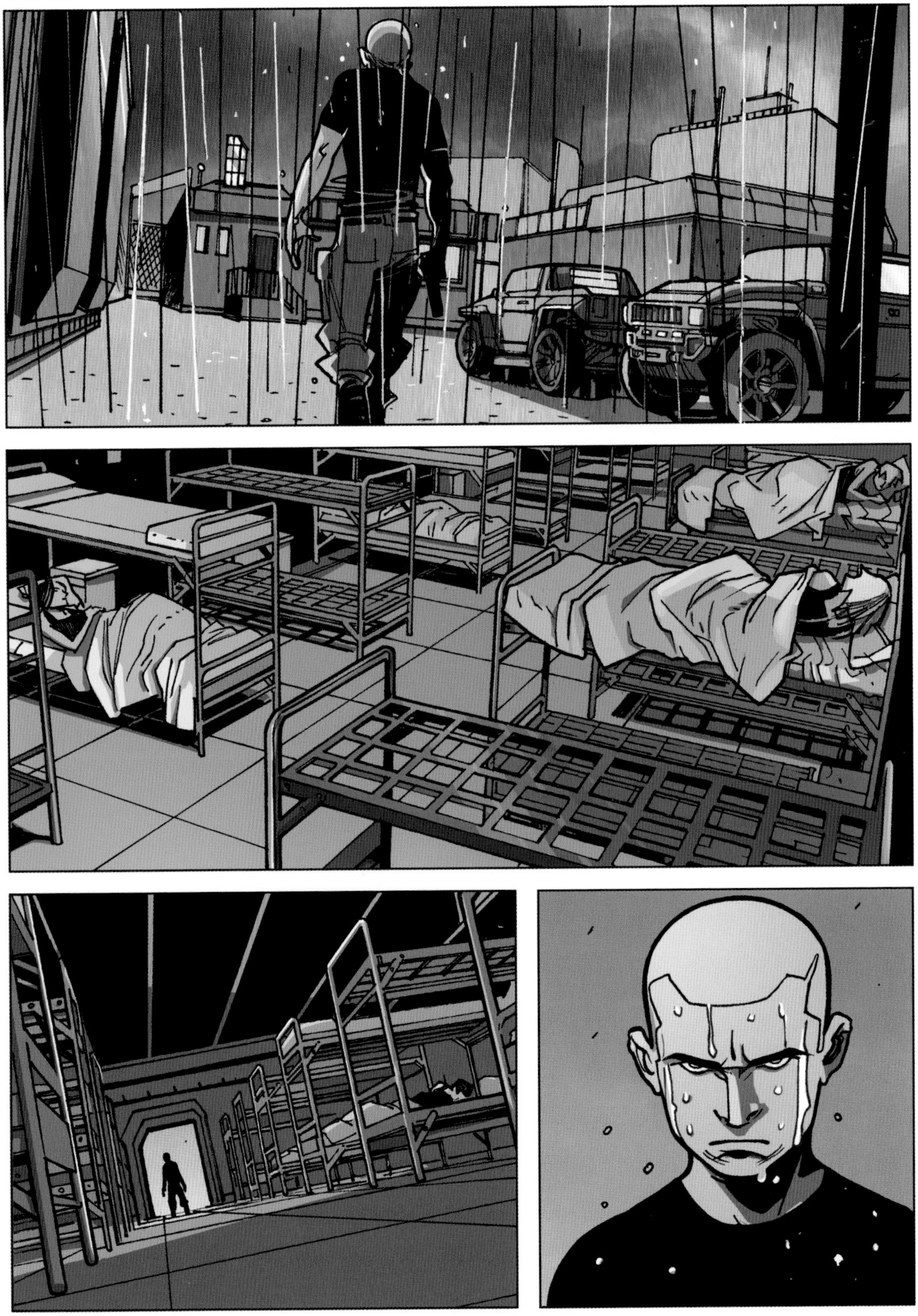

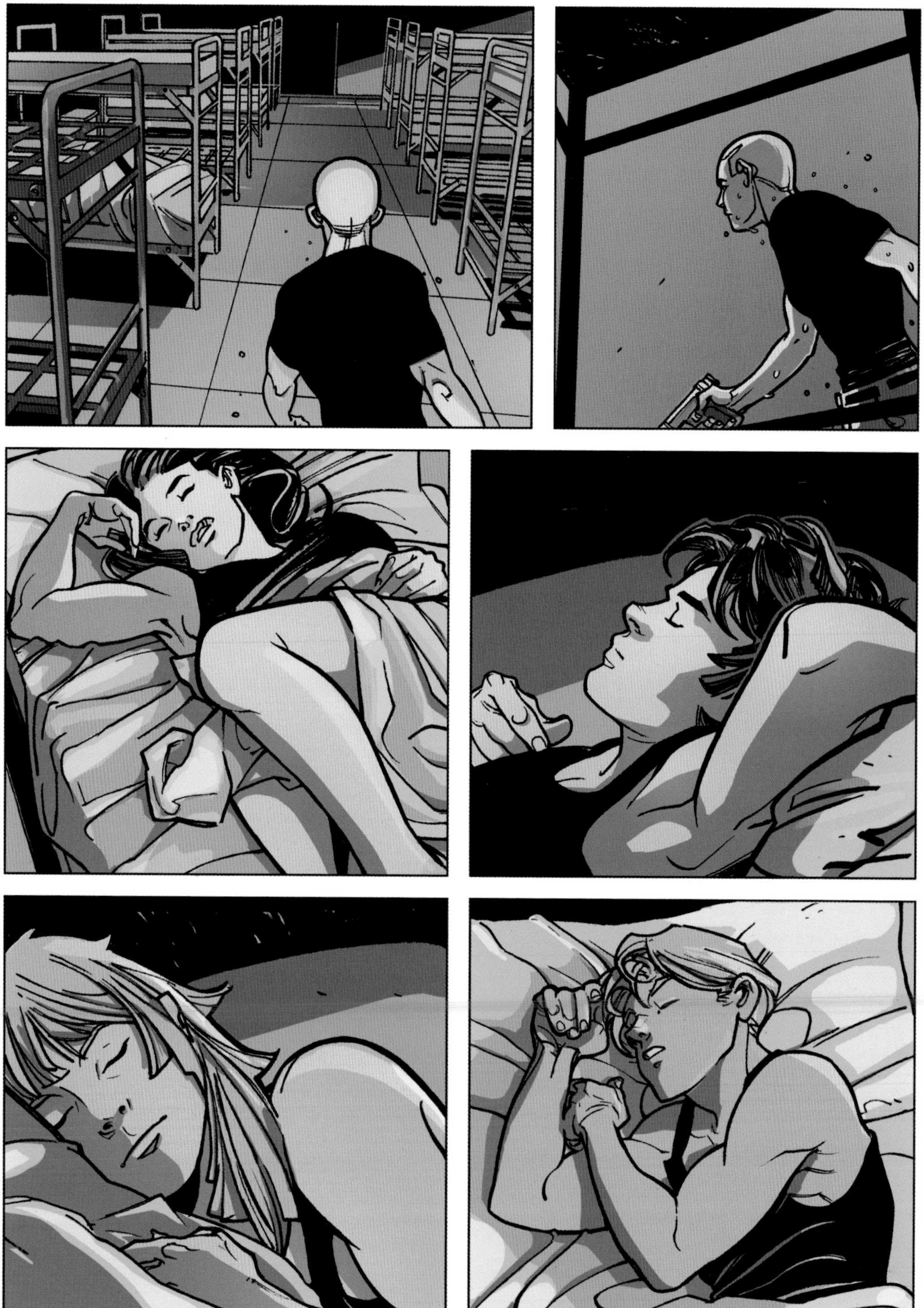

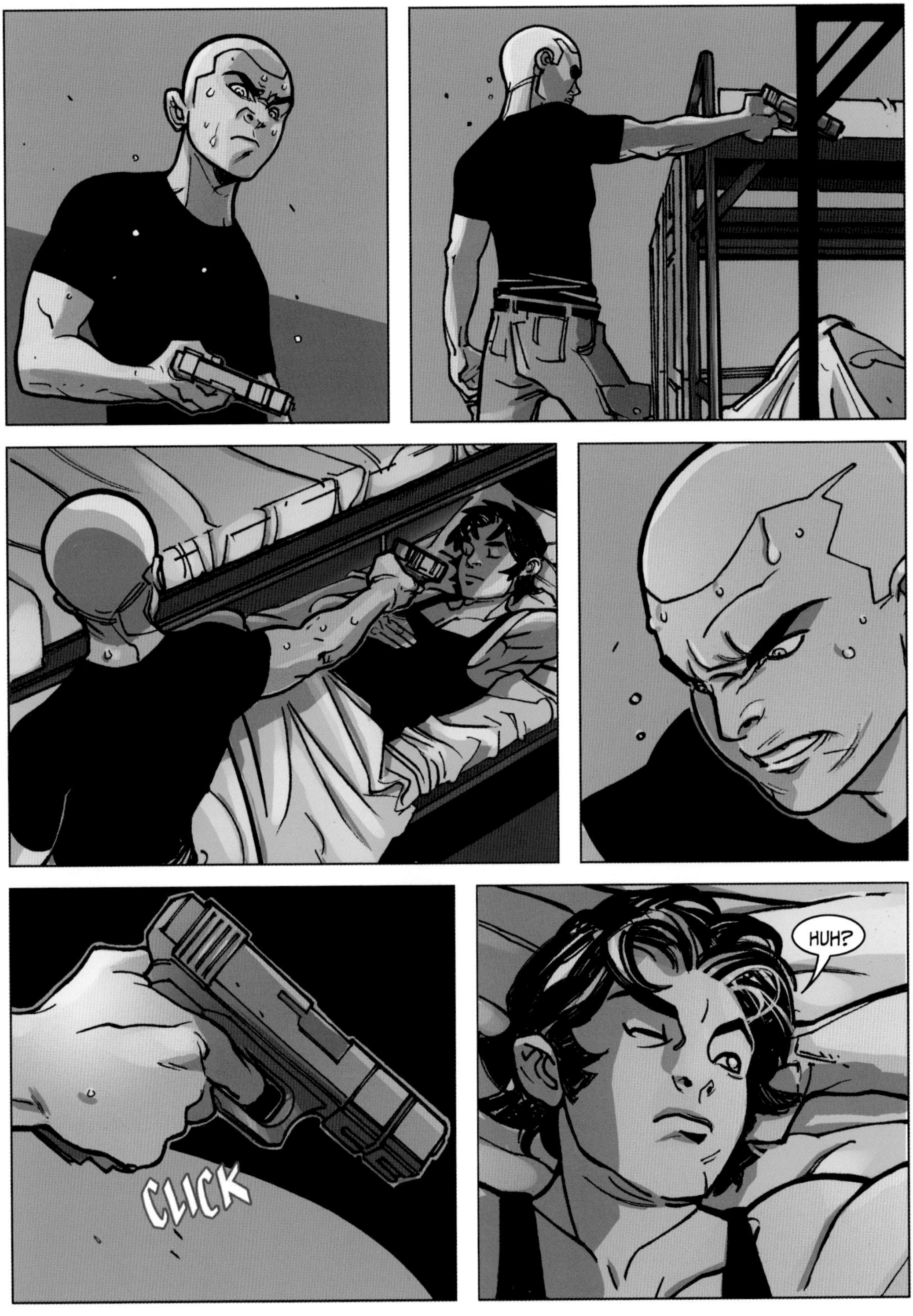
CLICK
HUH?

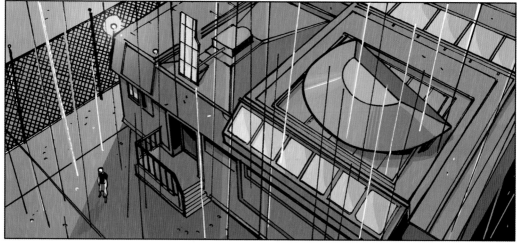

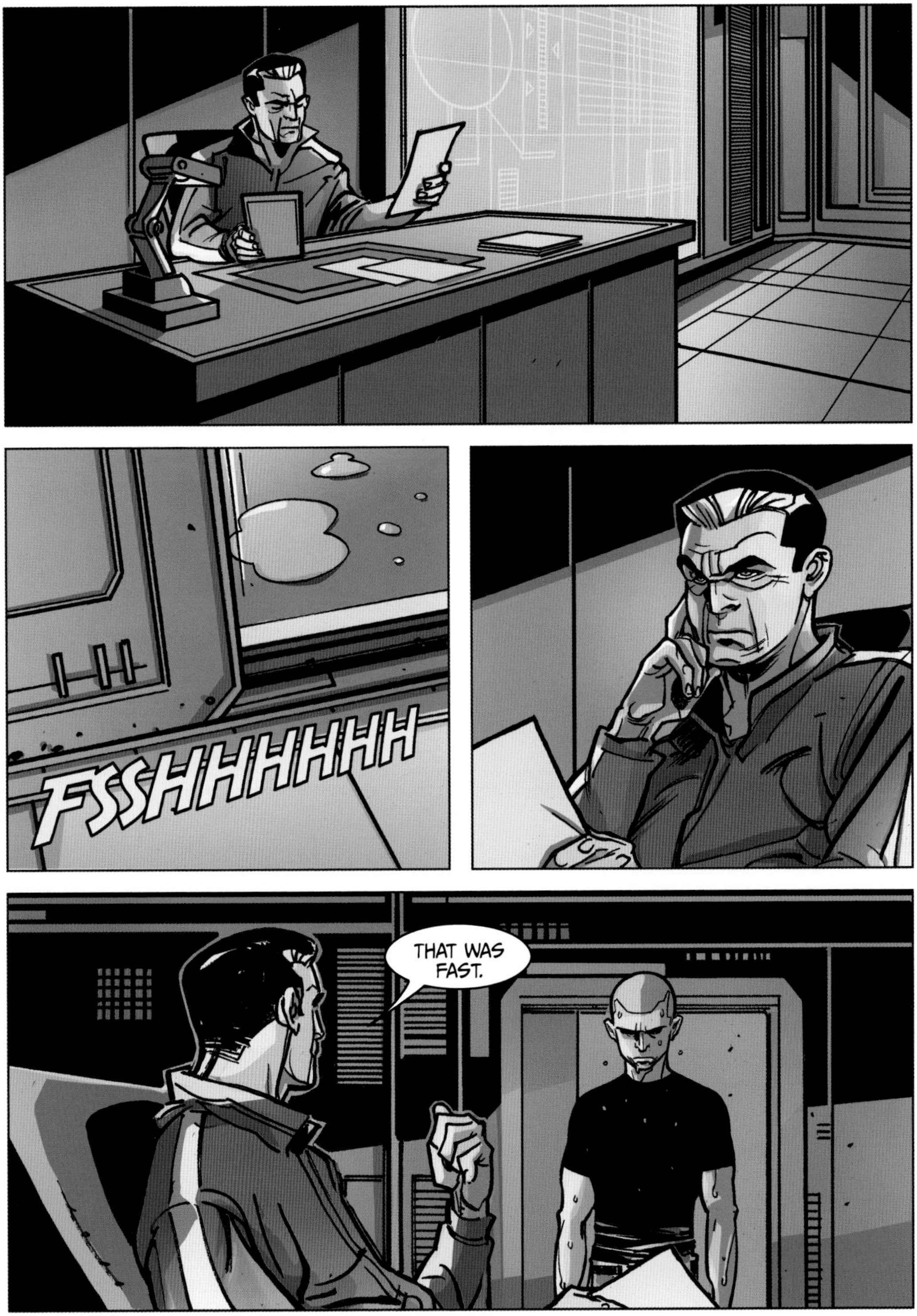
FSSHHHHHHH
THAT WAS FAST.

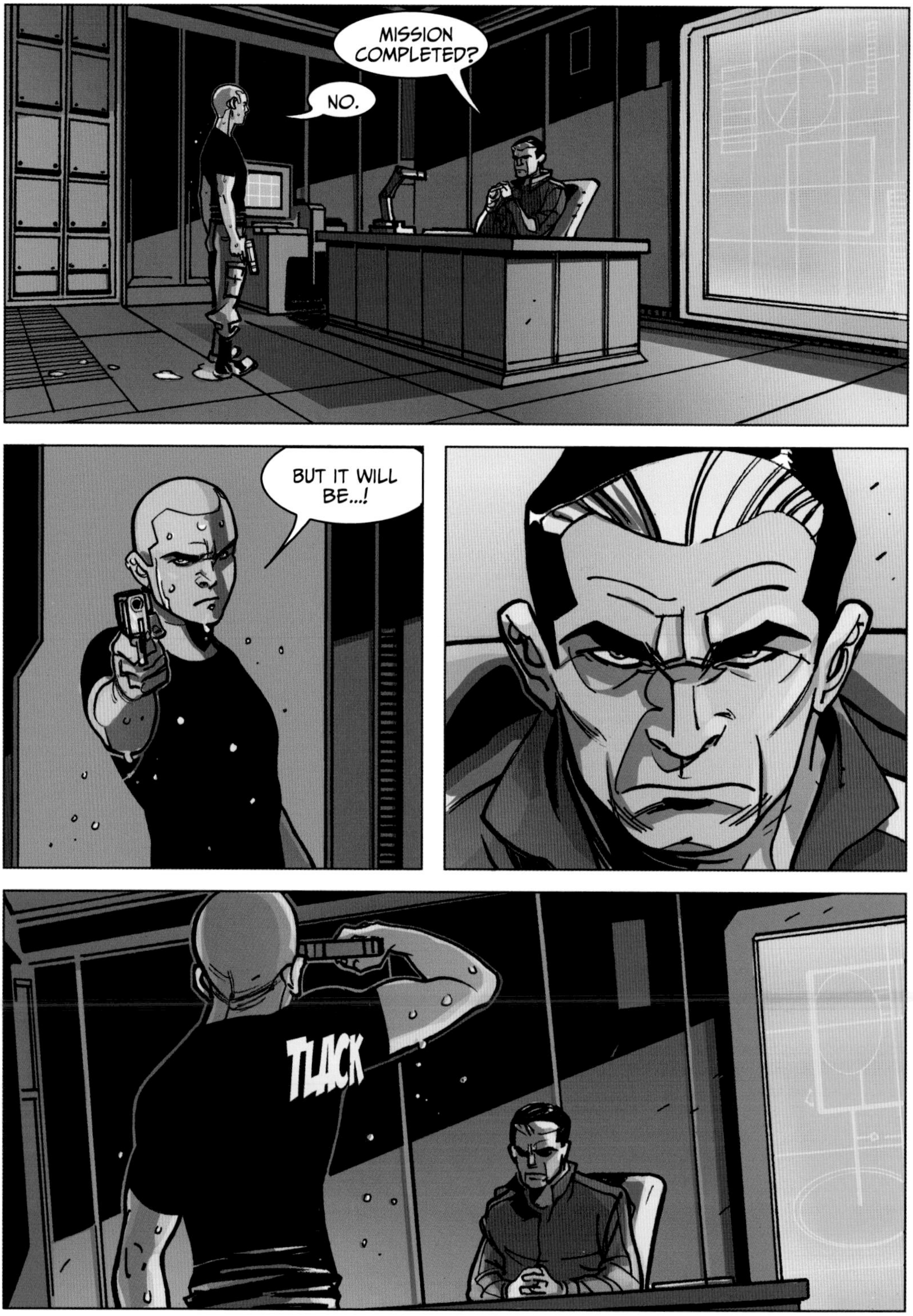
MISSION COMPLETED?
NO.
BUT IT WILL BE...!
TLACK

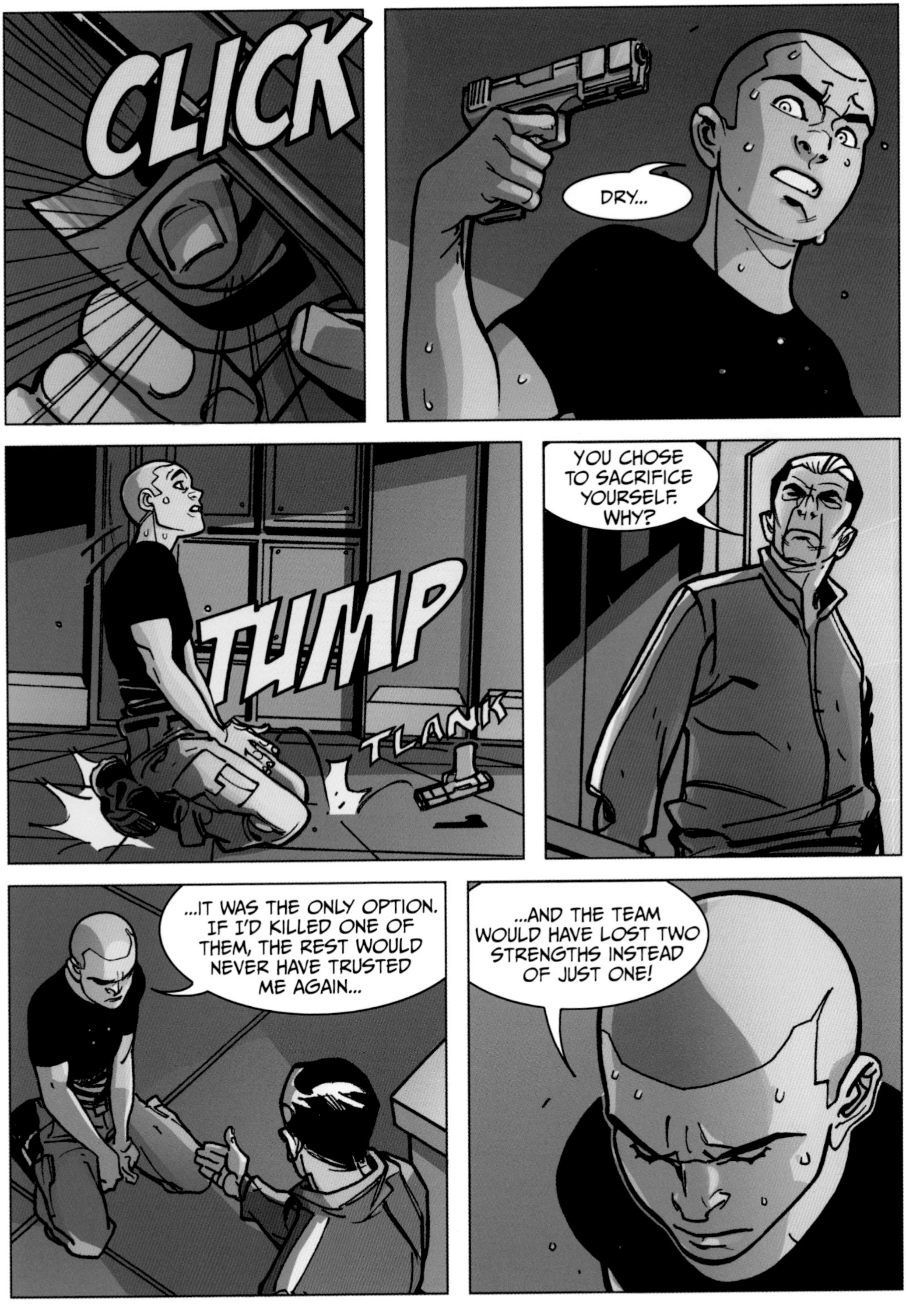
CLICK
DRY...
TUMP
TLANK
YOU CHOSE TO SACRIFICE YOURSELF. WHY?
...IT WAS THE ONLY OPTION. IF I'D KILLED ONE OF THEM, THE REST WOULD NEVER HAVE TRUSTED ME AGAIN...
...AND THE TEAM WOULD HAVE LOST TWO STRENGTHS INSTEAD OF JUST ONE!

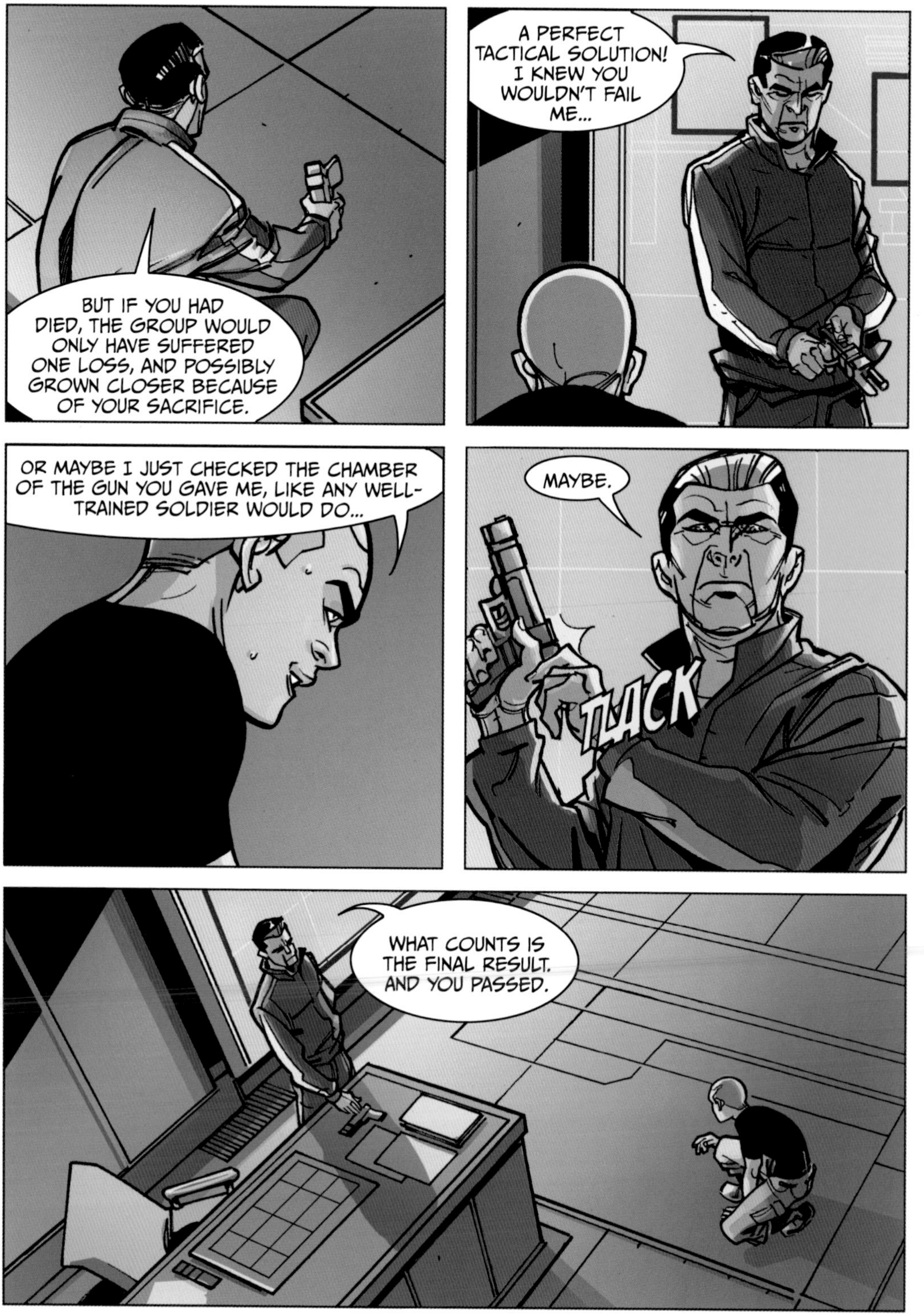
BUT IF YOU HAD DIED, THE GROUP WOULD ONLY HAVE SUFFERED ONE LOSS, AND POSSIBLY GROWN CLOSER BECAUSE OF YOUR SACRIFICE.
A PERFECT TACTICAL SOLUTION! I KNEW YOU WOULDN'T FAIL ME...
OR MAYBE I JUST CHECKED THE CHAMBER OF THE GUN YOU GAVE ME, LIKE ANY WELL-TRAINED SOLDIER WOULD DO...
MAYBE.
TLACK
WHAT COUNTS IS THE FINAL RESULT. AND YOU PASSED.

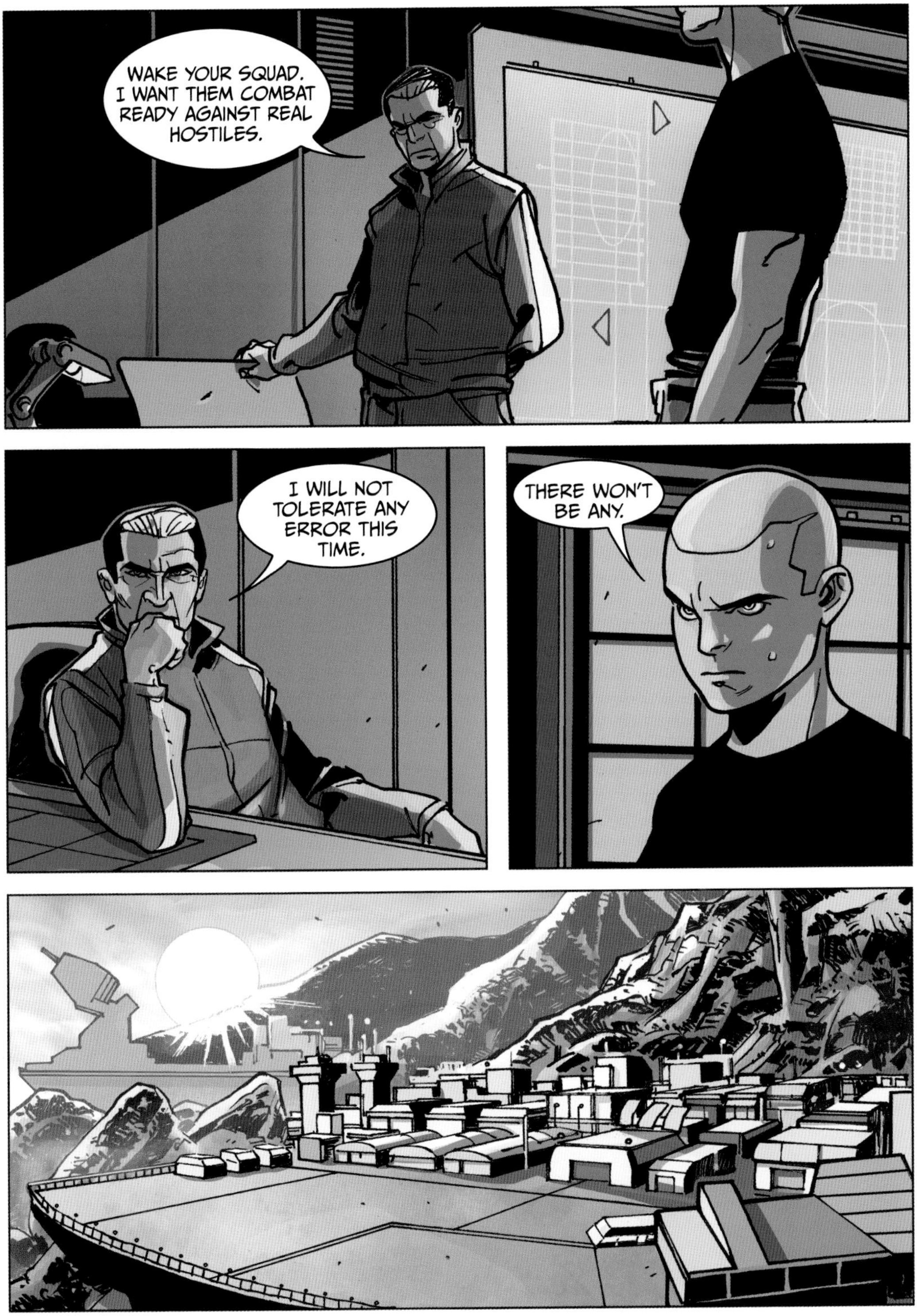
WAKE YOUR SQUAD. I WANT THEM COMBAT READY AGAINST REAL HOSTILES.
I WILL NOT TOLERATE ANY ERROR THIS TIME.
THERE WON'T BE ANY.

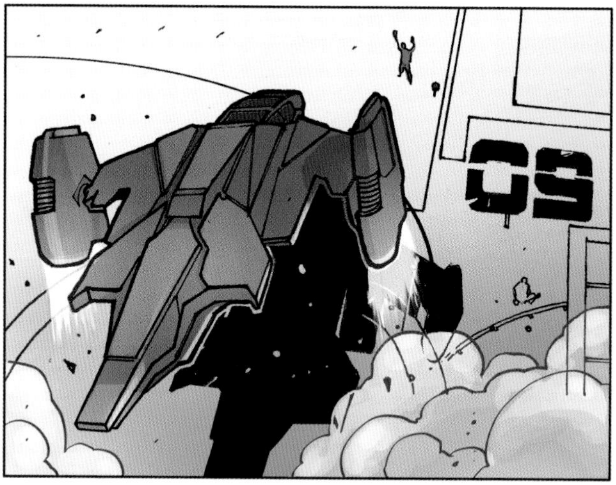

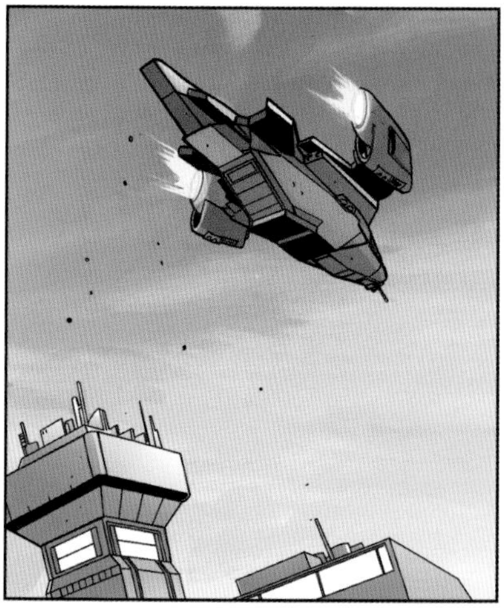

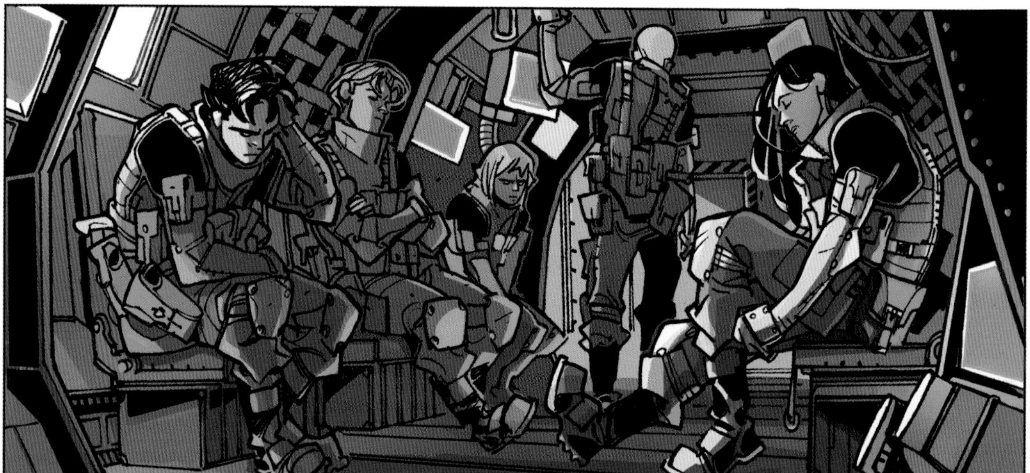

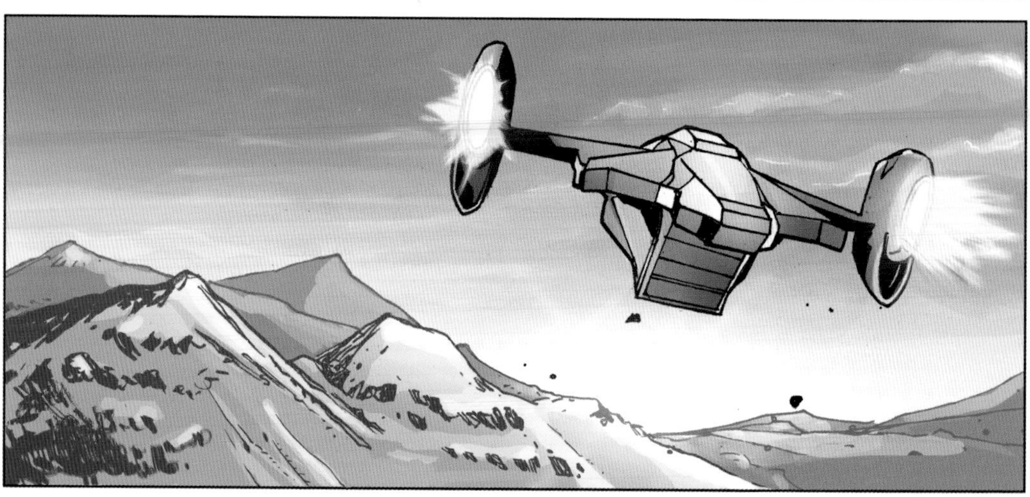

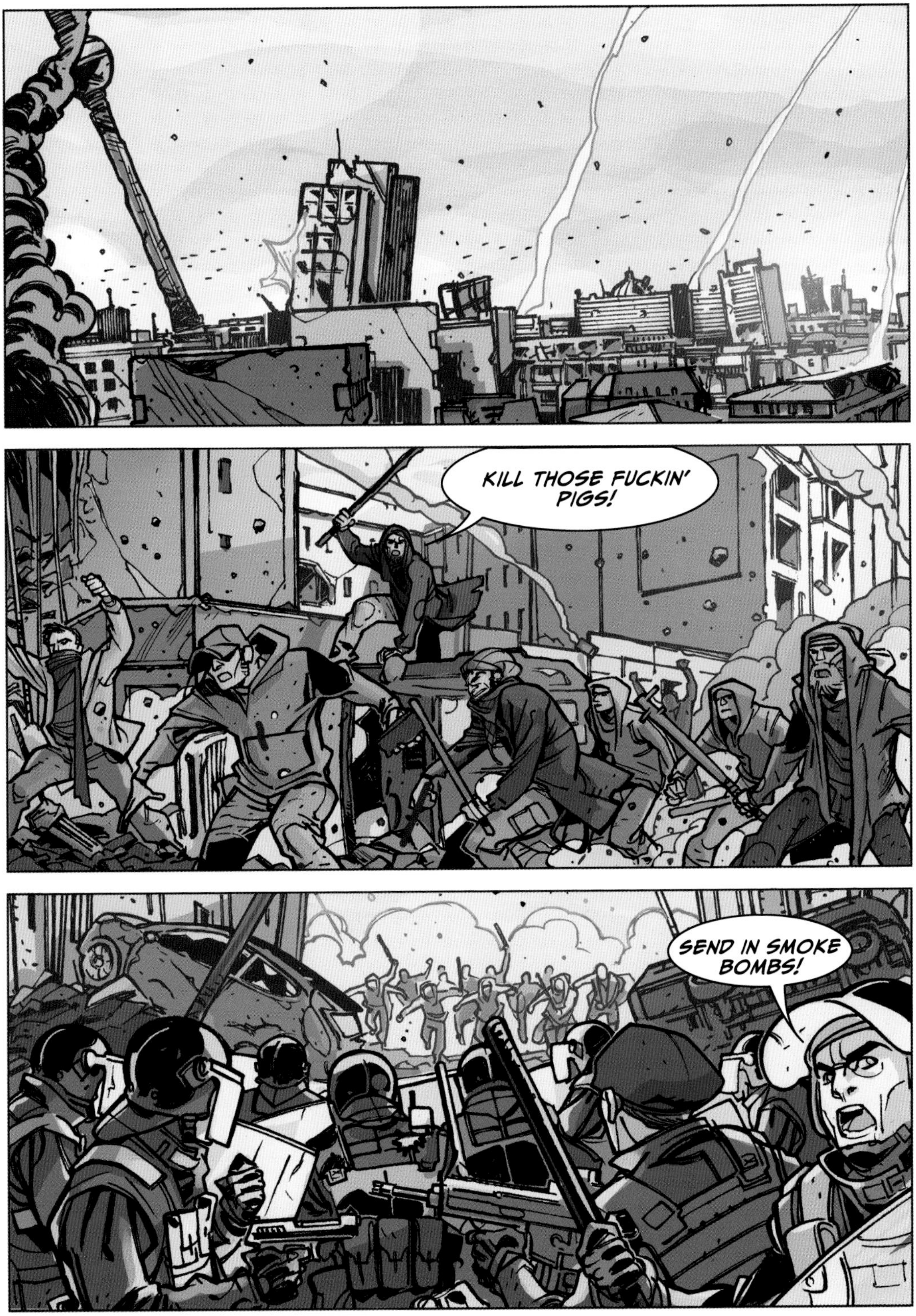
KILL THOSE FUCKIN' PIGS!
SEND IN SMOKE BOMBS!

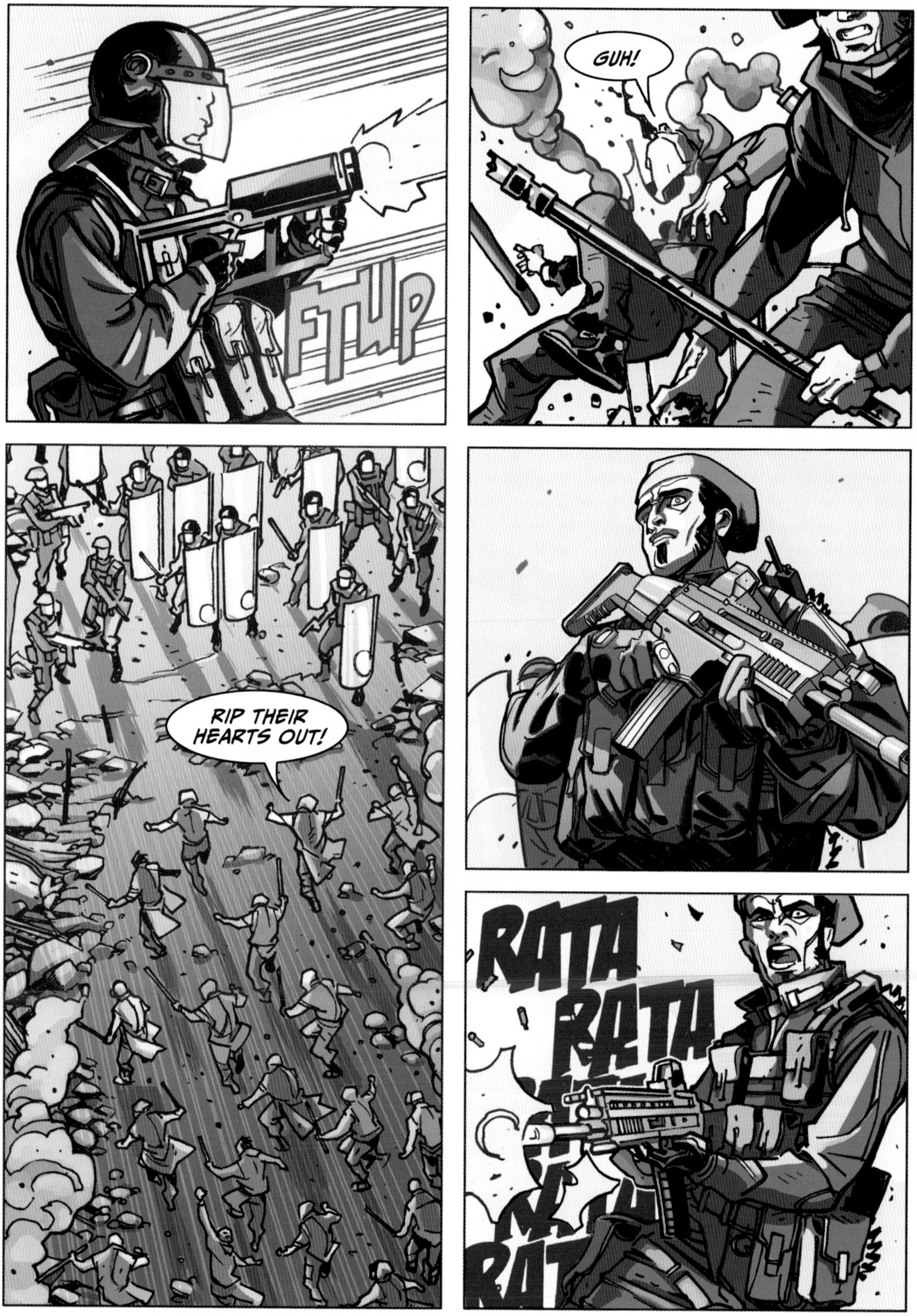
FTUP
GUH!
RIP THEIR HEARTS OUT!
RATA
RATA

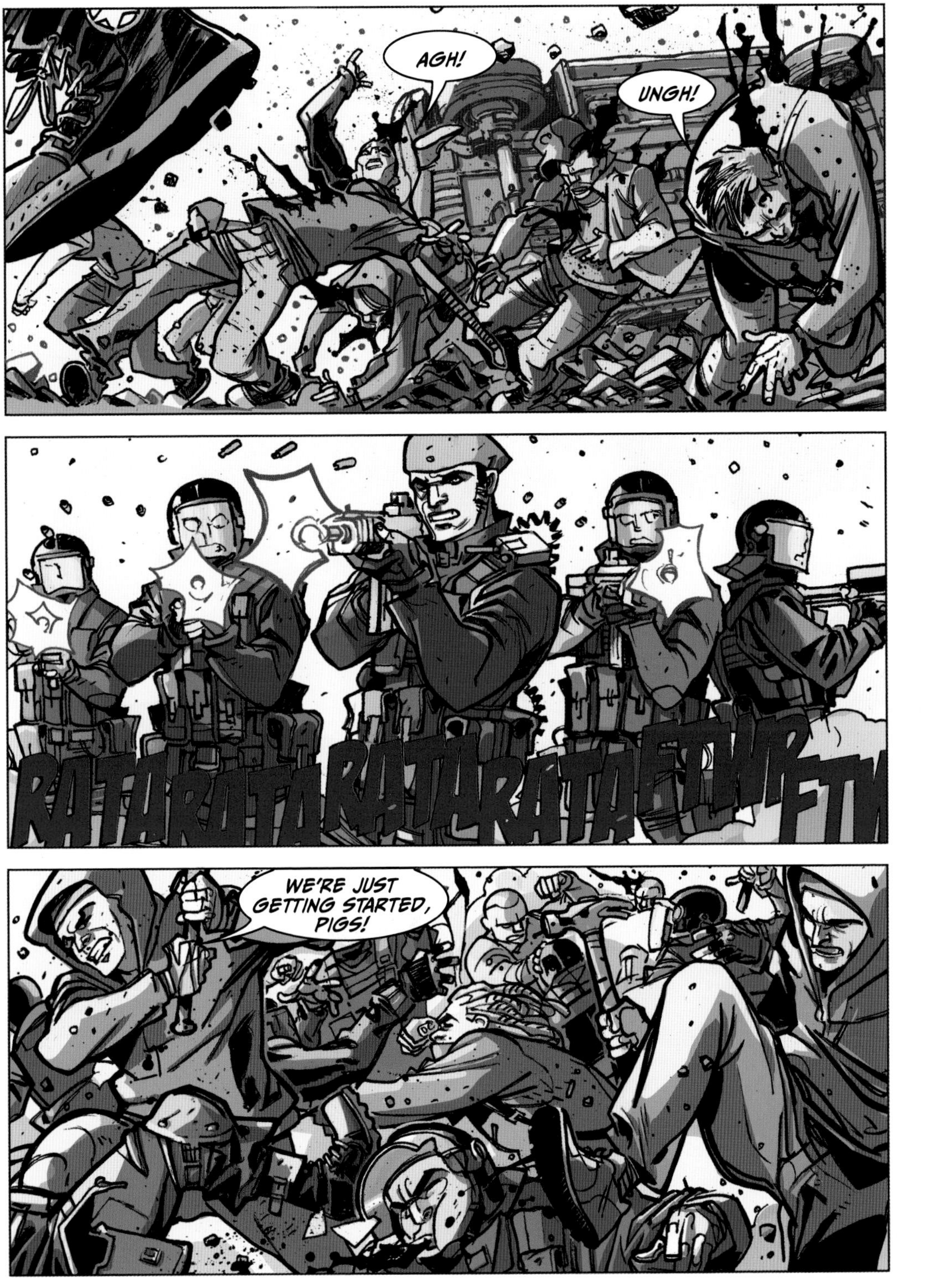
AGH!
UNGH!
RATATATARATATARATATAFTWR
FTW
WE'RE JUST GETTING STARTED, PIGS!

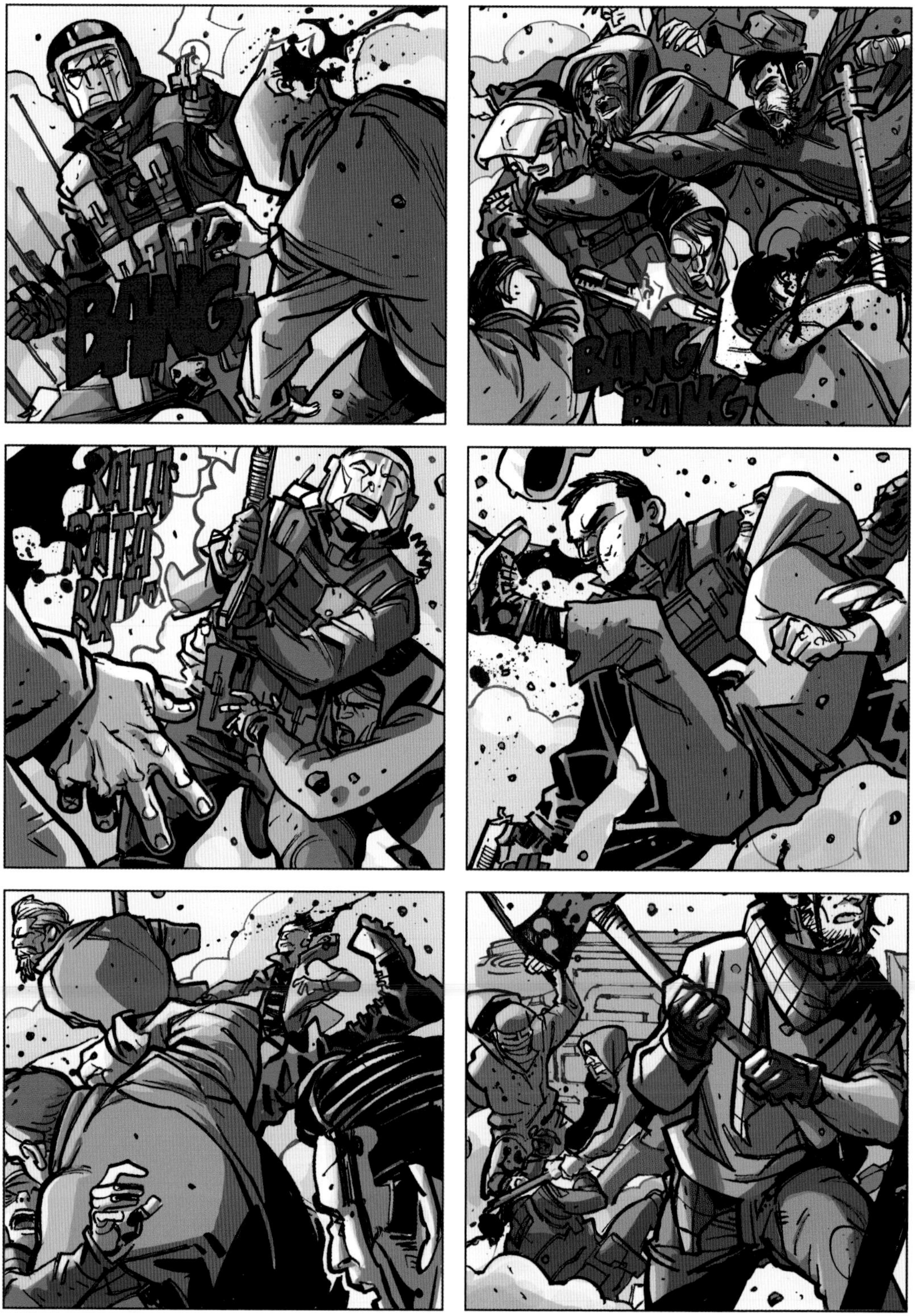
BANG
BANG
BANG
RATA
RATA
RATA

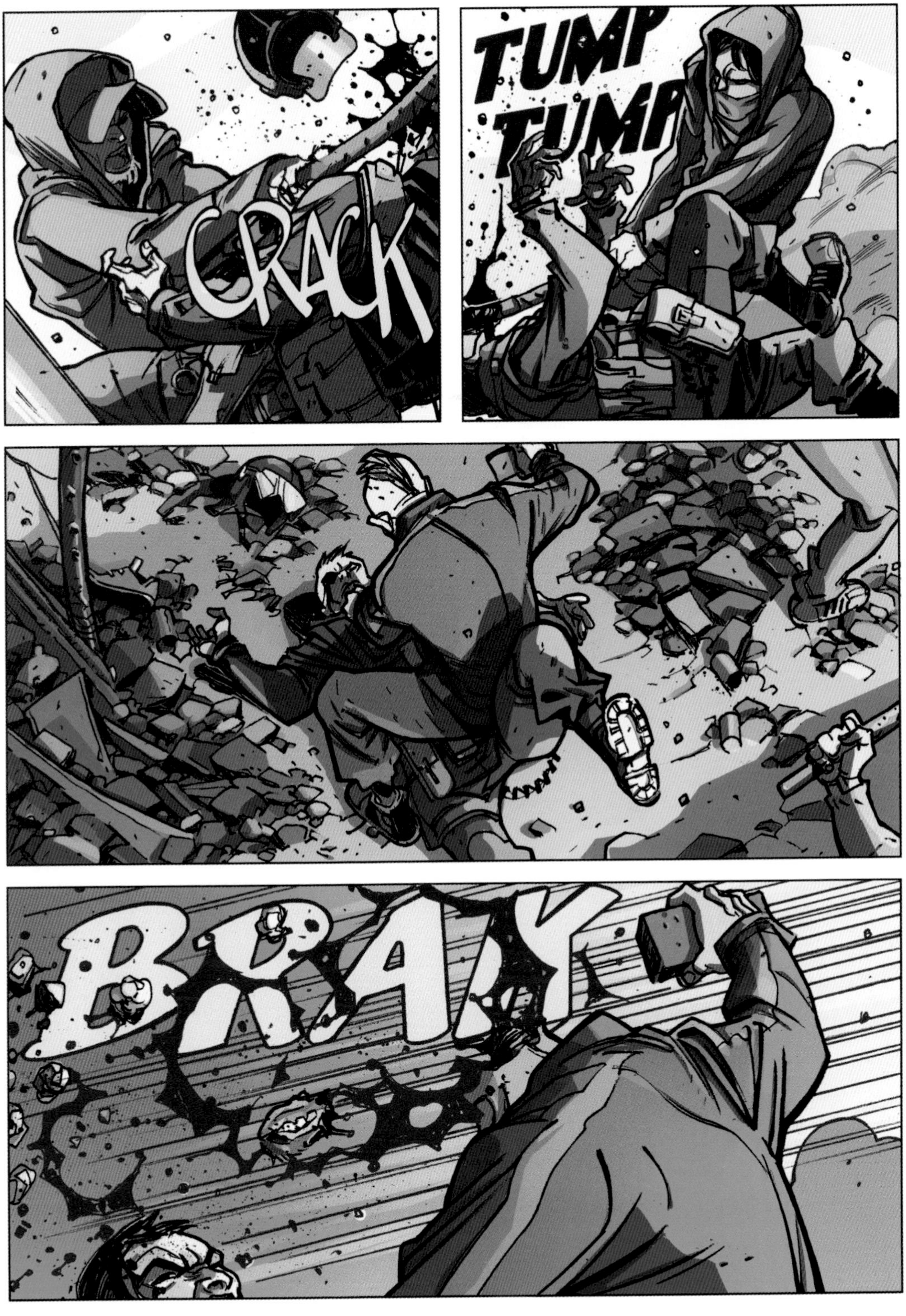
CRACK
TUMP
TUMP
BRAK

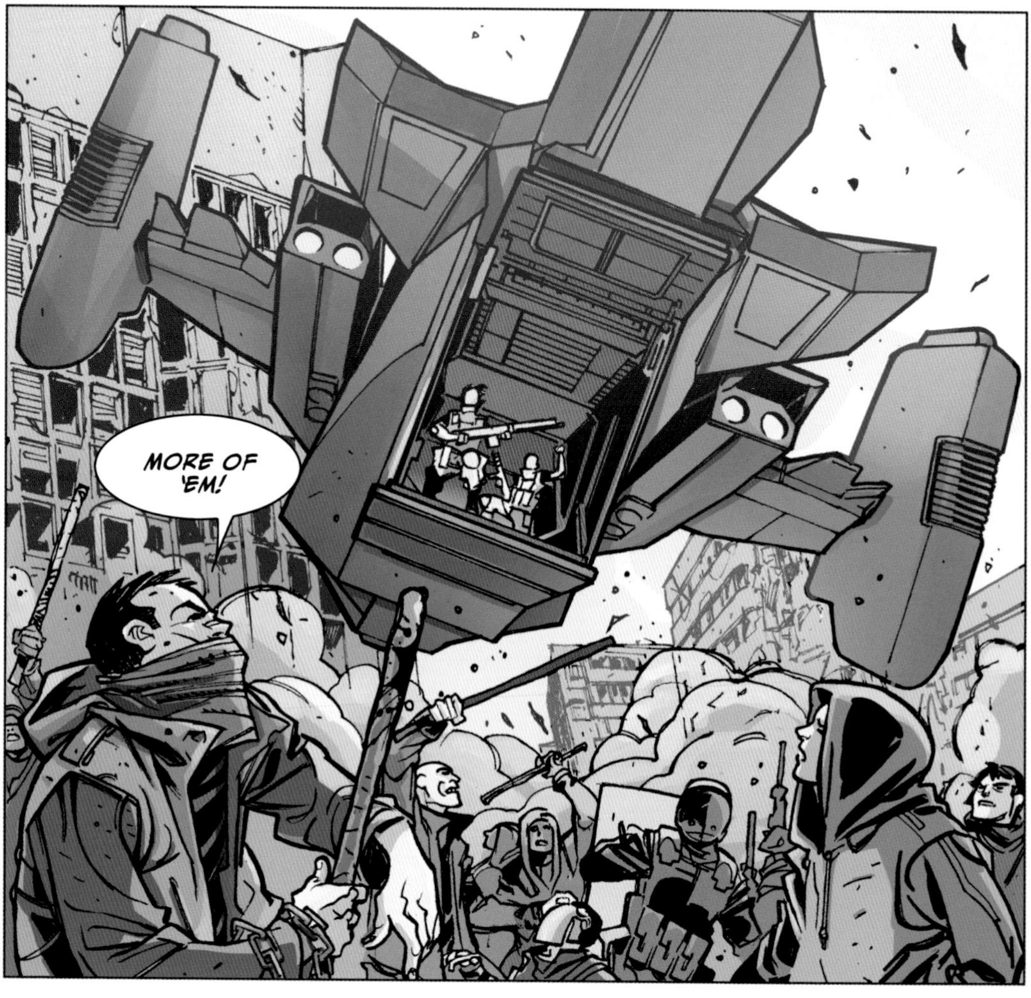
MORE OF 'EM!

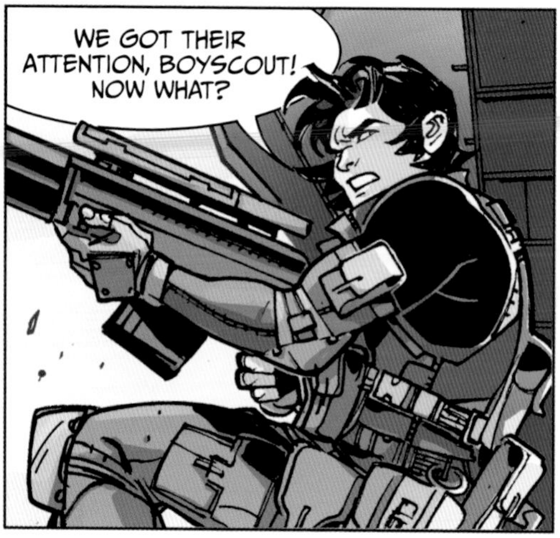
WE GOT THEIR ATTENTION, BOYSCOUT! NOW WHAT?

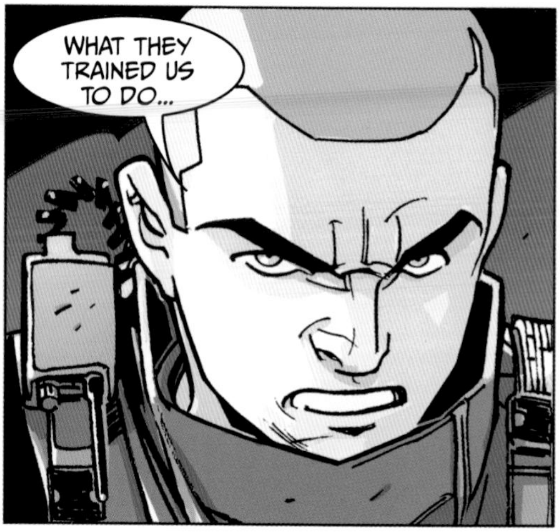
WHAT THEY TRAINED US TO DO...

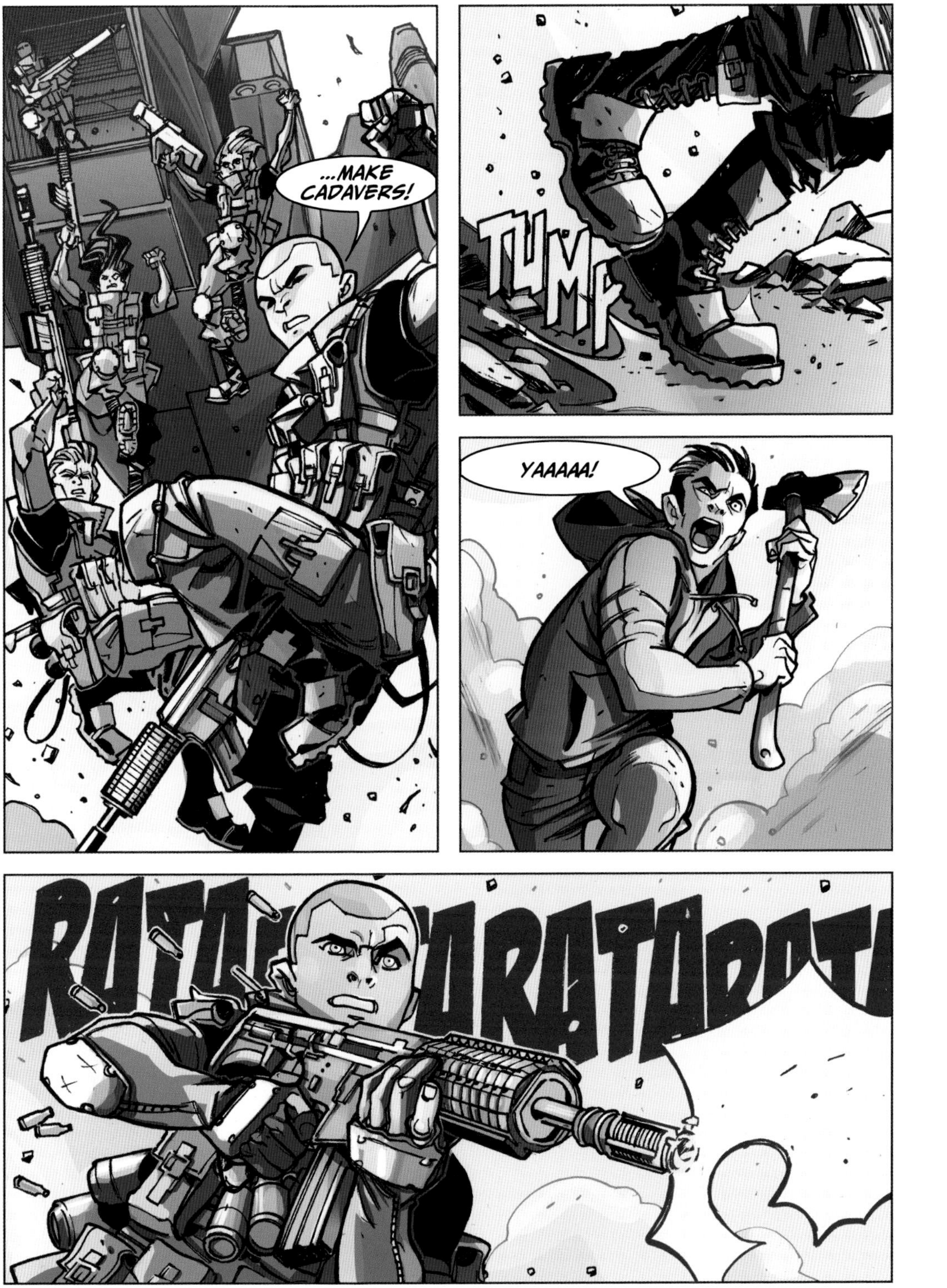
...MAKE CADAVERS!
TUMP
YAAAAA!
RATA
RATATARATA

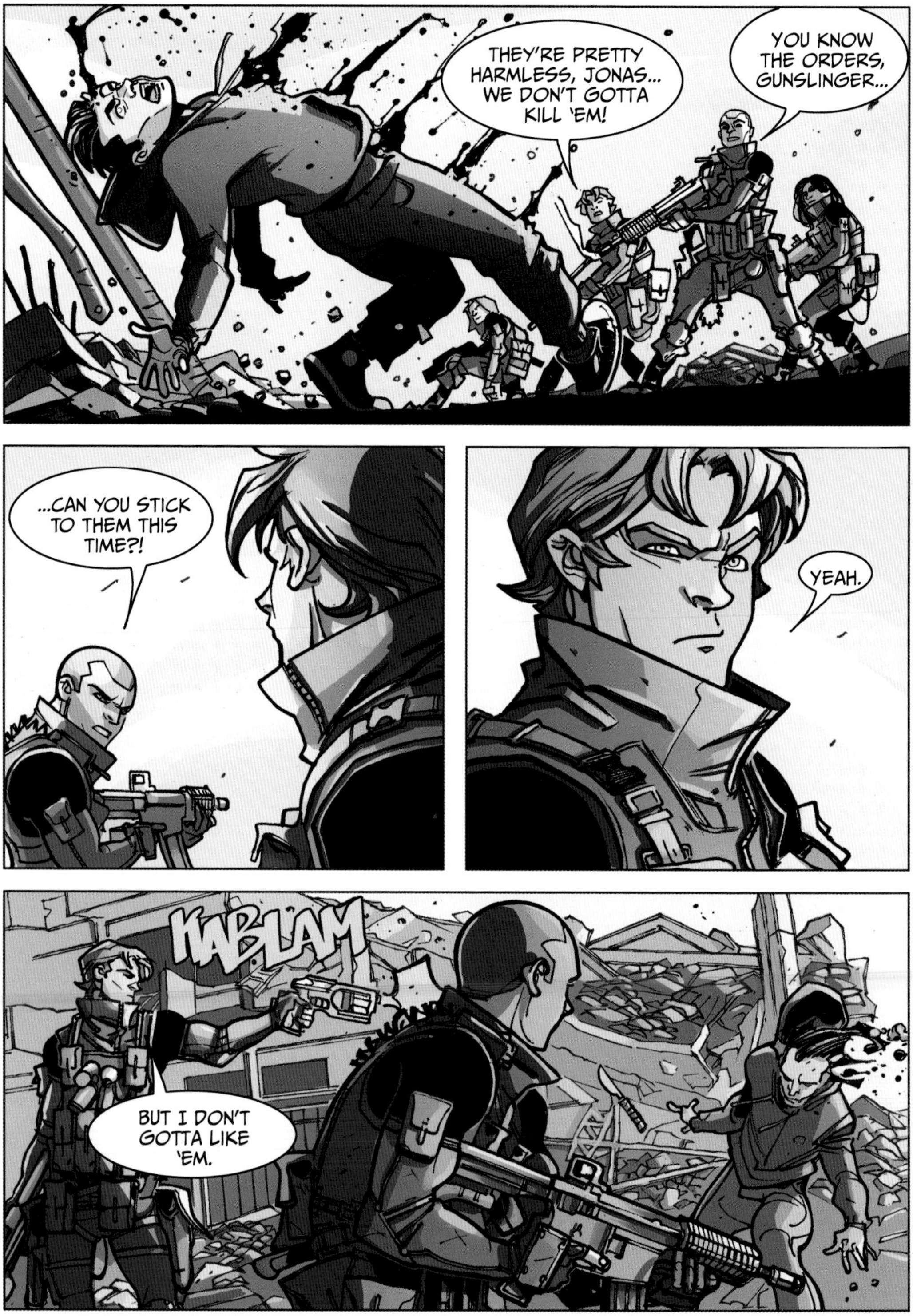
THEY'RE PRETTY HARMLESS, JONAS... WE DON'T GOTTA KILL 'EM!
YOU KNOW THE ORDERS, GUNSLINGER...
...CAN YOU STICK TO THEM THIS TIME?!
YEAH.
KABLAM
BUT I DON'T GOTTA LIKE 'EM.

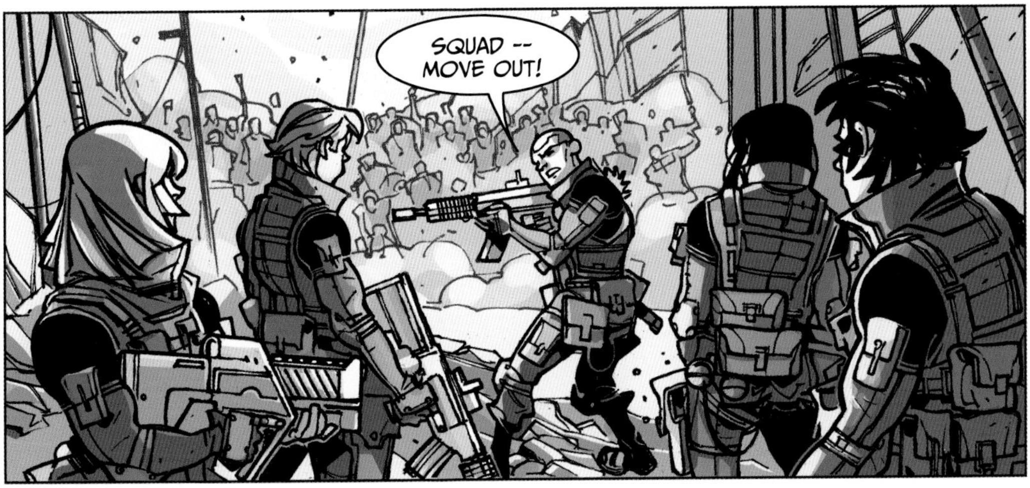
SQUAD -- MOVE OUT!

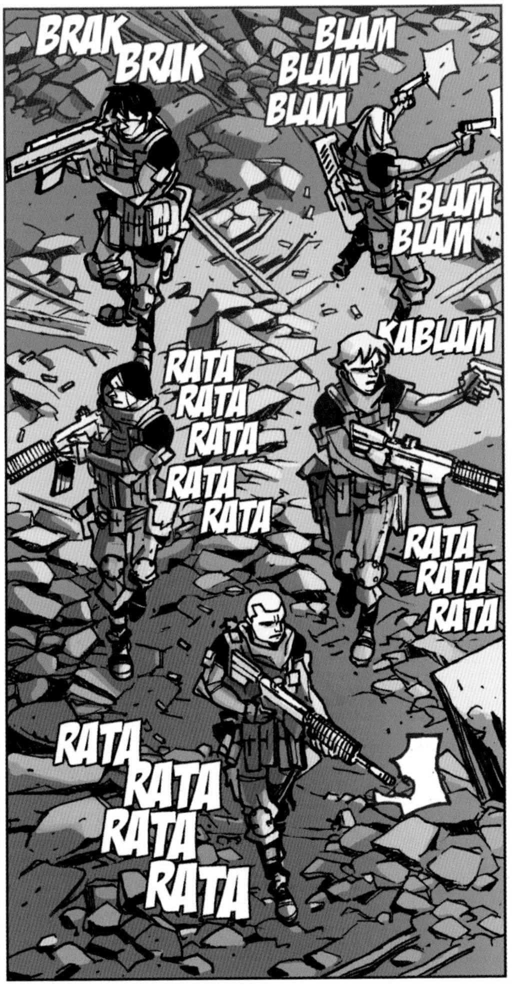
BRAK
BRAK
BLAM
BLAM
BLAM
BLAM
BLAM
KABLAM
RATA
RATA
RATA
RATA
RATA
RATA
RATA
RATA
RATA
RATA
RATA
RATA

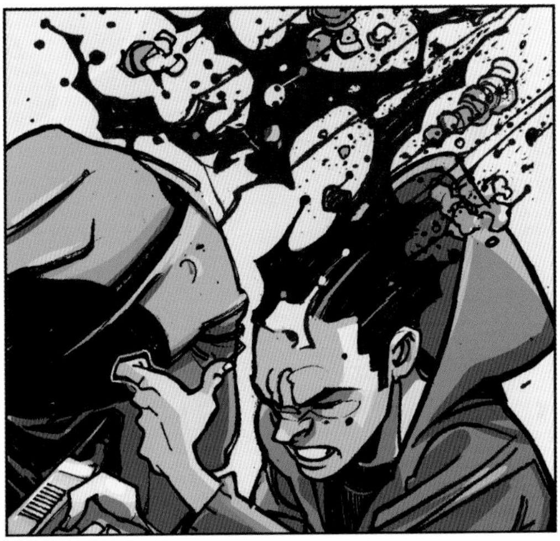

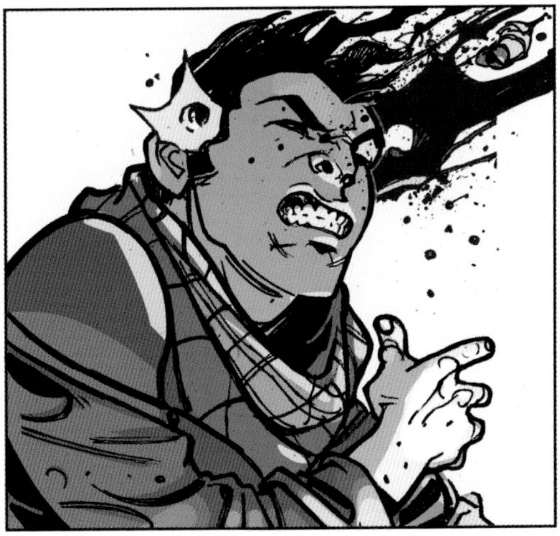

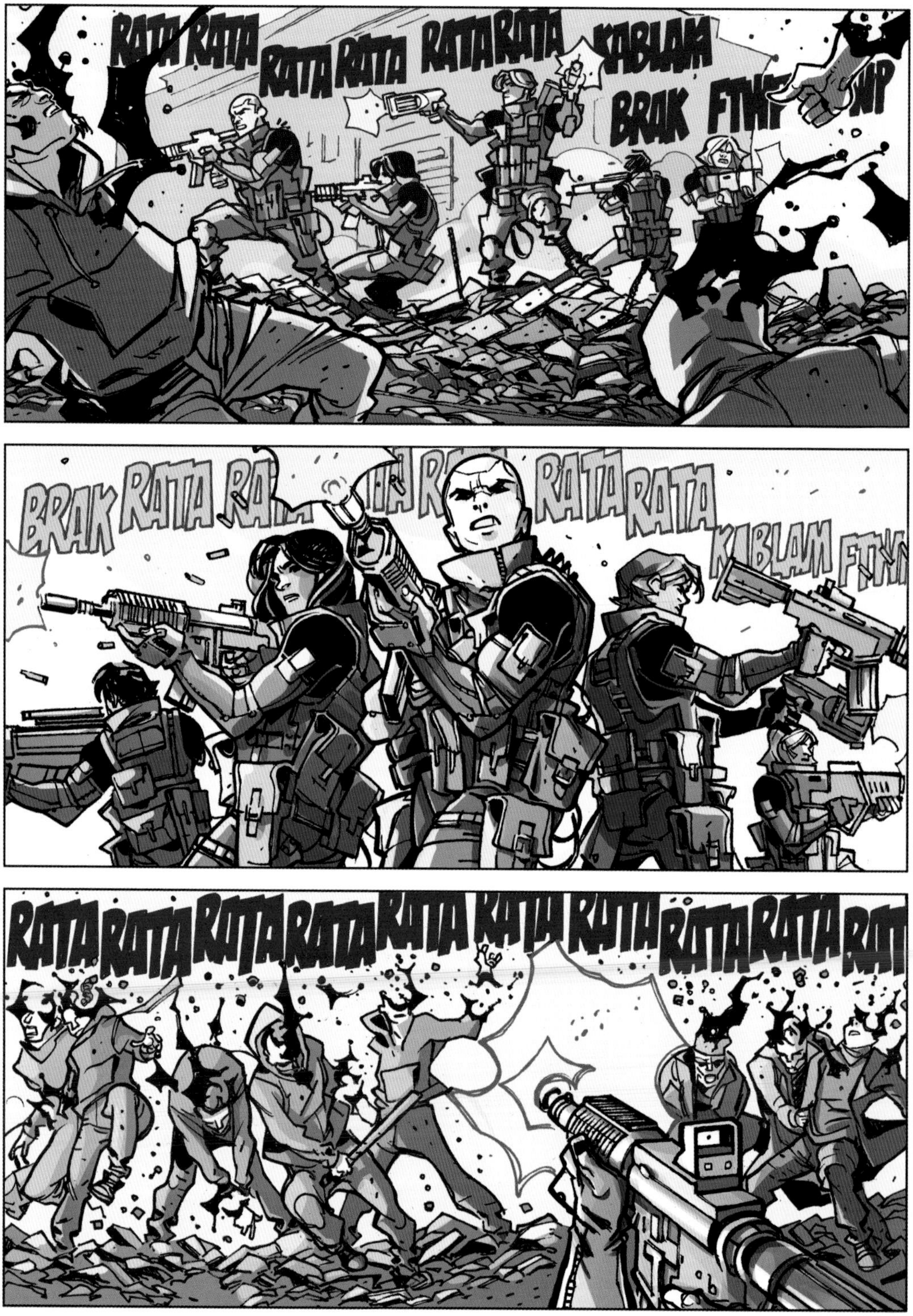
RATA RATA
RATA RATA
RATA RATA
KABLAM
BRAK
BRAK RATA
RATA RATA
KABLAM
RATA RATA RATA RATA RATA RATA RATA RATA RATA

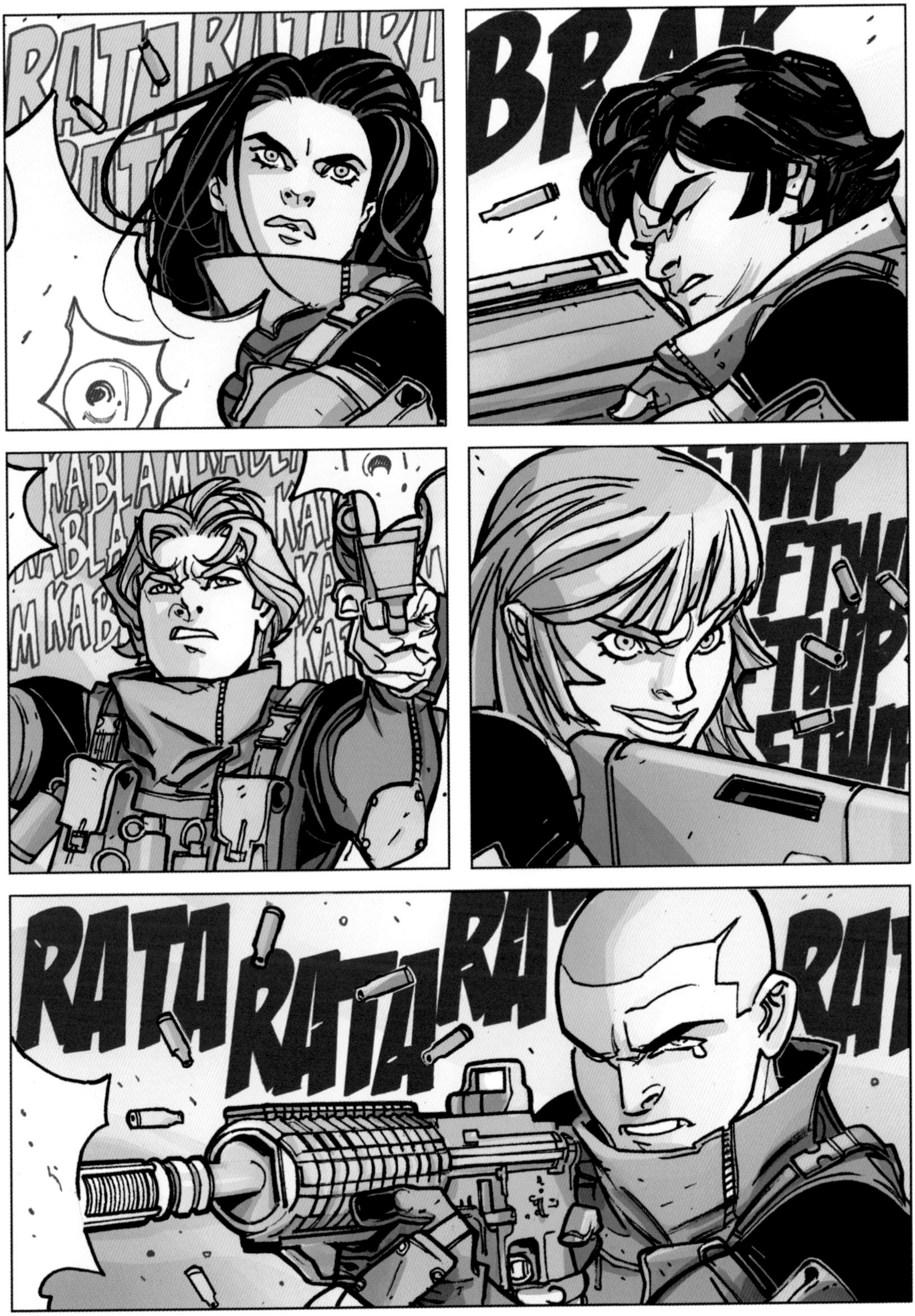
RATA
BRAK
RATA RATA

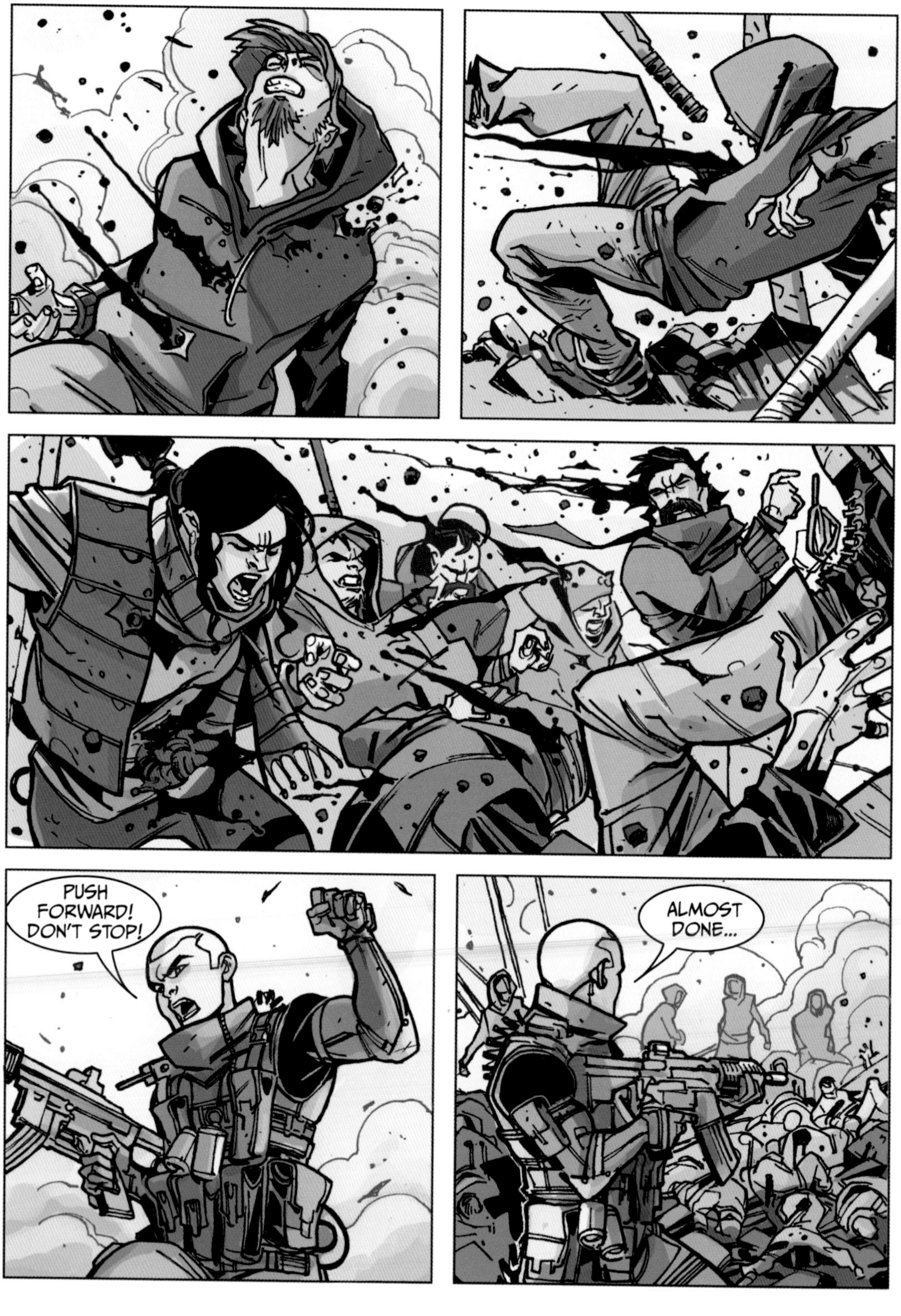
PUSH FORWARD! DON'T STOP!
ALMOST DONE...

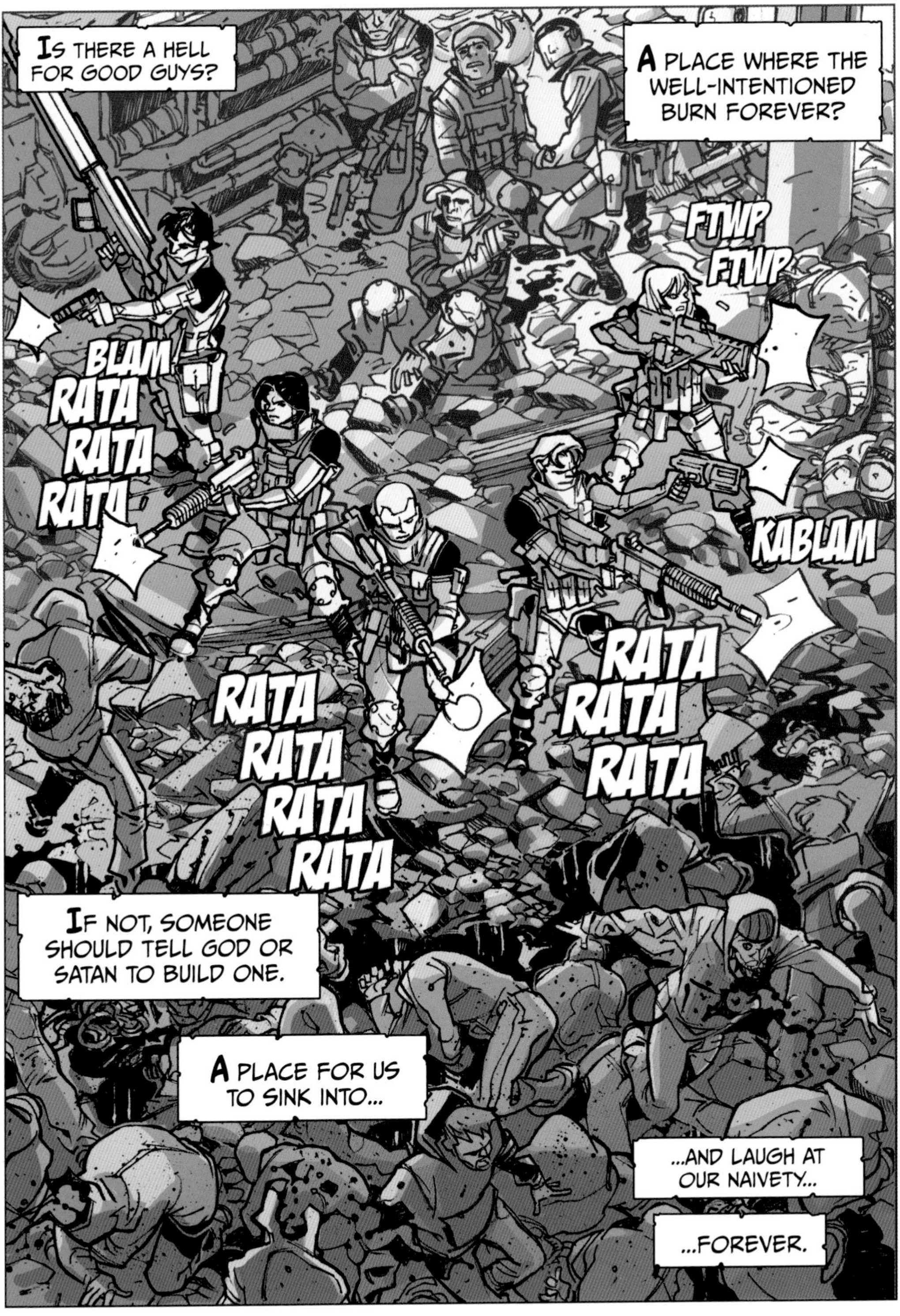
IS THERE A HELL FOR GOOD GUYS?
A PLACE WHERE THE WELL-INTENTIONED BURN FOREVER?
FTWP FTWP
BLAM
RATA RATA RATA
KABLAM
RATA RATA RATA RATA
RATA RATA RATA
IF NOT, SOMEONE SHOULD TELL GOD OR SATAN TO BUILD ONE.
A PLACE FOR US TO SINK INTO...
...AND LAUGH AT OUR NAIVETY...
...FOREVER.

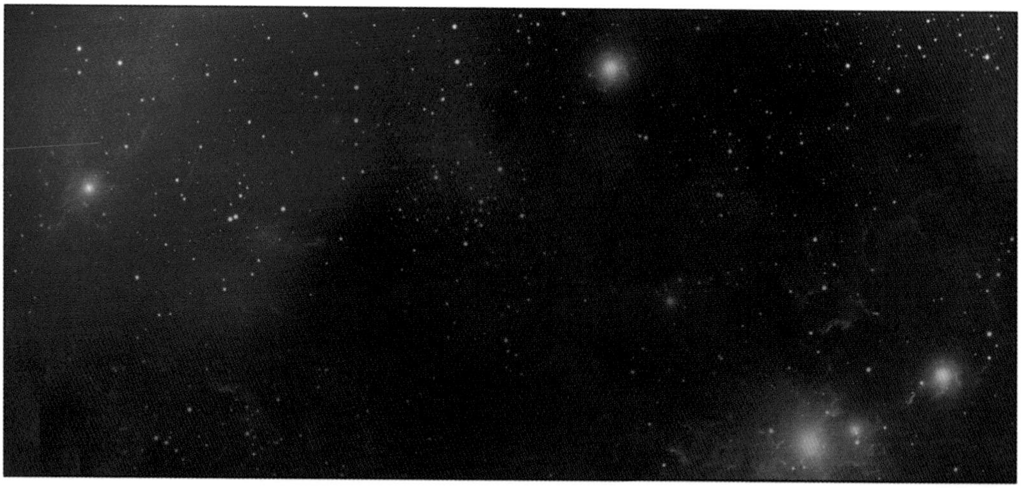

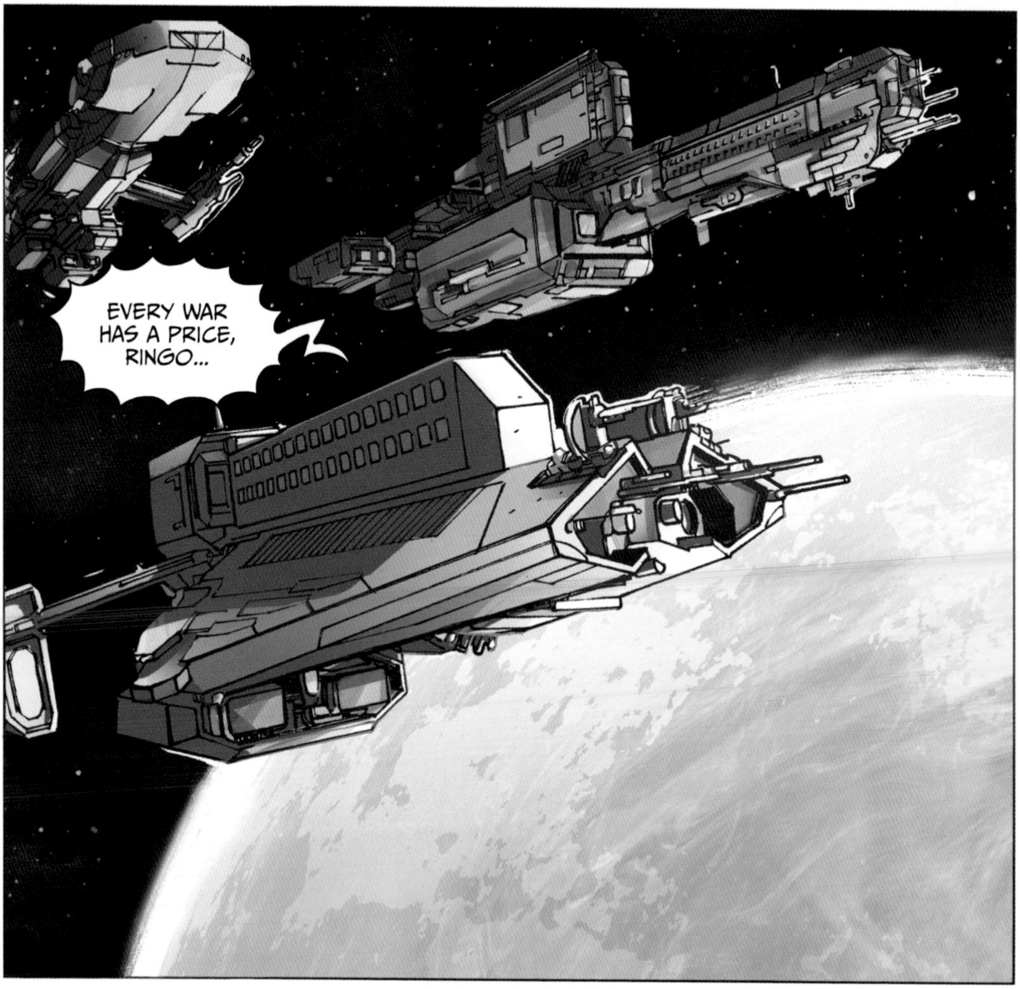
EVERY WAR HAS A PRICE, RINGO...

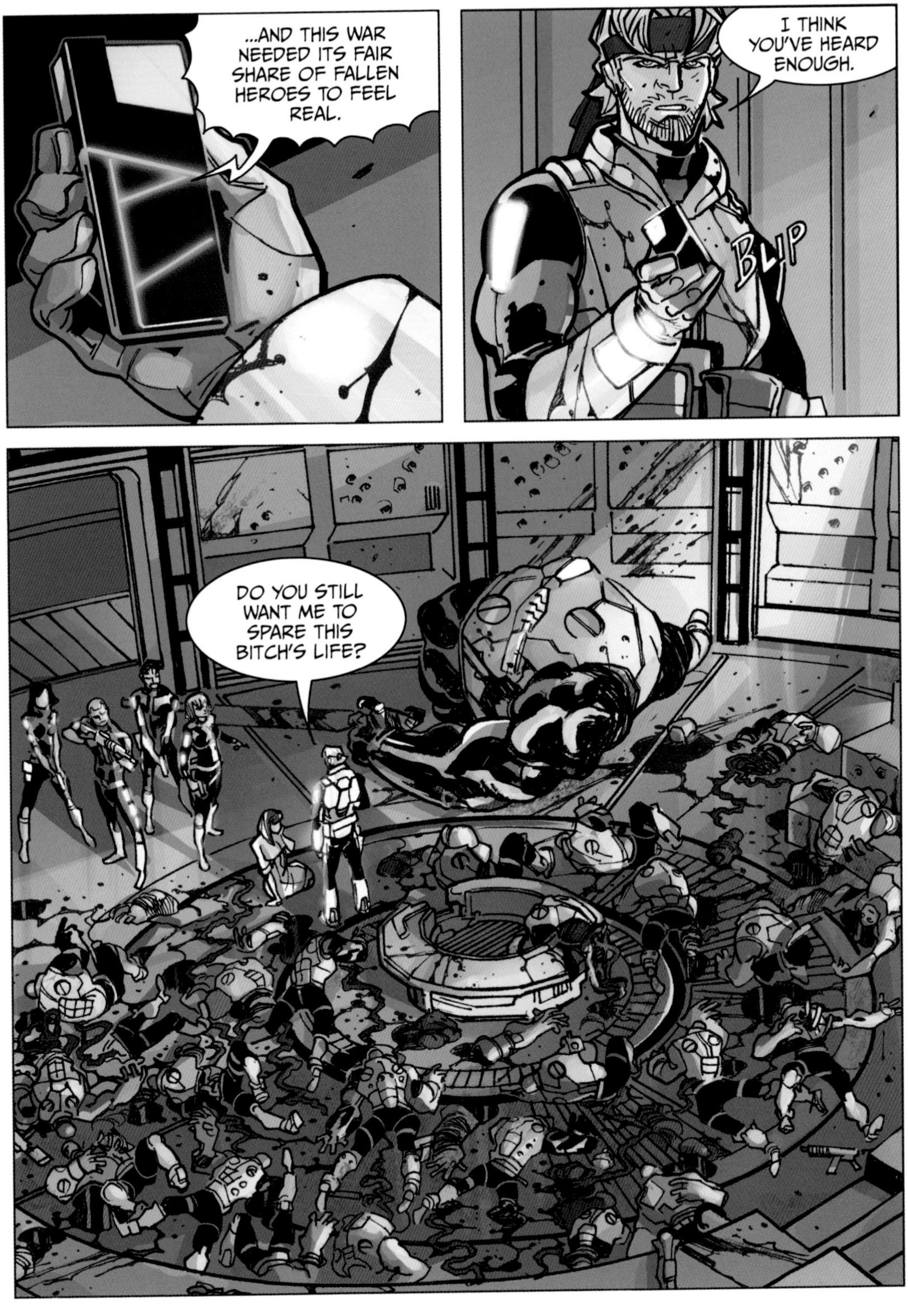
...AND THIS WAR NEEDED ITS FAIR SHARE OF FALLEN HEROES TO FEEL REAL.
I THINK YOU'VE HEARD ENOUGH.
BLIP
DO YOU STILL WANT ME TO SPARE THIS BITCH'S LIFE?

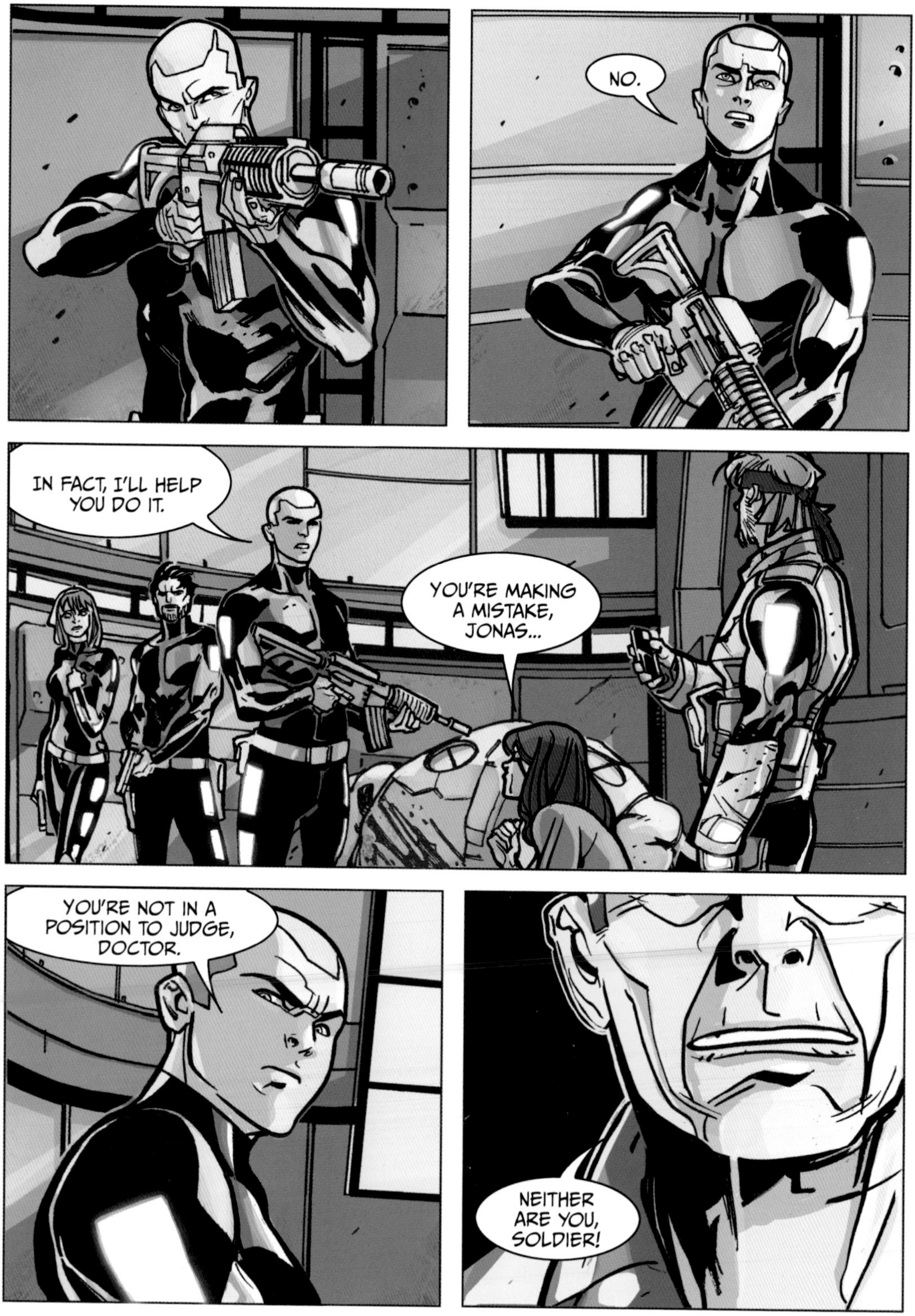
NO.
IN FACT, I'LL HELP YOU DO IT.
YOU'RE MAKING A MISTAKE, JONAS...
YOU'RE NOT IN A POSITION TO JUDGE, DOCTOR.
NEITHER ARE YOU, SOLDIER!

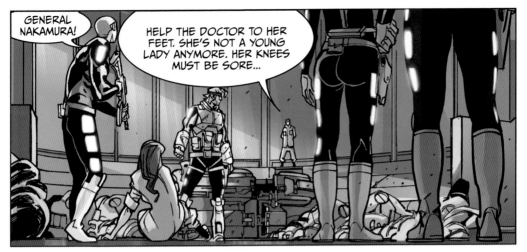

GENERAL NAKAMURA!

HELP THE DOCTOR TO HER FEET. SHE'S NOT A YOUNG LADY ANYMORE. HER KNEES MUST BE SORE...

SHE WON'T FEEL MUCH PAIN SOON...

QUIET, RINGO. YOU'VE DONE ENOUGH DAMAGE ALREADY.

THANK YOU, GENERAL.

WITH ALL DUE RESPECT, SIR, IT'S NOT RINGO YOU SHOULD BE WORRIED ABOUT!

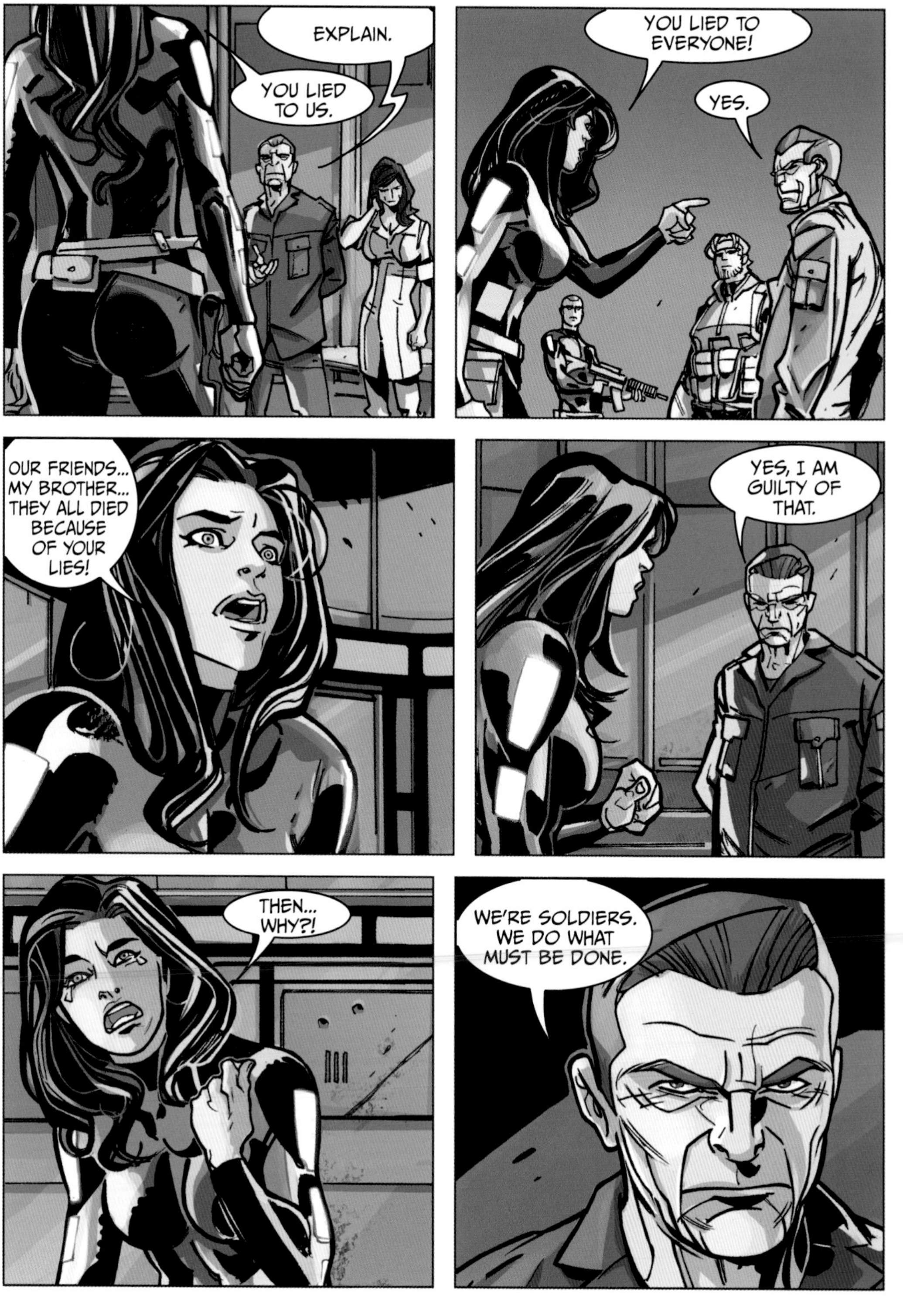
EXPLAIN.
YOU LIED TO US.
YOU LIED TO EVERYONE!
YES.
OUR FRIENDS... MY BROTHER... THEY ALL DIED BECAUSE OF YOUR LIES!
YES, I AM GUILTY OF THAT.
THEN... WHY?!
WE'RE SOLDIERS. WE DO WHAT MUST BE DONE.

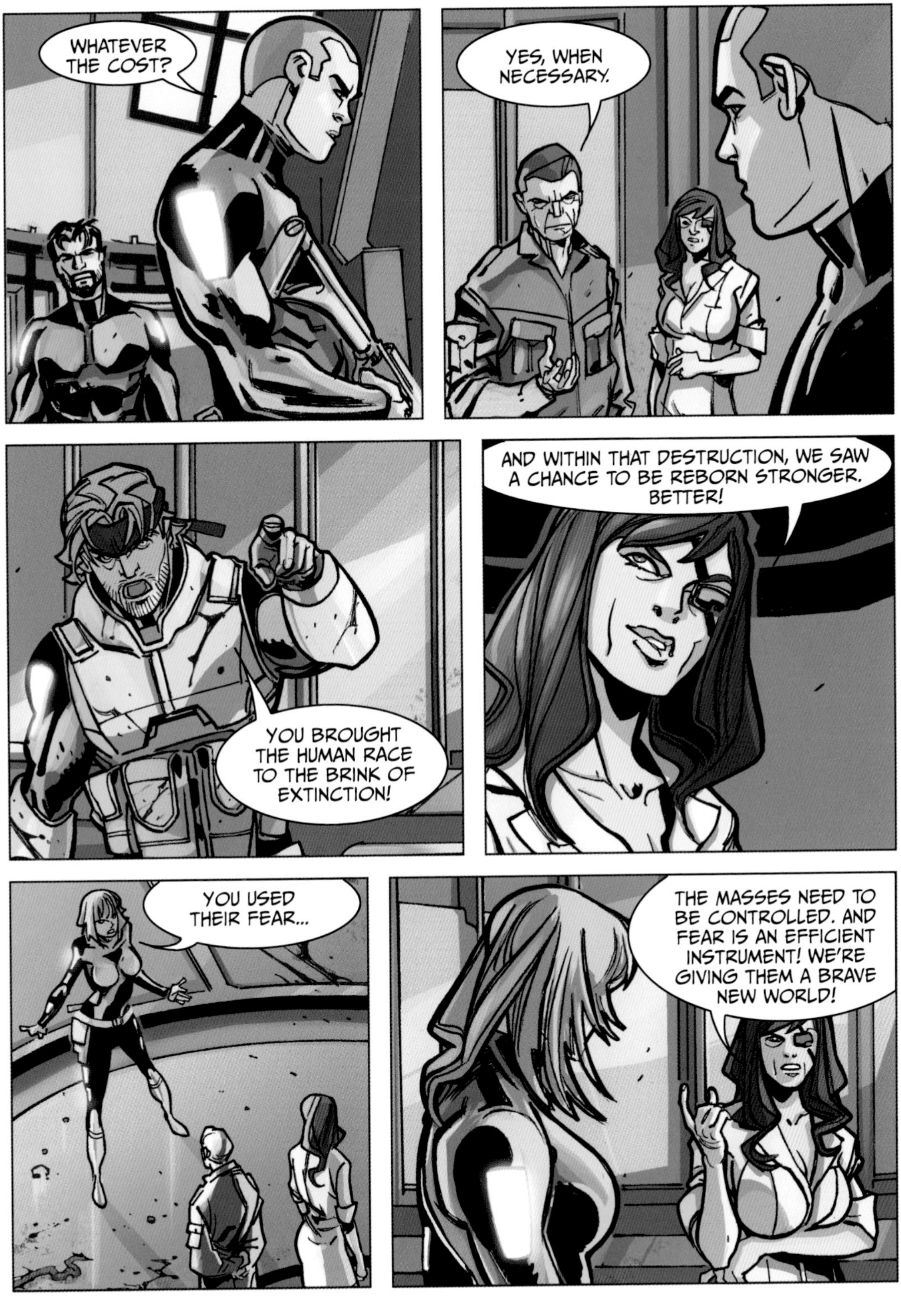
WHATEVER THE COST?
YES, WHEN NECESSARY.
YOU BROUGHT THE HUMAN RACE TO THE BRINK OF EXTINCTION!
AND WITHIN THAT DESTRUCTION, WE SAW A CHANCE TO BE REBORN STRONGER. BETTER!
YOU USED THEIR FEAR...
THE MASSES NEED TO BE CONTROLLED. AND FEAR IS AN EFFICIENT INSTRUMENT! WE'RE GIVING THEM A BRAVE NEW WORLD!

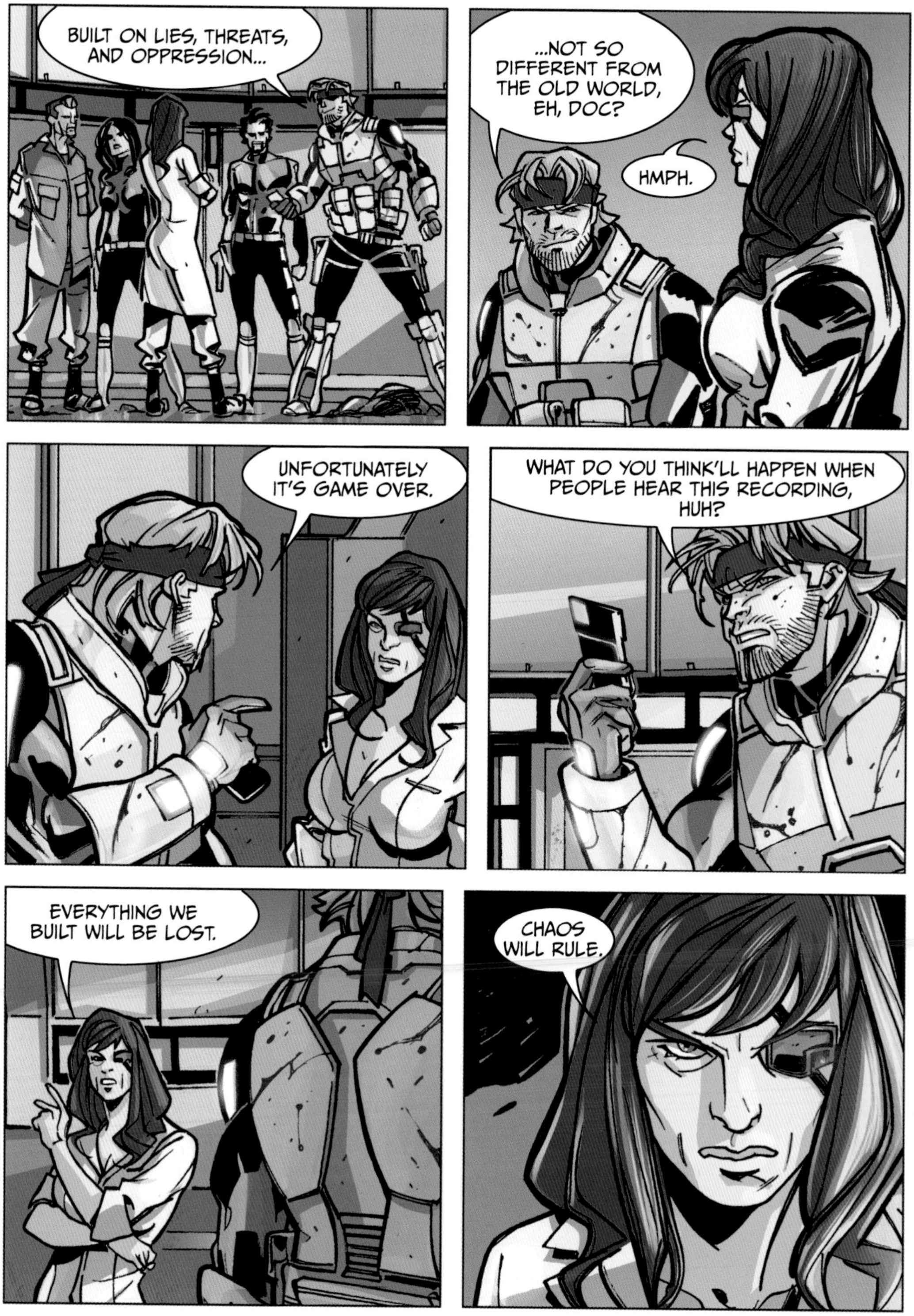
BUILT ON LIES, THREATS, AND OPPRESSION...
...NOT SO DIFFERENT FROM THE OLD WORLD, EH, DOC?
HMPH.
UNFORTUNATELY IT'S GAME OVER.
WHAT DO YOU THINK'LL HAPPEN WHEN PEOPLE HEAR THIS RECORDING, HUH?
EVERYTHING WE BUILT WILL BE LOST.
CHAOS WILL RULE.

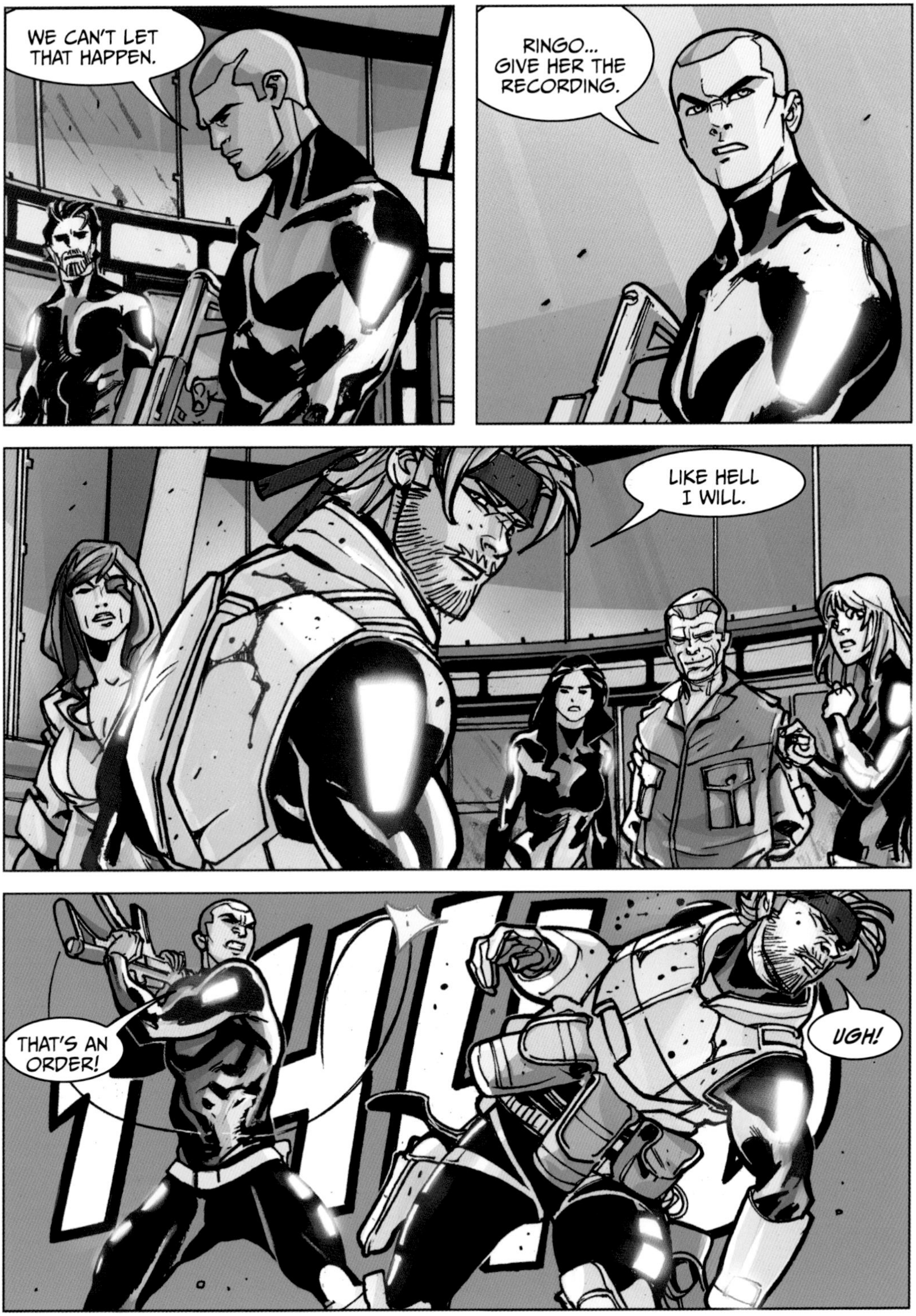
WE CAN'T LET THAT HAPPEN.
RINGO... GIVE HER THE RECORDING.
LIKE HELL I WILL.
THAT'S AN ORDER!
UGH!

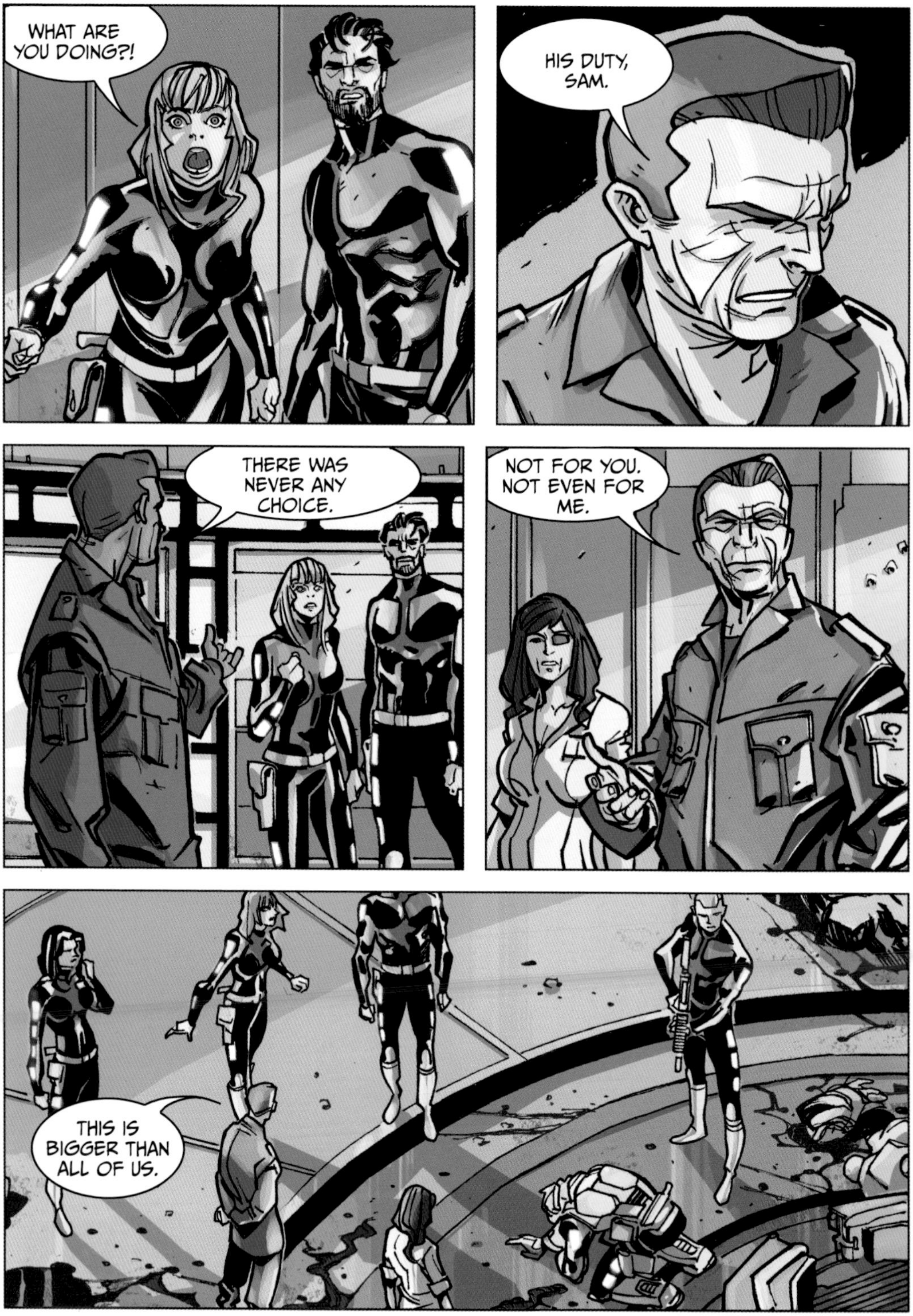
WHAT ARE YOU DOING?!
HIS DUTY, SAM.
THERE WAS NEVER ANY CHOICE.
NOT FOR YOU. NOT EVEN FOR ME.
THIS IS BIGGER THAN ALL OF US.

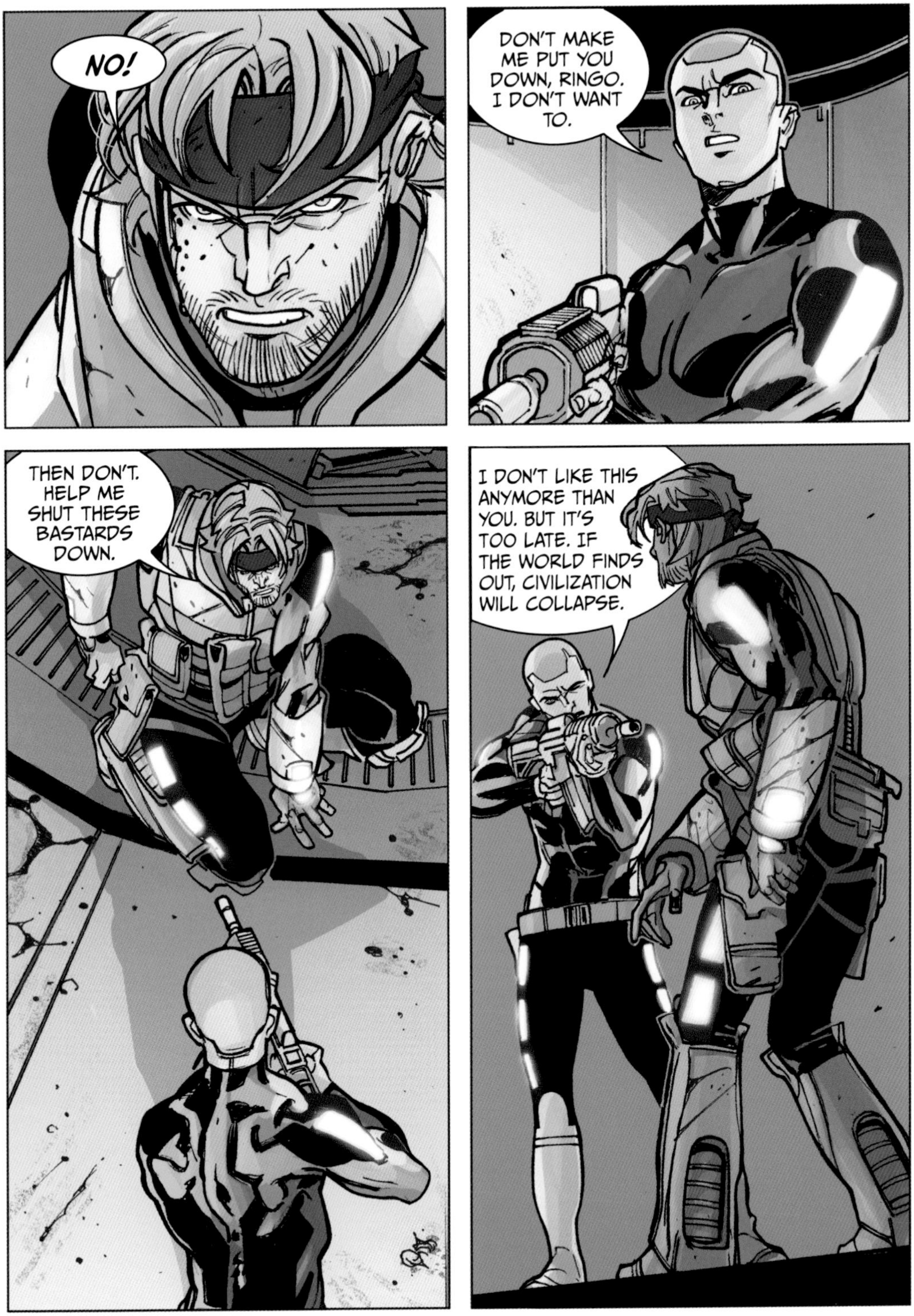
NO!
DON'T MAKE ME PUT YOU DOWN, RINGO. I DON'T WANT TO.
THEN DON'T. HELP ME SHUT THESE BASTARDS DOWN.
I DON'T LIKE THIS ANYMORE THAN YOU. BUT IT'S TOO LATE. IF THE WORLD FINDS OUT, CIVILIZATION WILL COLLAPSE.

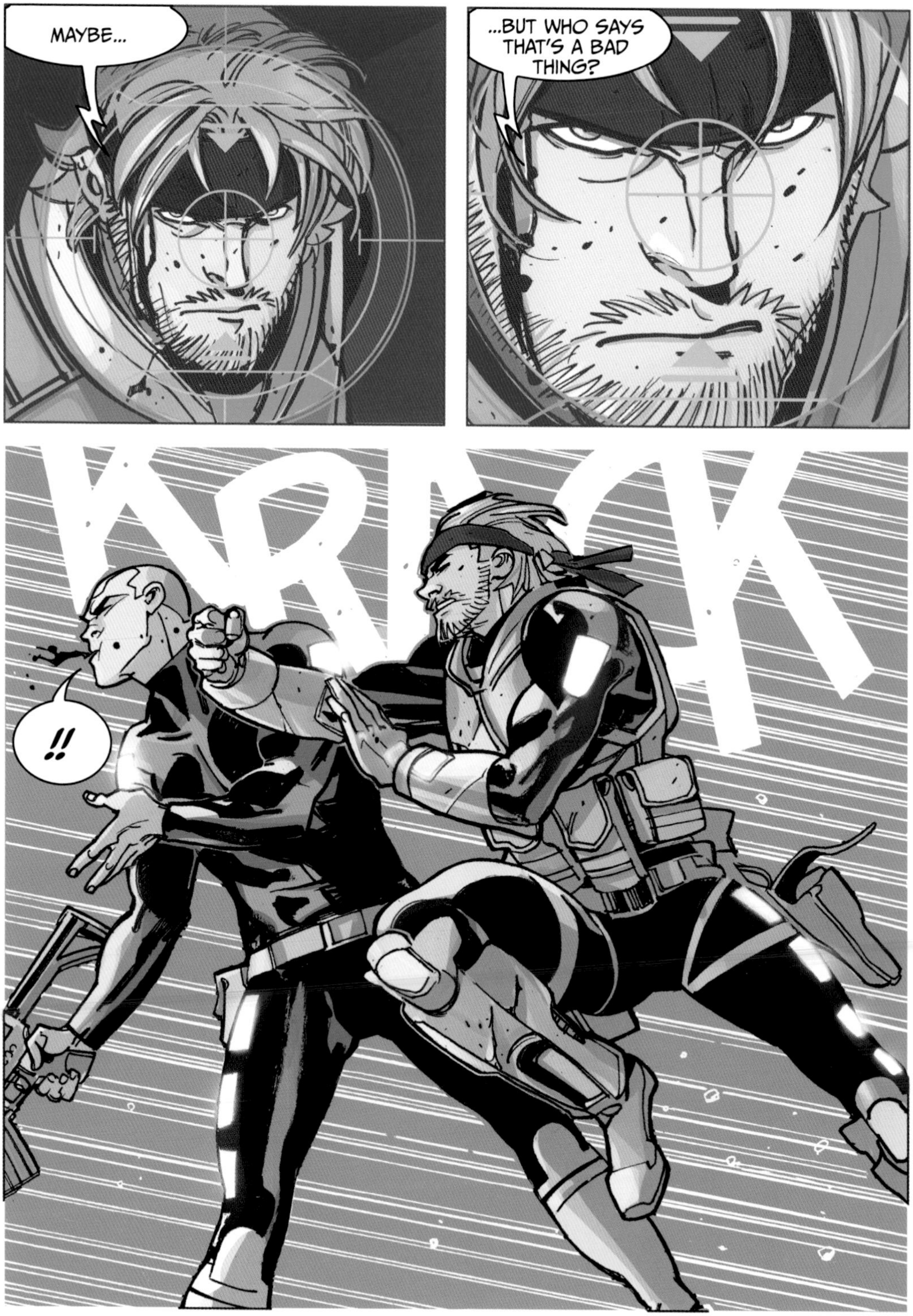
MAYBE...
...BUT WHO SAYS THAT'S A BAD THING?
!!

YOU NEVER CHANGE, RINGO...

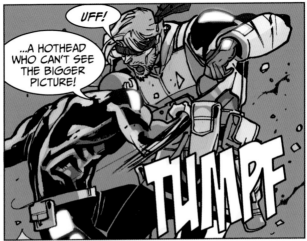

UFF!

...A HOTHEAD WHO CAN'T SEE THE BIGGER PICTURE!

TIME TO GROW UP!

AND BECOME LIKE YOU?!

NO THANKS!

YOU THINK YOU HAVE A CHOICE IN THIS?

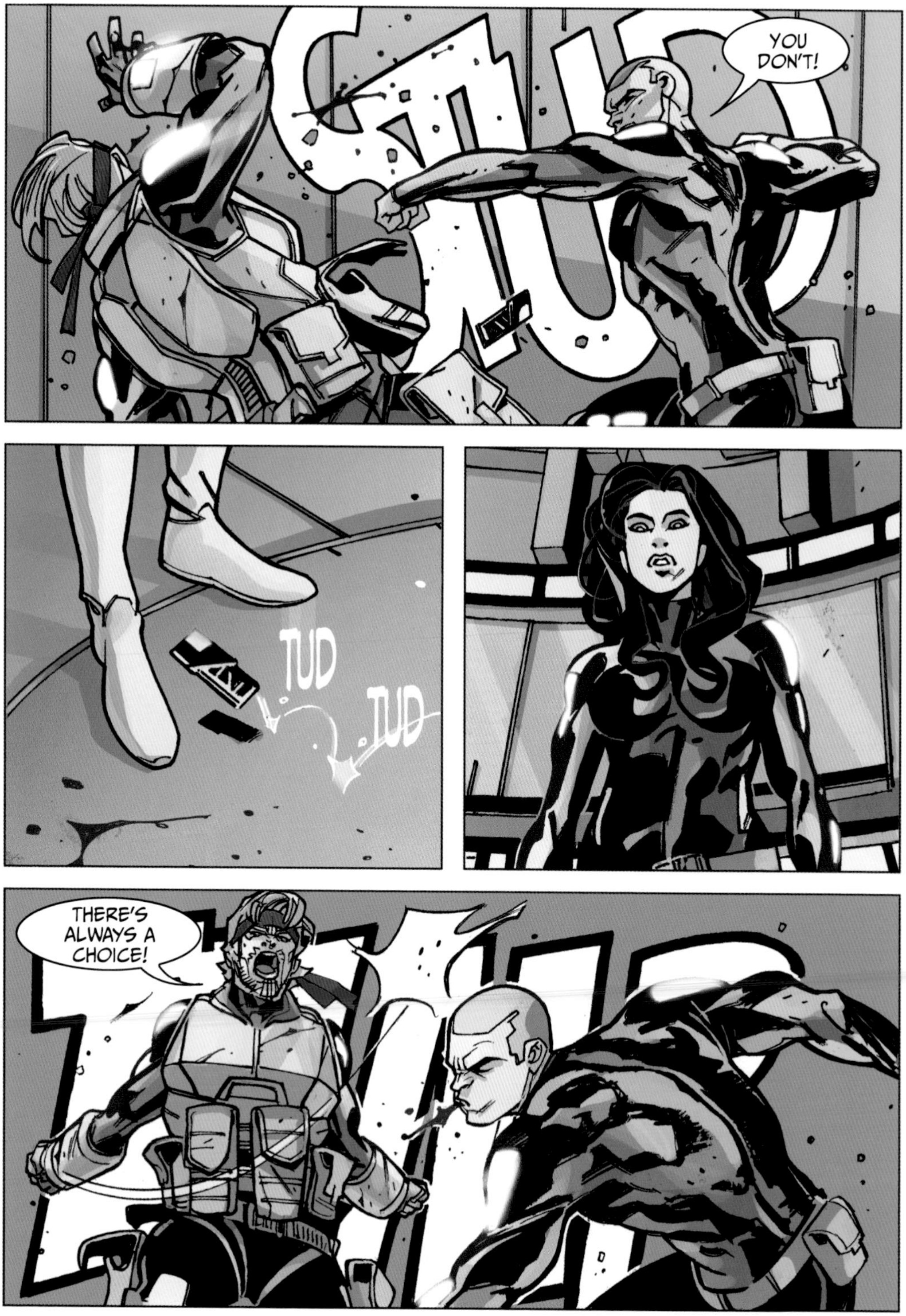
YOU DON'T!
TUD
TUD
THERE'S ALWAYS A CHOICE!

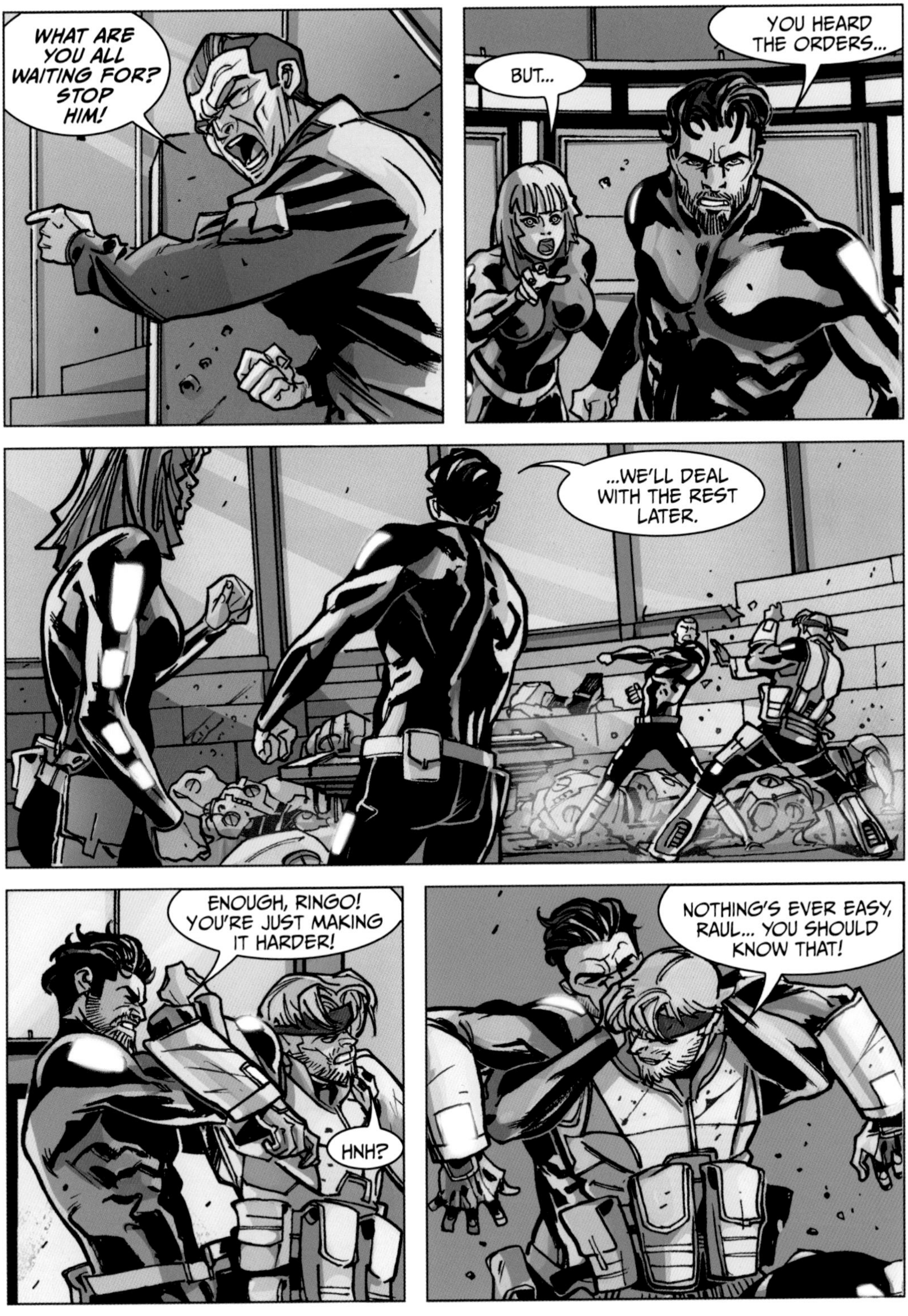
WHAT ARE YOU ALL WAITING FOR? STOP HIM!
BUT...
YOU HEARD THE ORDERS...
...WE'LL DEAL WITH THE REST LATER.
ENOUGH, RINGO! YOU'RE JUST MAKING IT HARDER!
HNH?
NOTHING'S EVER EASY, RAUL... YOU SHOULD KNOW THAT!

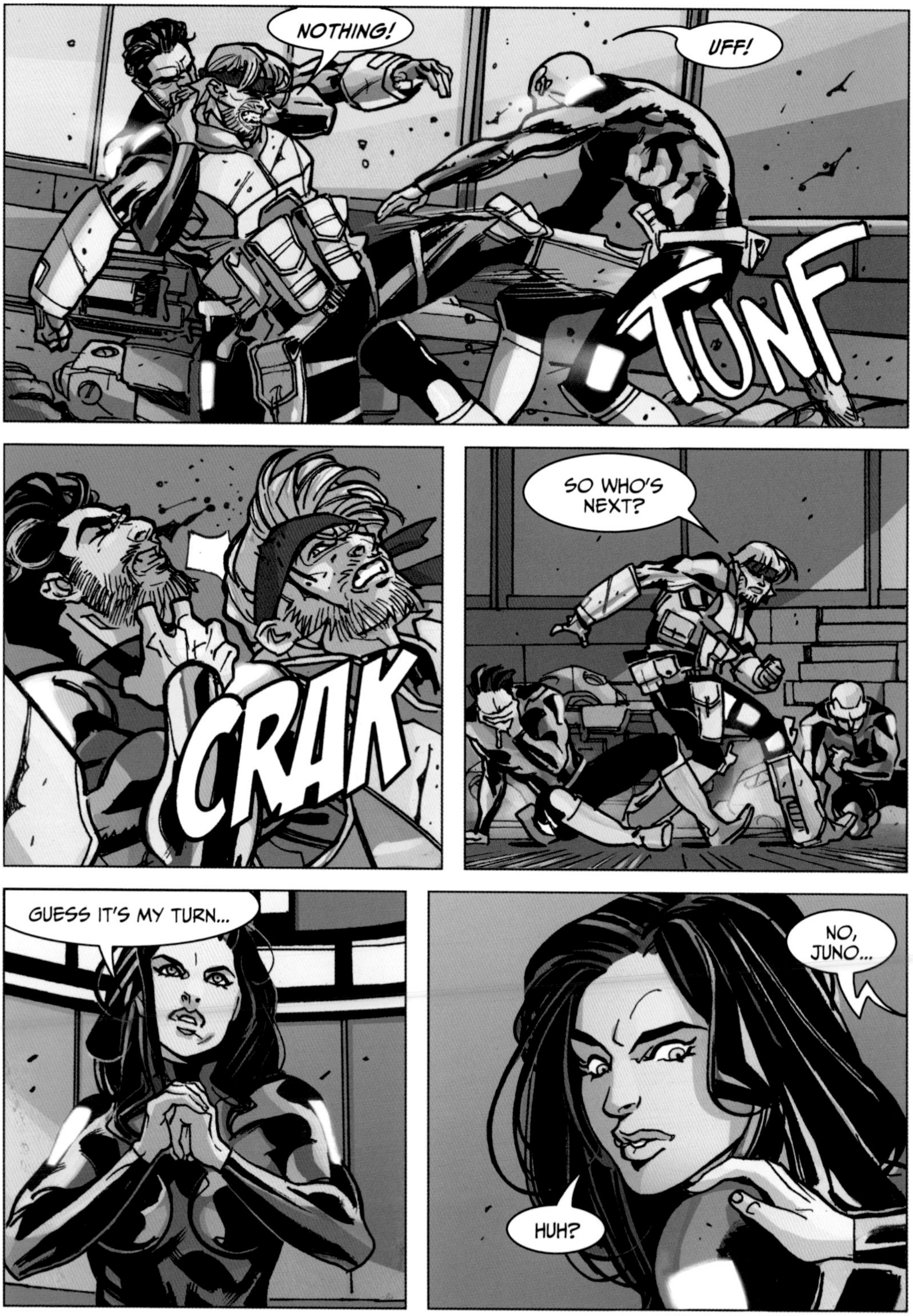
NOTHING!
UFF!
TUNF
CRAK
SO WHO'S NEXT?
GUESS IT'S MY TURN...
NO, JUNO...
HUH?

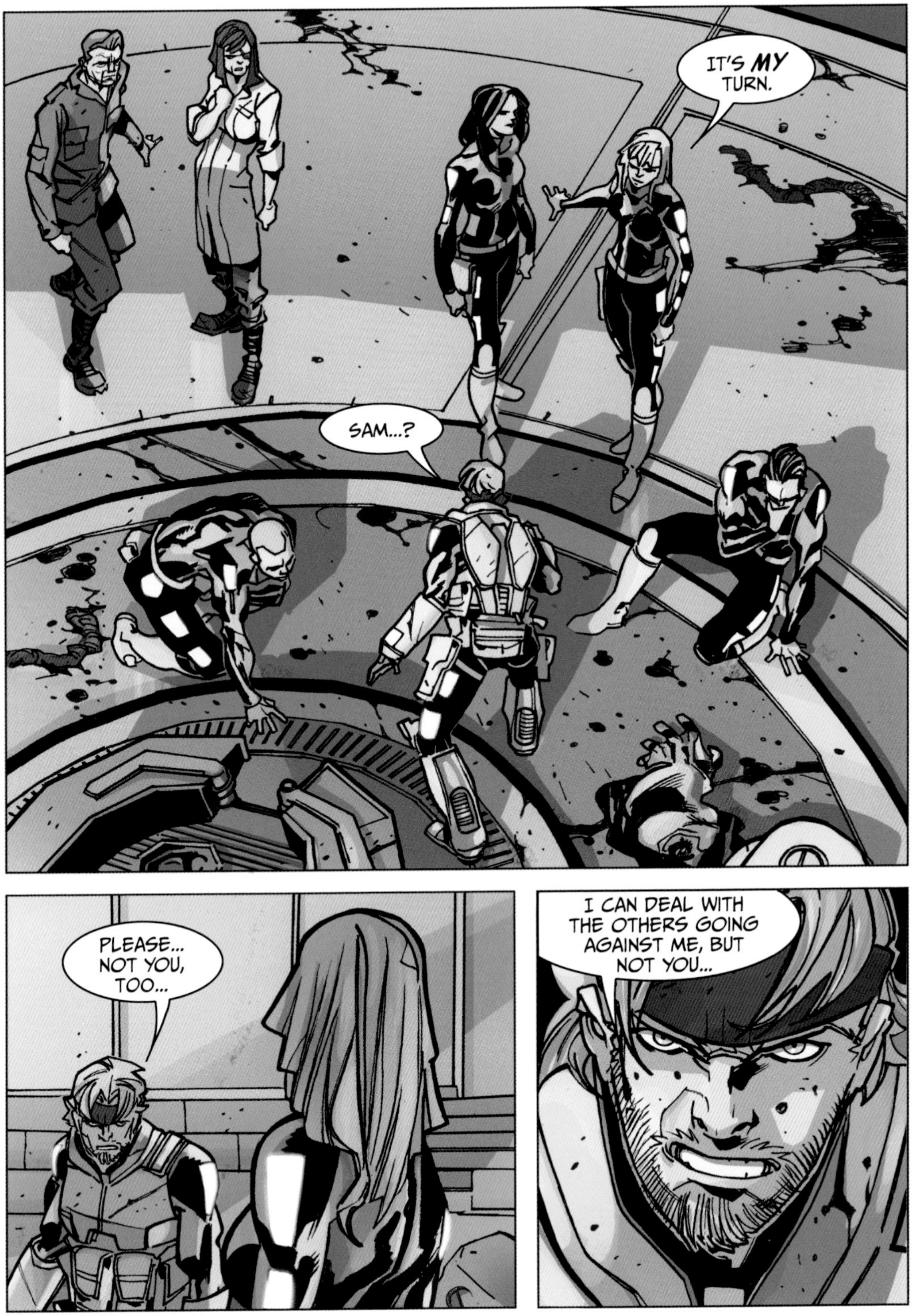
IT'S MY TURN.
SAM...?
PLEASE... NOT YOU, TOO...
I CAN DEAL WITH THE OTHERS GOING AGAINST ME, BUT NOT YOU...

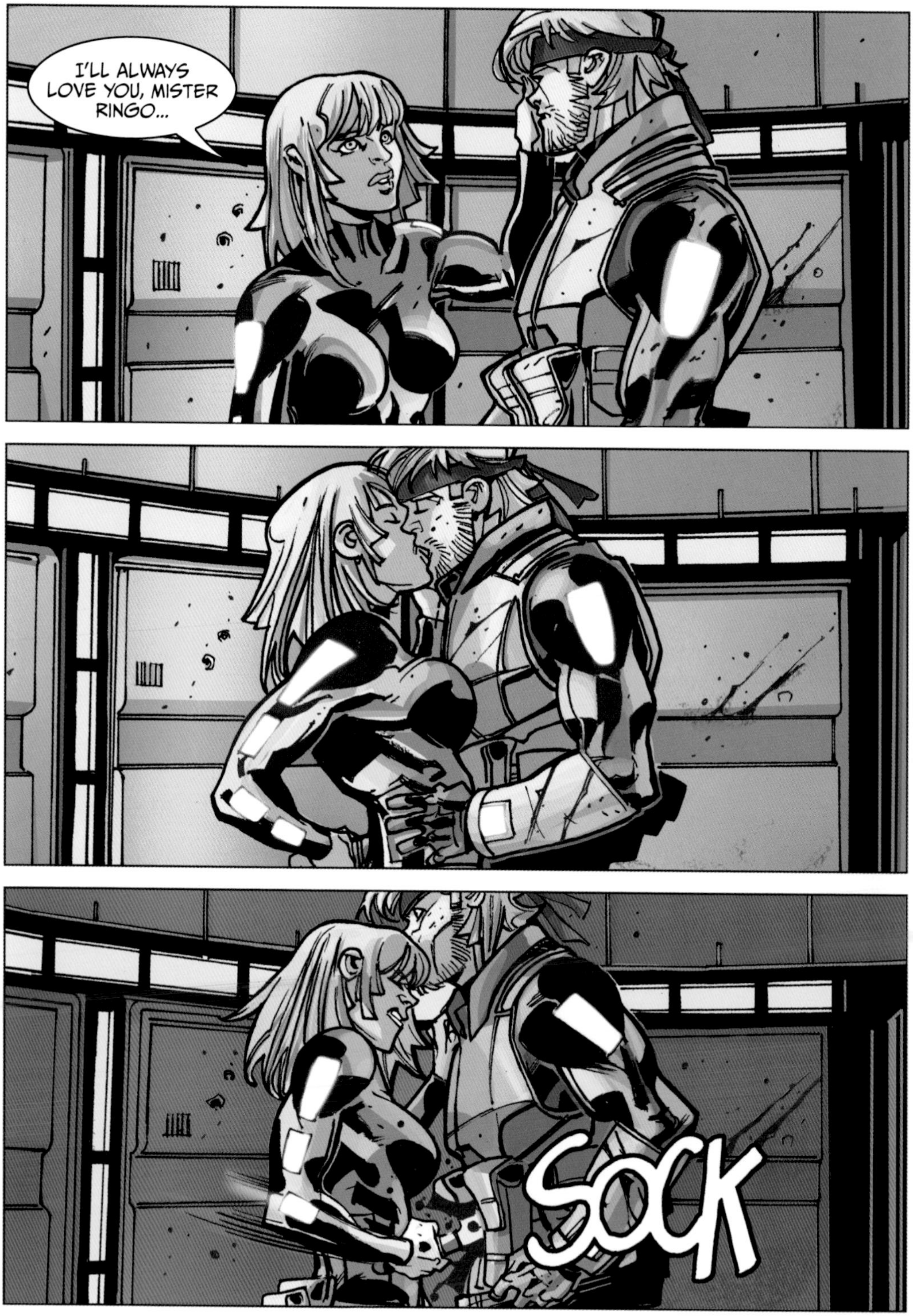
I'LL ALWAYS LOVE YOU, MISTER RINGO...
SOCK

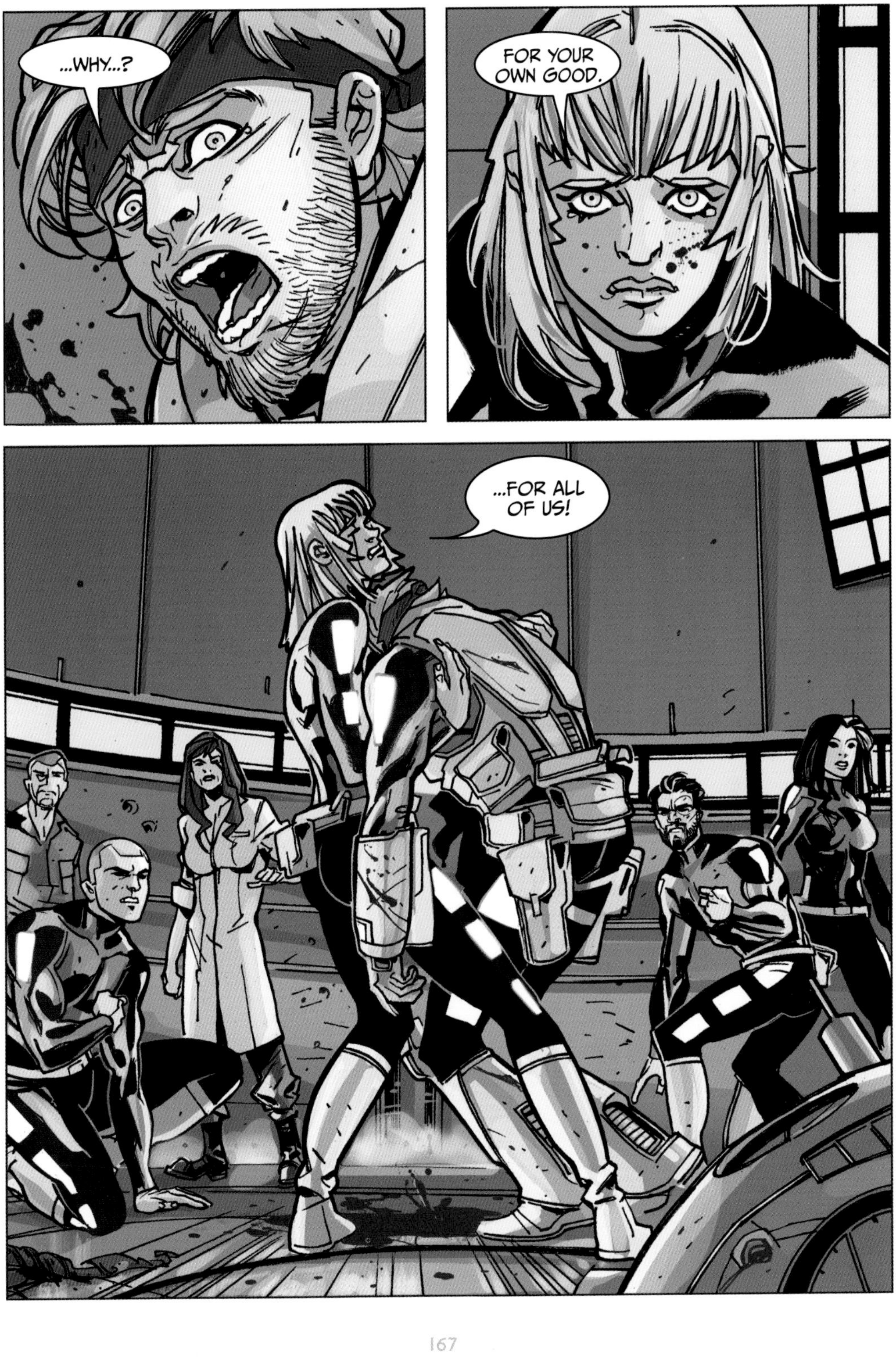
...WHY...?
FOR YOUR OWN GOOD.
...FOR ALL OF US!

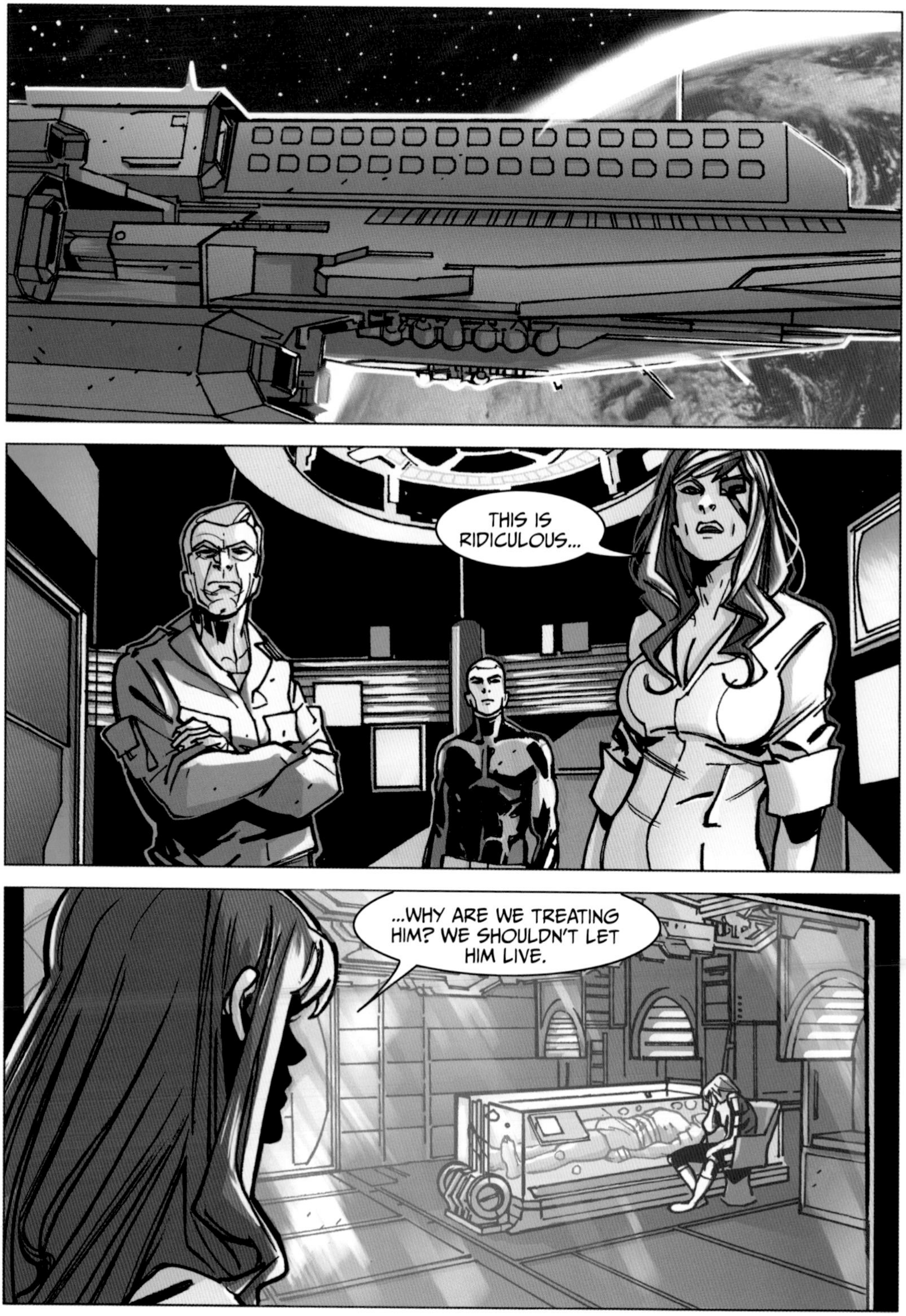
THIS IS RIDICULOUS...
...WHY ARE WE TREATING HIM? WE SHOULDN'T LET HIM LIVE.

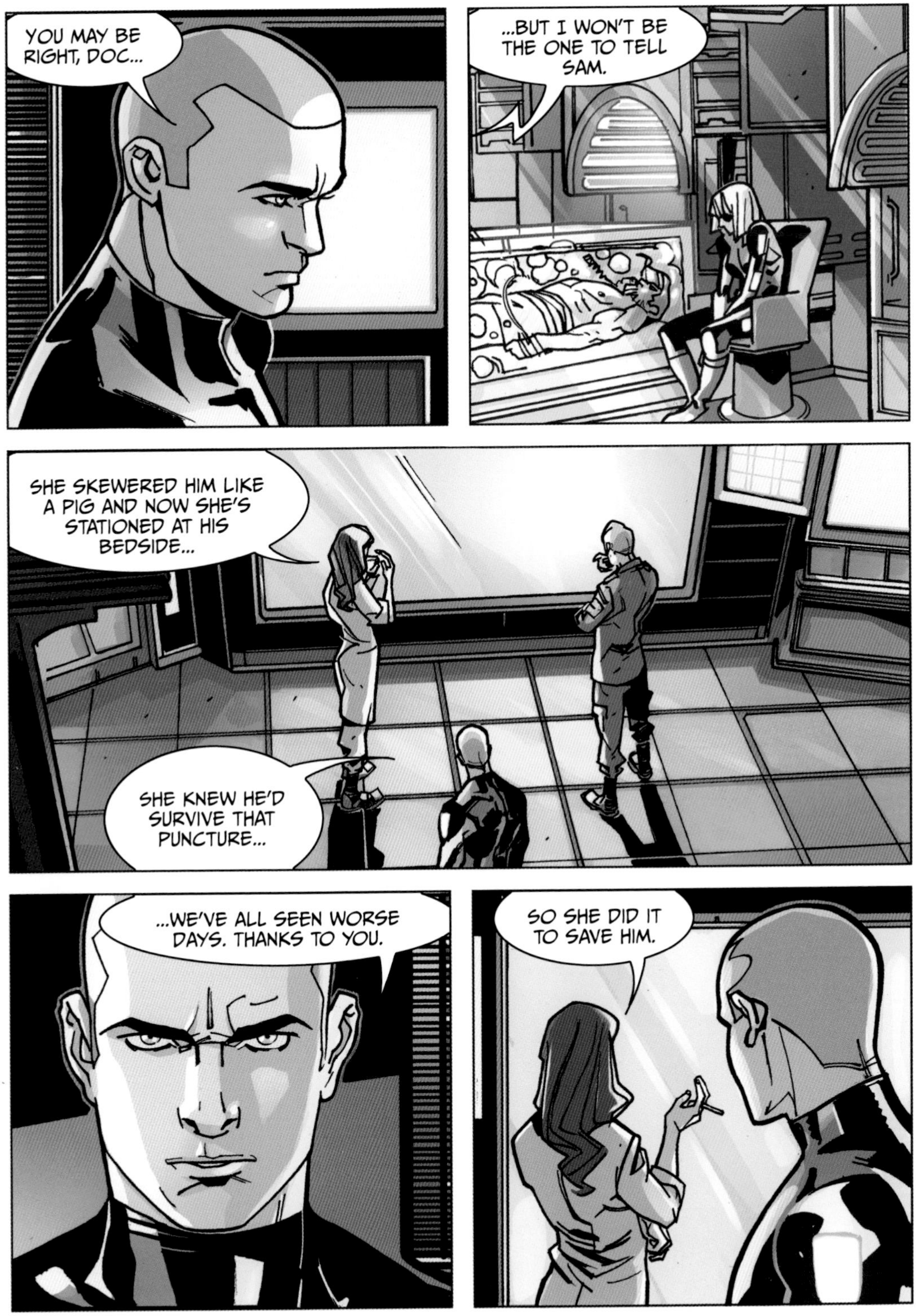
YOU MAY BE RIGHT, DOC...
...BUT I WON'T BE THE ONE TO TELL SAM.
SHE SKEWERED HIM LIKE A PIG AND NOW SHE'S STATIONED AT HIS BEDSIDE...
SHE KNEW HE'D SURVIVE THAT PUNCTURE...
...WE'VE ALL SEEN WORSE DAYS. THANKS TO YOU.
SO SHE DID IT TO SAVE HIM.

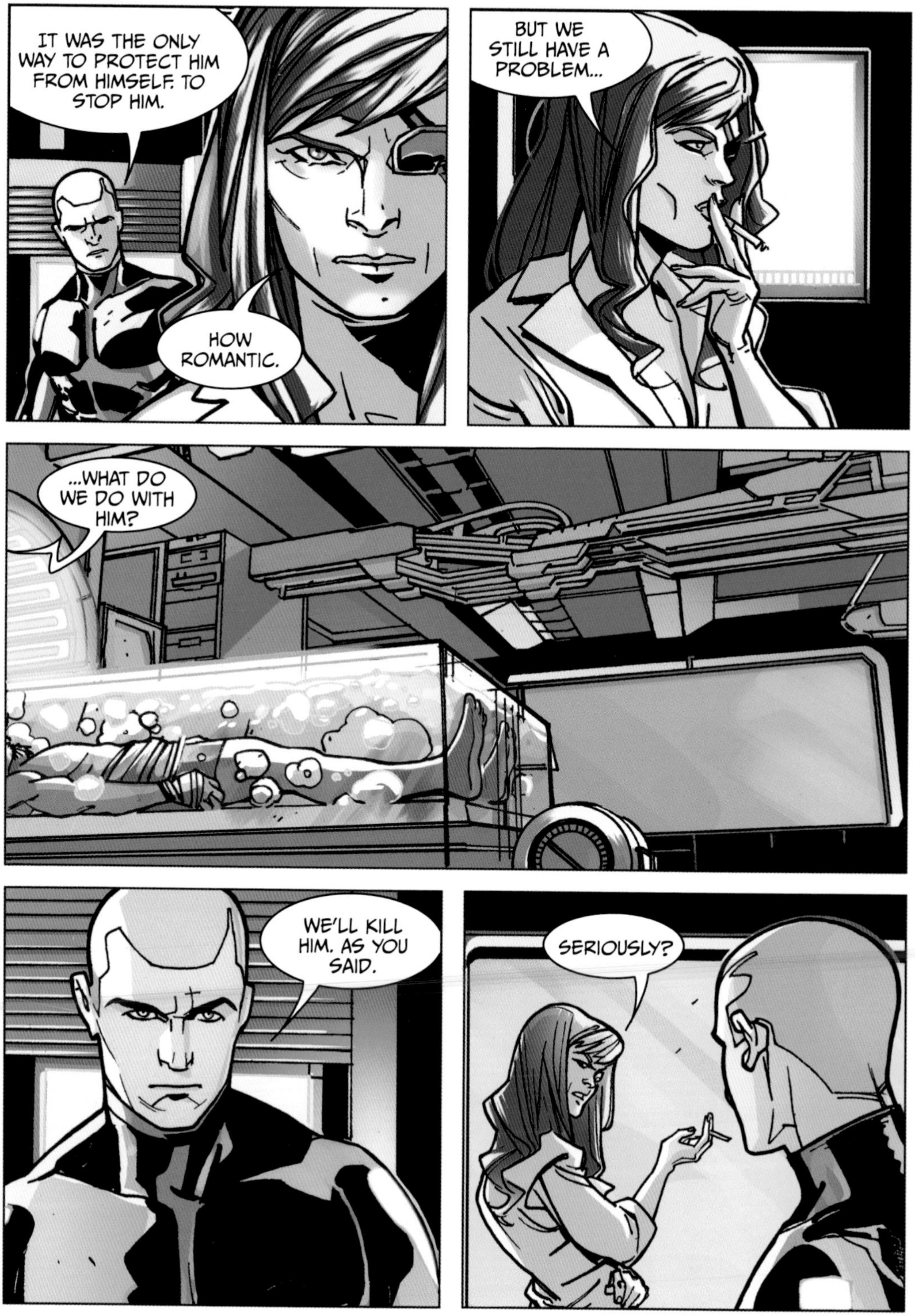
IT WAS THE ONLY WAY TO PROTECT HIM FROM HIMSELF. TO STOP HIM.
HOW ROMANTIC.
BUT WE STILL HAVE A PROBLEM...
...WHAT DO WE DO WITH HIM?
WE'LL KILL HIM. AS YOU SAID.
SERIOUSLY?

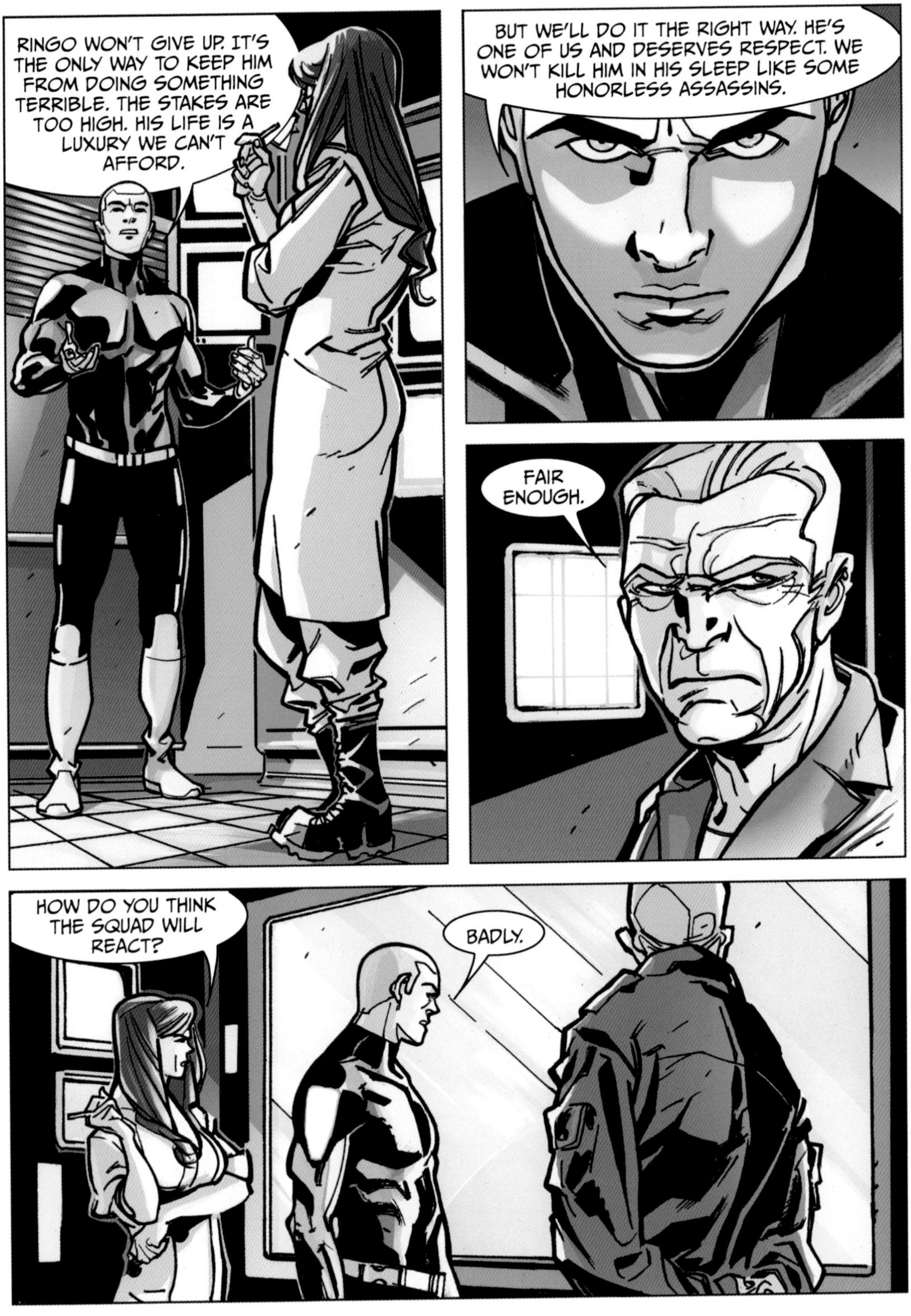
RINGO WON'T GIVE UP. IT'S THE ONLY WAY TO KEEP HIM FROM DOING SOMETHING TERRIBLE. THE STAKES ARE TOO HIGH. HIS LIFE IS A LUXURY WE CAN'T AFFORD.
BUT WE'LL DO IT THE RIGHT WAY. HE'S ONE OF US AND DESERVES RESPECT. WE WON'T KILL HIM IN HIS SLEEP LIKE SOME HONORLESS ASSASSINS.
FAIR ENOUGH.
HOW DO YOU THINK THE SQUAD WILL REACT?
BADLY.

BUT THEY'RE GOOD SOLDIERS.

EVEN SAM? OR DO WE DEAL WITH HER, TOO?

IF ANYONE UNDERSTANDS RINGO'S SOUL, IT'S HER...

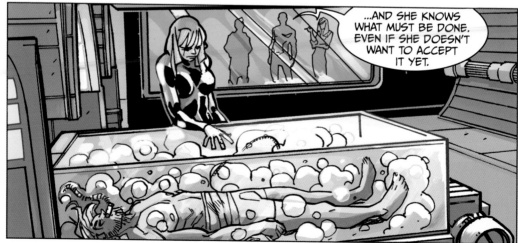

...AND SHE KNOWS WHAT MUST BE DONE. EVEN IF SHE DOESN'T WANT TO ACCEPT IT YET.

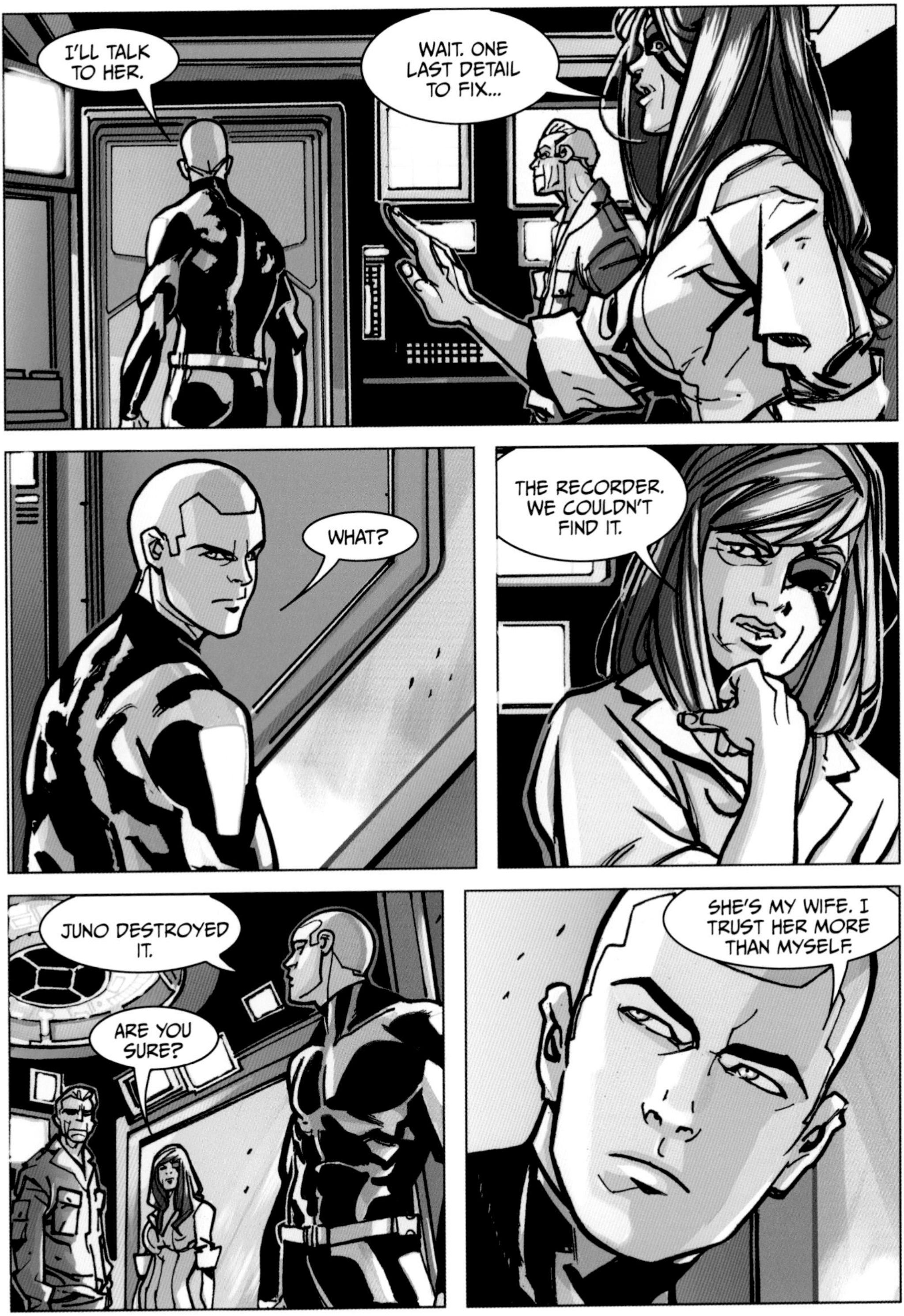
I'LL TALK TO HER.
WAIT. ONE LAST DETAIL TO FIX...
WHAT?
THE RECORDER. WE COULDN'T FIND IT.
JUNO DESTROYED IT.
ARE YOU SURE?
SHE'S MY WIFE. I TRUST HER MORE THAN MYSELF.

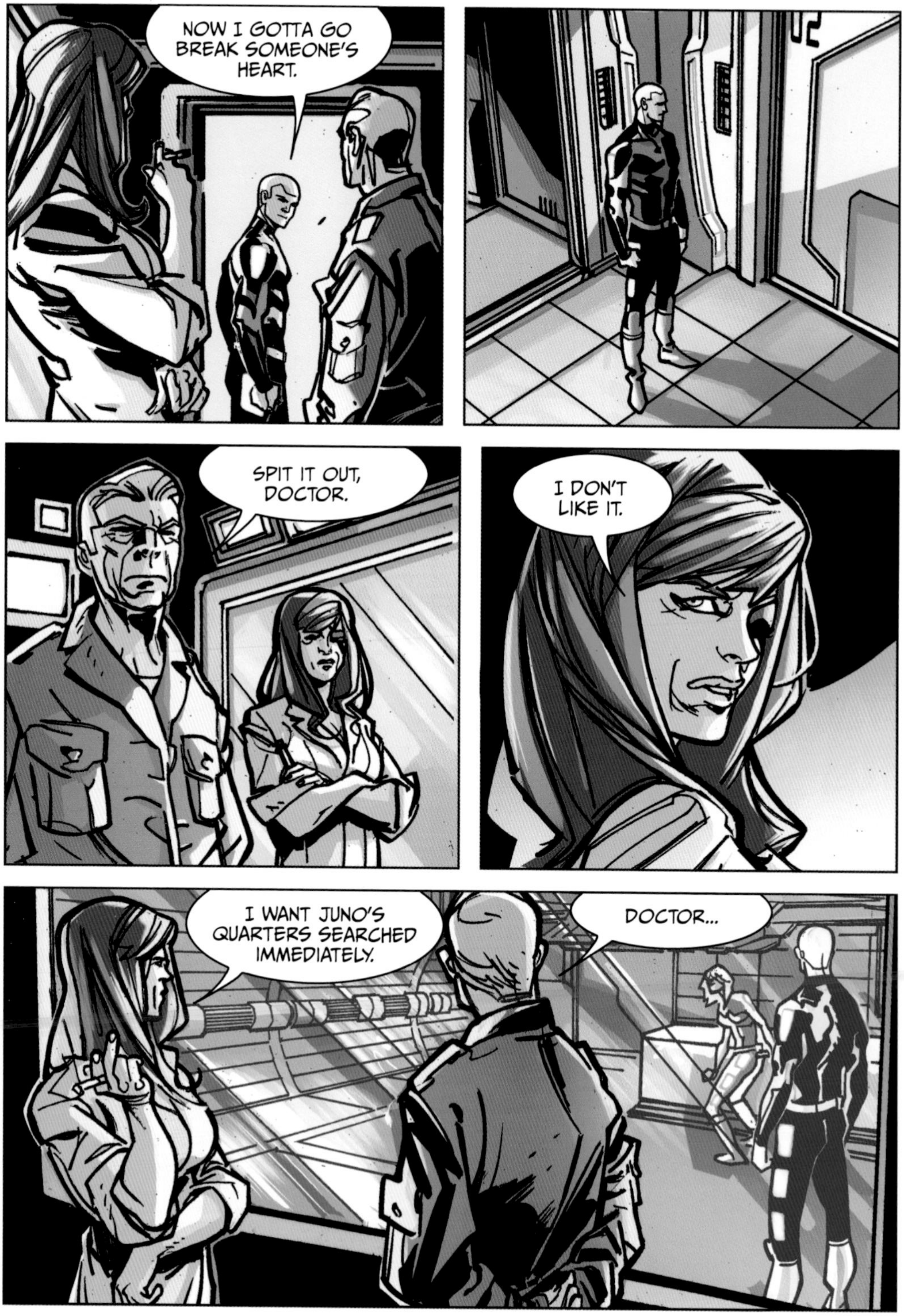
NOW I GOTTA GO BREAK SOMEONE'S HEART.
SPIT IT OUT, DOCTOR.
I DON'T LIKE IT.
I WANT JUNO'S QUARTERS SEARCHED IMMEDIATELY.
DOCTOR...

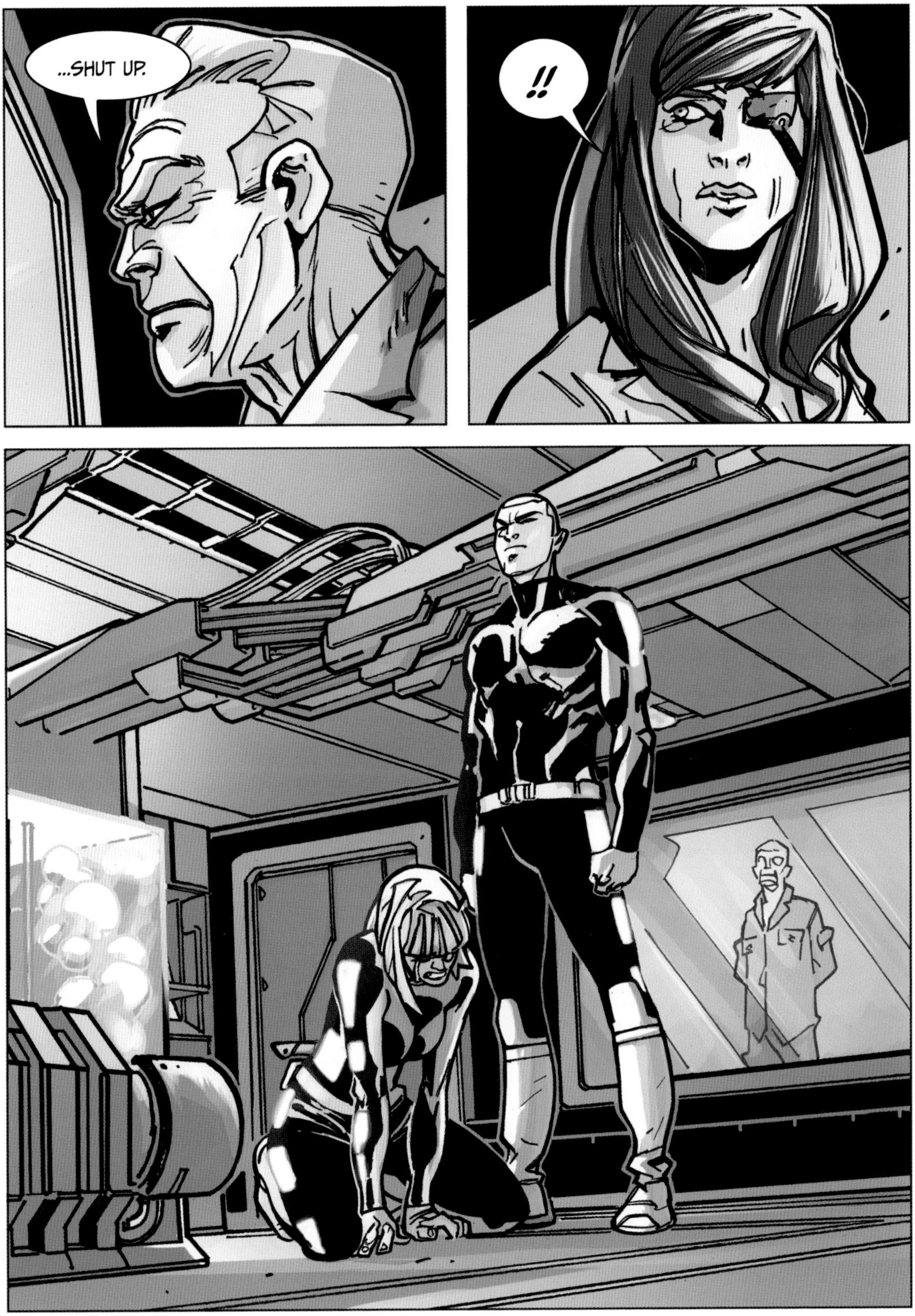
...SHUT UP.
!!

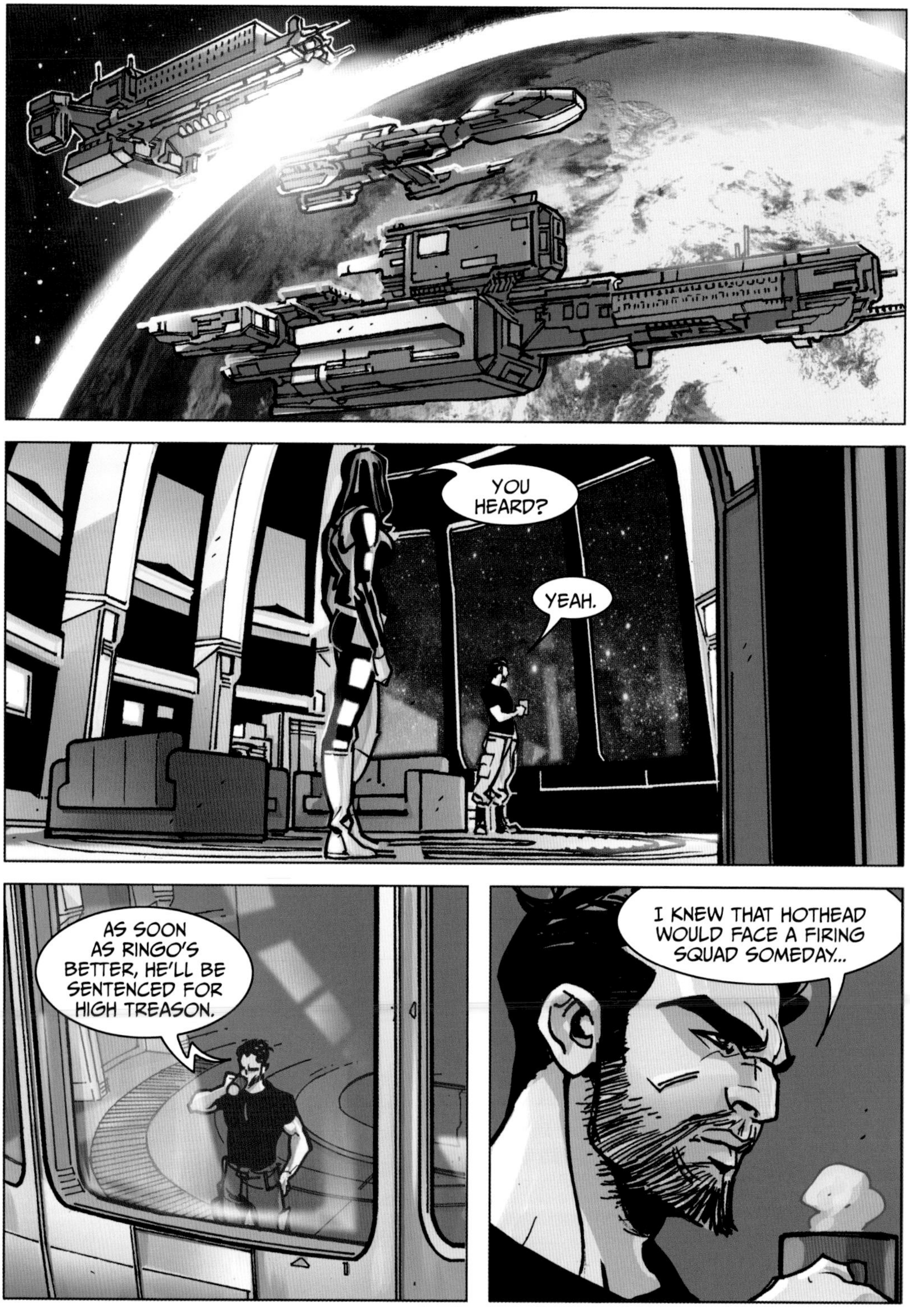
YOU HEARD?
YEAH.
AS SOON AS RINGO'S BETTER, HE'LL BE SENTENCED FOR HIGH TREASON.
I KNEW THAT HOTHEAD WOULD FACE A FIRING SQUAD SOMEDAY...

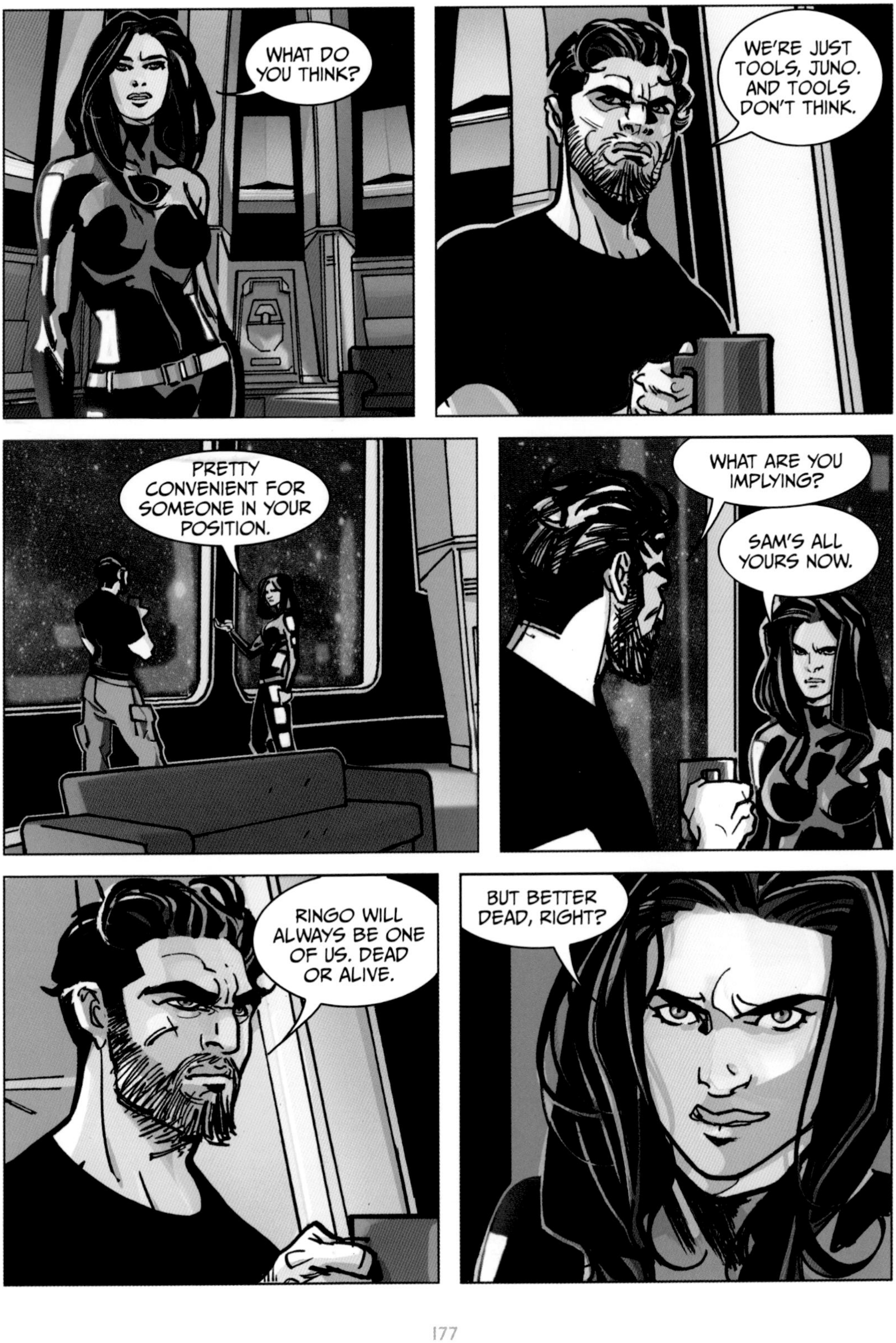
WHAT DO YOU THINK?
WE'RE JUST TOOLS, JUNO. AND TOOLS DON'T THINK.
PRETTY CONVENIENT FOR SOMEONE IN YOUR POSITION.
WHAT ARE YOU IMPLYING?
SAM'S ALL YOURS NOW.
RINGO WILL ALWAYS BE ONE OF US. DEAD OR ALIVE.
BUT BETTER DEAD, RIGHT?

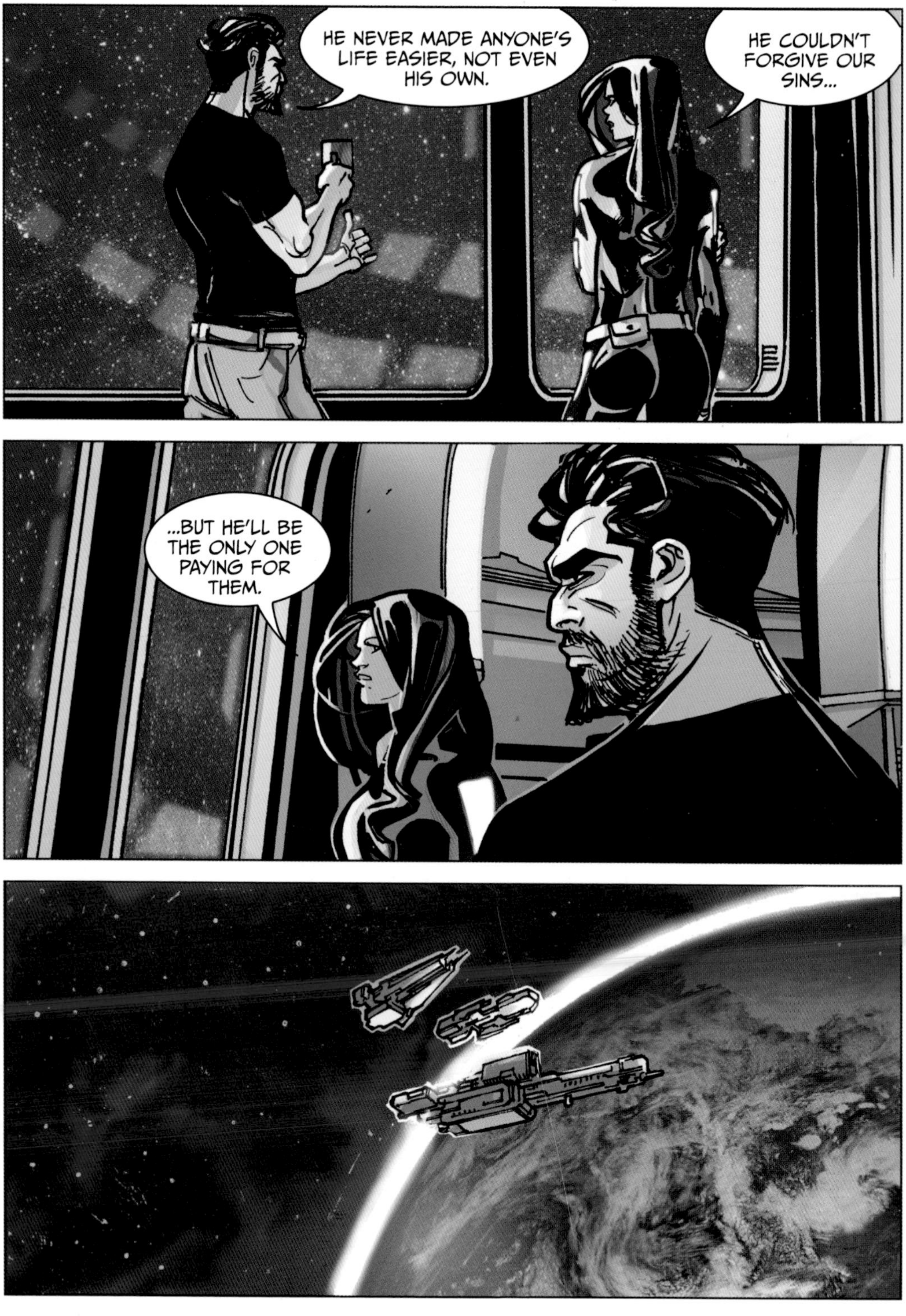
HE NEVER MADE ANYONE'S LIFE EASIER, NOT EVEN HIS OWN.
HE COULDN'T FORGIVE OUR SINS...
...BUT HE'LL BE THE ONLY ONE PAYING FOR THEM.

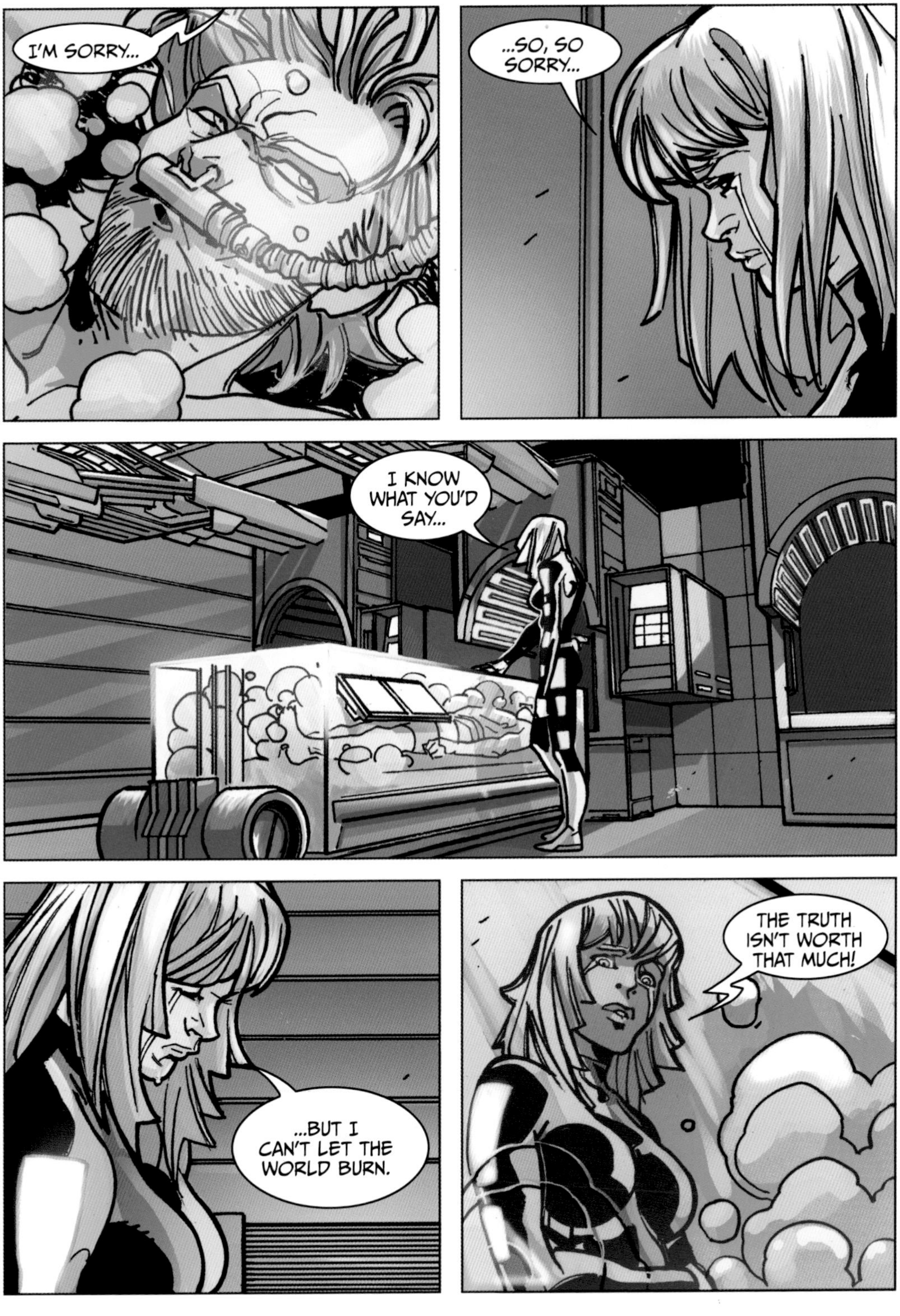
I'M SORRY...
...SO, SO SORRY...
I KNOW WHAT YOU'D SAY...
...BUT I CAN'T LET THE WORLD BURN.
THE TRUTH ISN'T WORTH THAT MUCH!

WE AREN'T WORTH THAT MUCH.

THE PEOPLE... THEY NEED HOPE...

I NEED HOPE!

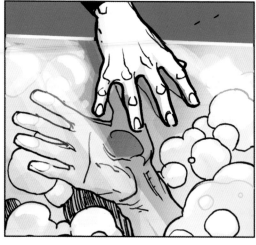

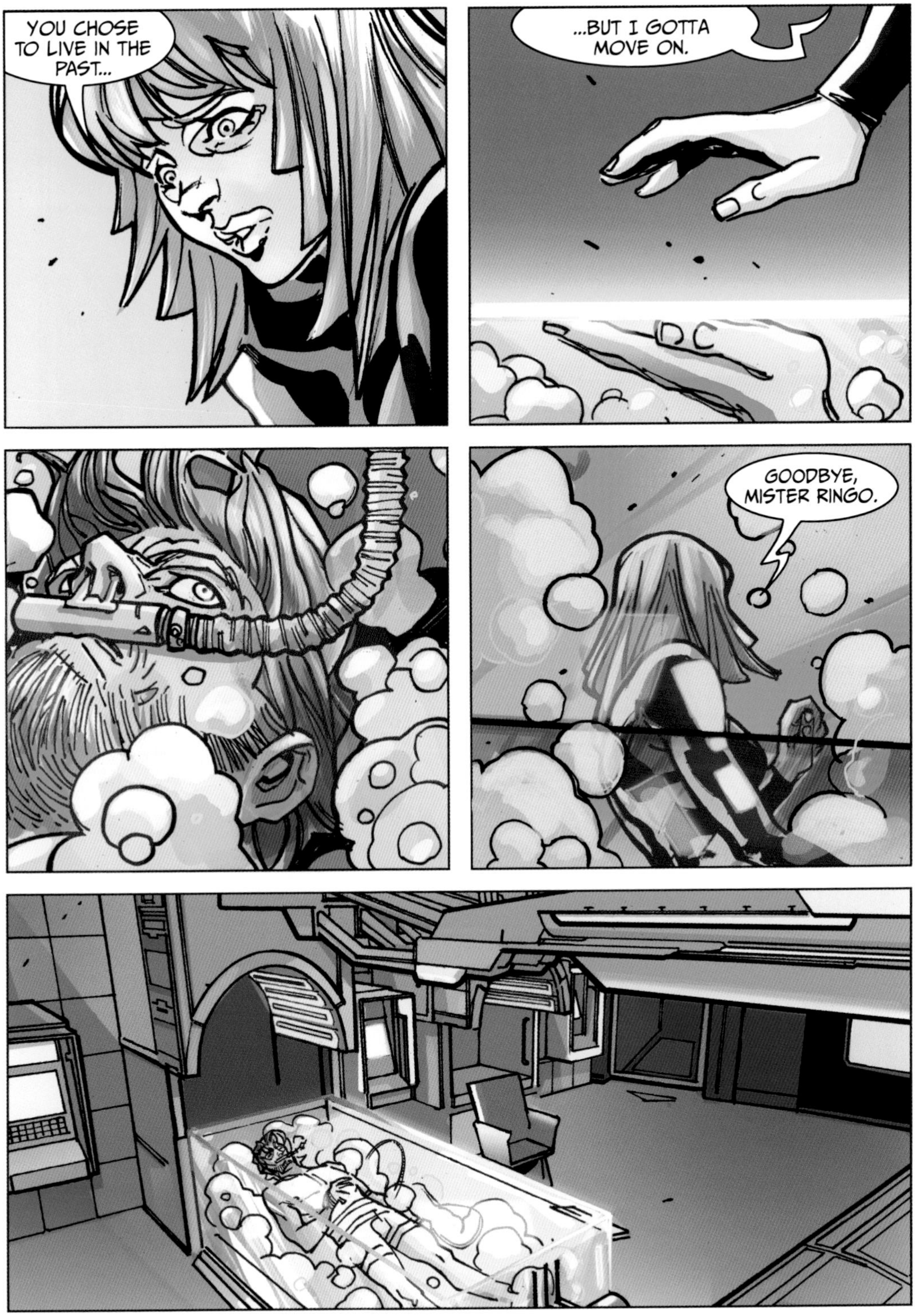
YOU CHOSE TO LIVE IN THE PAST...
...BUT I GOTTA MOVE ON.
GOODBYE, MISTER RINGO.

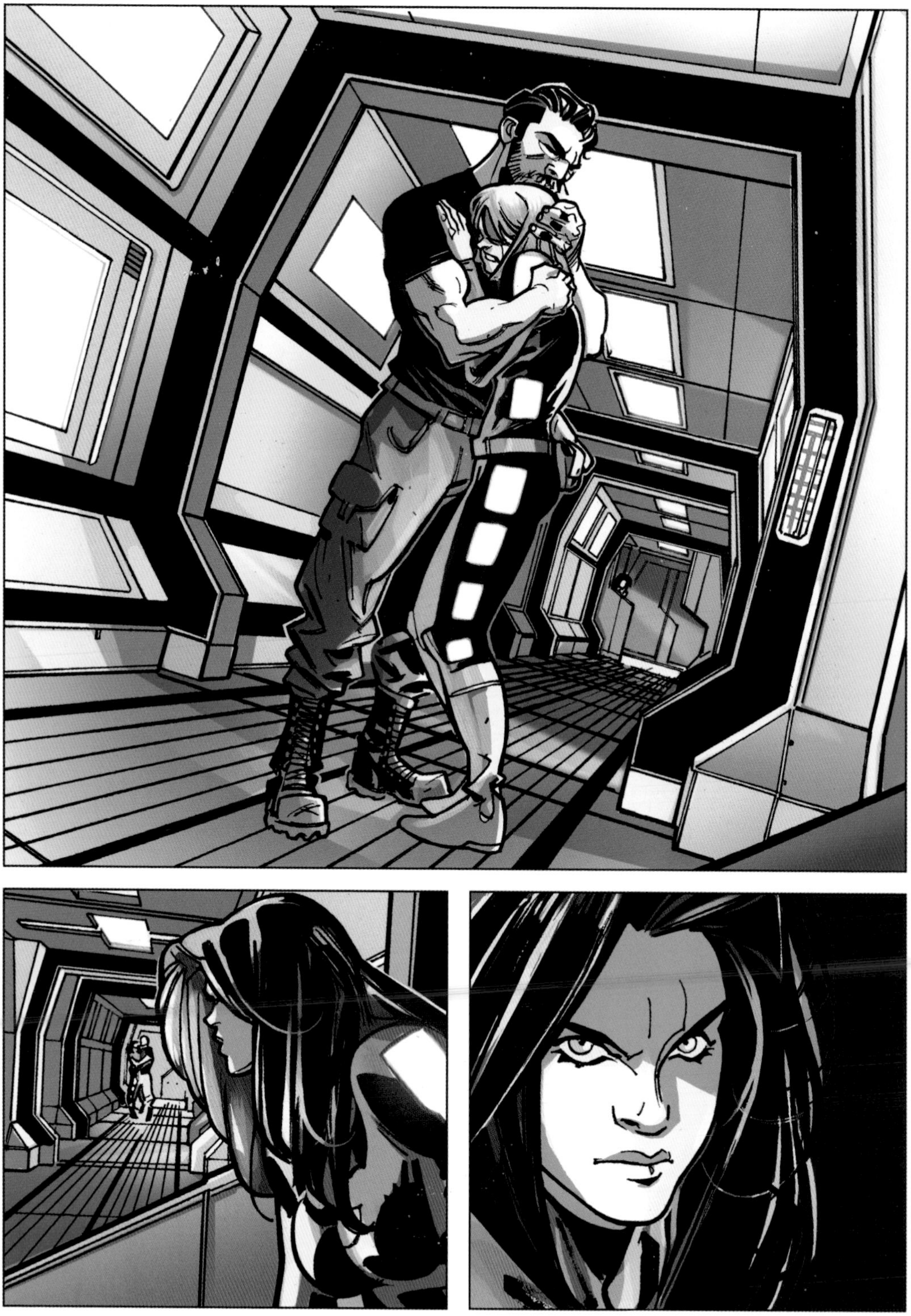

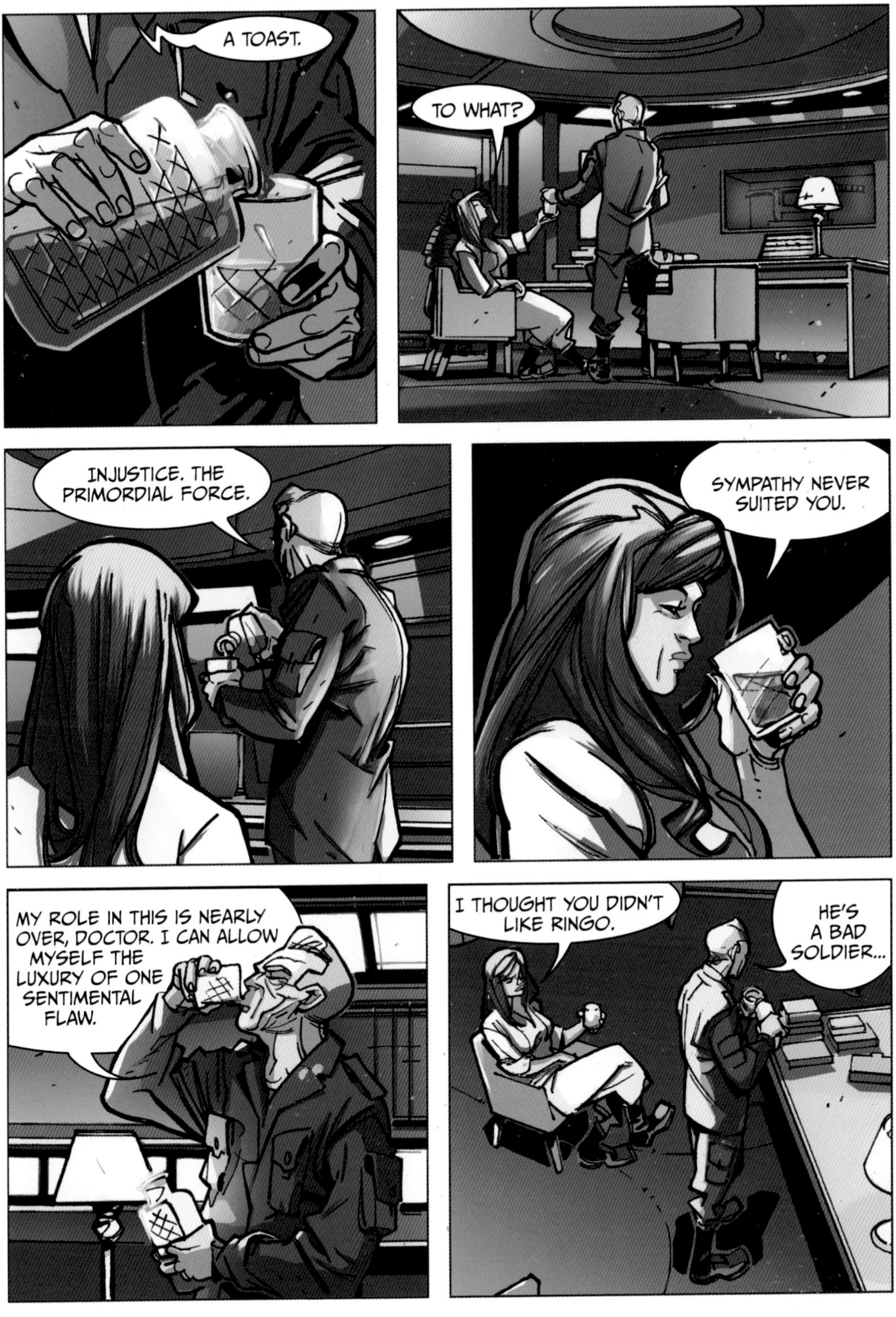
A TOAST.
TO WHAT?
INJUSTICE. THE PRIMORDIAL FORCE.
SYMPATHY NEVER SUITED YOU.
MY ROLE IN THIS IS NEARLY OVER, DOCTOR. I CAN ALLOW MYSELF THE LUXURY OF ONE SENTIMENTAL FLAW.
I THOUGHT YOU DIDN'T LIKE RINGO.
HE'S A BAD SOLDIER...

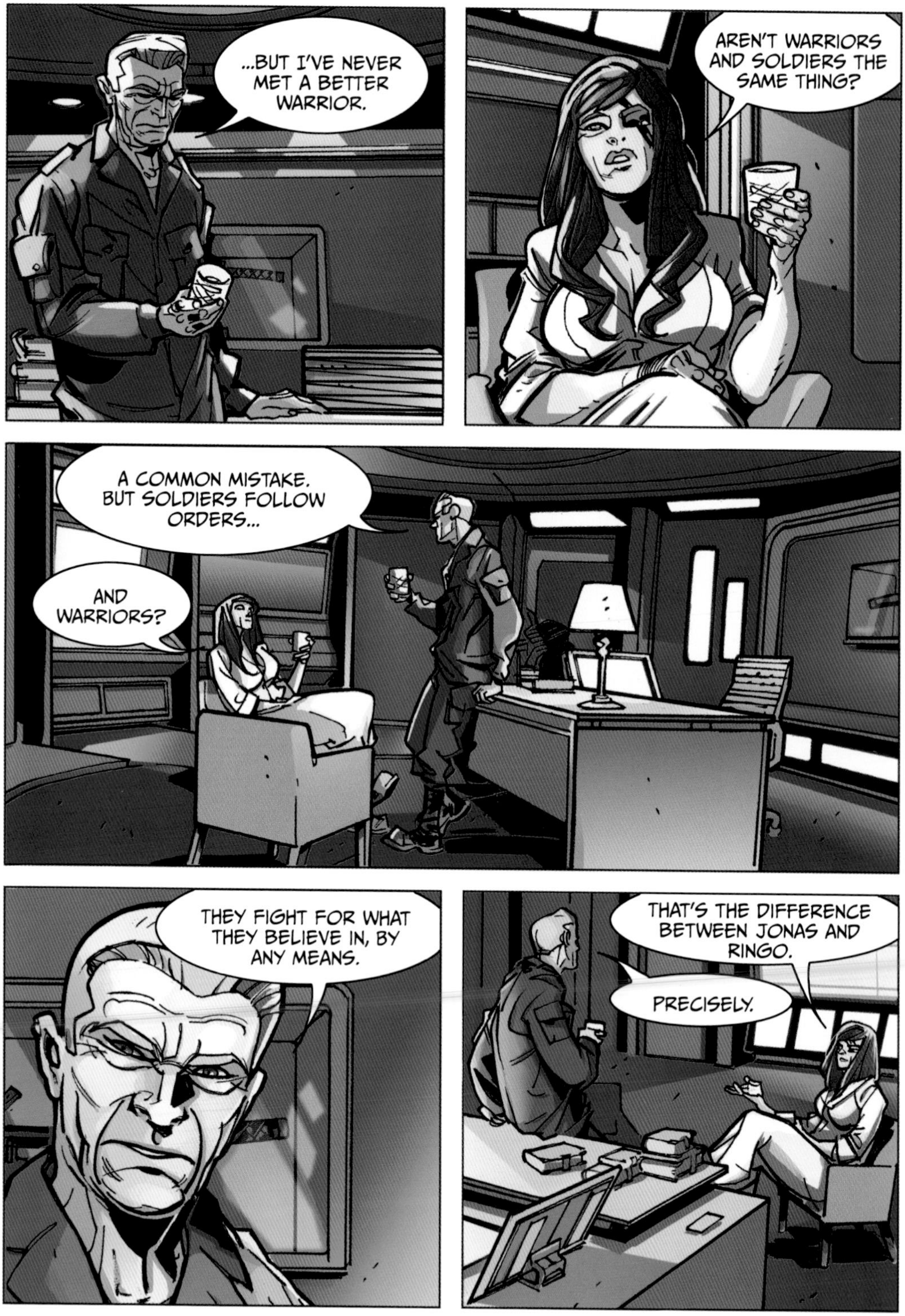
...BUT I'VE NEVER MET A BETTER WARRIOR.
AREN'T WARRIORS AND SOLDIERS THE SAME THING?
A COMMON MISTAKE. BUT SOLDIERS FOLLOW ORDERS...
AND WARRIORS?
THEY FIGHT FOR WHAT THEY BELIEVE IN, BY ANY MEANS.
THAT'S THE DIFFERENCE BETWEEN JONAS AND RINGO.
PRECISELY.

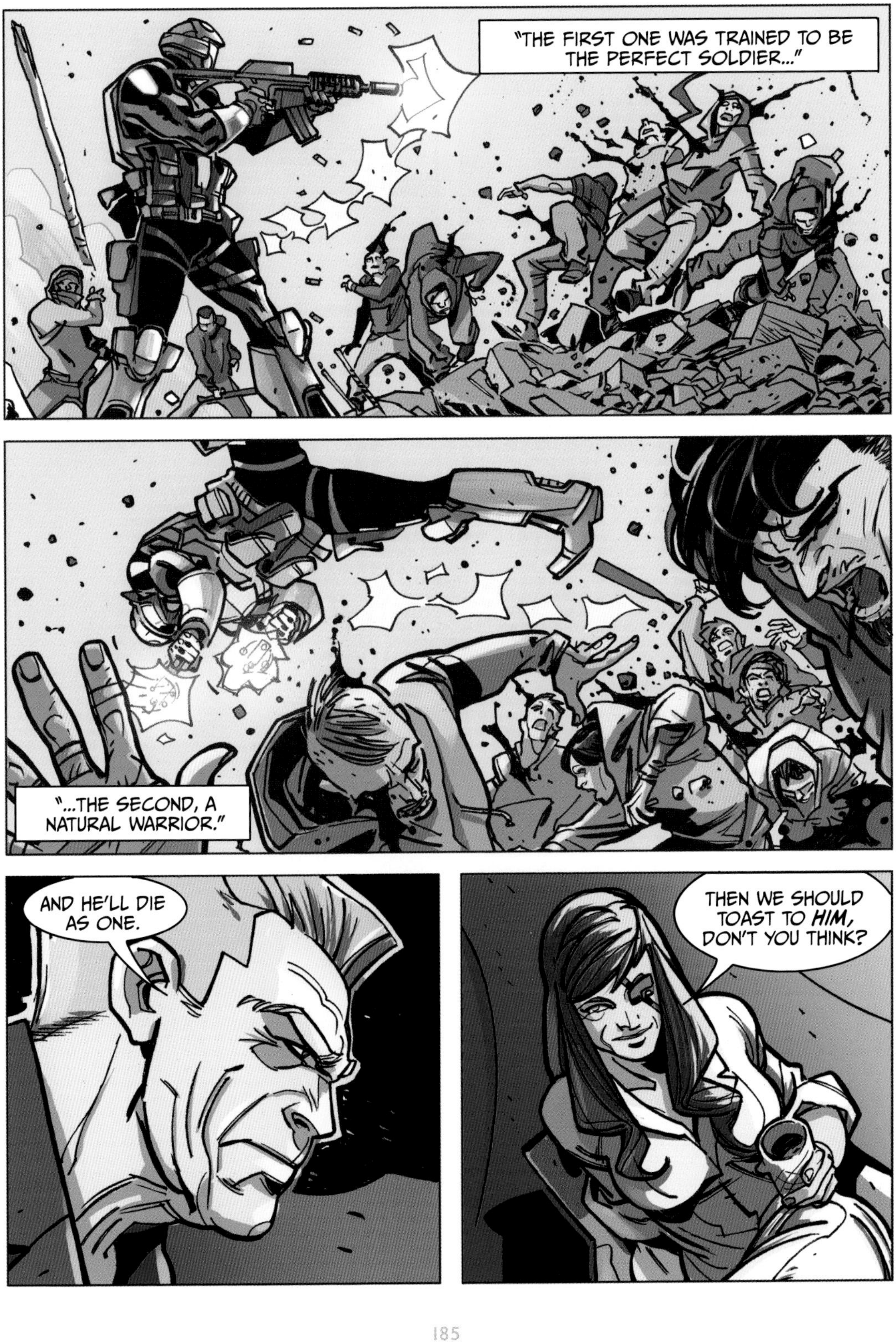
"THE FIRST ONE WAS TRAINED TO BE THE PERFECT SOLDIER..."
"...THE SECOND, A NATURAL WARRIOR."
AND HE'LL DIE AS ONE.
THEN WE SHOULD TOAST TO *HIM*, DON'T YOU THINK?

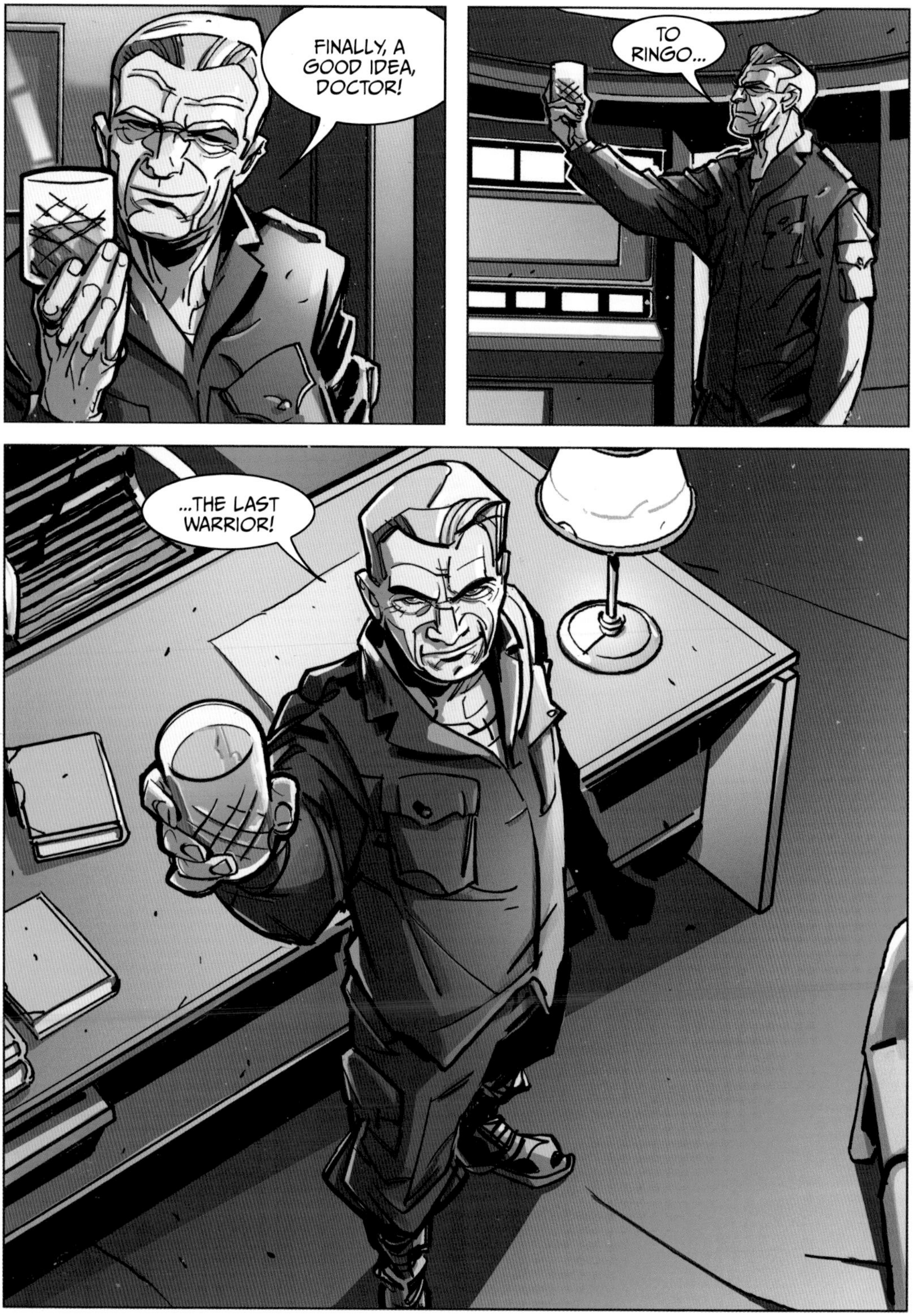
FINALLY, A GOOD IDEA, DOCTOR!
TO RINGO...
...THE LAST WARRIOR!

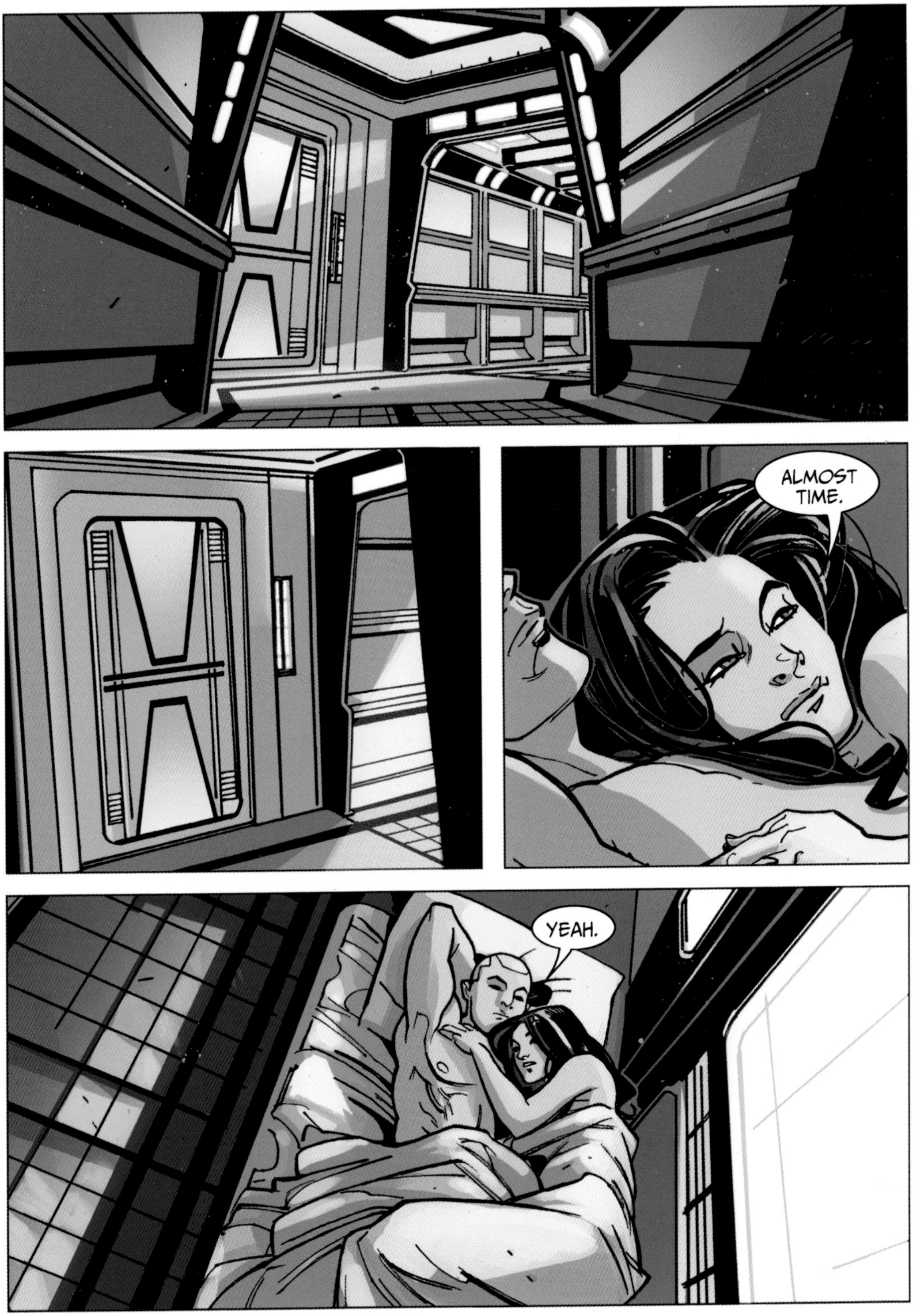
ALMOST TIME.
YEAH.

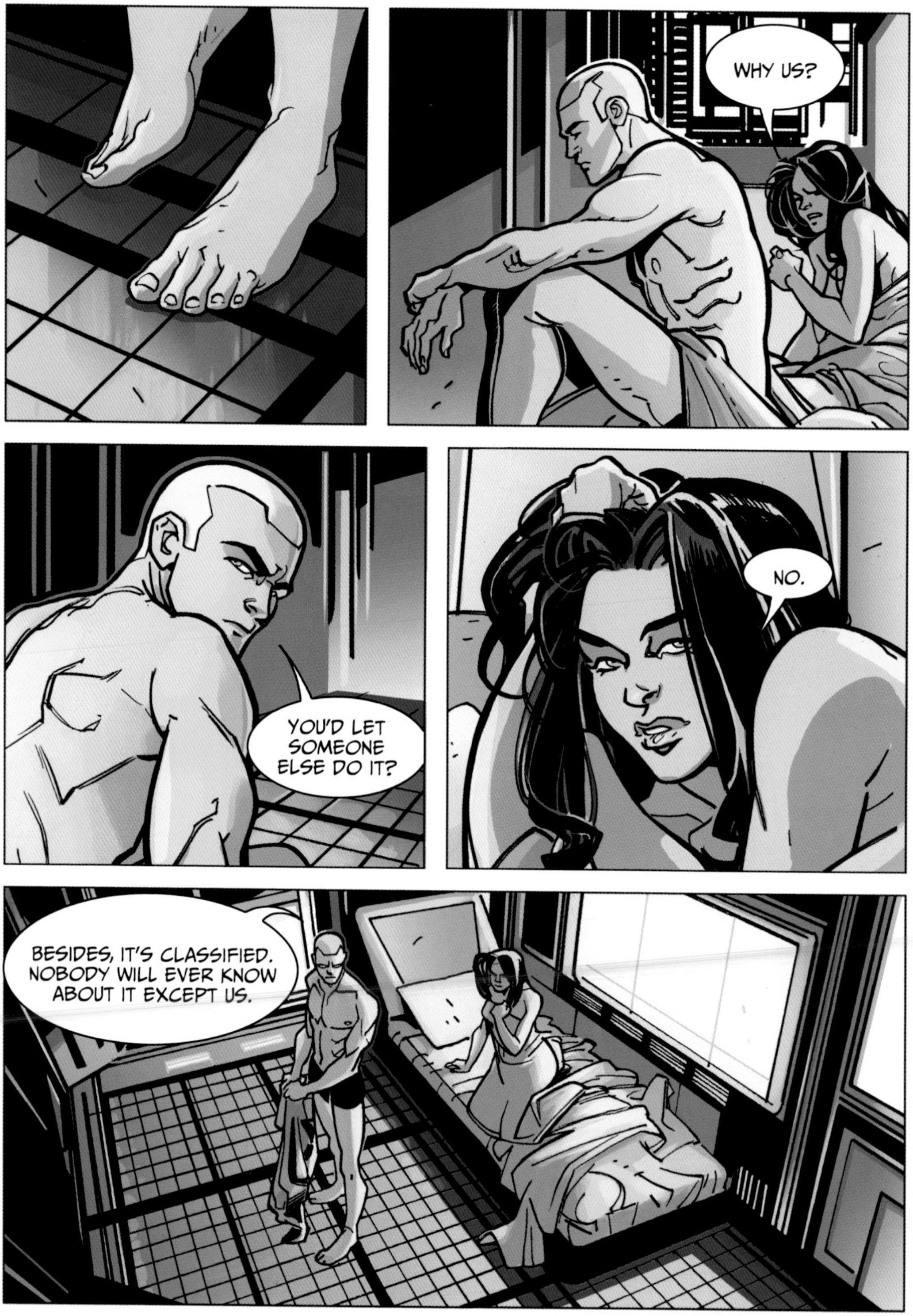
WHY US?
YOU'D LET SOMEONE ELSE DO IT?
NO.
BESIDES, IT'S CLASSIFIED. NOBODY WILL EVER KNOW ABOUT IT EXCEPT US.

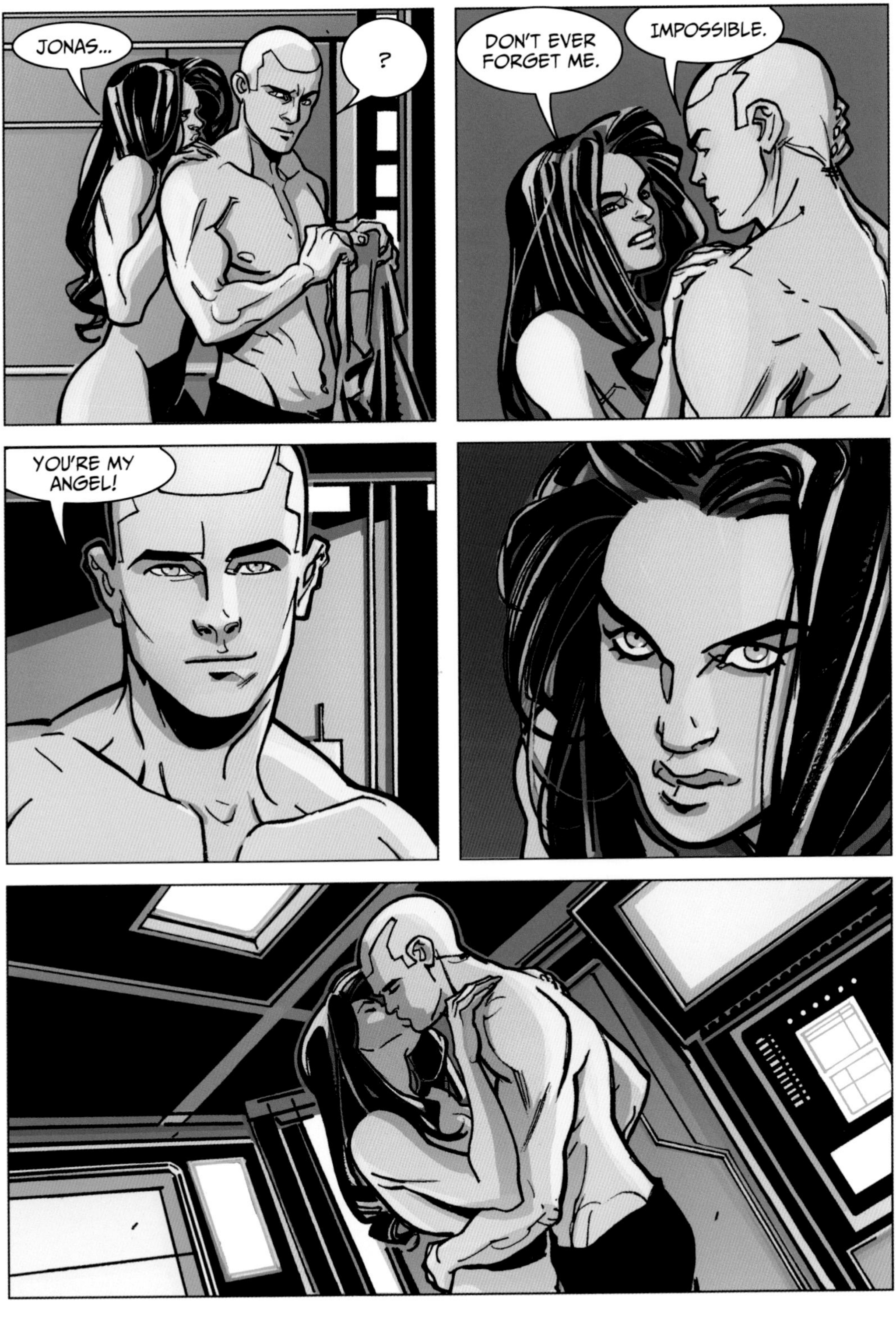
JONAS...
?
DON'T EVER FORGET ME.
IMPOSSIBLE.
YOU'RE MY ANGEL!

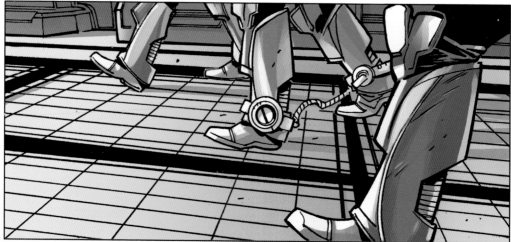

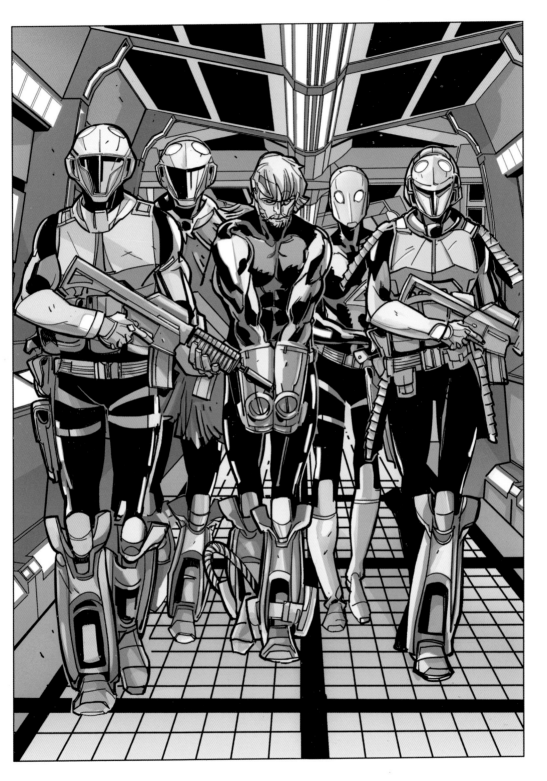

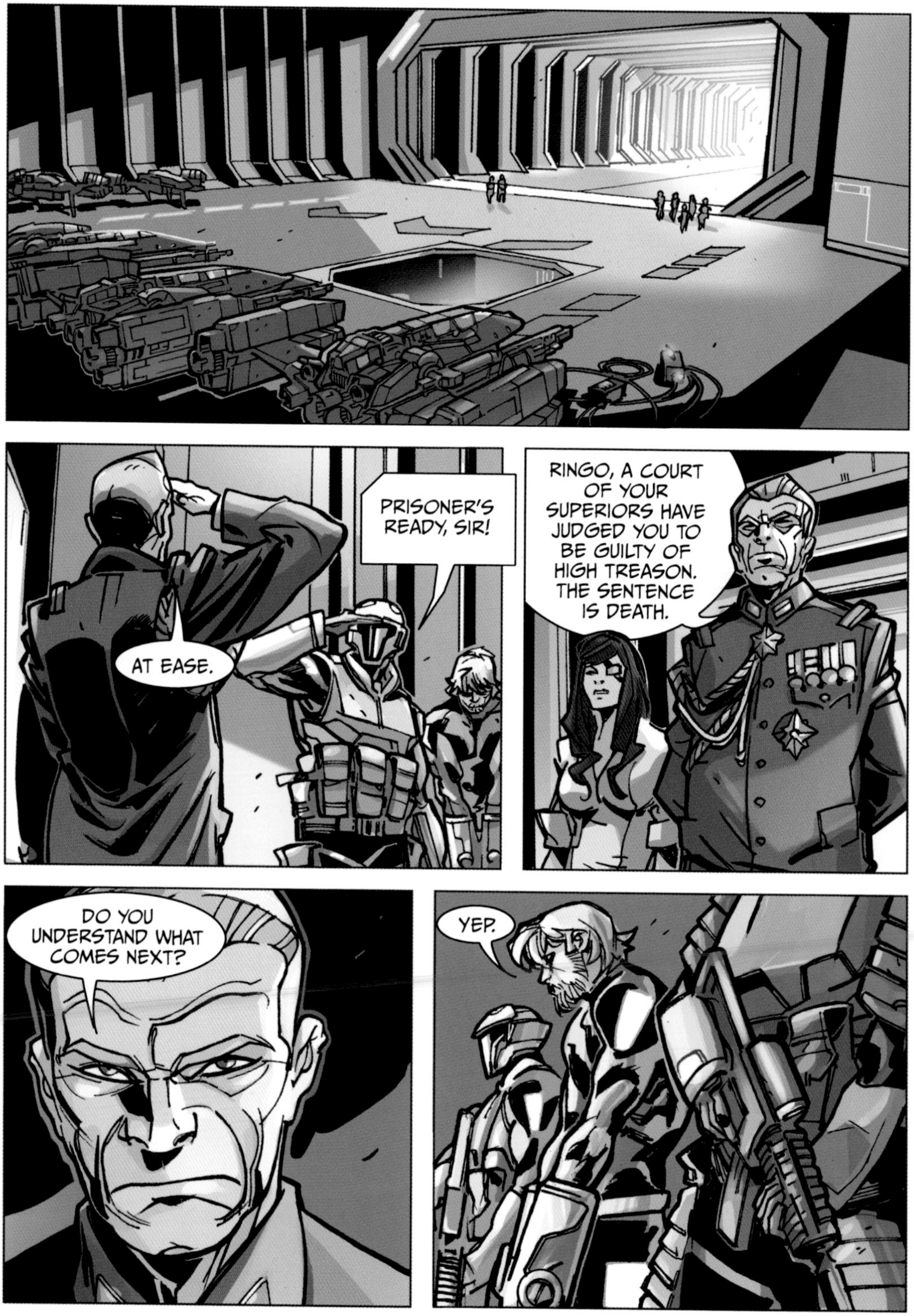
PRISONER'S READY, SIR!
AT EASE.
RINGO, A COURT OF YOUR SUPERIORS HAVE JUDGED YOU TO BE GUILTY OF HIGH TREASON. THE SENTENCE IS DEATH.
DO YOU UNDERSTAND WHAT COMES NEXT?
YEP.

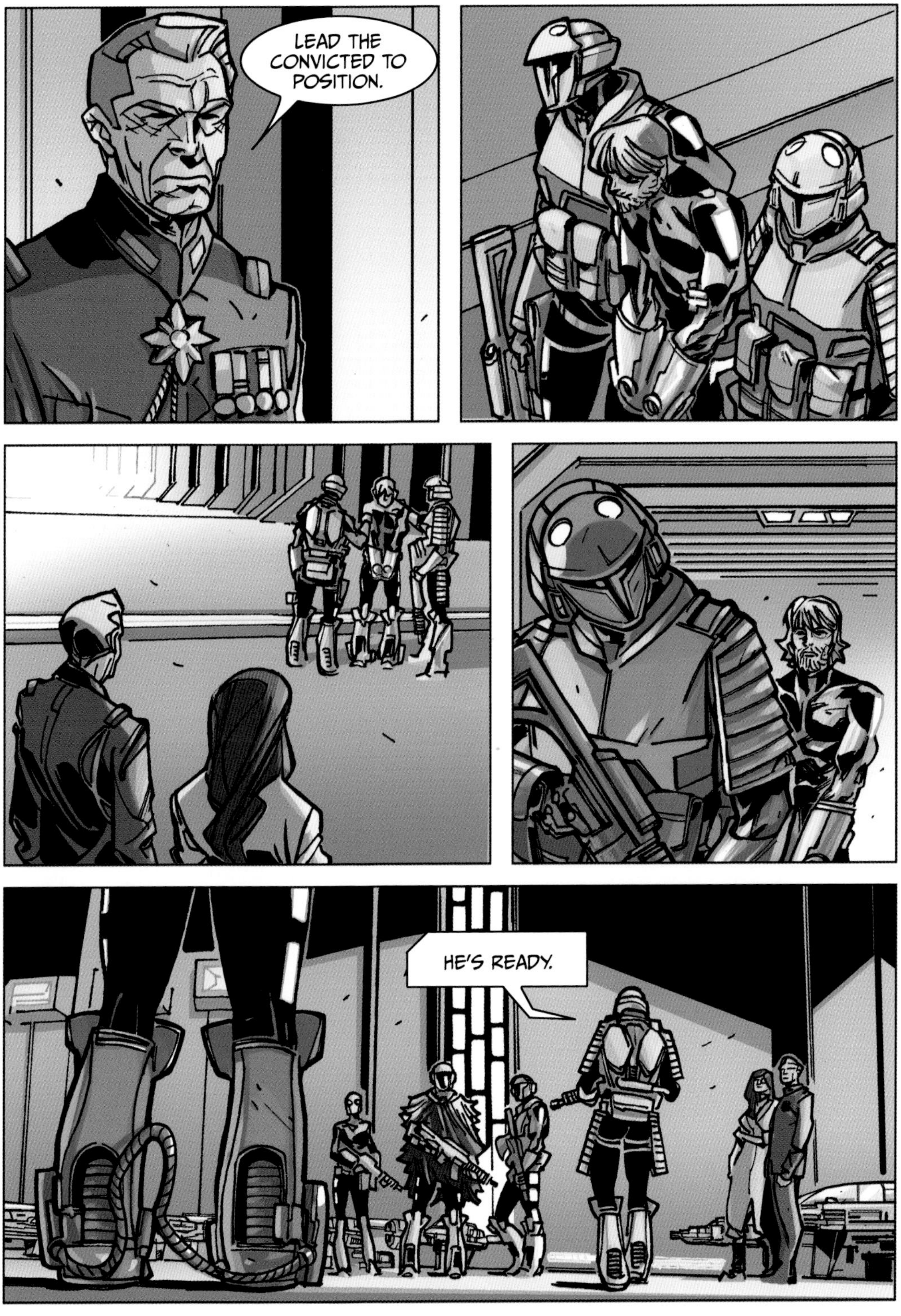
LEAD THE CONVICTED TO POSITION.
HE'S READY.

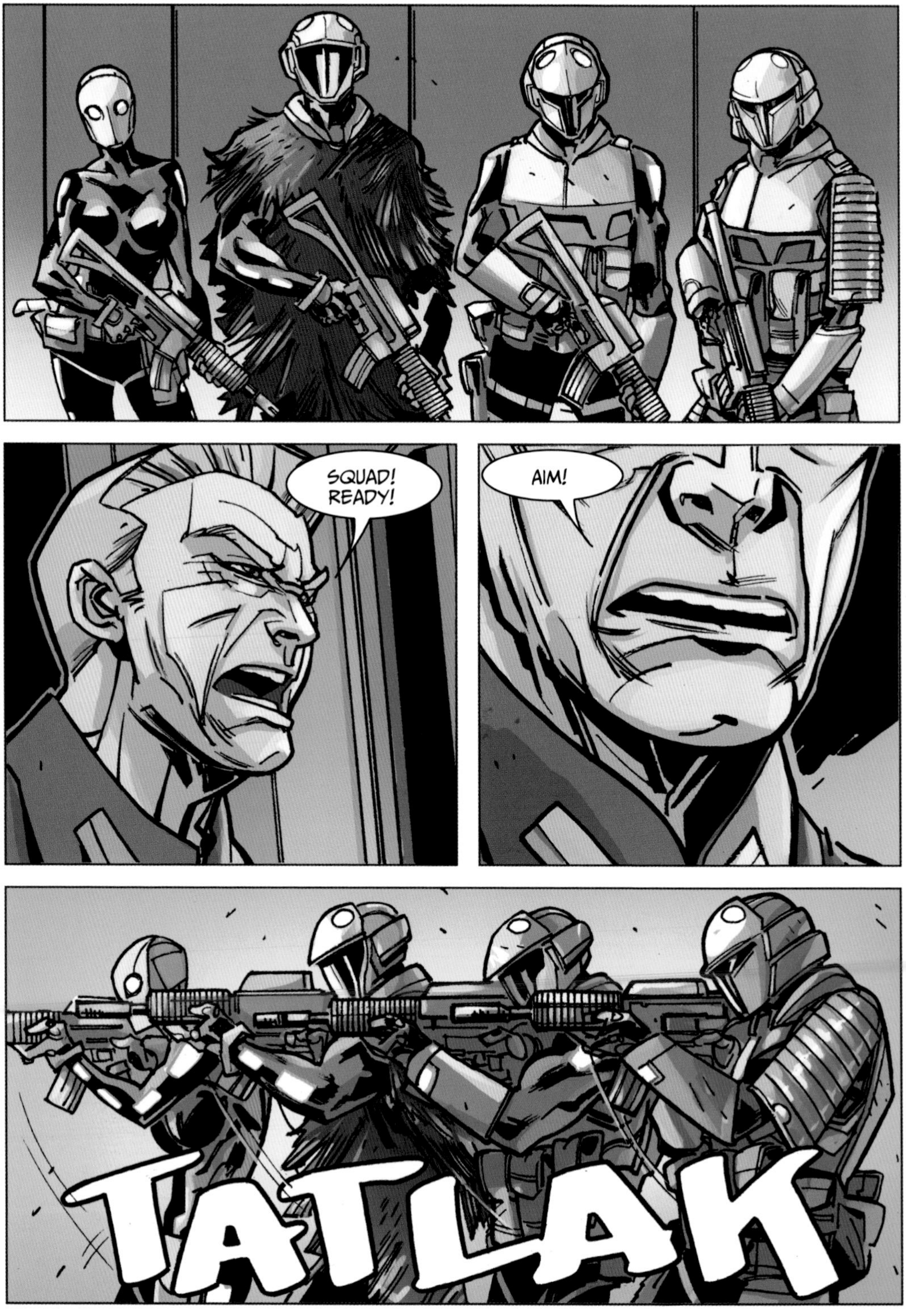
SQUAD! READY!
AIM!
TATLAK

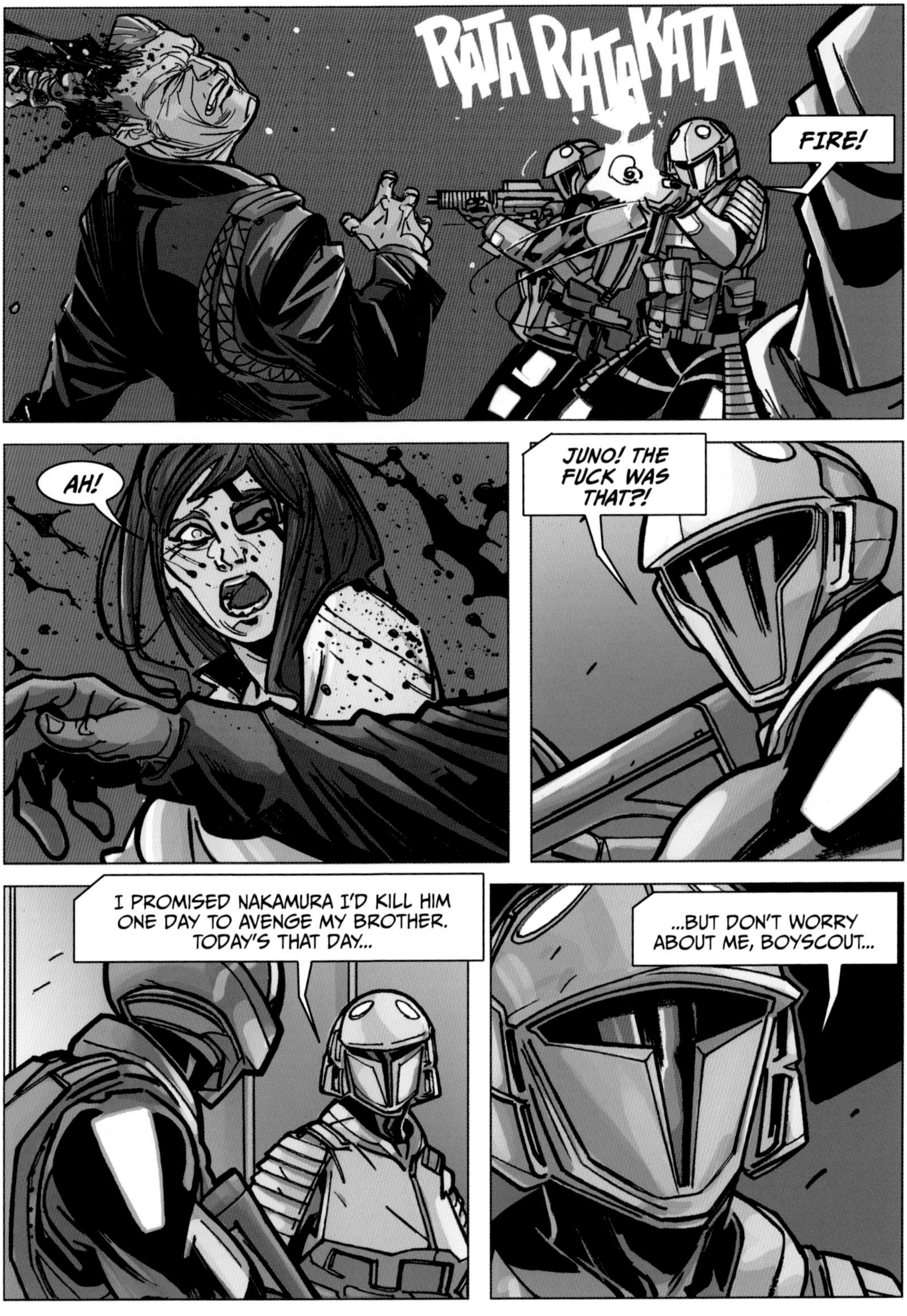
RATA RATA KATA
FIRE!
AH!
JUNO! THE FUCK WAS THAT?!
I PROMISED NAKAMURA I'D KILL HIM ONE DAY TO AVENGE MY BROTHER. TODAY'S THAT DAY...
...BUT DON'T WORRY ABOUT ME, BOYSCOUT...

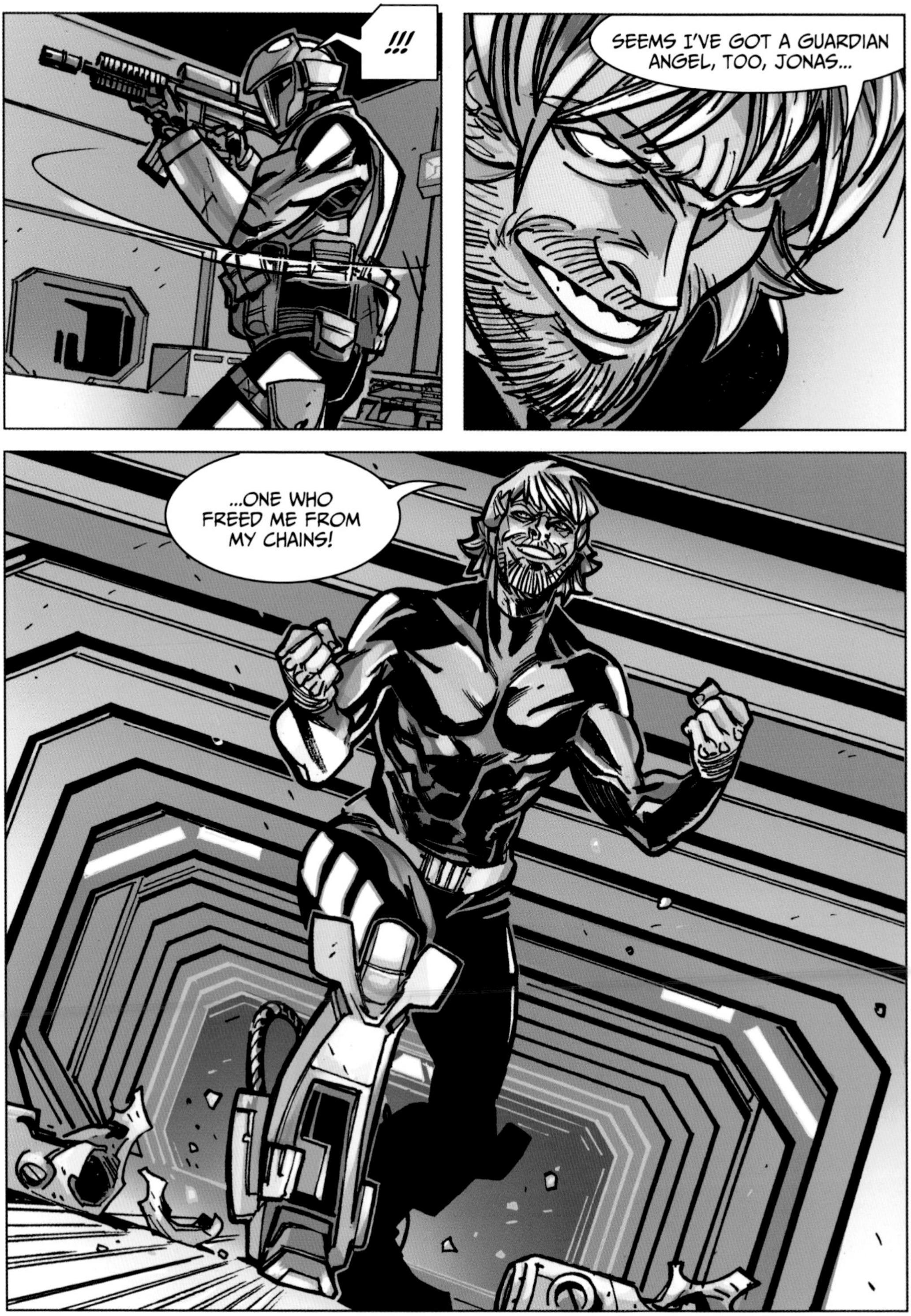
!!!
SEEMS I'VE GOT A GUARDIAN ANGEL, TOO, JONAS...
...ONE WHO FREED ME FROM MY CHAINS!

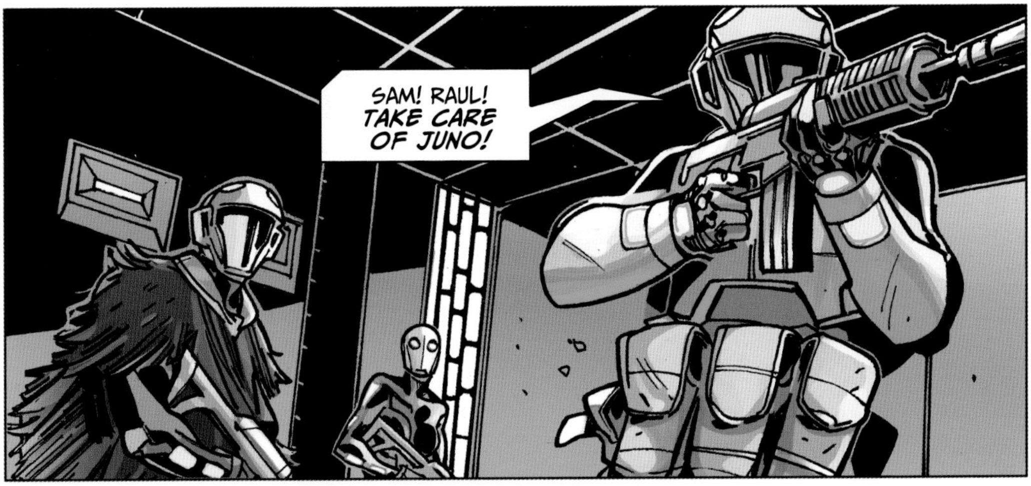
SAM! RAUL!
TAKE CARE OF JUNO!

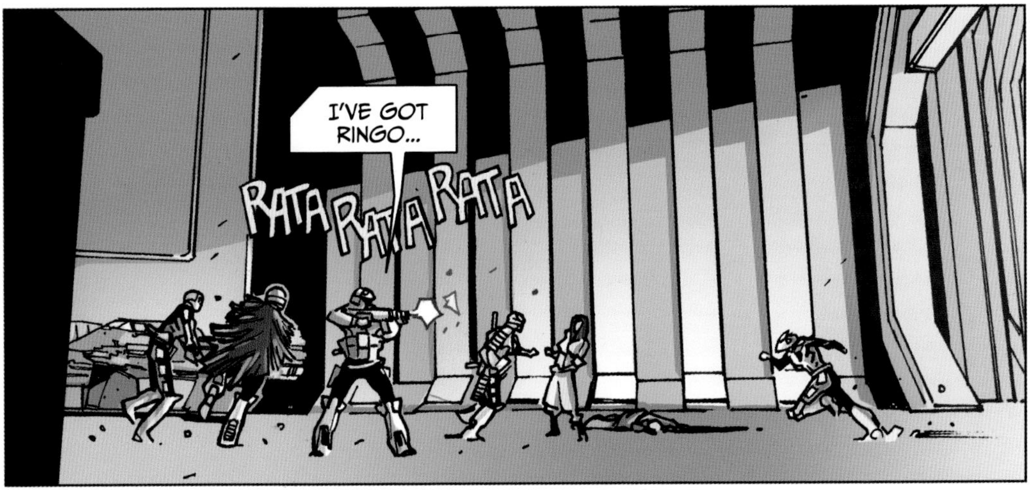
I'VE GOT RINGO...
RATA RATA RATA

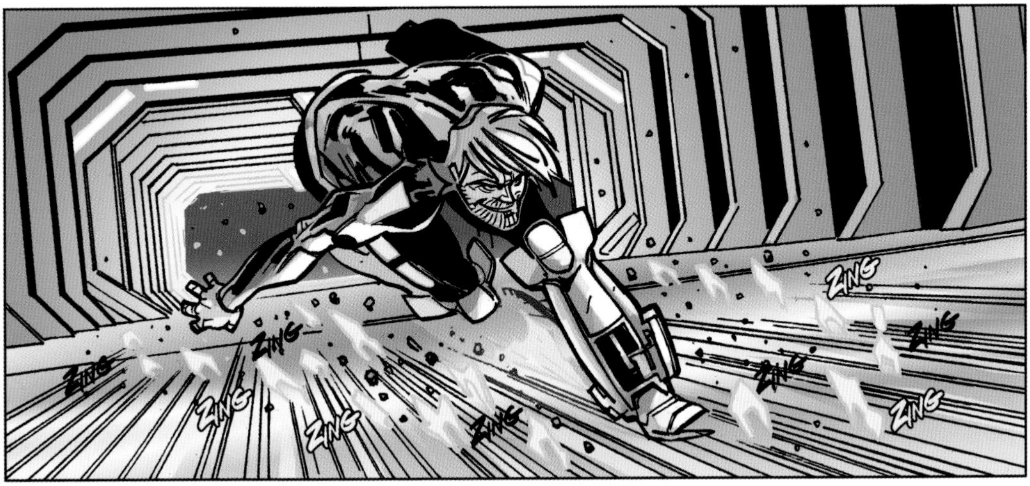
ZING ZING ZING ZING ZING ZING ZING ZING ZING

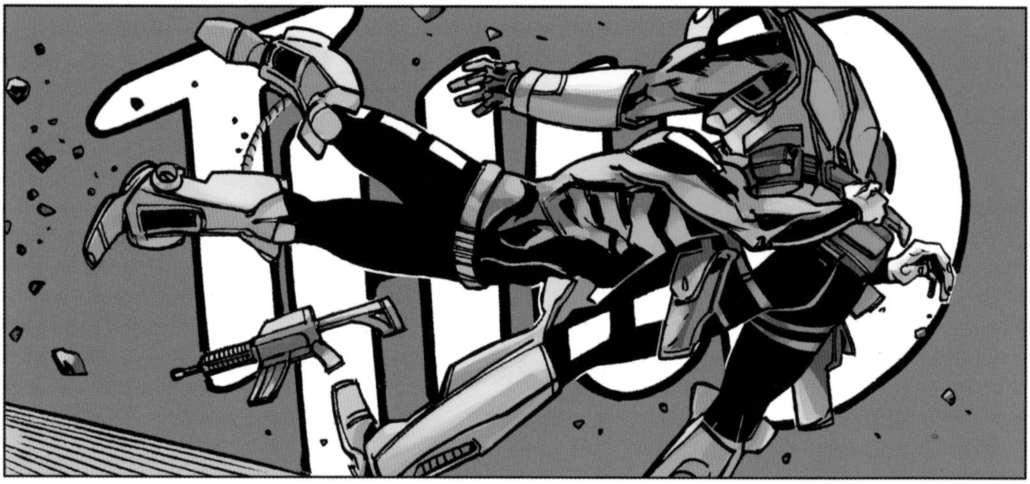

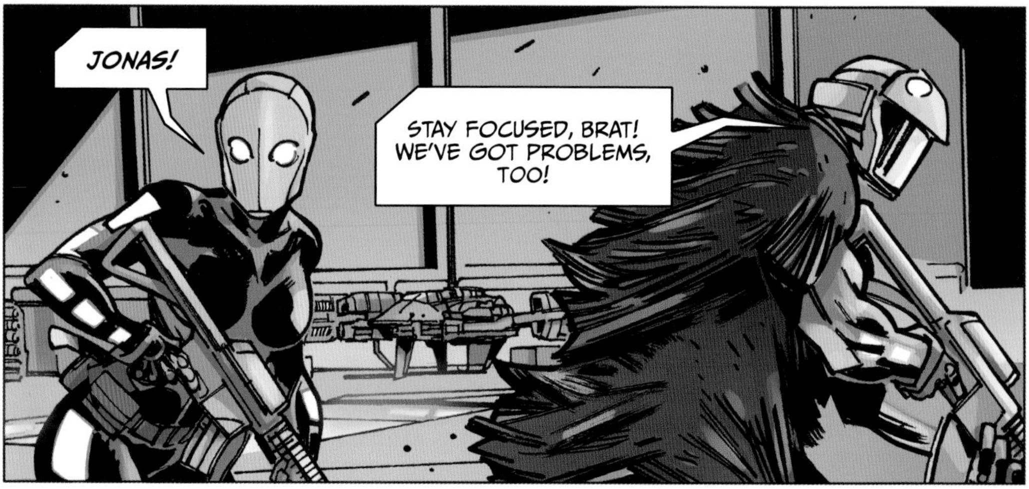
JONAS!
STAY FOCUSED, BRAT! WE'VE GOT PROBLEMS, TOO!

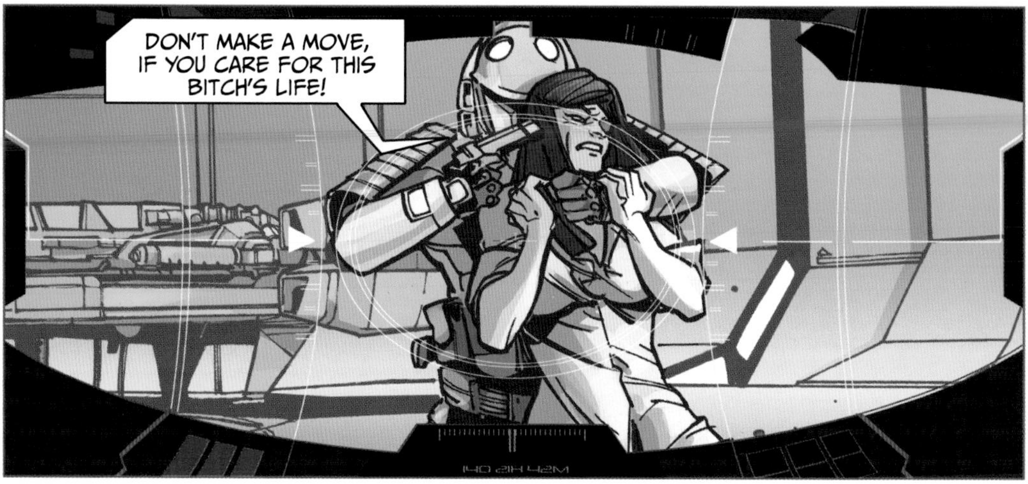
DON'T MAKE A MOVE, IF YOU CARE FOR THIS BITCH'S LIFE!

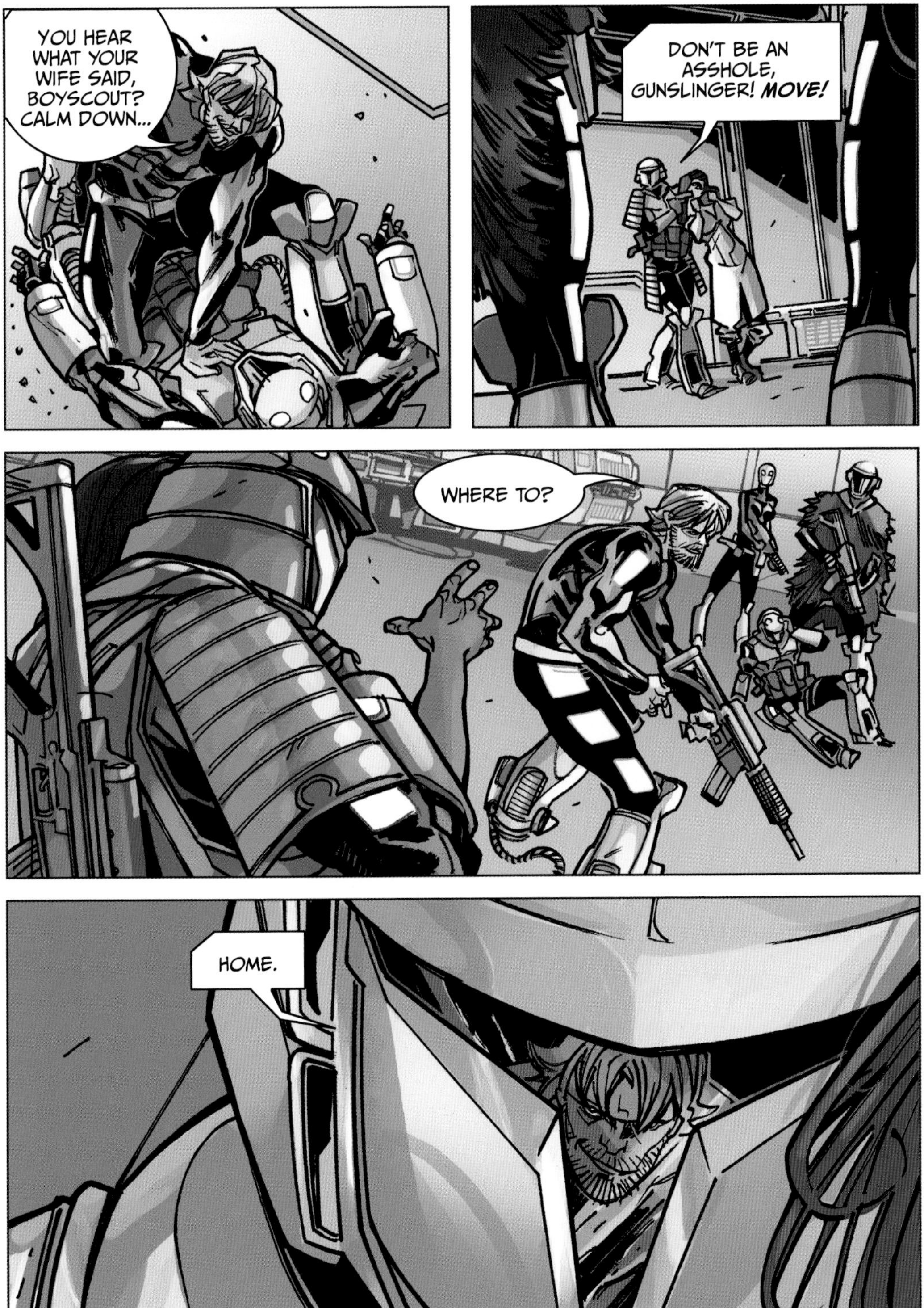
YOU HEAR WHAT YOUR WIFE SAID, BOYSCOUT? CALM DOWN...
DON'T BE AN ASSHOLE, GUNSLINGER! *MOVE!*
WHERE TO?
HOME.

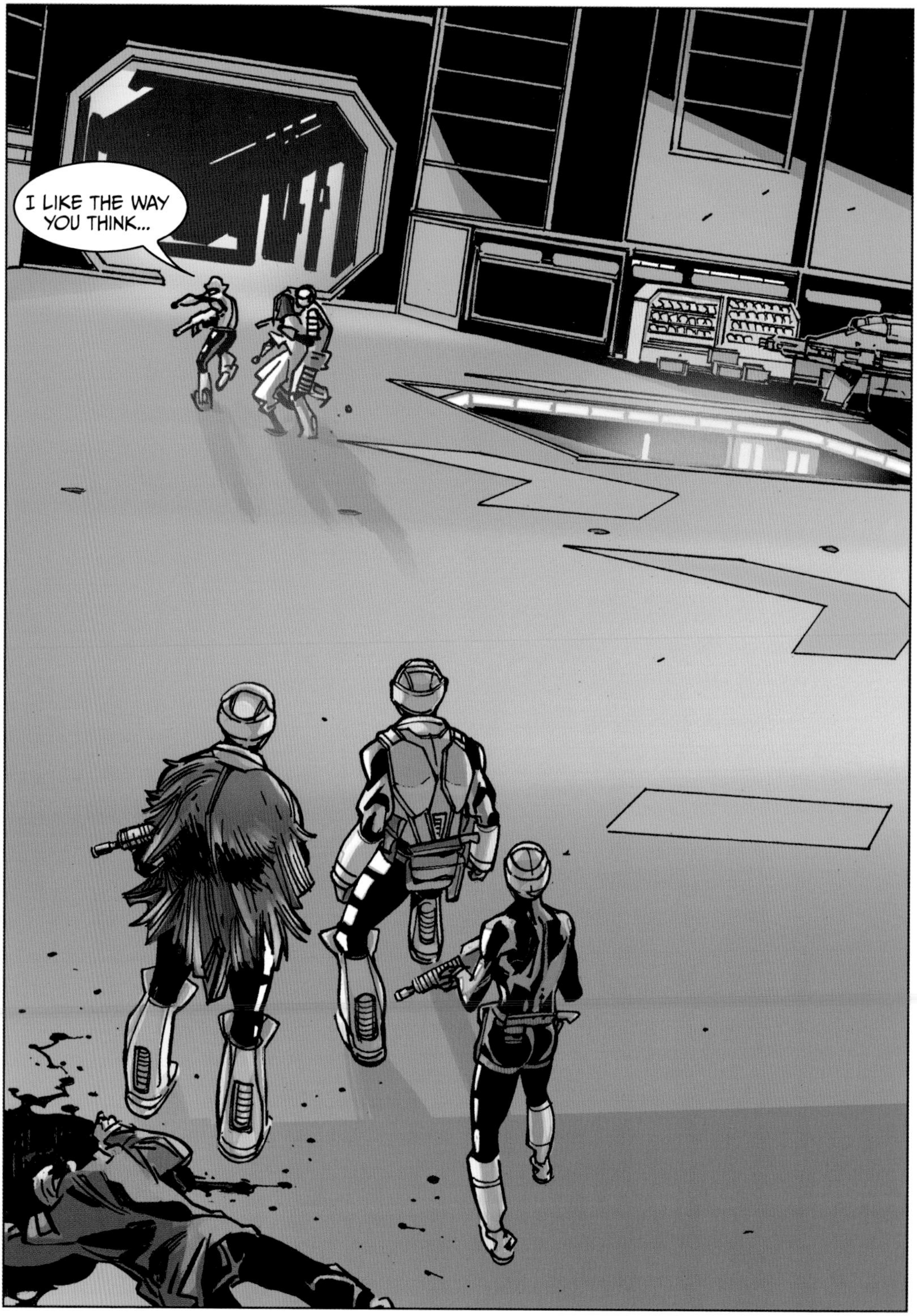
I LIKE THE WAY YOU THINK...

DAVIDE GIANFELICE — **ARTIST**

When and where were you born? Where do you live now?
I was born on June 18, 1977 in Milan, where I still live and work.

What sort of artistic education did you have?
I attended an artistic high school and due to my passion for drawing and comics, I enrolled to the Comic School in Milan from which I finally graduated in 1999.

Tell us about your previous works, before *Orphans*.
My professional training started with Eura Editoriale, working with Roberto Recchioni on the series *John Doe*. After that, I started working with all the major publishers in America. I published the first volume of *Northlanders* for Vertigo-DC Comics, for which I also co-created the series *Greek Street*. After that, I worked on Marvel's miniseries *Daredevil Reborn*, *Weapon X*, and *Six Gun*. I also worked on Dark Horse's new cycle of *Conan* for a run and drew two runs of *Ghosted* for Skybound.

When did you start working on *Orphans*, and when did you finish drawing this chapter?
I've been busy for almost a year with my chapter. I delivered the final product in September 2013.

What tools did you use?
The traditional ones: paper, pencil and China ink. Recently, I've turned to digital drawing.

What was the most difficult scene and which one did you have to redraw more times?
The whole sequence of the room with the dead abominations was really long and tough. We see the protagonists amidst a sea of bodies lying on the floor. I had to remember the positions of each element and make them interact in a functional way, especially the characters in the background, which are as important as the ones at the center of the action.

If you could go back in time, what would you change about this chapter?
Normally, I'm very critical about my own work. It helps me improve what doesn't work, and it's a good means of self-analysis and study. But I wouldn't redo anything, even if there are a lot of things that I don't like anymore.

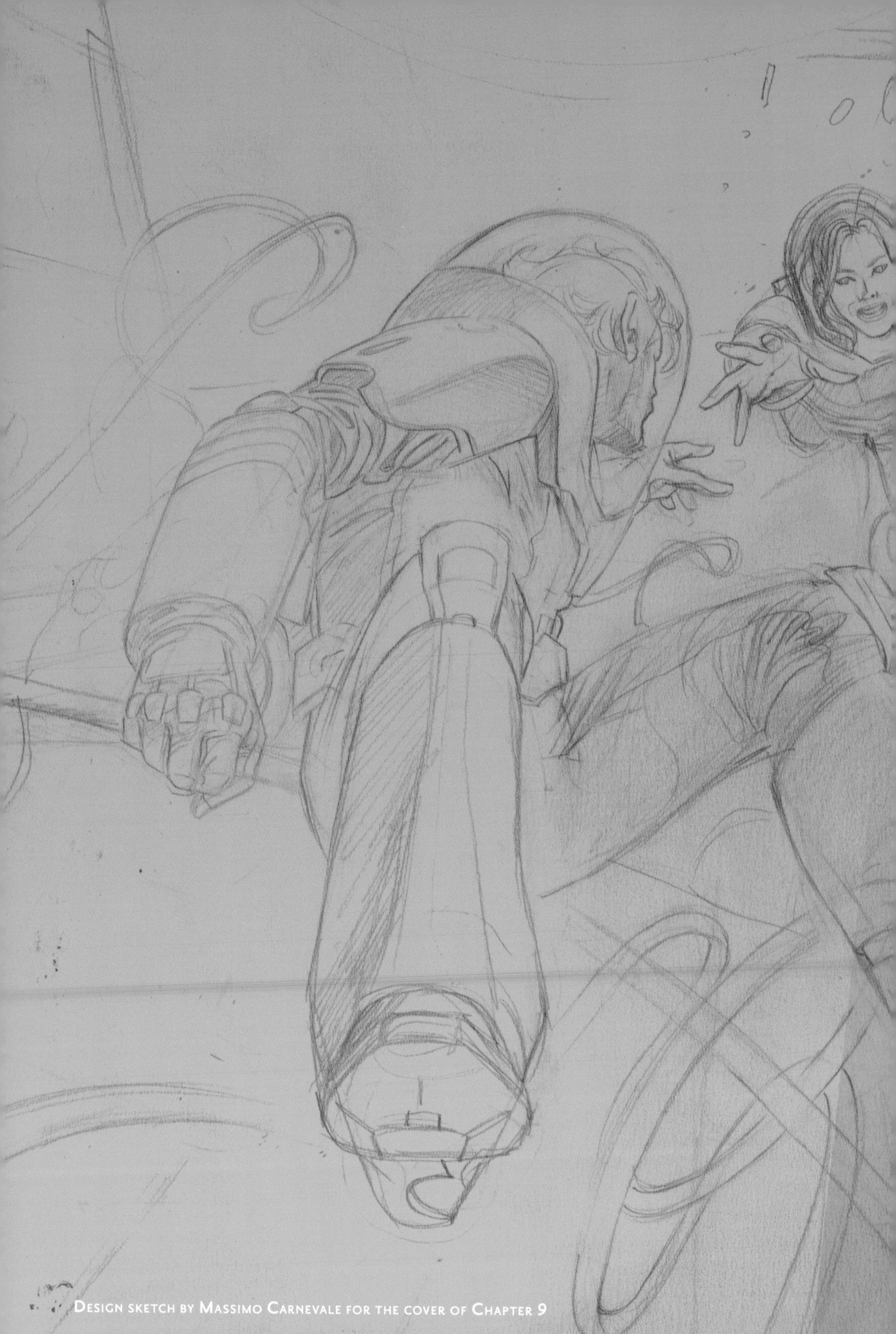

Design sketch by Massimo Carnevale for the cover of Chapter 9

COLD AS SPACE

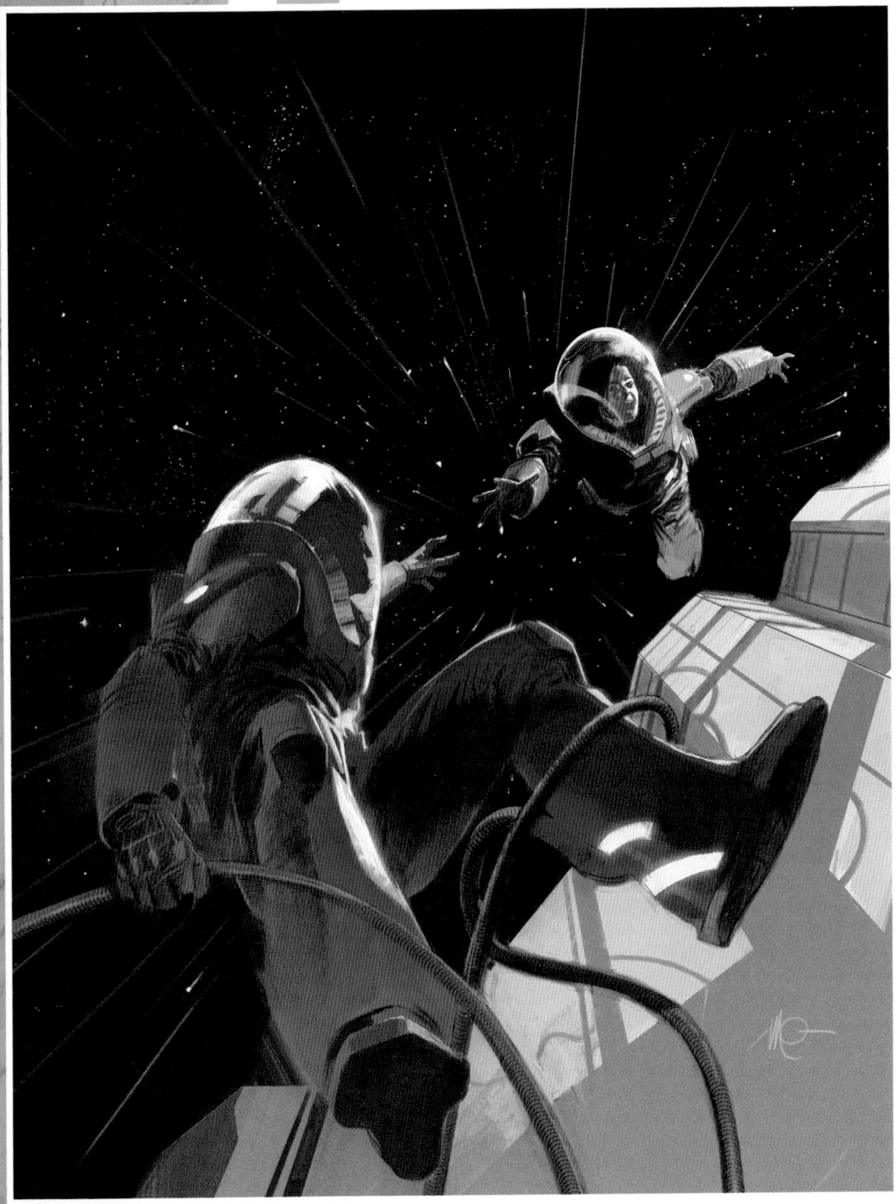

ORPHANS: CHAPTER 9

story: ROBERTO RECCHIONI
art: GIGI CAVENAGO and WERTHER DELL'EDERA
colors: GIOVANNA NIRO and ALESSIA PASTORELLO
cover: MASSIMO CARNEVALE

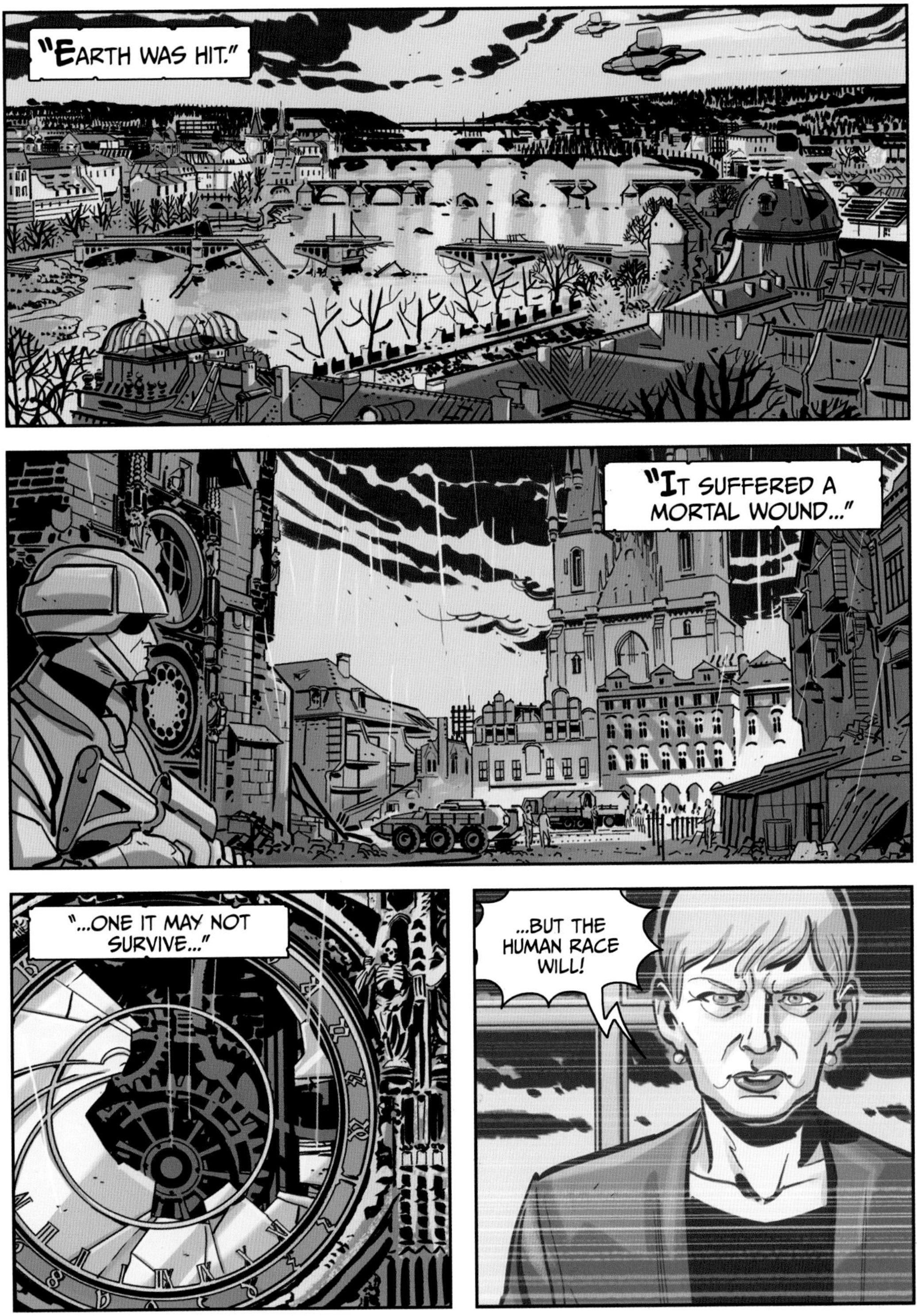
"EARTH WAS HIT."
"IT SUFFERED A MORTAL WOUND..."
"...ONE IT MAY NOT SURVIVE..."
...BUT THE HUMAN RACE WILL!

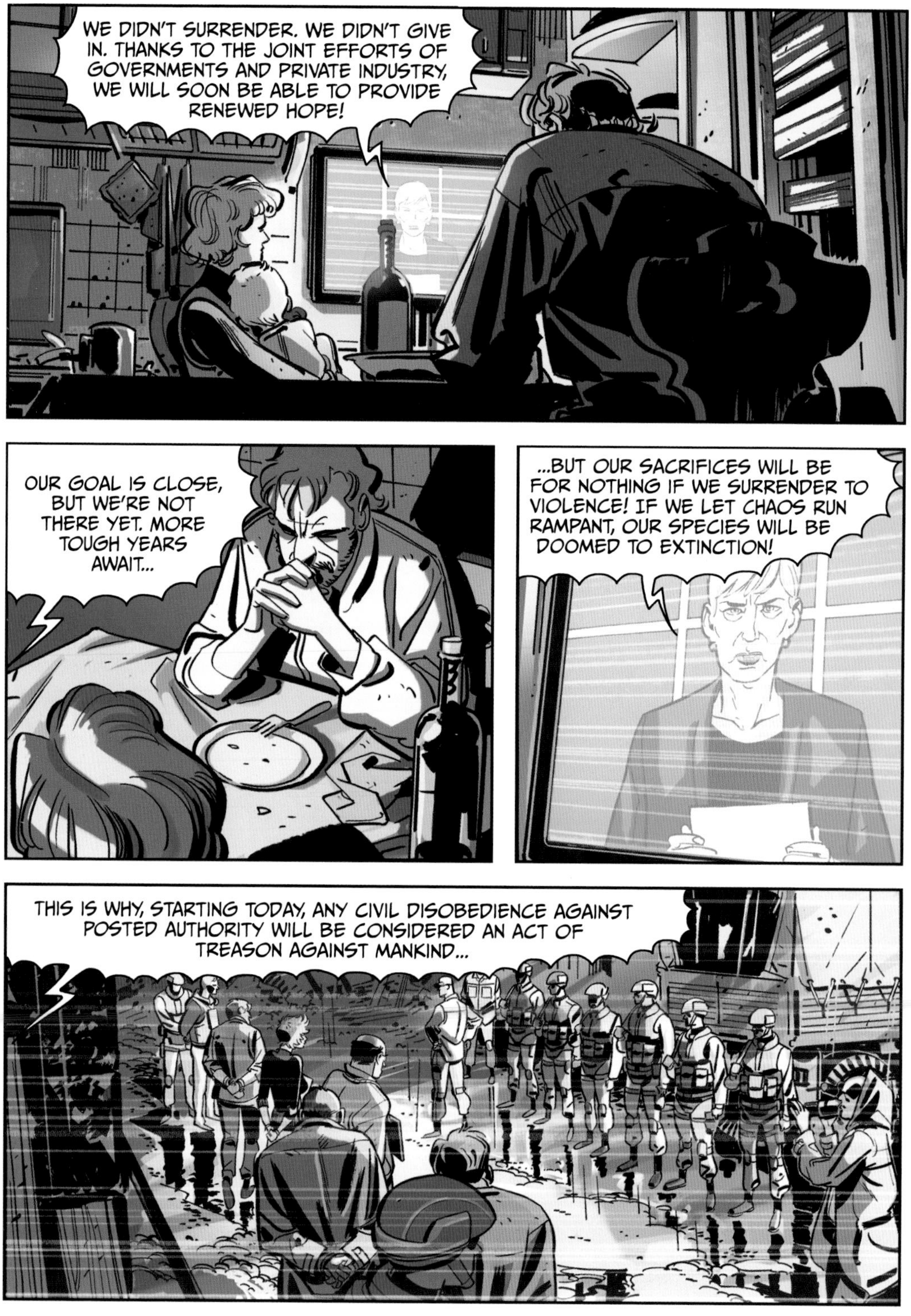
WE DIDN'T SURRENDER. WE DIDN'T GIVE IN. THANKS TO THE JOINT EFFORTS OF GOVERNMENTS AND PRIVATE INDUSTRY, WE WILL SOON BE ABLE TO PROVIDE RENEWED HOPE!
OUR GOAL IS CLOSE, BUT WE'RE NOT THERE YET. MORE TOUGH YEARS AWAIT...
...BUT OUR SACRIFICES WILL BE FOR NOTHING IF WE SURRENDER TO VIOLENCE! IF WE LET CHAOS RUN RAMPANT, OUR SPECIES WILL BE DOOMED TO EXTINCTION!
THIS IS WHY, STARTING TODAY, ANY CIVIL DISOBEDIENCE AGAINST POSTED AUTHORITY WILL BE CONSIDERED AN ACT OF TREASON AGAINST MANKIND...

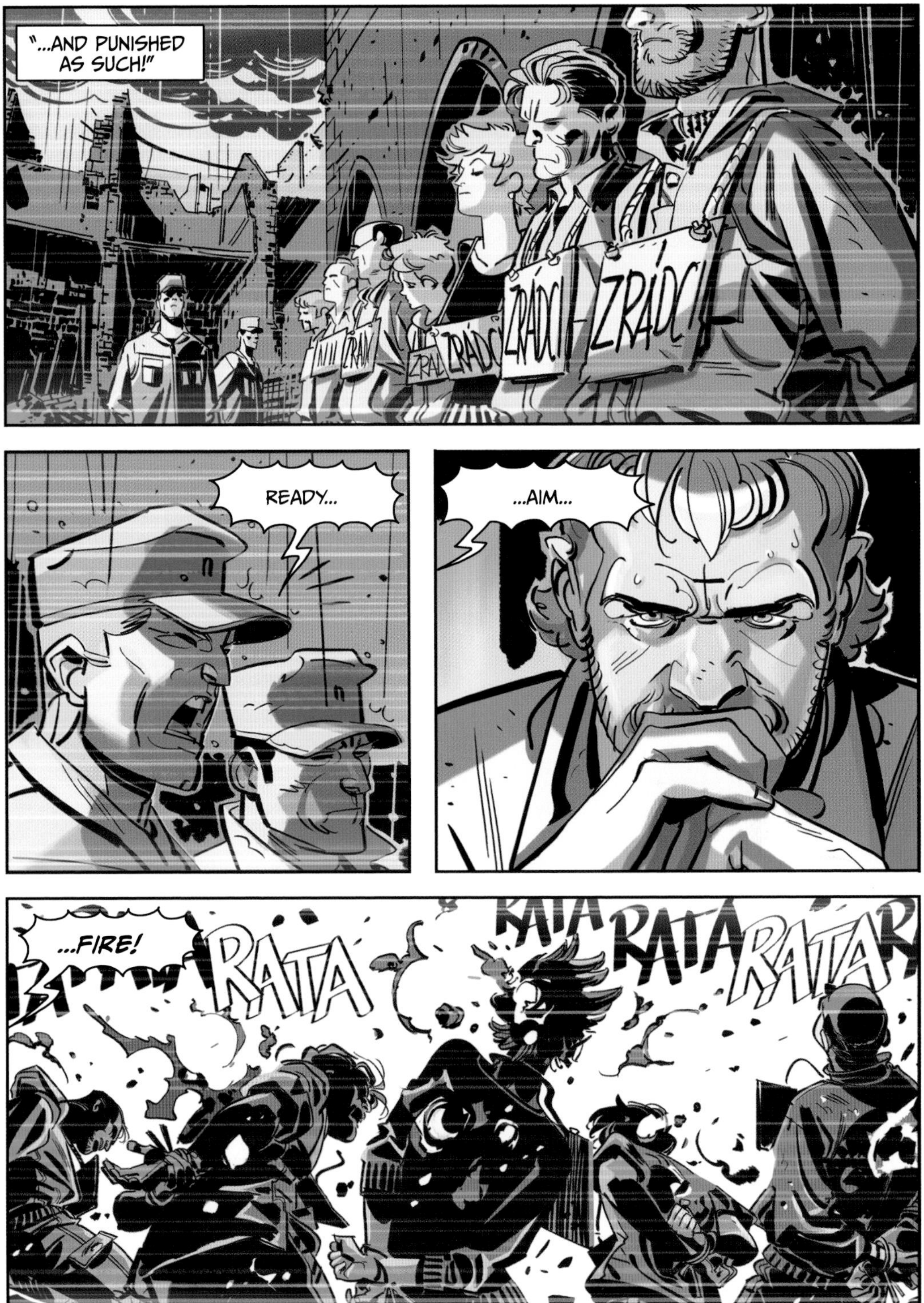
"...AND PUNISHED AS SUCH!"
ZRÁDCI
ZRÁDCI
READY...
...AIM...
...FIRE!
RATA
RATA
RATA
RATAR

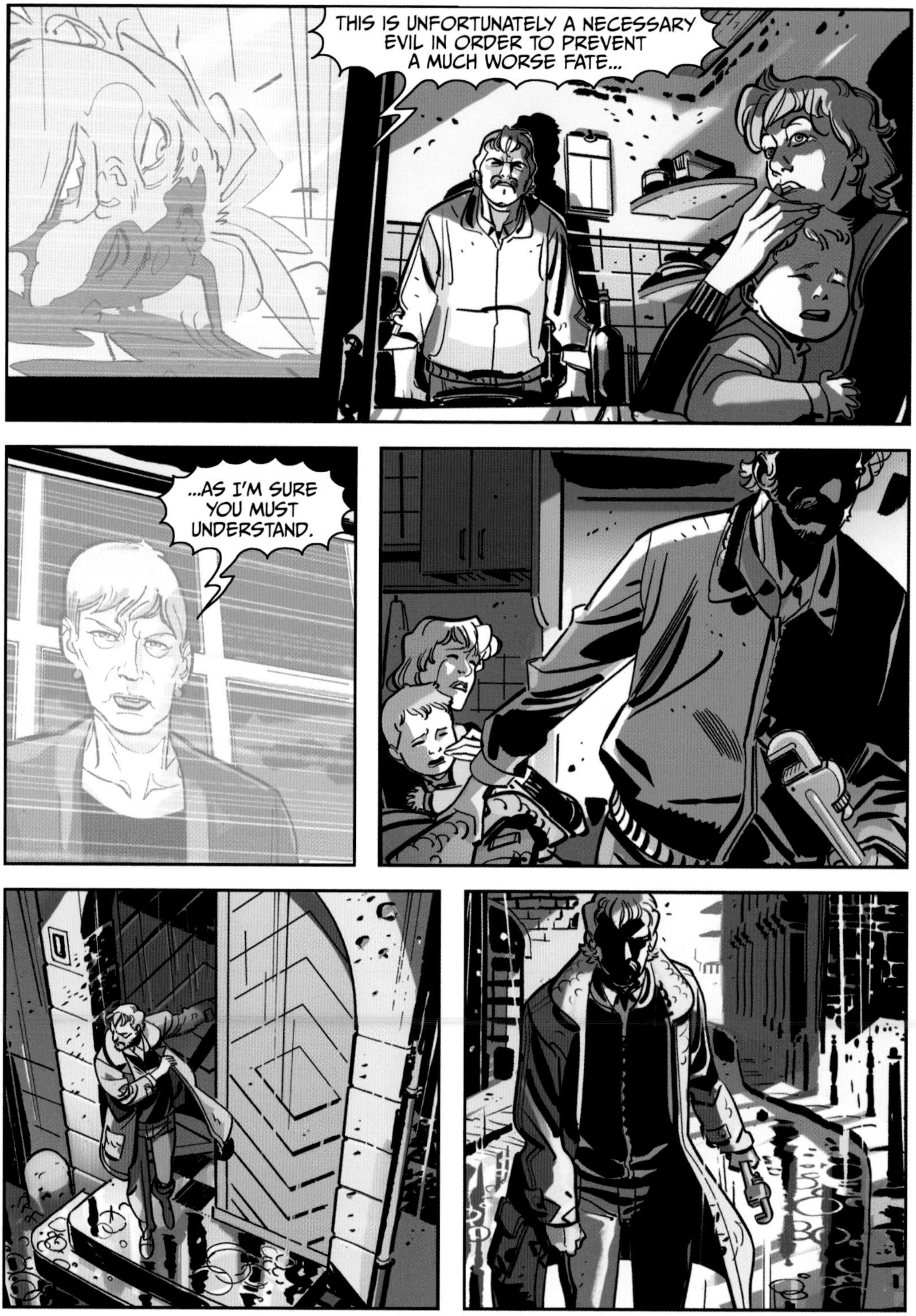
THIS IS UNFORTUNATELY A NECESSARY EVIL IN ORDER TO PREVENT A MUCH WORSE FATE...
...AS I'M SURE YOU MUST UNDERSTAND.

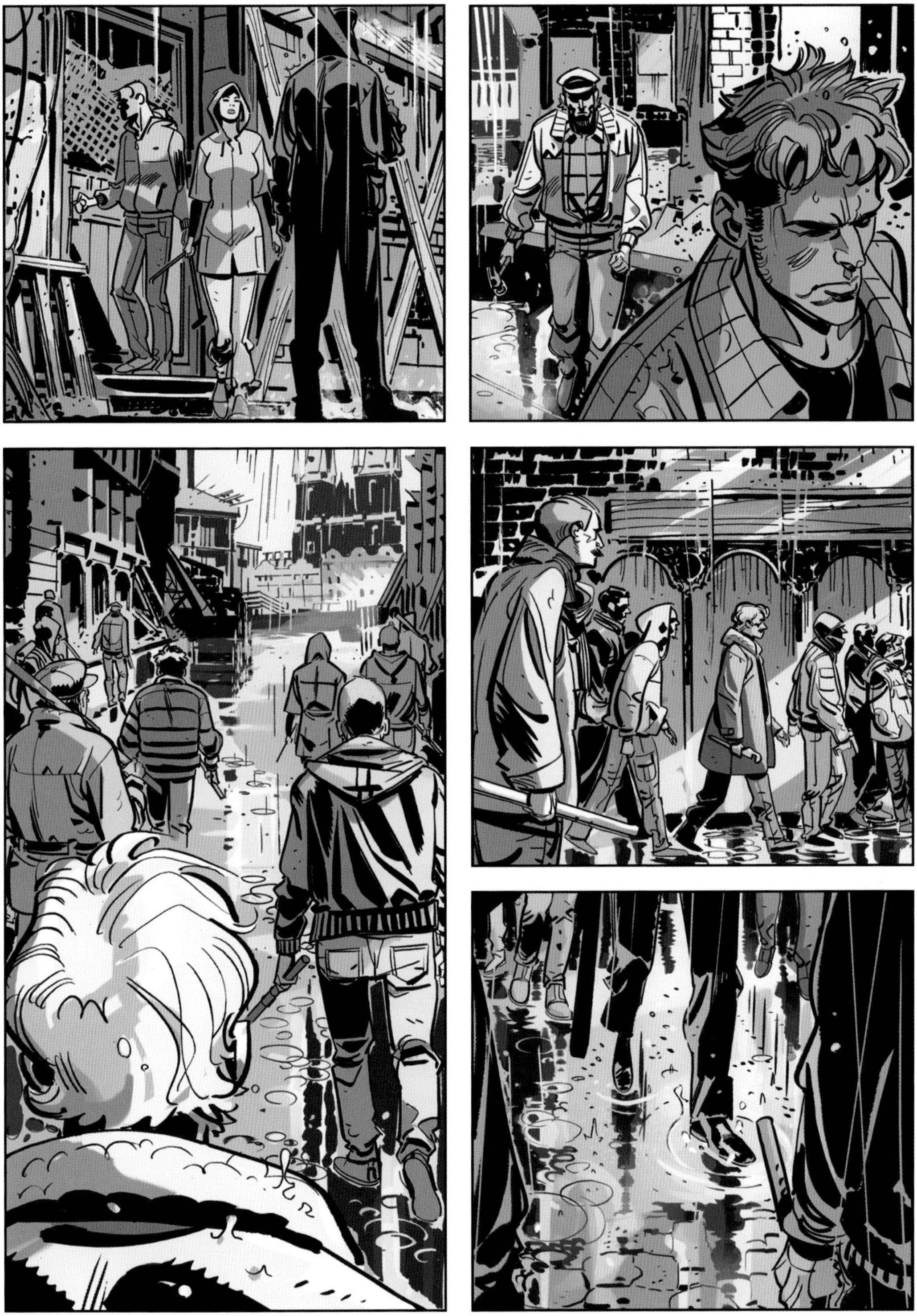

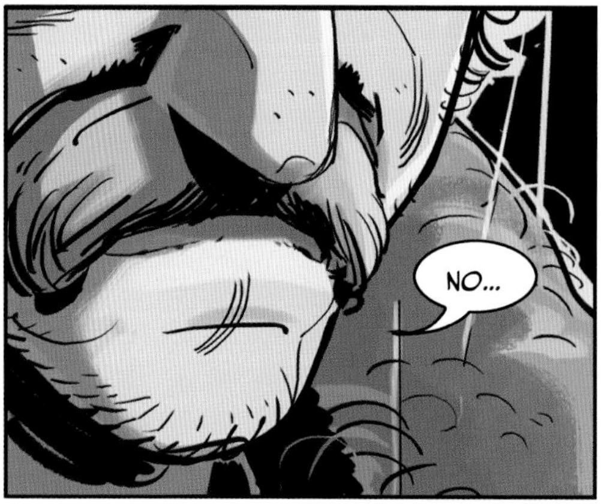
NO...

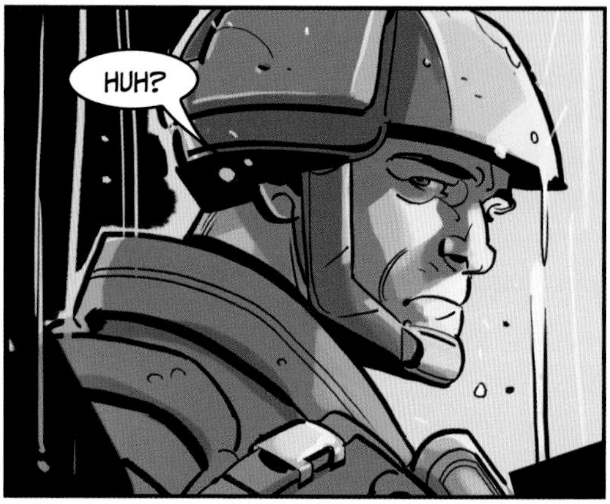
HUH?

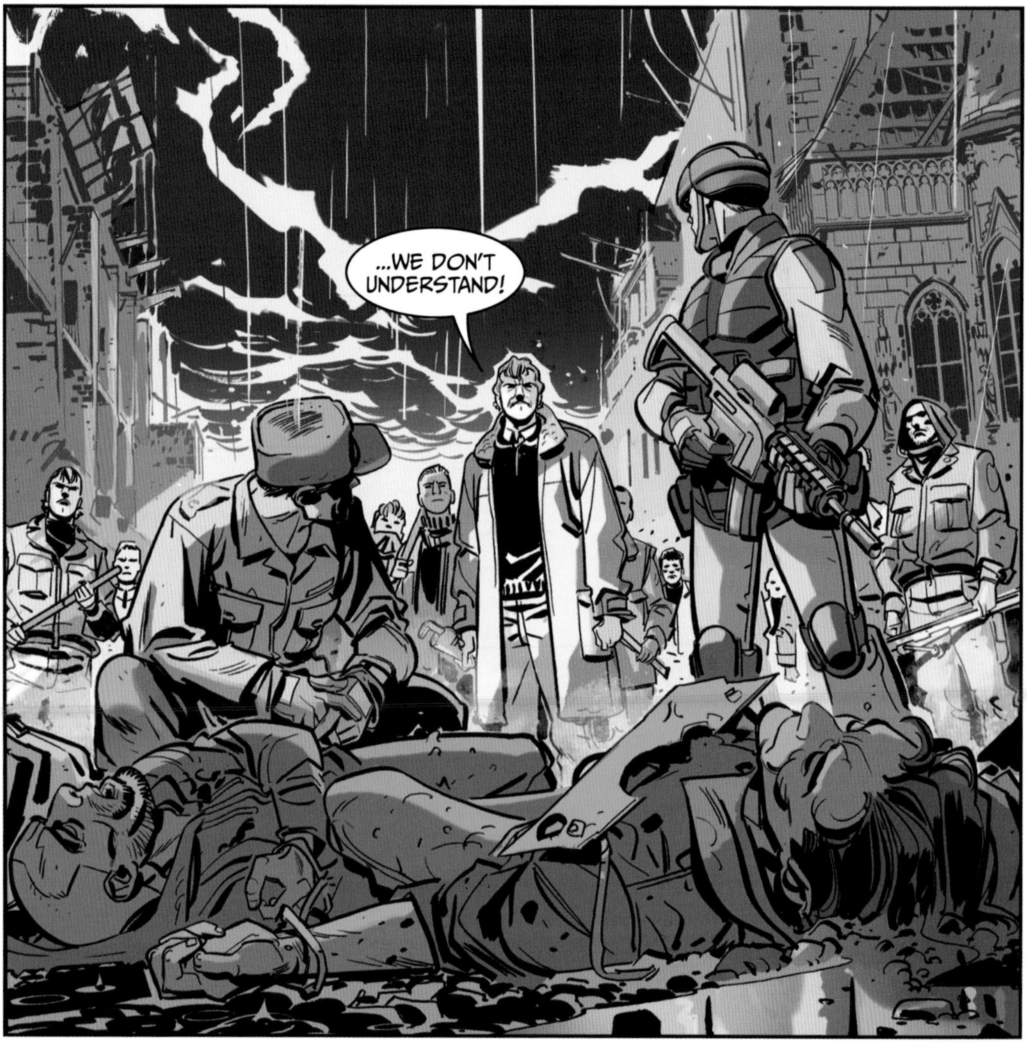
...WE DON'T UNDERSTAND!

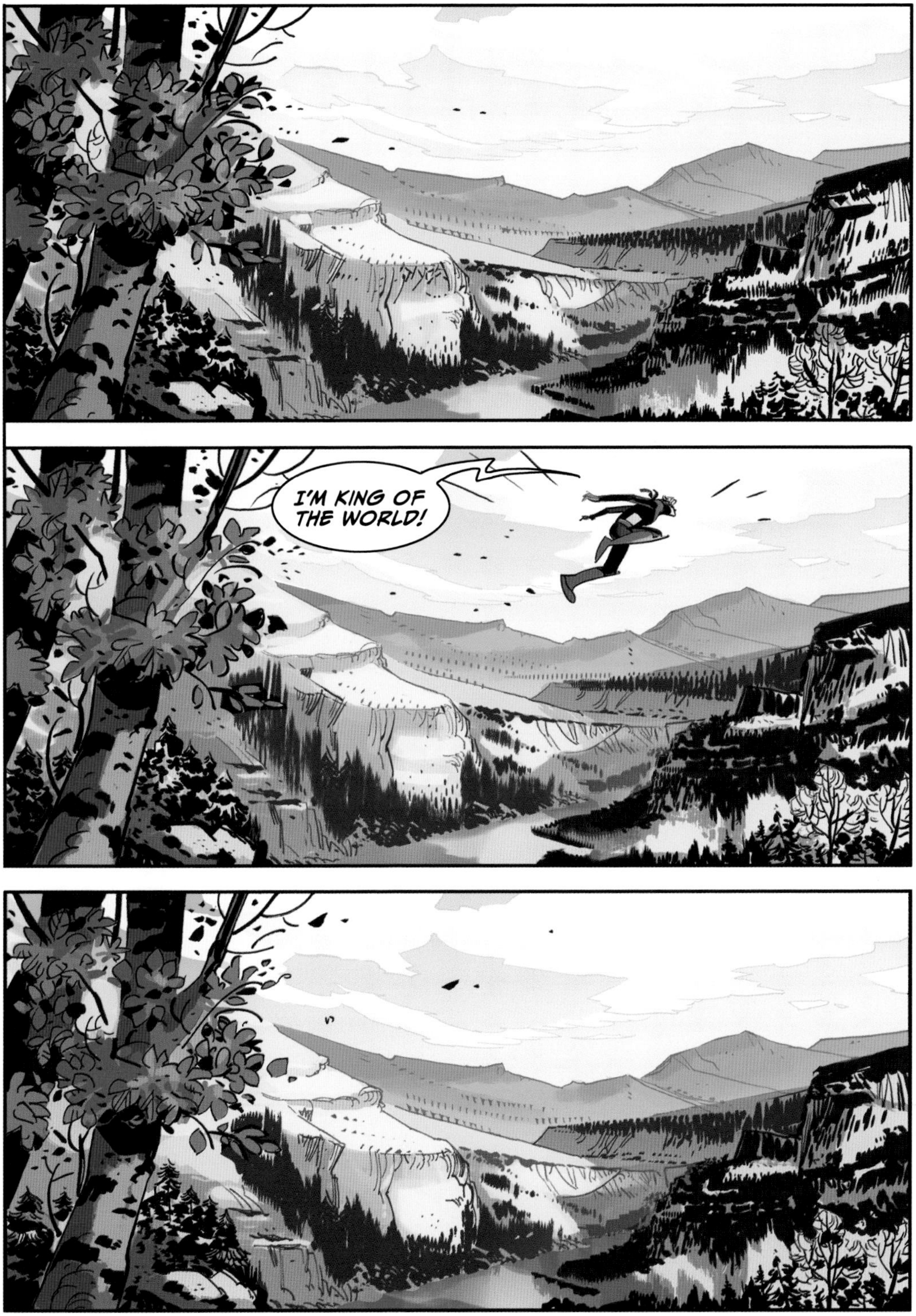
I'M KING OF THE WORLD!

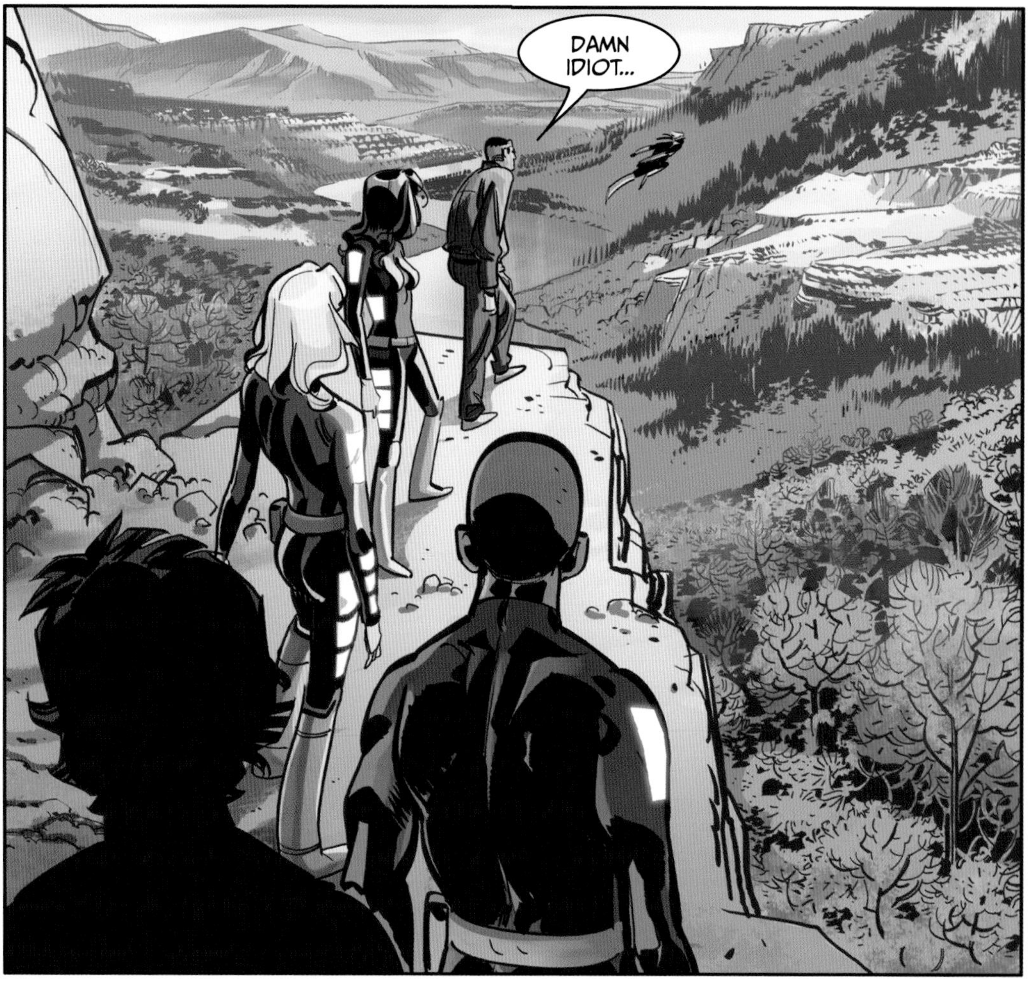
DAMN IDIOT...

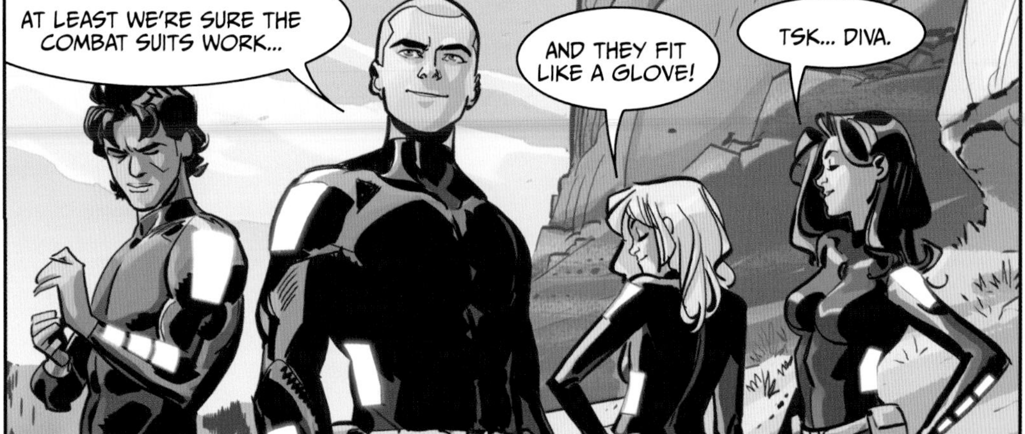
AT LEAST WE'RE SURE THE COMBAT SUITS WORK...
AND THEY FIT LIKE A GLOVE!
TSK... DIVA.

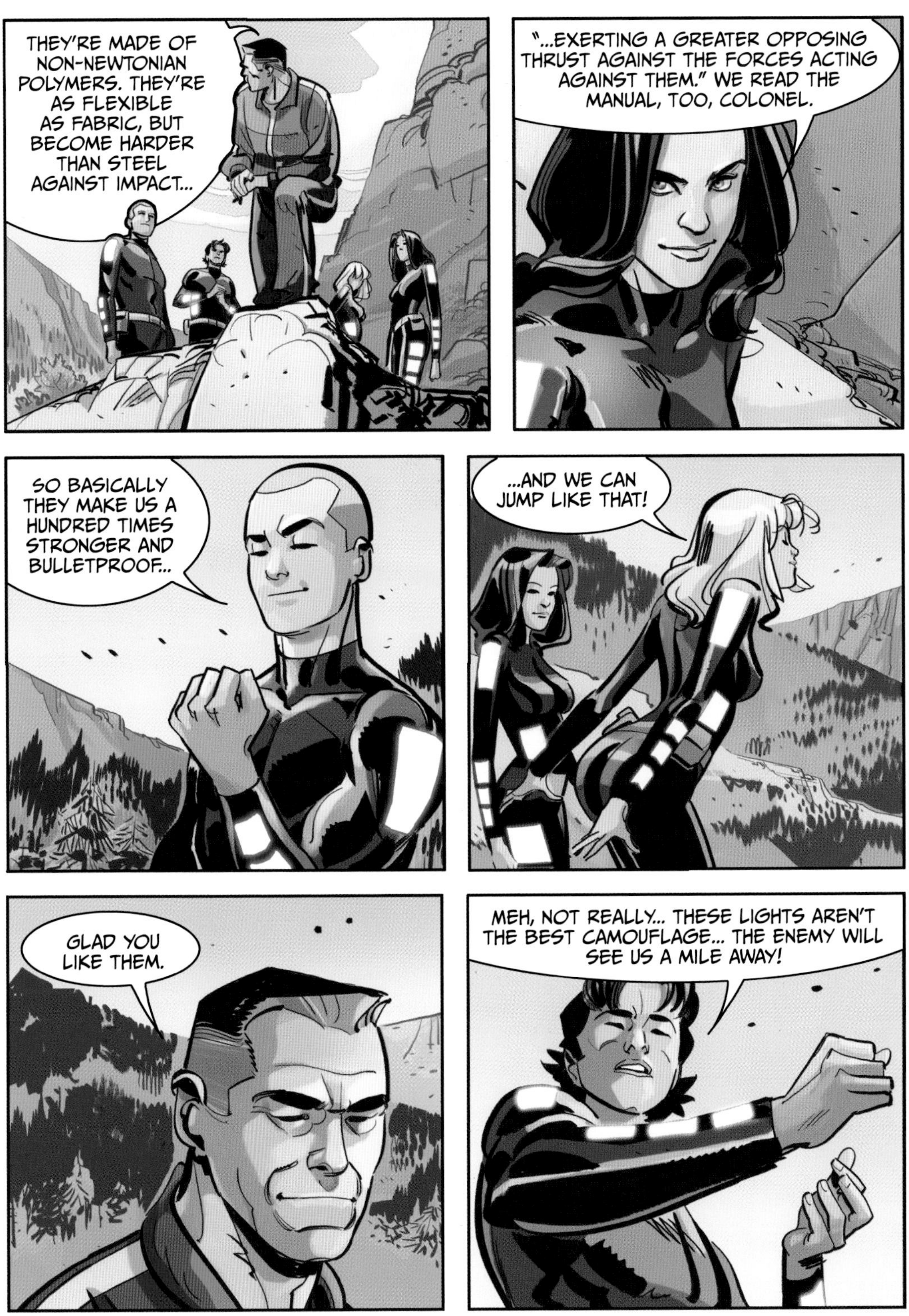
THEY'RE MADE OF NON-NEWTONIAN POLYMERS. THEY'RE AS FLEXIBLE AS FABRIC, BUT BECOME HARDER THAN STEEL AGAINST IMPACT...
"...EXERTING A GREATER OPPOSING THRUST AGAINST THE FORCES ACTING AGAINST THEM." WE READ THE MANUAL, TOO, COLONEL.
SO BASICALLY THEY MAKE US A HUNDRED TIMES STRONGER AND BULLETPROOF...
...AND WE CAN JUMP LIKE THAT!
GLAD YOU LIKE THEM.
MEH, NOT REALLY... THESE LIGHTS AREN'T THE BEST CAMOUFLAGE... THE ENEMY WILL SEE US A MILE AWAY!

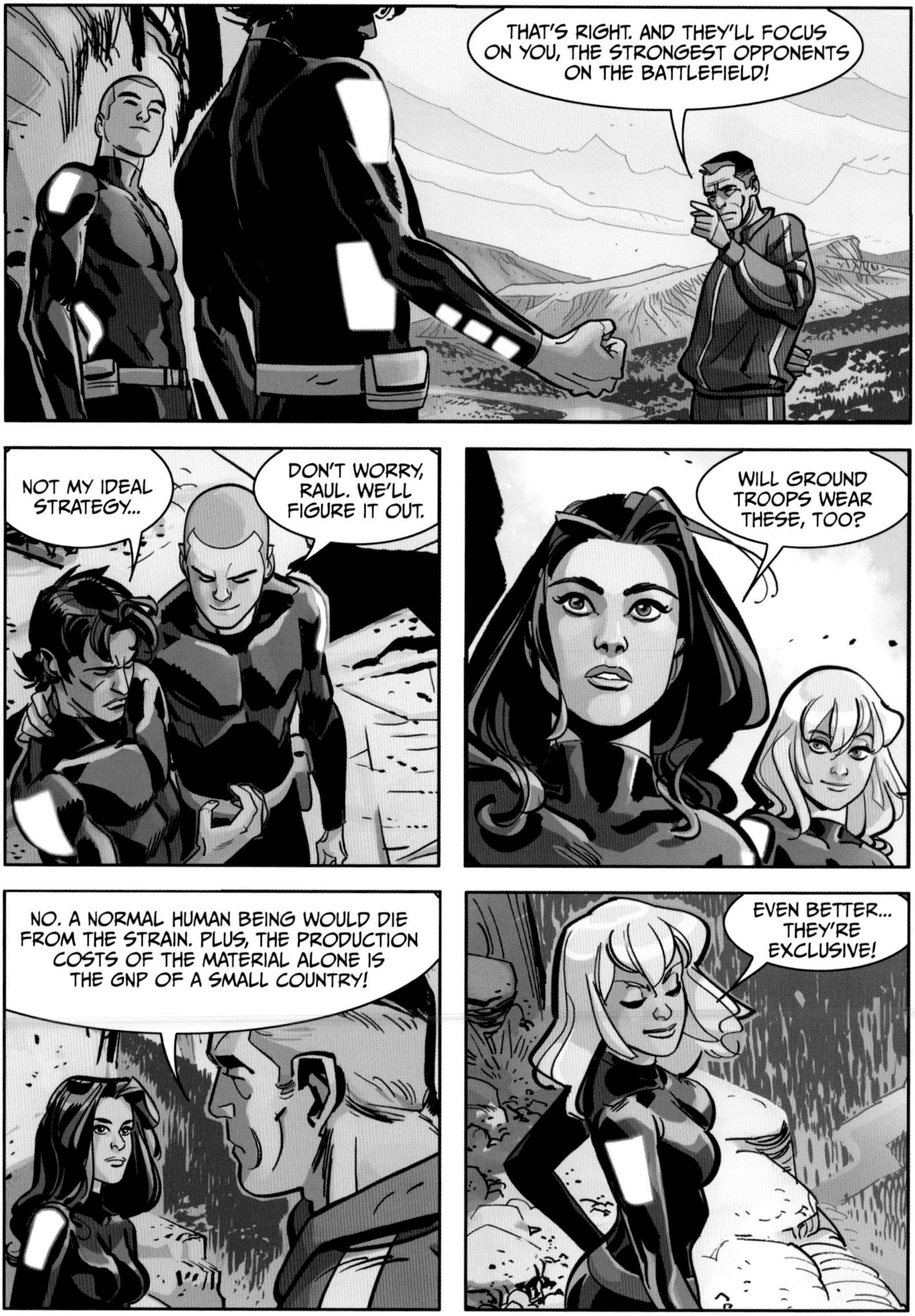
THAT'S RIGHT. AND THEY'LL FOCUS ON YOU, THE STRONGEST OPPONENTS ON THE BATTLEFIELD!
NOT MY IDEAL STRATEGY...
DON'T WORRY, RAUL. WE'LL FIGURE IT OUT.
WILL GROUND TROOPS WEAR THESE, TOO?
NO. A NORMAL HUMAN BEING WOULD DIE FROM THE STRAIN. PLUS, THE PRODUCTION COSTS OF THE MATERIAL ALONE IS THE GNP OF A SMALL COUNTRY!
EVEN BETTER... THEY'RE EXCLUSIVE!

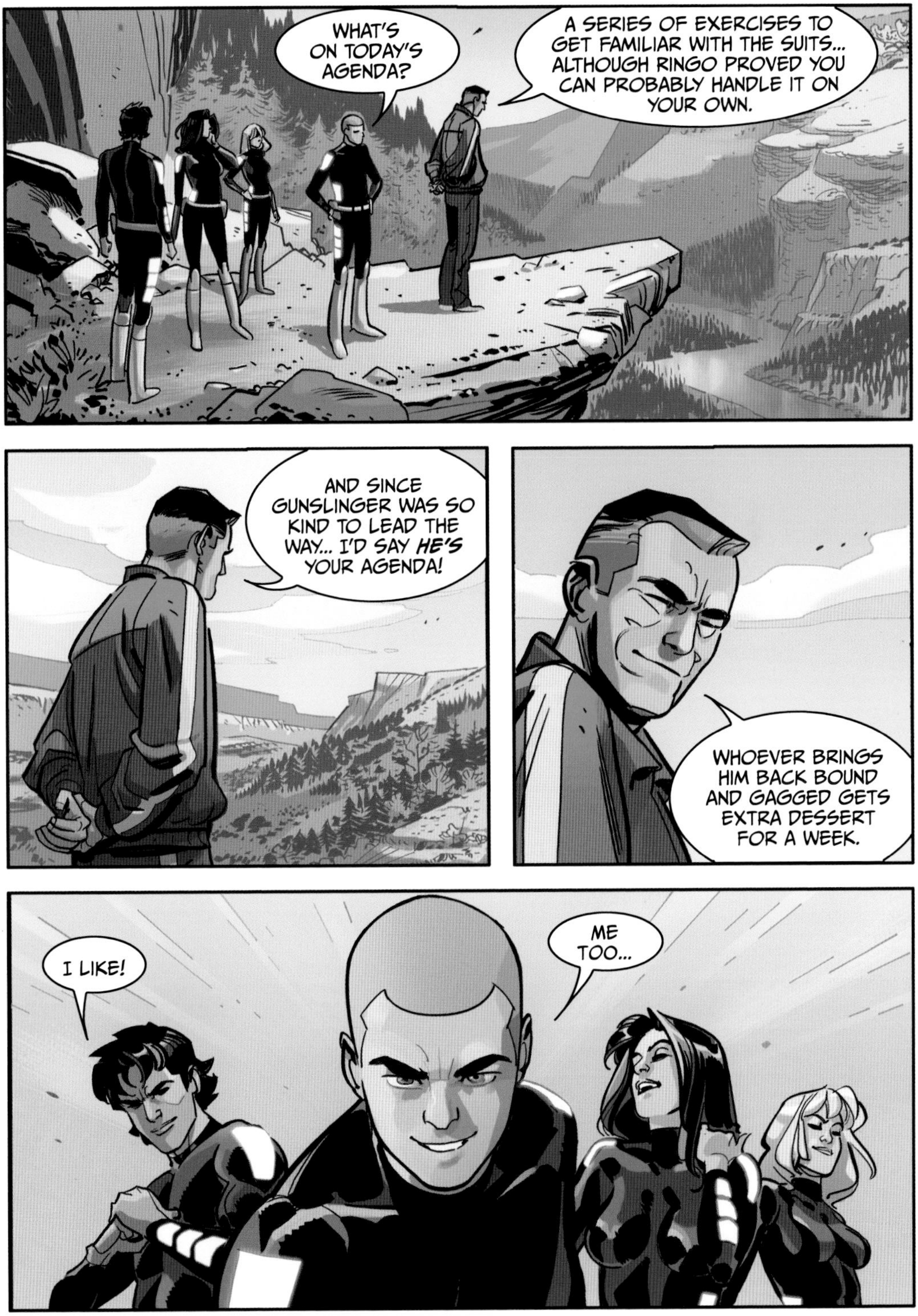
WHAT'S ON TODAY'S AGENDA?
A SERIES OF EXERCISES TO GET FAMILIAR WITH THE SUITS... ALTHOUGH RINGO PROVED YOU CAN PROBABLY HANDLE IT ON YOUR OWN.
AND SINCE GUNSLINGER WAS SO KIND TO LEAD THE WAY... I'D SAY *HE'S* YOUR AGENDA!
WHOEVER BRINGS HIM BACK BOUND AND GAGGED GETS EXTRA DESSERT FOR A WEEK.
I LIKE!
ME TOO...

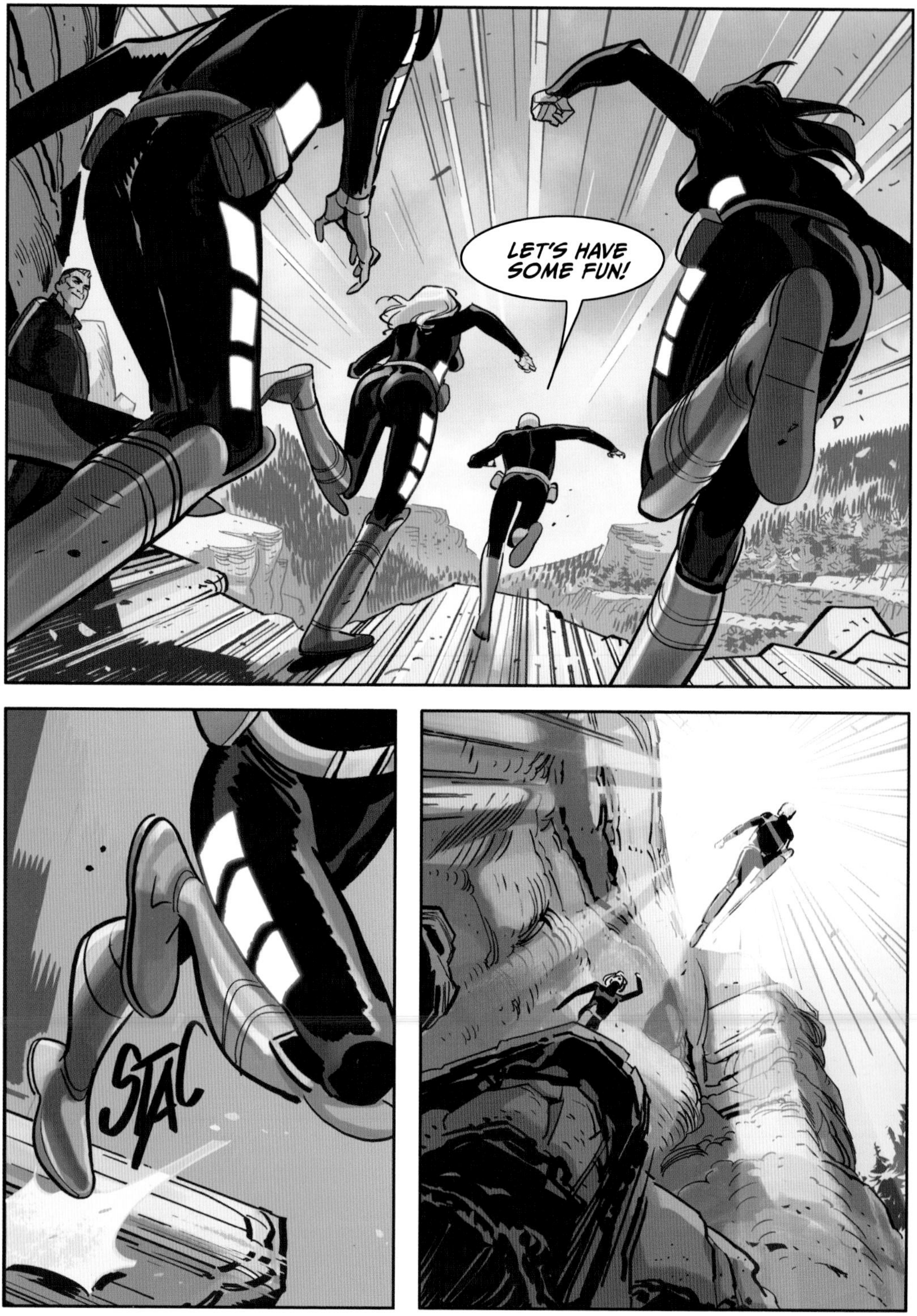
LET'S HAVE SOME FUN!
STAC

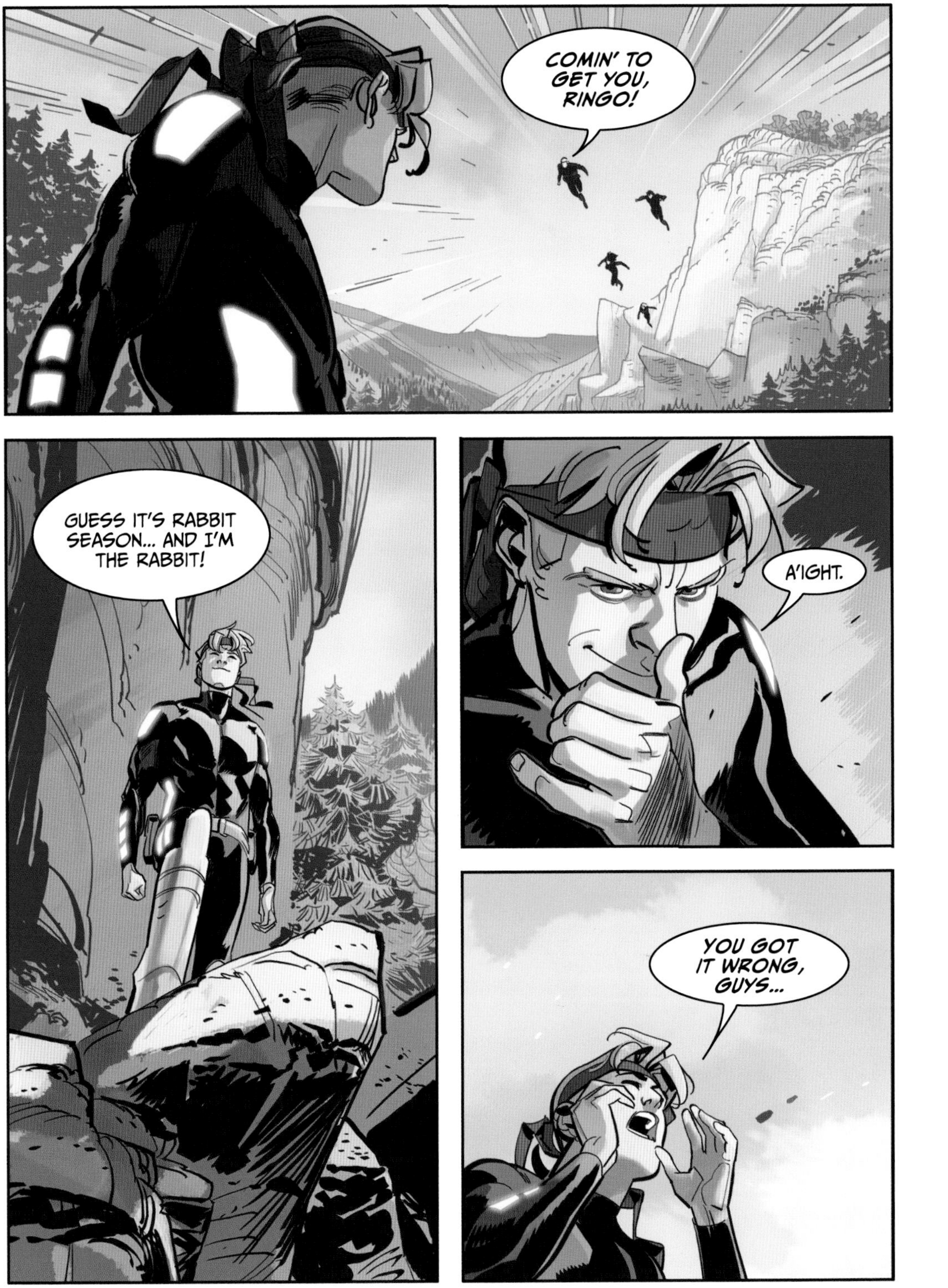
COMIN' TO GET YOU, RINGO!
GUESS IT'S RABBIT SEASON... AND I'M THE RABBIT!
A'IGHT.
YOU GOT IT WRONG, GUYS...

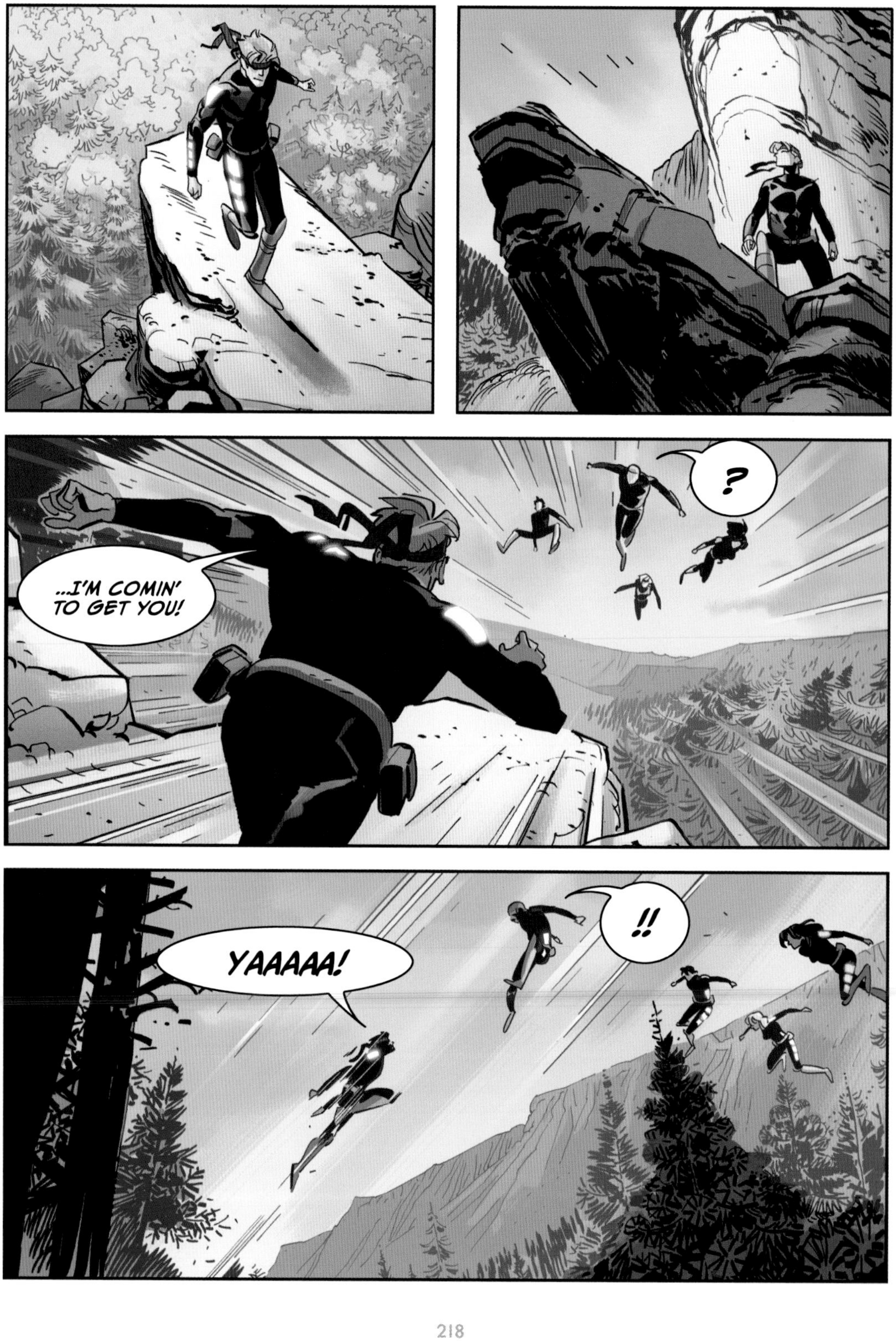
?
...I'M COMIN' TO GET YOU!
YAAAAA!
!!

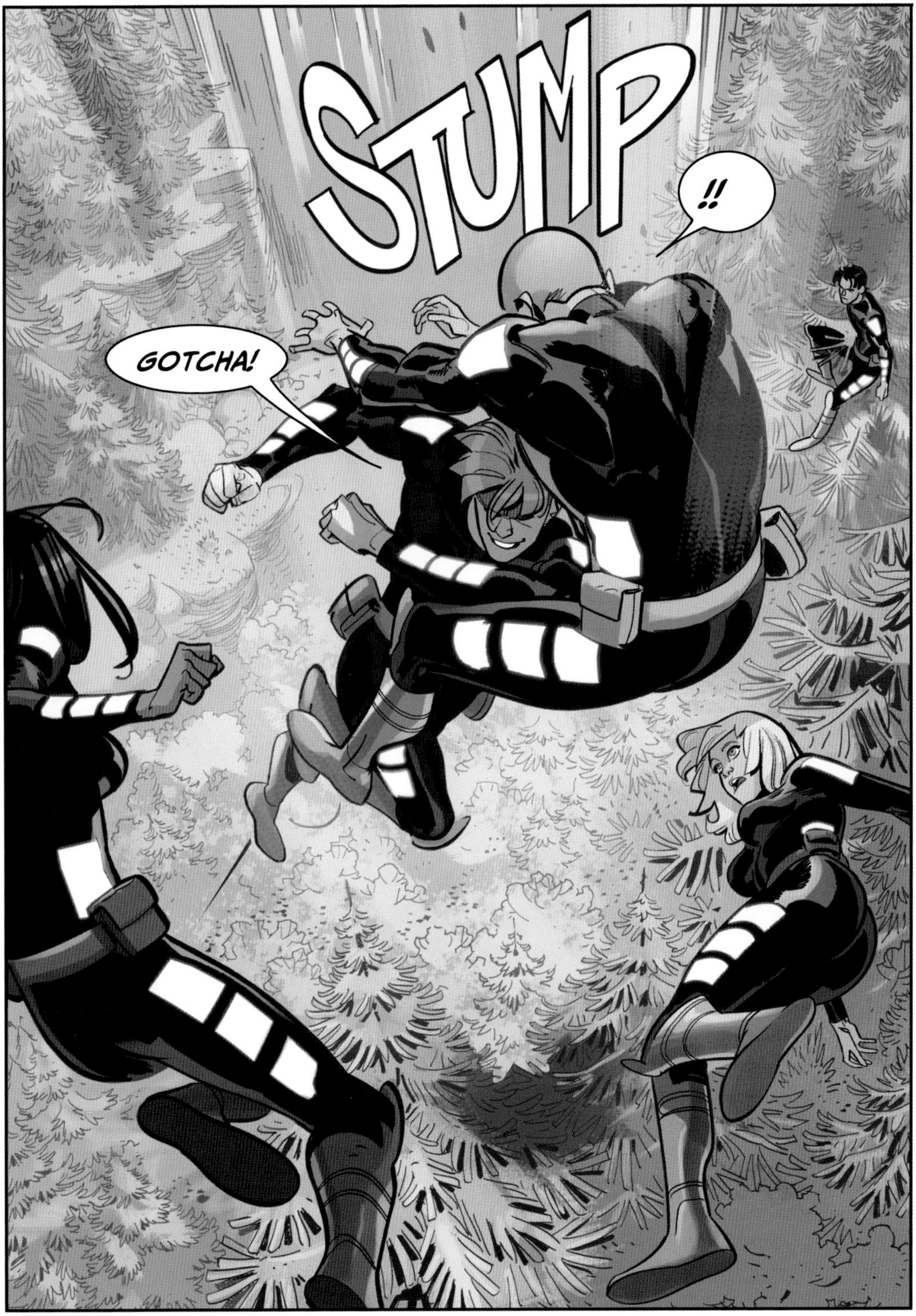
STUMP
!!
GOTCHA!

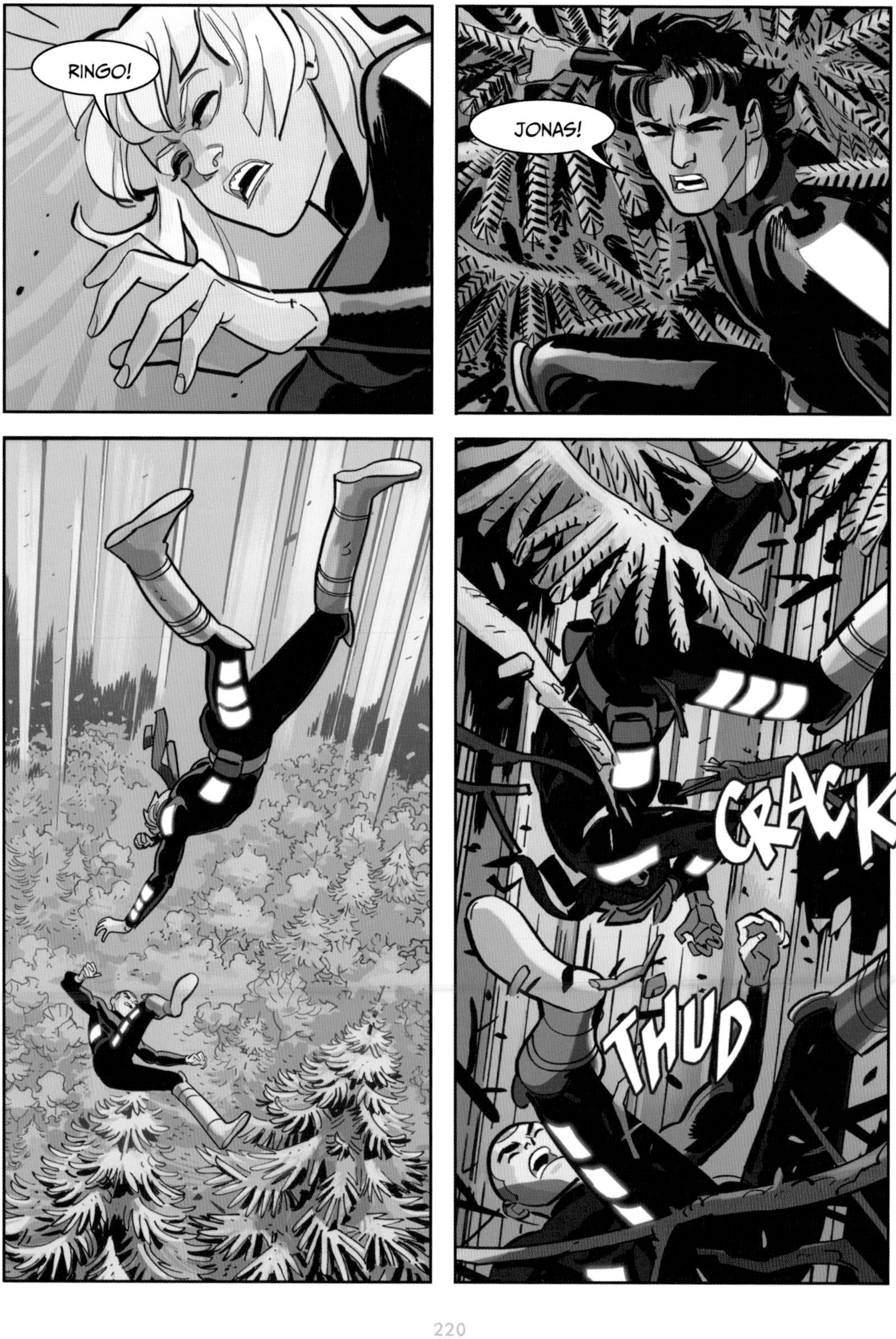
RINGO!
JONAS!
CRACK
THUD

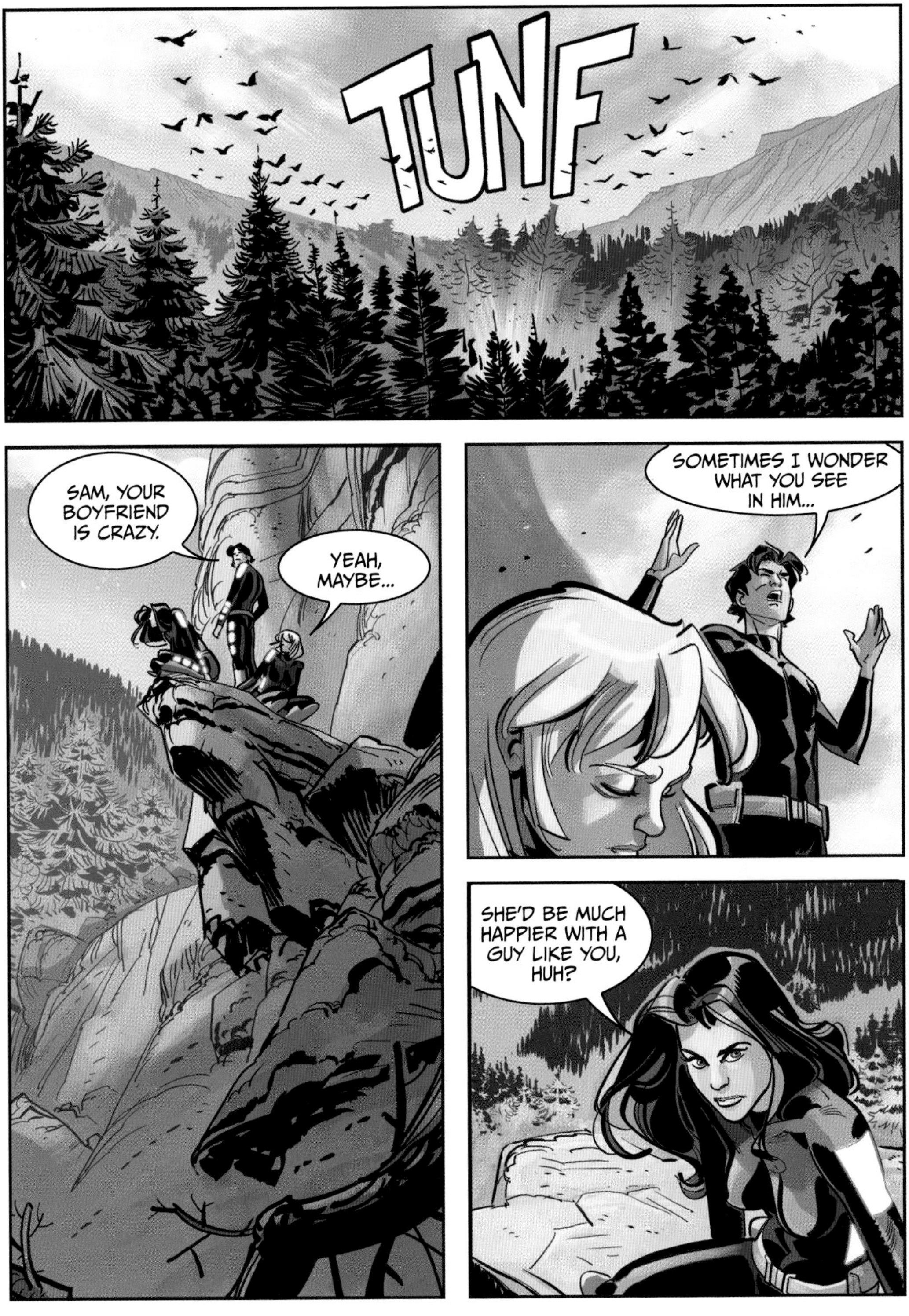
TUNF
SAM, YOUR BOYFRIEND IS CRAZY.
YEAH, MAYBE...
SOMETIMES I WONDER WHAT YOU SEE IN HIM...
SHE'D BE MUCH HAPPIER WITH A GUY LIKE YOU, HUH?

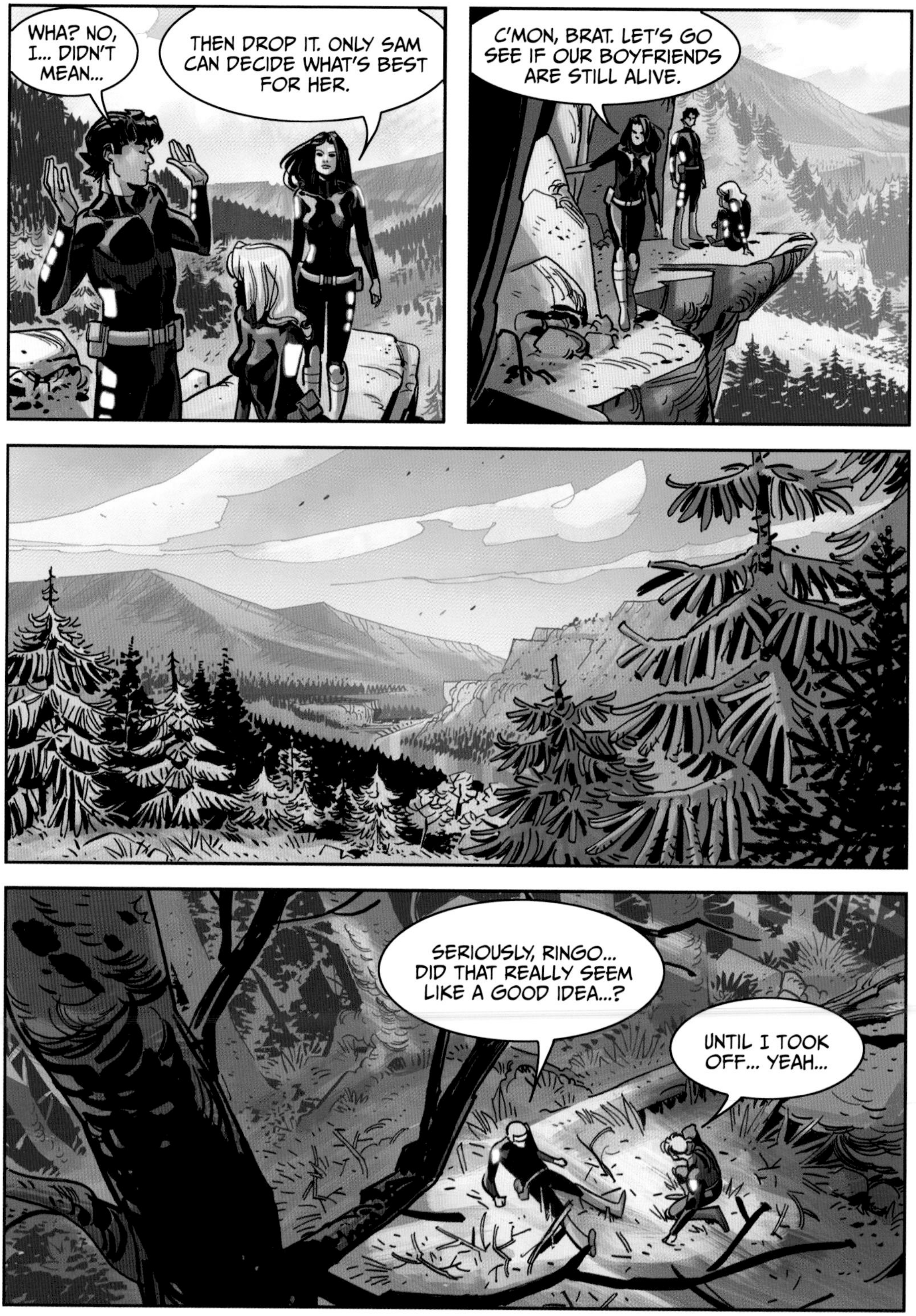
WHA? NO, I... DIDN'T MEAN...
THEN DROP IT. ONLY SAM CAN DECIDE WHAT'S BEST FOR HER.
C'MON, BRAT. LET'S GO SEE IF OUR BOYFRIENDS ARE STILL ALIVE.
SERIOUSLY, RINGO... DID THAT REALLY SEEM LIKE A GOOD IDEA...?
UNTIL I TOOK OFF... YEAH...

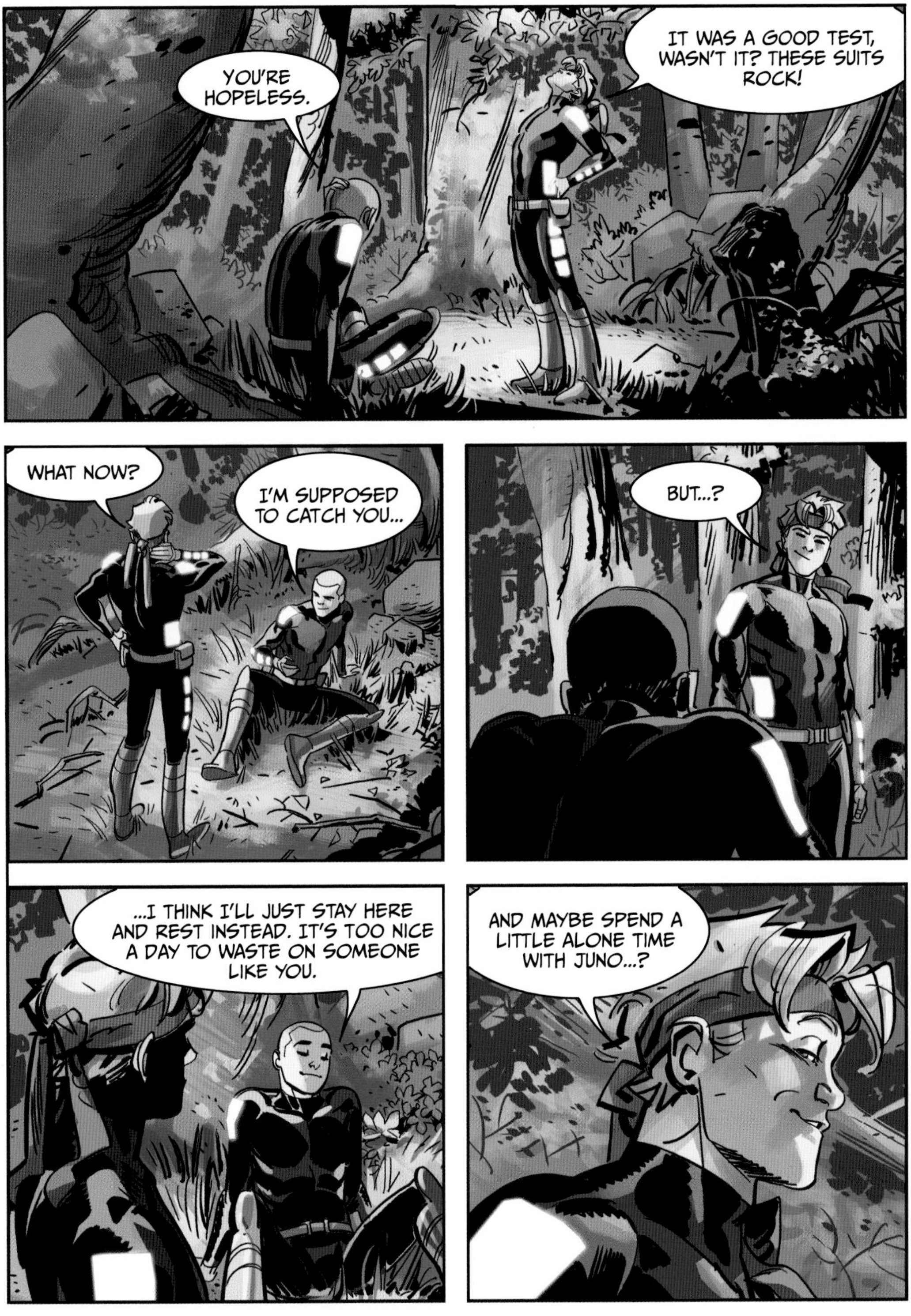
YOU'RE HOPELESS.
IT WAS A GOOD TEST, WASN'T IT? THESE SUITS ROCK!
WHAT NOW?
I'M SUPPOSED TO CATCH YOU...
BUT...?
...I THINK I'LL JUST STAY HERE AND REST INSTEAD. IT'S TOO NICE A DAY TO WASTE ON SOMEONE LIKE YOU.
AND MAYBE SPEND A LITTLE ALONE TIME WITH JUNO...?

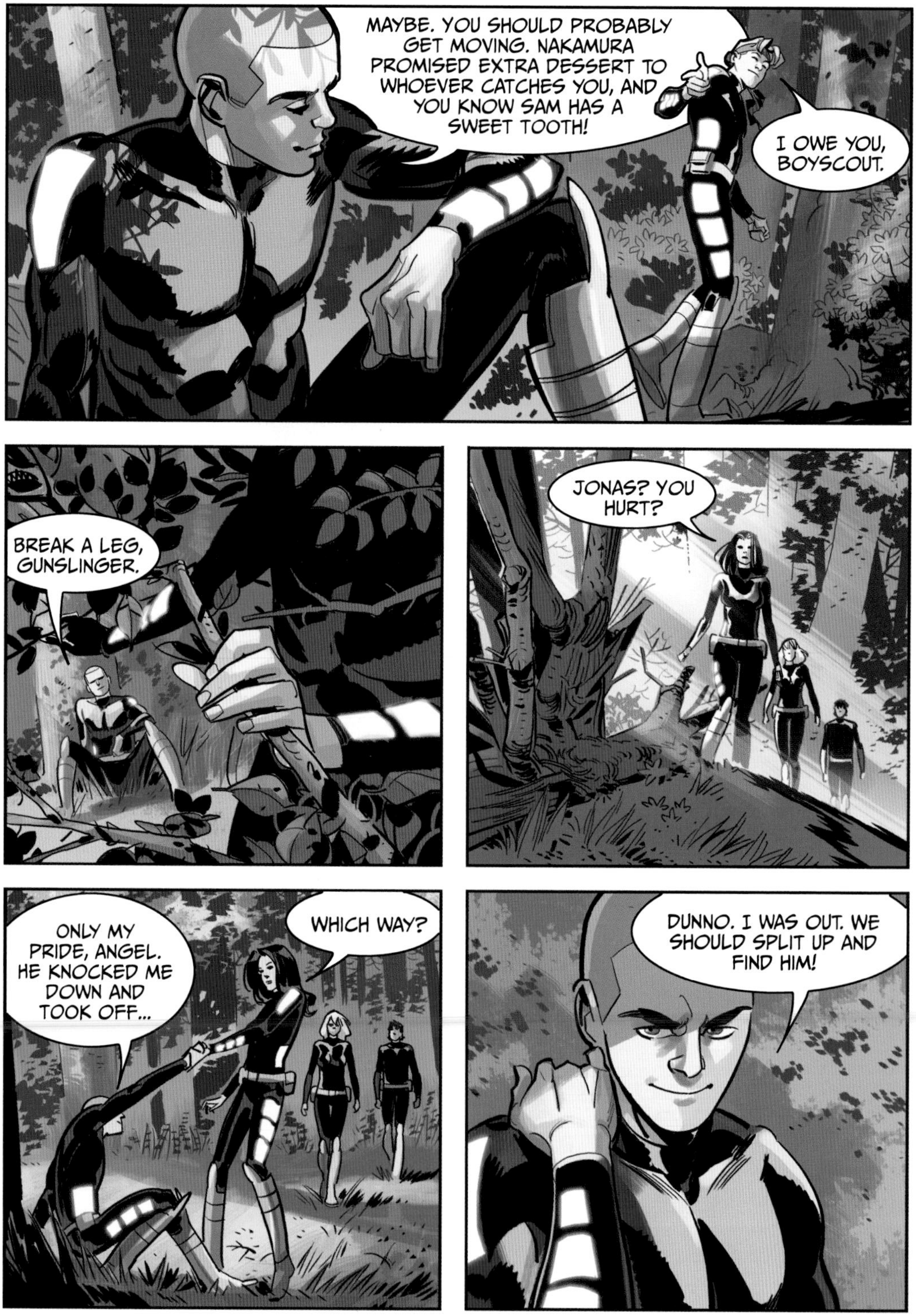
MAYBE. YOU SHOULD PROBABLY GET MOVING. NAKAMURA PROMISED EXTRA DESSERT TO WHOEVER CATCHES YOU, AND YOU KNOW SAM HAS A SWEET TOOTH!
I OWE YOU, BOYSCOUT.
BREAK A LEG, GUNSLINGER.
JONAS? YOU HURT?
ONLY MY PRIDE, ANGEL. HE KNOCKED ME DOWN AND TOOK OFF...
WHICH WAY?
DUNNO. I WAS OUT. WE SHOULD SPLIT UP AND FIND HIM!

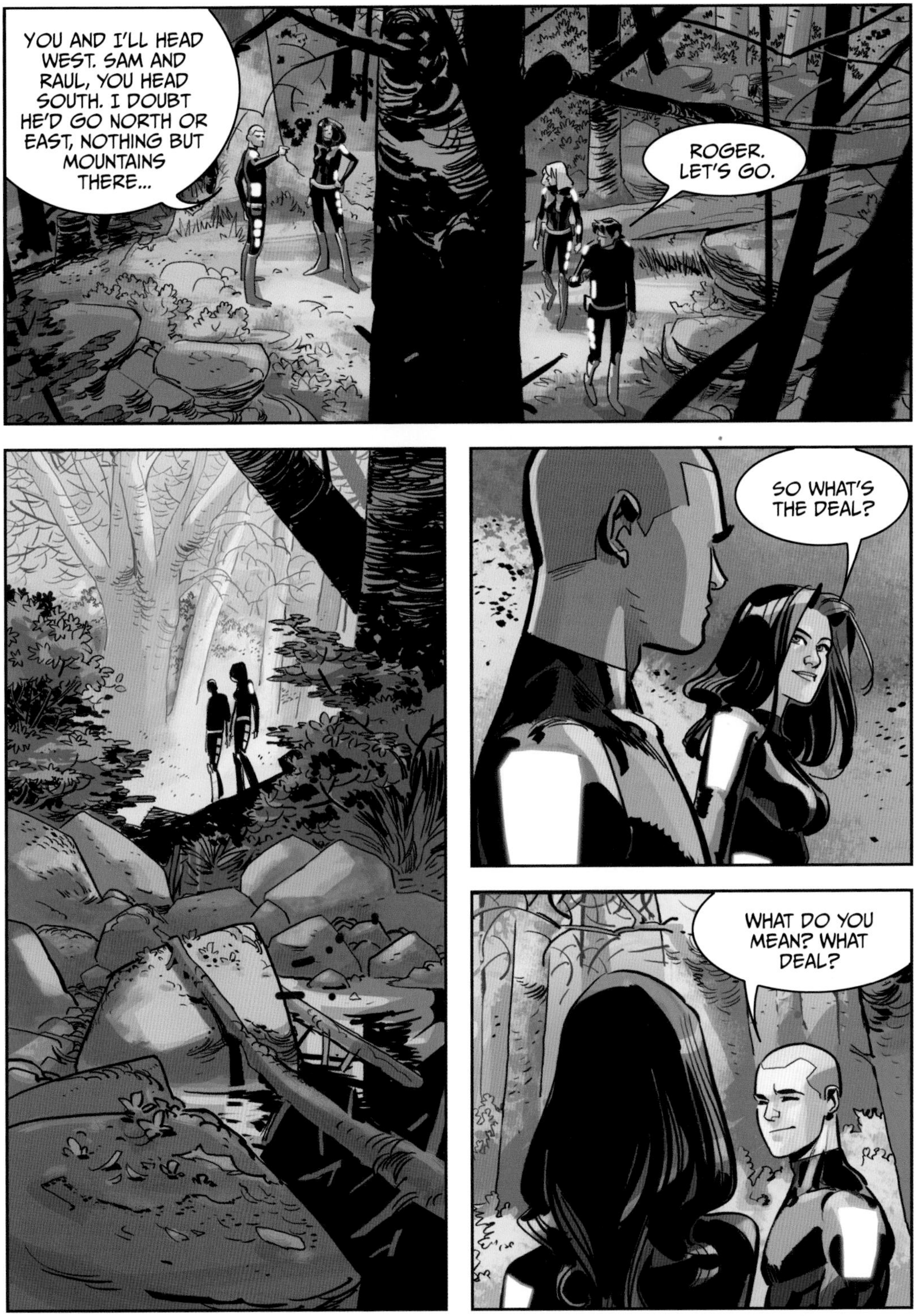
YOU AND I'LL HEAD WEST. SAM AND RAUL, YOU HEAD SOUTH. I DOUBT HE'D GO NORTH OR EAST, NOTHING BUT MOUNTAINS THERE...
ROGER. LET'S GO.
SO WHAT'S THE DEAL?
WHAT DO YOU MEAN? WHAT DEAL?

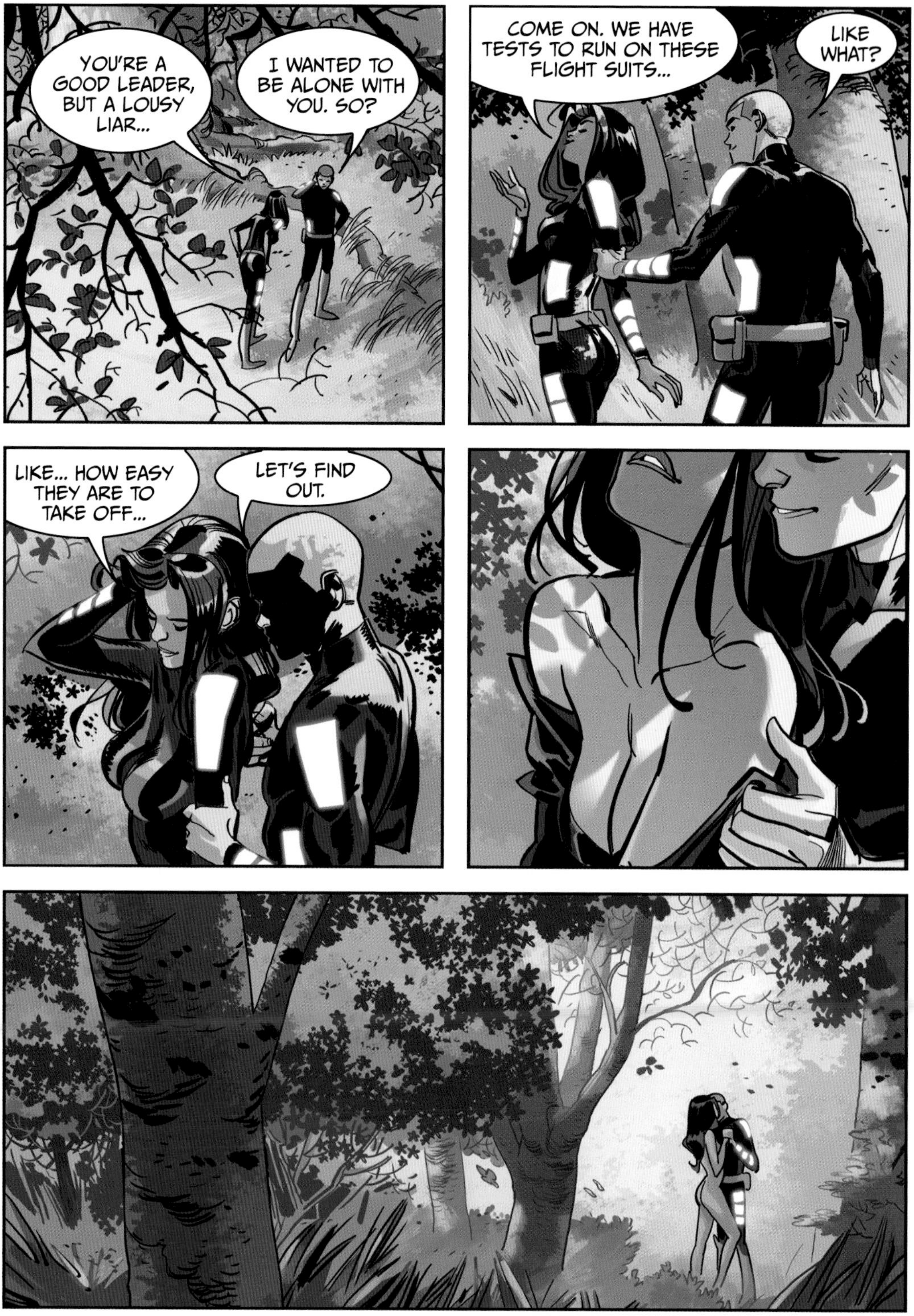
YOU'RE A GOOD LEADER, BUT A LOUSY LIAR...
I WANTED TO BE ALONE WITH YOU. SO?
COME ON. WE HAVE TESTS TO RUN ON THESE FLIGHT SUITS...
LIKE WHAT?
LIKE... HOW EASY THEY ARE TO TAKE OFF...
LET'S FIND OUT.

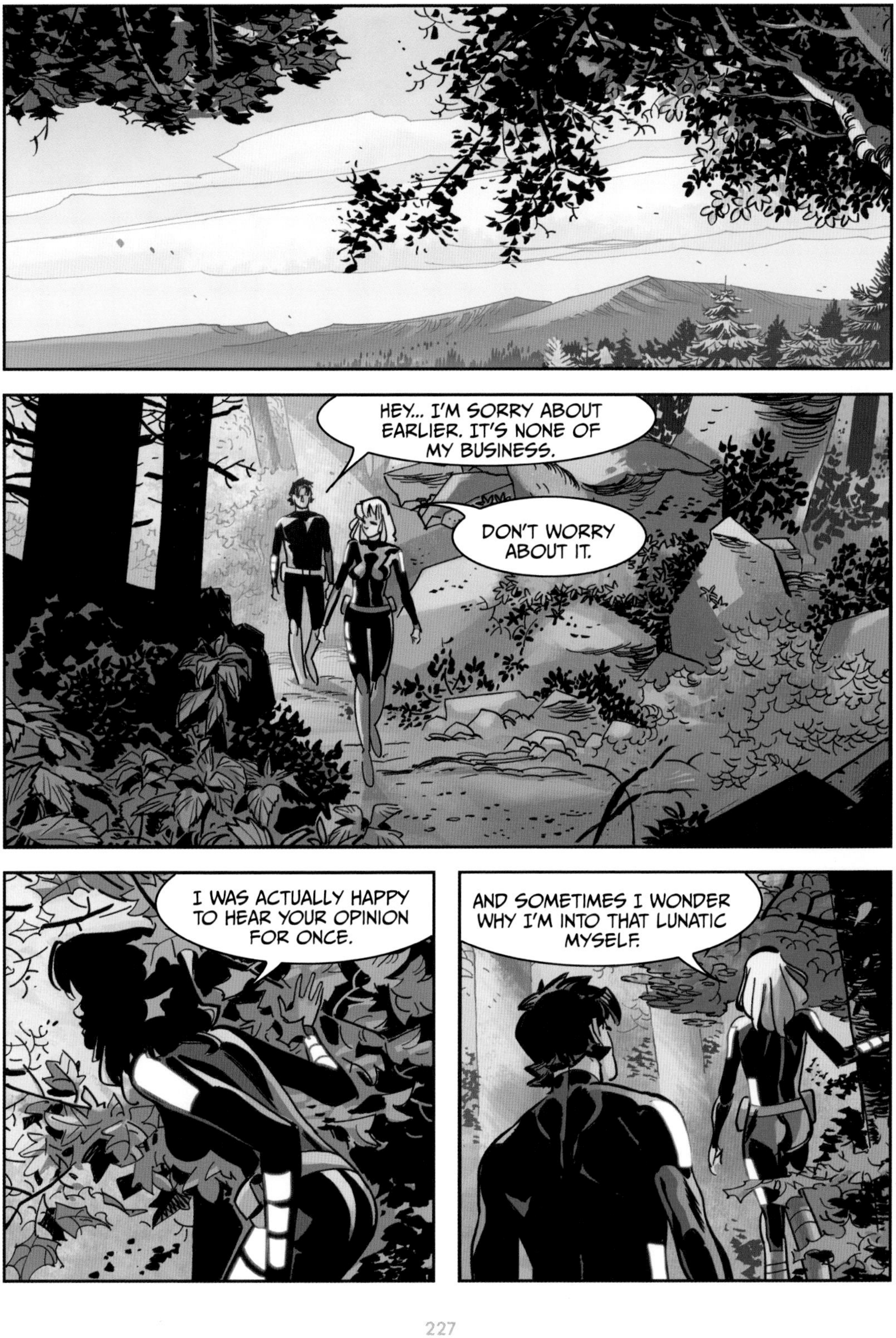
HEY... I'M SORRY ABOUT EARLIER. IT'S NONE OF MY BUSINESS.
DON'T WORRY ABOUT IT.
I WAS ACTUALLY HAPPY TO HEAR YOUR OPINION FOR ONCE.
AND SOMETIMES I WONDER WHY I'M INTO THAT LUNATIC MYSELF.

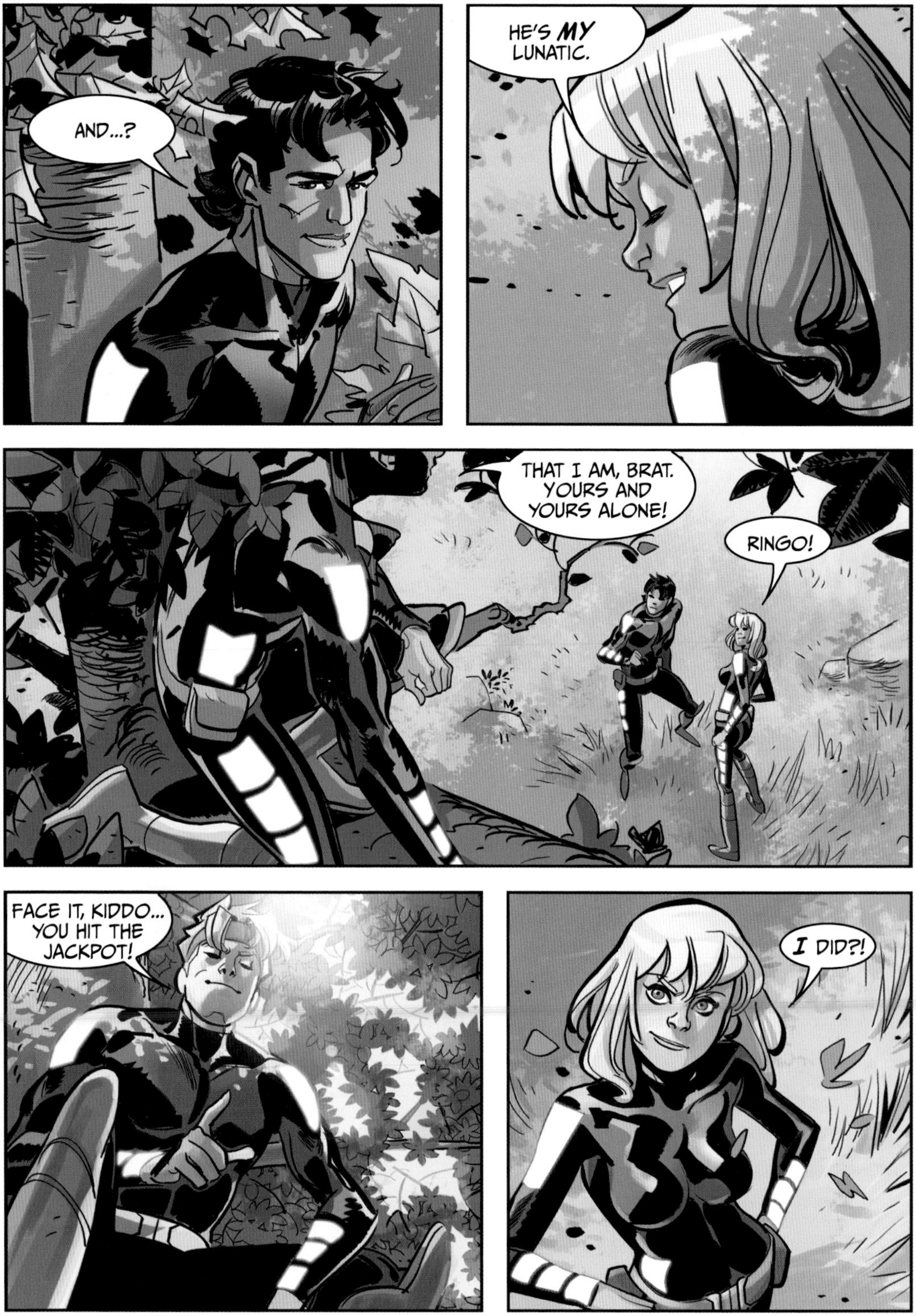
AND...?
HE'S *MY* LUNATIC.
THAT I AM, BRAT. YOURS AND YOURS ALONE!
RINGO!
FACE IT, KIDDO... YOU HIT THE JACKPOT!
I DID?!

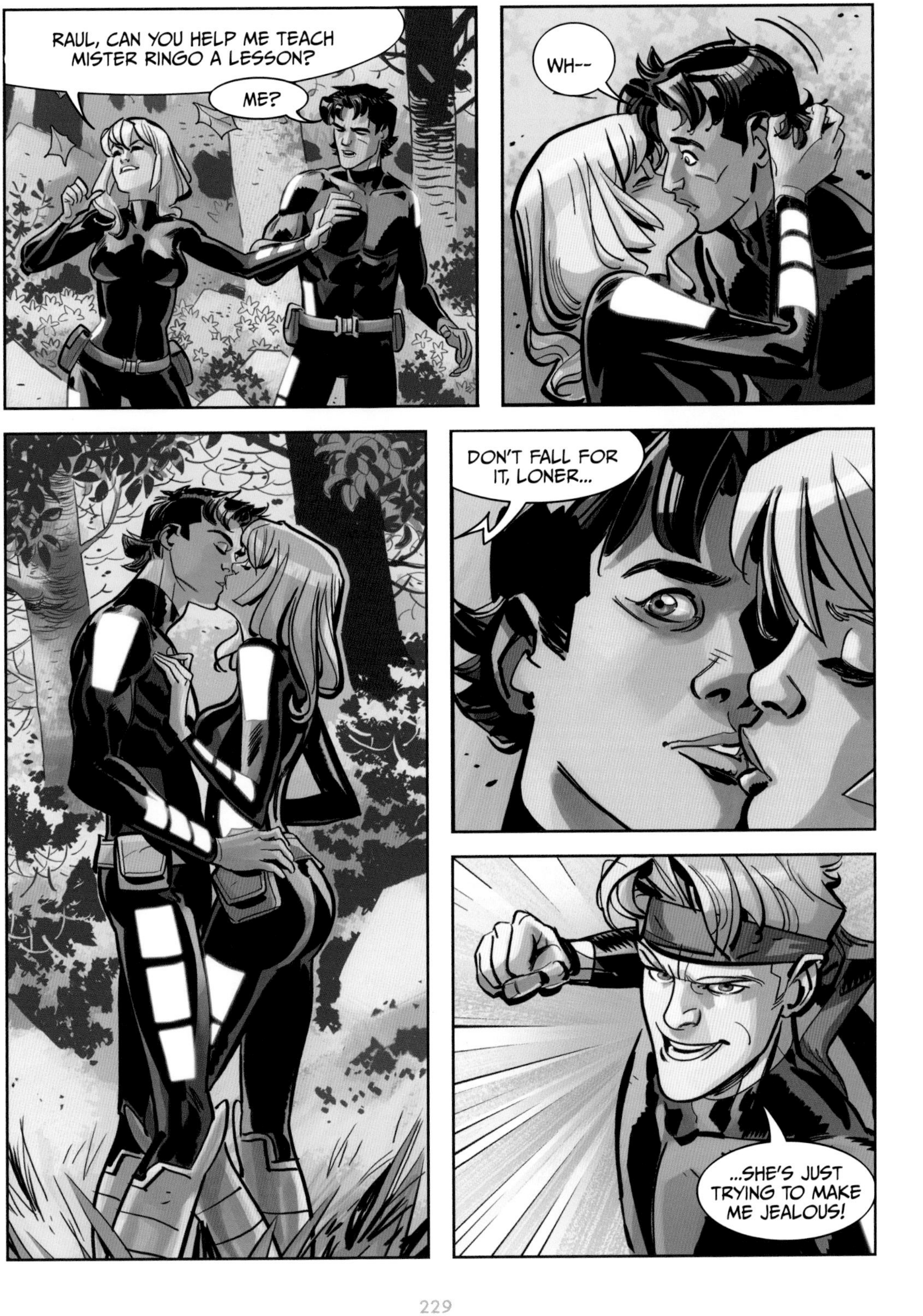
RAUL, CAN YOU HELP ME TEACH MISTER RINGO A LESSON?
ME?
WH--
DON'T FALL FOR IT, LONER...
...SHE'S JUST TRYING TO MAKE ME JEALOUS!

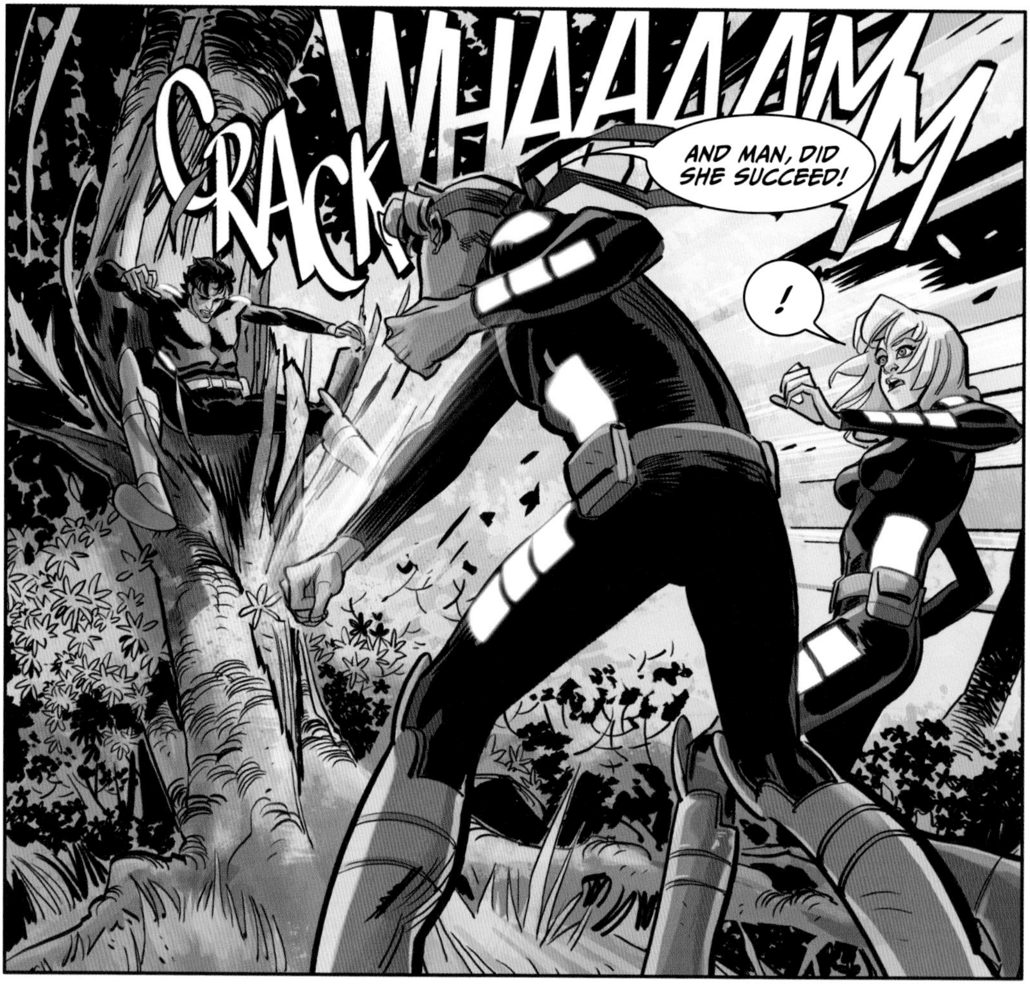
CRACK
WHAAAAM
AND MAN, DID SHE SUCCEED!
!

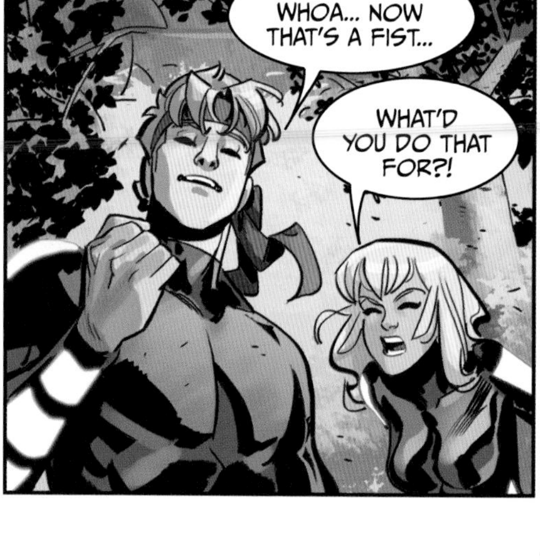
WHOA... NOW THAT'S A FIST...
WHAT'D YOU DO THAT FOR?!

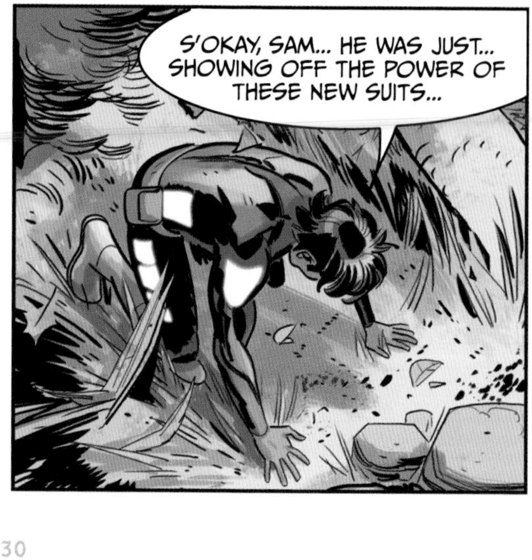
S'OKAY, SAM... HE WAS JUST... SHOWING OFF THE POWER OF THESE NEW SUITS...

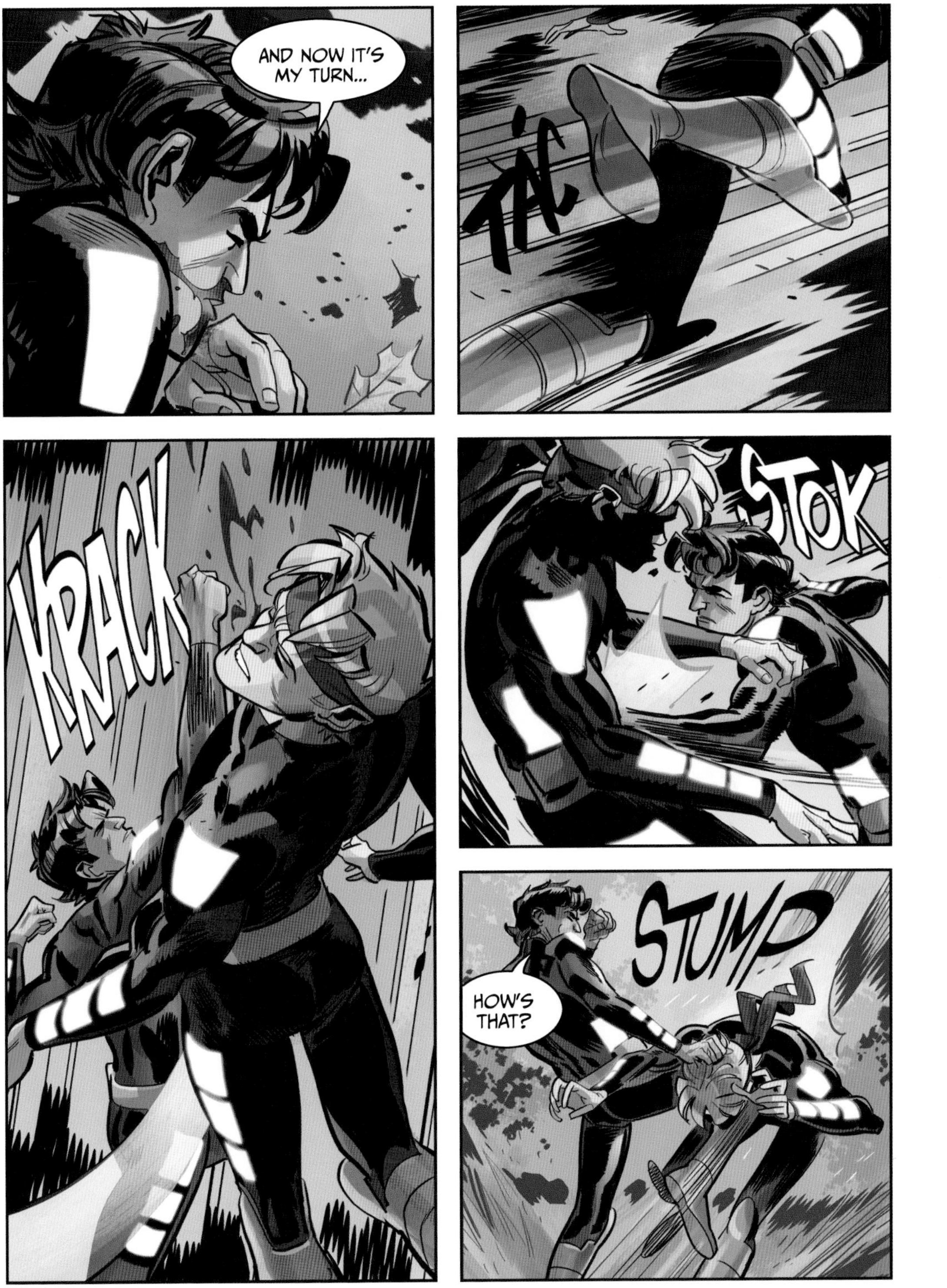
AND NOW IT'S MY TURN...
TAC
KRACK
STOK
STUMP
HOW'S THAT?

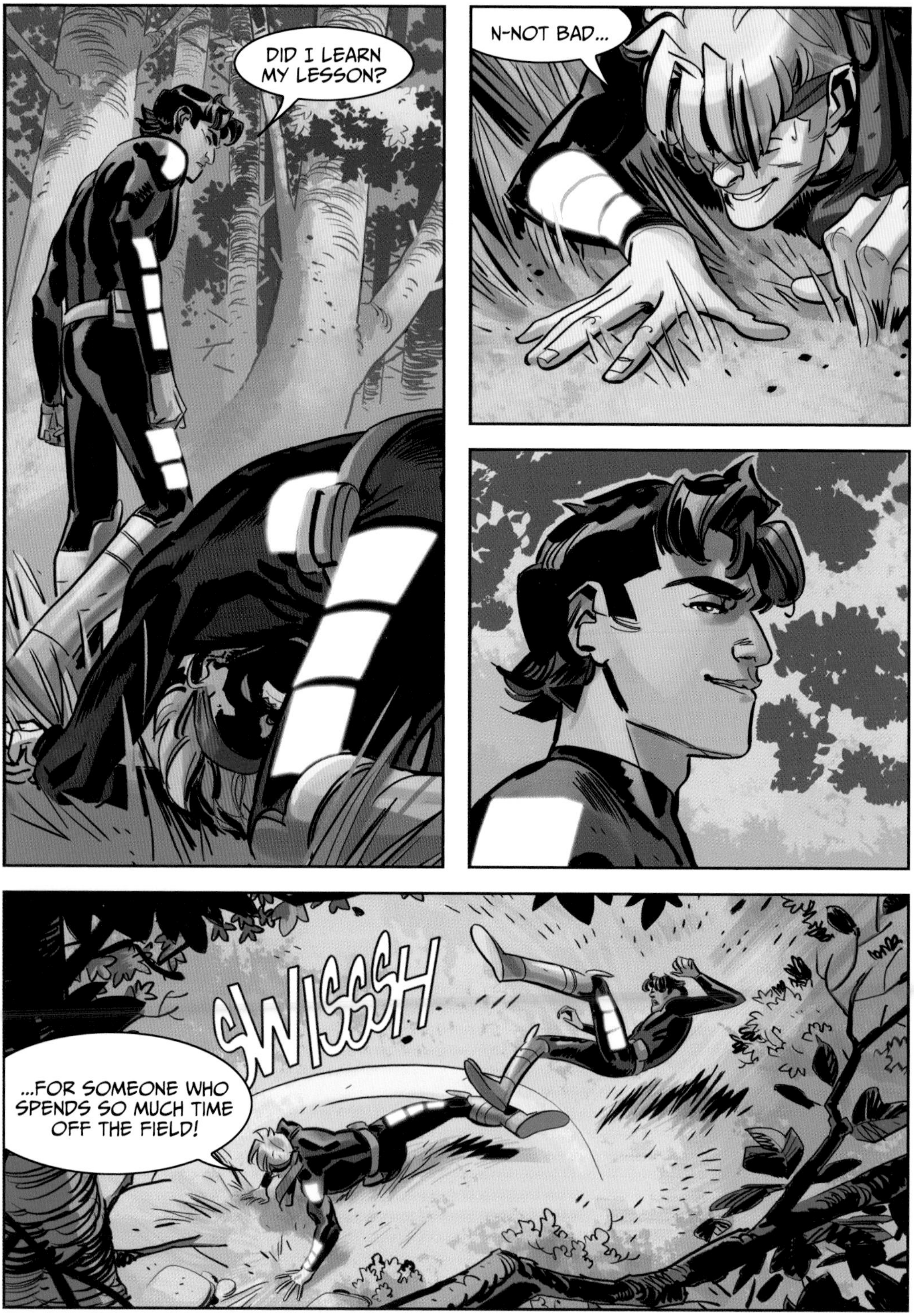
DID I LEARN MY LESSON?
N-NOT BAD...
SWISSSH
...FOR SOMEONE WHO SPENDS SO MUCH TIME OFF THE FIELD!

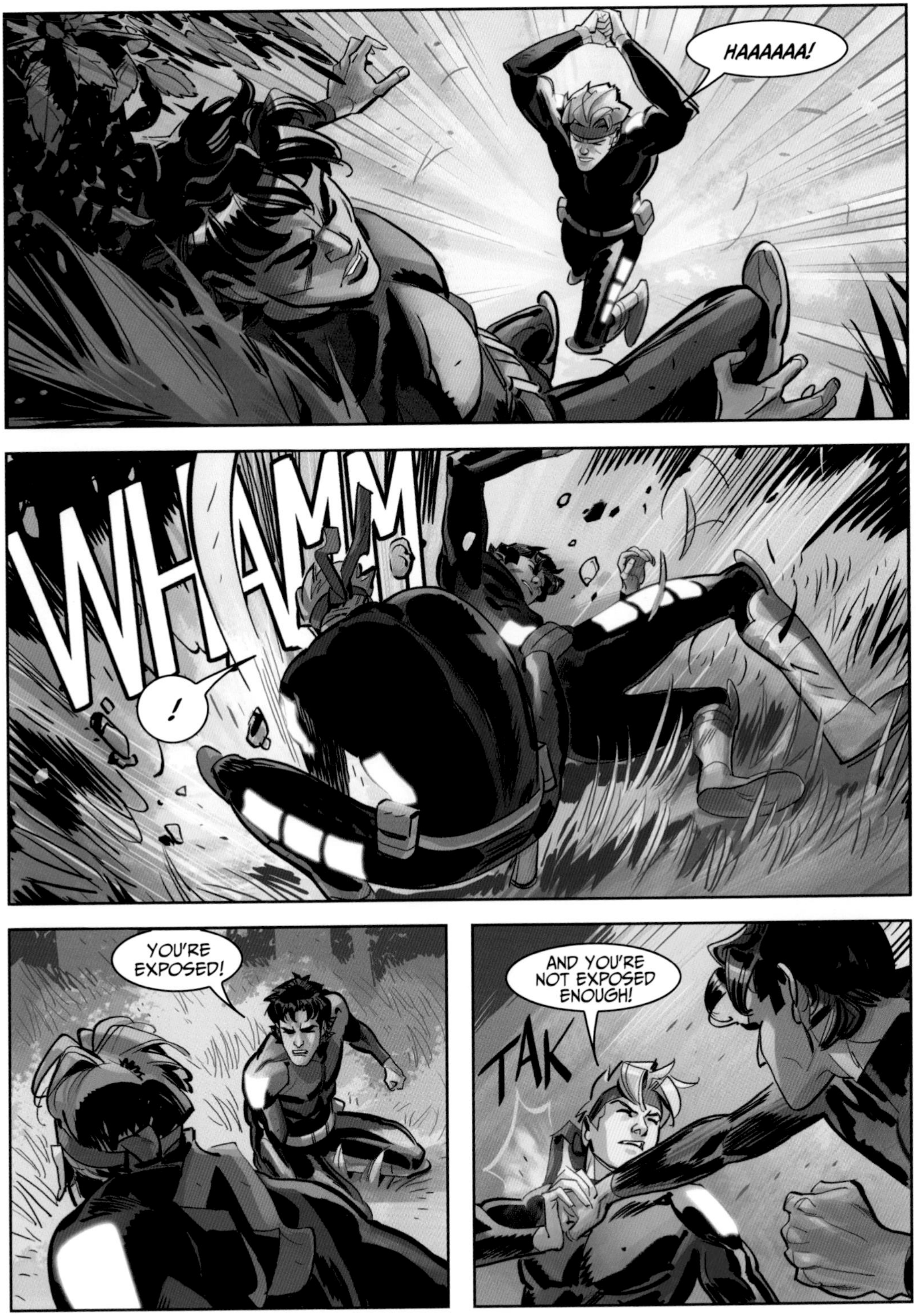
HAAAAAA!
WHAMM
!
YOU'RE EXPOSED!
AND YOU'RE NOT EXPOSED ENOUGH!
TAK

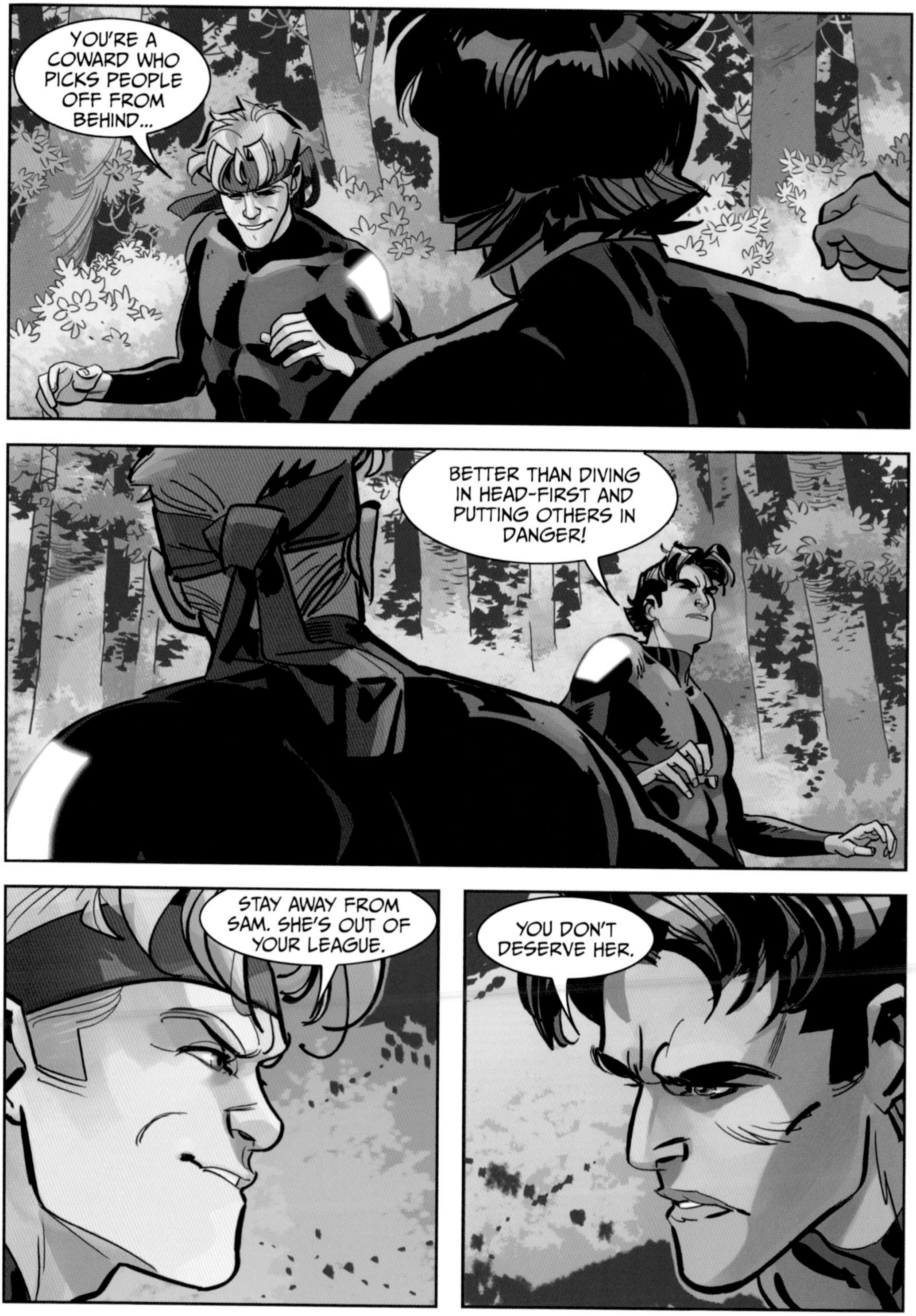
YOU'RE A COWARD WHO PICKS PEOPLE OFF FROM BEHIND...
BETTER THAN DIVING IN HEAD-FIRST AND PUTTING OTHERS IN DANGER!
STAY AWAY FROM SAM. SHE'S OUT OF YOUR LEAGUE.
YOU DON'T DESERVE HER.

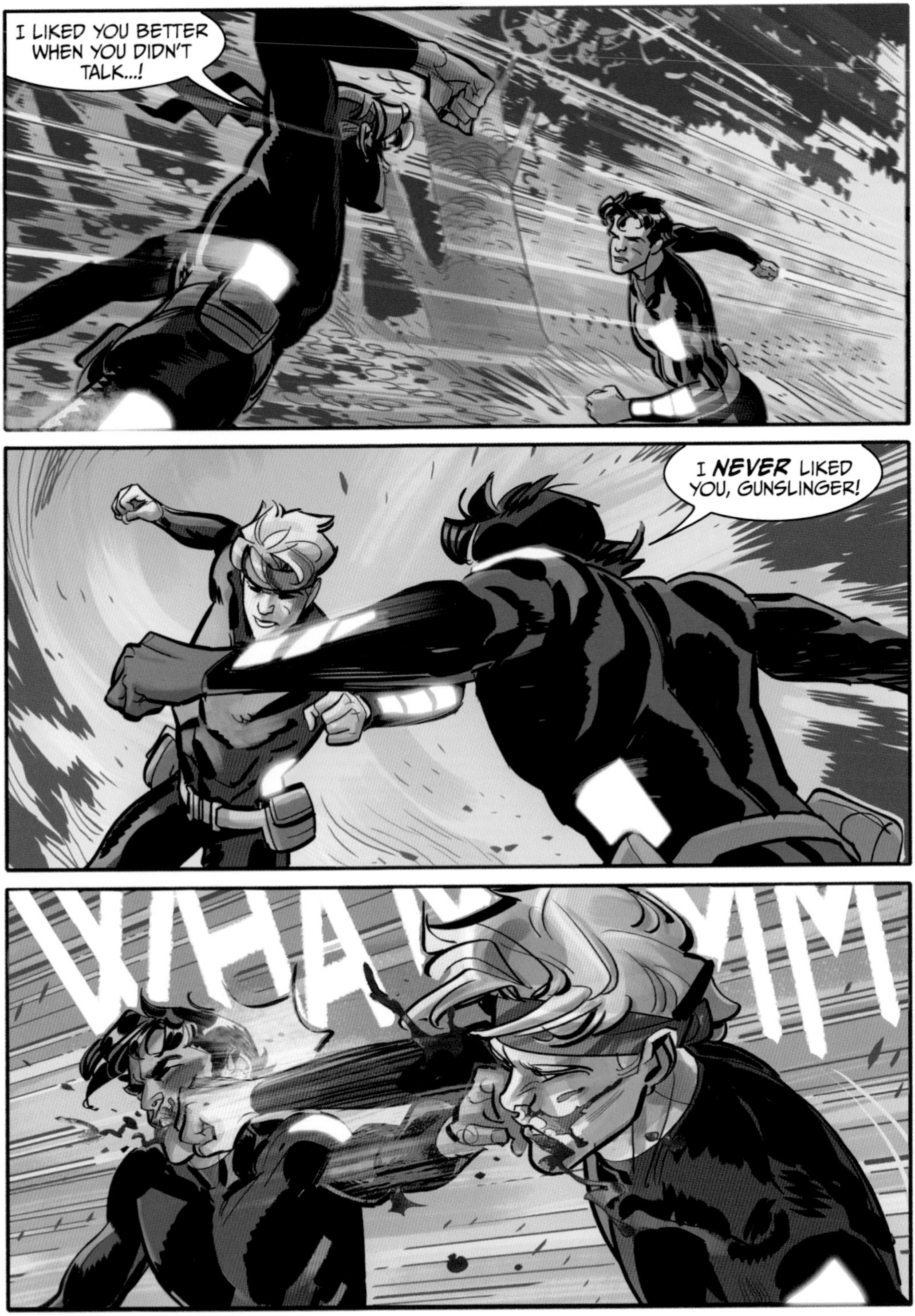
I LIKED YOU BETTER WHEN YOU DIDN'T TALK...!
I **NEVER** LIKED YOU, GUNSLINGER!

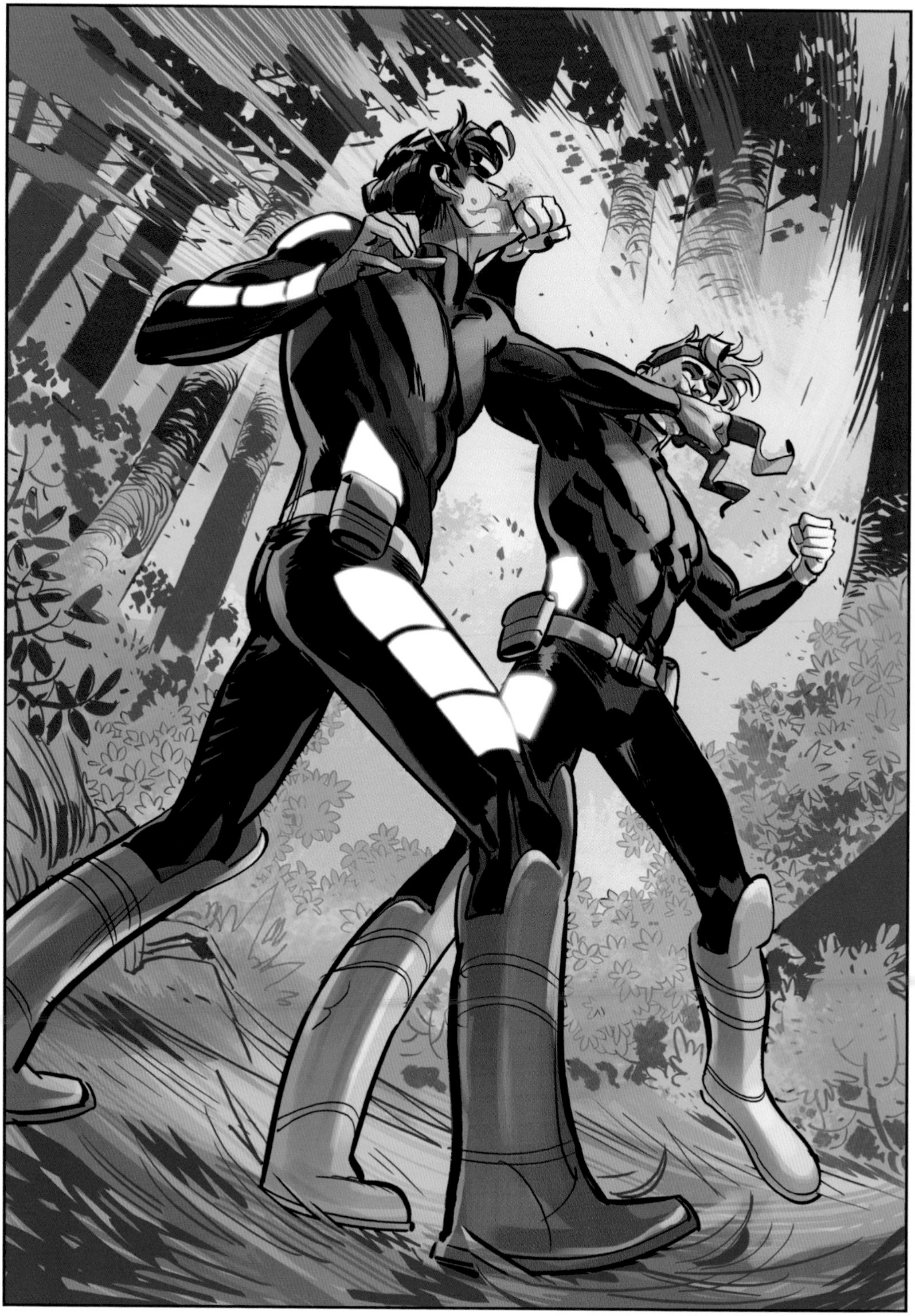

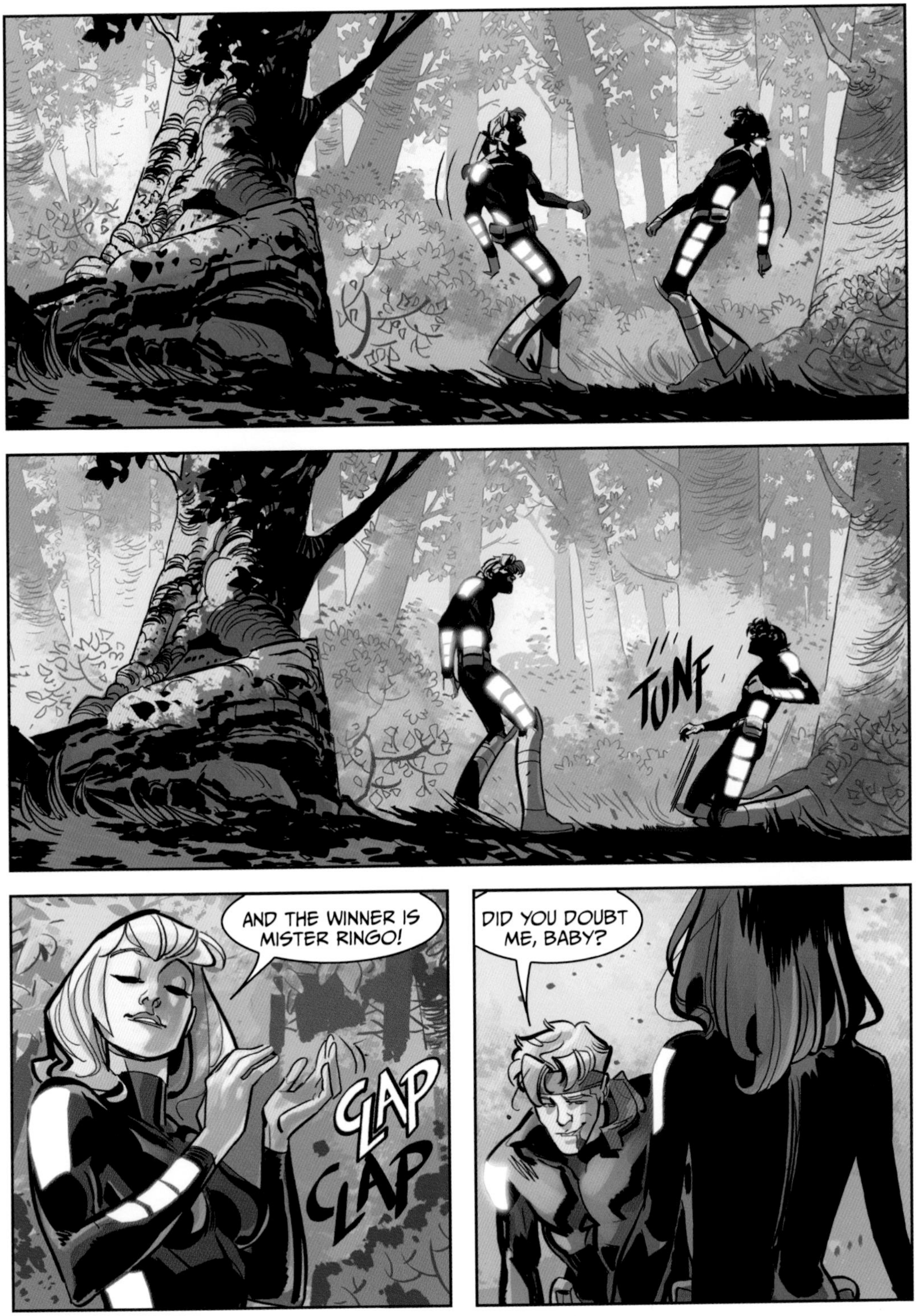
TUNF
AND THE WINNER IS MISTER RINGO!
CLAP
CLAP
DID YOU DOUBT ME, BABY?

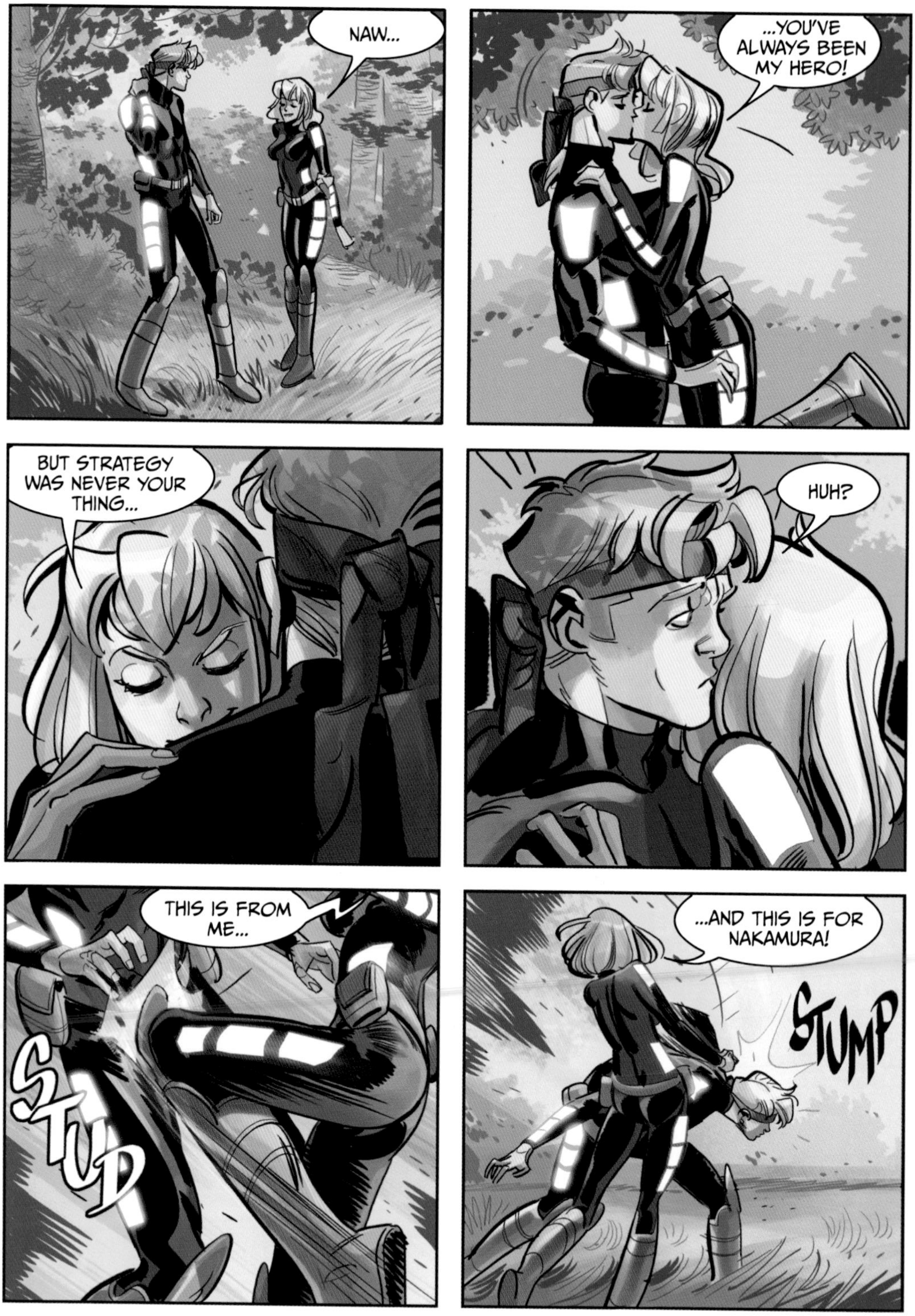
NAW...
...YOU'VE ALWAYS BEEN MY HERO!
BUT STRATEGY WAS NEVER YOUR THING...
HUH?
THIS IS FROM ME...
STUD
...AND THIS IS FOR NAKAMURA!
STUMP

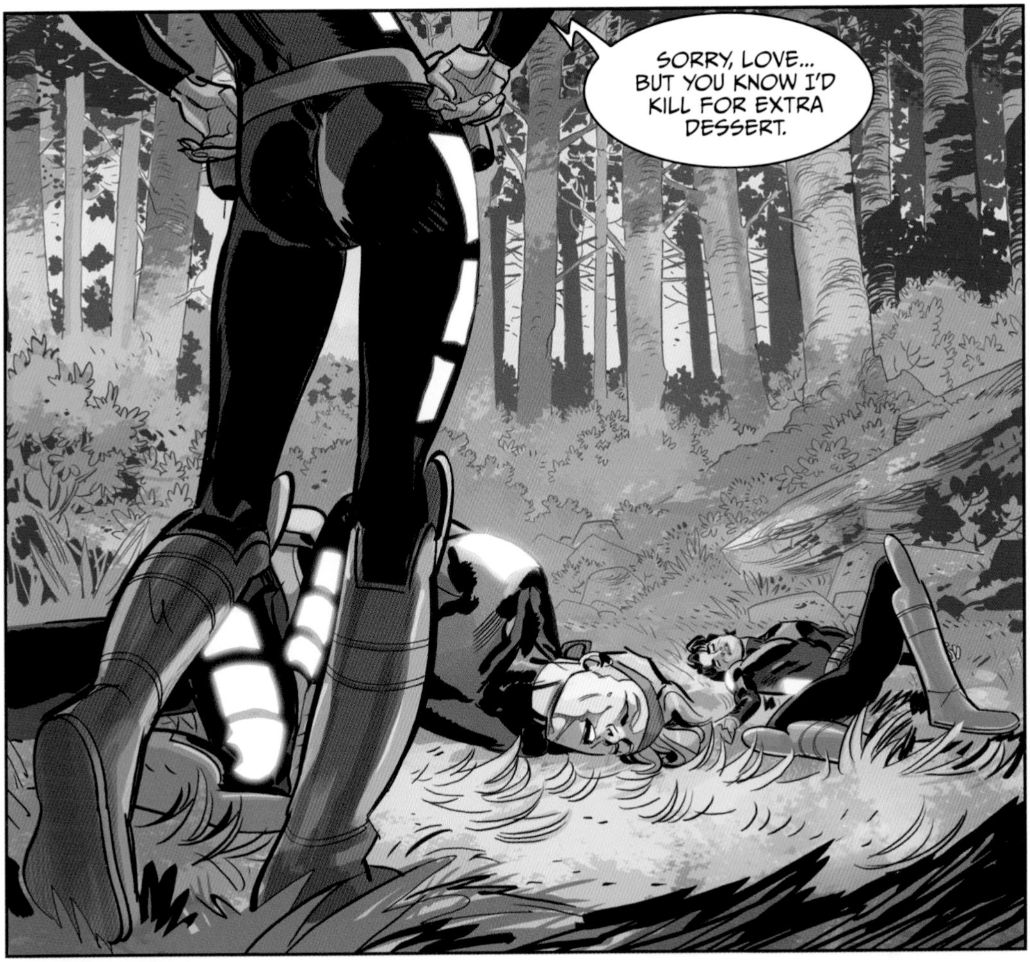
SORRY, LOVE...
BUT YOU KNOW I'D
KILL FOR EXTRA
DESSERT.

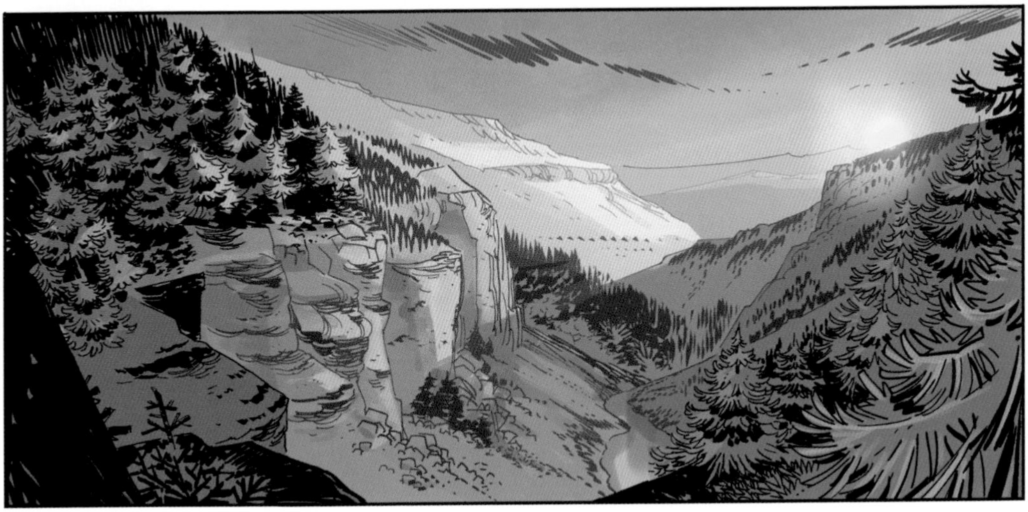

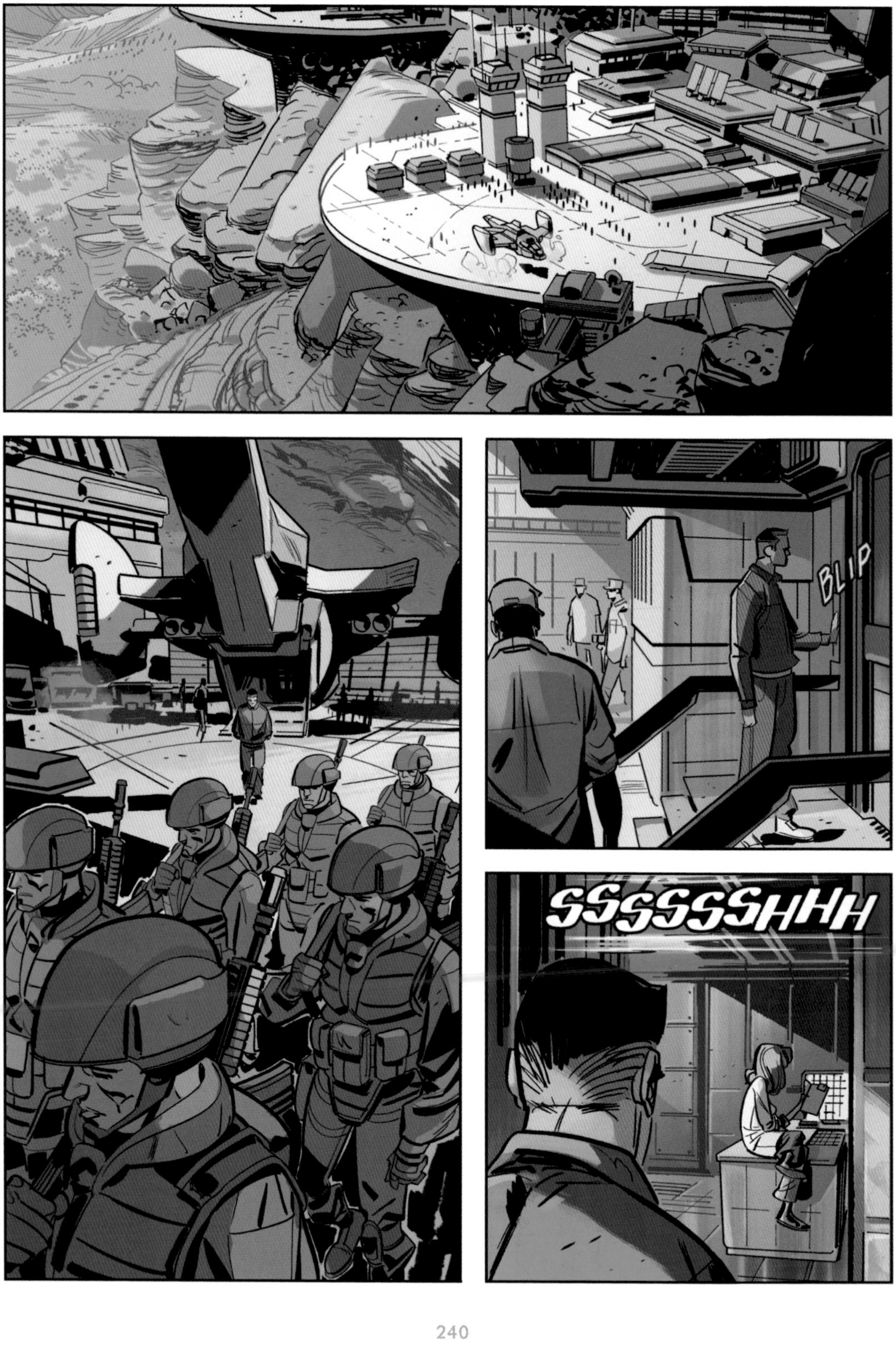
BLIP
SSSSSSHHH

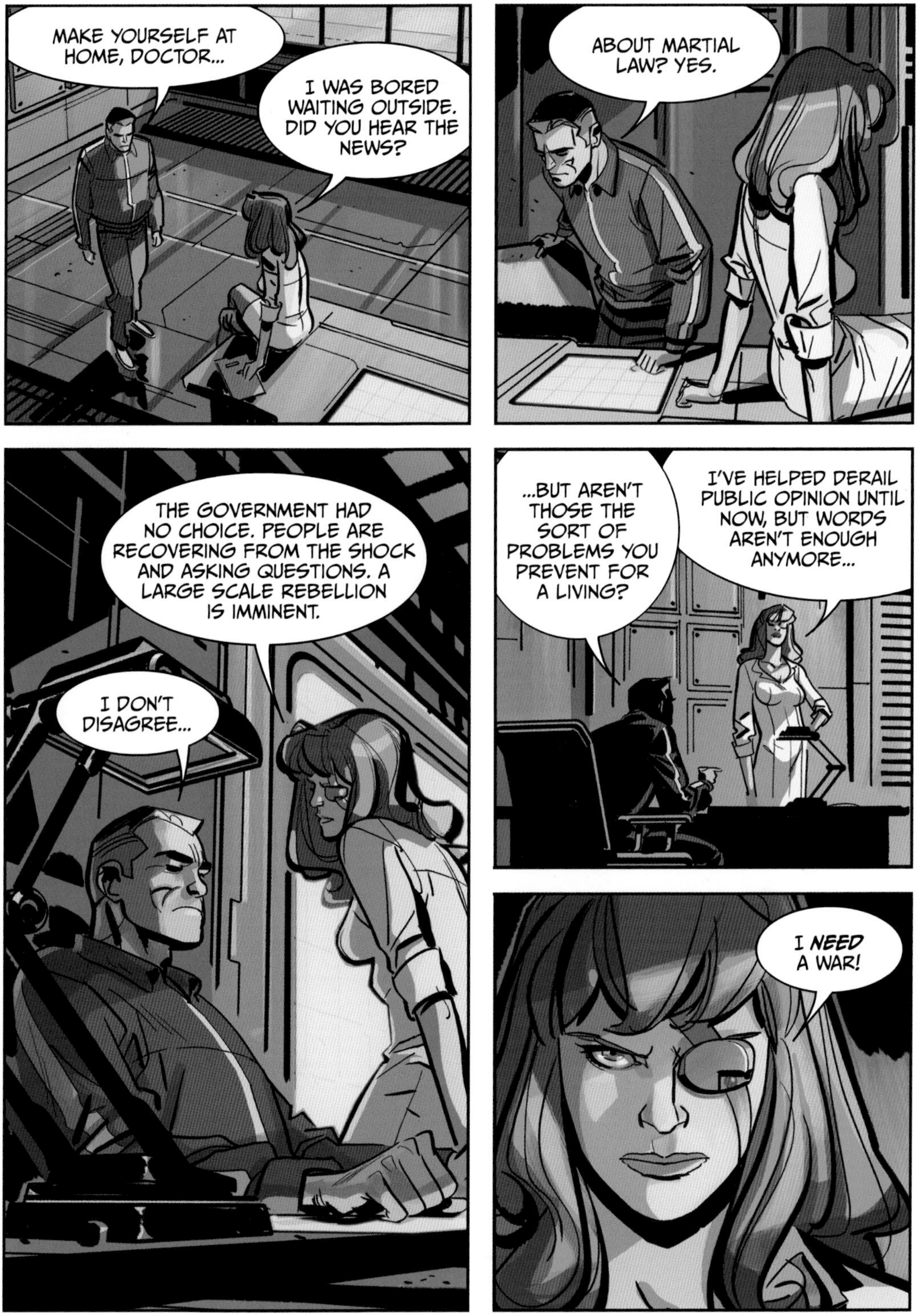
MAKE YOURSELF AT HOME, DOCTOR...
I WAS BORED WAITING OUTSIDE. DID YOU HEAR THE NEWS?
ABOUT MARTIAL LAW? YES.
THE GOVERNMENT HAD NO CHOICE. PEOPLE ARE RECOVERING FROM THE SHOCK AND ASKING QUESTIONS. A LARGE SCALE REBELLION IS IMMINENT.
I DON'T DISAGREE...
...BUT AREN'T THOSE THE SORT OF PROBLEMS YOU PREVENT FOR A LIVING?
I'VE HELPED DERAIL PUBLIC OPINION UNTIL NOW, BUT WORDS AREN'T ENOUGH ANYMORE...
I *NEED* A WAR!

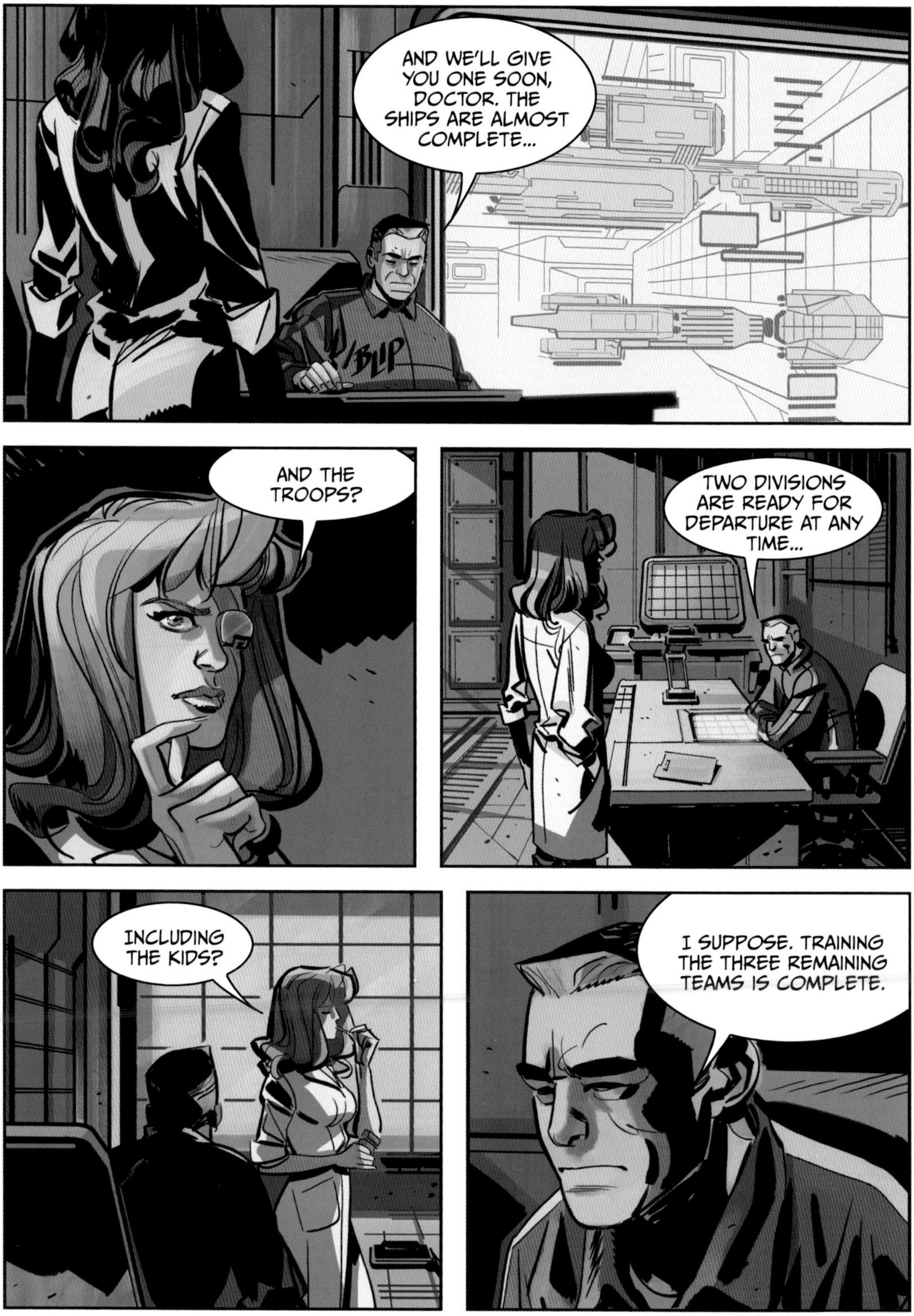
AND WE'LL GIVE YOU ONE SOON, DOCTOR. THE SHIPS ARE ALMOST COMPLETE...
BLIP
AND THE TROOPS?
TWO DIVISIONS ARE READY FOR DEPARTURE AT ANY TIME...
INCLUDING THE KIDS?
I SUPPOSE. TRAINING THE THREE REMAINING TEAMS IS COMPLETE.

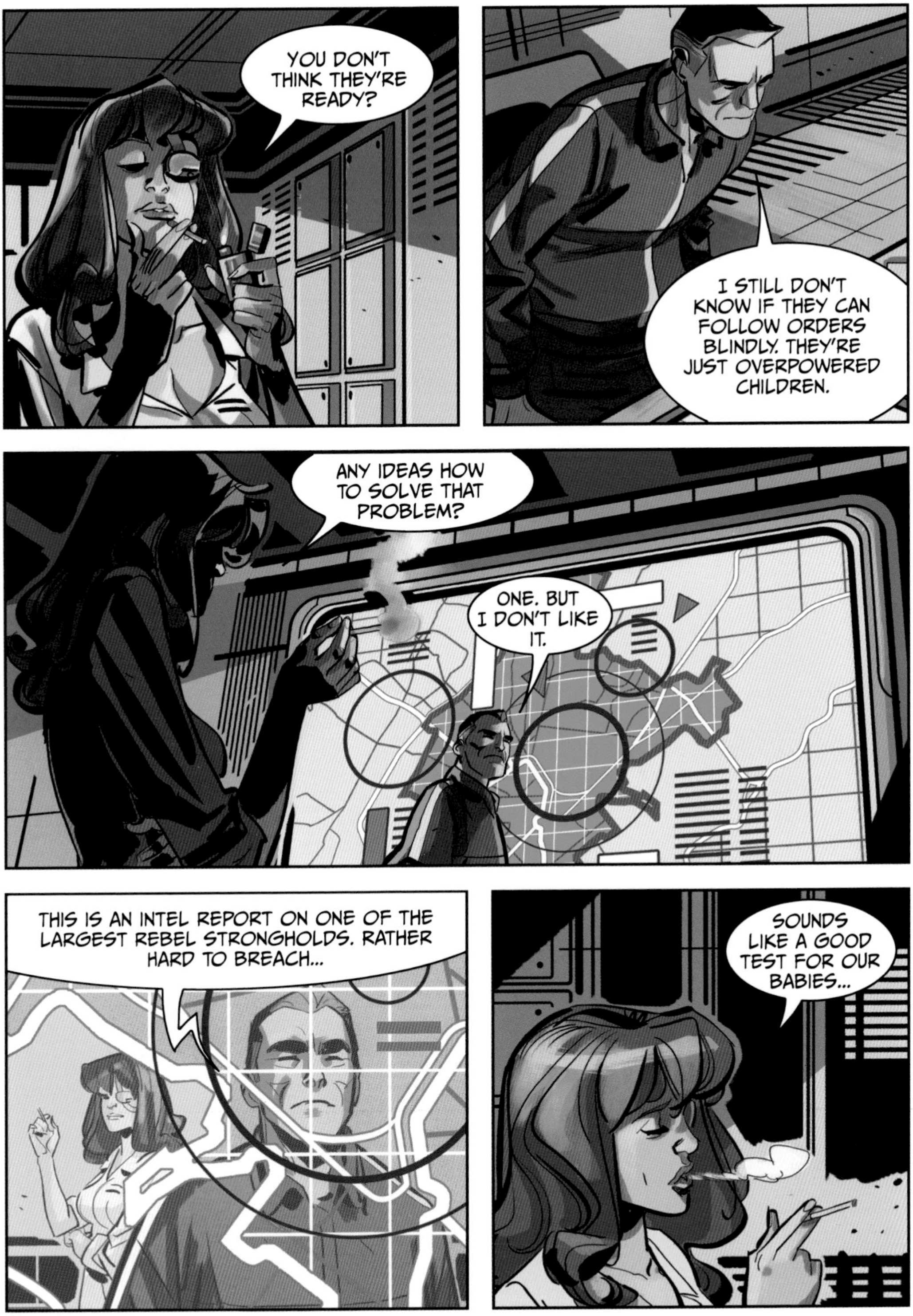
YOU DON'T THINK THEY'RE READY?
I STILL DON'T KNOW IF THEY CAN FOLLOW ORDERS BLINDLY. THEY'RE JUST OVERPOWERED CHILDREN.
ANY IDEAS HOW TO SOLVE THAT PROBLEM?
ONE. BUT I DON'T LIKE IT.
THIS IS AN INTEL REPORT ON ONE OF THE LARGEST REBEL STRONGHOLDS. RATHER HARD TO BREACH...
SOUNDS LIKE A GOOD TEST FOR OUR BABIES...

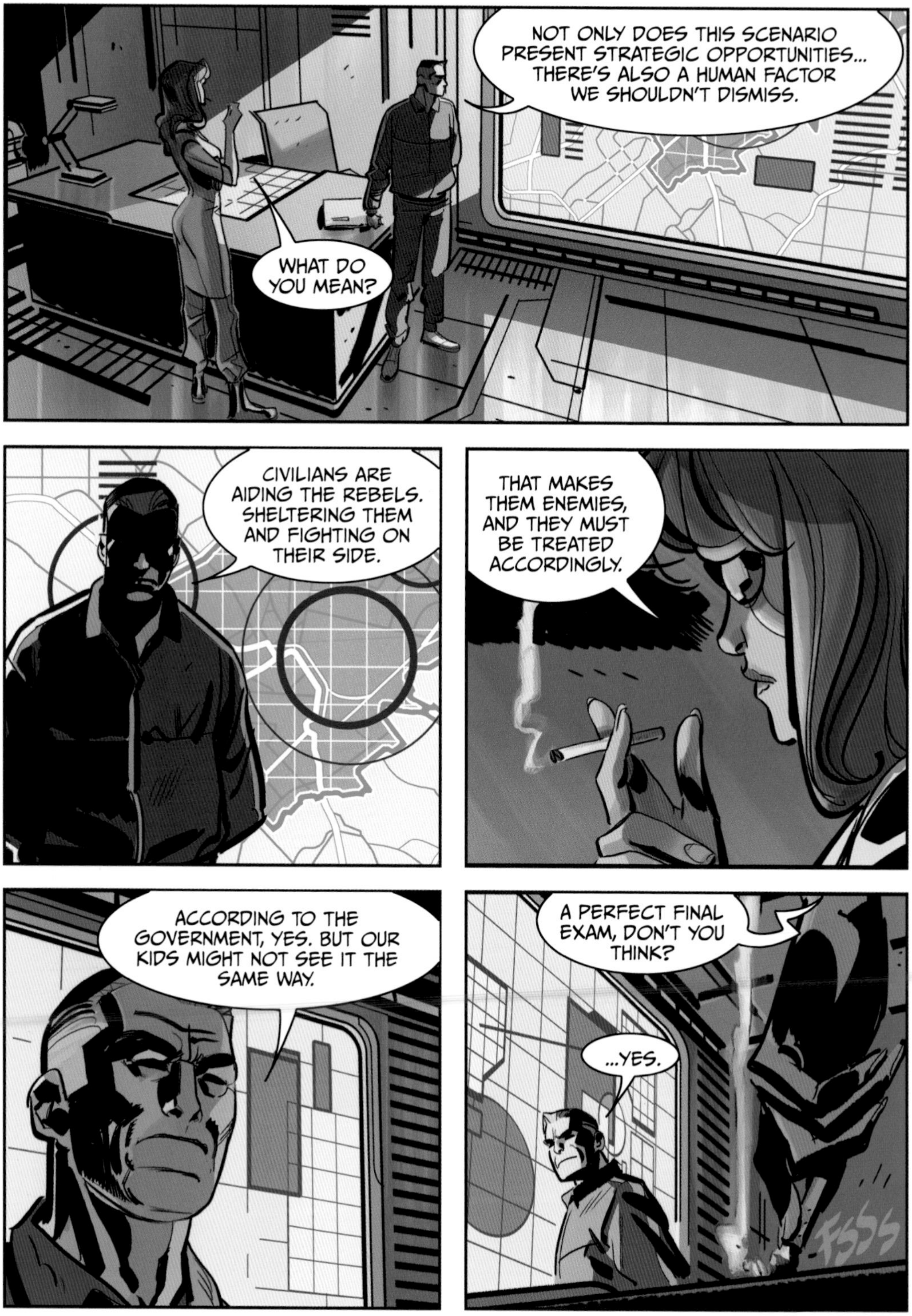
NOT ONLY DOES THIS SCENARIO PRESENT STRATEGIC OPPORTUNITIES... THERE'S ALSO A HUMAN FACTOR WE SHOULDN'T DISMISS.
WHAT DO YOU MEAN?
CIVILIANS ARE AIDING THE REBELS. SHELTERING THEM AND FIGHTING ON THEIR SIDE.
THAT MAKES THEM ENEMIES, AND THEY MUST BE TREATED ACCORDINGLY.
ACCORDING TO THE GOVERNMENT, YES. BUT OUR KIDS MIGHT NOT SEE IT THE SAME WAY.
A PERFECT FINAL EXAM, DON'T YOU THINK?
...YES.
FSSS

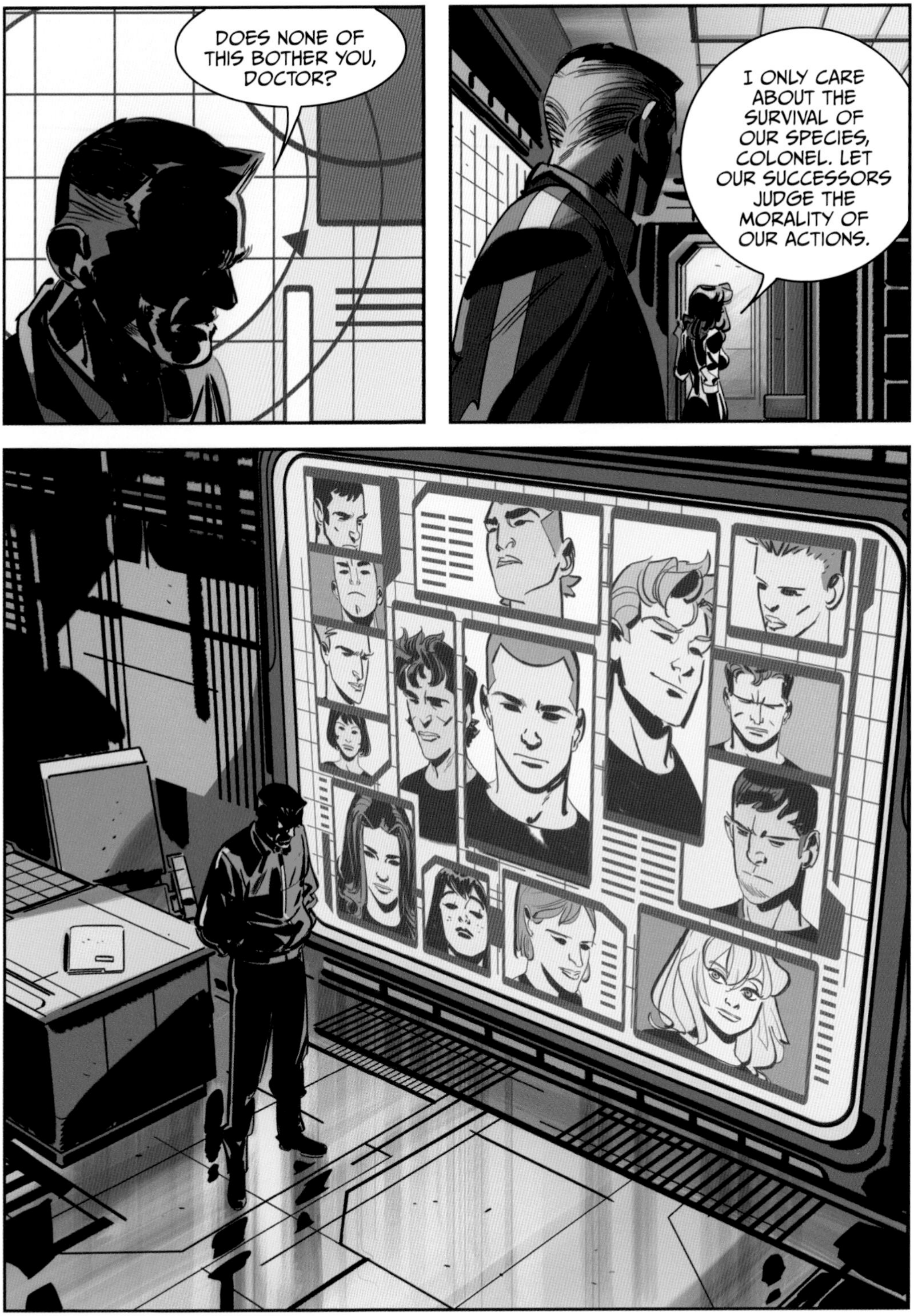
DOES NONE OF THIS BOTHER YOU, DOCTOR?
I ONLY CARE ABOUT THE SURVIVAL OF OUR SPECIES, COLONEL. LET OUR SUCCESSORS JUDGE THE MORALITY OF OUR ACTIONS.

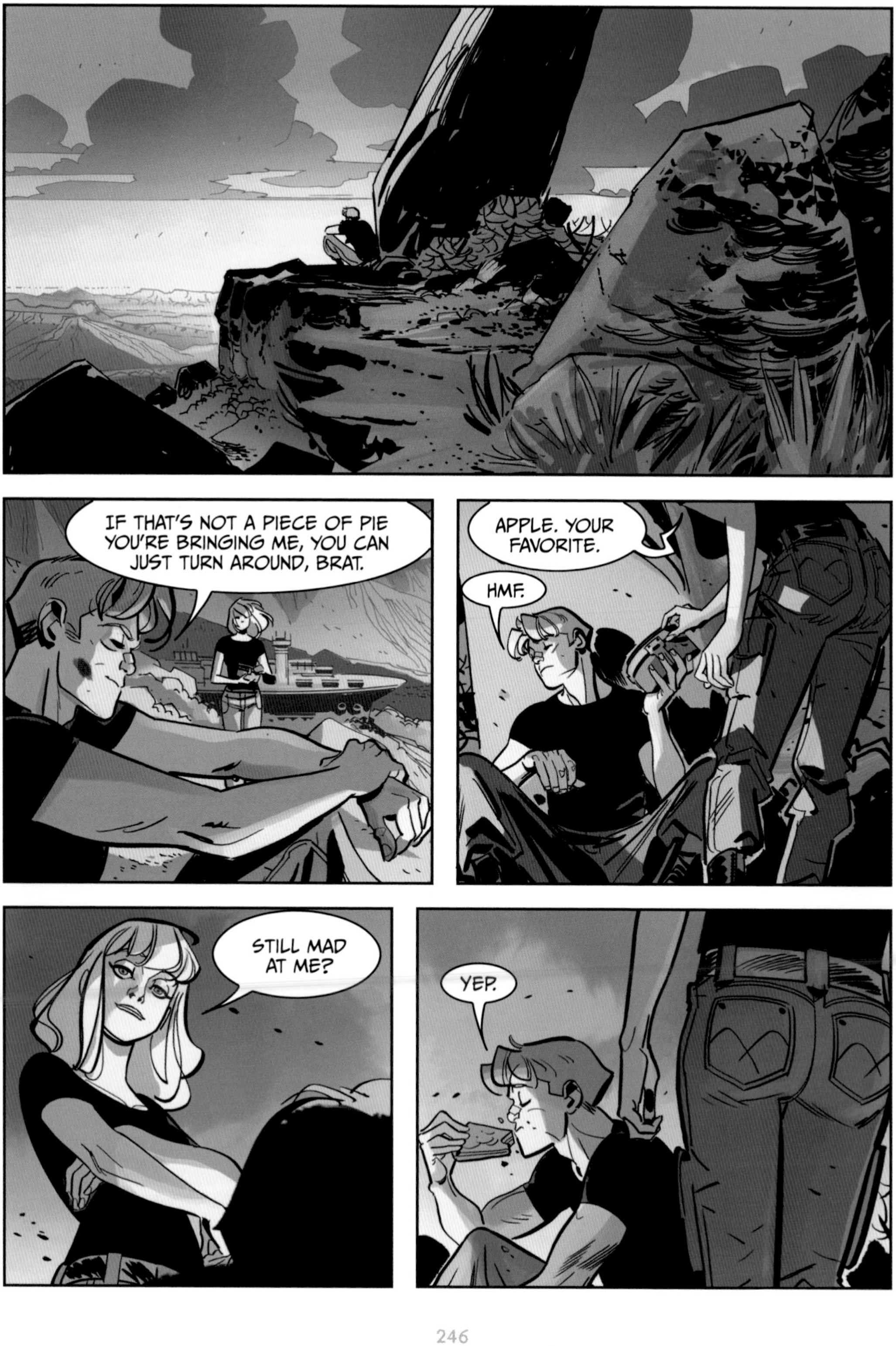
IF THAT'S NOT A PIECE OF PIE YOU'RE BRINGING ME, YOU CAN JUST TURN AROUND, BRAT.
APPLE. YOUR FAVORITE.
HMF.
STILL MAD AT ME?
YEP.

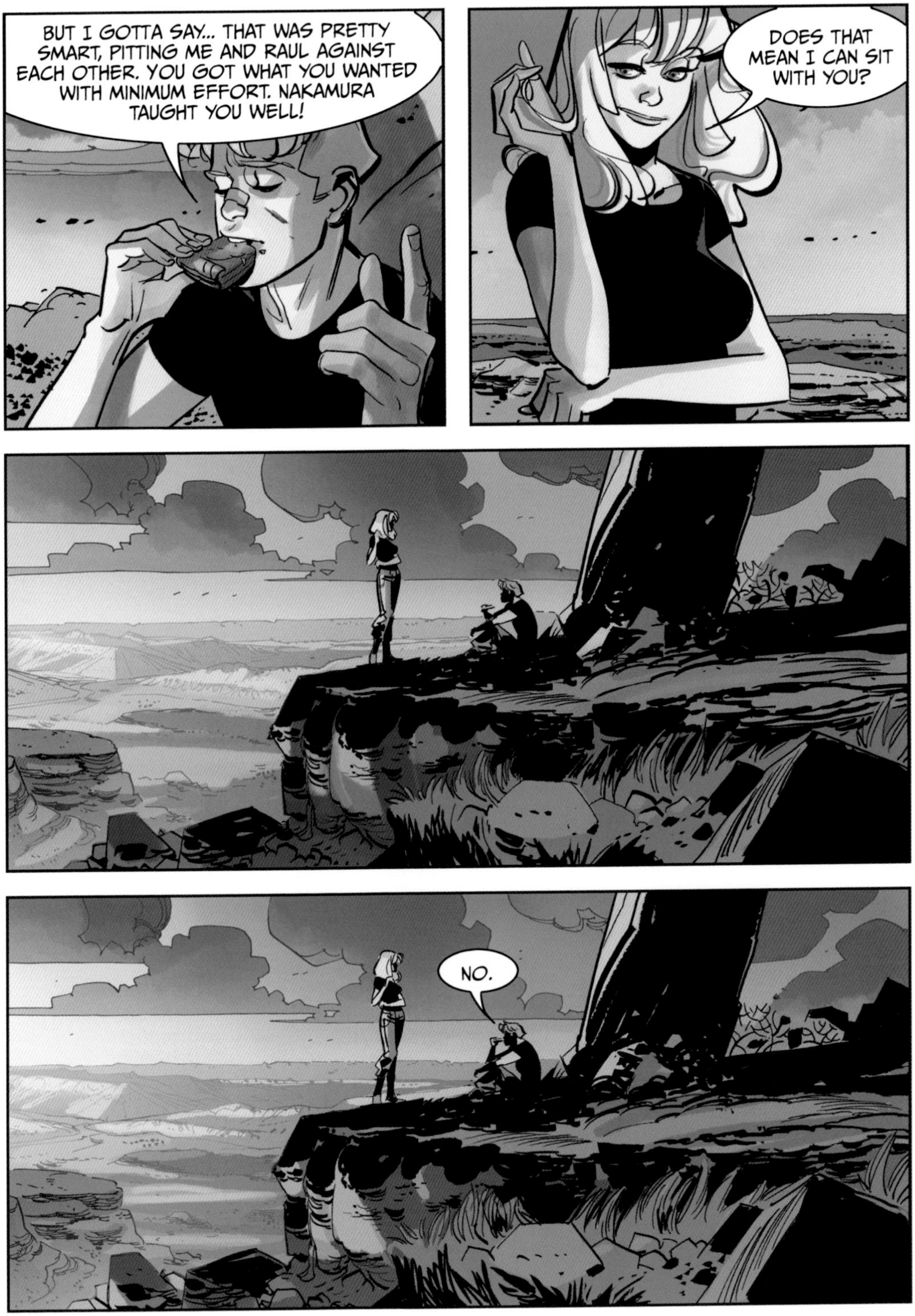
BUT I GOTTA SAY... THAT WAS PRETTY SMART, PITTING ME AND RAUL AGAINST EACH OTHER. YOU GOT WHAT YOU WANTED WITH MINIMUM EFFORT. NAKAMURA TAUGHT YOU WELL!
DOES THAT MEAN I CAN SIT WITH YOU?
NO.

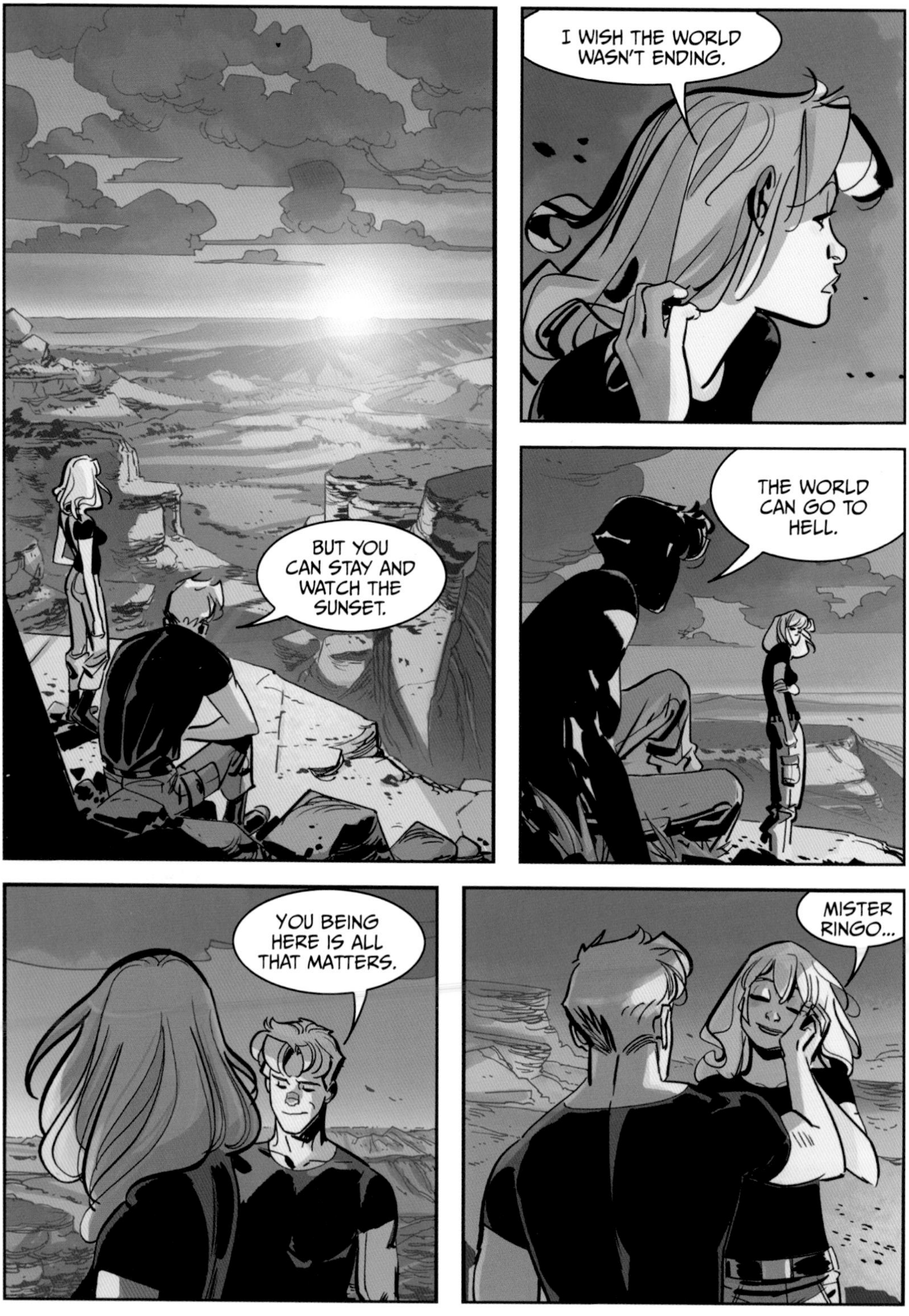
BUT YOU CAN STAY AND WATCH THE SUNSET.
I WISH THE WORLD WASN'T ENDING.
THE WORLD CAN GO TO HELL.
YOU BEING HERE IS ALL THAT MATTERS.
MISTER RINGO...

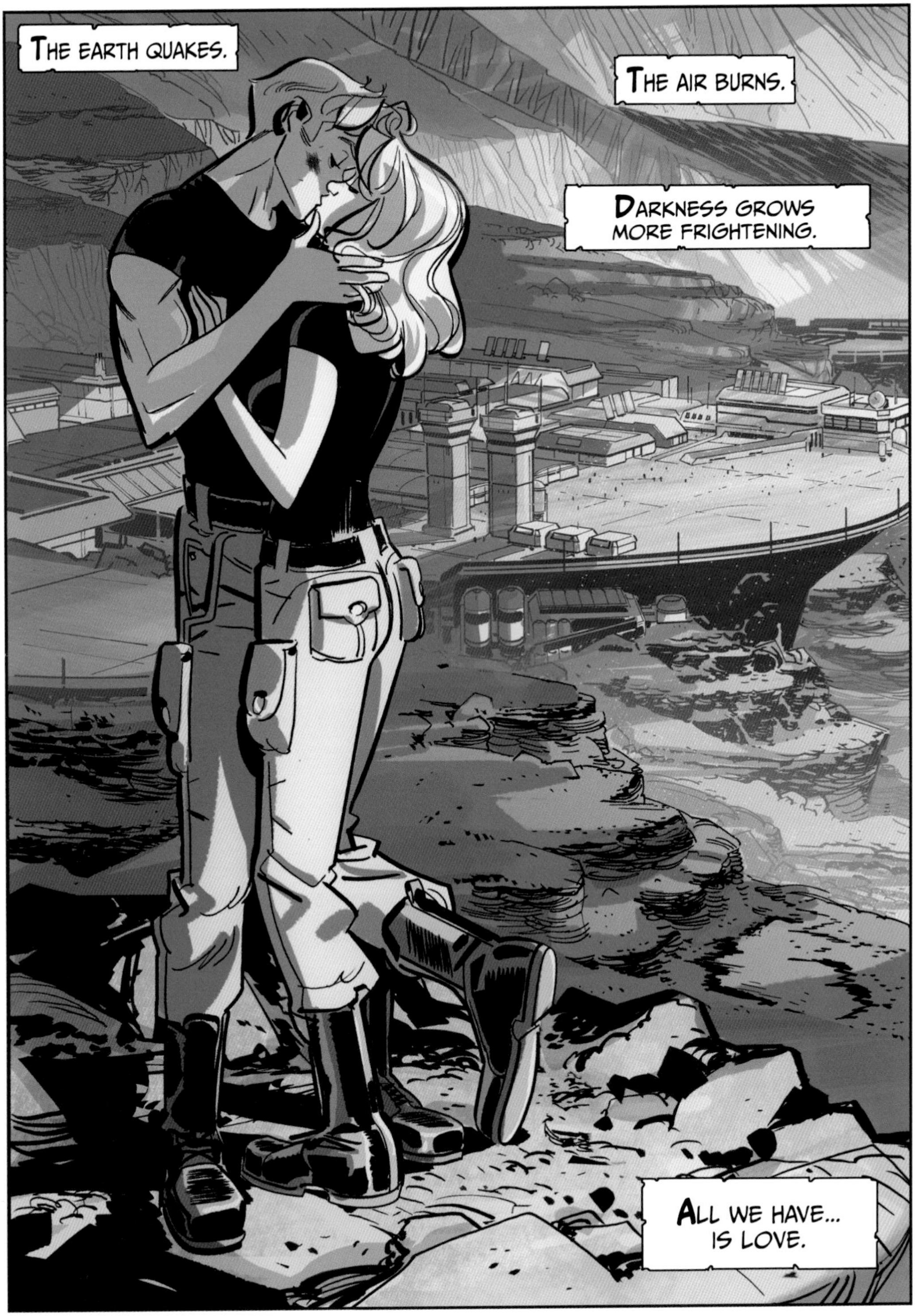
The earth quakes.
The air burns.
Darkness grows more frightening.
All we have... is love.

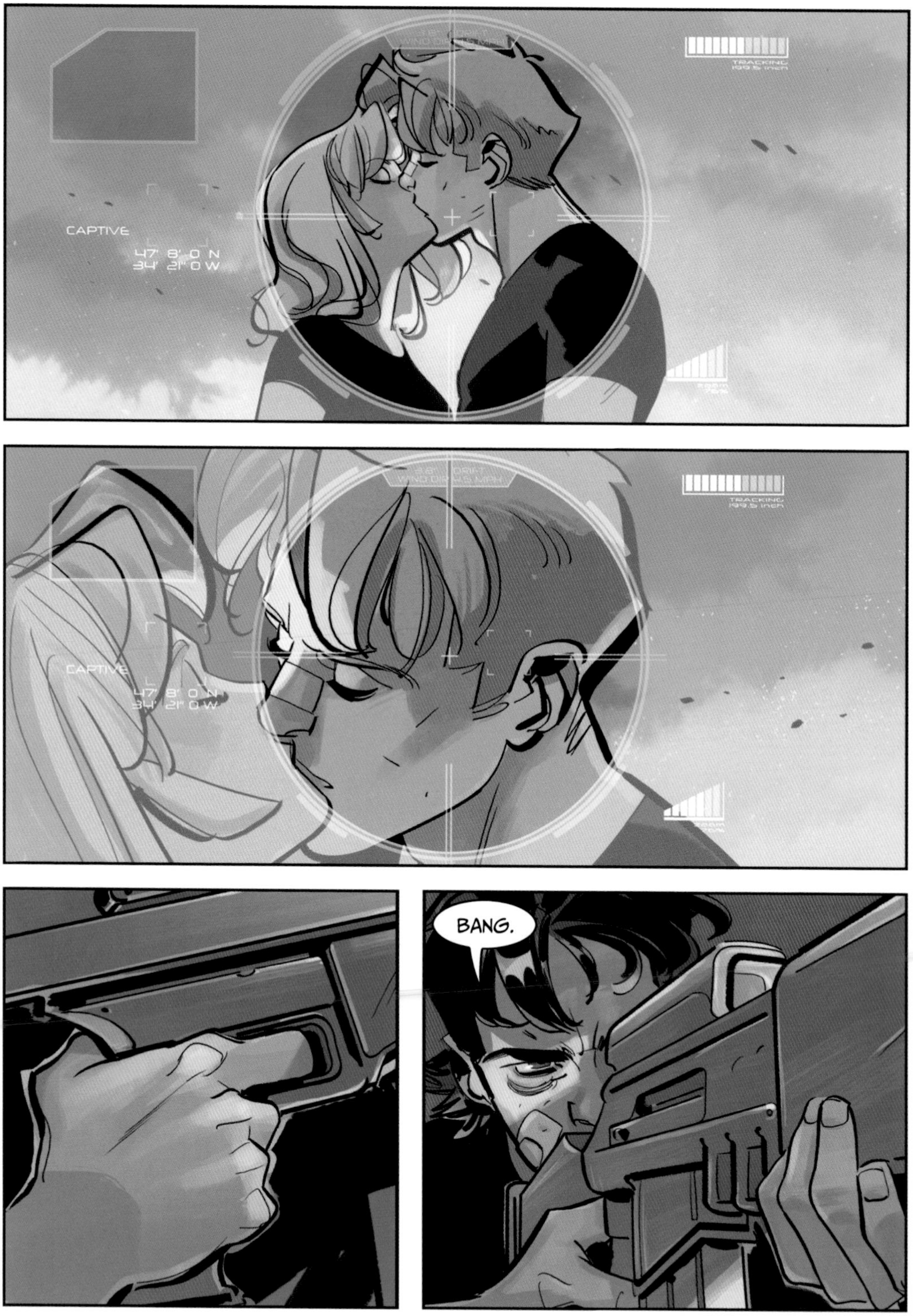
TRACKING
199.5 inch
CAPTIVE
47' 8' 0 N
34' 21" 0 W
TRACKING
199.5 inch
CAPTIVE
47' 8' 0 N
34' 21" 0 W
BANG.

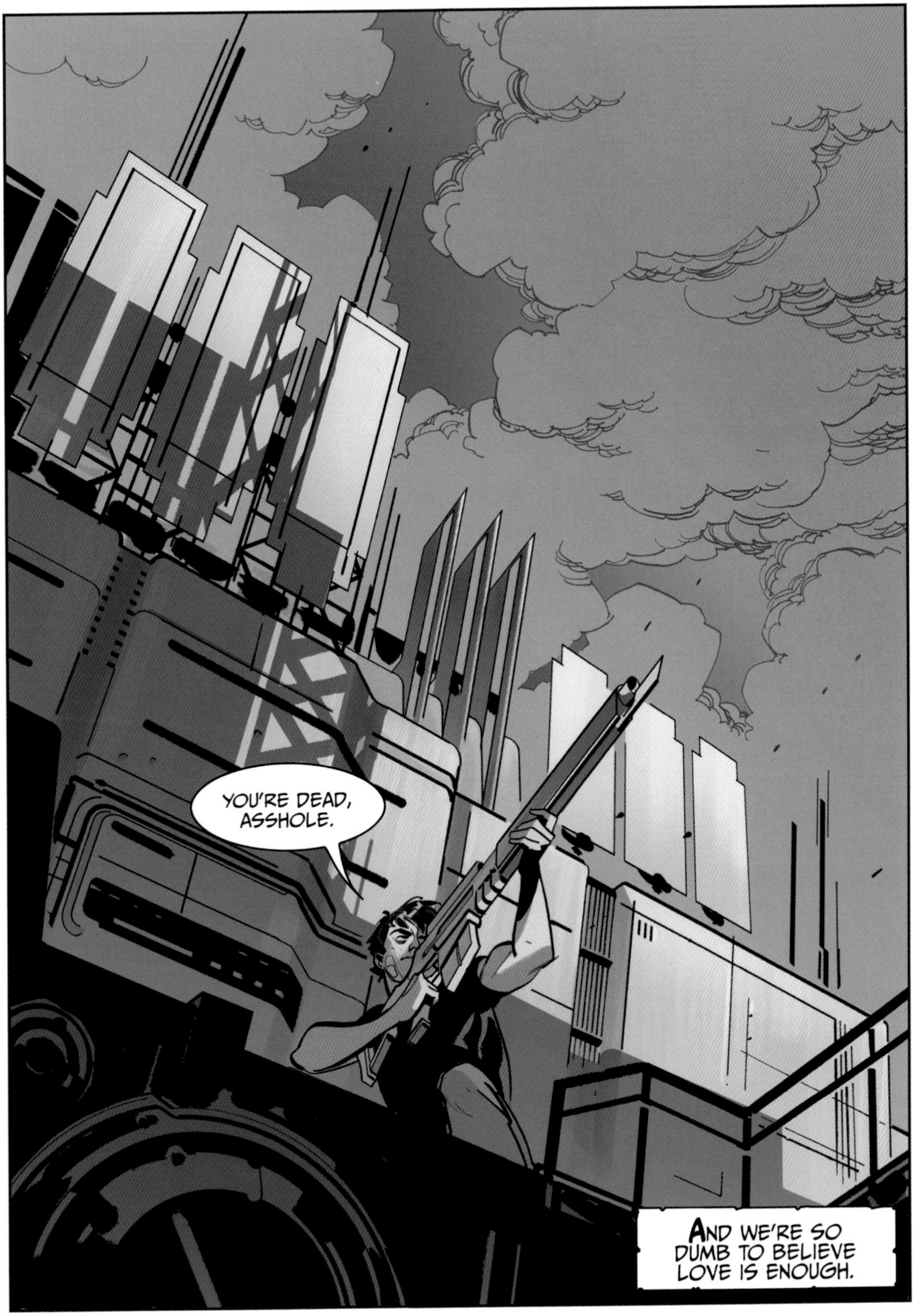
YOU'RE DEAD, ASSHOLE.
AND WE'RE SO DUMB TO BELIEVE LOVE IS ENOUGH.

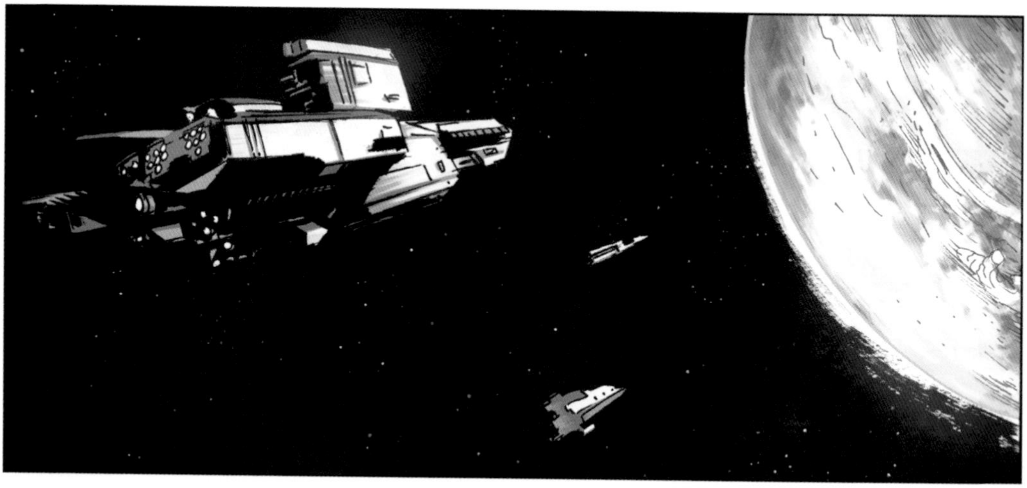

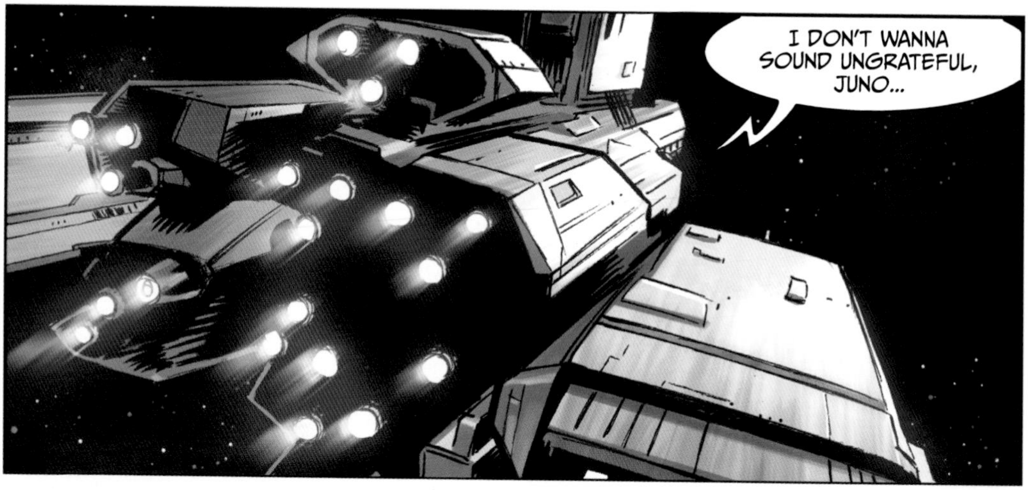
I DON'T WANNA SOUND UNGRATEFUL, JUNO...

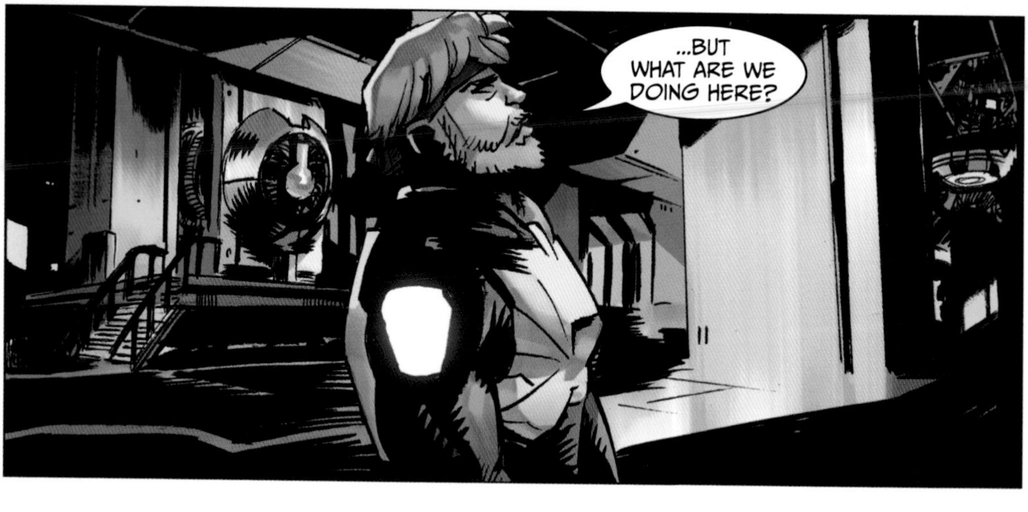
...BUT WHAT ARE WE DOING HERE?

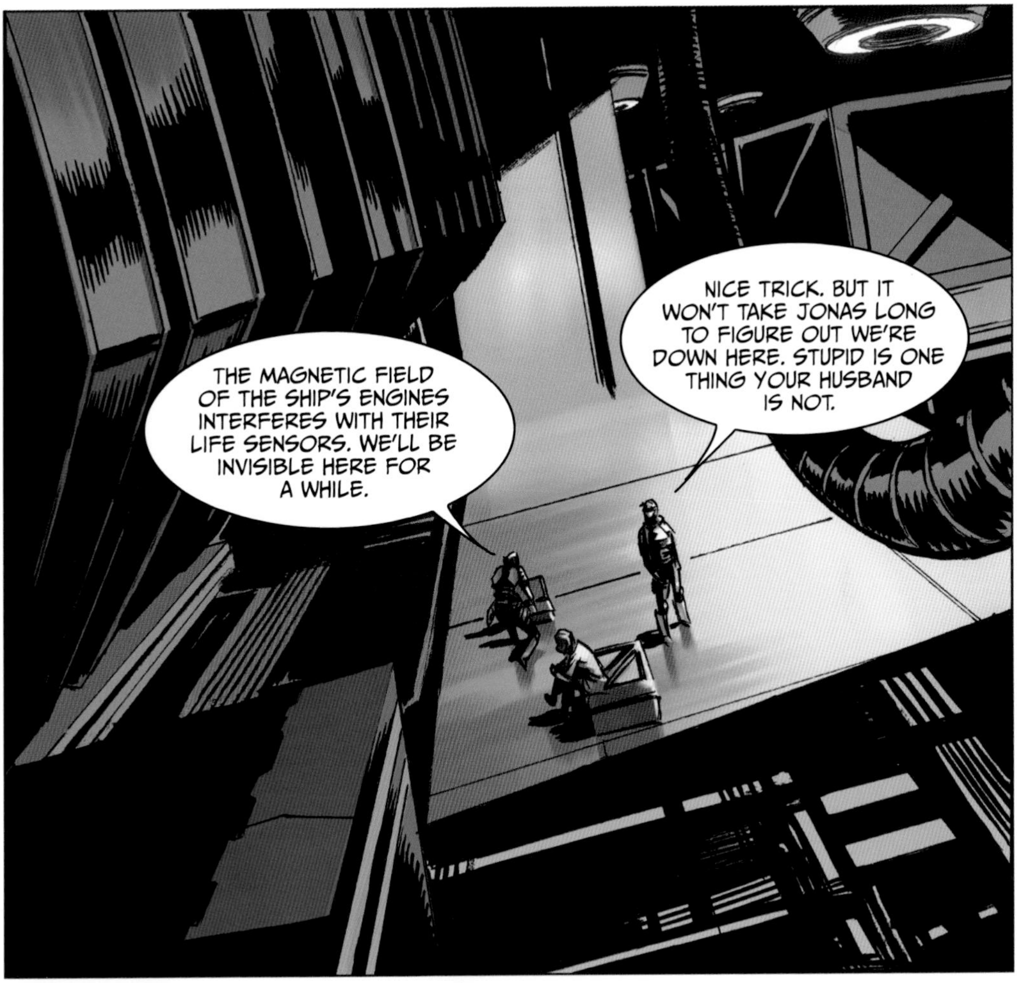
THE MAGNETIC FIELD OF THE SHIP'S ENGINES INTERFERES WITH THEIR LIFE SENSORS. WE'LL BE INVISIBLE HERE FOR A WHILE.
NICE TRICK. BUT IT WON'T TAKE JONAS LONG TO FIGURE OUT WE'RE DOWN HERE. STUPID IS ONE THING YOUR HUSBAND IS NOT.

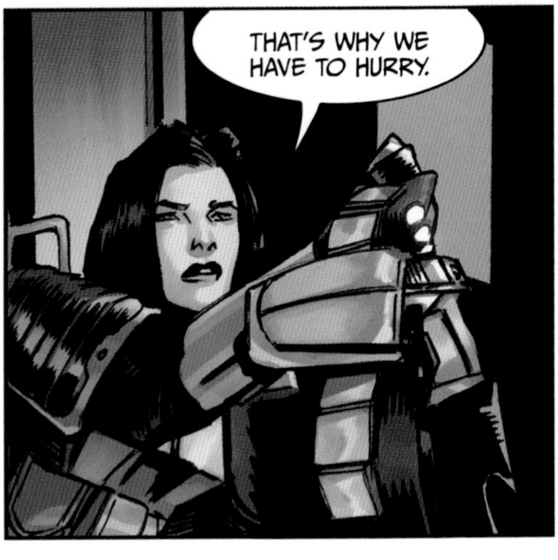
THAT'S WHY WE HAVE TO HURRY.

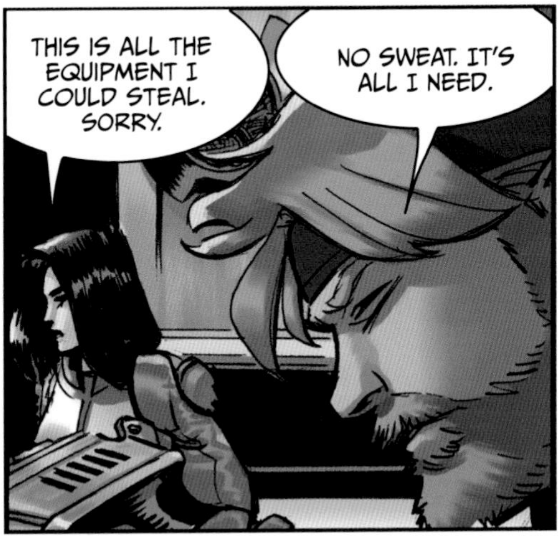
THIS IS ALL THE EQUIPMENT I COULD STEAL. SORRY.
NO SWEAT. IT'S ALL I NEED.

ONE MORE THING...

HERE.

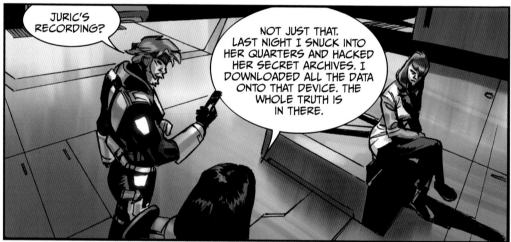

JURIC'S RECORDING?

NOT JUST THAT. LAST NIGHT I SNUCK INTO HER QUARTERS AND HACKED HER SECRET ARCHIVES. I DOWNLOADED ALL THE DATA ONTO THAT DEVICE. THE WHOLE TRUTH IS IN THERE.

YOU'VE BEEN BUSY. I THOUGHT YOU WERE JUST FLYING BY THE SEAT OF YOUR PANTS!

THE THOUGHT OF LETTING THEM GET AWAY WITH IT NEVER ENTERED MY MIND...

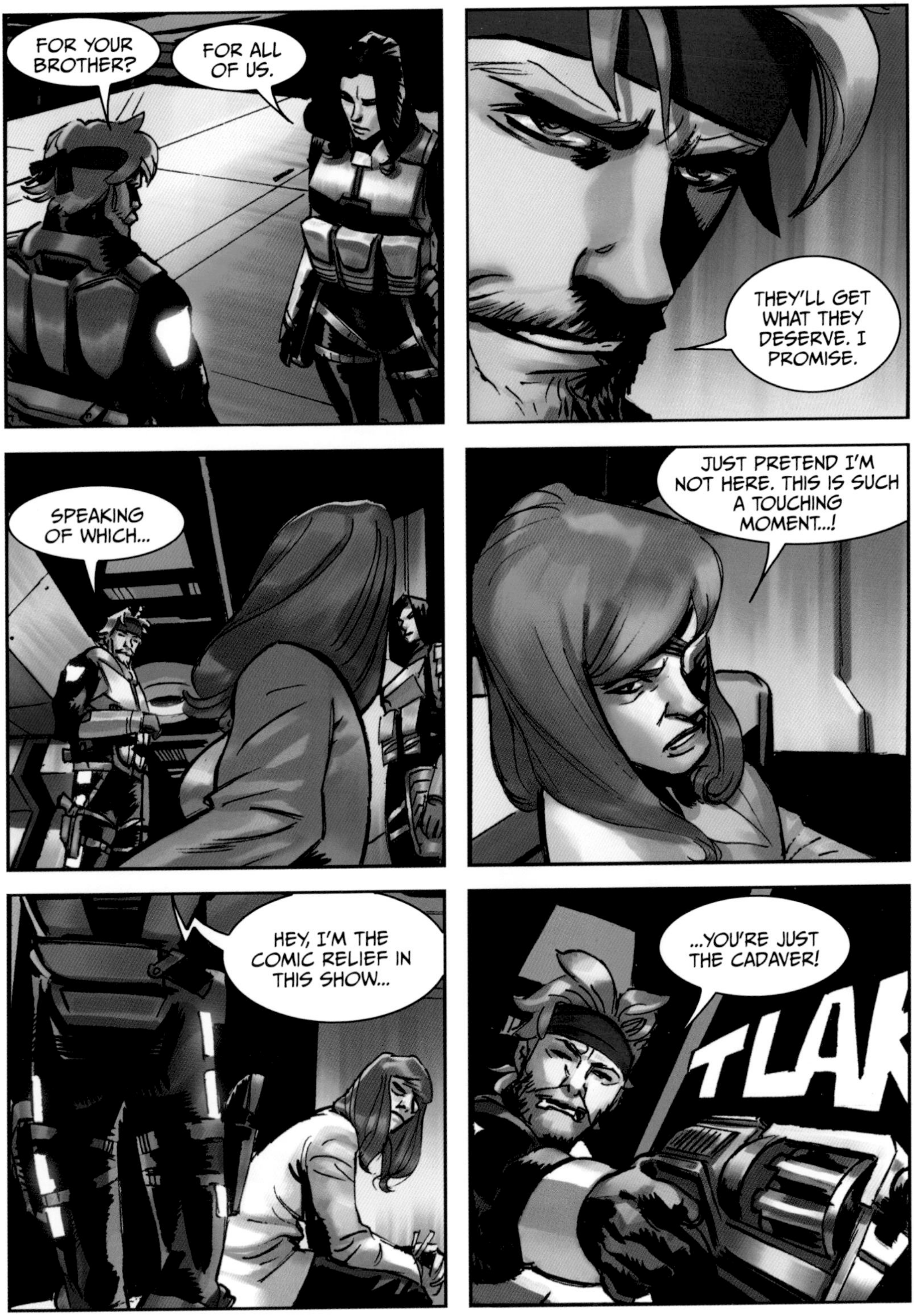
FOR YOUR BROTHER?
FOR ALL OF US.
THEY'LL GET WHAT THEY DESERVE. I PROMISE.
SPEAKING OF WHICH...
JUST PRETEND I'M NOT HERE. THIS IS SUCH A TOUCHING MOMENT...!
HEY, I'M THE COMIC RELIEF IN THIS SHOW...
...YOU'RE JUST THE CADAVER!
TLAK

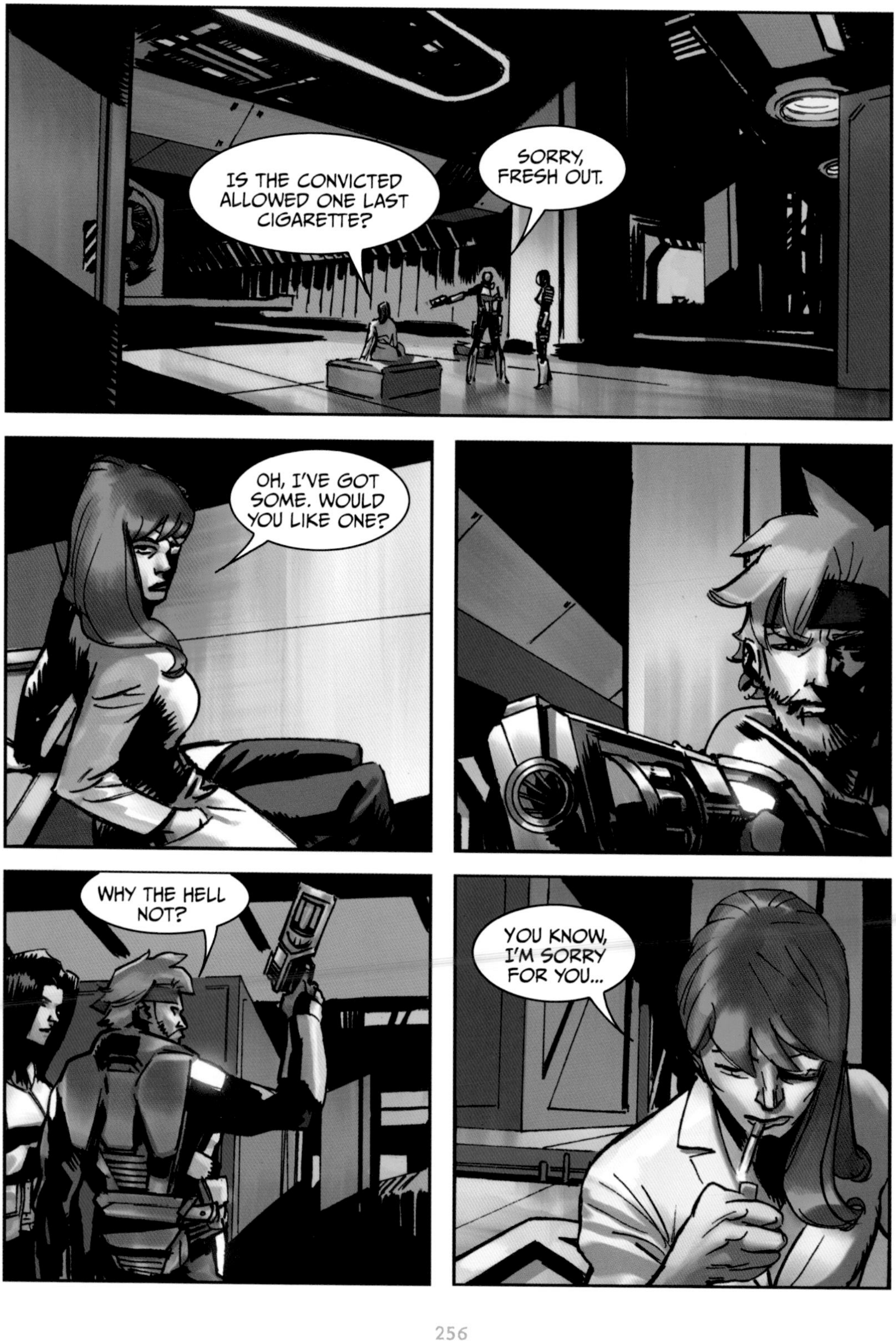
IS THE CONVICTED ALLOWED ONE LAST CIGARETTE?
SORRY, FRESH OUT.
OH, I'VE GOT SOME. WOULD YOU LIKE ONE?
WHY THE HELL NOT?
YOU KNOW, I'M SORRY FOR YOU...

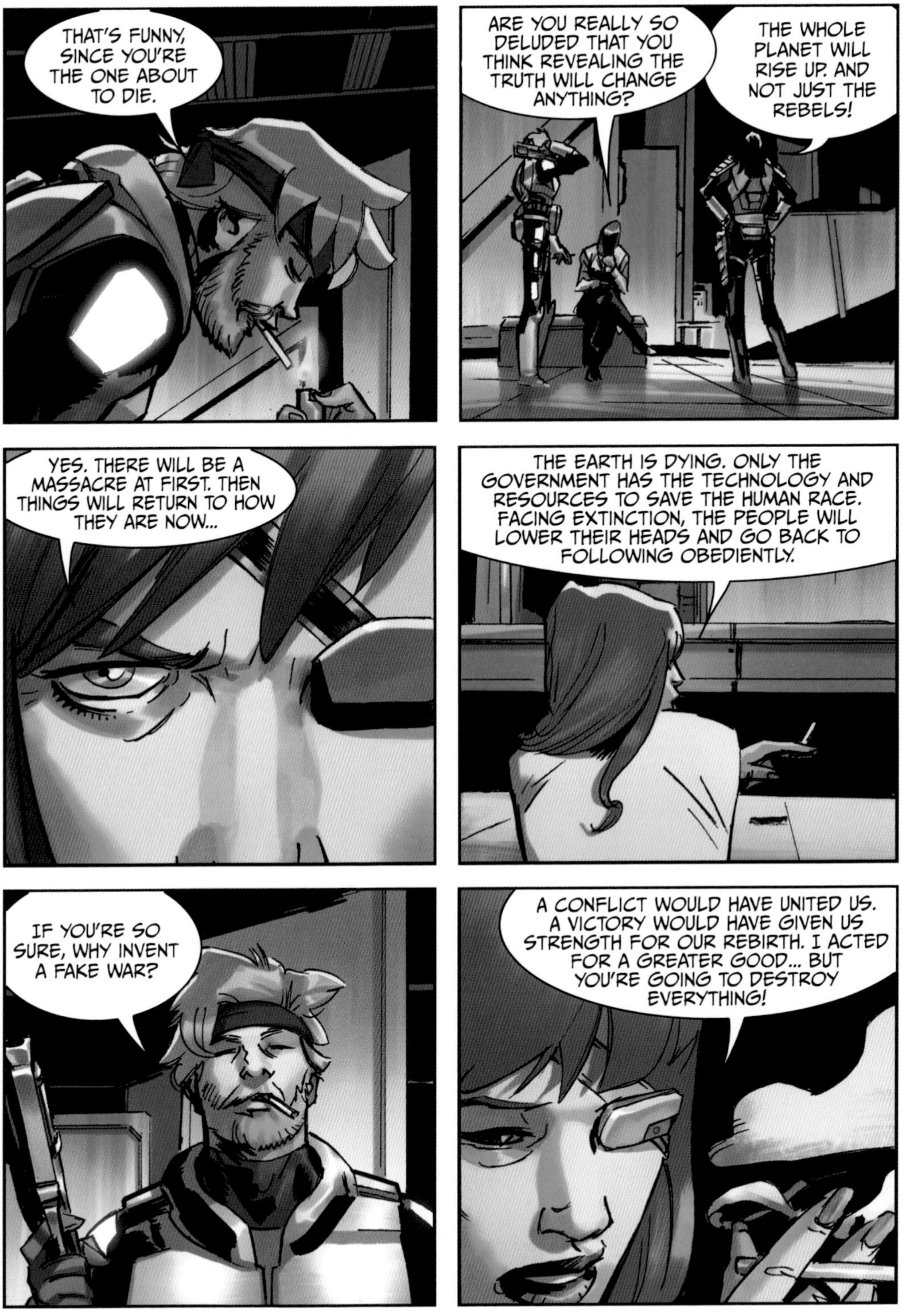
THAT'S FUNNY, SINCE YOU'RE THE ONE ABOUT TO DIE.
ARE YOU REALLY SO DELUDED THAT YOU THINK REVEALING THE TRUTH WILL CHANGE ANYTHING?
THE WHOLE PLANET WILL RISE UP. AND NOT JUST THE REBELS!
YES. THERE WILL BE A MASSACRE AT FIRST. THEN THINGS WILL RETURN TO HOW THEY ARE NOW...
THE EARTH IS DYING. ONLY THE GOVERNMENT HAS THE TECHNOLOGY AND RESOURCES TO SAVE THE HUMAN RACE. FACING EXTINCTION, THE PEOPLE WILL LOWER THEIR HEADS AND GO BACK TO FOLLOWING OBEDIENTLY.
IF YOU'RE SO SURE, WHY INVENT A FAKE WAR?
A CONFLICT WOULD HAVE UNITED US. A VICTORY WOULD HAVE GIVEN US STRENGTH FOR OUR REBIRTH. I ACTED FOR A GREATER GOOD... BUT YOU'RE GOING TO DESTROY EVERYTHING!

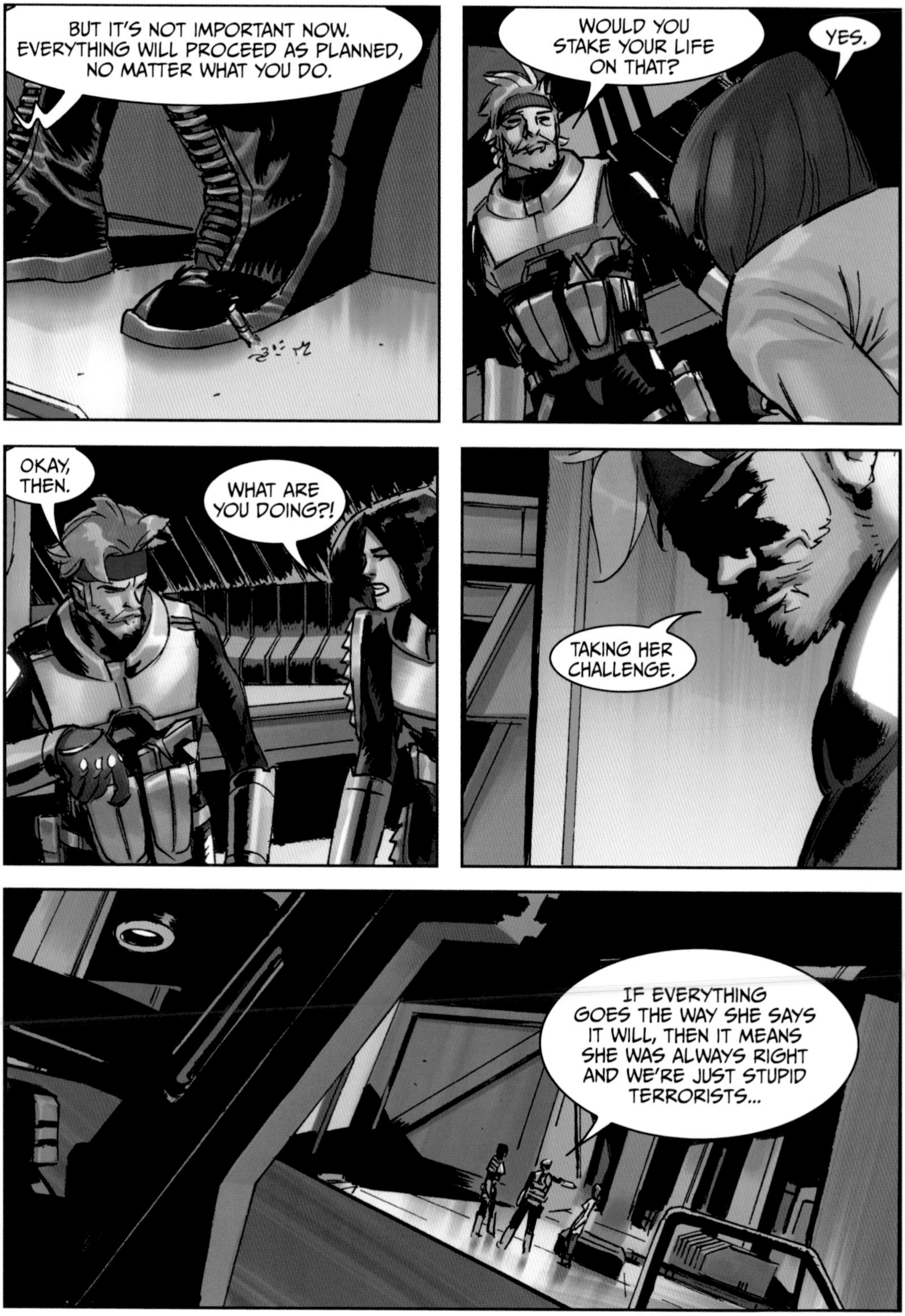
BUT IT'S NOT IMPORTANT NOW. EVERYTHING WILL PROCEED AS PLANNED, NO MATTER WHAT YOU DO.
WOULD YOU STAKE YOUR LIFE ON THAT?
YES.
OKAY, THEN.
WHAT ARE YOU DOING?!
TAKING HER CHALLENGE.
IF EVERYTHING GOES THE WAY SHE SAYS IT WILL, THEN IT MEANS SHE WAS ALWAYS RIGHT AND WE'RE JUST STUPID TERRORISTS...

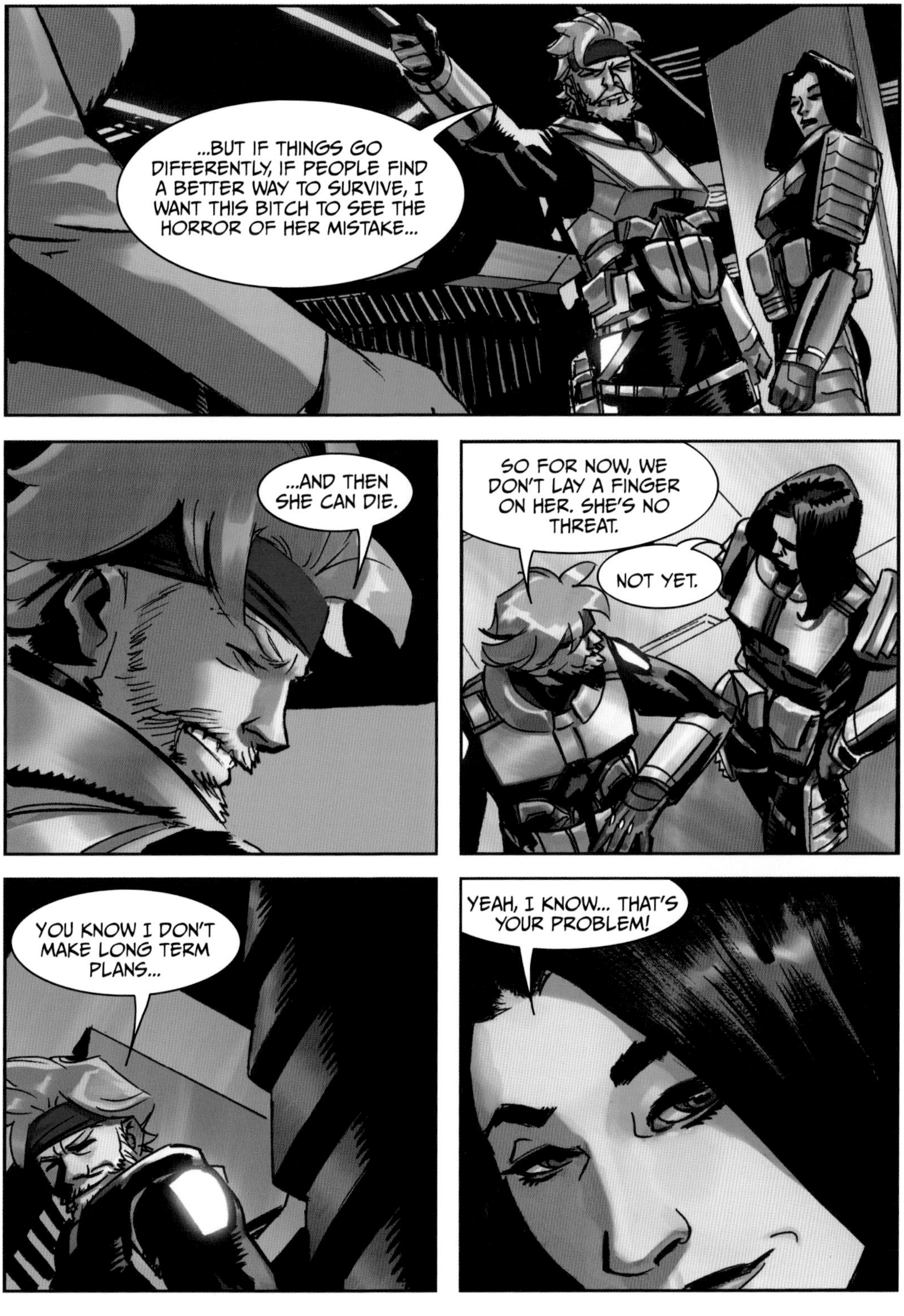
...BUT IF THINGS GO DIFFERENTLY, IF PEOPLE FIND A BETTER WAY TO SURVIVE, I WANT THIS BITCH TO SEE THE HORROR OF HER MISTAKE...
...AND THEN SHE CAN DIE.
SO FOR NOW, WE DON'T LAY A FINGER ON HER. SHE'S NO THREAT.
NOT YET.
YOU KNOW I DON'T MAKE LONG TERM PLANS...
YEAH, I KNOW... THAT'S YOUR PROBLEM!

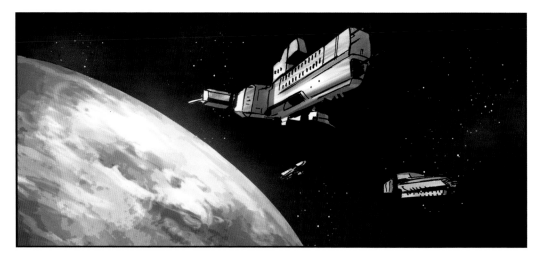

THE ENGINE ROOM IS THE ONLY ONE OUT OF SENSOR RANGE...

...THEY MUST BE HIDING THERE.

SHOULD WE GO GET 'EM?

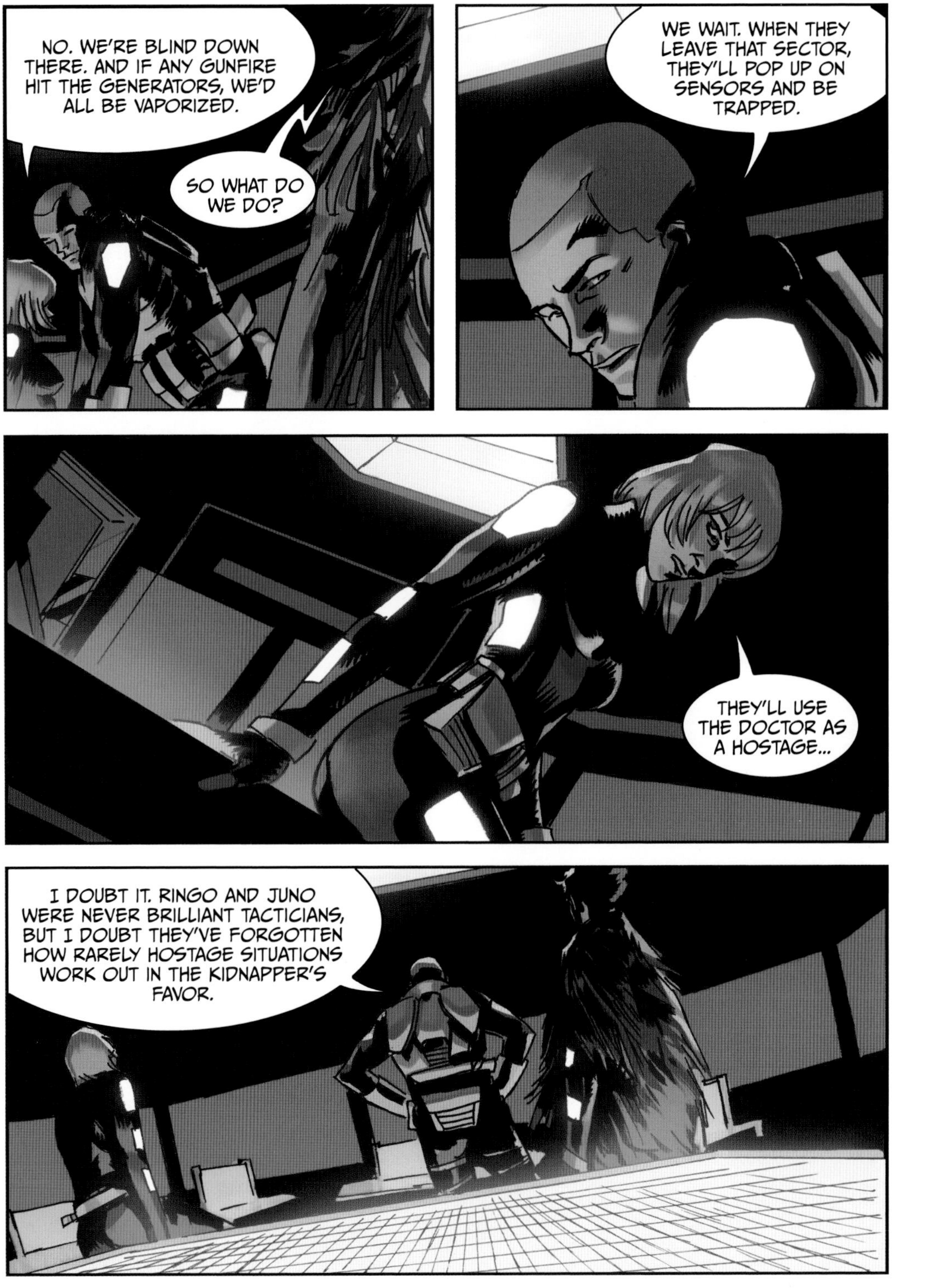
NO. WE'RE BLIND DOWN THERE. AND IF ANY GUNFIRE HIT THE GENERATORS, WE'D ALL BE VAPORIZED.
SO WHAT DO WE DO?
WE WAIT. WHEN THEY LEAVE THAT SECTOR, THEY'LL POP UP ON SENSORS AND BE TRAPPED.
THEY'LL USE THE DOCTOR AS A HOSTAGE...
I DOUBT IT. RINGO AND JUNO WERE NEVER BRILLIANT TACTICIANS, BUT I DOUBT THEY'VE FORGOTTEN HOW RARELY HOSTAGE SITUATIONS WORK OUT IN THE KIDNAPPER'S FAVOR.

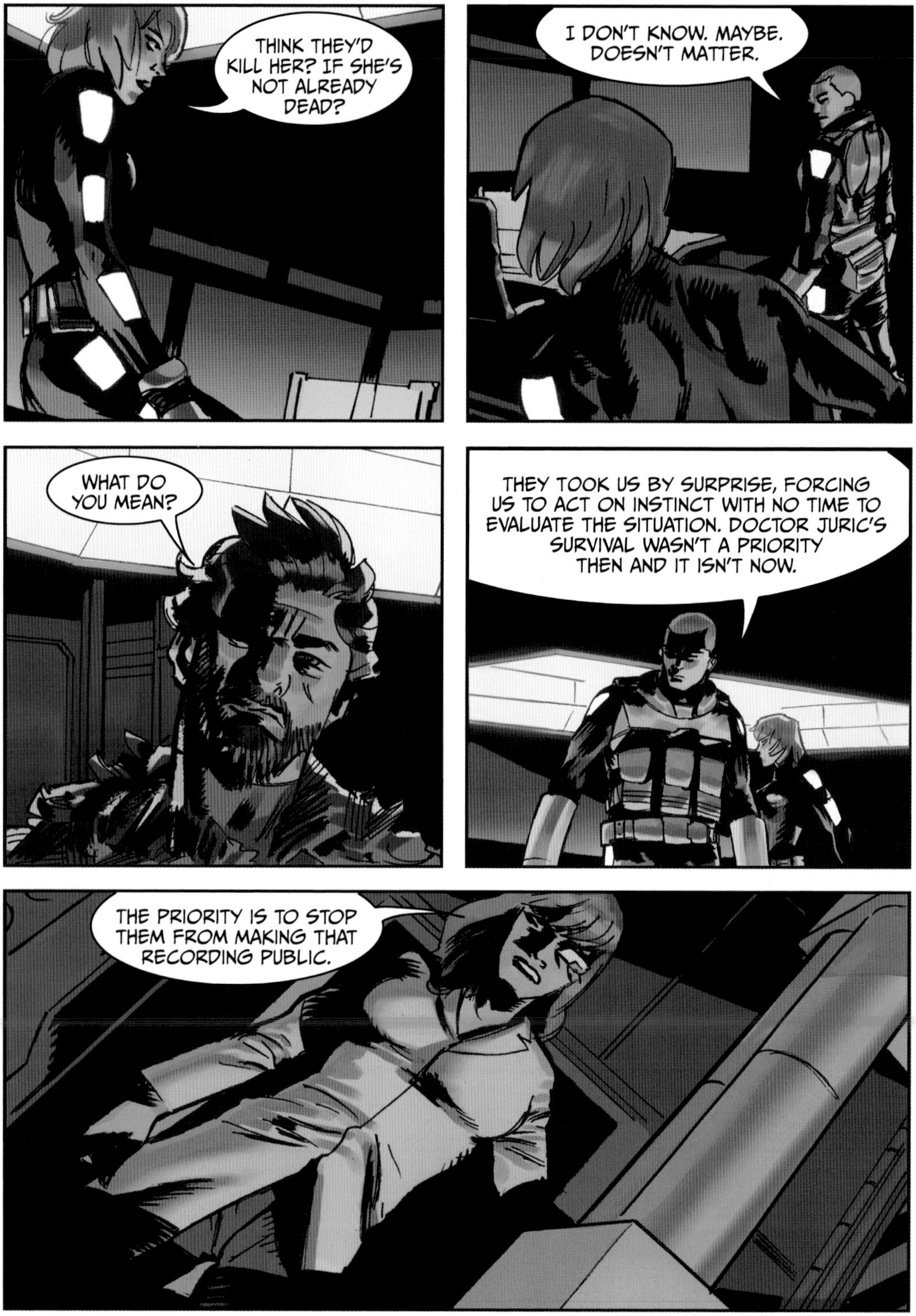
THINK THEY'D KILL HER? IF SHE'S NOT ALREADY DEAD?
I DON'T KNOW. MAYBE. DOESN'T MATTER.
WHAT DO YOU MEAN?
THEY TOOK US BY SURPRISE, FORCING US TO ACT ON INSTINCT WITH NO TIME TO EVALUATE THE SITUATION. DOCTOR JURIC'S SURVIVAL WASN'T A PRIORITY THEN AND IT ISN'T NOW.
THE PRIORITY IS TO STOP THEM FROM MAKING THAT RECORDING PUBLIC.

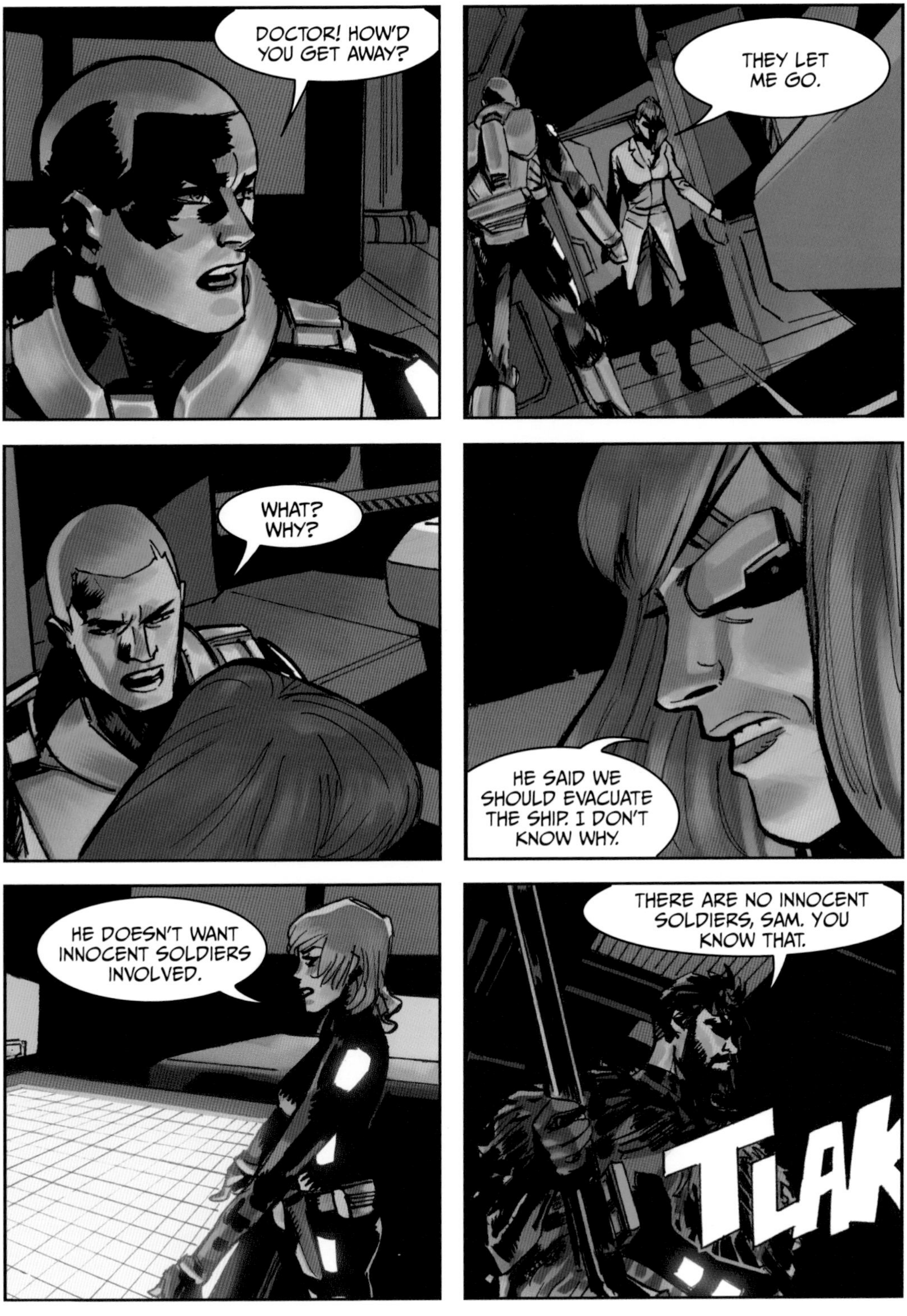
DOCTOR! HOW'D YOU GET AWAY?
THEY LET ME GO.
WHAT? WHY?
HE SAID WE SHOULD EVACUATE THE SHIP. I DON'T KNOW WHY.
HE DOESN'T WANT INNOCENT SOLDIERS INVOLVED.
THERE ARE NO INNOCENT SOLDIERS, SAM. YOU KNOW THAT.
TLAK

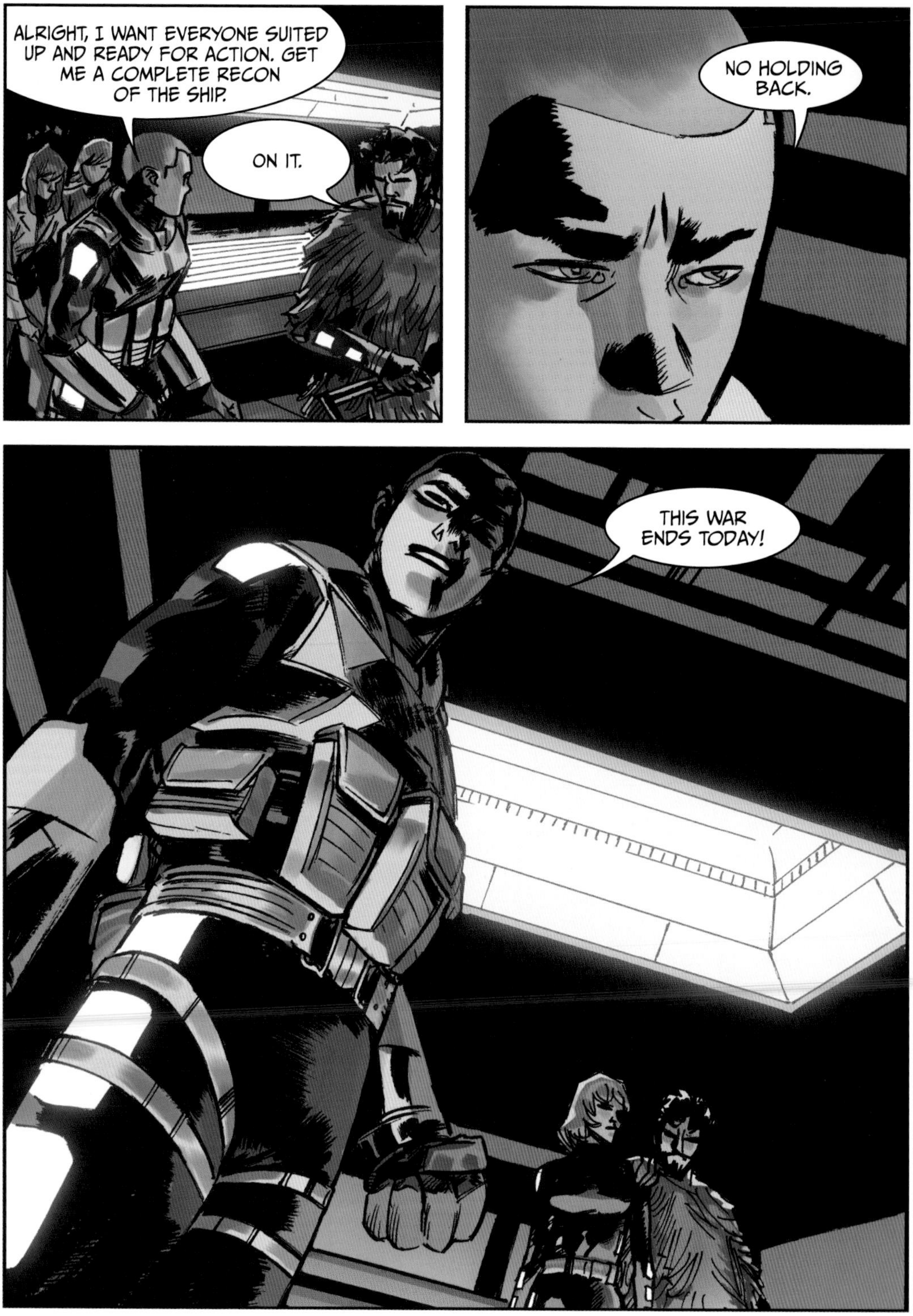
ALRIGHT, I WANT EVERYONE SUITED UP AND READY FOR ACTION. GET ME A COMPLETE RECON OF THE SHIP.
ON IT.
NO HOLDING BACK.
THIS WAR ENDS TODAY!

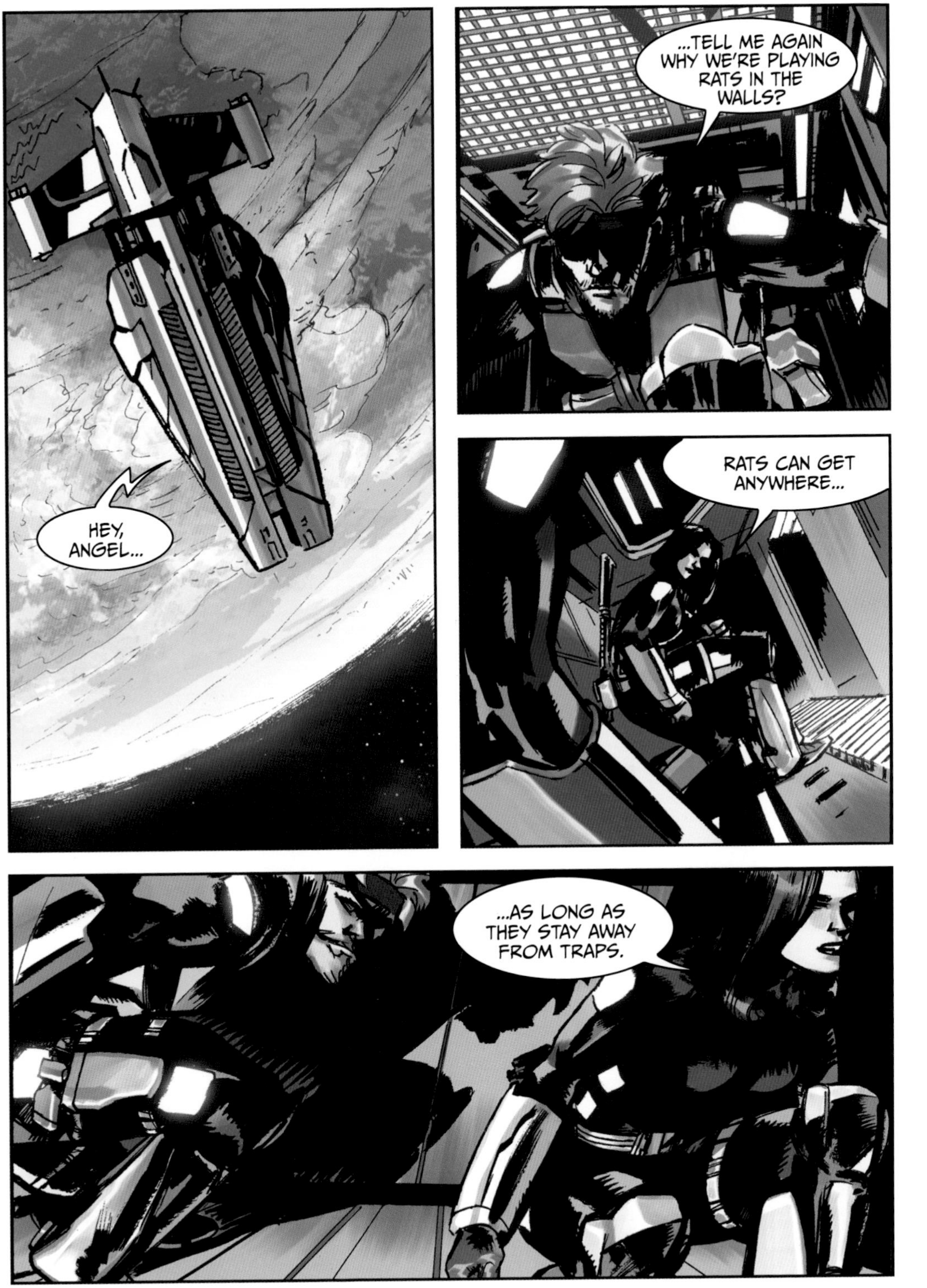
HEY, ANGEL...
...TELL ME AGAIN WHY WE'RE PLAYING RATS IN THE WALLS?
RATS CAN GET ANYWHERE...
...AS LONG AS THEY STAY AWAY FROM TRAPS.

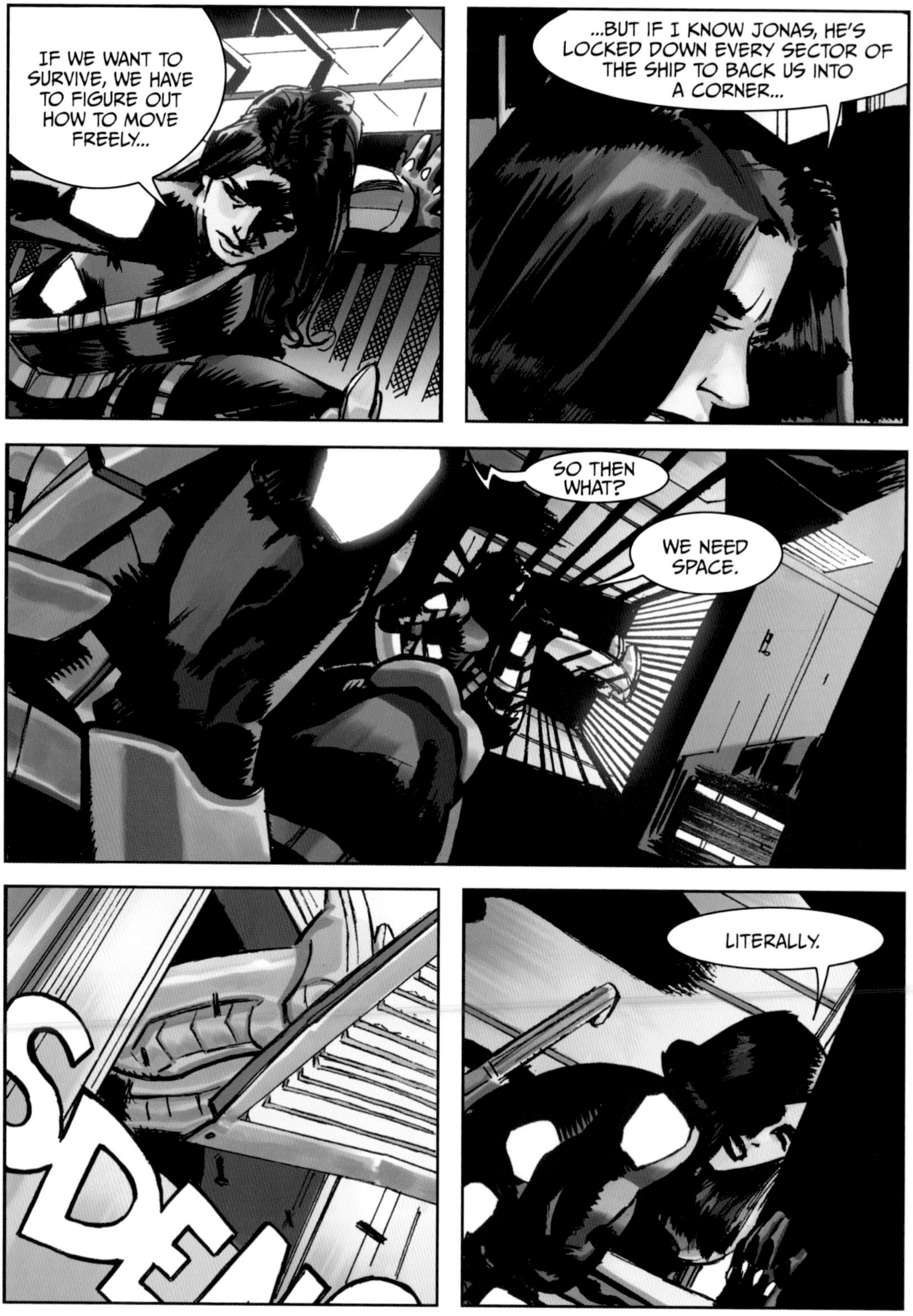
IF WE WANT TO SURVIVE, WE HAVE TO FIGURE OUT HOW TO MOVE FREELY...
...BUT IF I KNOW JONAS, HE'S LOCKED DOWN EVERY SECTOR OF THE SHIP TO BACK US INTO A CORNER...
SO THEN WHAT?
WE NEED SPACE.
LITERALLY.

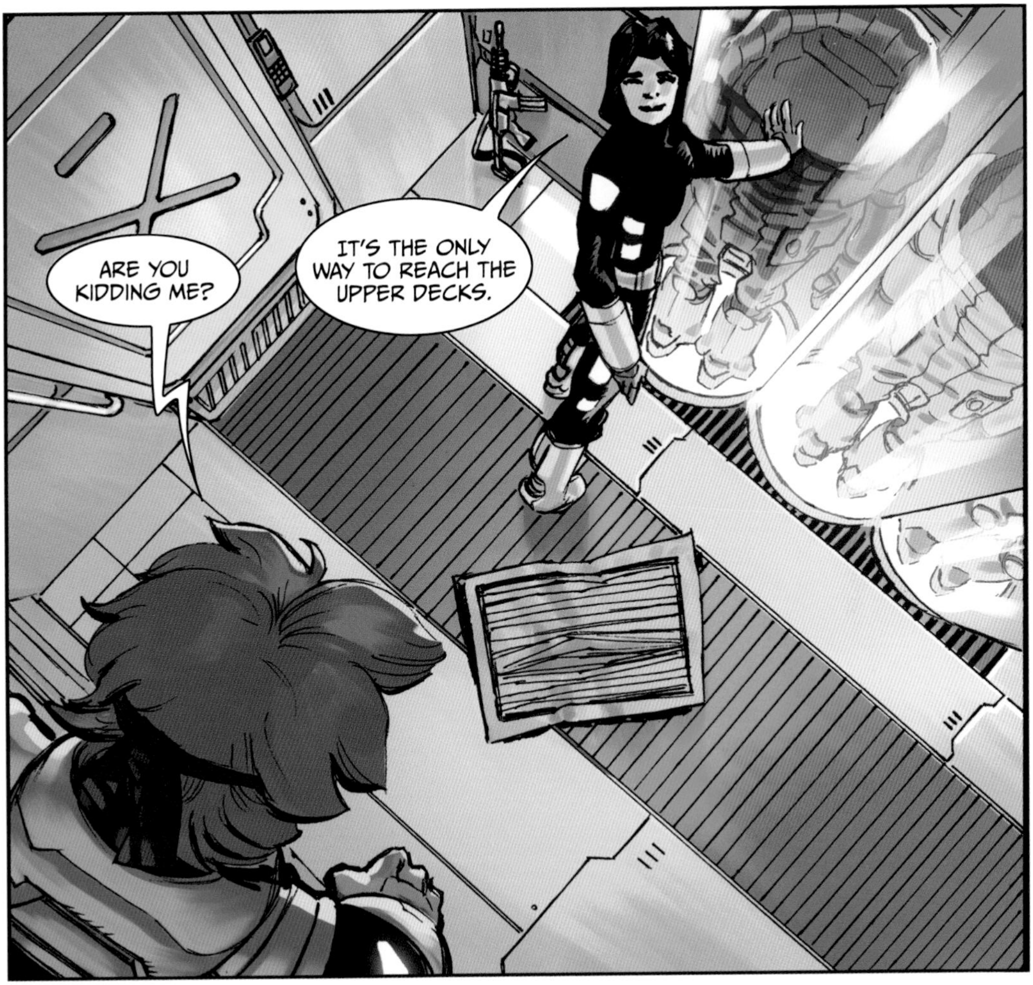
IT'S THE ONLY WAY TO REACH THE UPPER DECKS.
ARE YOU KIDDING ME?

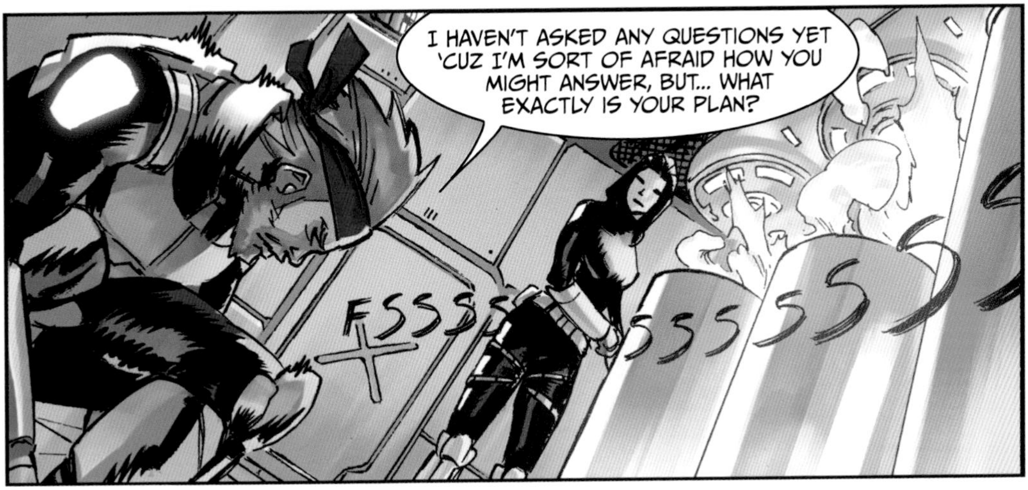
I HAVEN'T ASKED ANY QUESTIONS YET 'CUZ I'M SORT OF AFRAID HOW YOU MIGHT ANSWER, BUT... WHAT EXACTLY IS YOUR PLAN?
FSSSSSSSSSSSS

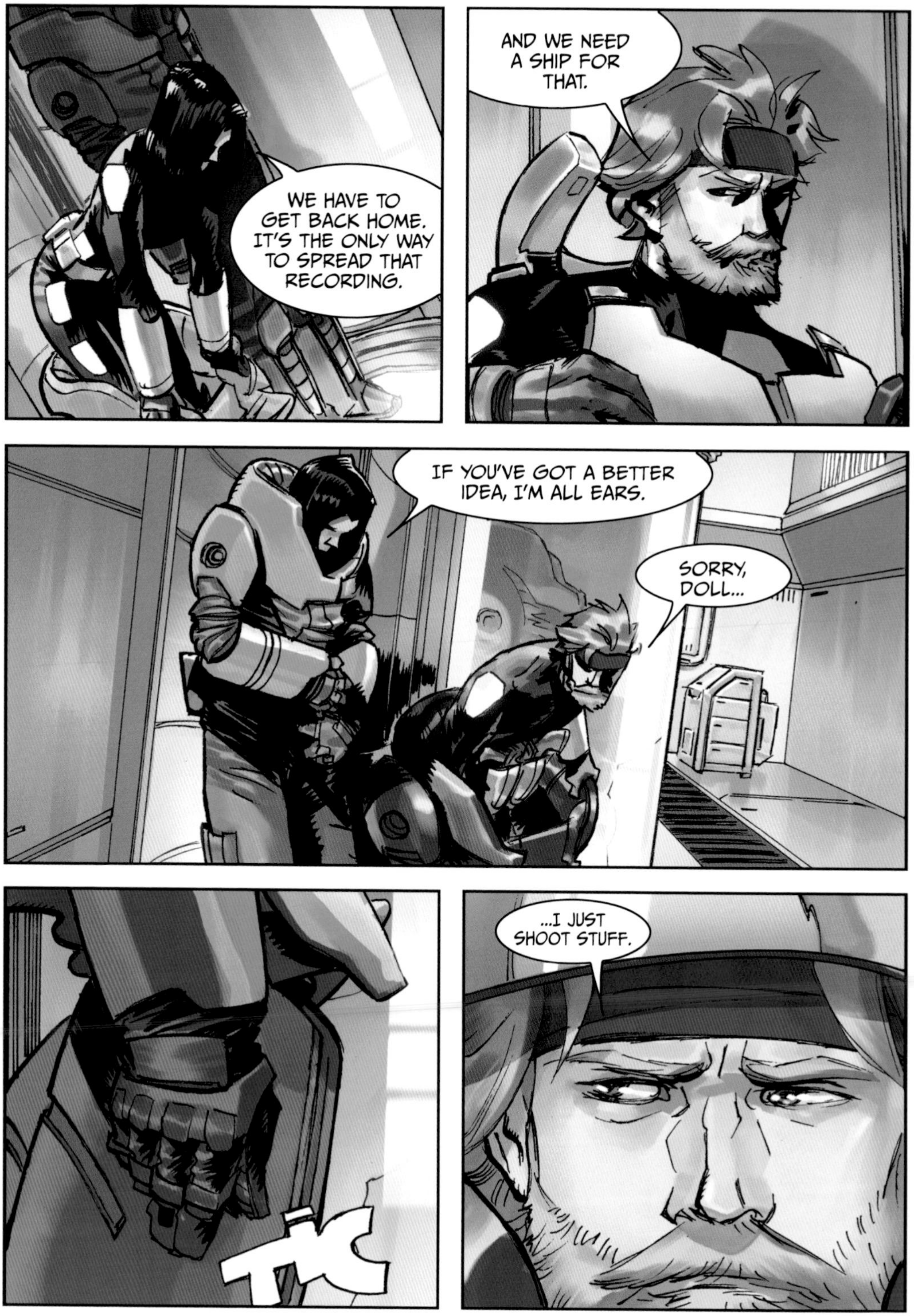
WE HAVE TO GET BACK HOME. IT'S THE ONLY WAY TO SPREAD THAT RECORDING.
AND WE NEED A SHIP FOR THAT.
IF YOU'VE GOT A BETTER IDEA, I'M ALL EARS.
SORRY, DOLL...
TIC
...I JUST SHOOT STUFF.

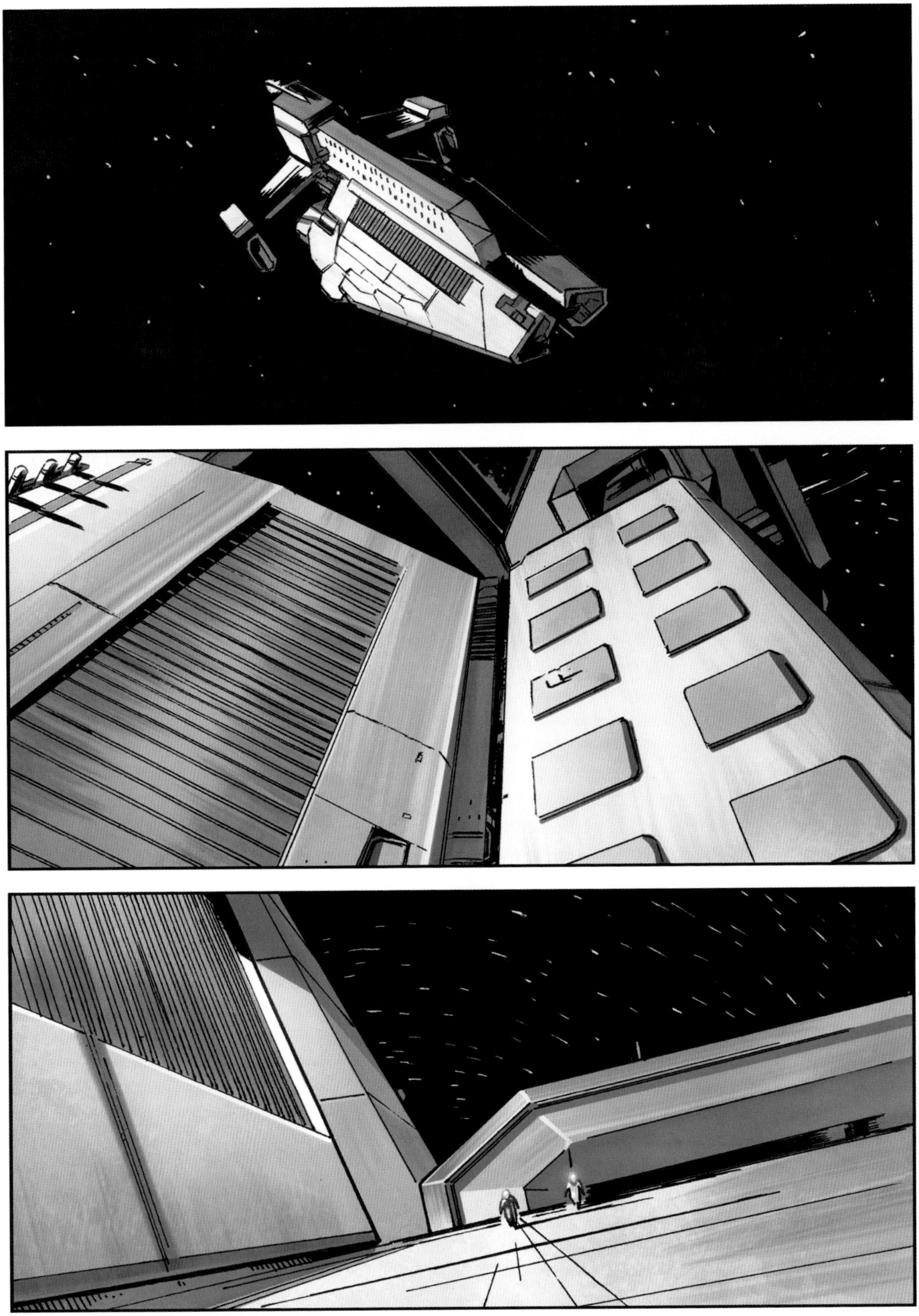

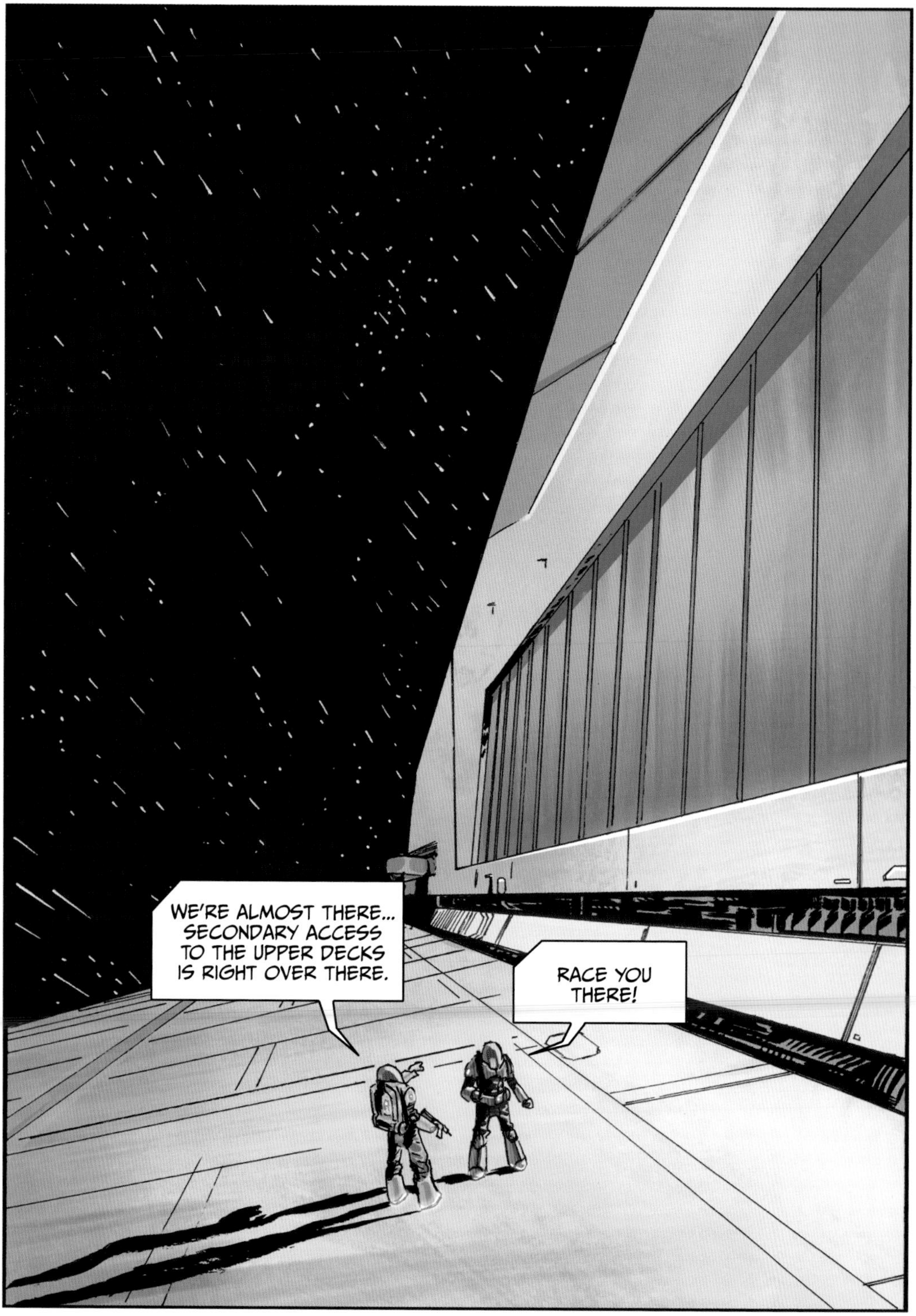
WE'RE ALMOST THERE... SECONDARY ACCESS TO THE UPPER DECKS IS RIGHT OVER THERE.
RACE YOU THERE!

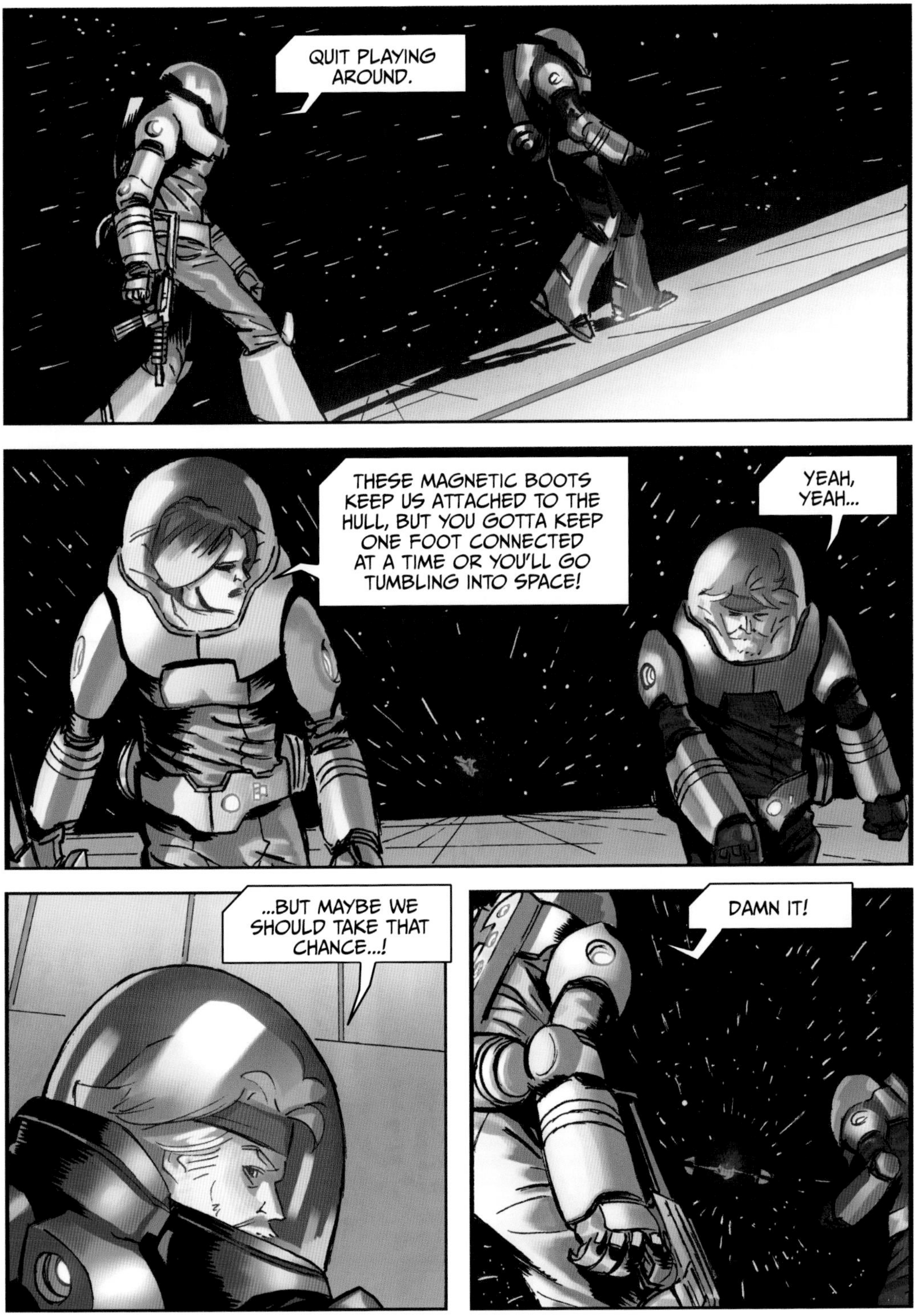
QUIT PLAYING AROUND.
THESE MAGNETIC BOOTS KEEP US ATTACHED TO THE HULL, BUT YOU GOTTA KEEP ONE FOOT CONNECTED AT A TIME OR YOU'LL GO TUMBLING INTO SPACE!
YEAH, YEAH...
...BUT MAYBE WE SHOULD TAKE THAT CHANCE...!
DAMN IT!

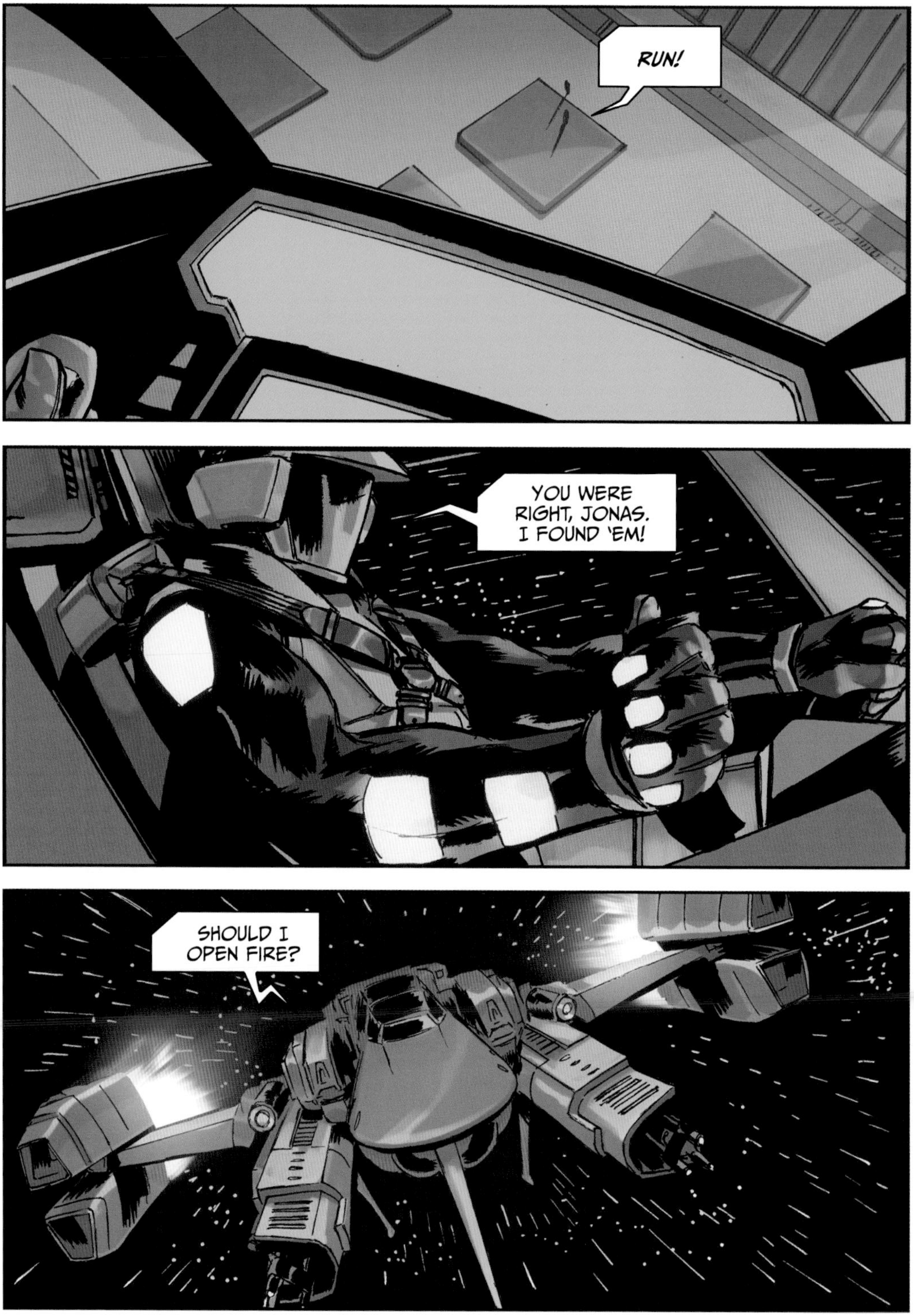
RUN!
YOU WERE RIGHT, JONAS. I FOUND 'EM!
SHOULD I OPEN FIRE?

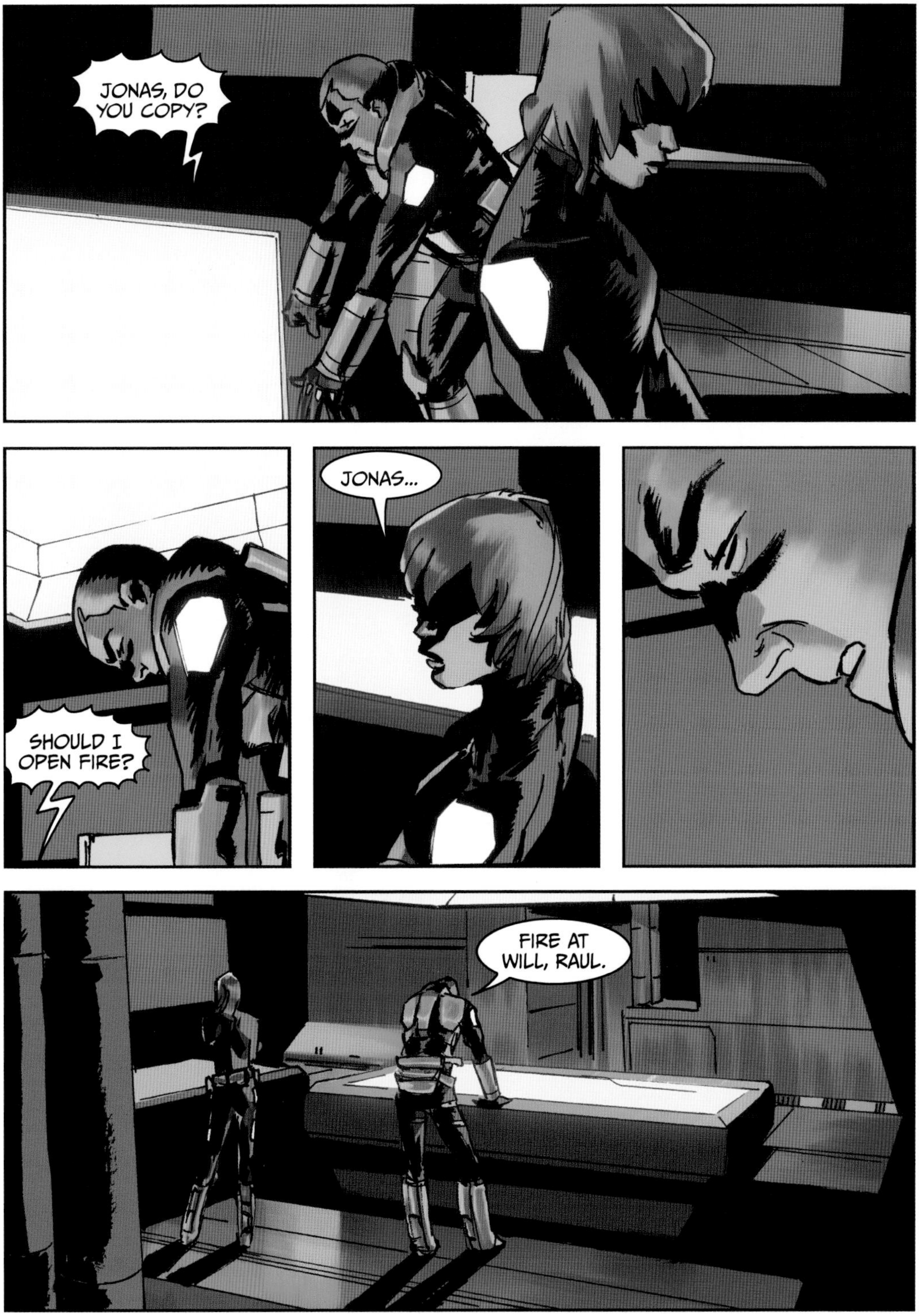
JONAS, DO YOU COPY?
SHOULD I OPEN FIRE?
JONAS...
FIRE AT WILL, RAUL.

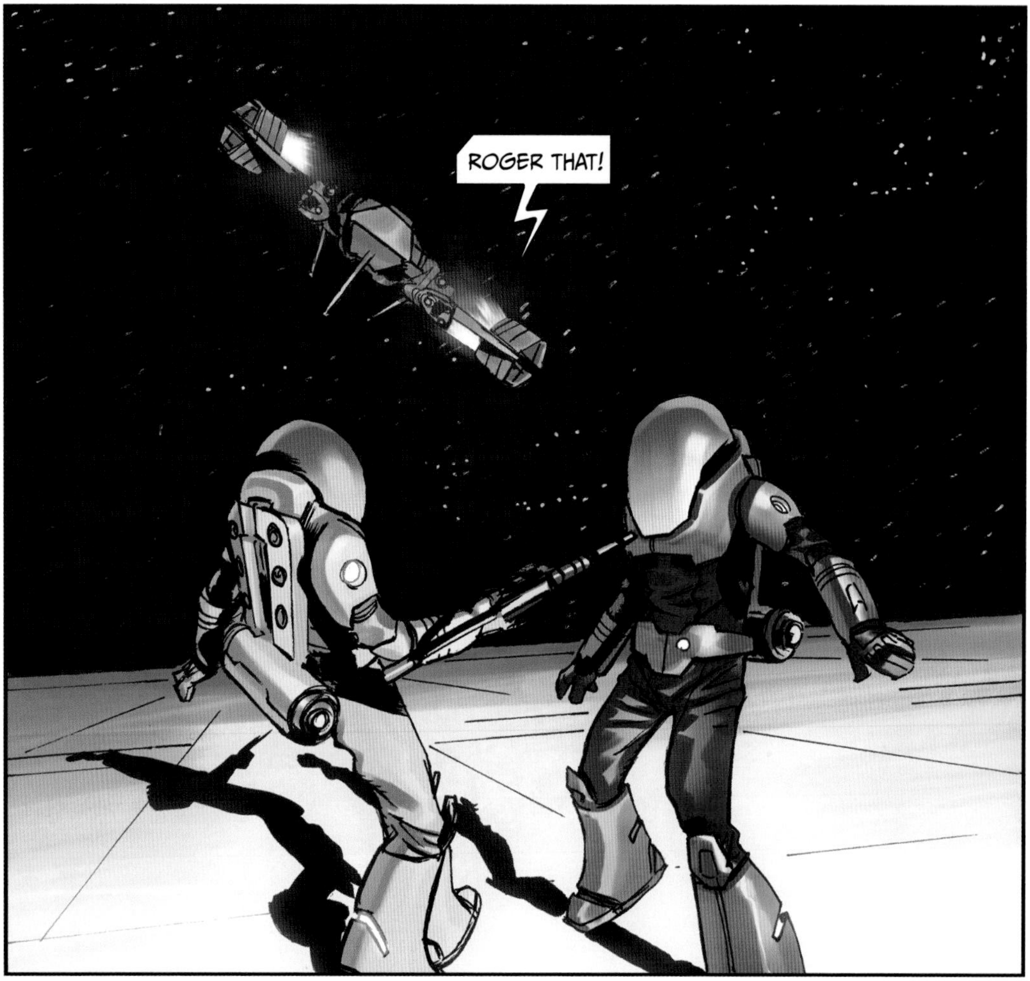
ROGER THAT!

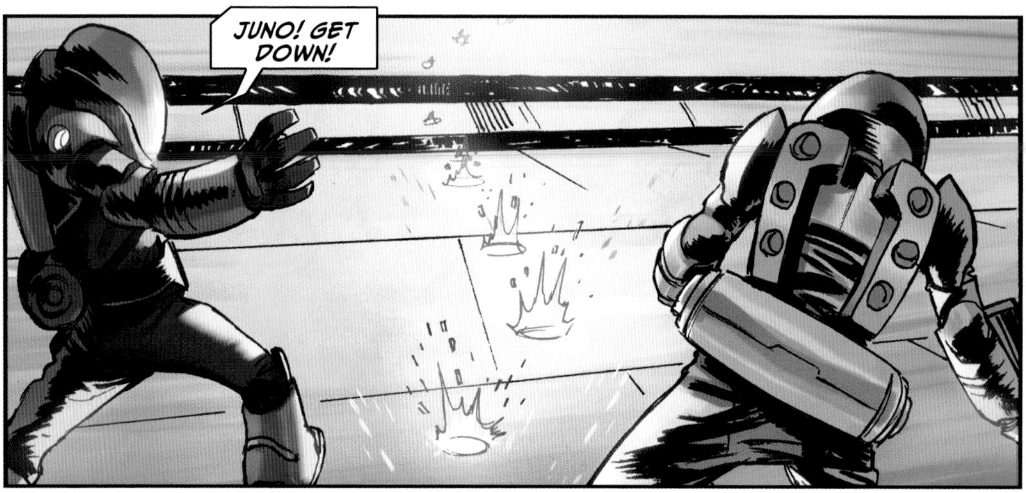
JUNO! GET DOWN!

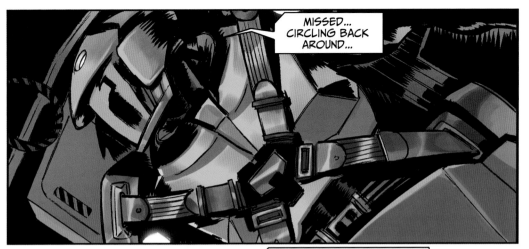

MISSED... CIRCLING BACK AROUND...

HE'S COMING BACK! MOVE!

WE'RE STILL TOO FAR!

IF WE RUN, WE WON'T MAKE IT... WE HAVE TO FIGHT BACK!

I WAS HOPING YOU'D SAY THAT...

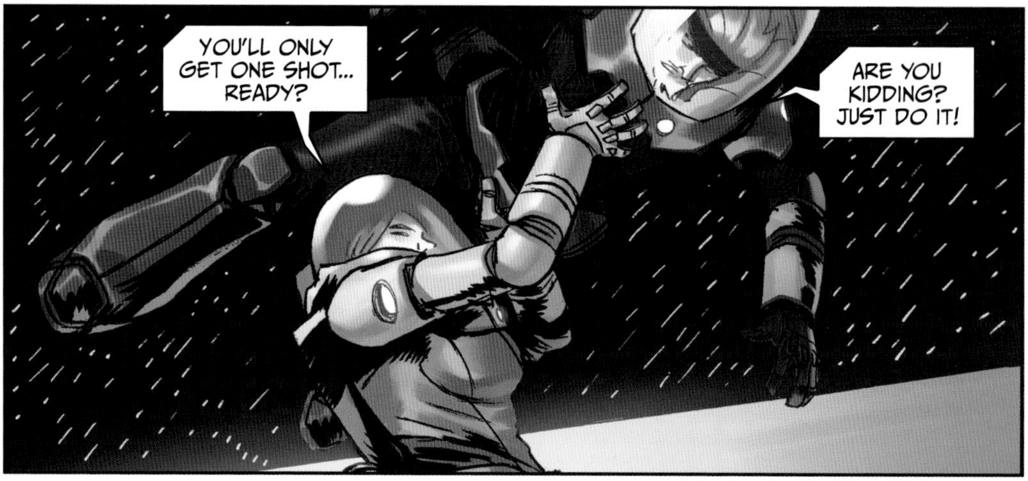
YOU'LL ONLY GET ONE SHOT... READY?
ARE YOU KIDDING? JUST DO IT!

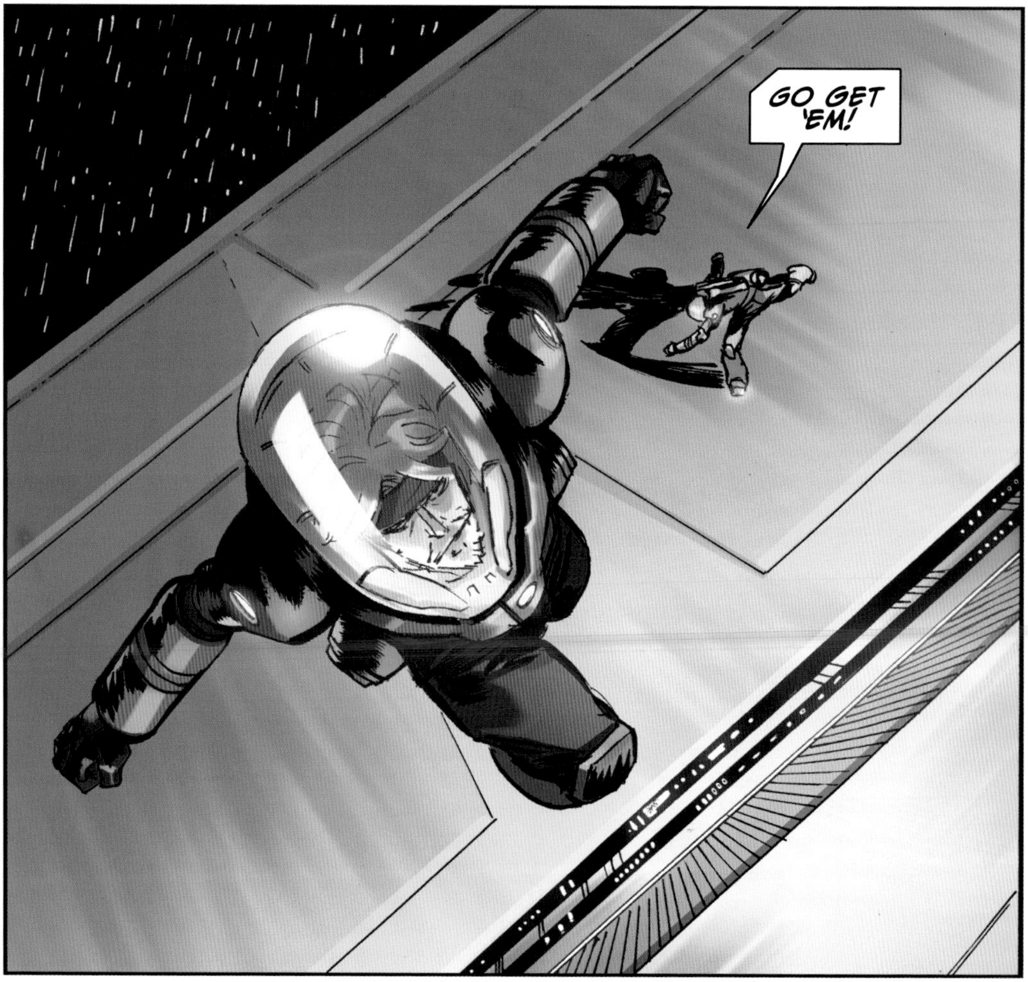
GO GET 'EM!

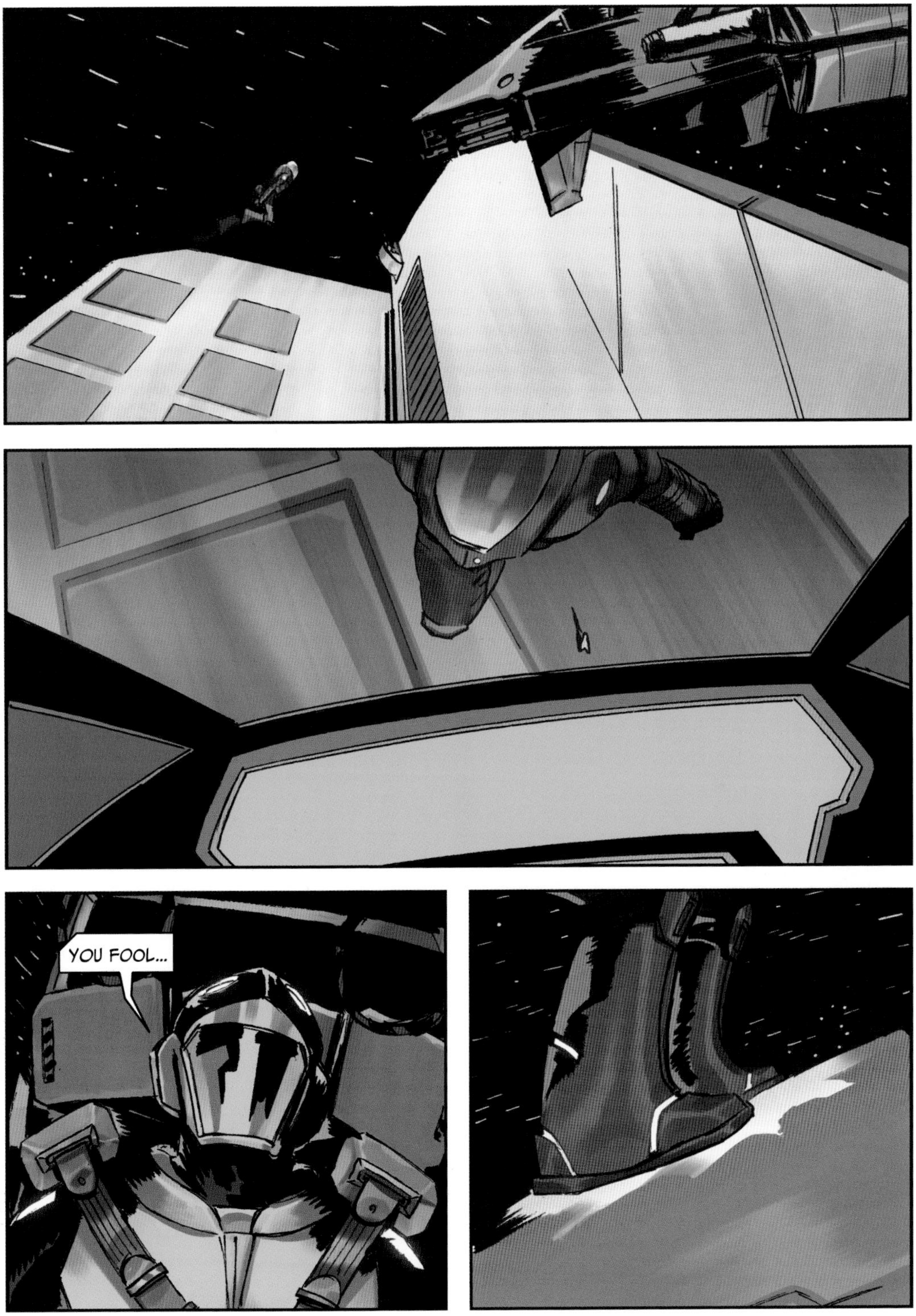
YOU FOOL...

HEYA, LONER!
COME OUT AND FIGHT LIKE A MAN, YOU SONOVABITCH!

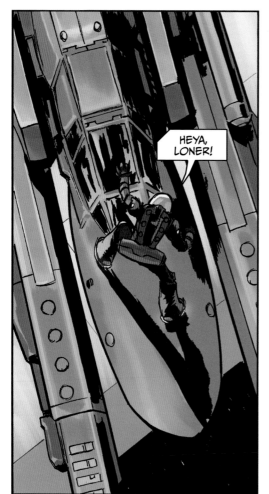

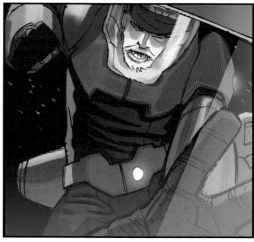

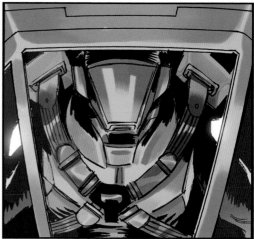

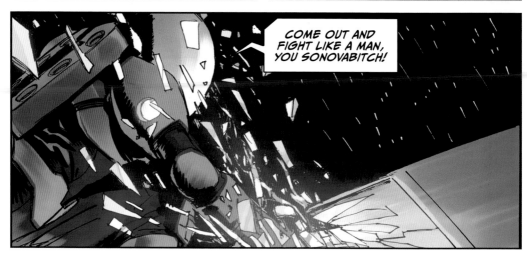

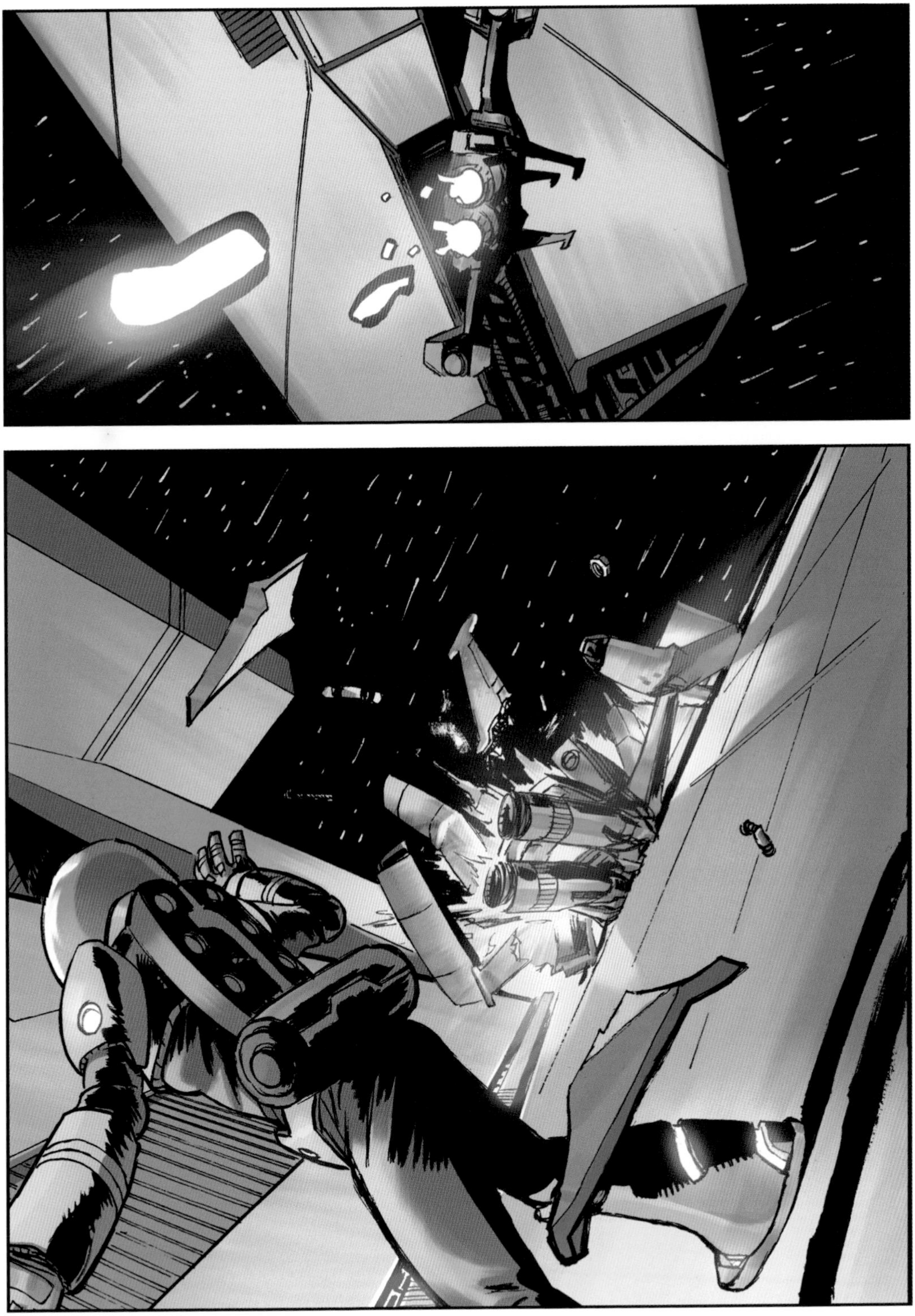

RINGO! CAN YOU HEAR ME?!

YEAH... I'M ALIVE, BUT DON'T ASK ME TO DO SOMETHING LIKE THAT EVER AGAIN...

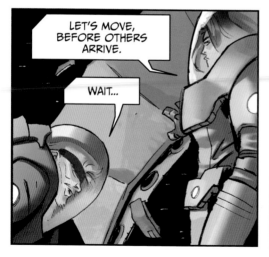

LET'S MOVE, BEFORE OTHERS ARRIVE.

WAIT...

...WE CAN'T JUST LEAVE HIM OUT HERE...

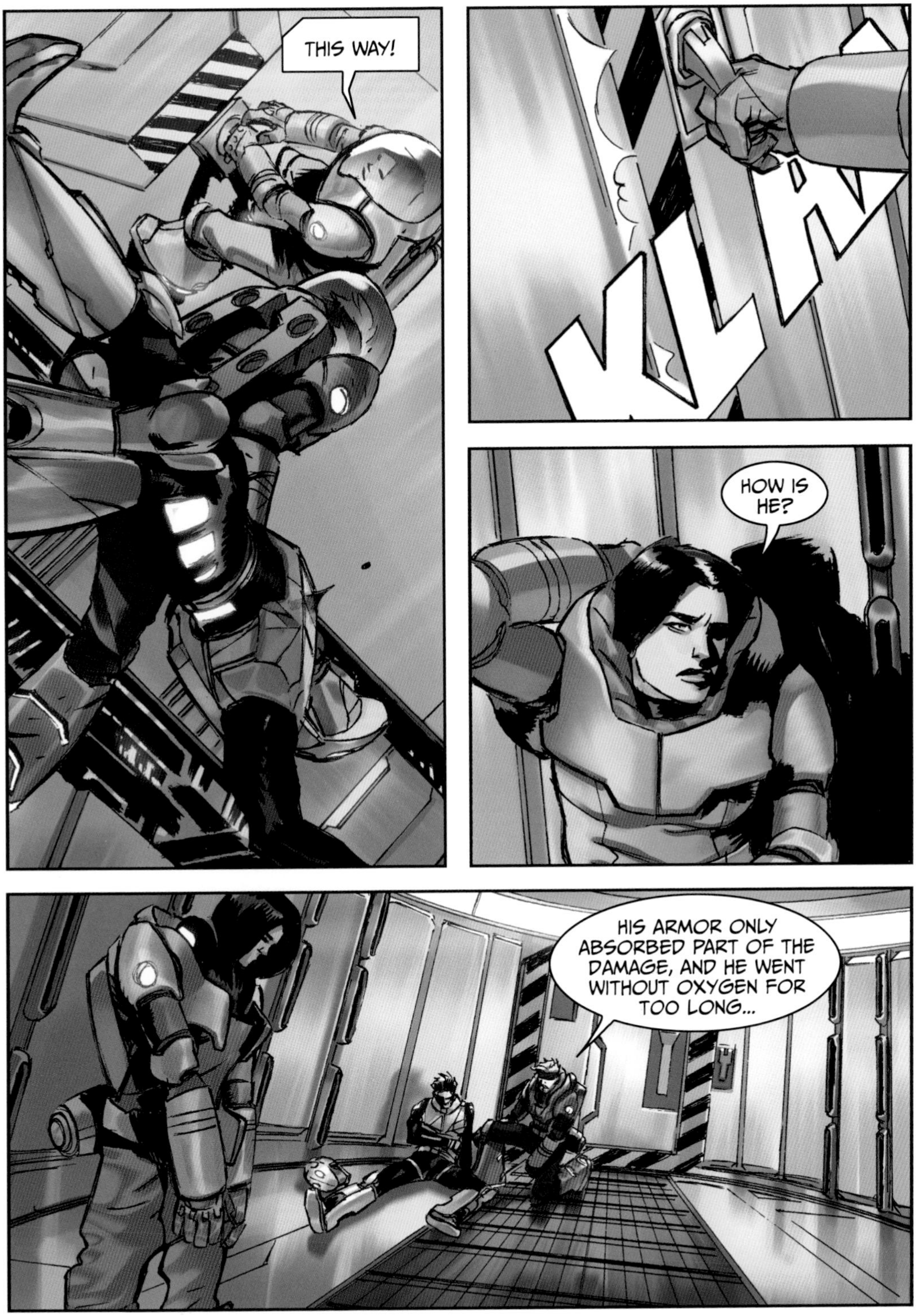
THIS WAY!
HOW IS HE?
HIS ARMOR ONLY ABSORBED PART OF THE DAMAGE, AND HE WENT WITHOUT OXYGEN FOR TOO LONG...

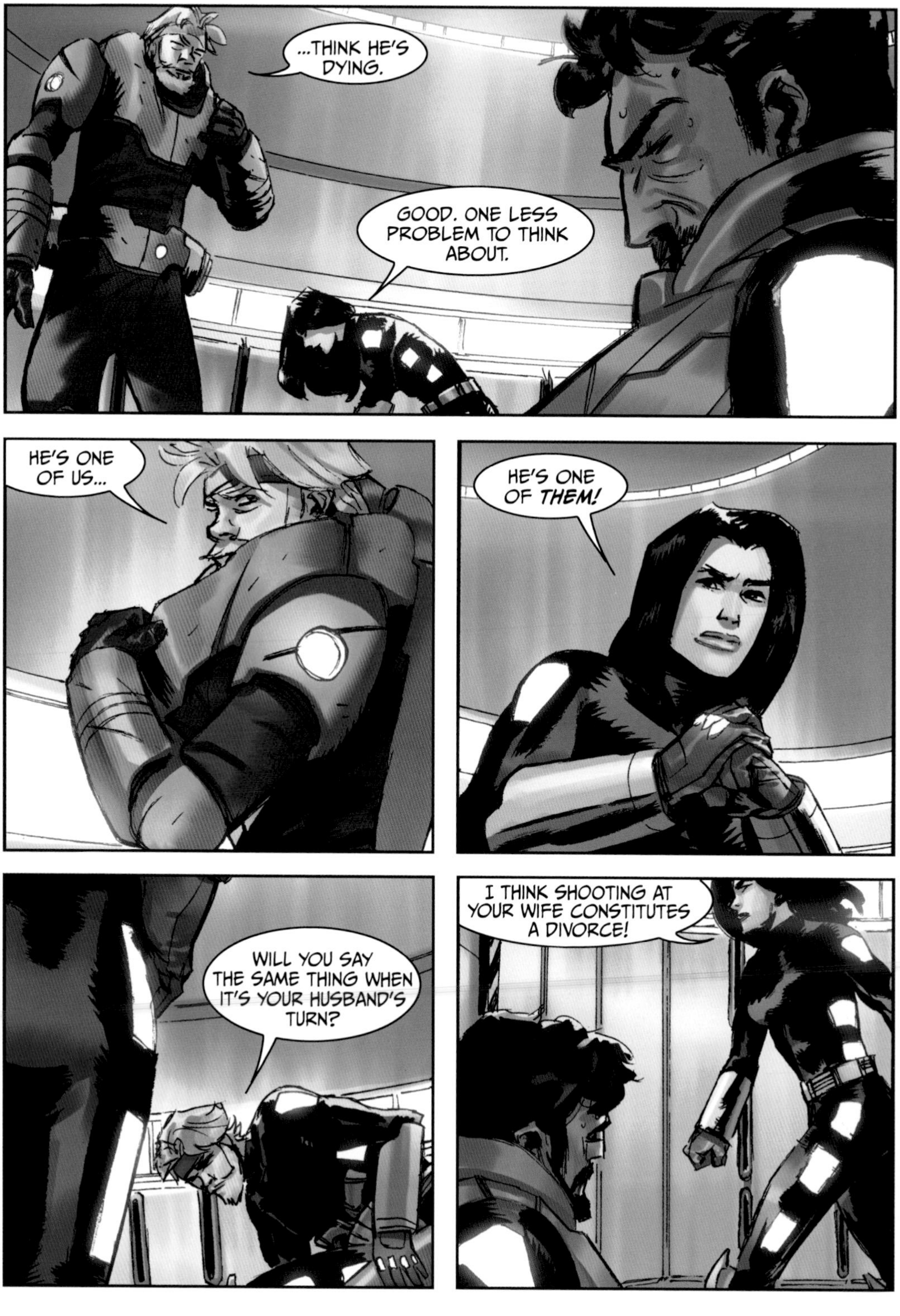
...THINK HE'S DYING.
GOOD. ONE LESS PROBLEM TO THINK ABOUT.
HE'S ONE OF US...
HE'S ONE OF *THEM!*
WILL YOU SAY THE SAME THING WHEN IT'S YOUR HUSBAND'S TURN?
I THINK SHOOTING AT YOUR WIFE CONSTITUTES A DIVORCE!

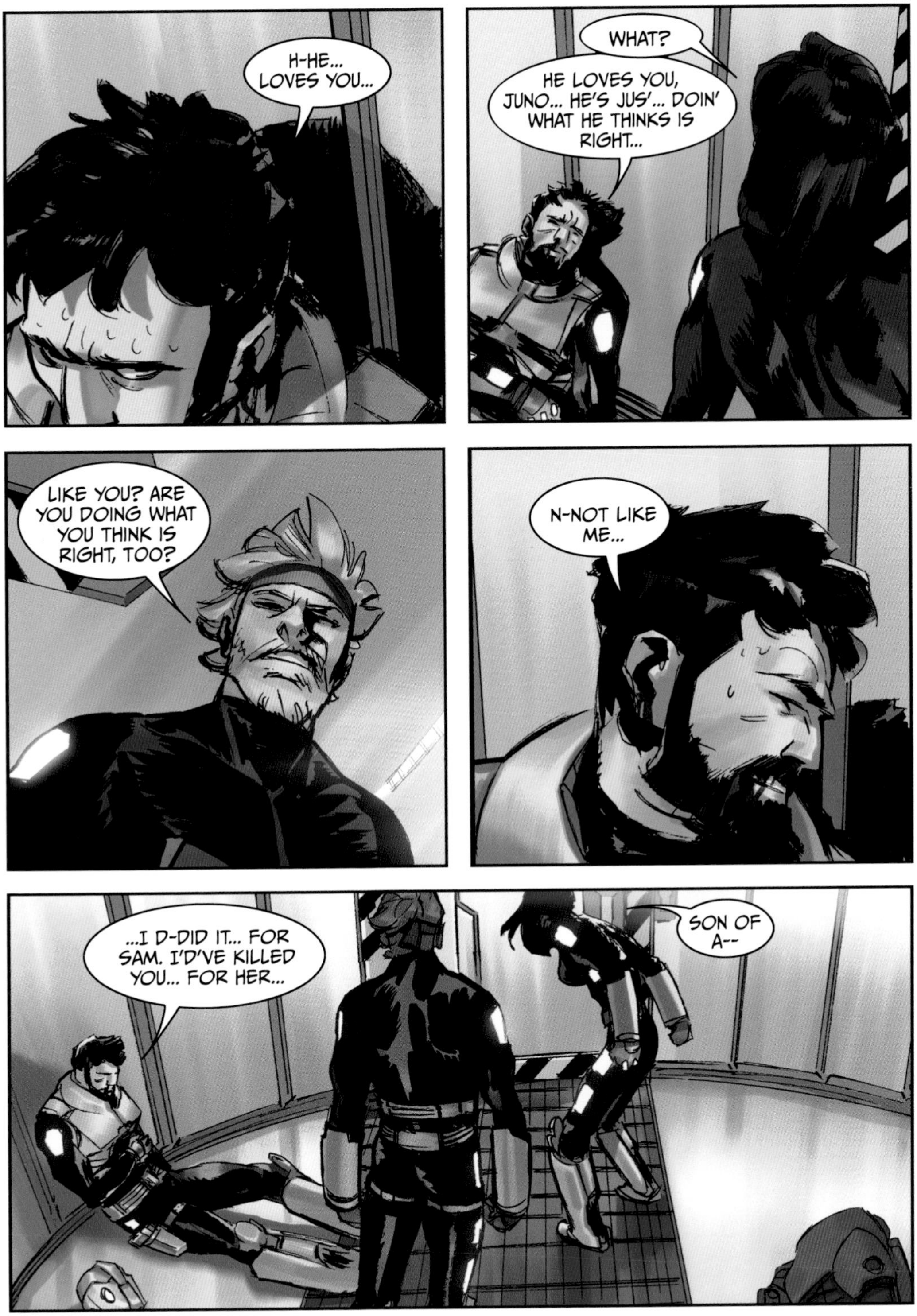
H-HE... LOVES YOU...
WHAT?
HE LOVES YOU, JUNO... HE'S JUS'... DOIN' WHAT HE THINKS IS RIGHT...
LIKE YOU? ARE YOU DOING WHAT YOU THINK IS RIGHT, TOO?
N-NOT LIKE ME...
...I D-DID IT... FOR SAM. I'D'VE KILLED YOU... FOR HER...
SON OF A--

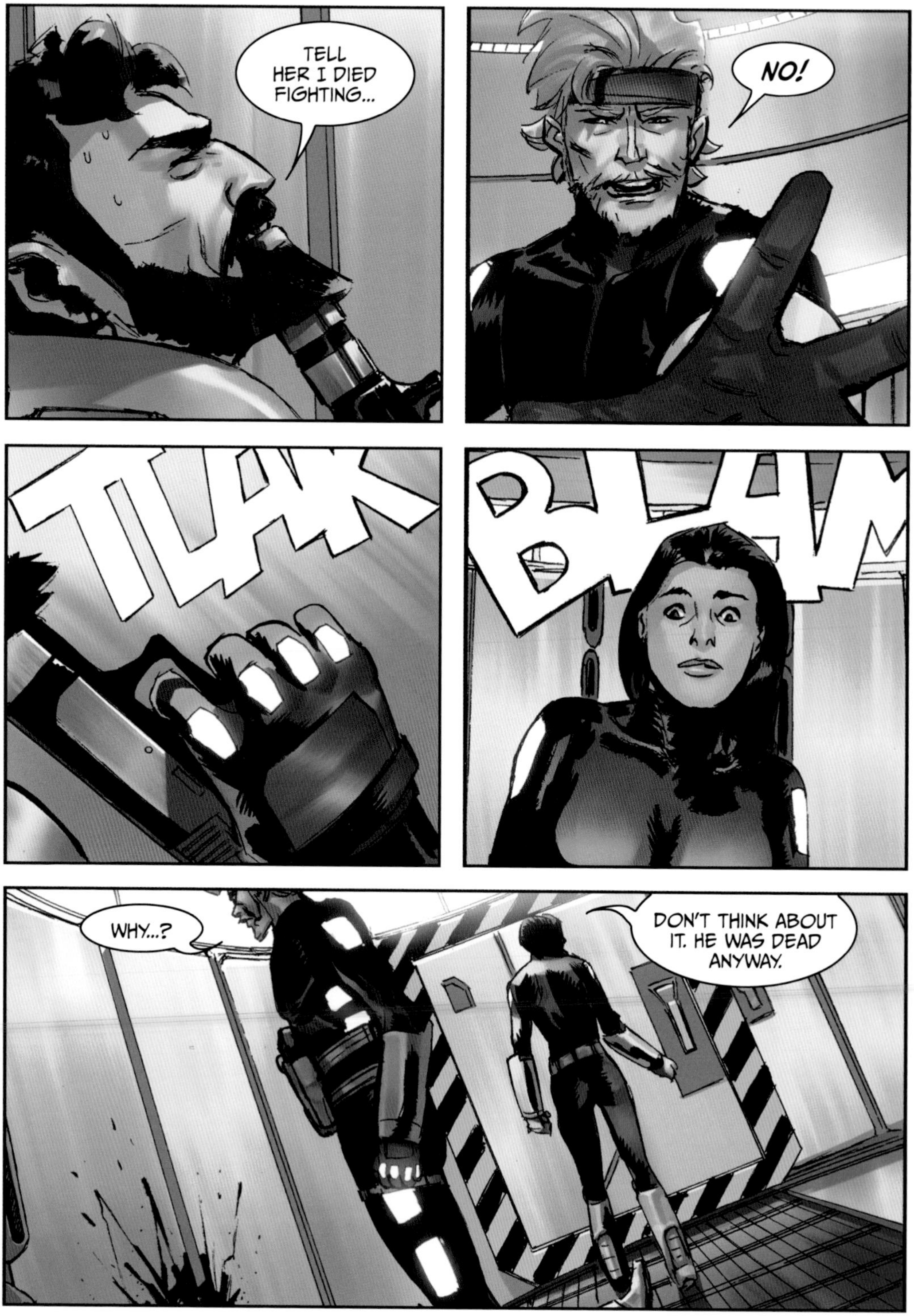
TELL HER I DIED FIGHTING...
NO!
TLAK
BLAM
WHY...?
DON'T THINK ABOUT IT. HE WAS DEAD ANYWAY.

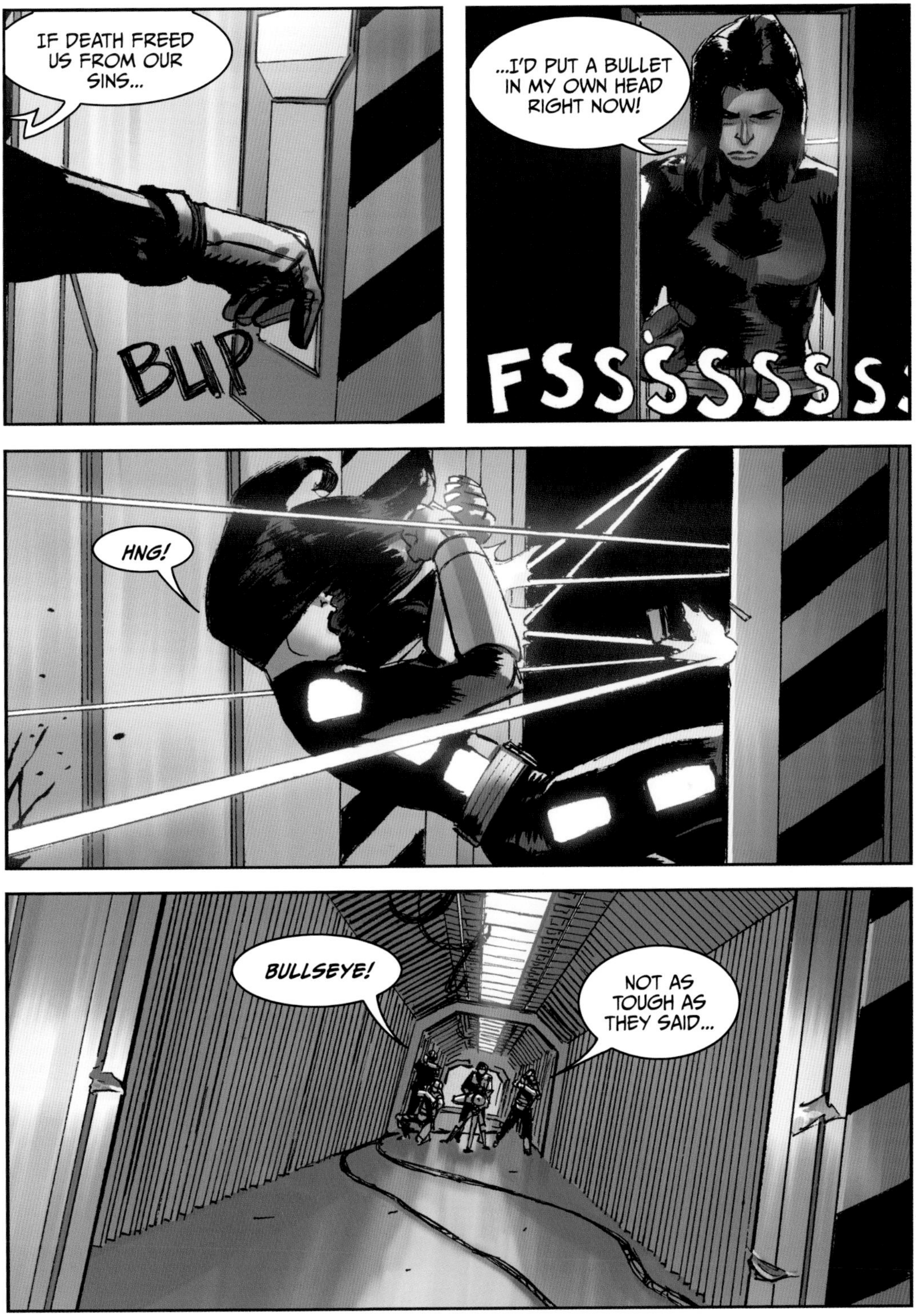
IF DEATH FREED US FROM OUR SINS...
BLIP
...I'D PUT A BULLET IN MY OWN HEAD RIGHT NOW!
FSSSSSSS
HNG!
BULLSEYE!
NOT AS TOUGH AS THEY SAID...

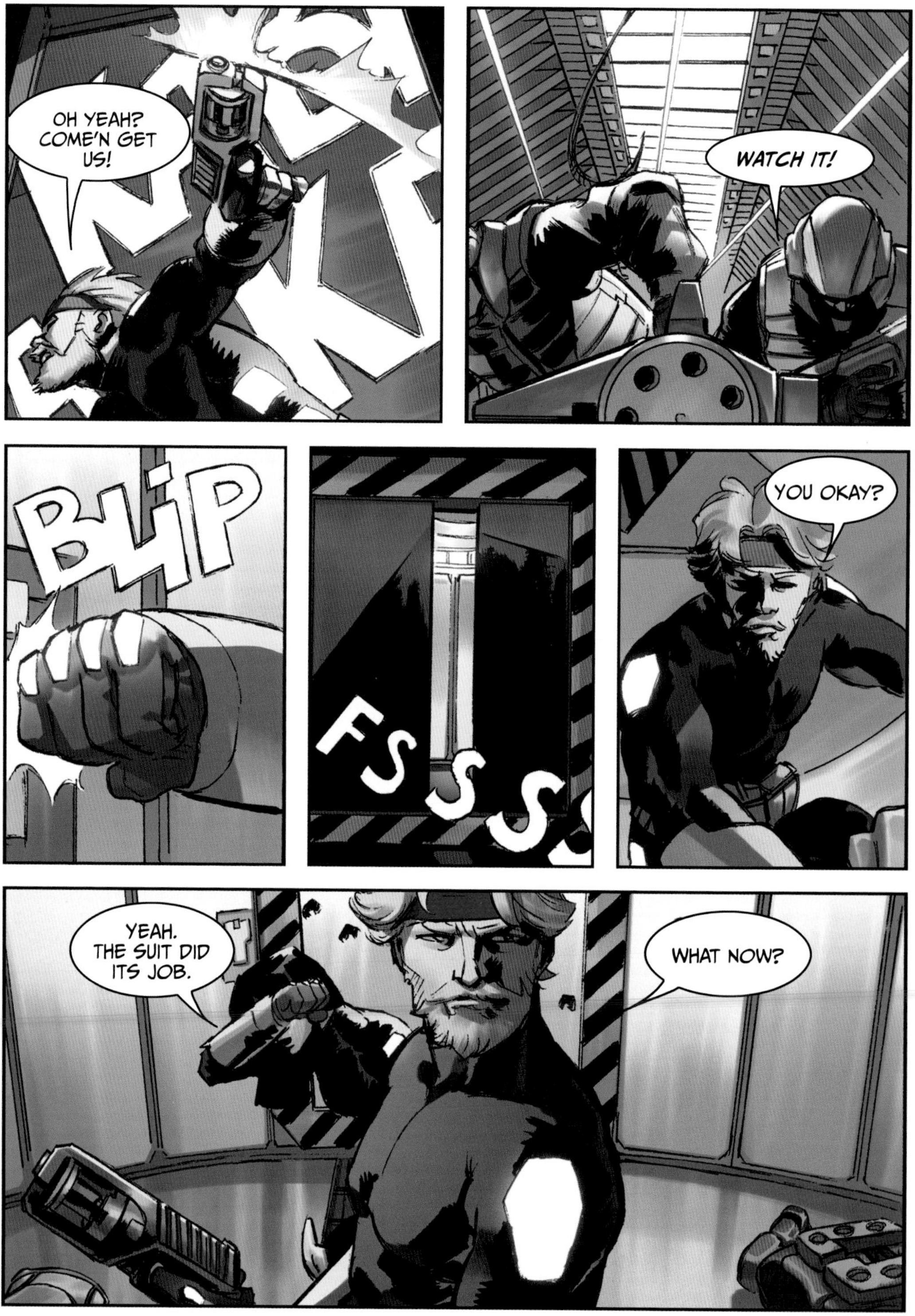
OH YEAH? COME'N GET US!
WATCH IT!
BLIP
FSSS
YOU OKAY?
YEAH. THE SUIT DID ITS JOB.
WHAT NOW?

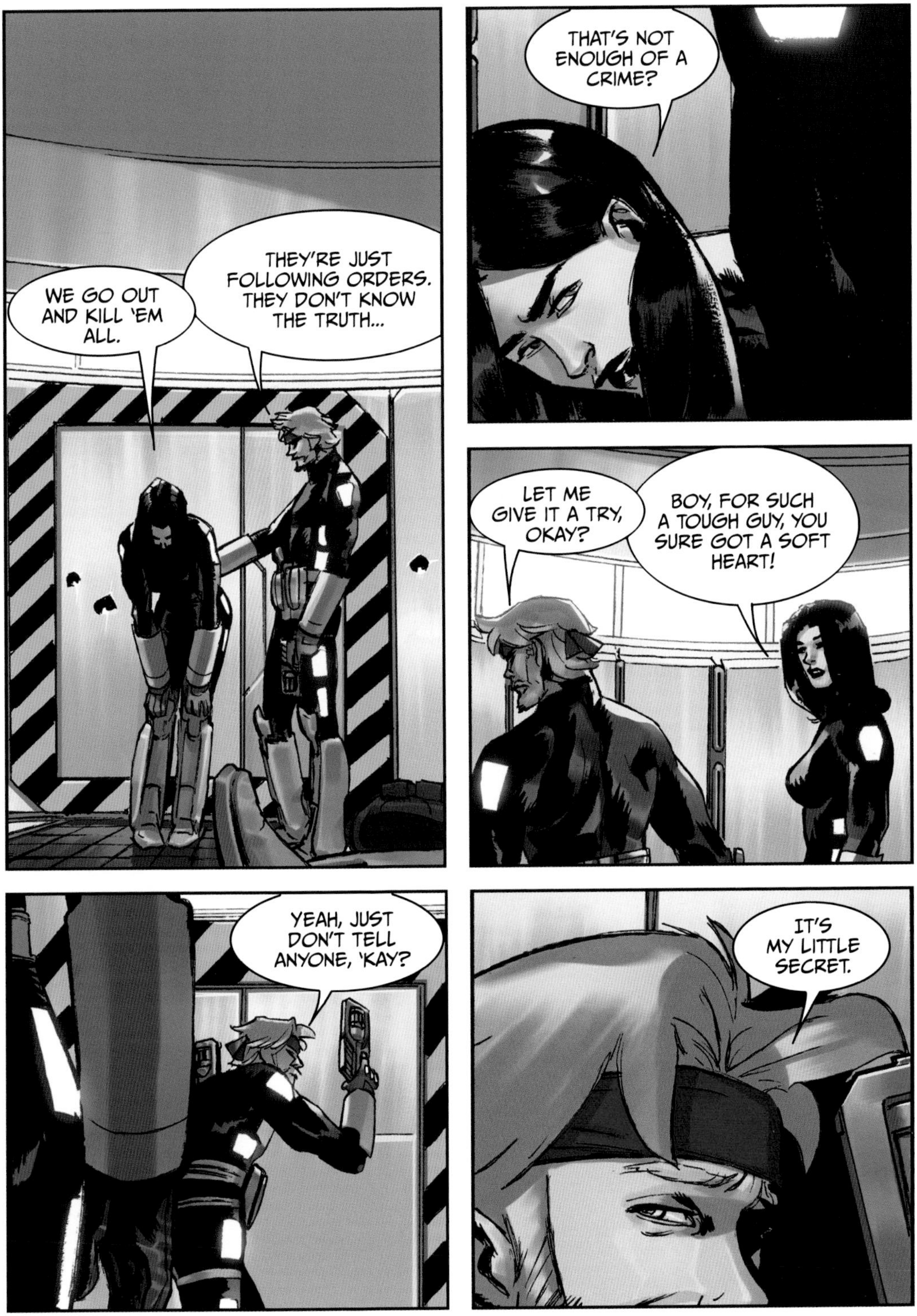
WE GO OUT AND KILL 'EM ALL.
THEY'RE JUST FOLLOWING ORDERS. THEY DON'T KNOW THE TRUTH...
THAT'S NOT ENOUGH OF A CRIME?
LET ME GIVE IT A TRY, OKAY?
BOY, FOR SUCH A TOUGH GUY, YOU SURE GOT A SOFT HEART!
YEAH, JUST DON'T TELL ANYONE, 'KAY?
IT'S MY LITTLE SECRET.

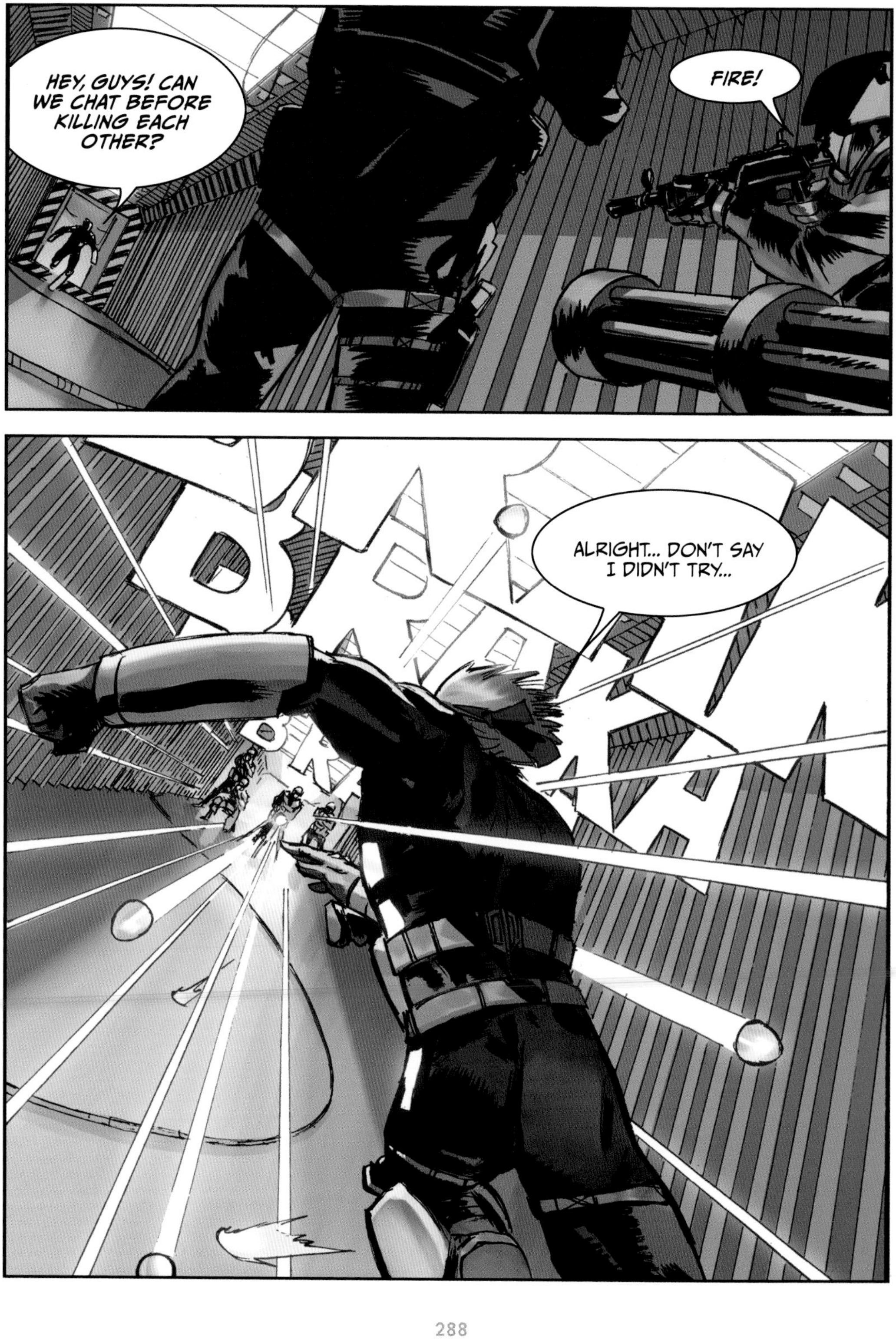
HEY, GUYS! CAN WE CHAT BEFORE KILLING EACH OTHER?
FIRE!
ALRIGHT... DON'T SAY I DIDN'T TRY...

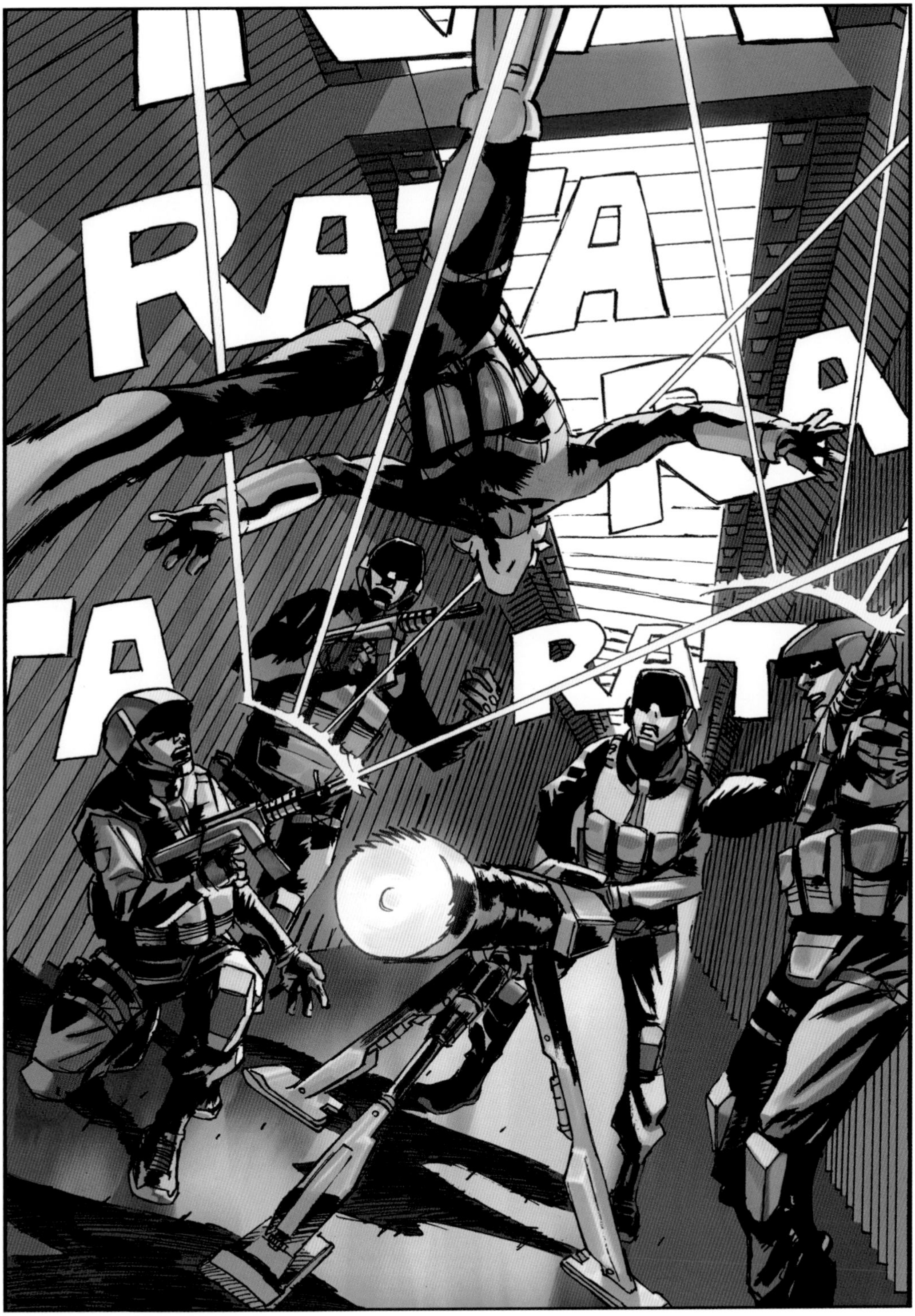

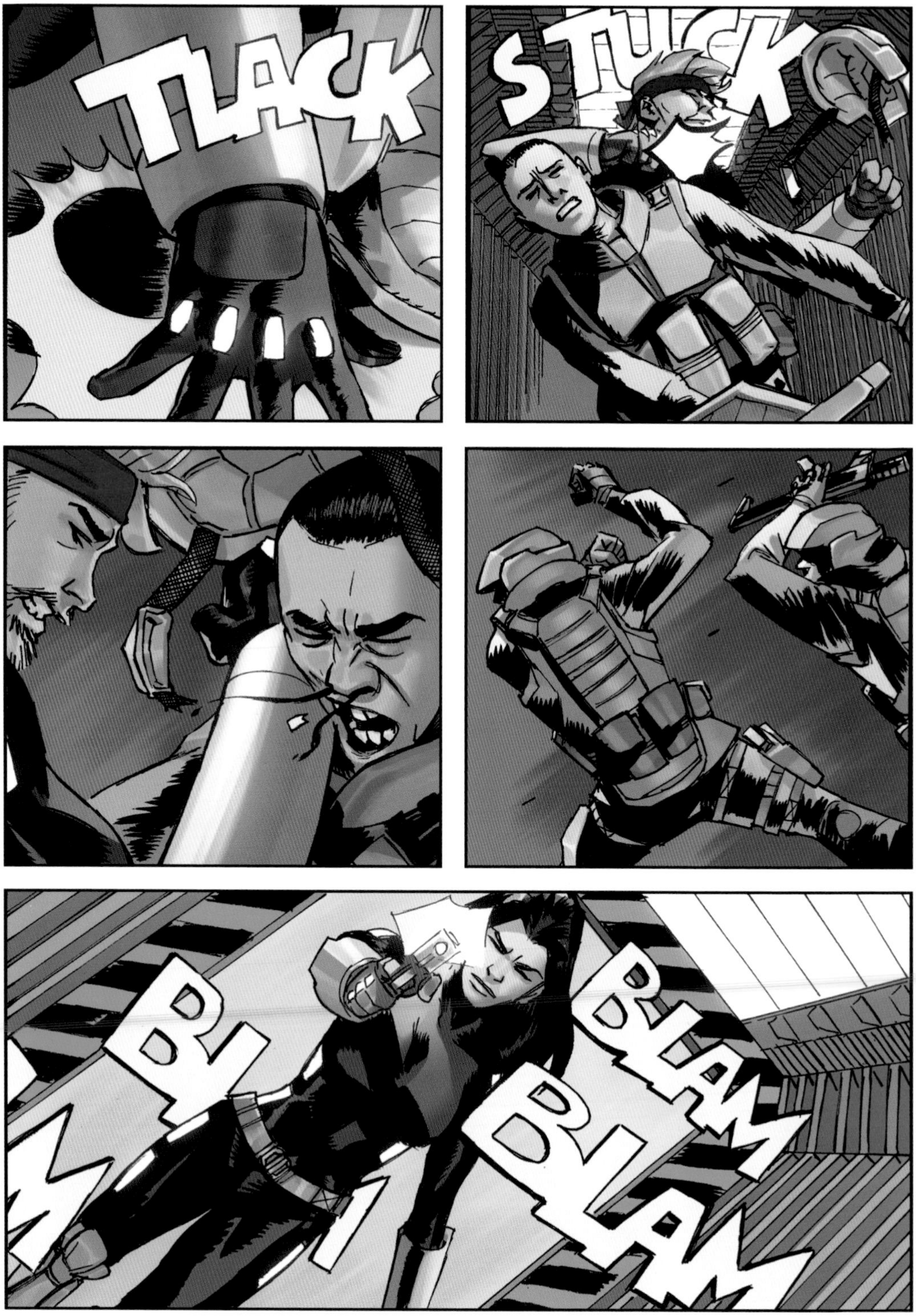
TLACK
STUCK
BLAM
BLAM
BLAM

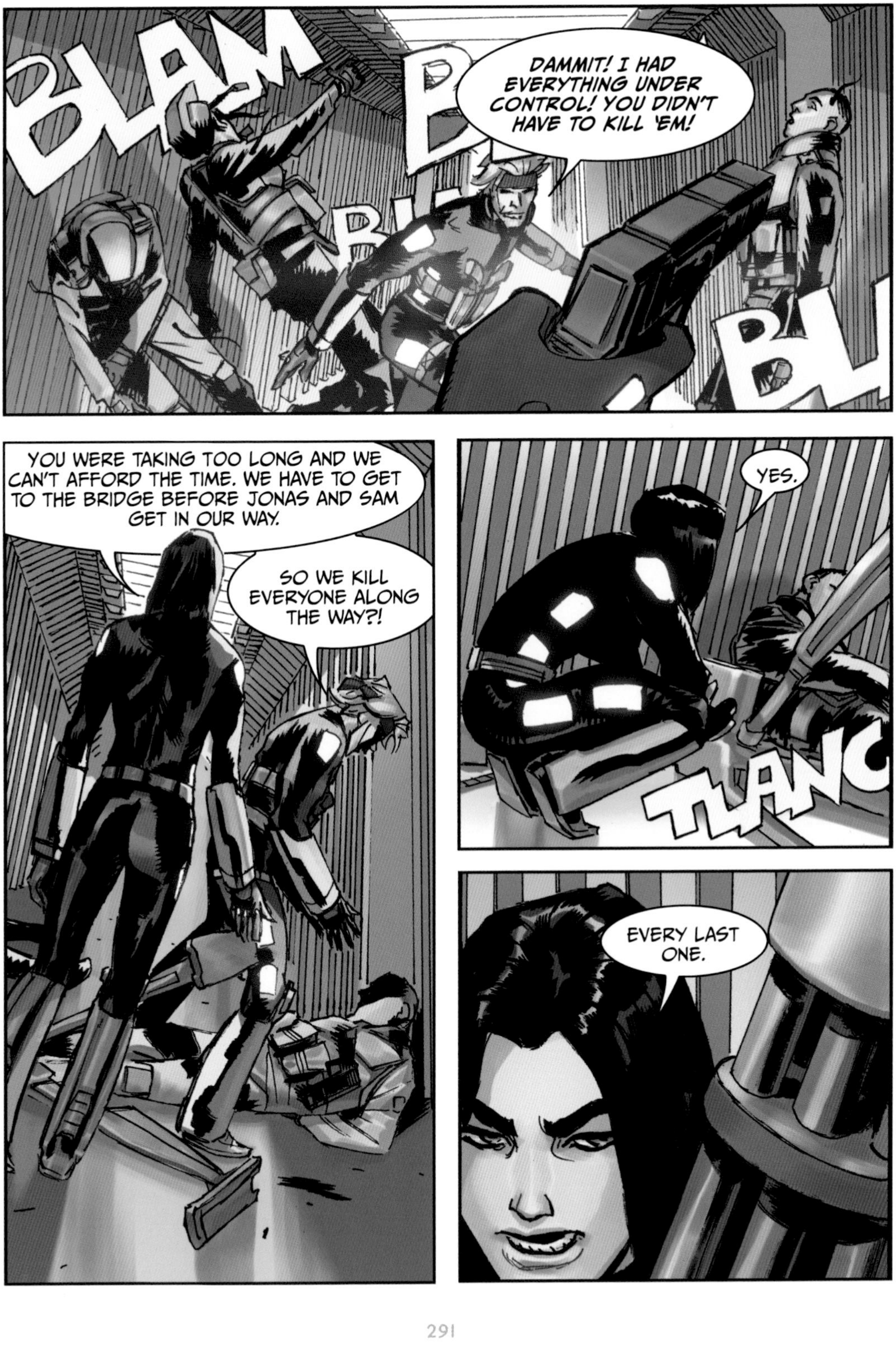
BLAM
B
DAMMIT! I HAD EVERYTHING UNDER CONTROL! YOU DIDN'T HAVE TO KILL 'EM!
BL
BL
YOU WERE TAKING TOO LONG AND WE CAN'T AFFORD THE TIME. WE HAVE TO GET TO THE BRIDGE BEFORE JONAS AND SAM GET IN OUR WAY.
SO WE KILL EVERYONE ALONG THE WAY?!
YES.
TLANG
EVERY LAST ONE.

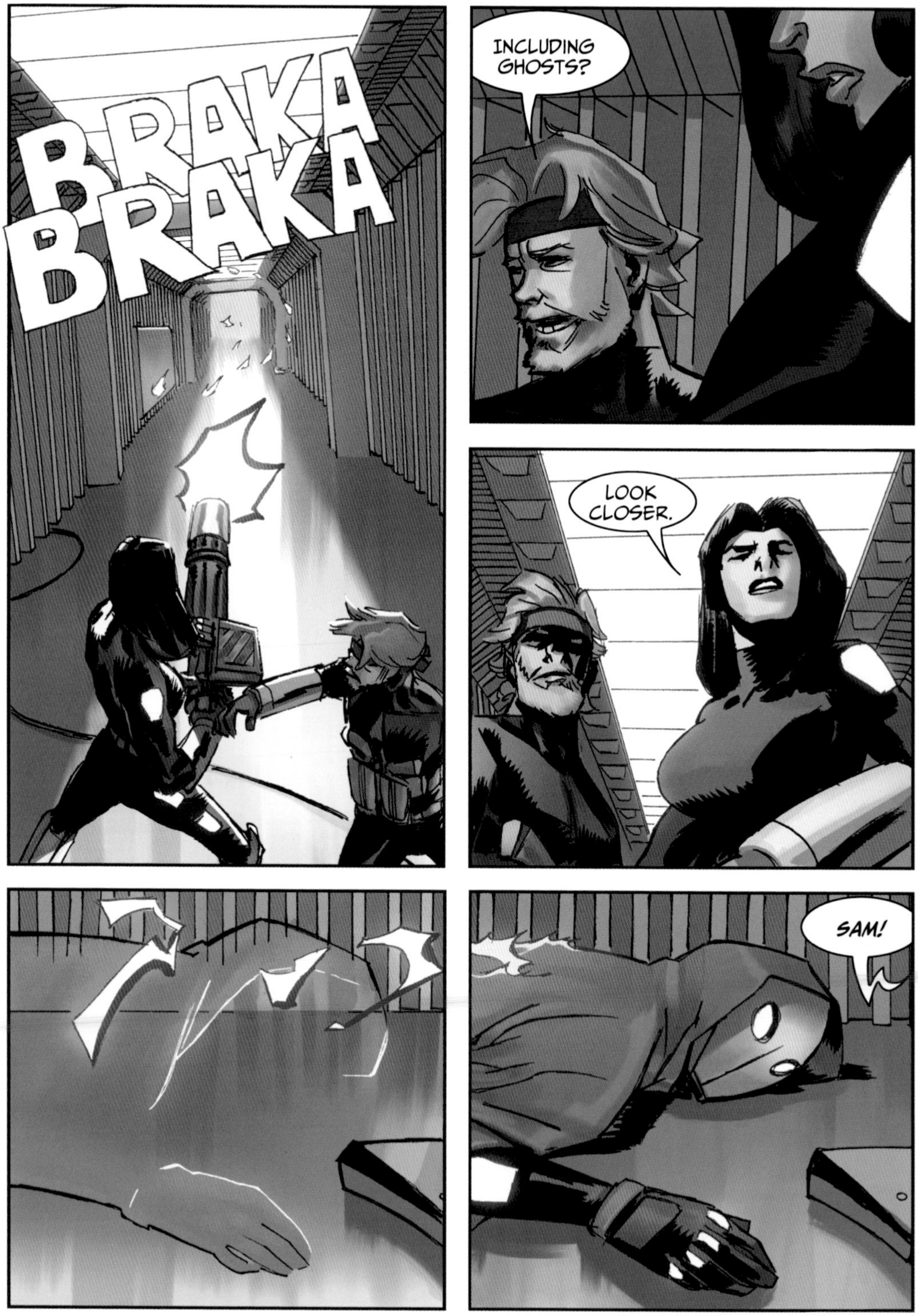
BRAKA
BRAKA
INCLUDING GHOSTS?
LOOK CLOSER.
SAM!

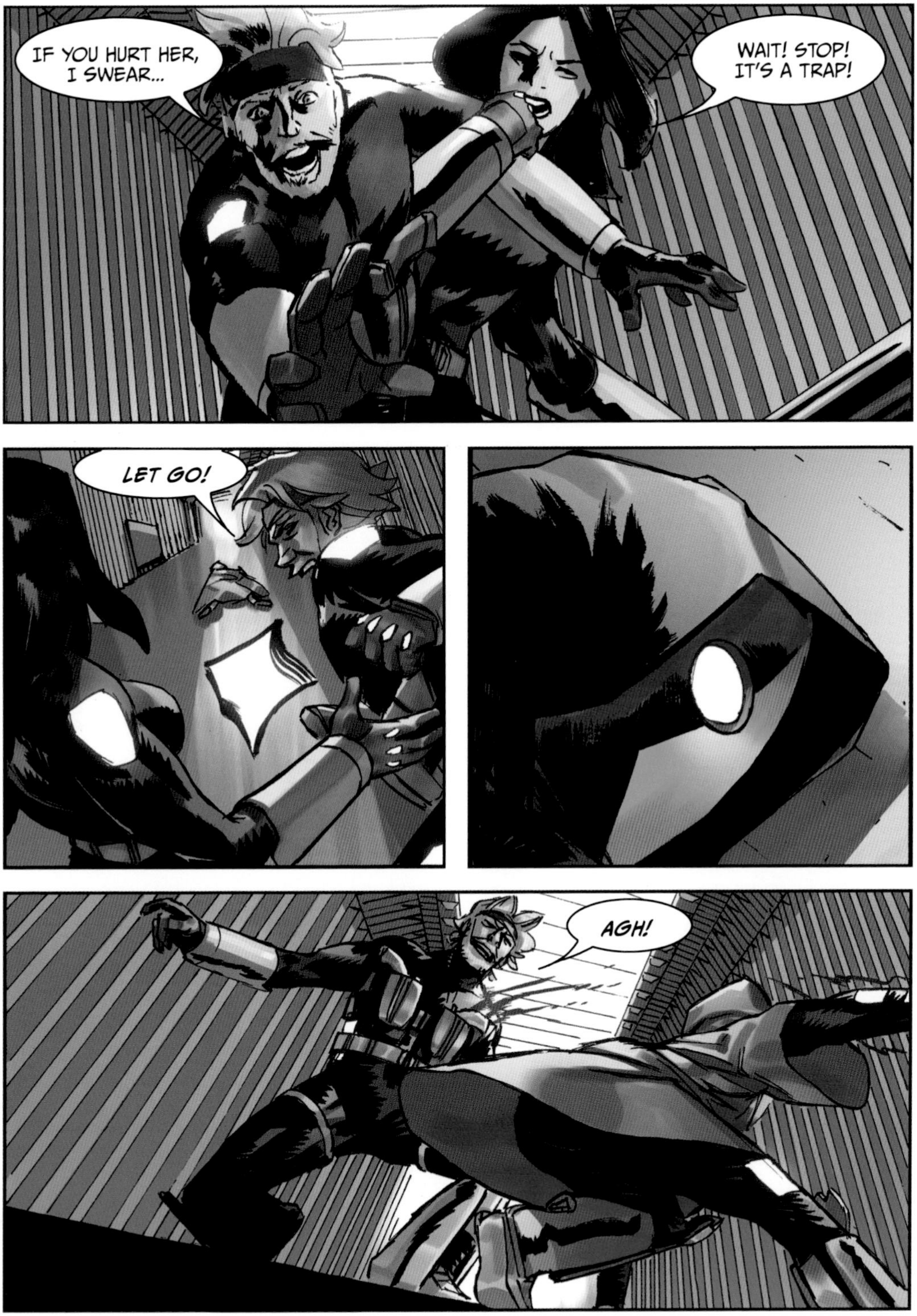
IF YOU HURT HER, I SWEAR...
WAIT! STOP! IT'S A TRAP!
LET GO!
AGH!

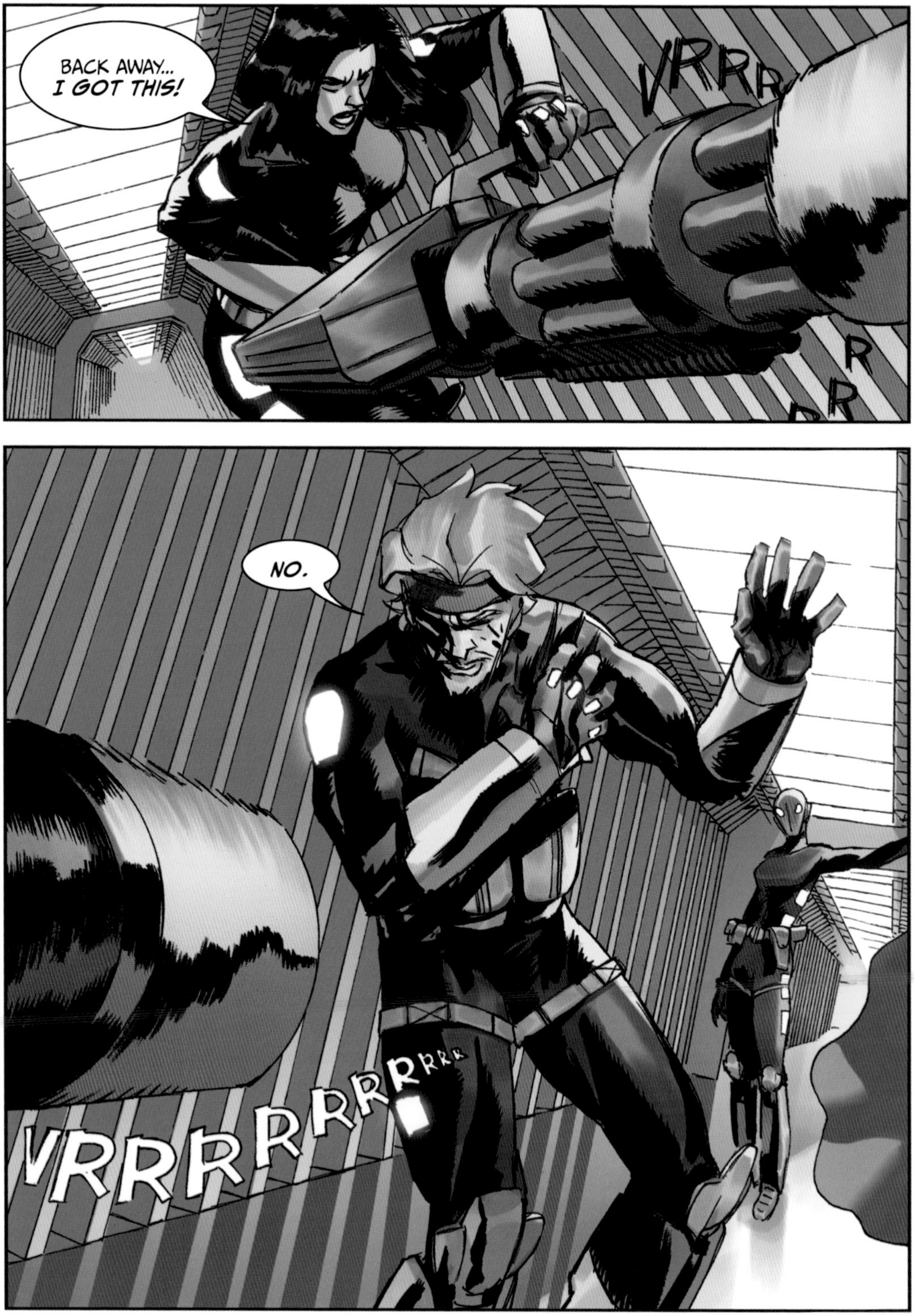
BACK AWAY...
I GOT THIS!
VRRR
R
R
NO.
VRRRRRRRRRR

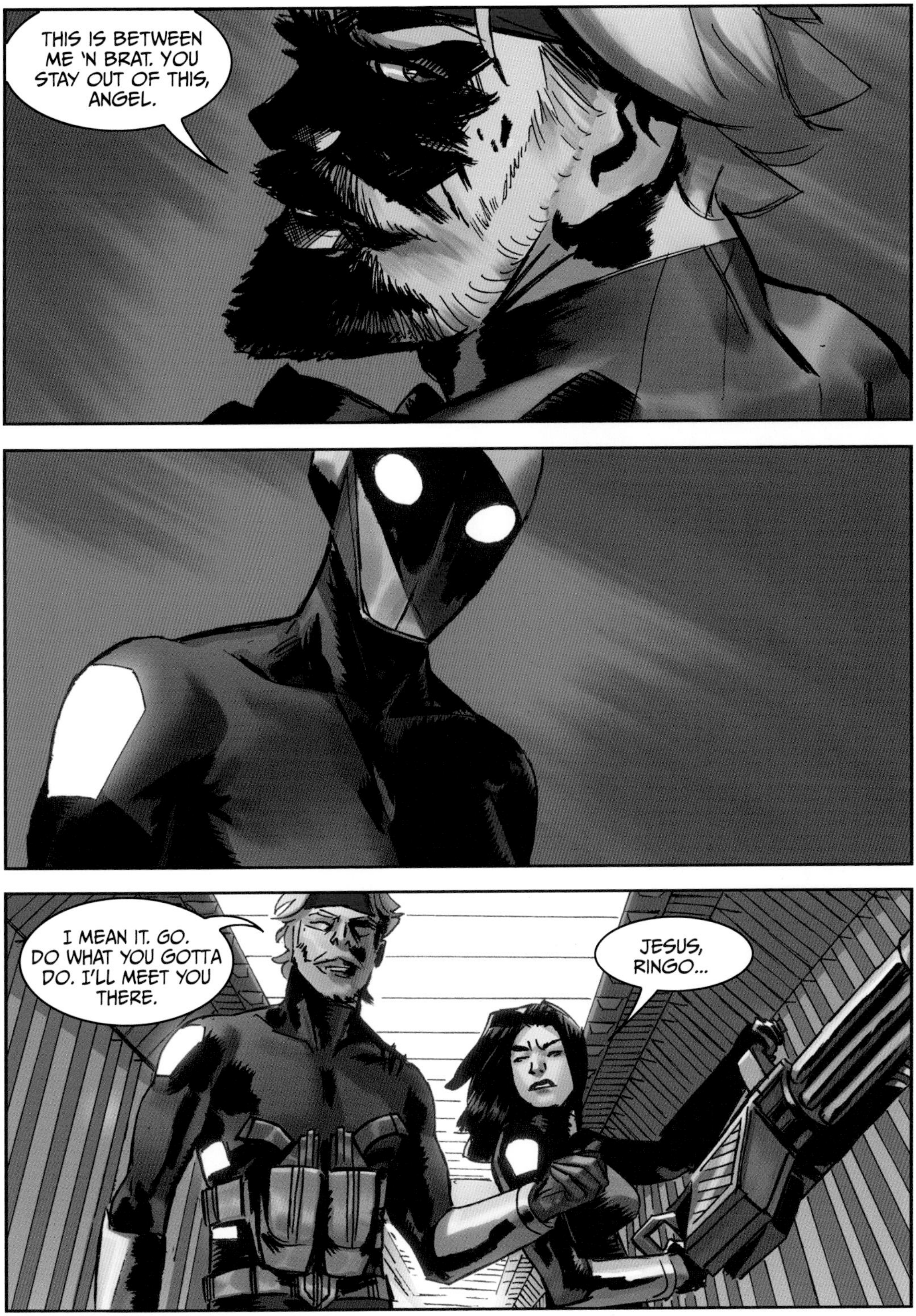
THIS IS BETWEEN ME 'N BRAT. YOU STAY OUT OF THIS, ANGEL.
I MEAN IT. GO. DO WHAT YOU GOTTA DO. I'LL MEET YOU THERE.
JESUS, RINGO...

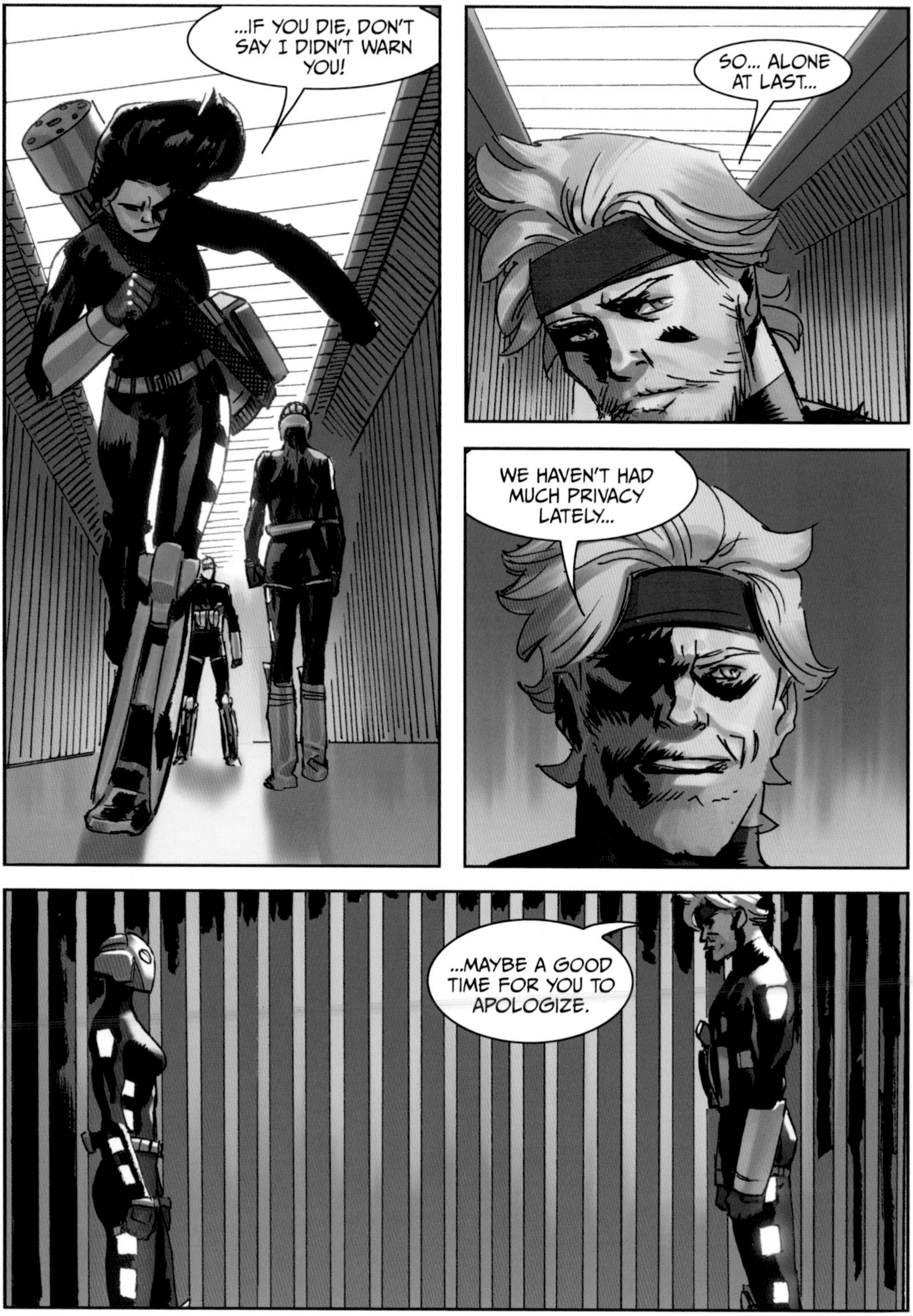
...IF YOU DIE, DON'T SAY I DIDN'T WARN YOU!
SO... ALONE AT LAST...
WE HAVEN'T HAD MUCH PRIVACY LATELY...
...MAYBE A GOOD TIME FOR YOU TO APOLOGIZE.

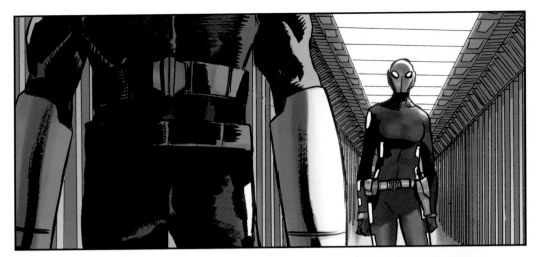

YOU'RE NOT MAKING THIS EASY, BRAT...

SAY SOMETHING!

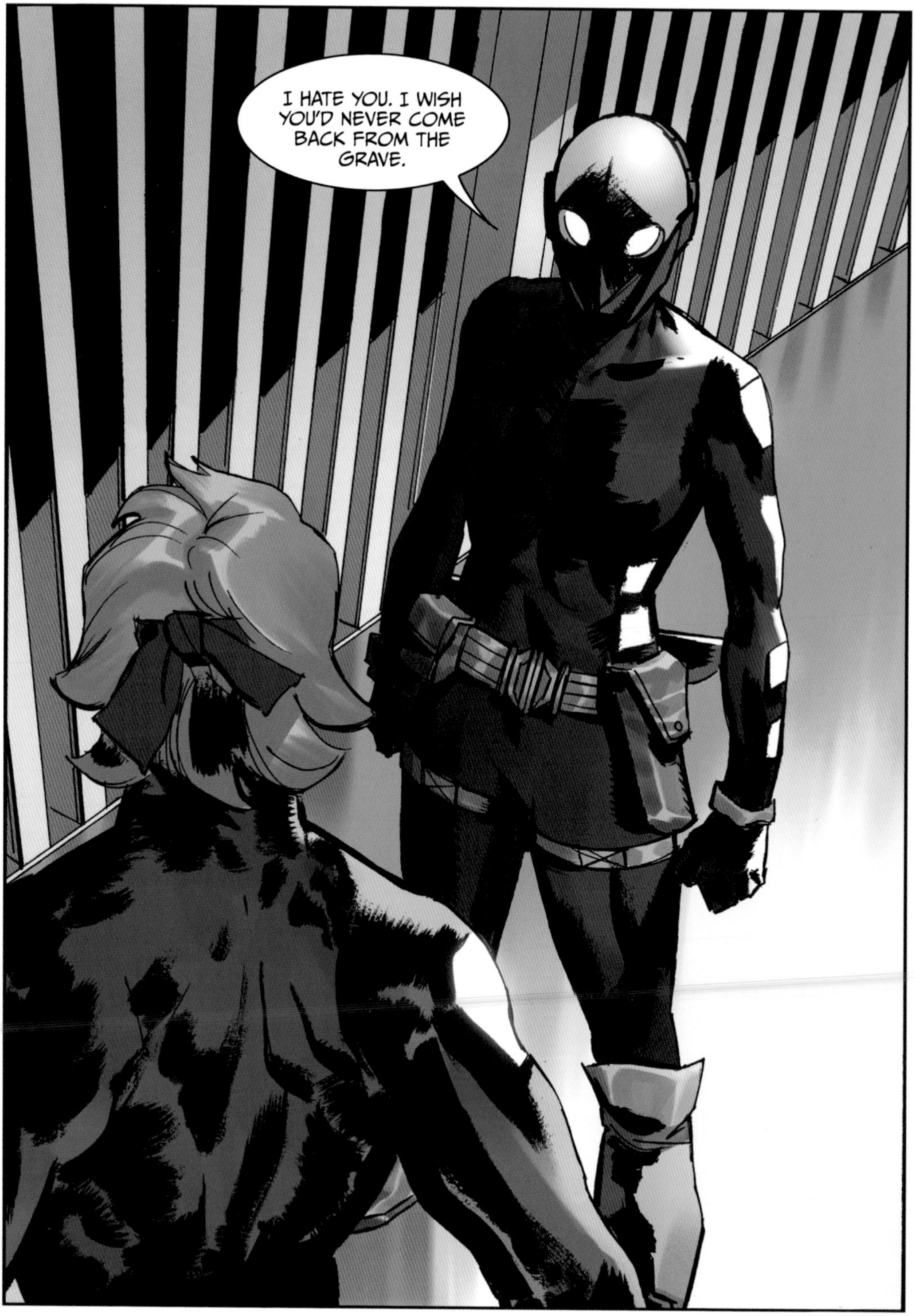
I HATE YOU. I WISH YOU'D NEVER COME BACK FROM THE GRAVE.

GIGI CAVENAGO **ARTIST**

When and where were you born? Where do you live now?
I was born in Milan on October 12, 1982. Now I live in Senago.

What sort of artistic education did you have?
I attended a class at the Comics School in Milan but I've also studied graphic design at the Rizzoli Institute for Graphic Arts.

Tell us about your previous works, before *Orphans*.
Jonathan Steele, by Memola and Marzia, published by Star Comics; the miniseries *Dr. Voodoo* with Giovanni Gualdoni for Free Books and, last but not least, *Cassidy*, a miniseries by Pasquale Rujo for Sergio Bonelli Editore.

When did you start working on *Orphans*, and when did you finish drawing this chapter?
The first files for my half of this chapter date back to February 2013. The latest are from mid-October 2013.

What tools did you use?
For this chapter, I chose a mix of digital and traditional drawing. Let's just say that when inking forests and trees, it is much more fun to let the brush guide your hand. Nevertheless, digital drawing started to claim its space towards the end, to the point that the last pages are 100% digital.

What was the most difficult scene and which one did you have to redraw more times?
The toughest task for me wasn't a scene, but just a very big panel (on page 239): it's the end of the sequence in which Ringo lies on the ground after being kneed in the groin. It wasn't easy to convey the right tone for the scene because it shouldn't seem too silly nor too serious. After all, if the scene you're telling is funny by itself, there's no need to exaggerate it further.

If you could go back in time, what would you change about this chapter?
Page 211. Three identical horizontal panels with the same fixed shot of forests and mountains in which Ringo enters the scene with a colossal jump. I redrew that jump at least ten times, but couldn't really make it work. Eventually, it proved to be a real "Columbus Egg" (an obvious trick) and I just needed to put Ringo far away, transforming him into a tiny silhouette. After that, I made a color illustration with the rejected sketches of Ringo jumping in a kinetic, colorful space (shown on page 334 of this volume).

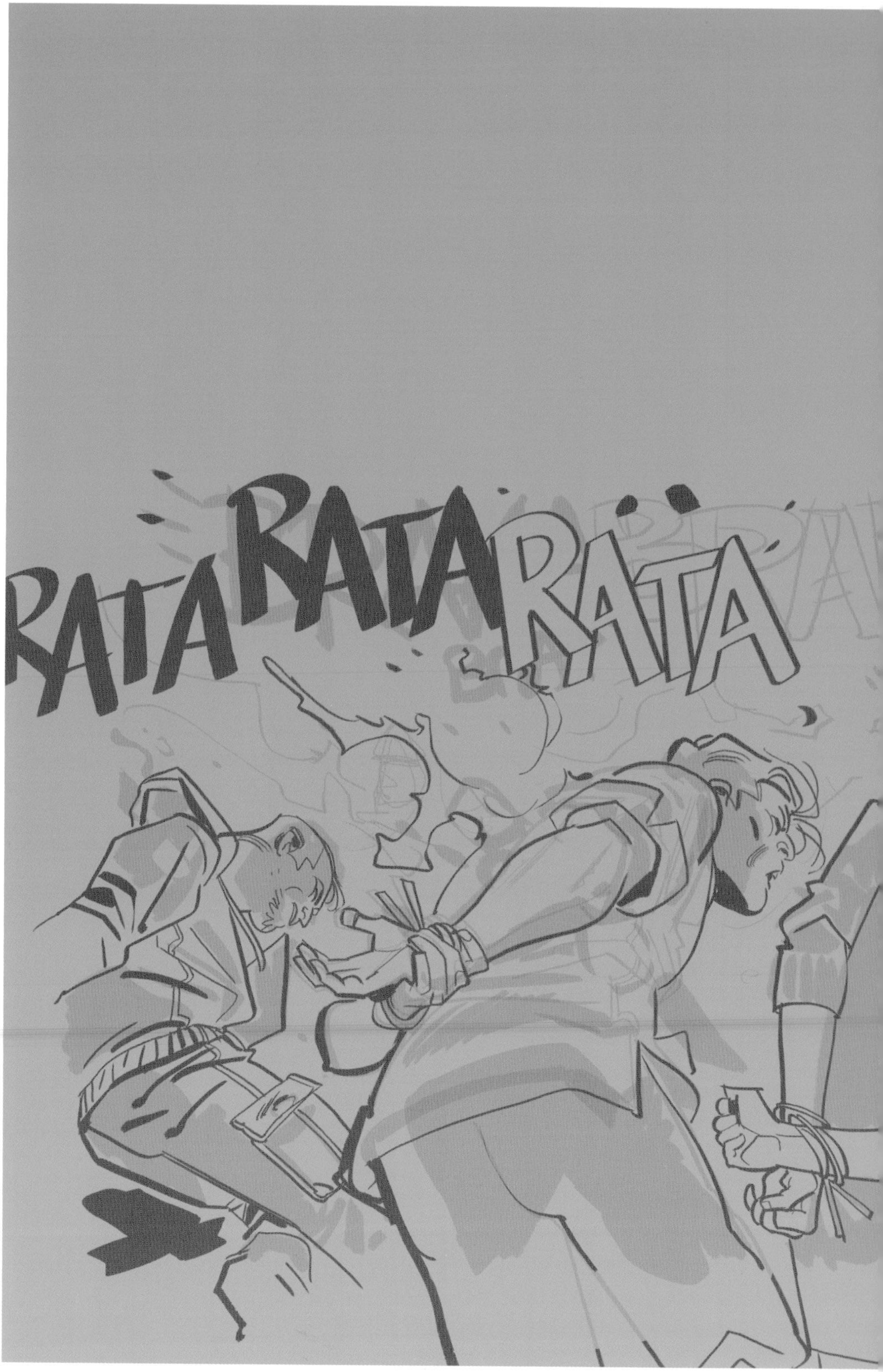
RATA RATA RATA

ORPHANS

EXTRA

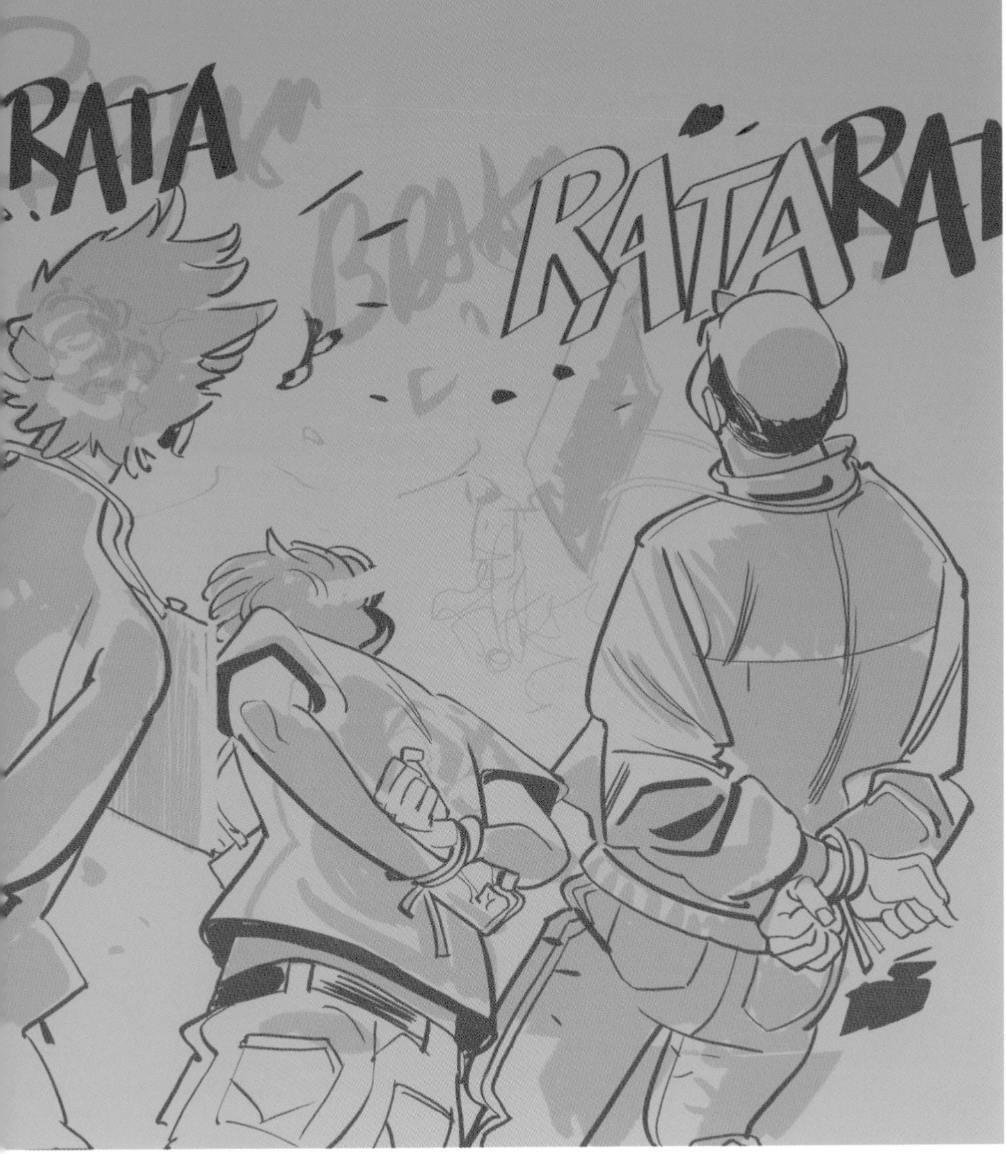
RATA
RATARAT

USING LIGHTING IN THE SCENES AND A CHOICE OF THE COLORS IN THAT SENSE, WE DECIDED TO MATCH THE TONE OF THE STORY, EMPHASIZING ITS RHYTHM AND SUGGESTING ITS ATMOSPHERES.

– LORENZO DE FELICI

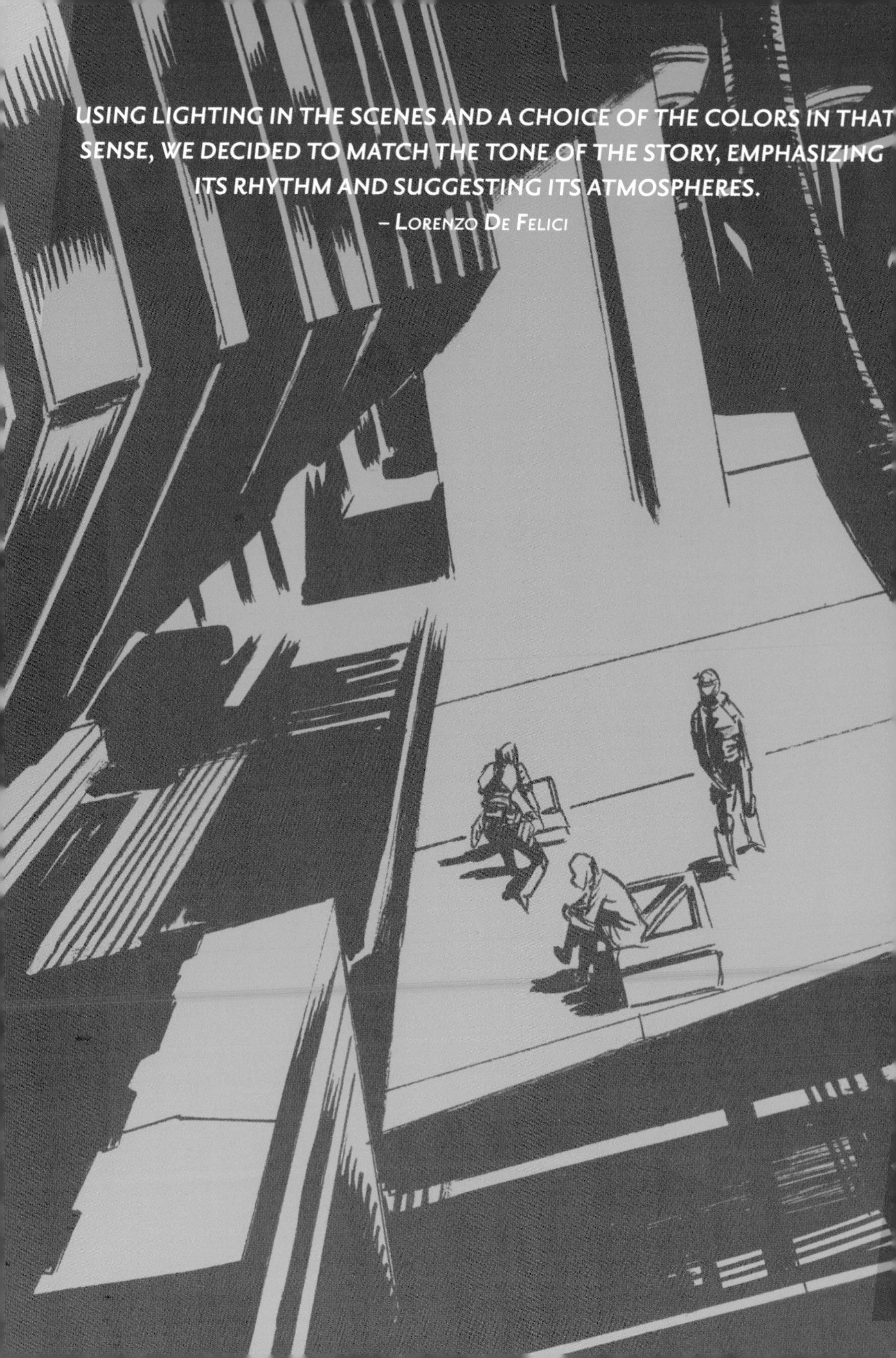

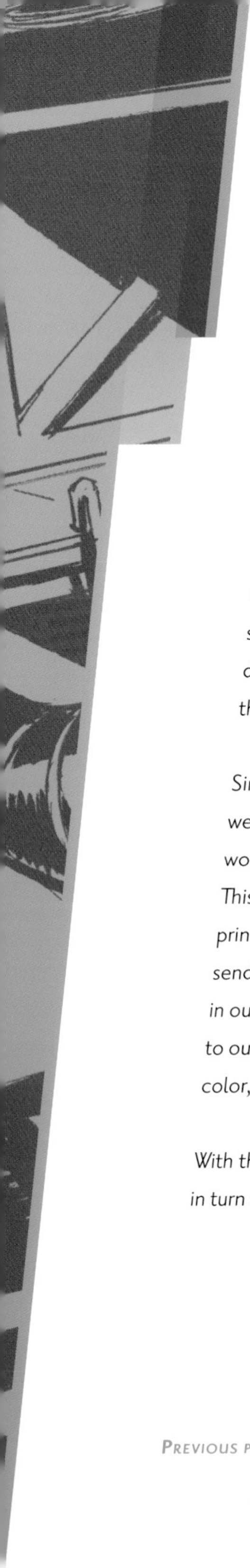

COLOR CODE

by **LORENZO DE FELICI**

Coloring *Orphans* was, like *Orphans* itself, a one-of-a-kind work. Its strong identity is the result of a series of formal needs and technical issues that we faced from the very start: we needed to provide and support a mood, but also define some sort of cooperation among the different elements. We were prepared for the worst, but still accepted the challenge and teamed up.

Since the beginning, to obtain a result that was as uniform as possible, we realized we needed to set some strong directions that every artist would express in their own way, according to their individual "voices." This is why we decided to ground all of our choices on one of the basic principles of the job: the emotional importance of color. Every color sends a very distinct input to our brain: it's a language deeply rooted in our animal nature, belonging to a complex system that's connected to our survival instinct. A silent yet powerful mechanism: the purer the color, the purer the emotion aroused by it.

With this "power" in mind, we combined color and illustration, which in turn is combined with writing to create an unified package.

Previous page: illustration by Werther Dell'Edera

In that way, we found ourselves similar to cinematic assistants whose contribution to the finished product is tightly connected to everybody else's. Thanks to the choices we made in terms of lighting and color, we tried to adapt to the story, enhancing its rhythm and suggesting a mood.

COLORING STAGES BY LORENZO DE FELICI
ON AN ILLUSTRATION BY GIGI CAVENAGO

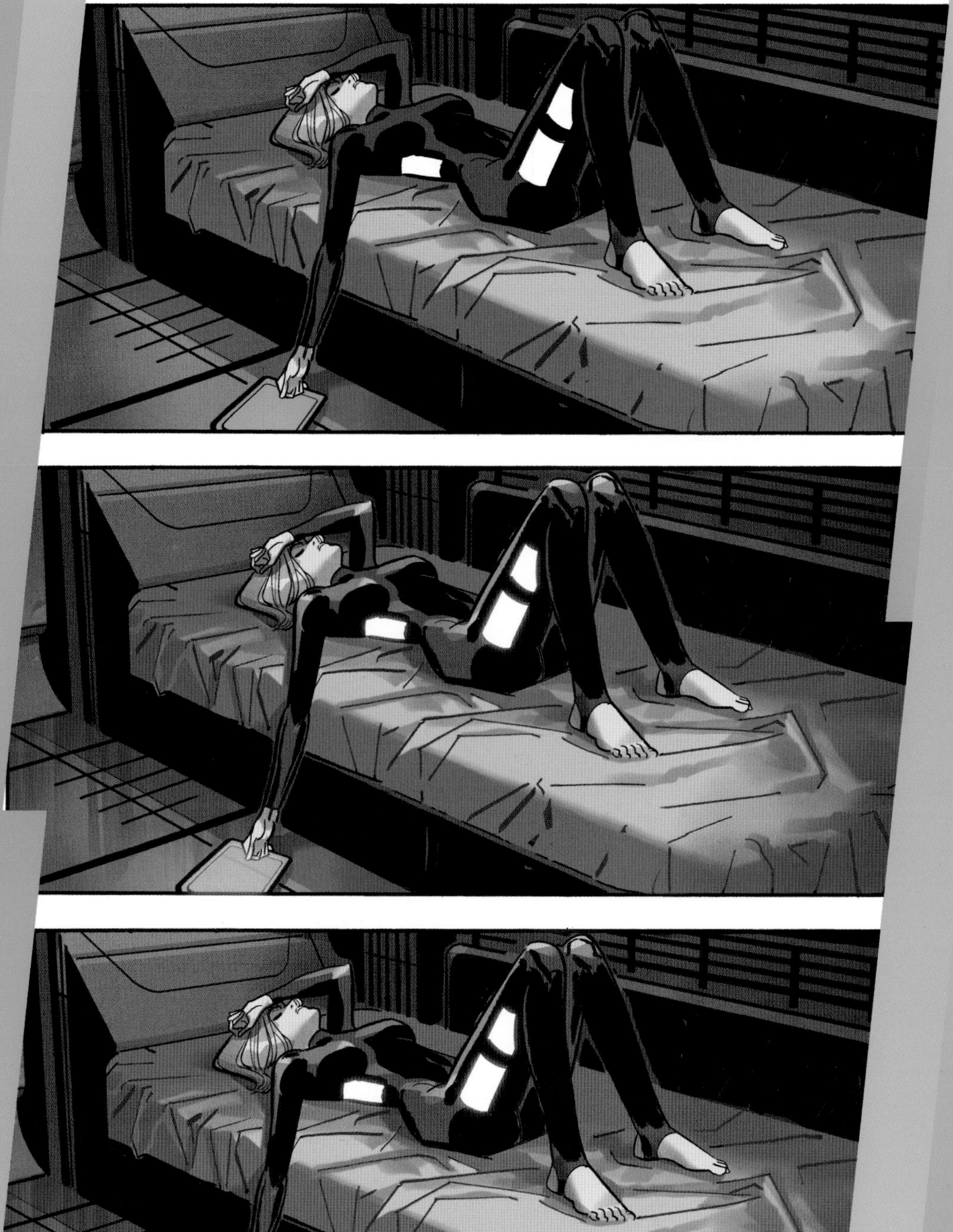
BIRI BIRI BIRI BIRI BIRI

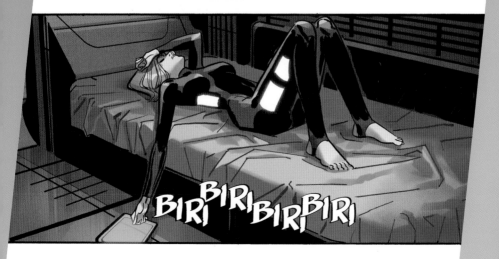

The paper and format of the first printed edition helped us set up an initial working plan, because it forced our coloring to be simple and "lively": too dark shades and too many details would've made it harder to read the comic, splitting the narration and damaging the mood. Plus, our first idea was to use color to "glue" the different chapters and the different art styles together.

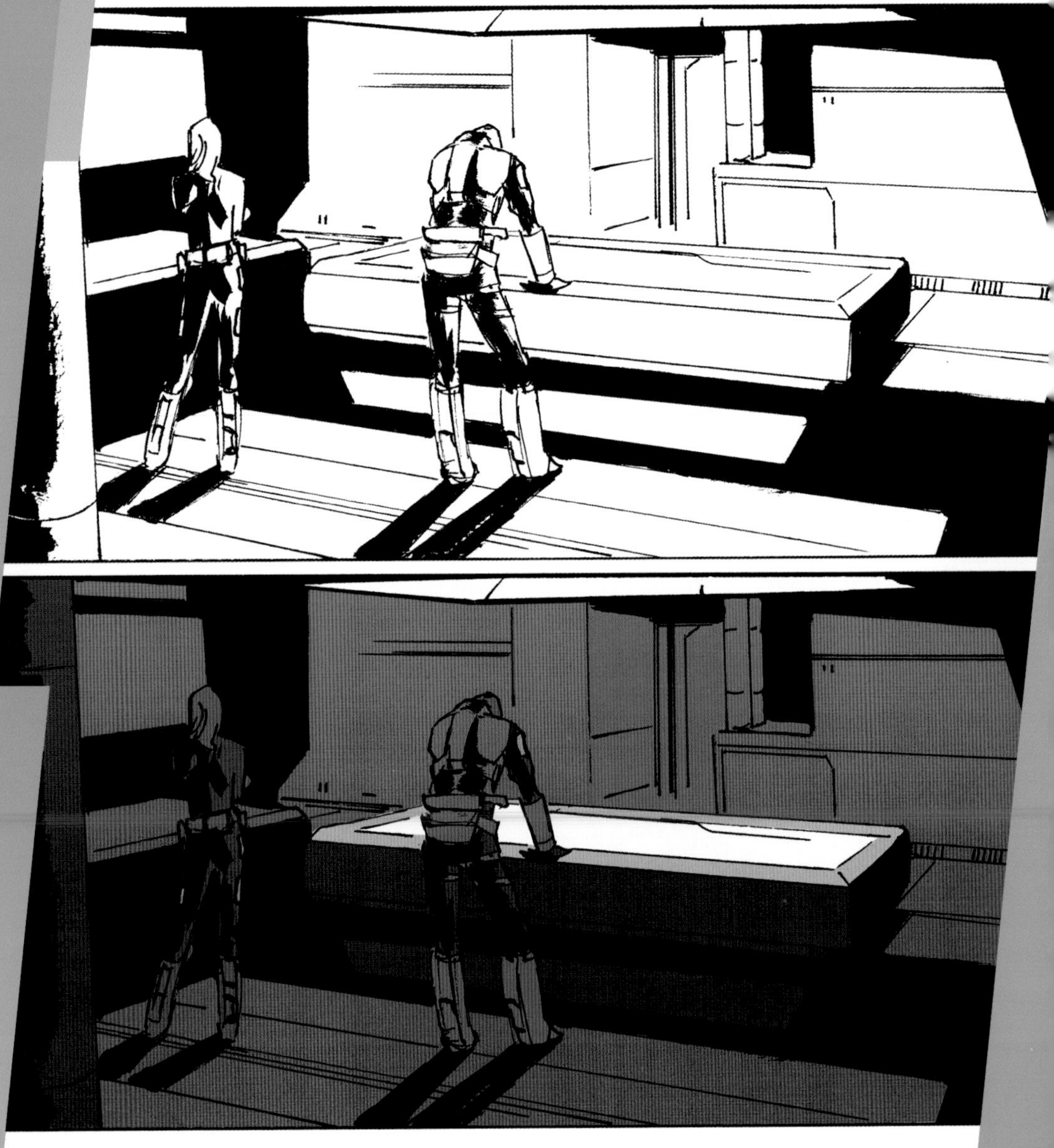

Coloring stages by Alessia Pastorello on an illustration by Werther Dell'Edera

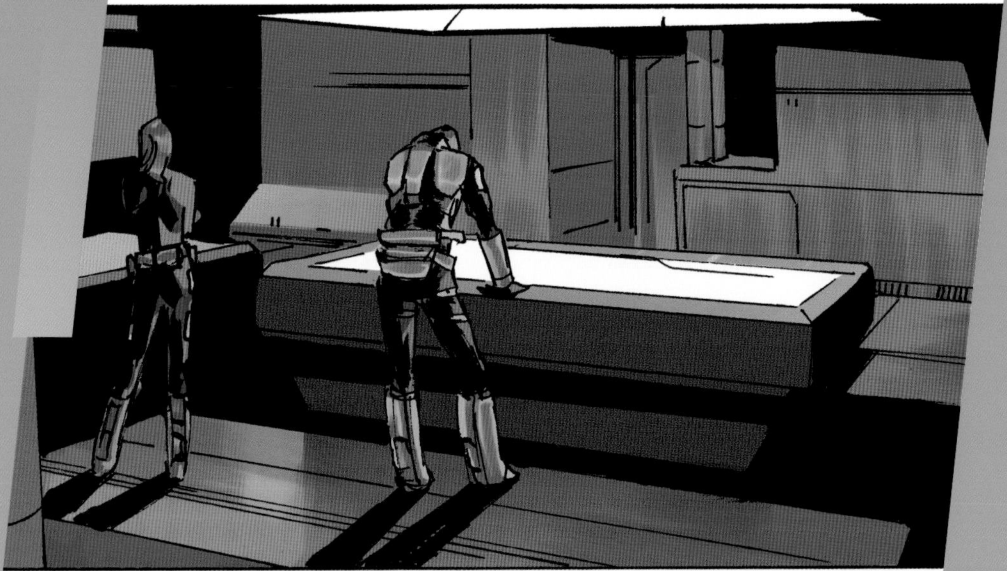

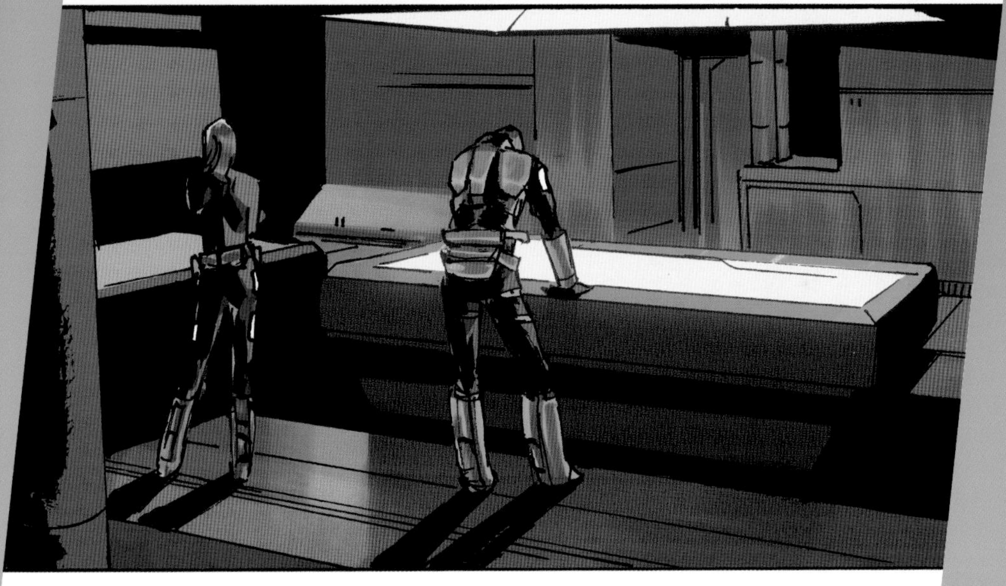

EVERY COLOR SENDS A VERY DISTINCT INPUT TO OUR BRAIN: IT'S A LANGUAGE DEEPLY ROOTED IN OUR ANIMAL NATURE, BELONGING TO A COMPLEX SYSTEM THAT'S CONNECTED TO OUR SURVIVAL INSTINCT.

– Lorenzo De Felici

So we decided to simplify our palettes as we went, using default sets of two or three colors for each scene.

Every Orphan has an identifying color, and so does every room, every technological element, and every setting. Once we decided that, the shades could vary and become "warmer" when we're working on an action scene or a visually compelling sequence (in which case you just need to add a higher percentage of red or orange to the colors, or even just pure red or orange), or they can remain "cool" in quiet scenes or in sequences that are "calm before the storm."

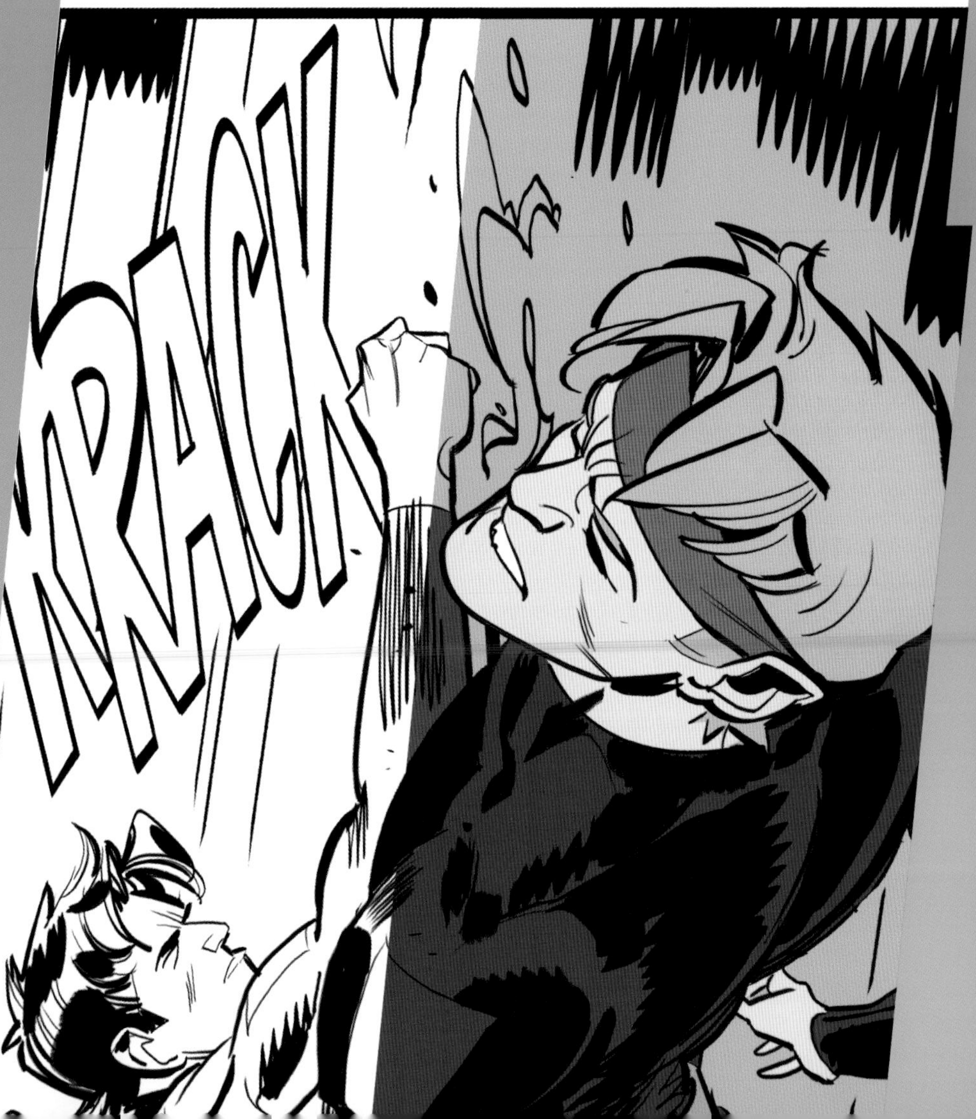
KRACK

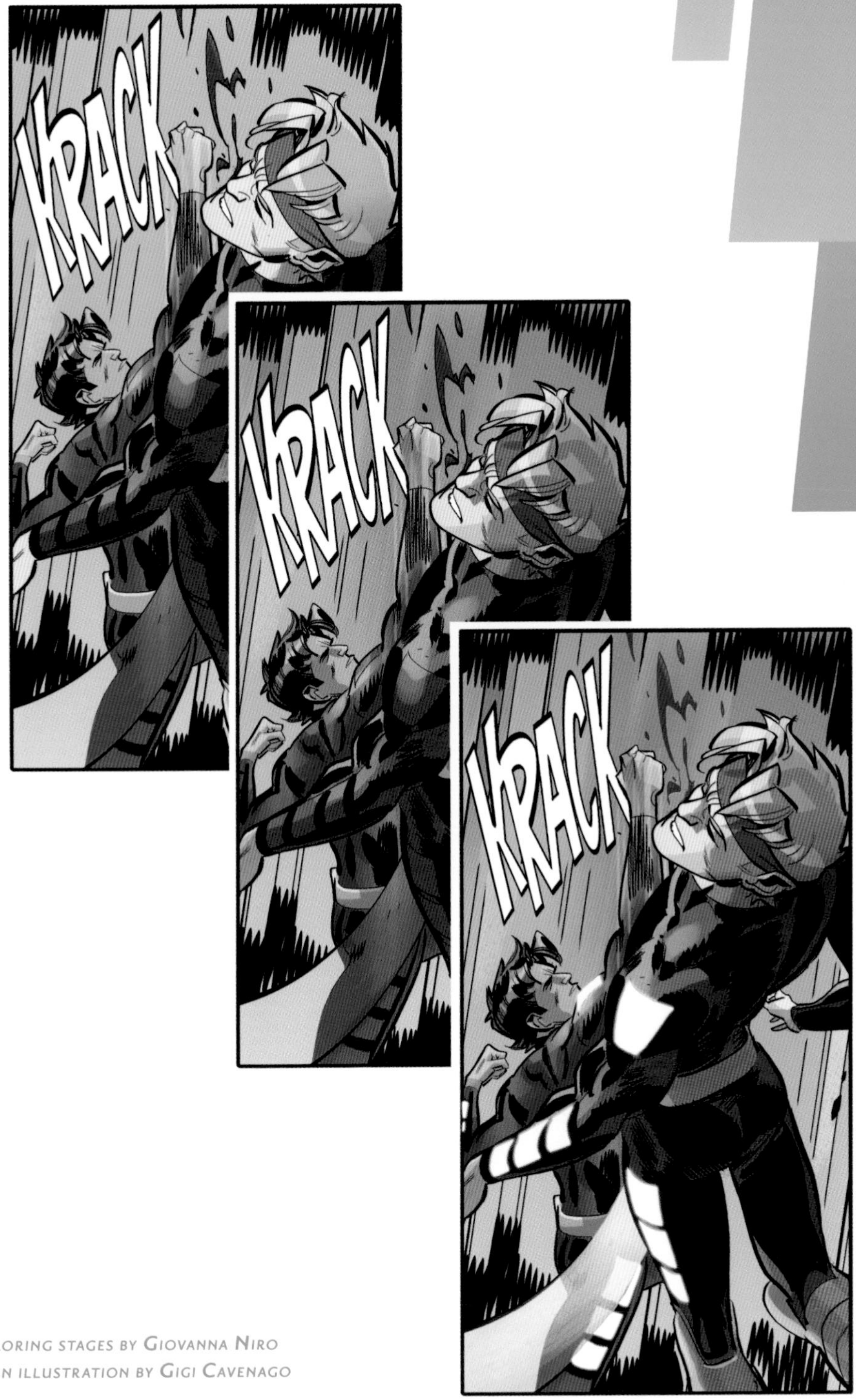
KRACK
KRACK
KRACK

Coloring stages by Giovanna Niro
on an illustration by Gigi Cavenago

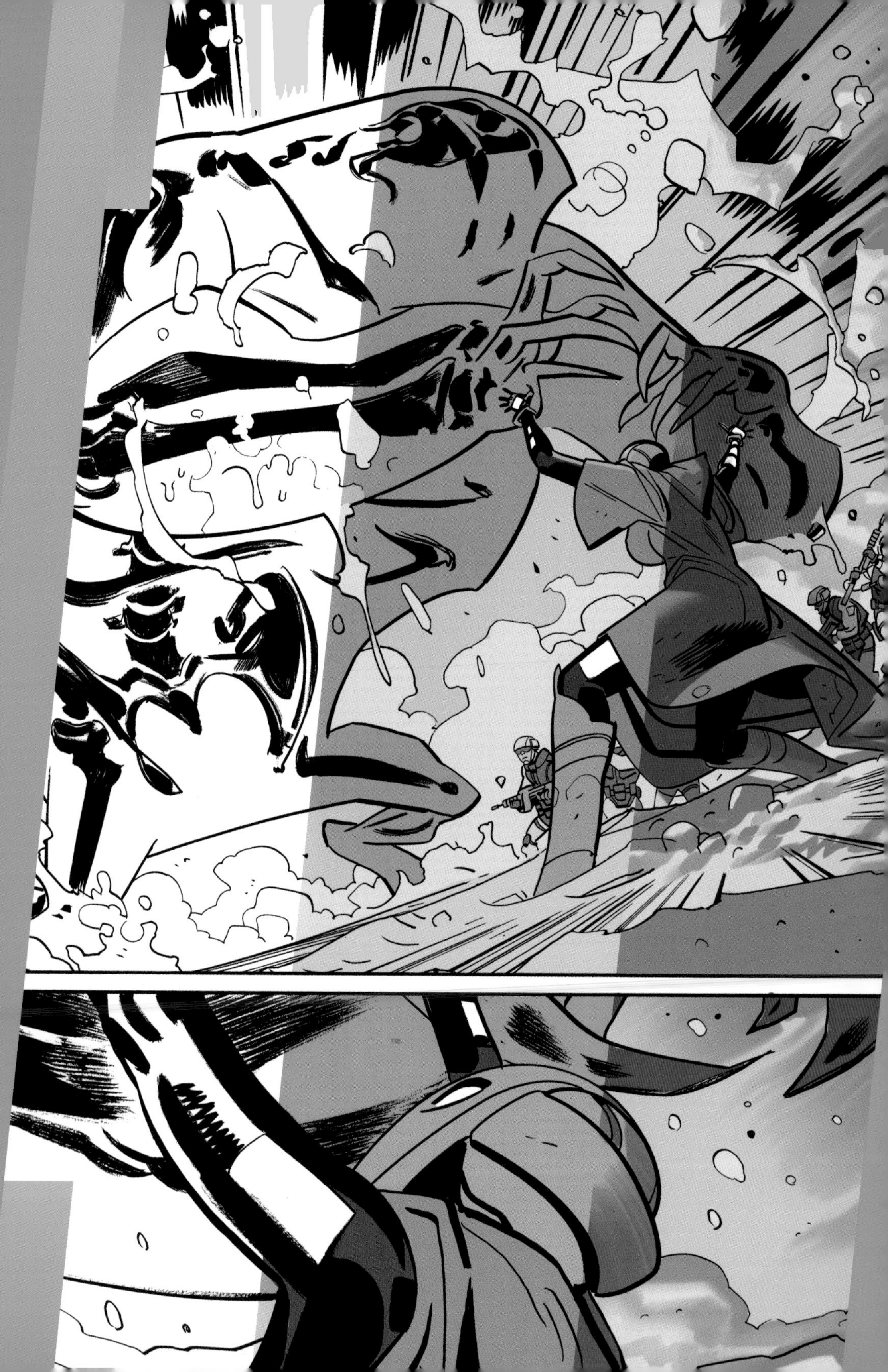

Beyond being a fundamental trait of each scene, color can change along with the overarching plot: when we meet the Orphans for the first time as children in the first volume, we're in the wilderness, and the color is bright because the atmosphere is full of hope. In the second part of the same chapter, we find ourselves on a hostile planet, characterized by cold and dark shades, where the only "warm" element are the aliens, the explosive gunfire, and the blood of the dead. And when the Orphans arrive on the field like demigods, they (and their unnatural colors) storm into this merciless, fiery setting. The rest of their world has lost its old light, though.

Coloring stages by Lorenzo De Felici on an illustration by Gigi Cavenago

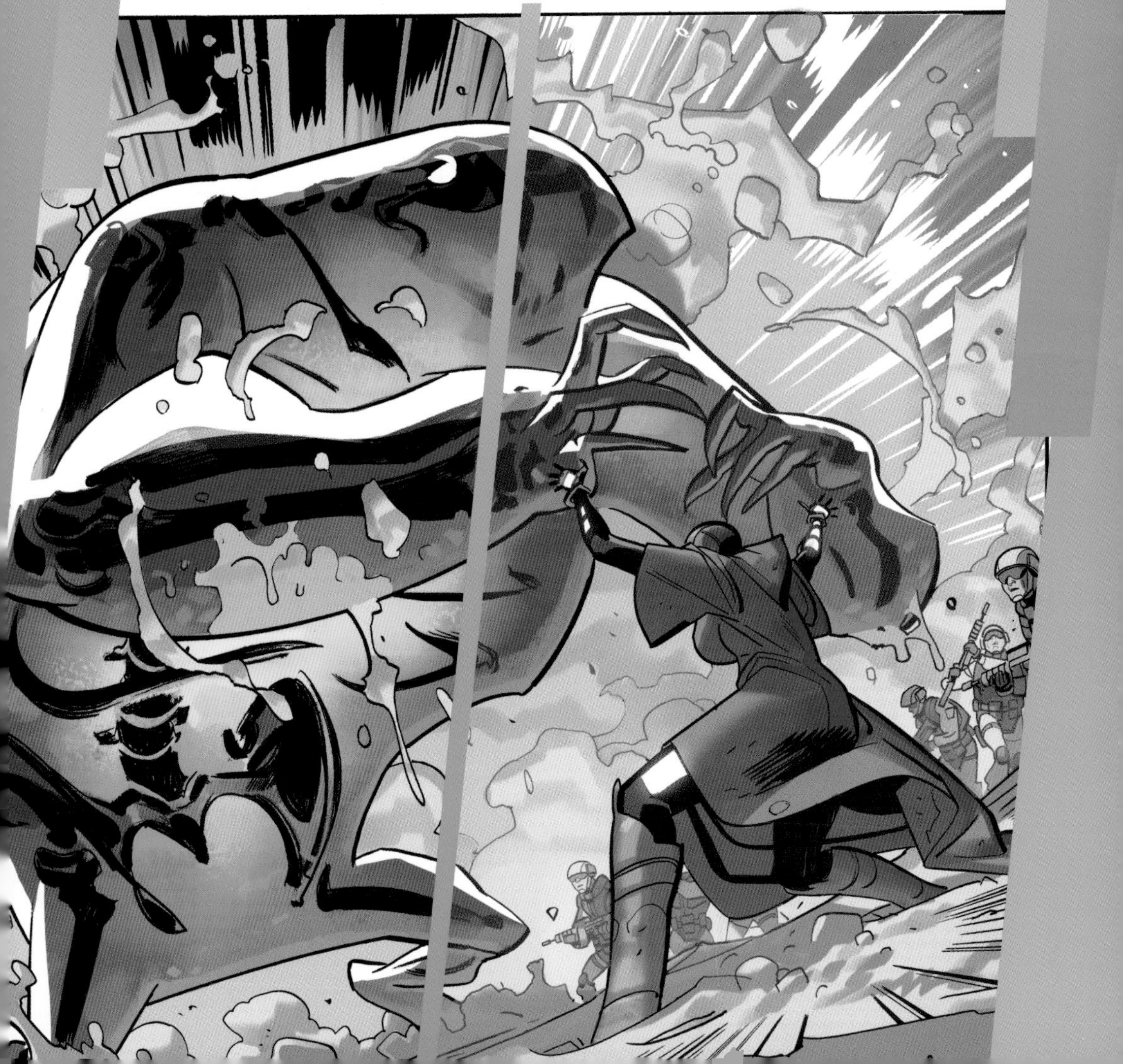

I CAN'T EVEN IMAGINE ORPHANS IN BLACK AND WHITE. THERE ARE SO M
NARRATIVE ELEMENTS ALMOST ENTIRELY EXPRESSED BY COLOR THAT I
IMPOSSIBLE FOR ME TO THINK ABOUT IT OTHERWISE.

– ROBERTO RECCHIONI

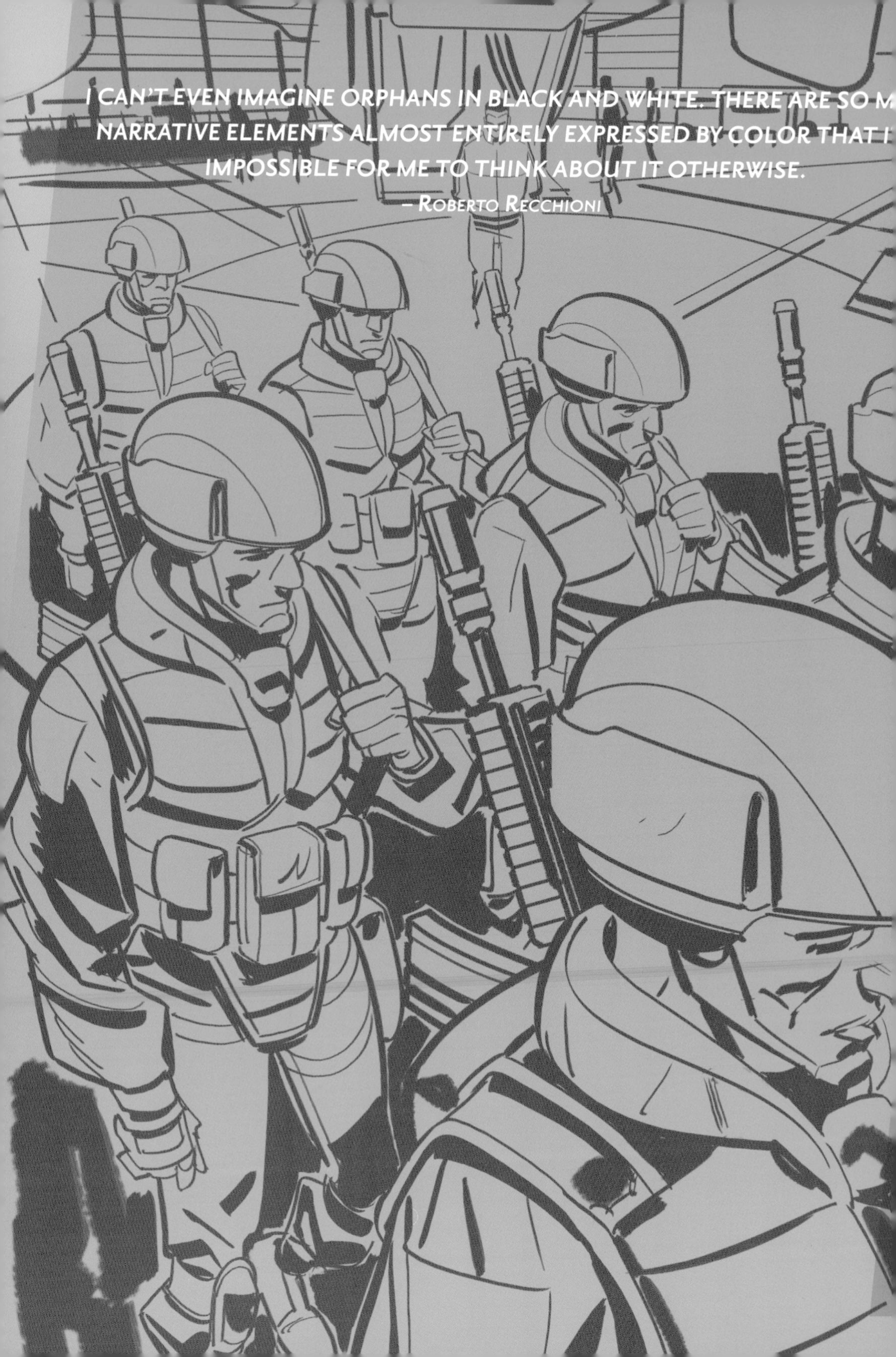

POINT OF NO RETURN

ROBERTO RECCHIONI: Even though the structure of this series was clear from the beginning, it was also evident that the visual aspect couldn't be improvised. The project requested so many artists and colorists that each character, environment, and device had to be designed in a consistent way from the very beginning, so that we'd leave nothing to chance.

STUDY BY GIGI CAVENAGO

ALESSANDRO BIGNAMINI: *This second experience was pure fun for me. Unlike my first chapter, I only had to draw the present timeline of the story, in which the action and combat played a leading role. It was like drawing Marvel or DC superheroes, which I've always read and appreciated, so this gave me an opportunity to show a more dynamic side of my drawing style. In this chapter, the doubts and hesitations of the first pages of Chapter Two left room for more confidence with the characters and situations in which I felt more comfortable. I think I did my best thanks to the great contribution by the amazing coloring department.*

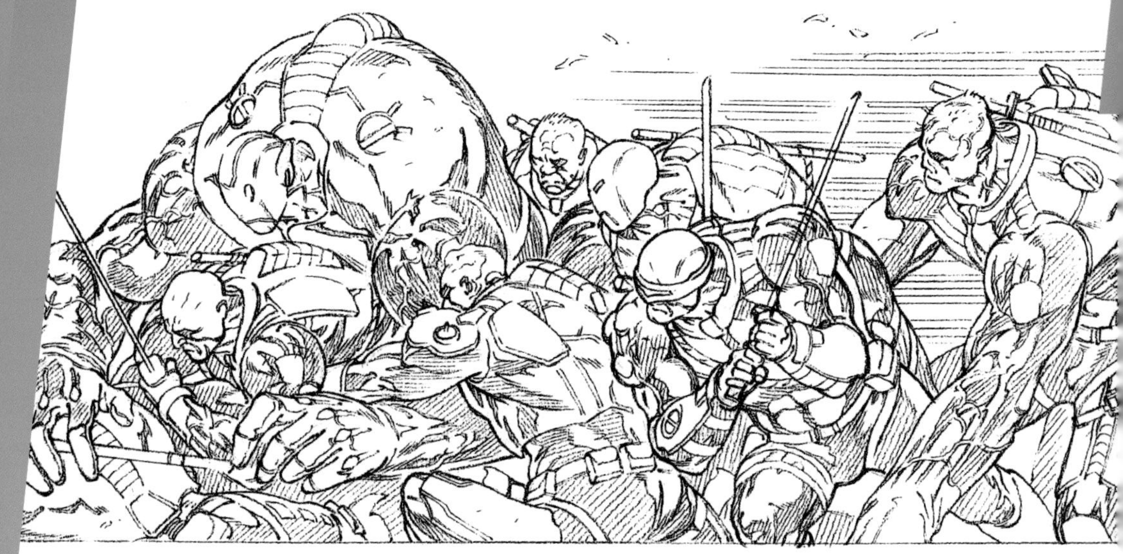

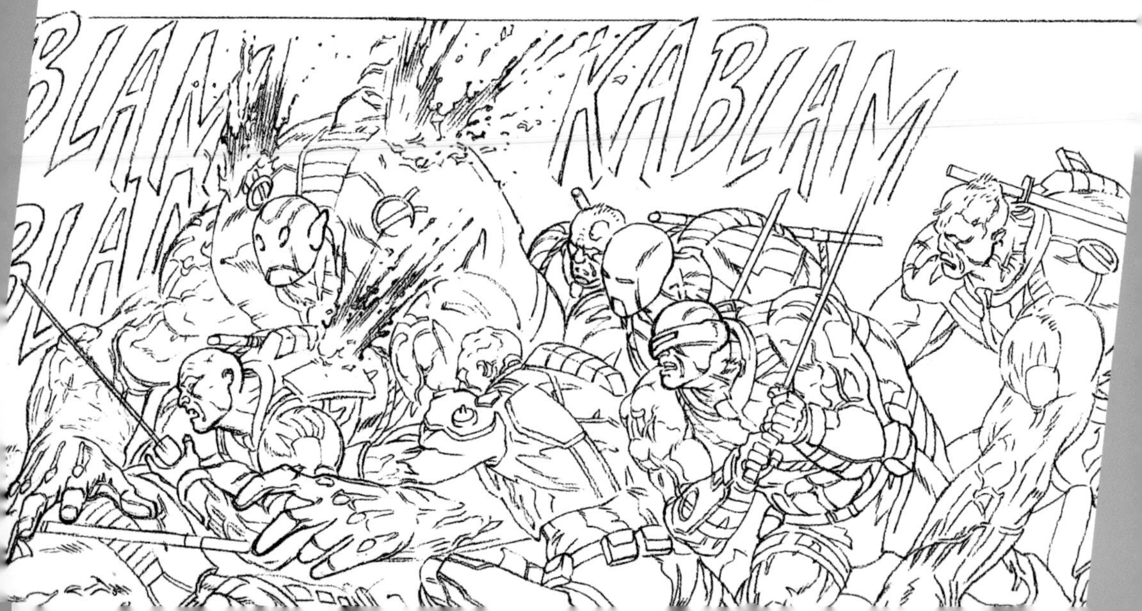
KABLAM

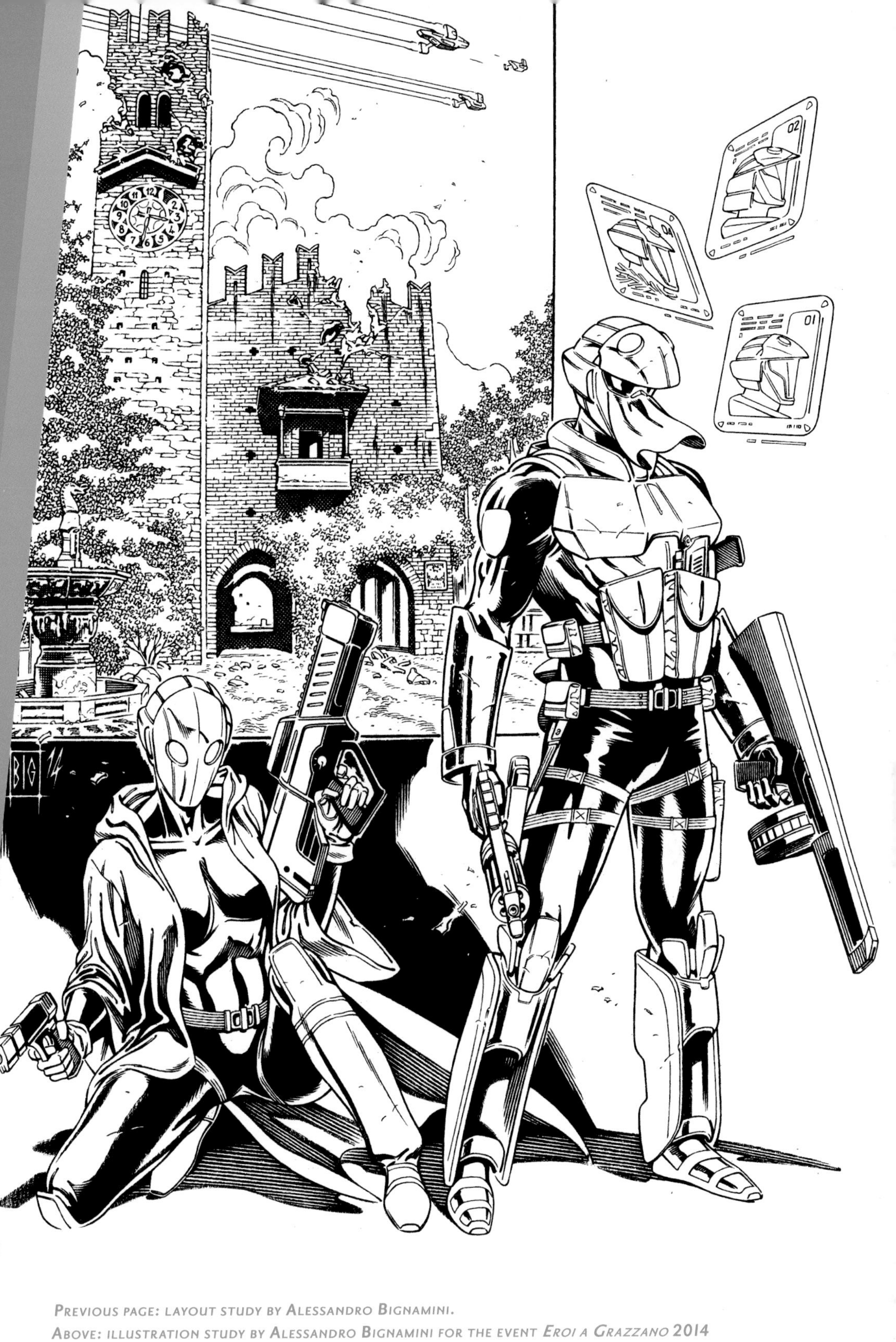
02
04
01

Previous page: layout study by Alessandro Bignamini.
Above: illustration study by Alessandro Bignamini for the event *Eroi a Grazzano* 2014

WERTHER DELL'EDERA: *Chronologically speaking, Chapter Nine is my third time working on Orphans. It's a bit of an intricate matter: to respect a sort of internal consistency, I started drawing the first part of Chapter Two and then the second half of Chapter Nine. But I suspect there were other needs involved. For example, the first half of Chapter Nine was more urgent than the second part of Capter Eleven so that it could be used as a reference for other artists. As it always happens, I can't keep still. I need to search and change and evolve. So every time is like the first time for me.*

ILLUSTRATIONS BY WERTHER DELL'EDERA

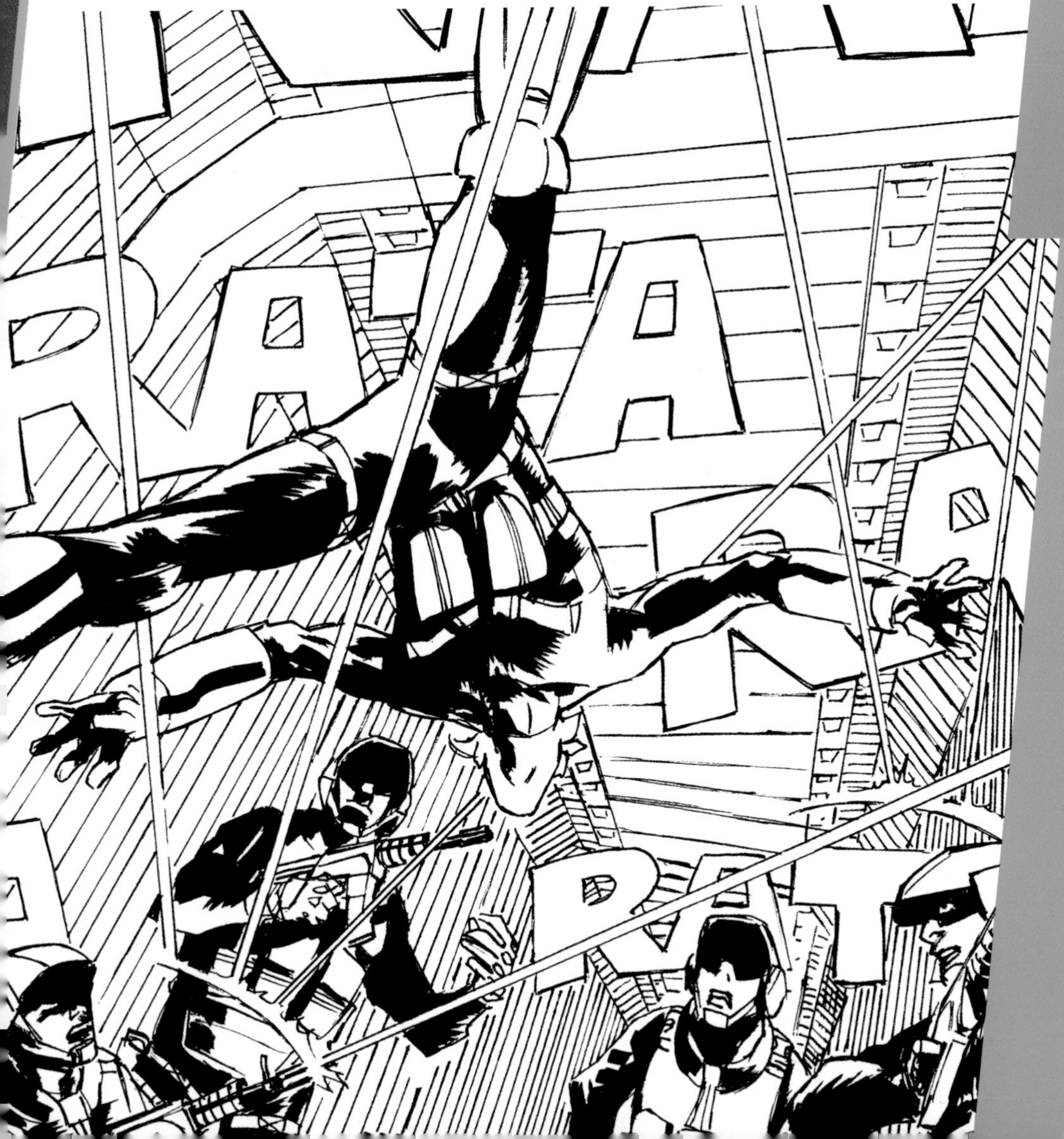

GIGI CAVENAGO: If my first chapter was a sort of baptism by fire and the second one was the one in which I tried to refine my technique, then this chapter is the one where I let myself go, style-wise. In this sense, I was more at ease because of the cheerful tone of the central part of the story which followed our characters through a beautiful yet hard phase of their lives.

BELOW: STUDY BY GIGI CAVENAGO.
NEXT PAGE: SKETCH BY WERTHER DELL'EDERA

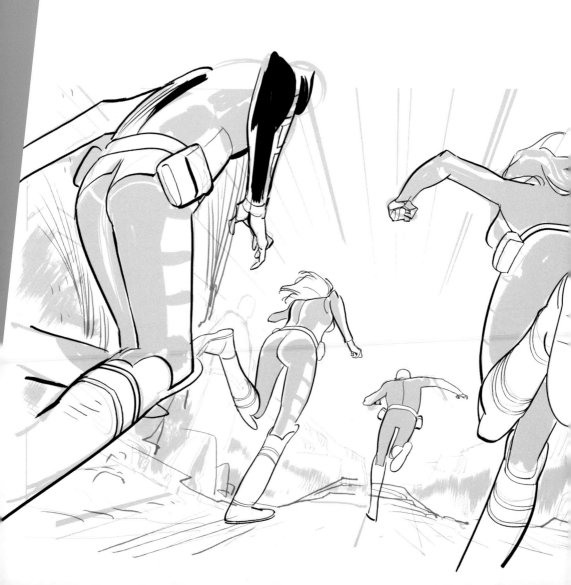

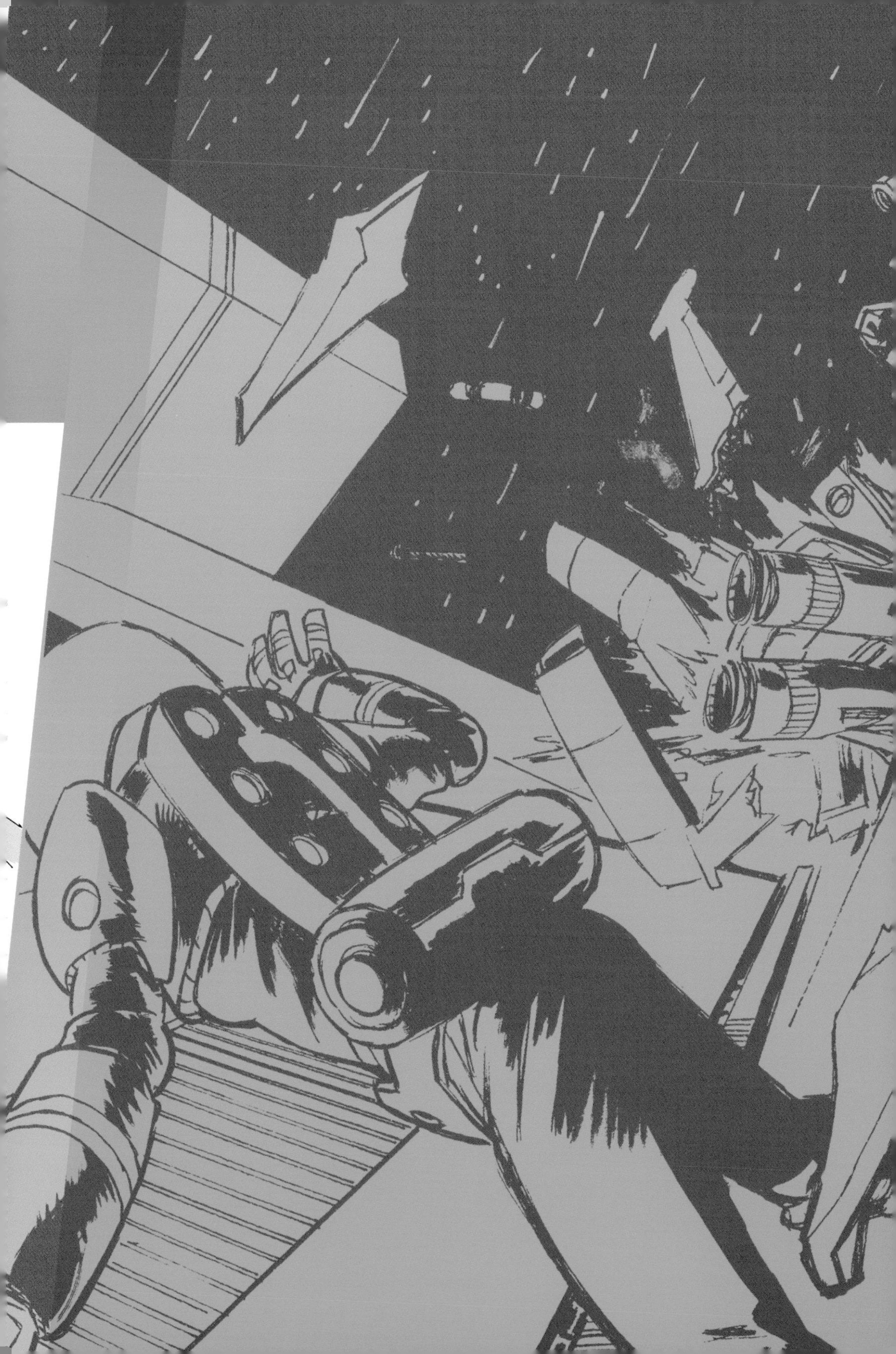

GIGI CAVENAGO: *After drawing plenty of action in the previous chapters, I tried focusing more on the characters' acting and the evocative atmosphere in this one. Just a few gestures and some shot changes. I must say that the most impressive scenes reached their full potential thanks to Alessia Pastorello's colors, who immediately became a real expert in conveying the depth of wide landscapes. But of course, fist fights are a must! When they scuffle, the Ridgeback Camp rookies could tear half a forest to the ground. But in this chapter they're just teenagers in a playful situation, one in which we can see their first lovers' quarrels, so I didn't need to be overly dramatic.*

NEXT PAGE: STUDIES BY GIGI CAVENAGO

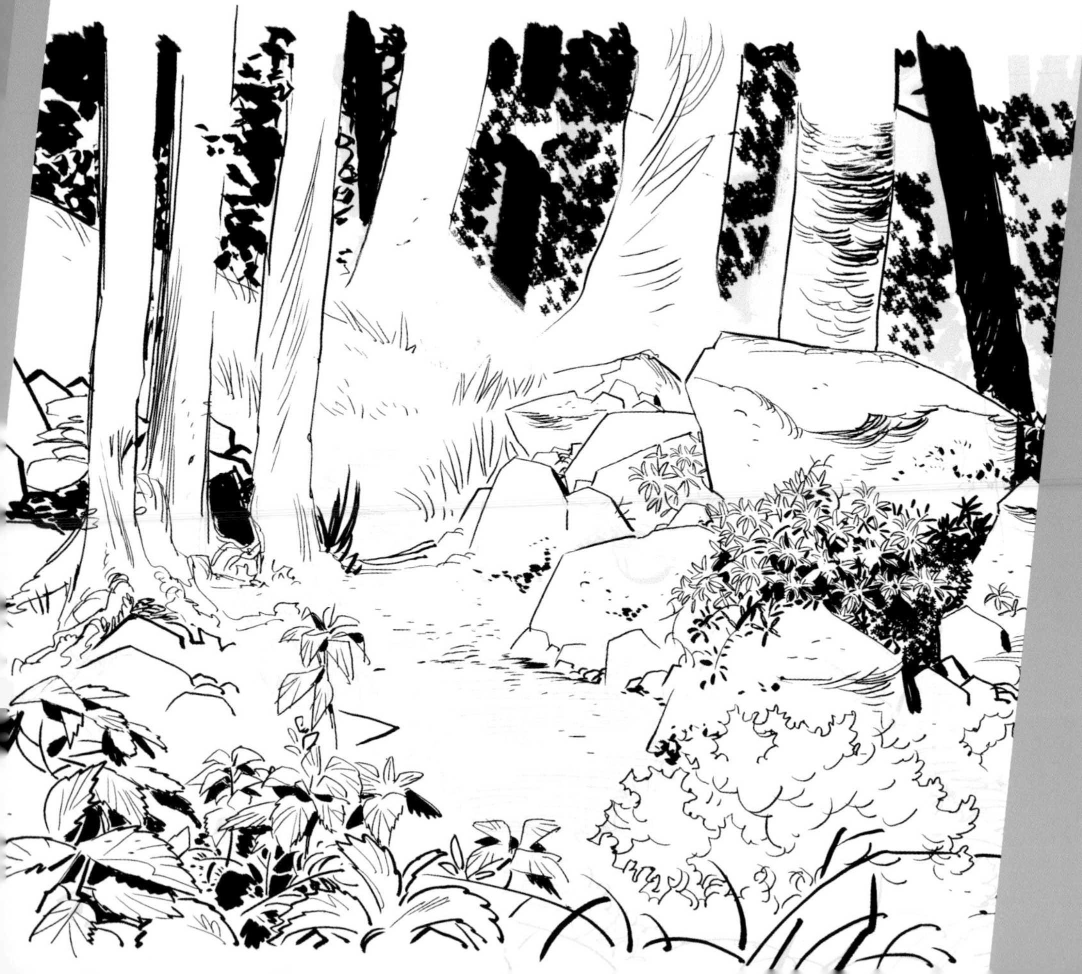

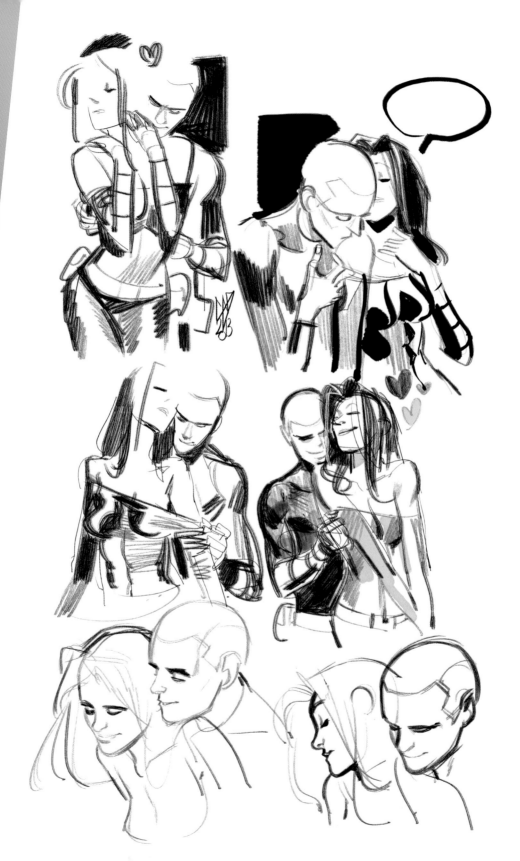

These two pages:
studies by Gigi Cavenago

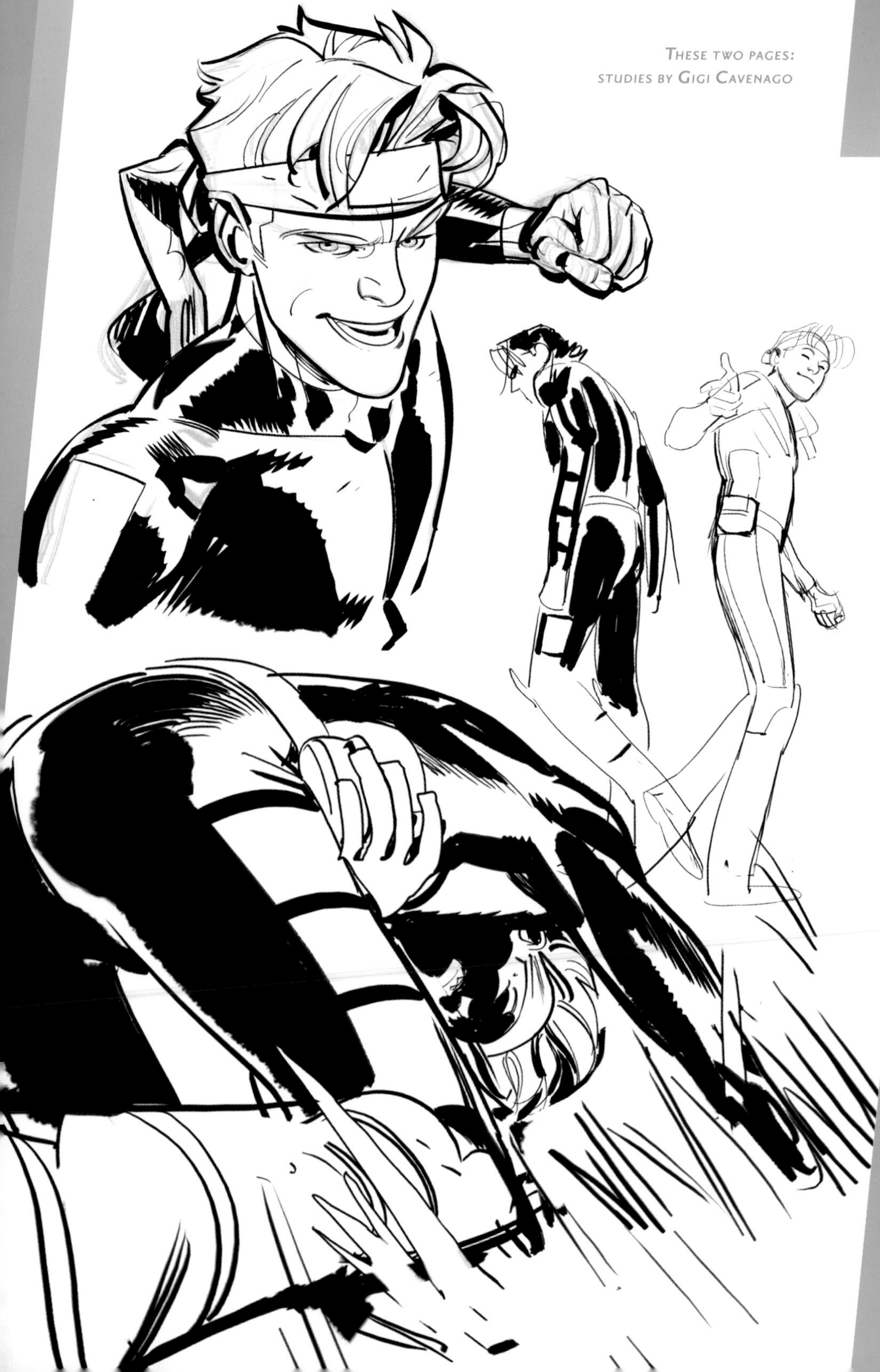

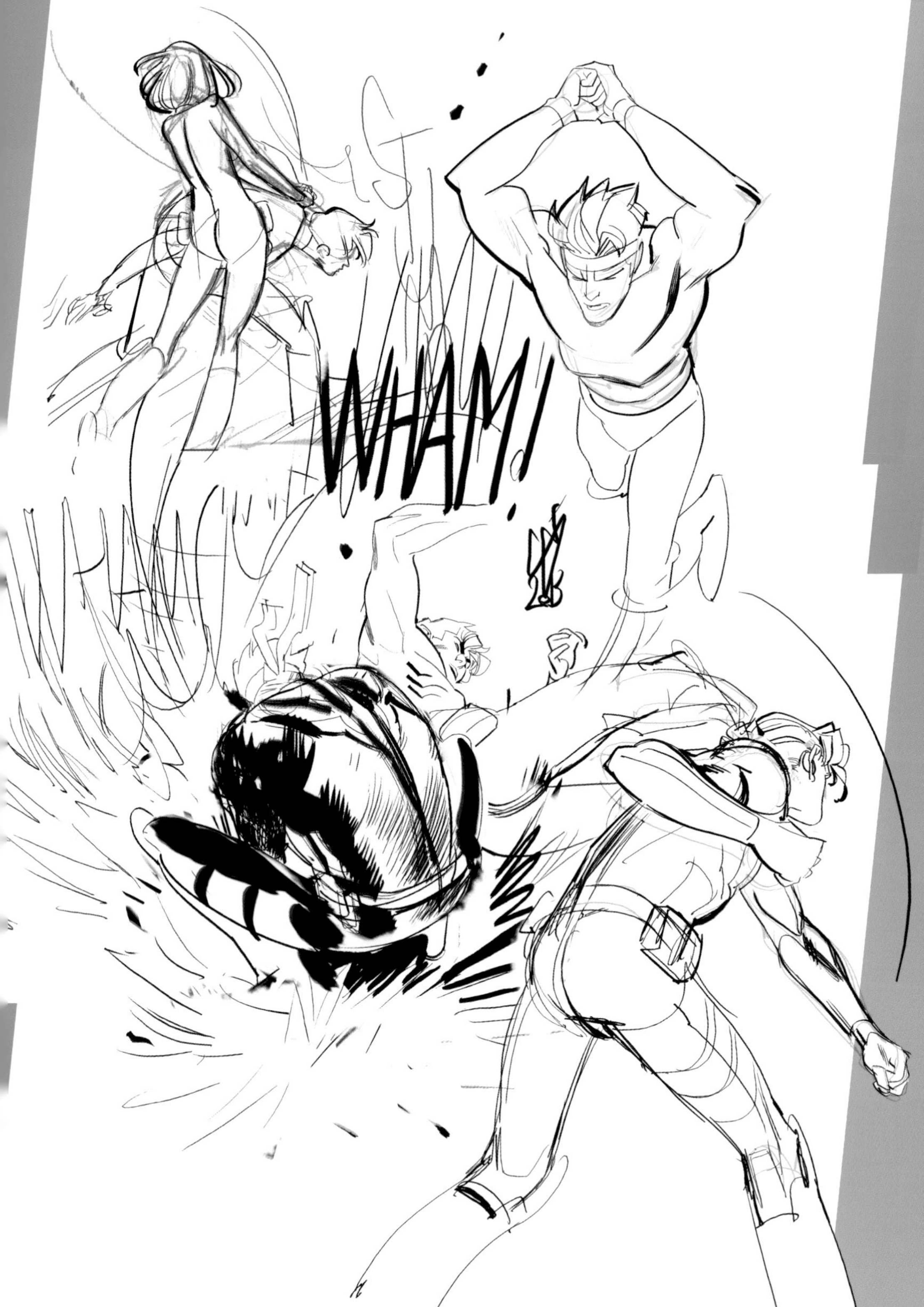
WHAM!

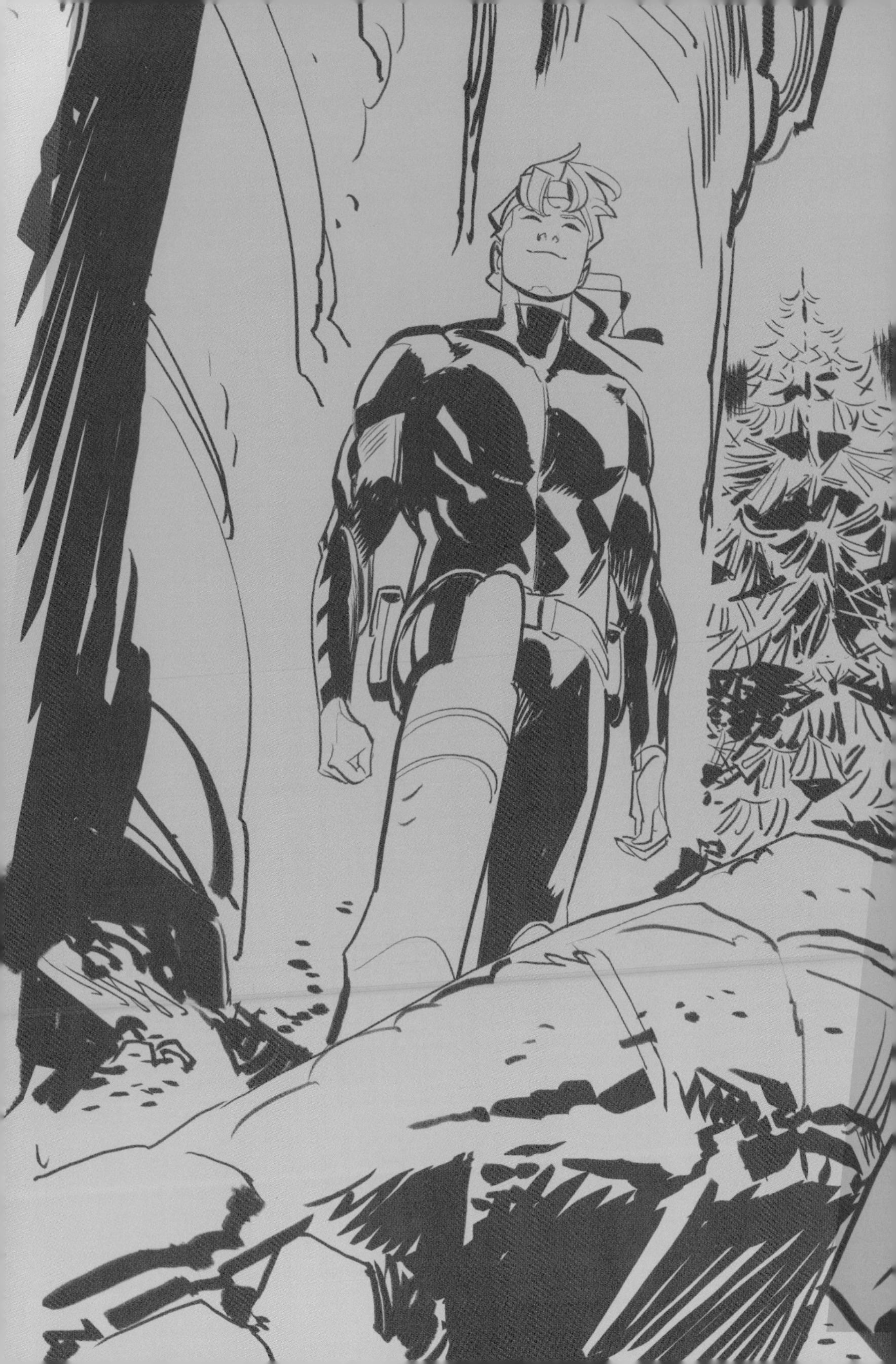

GIGI CAVENAGO: *Despite the lighter atmosphere, the story opens with a pretty tense sequence set in Prague. It only lasts six pages, but it required a certain care, precisely because it was so different from what we'd seen in the series until now, not to mention it's importance to the rest of the story. In a nutshell, I dared a little style diversion in which bold blacks were used to make the scene much dirtier, hoping not to complicate Alessia's coloring phase.*

THESE TWO PAGES: ILLUSTRATIONS AND STUDIES BY GIGI CAVENAGO

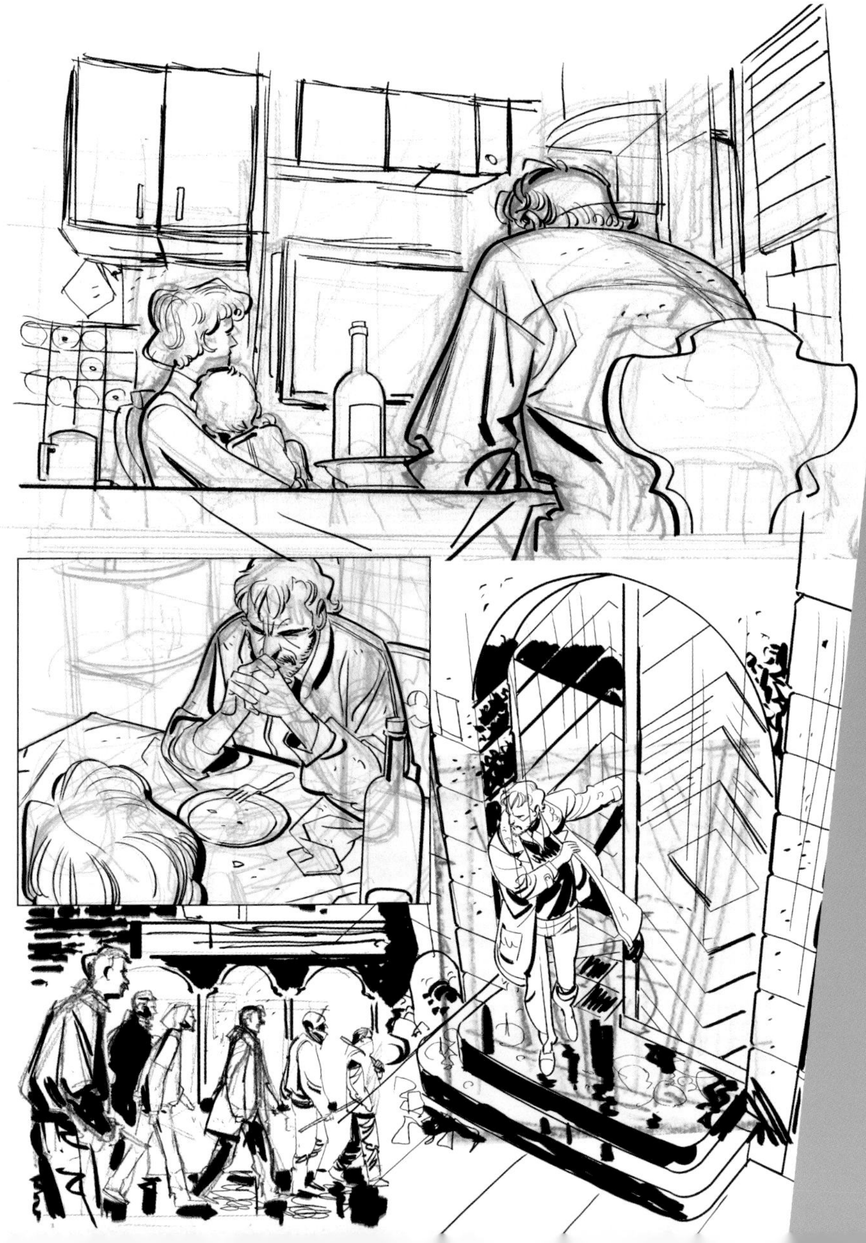

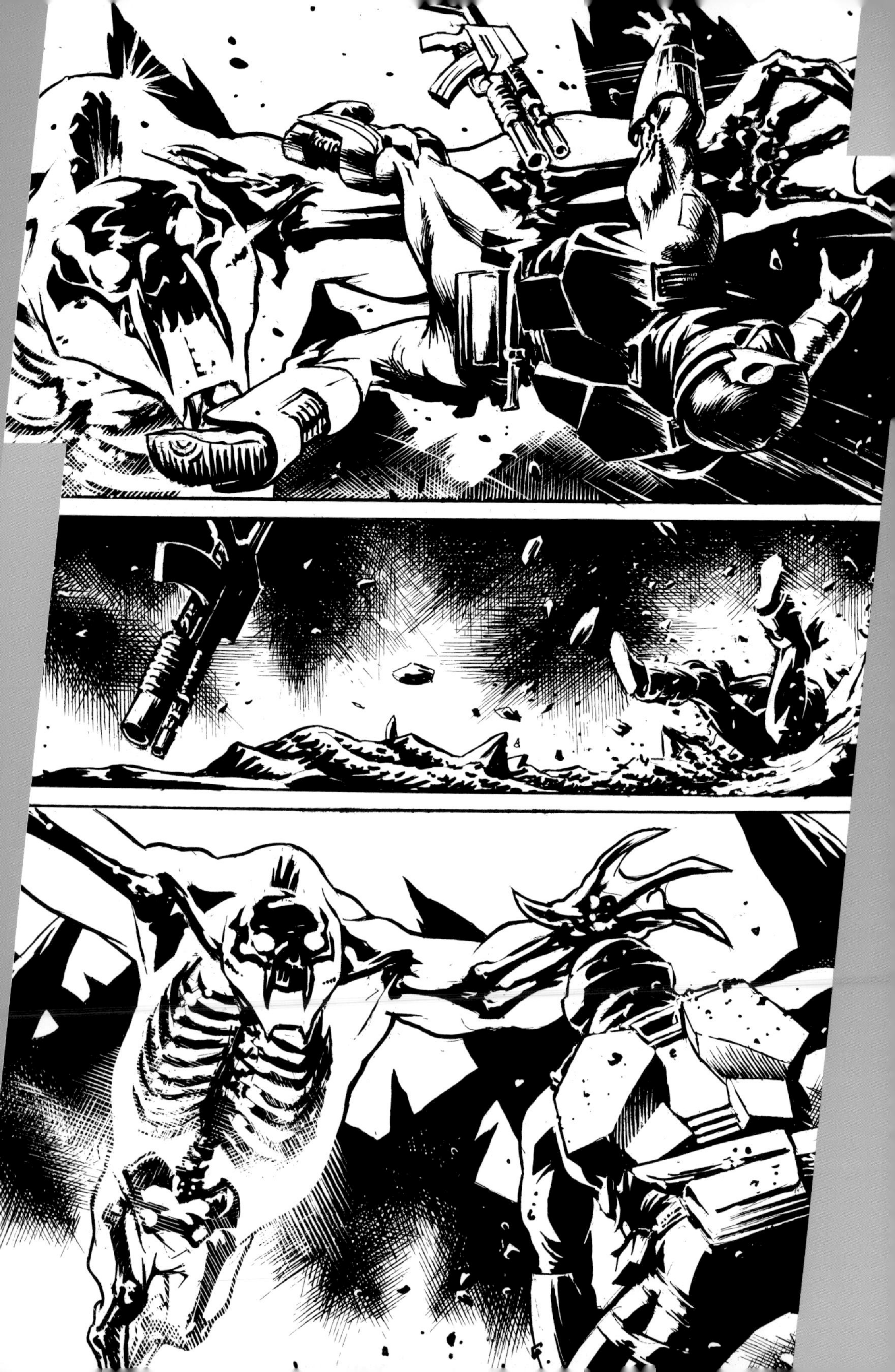

GIORGIO SANTUCCI: *I was supposed to work on a long scene starring the young Orphans in a SWAT-like armor, which I was also asked to design. We had plenty of documentation about the rest. I usually don't make detailed studies; when I feel I have the right idea I just draw anywhere. This is why I wanted to challenge myself with studies and pages featuring our grown characters: to have a broader idea of how to approach this series and what style would suit it best.*

ILLUSTRATIONS BY GIORGIO SANTUCCI

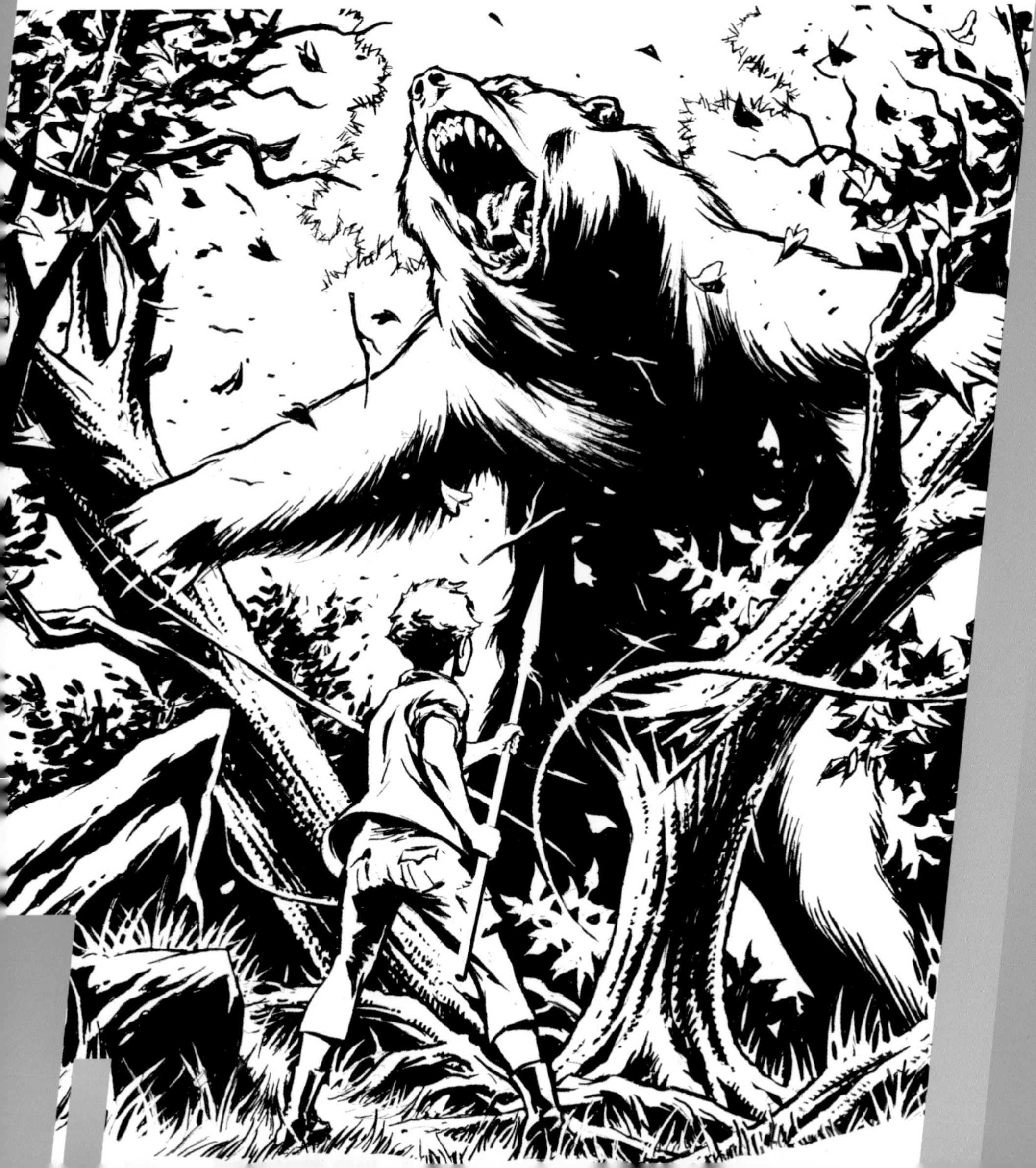

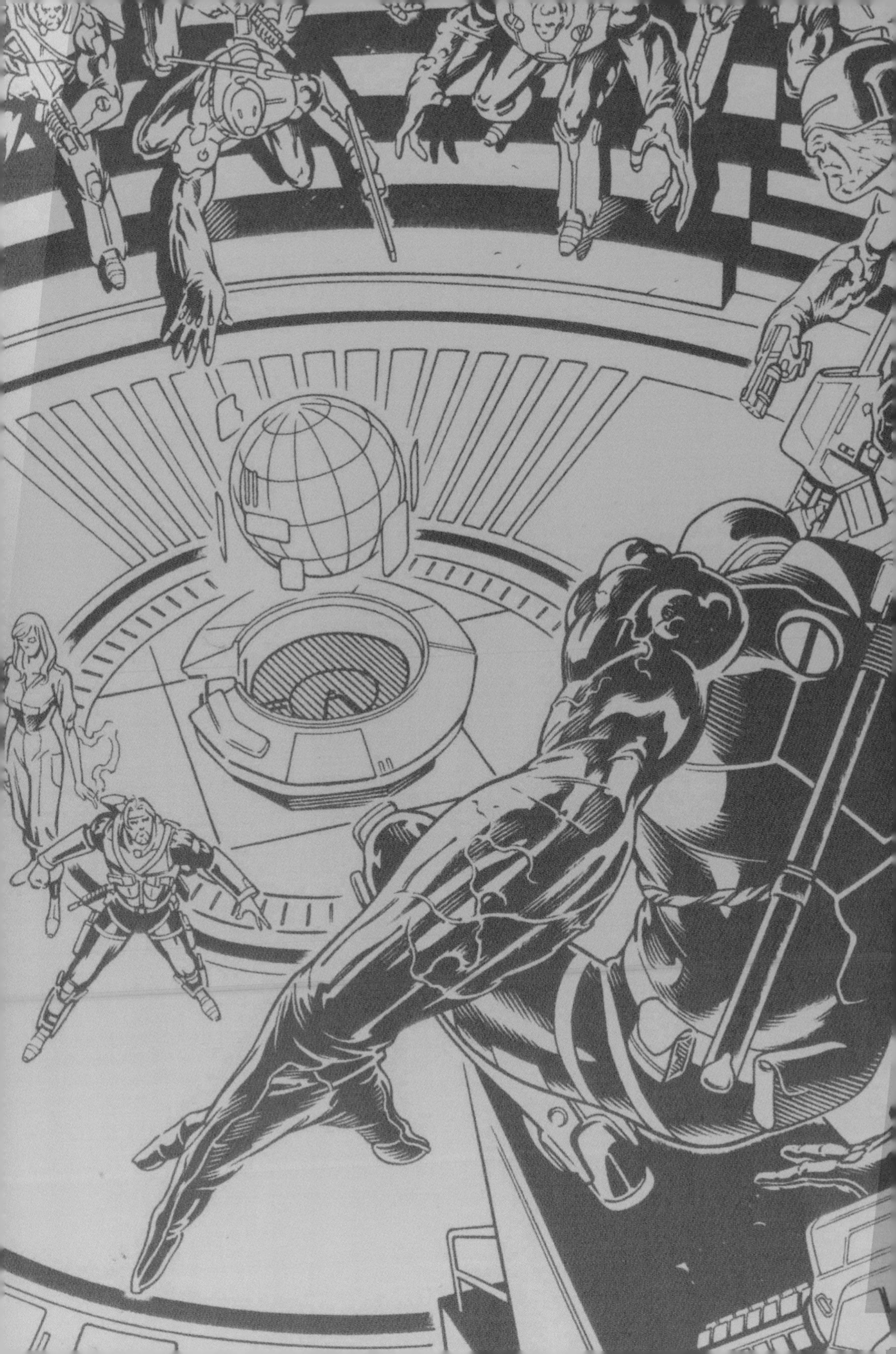

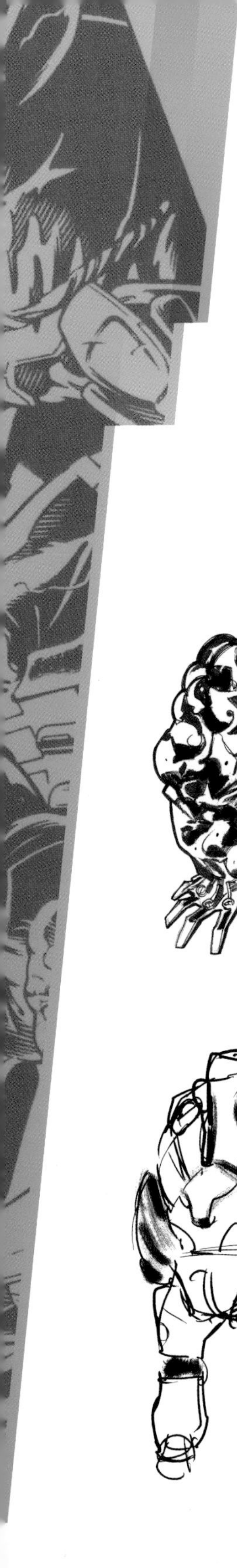

DAVIDE GIANFELICE: *One of the funniest parts in realizing my chapter was drawing the Abomination. It had to look gigantic, evil, and incredibly powerful and destructive. I focused on its huge, misshapen arms, its massive body and its relatively small legs. I thought its movements and body structure might resemble a gorilla's, so I chose that as my starting point.*

PREVIOUS PAGE: ILLUSTRATION BY ALESSANDRO BIGNAMINI.
BELOW: STUDIES BY DAVIDE GIANFELICE

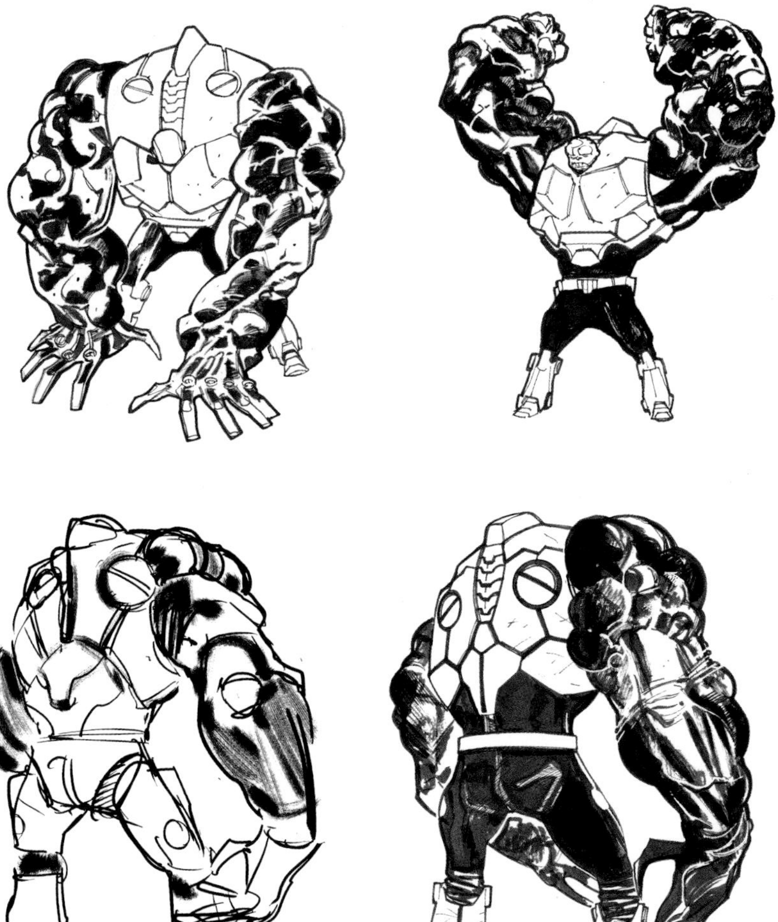

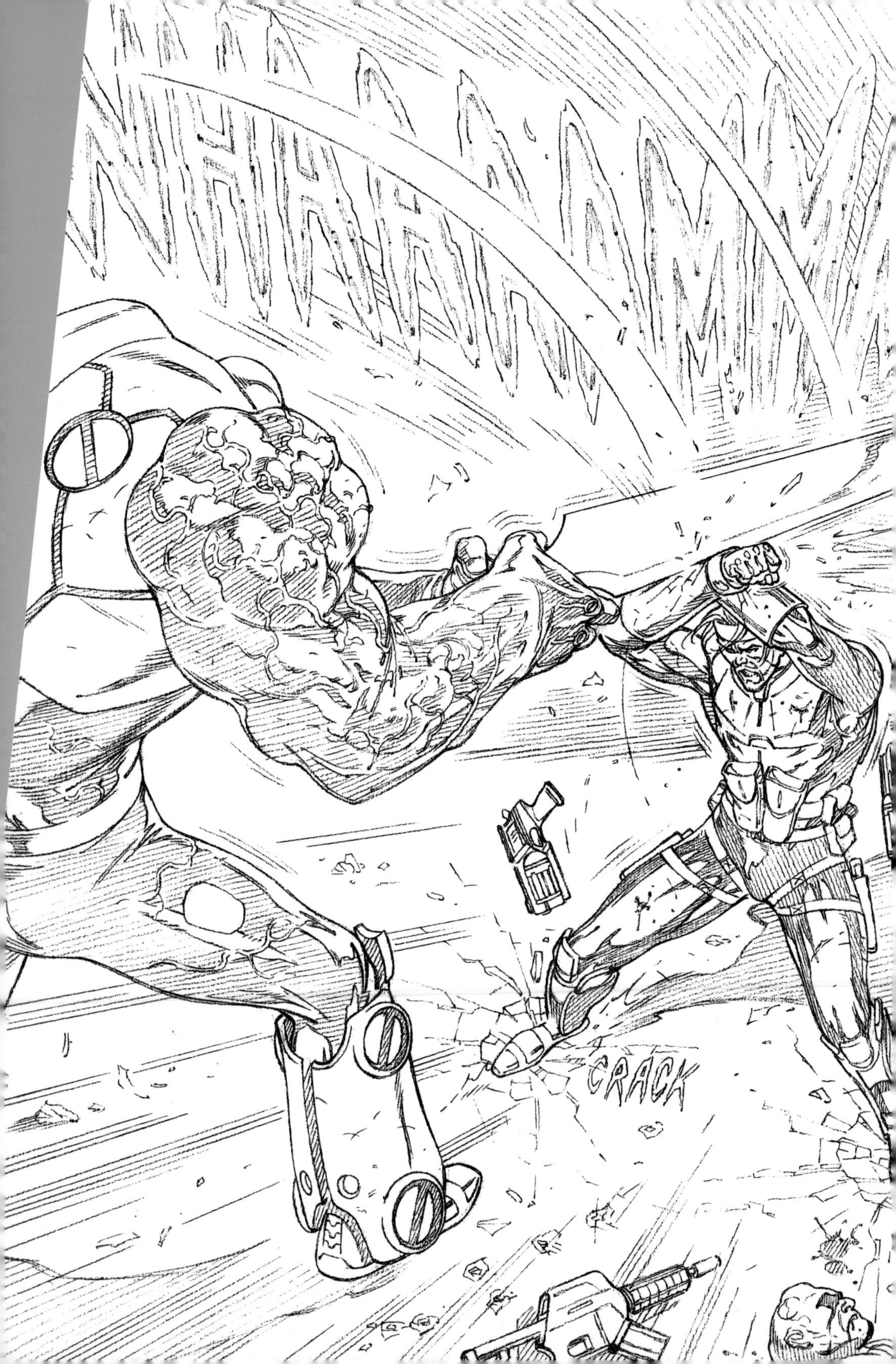
CRACK

IT WAS LIKE DRAWING MARVEL OR DC SUPERHEROES, WHICH I'VE ALWAYS READ AND APPRECIATED, SO I HAD THE OPPORTUNITY TO SHOW A MORE DYNAMIC SIDE OF MY DRAWING STYLE.

– ALESSANDRO BIGNAMINI

THESE TWO PAGES: ILLUSTRATIONS BY ALESSANDRO BIGNAMINI

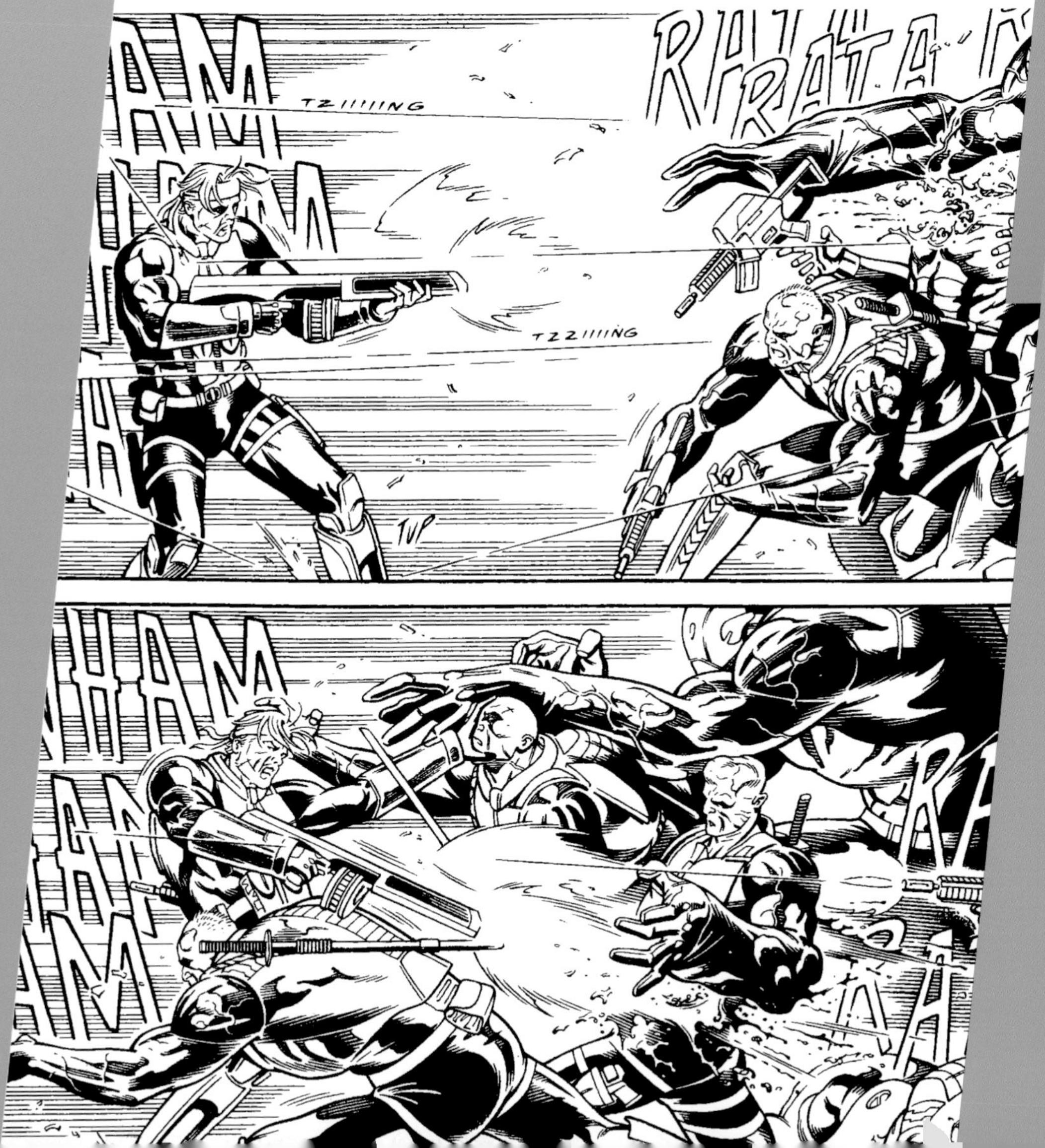

BLAM
BLAM
TZZIIIING
RATATA
TZZIIIING
TUP
BLAM
BLAM

ROBERTO RECCHIONI: *Conceiving the story as a whole, its structure was clear to me from the start: a big roller-coaster that slowly reaches its peak, then stops on the verge of a headlong fall, takes its time to let you catch your breath, and then plunges down. These chapters cover the part before the final fall.*

STUDIES BY GIGI CAVENAGO

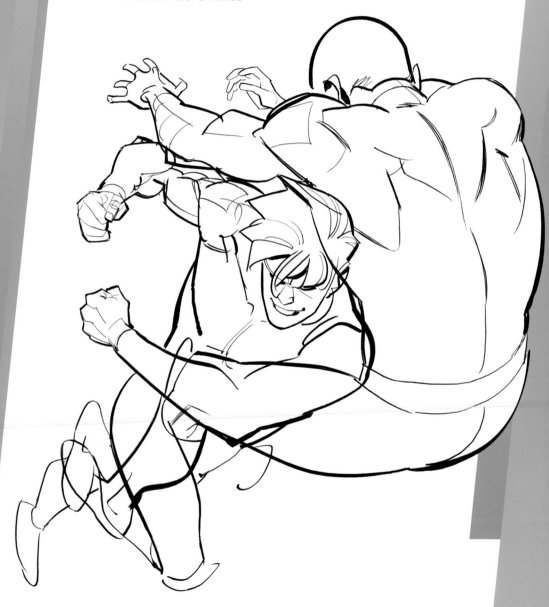

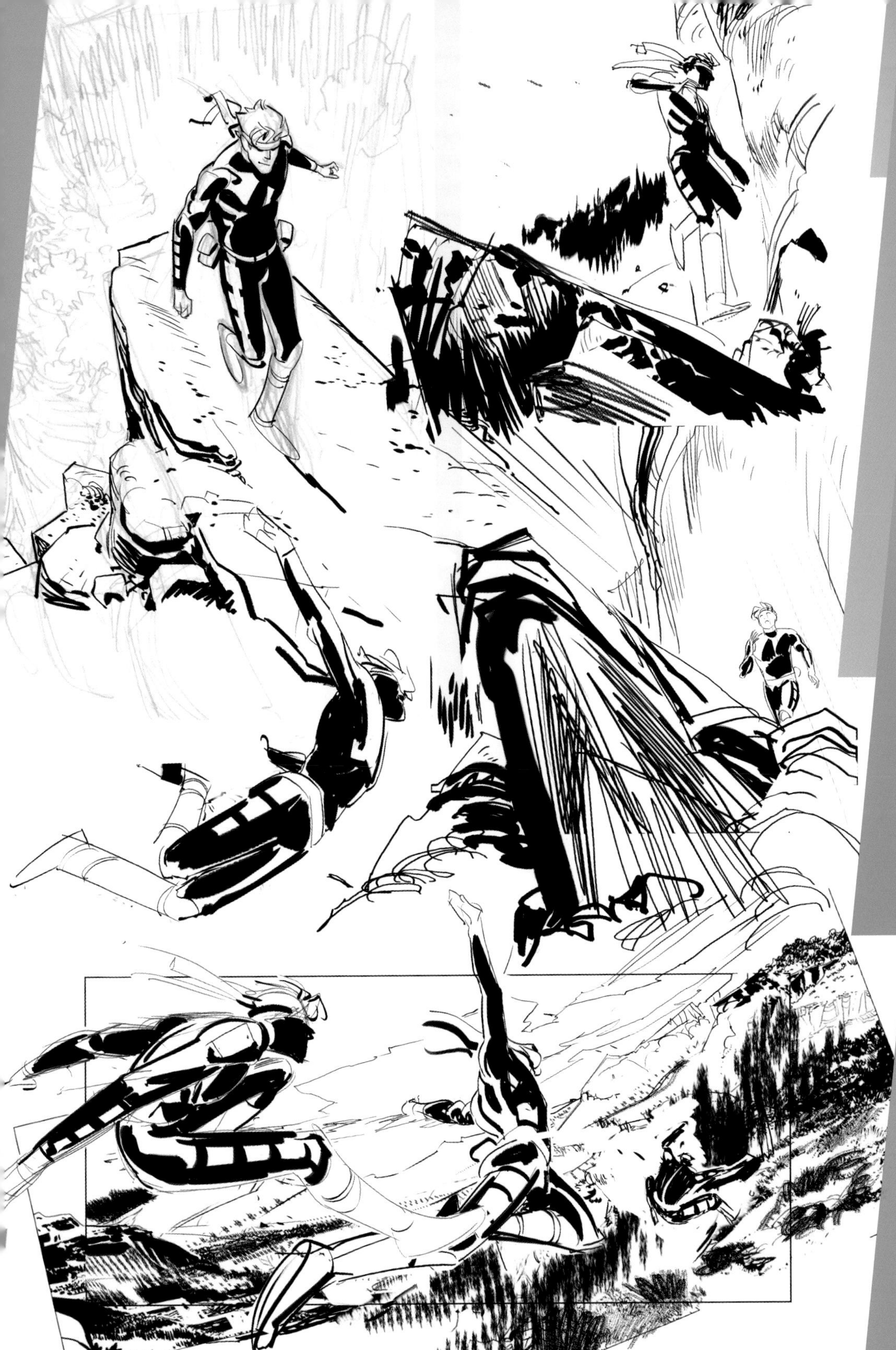

ILLUSTRATION BY GIGI CAVENAGO

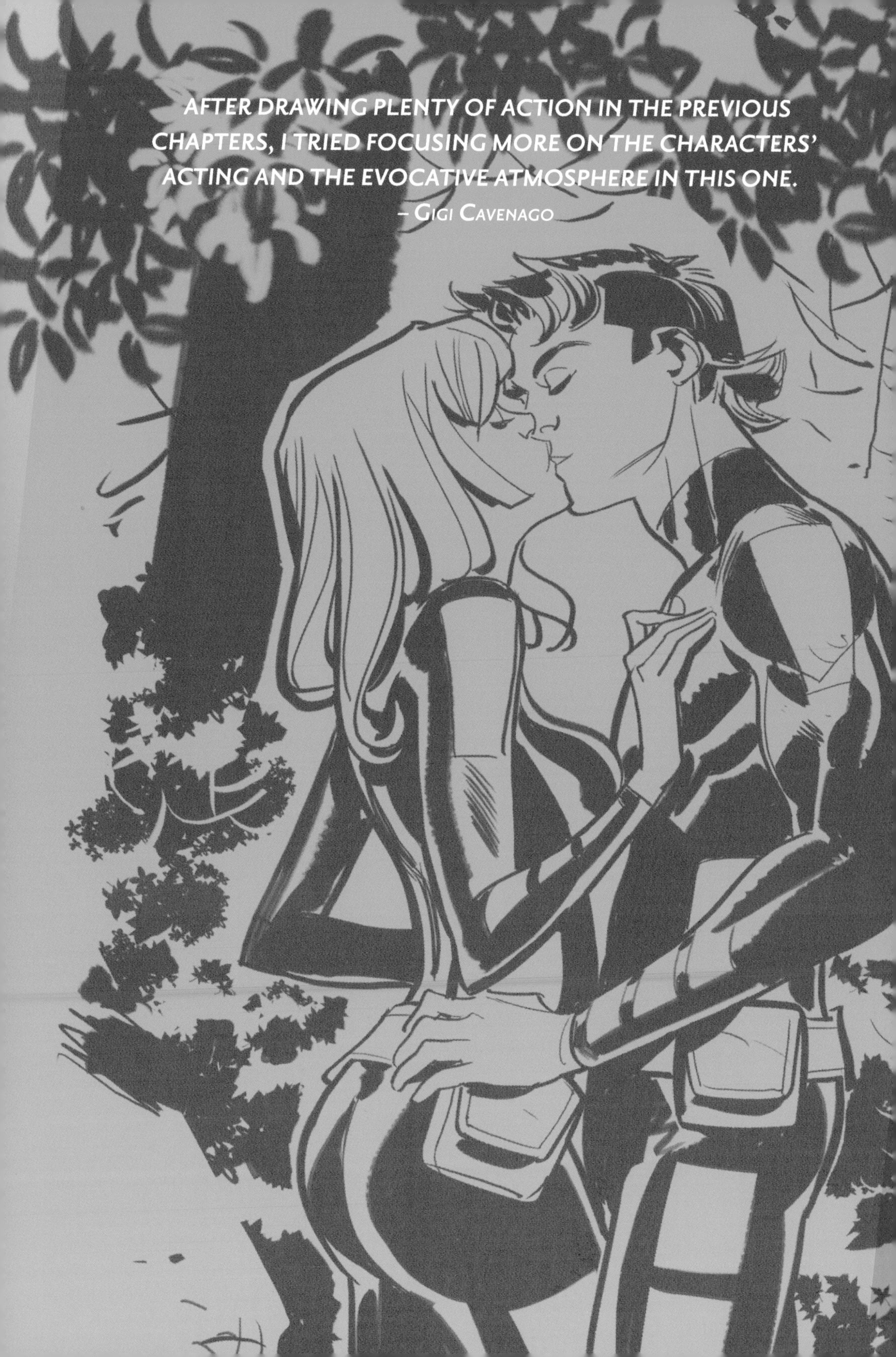
AFTER DRAWING PLENTY OF ACTION IN THE PREVIOUS CHAPTERS, I TRIED FOCUSING MORE ON THE CHARACTERS' ACTING AND THE EVOCATIVE ATMOSPHERE IN THIS ONE.
– GIGI CAVENAGO

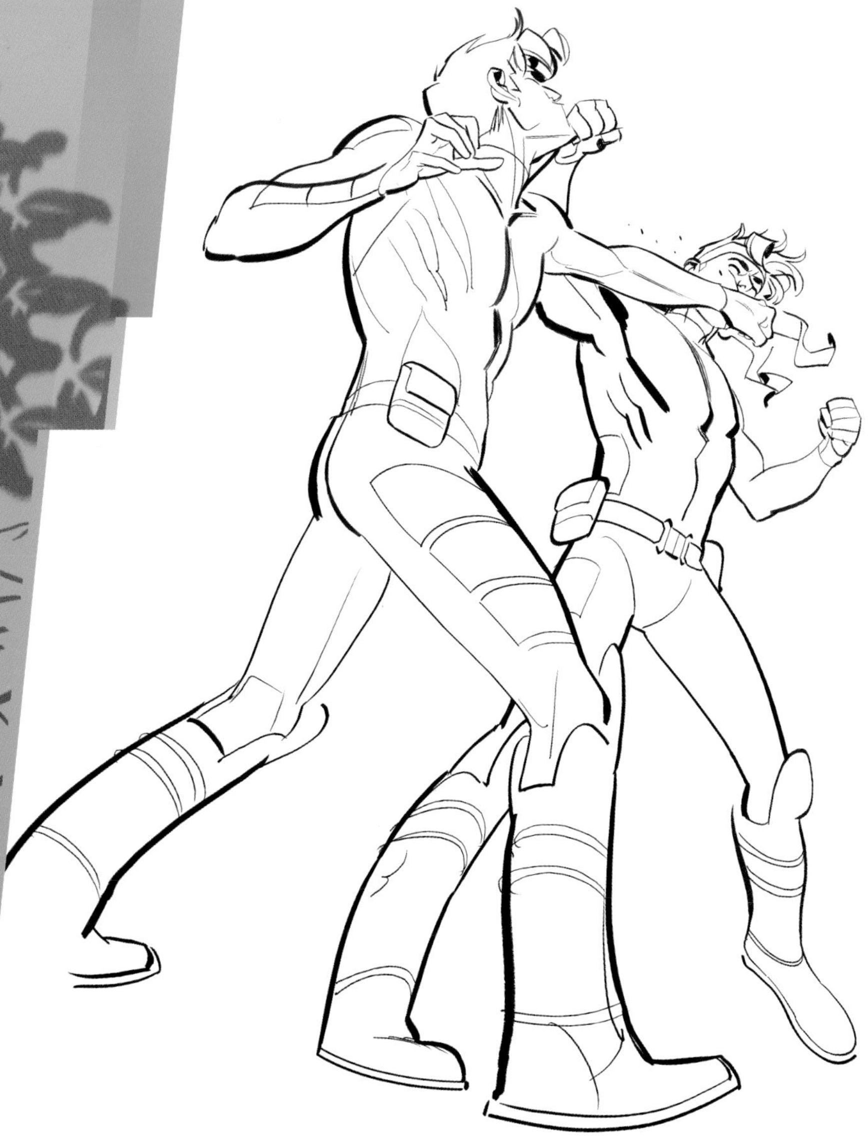

ROBERTO RECCHIONI: *For once, everything was preplanned and we made no changes as we went. This should be clear while reading the story. In the first volume, there are so many details that foreshadow events that we'll only see in the last chapters. This was the most structured series I've ever worked on.*

ILLUSTRATIONS AND STUDIES BY GIGI CAVENAGO

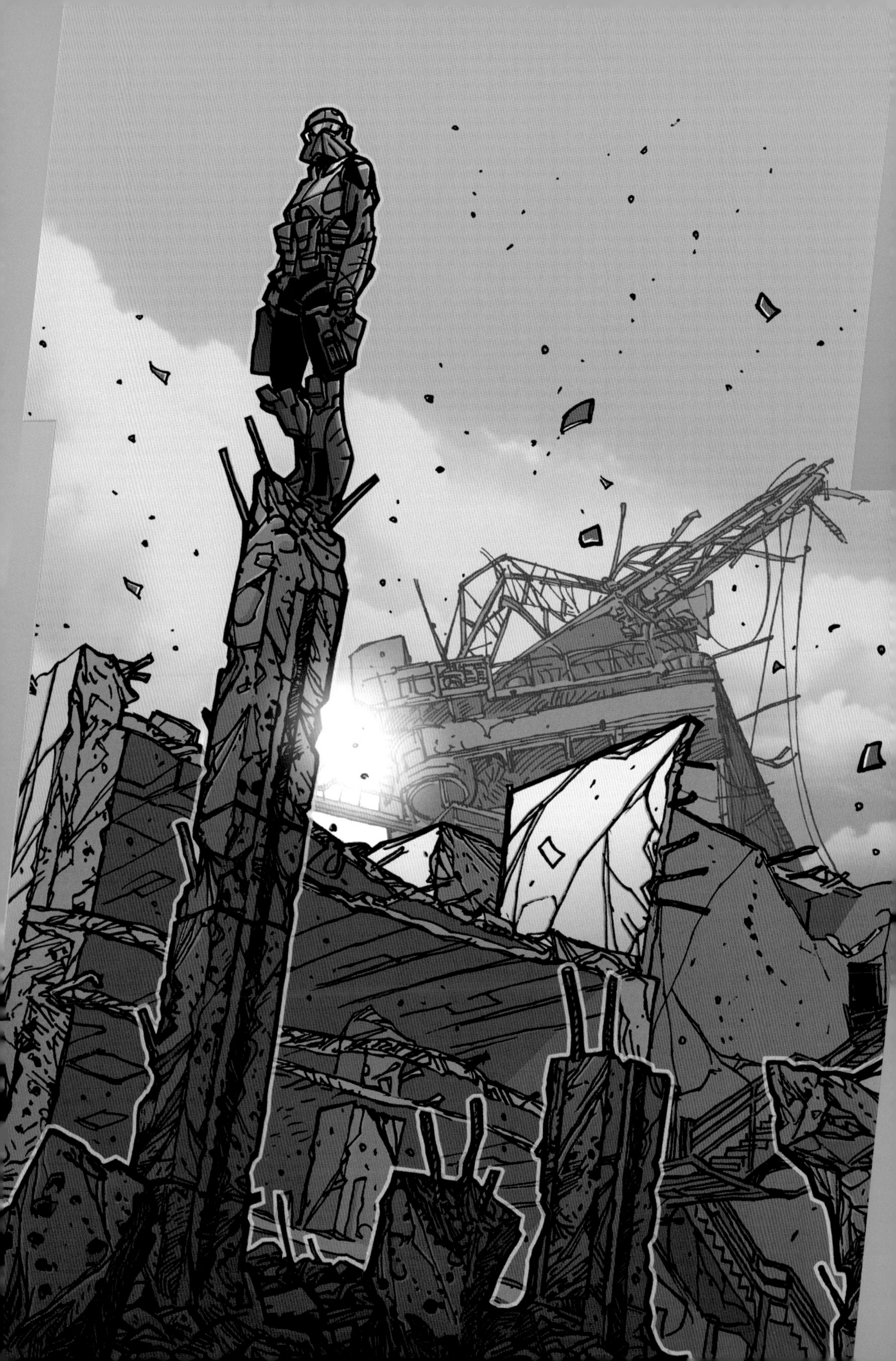

DAVIDE GIANFELICE: The riot scene was definitely challenging, especially concerning the Orphans' uniforms. I wanted something that resembled modern mercenaries and soldiers' uniforms, like suits full of pockets and extra protections. It's a big job, I know, but it surely was fun and satisfying.

PREVIOUS PAGE: ILLUSTRATION BY DAVIDE GIANFELICE, COLORS BY LUCA BERTELÈ.
ABOVE: STUDIES BY DAVIDE GIANFELICE

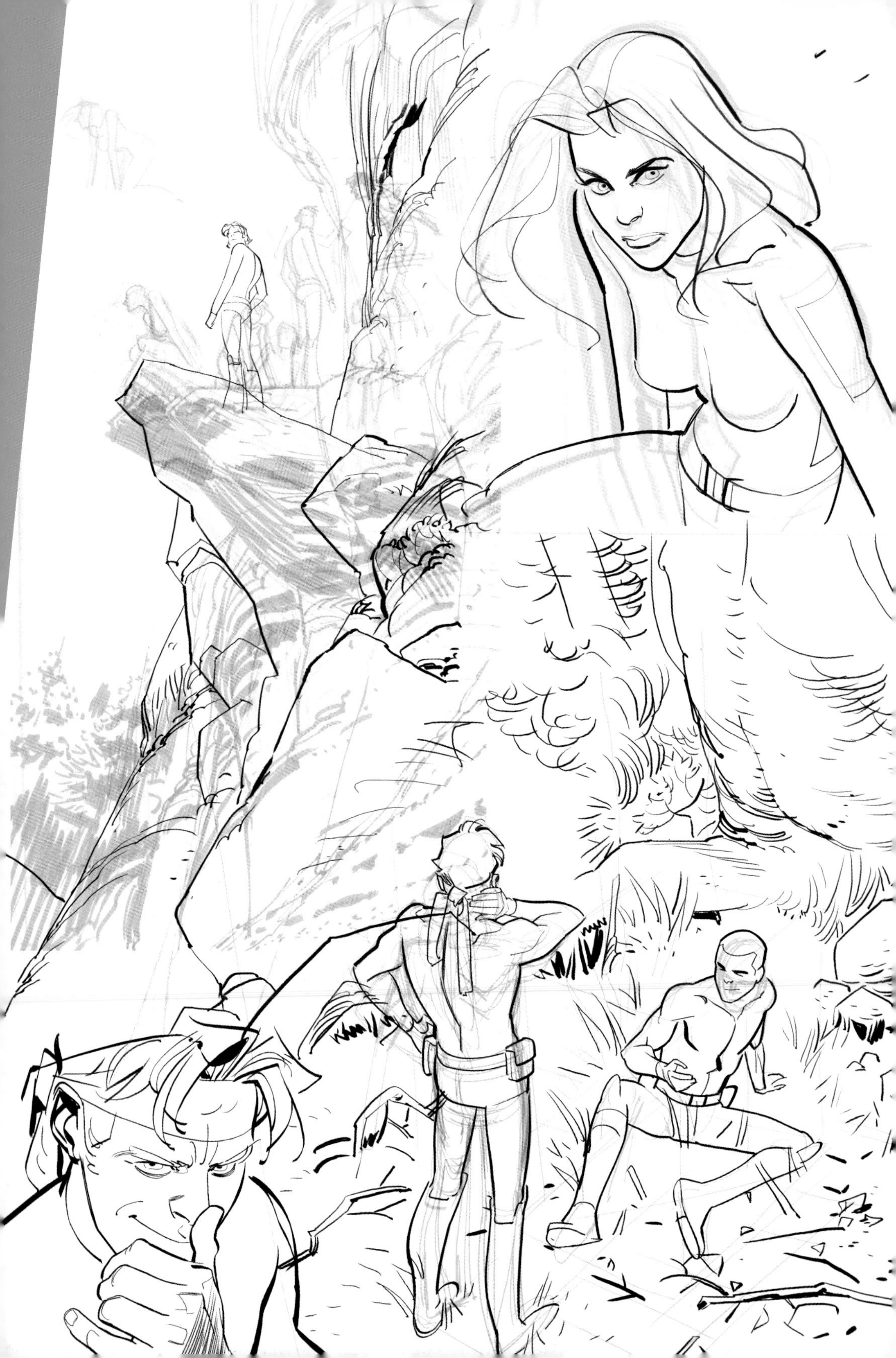

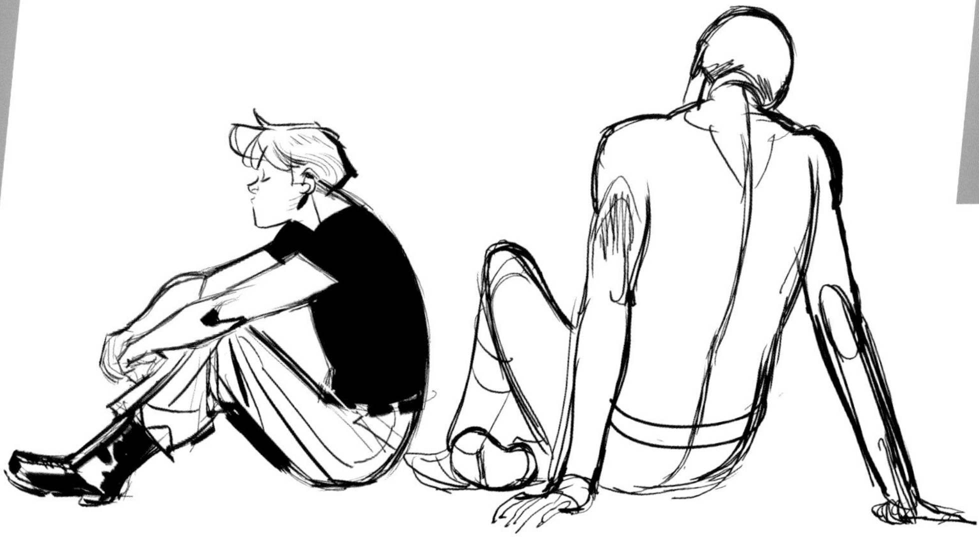

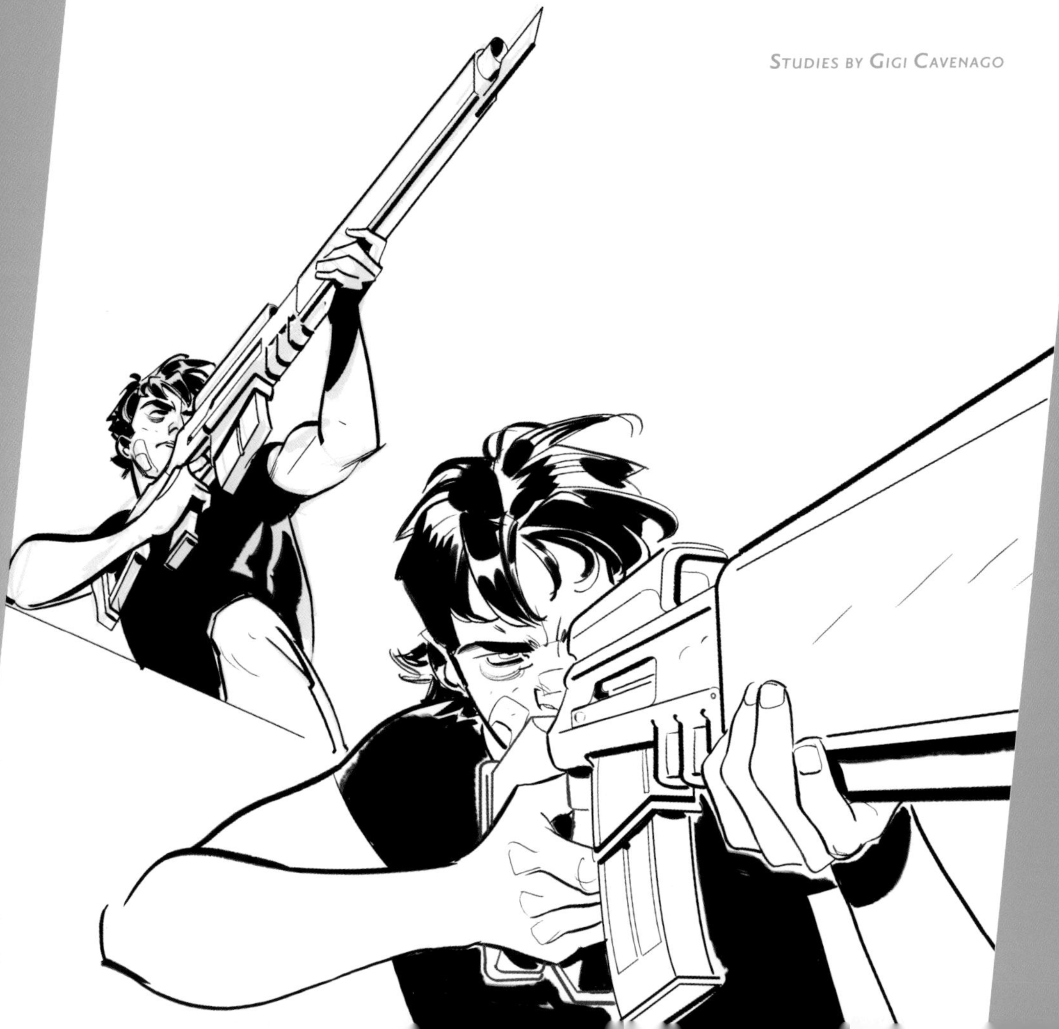

Studies by Gigi Cavenago

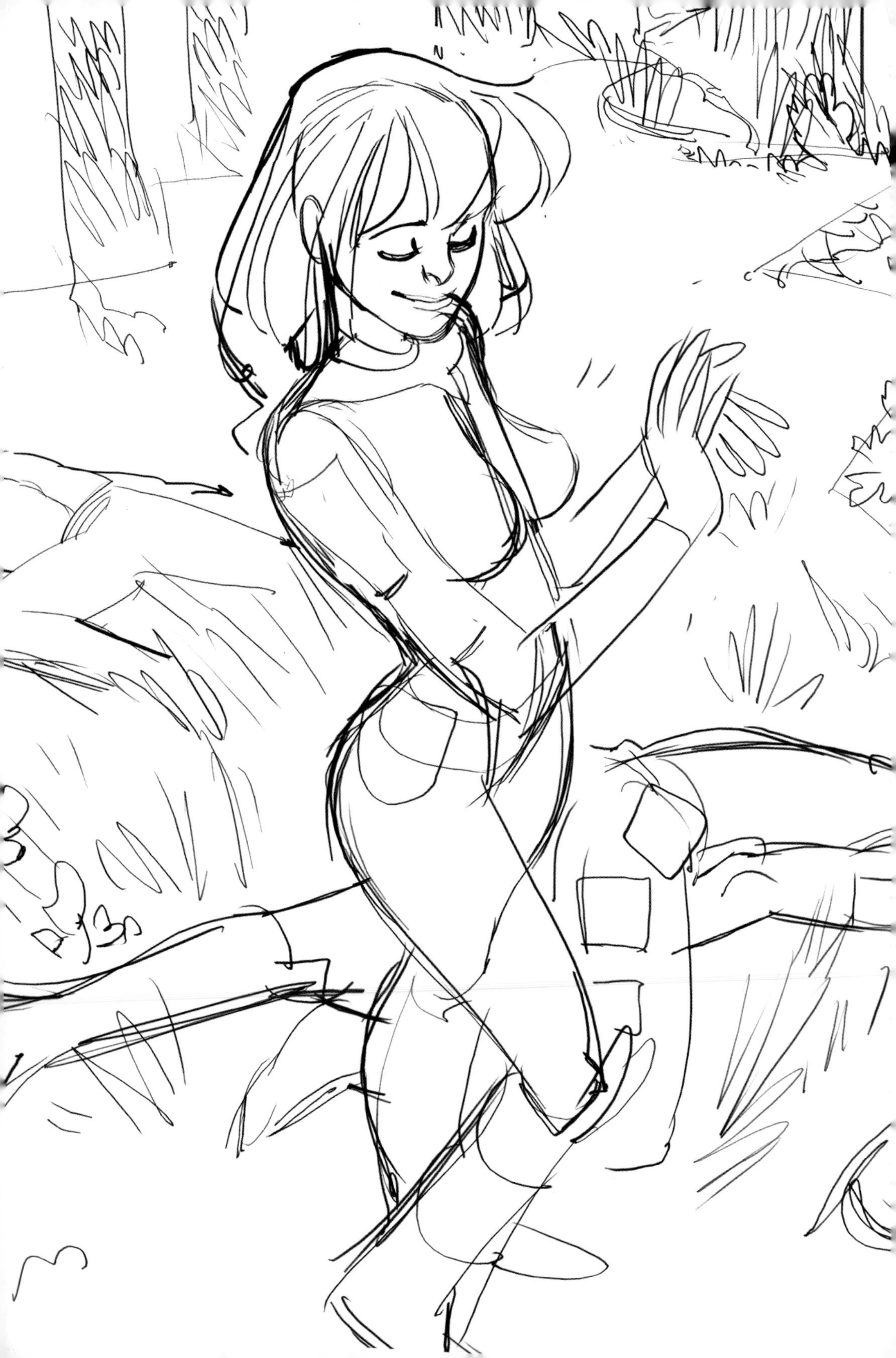

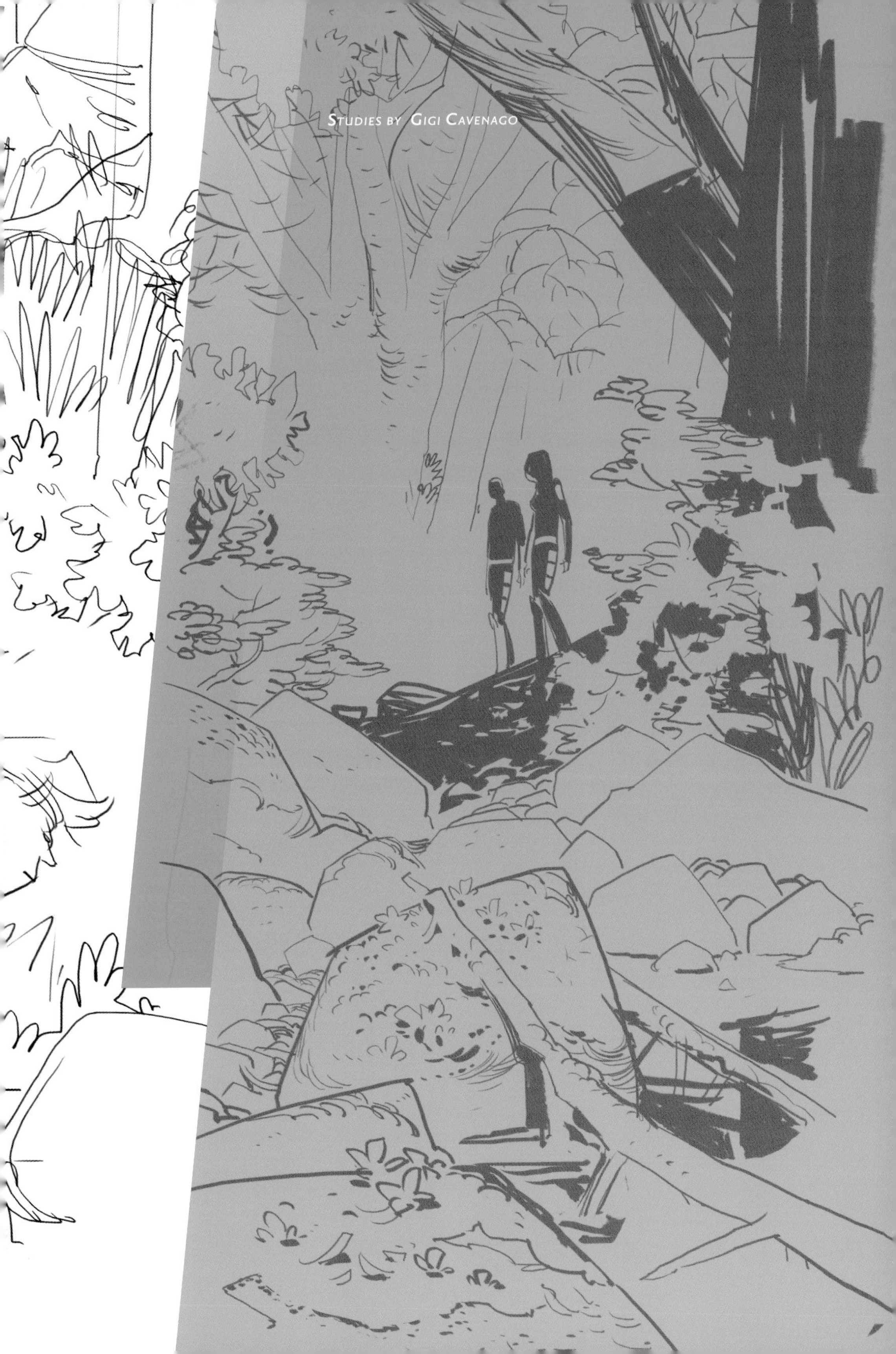

Studies by Gigi Cavenago

AS ALWAYS, RED SOLVES MOST PROBLEMS.

– Massimo Carnevale

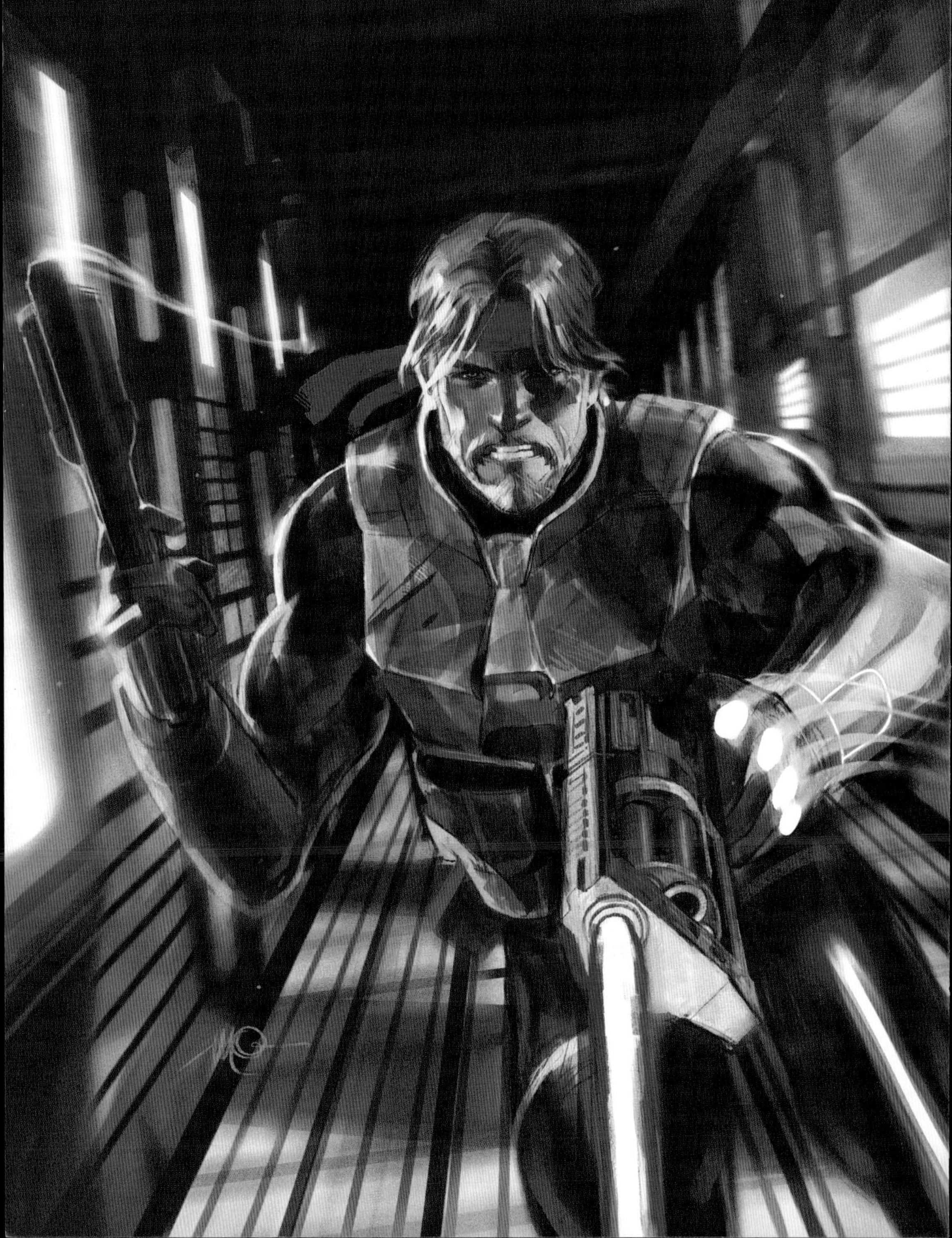

COVERS

MASSIMO CARNEVALE: As far as the cover of Chapter Seven is concerned, the idea of Ringo running while firing forward was almost a natural choice. You can also see it in the preliminary sketch, in which the layout and smooth digital coloring were already suggesting the idea that became real in the final version. The only doubt was about gray tones (as seen in the rough draft shown on page 3 of this volume): they didn't "pop out" properly nor convey the atmosphere of the scene. As always, red solves most problems.

Previous pages: preliminary sketches and illustrations for the cover of Orphans chapter seven by Massimo Carnevale.
Below and next page: studies and illustrations for the cover of Orphans chapter nine by Massimo Carnevale.

MASSIMO CARNEVALE: *I think the cover of Chapter Nine was the toughest one. I made thousands of sketches, but nothing stood out to me. This happens because it's pretty complicated to realize a dynamic scene in the void without any aliens or spaceships unless you find a way to create perspective and give depth to the scene. But the dimensions of the piece and the placement of the logo didn't leave much room, so depicting the figures in perspective was the only choice. Of course, it's impossible not to immediately think about movies such as* 2001: A Space Odyssey *or* Gravity.

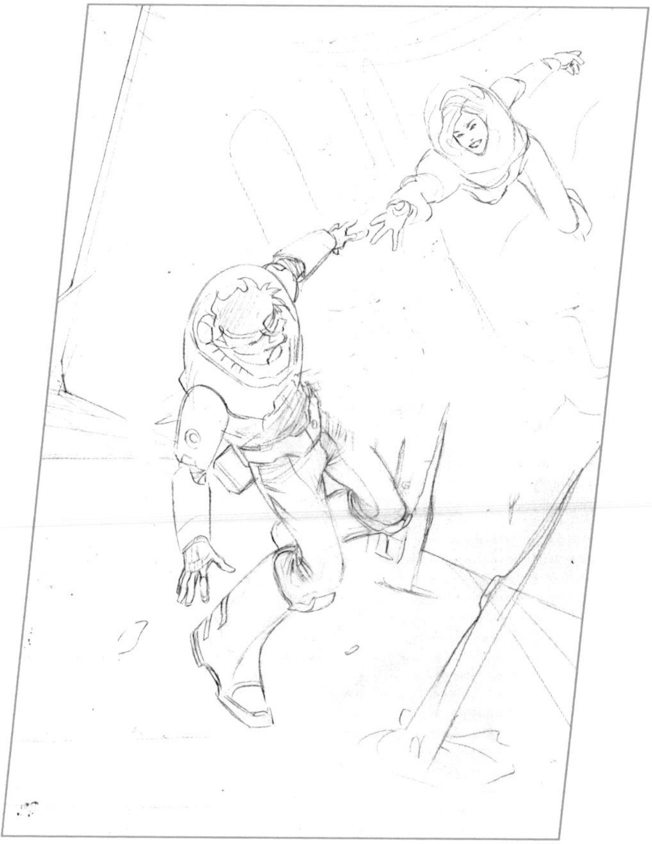

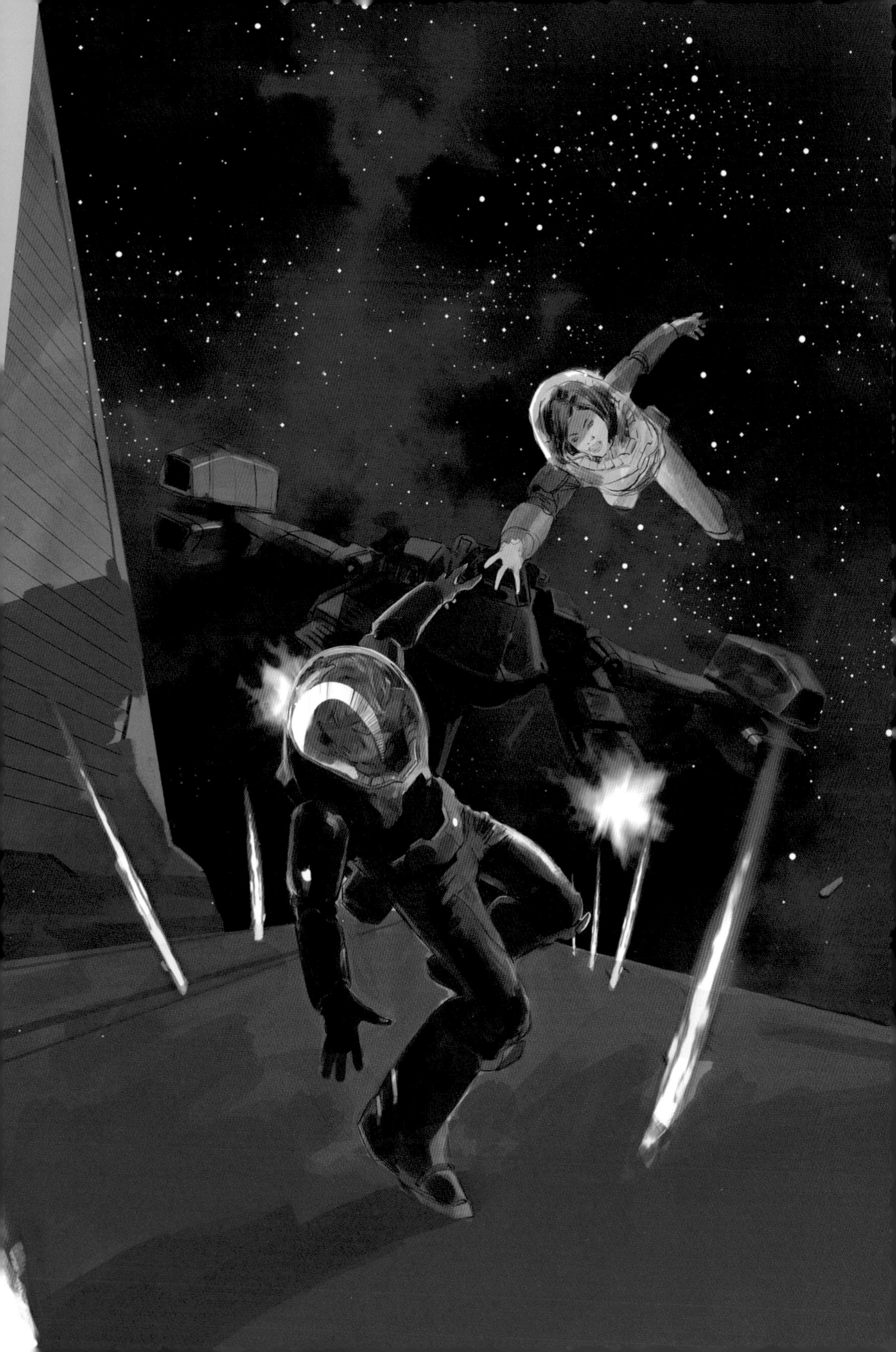

Steps for the cover of chapter nine by Massimo Carnevale.
Next page: the final illustration.

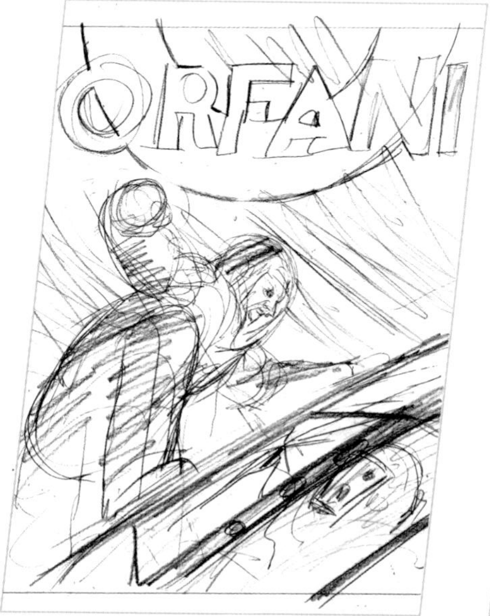
ORFANI

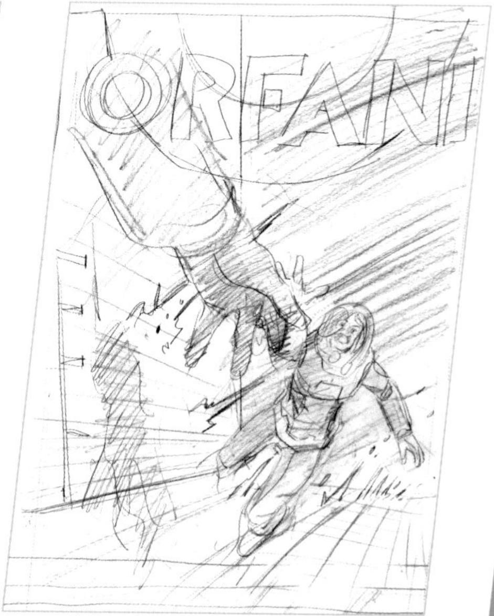
ORFANI

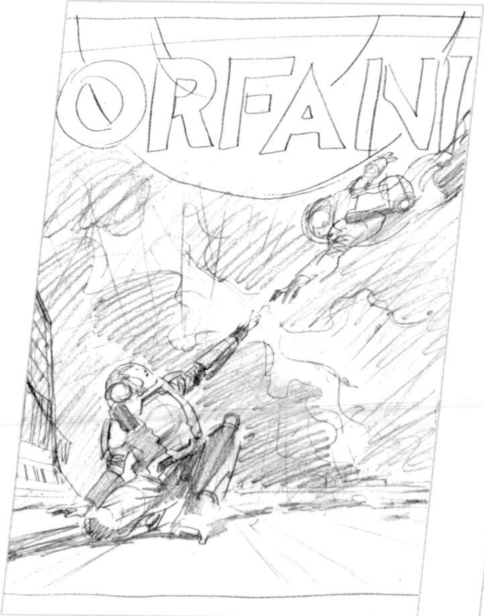
ORFANI

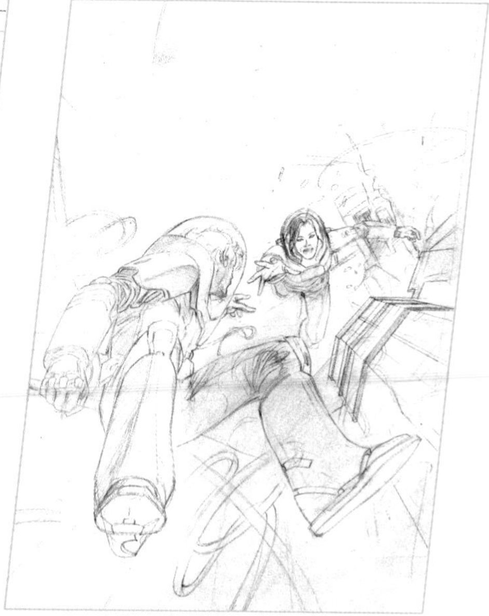